A

‘Astonishing, epic . . . a work of staggering scholarship, drawing on previously untapped sources locked away in European vaults and historical records . . . Green does not fall into the lazy assumption that Africa is one homogenous place . . . lays to rest centuries of biased scholarship’ Ben Okri, *Daily Telegraph*

‘Admirably complicates our understanding of Africa’s past and present . . . an extraordinary range of field research, archival material, and study of African oral traditions . . . One of its great strengths is that it reveals the often surprising success that Africans had throughout the first four hundred years of their encounter with Europe’
Howard W. French, *New York Review of Books*

‘A groundbreaking book. He brings together almost everything known about the economic history of the West African empires and peoples until the beginning of the nineteenth century in a coherent vision’
De Volkskrant

‘A work of staggering scholarship, peppered with astonishing facts’
Daily Telegraph, Summer Reading

‘Dismantles the racist myth of west African “backwardness” . . . The nineteenth-century imperial vision of Africa as somehow outside of history continues to mark even “world” histories, which often privilege the global north. *A Fistful of Shells* is an antidote to these histories, and to the master narrative of Africa as historical object, rather than subject’
Padraic Scanlan, *Guardian*

‘Uniquely valuable . . . represents an extraordinary and admirable archival and bibliographic undertaking’
Delinda J. Collier, *The Times Literary Supplement*

‘This meticulously researched book, based on archival research in nine countries, lays out a comprehensive overview of the economic history of West Africa and West-Central Africa before and after the slave trade . . . A valuable history written in an accessible style’ *Publishers Weekly*

'This impressive and welcome book engages with the new wave of studies on African economic history and places African societies at the centre of global events. Green interrogates and historicizes state failure, violence, corruption, military ideologies, commodification, and globalization, convincingly arguing that the roots of many of the current political and economic problems in Africa lie in the past. It is timely, relevant, and necessary in today's political and economic environment'
Mariana Candido, University of Notre Dame

'Toby Green's book restores the rich African history which she had been denied for too long. Here the author reveals that Africa was never at the margins of global commerce but was in fact a decisive player with the prowess to negotiate and also the goods – ivory, gum, gold – to supply' Hassoum Ceesay, National Museum, The Gambia

'Toby Green's transformative book repositions West African history in an entirely new light. It brings into focus the region's fundamental place in shaping the modern world as well as the powerful and also difficult legacy of this today' Paul Reid, Director, Black Cultural Archives

'Very seldom do I pick up a history book and wish I had written it myself. Toby Green's *A Fistful of Shells* is one such book. Brilliantly conceptualized, beautifully written, *A Fistful of Shells* breaks with colonially configured regional boundaries – which work to re-create unintended silos of knowledge – to imagine a West and West Central African Atlantic history of money, power, religion, and inequality that is as rich as it is sound'
Professor Nwando Achebe, Michigan State University

'Draws on a wide range of sources, from published histories, new statistics and first-hand travel accounts to fiction, poetry, traditional songs and newly discovered oral histories, much of which is revelatory . . . Green concludes by pointing to the lack of history being taught in schools and universities in West Africa and elsewhere; if it is taught at all, it tends to focus on the slave trade. *A Fistful of Shells* shows that there was so much more, and of so much relevance when looking at the issues of our own time' Anthony Sattin, *Spectator*

'A remarkable book . . . This original and thoughtful work is based on detailed first-hand knowledge of and collaboration with the cultures and peoples it depicts . . . Each page, even when the horrors are there too (Green doesn't shy away from them), is full of interest and humanity. The detail, too long and complicated to delineate here, is fascinating. I urge you to read it for yourself . . . this really *is* a "groundbreaking" work'
Ruth Finnegan, *Times Higher Education*

'Remarkable . . . *A Fistful of Shells* is principally an attempt to show how West Africa's precolonial histories are central to an understanding of the dilemmas of the present and to highlight the active role of its peoples in history, thereby transforming our view of the region . . . this is a hugely important book' *African Business*

'The range and depth of this book is simply stunning. By masterfully drawing on primary research and secondary sources in multiple languages, Green delivers a provocative book that is also a landmark of historical imagination and craftsmanship' Roquinaldo Ferreira, Henry Charles Lea Professor of History, University of Pennsylvania

ABOUT THE AUTHOR

Toby Green has worked widely with academics, musicians and writers across Africa, organizing events in collaboration with institutions in Angola, Ghana, Guinea-Bissau, Mozambique, Sierra Leone and the Gambia. He has written a number of previous books, and his work has been translated into twelve languages. Awarded a 2017 Philip Leverhulme Prize in History, he is Senior Lecturer in Lusophone African History and Culture at King's College, London. His 2019 book *A Fistful of Shells* won the Nayef Al-Rodhan Prize for global cultural understanding and was shortlisted for the Cundill History Prize and the inaugural Pius Adesanmi Memorial Award.

TOBY GREEN

A Fistful of Shells

West Africa from the Rise of the Slave Trade to the Age of Revolution

PENGUIN BOOKS

PENGUIN BOOKS

UK | USA | Canada | Ireland | Australia
India | New Zealand | South Africa

Penguin Books is part of the Penguin Random House group of companies whose addresses can be found at global.penguinrandomhouse.com

First published by Allen Lane 2019
Published in Penguin Books 2020
005

Set in 9.35/12.55 pt Sabon LT Std
Typeset by Jouve (UK), Milton Keynes
Printed and bound in Great Britain by Clays Ltd, Elcograf S.p.A.

A CIP catalogue record for this book is available from the British Library

ISBN: 978–0–141–97766–9

www.greenpenguin.co.uk

This book is dedicated to all those thanked in the Foreword, for their humanity and friendship.

Especially, it is for Aleida, Fatou and Ruby, and future generations of West African feminists; for Ben, Hassoum and Sam, and future generations of historians in West Africa.

It is for my much missed Uncle Niel, who would have loved reading and arguing about this book.

And it is for my dear wife Emily and my wonderful daughters, Lily and Flora – with love and gratitude.

A ko kolan siman gwɛlidi, jatigil'i fɛla

The stranger is like a dish, that the host can blow on

– Lansiné Diabaté[1]

I am spending what remains to me of life in investigation of the history of this age, and its turns of fortune, good and ill . . . Readers will derive pleasure from the narration and explanation. I go forward to add some ideas of my own . . . I have not stolen my fire from anyone's lamp.

– Sultan Mohammed Bello of the Sokoto Caliphate, *Infaku'l Maisuri* (1812)[2]

Contents

PART TWO
Consequences: Politics, Belief and Revolutions from Below

List of Maps

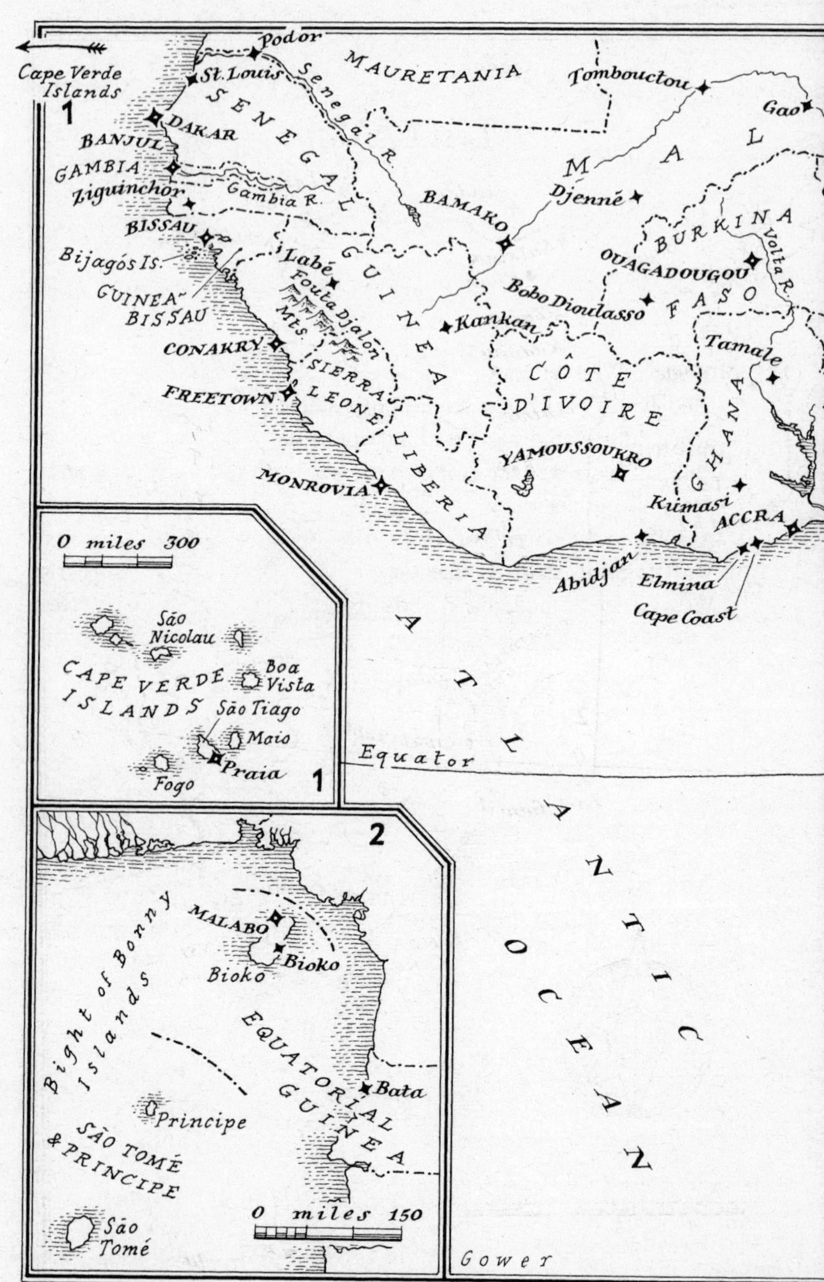

Modern West Africa

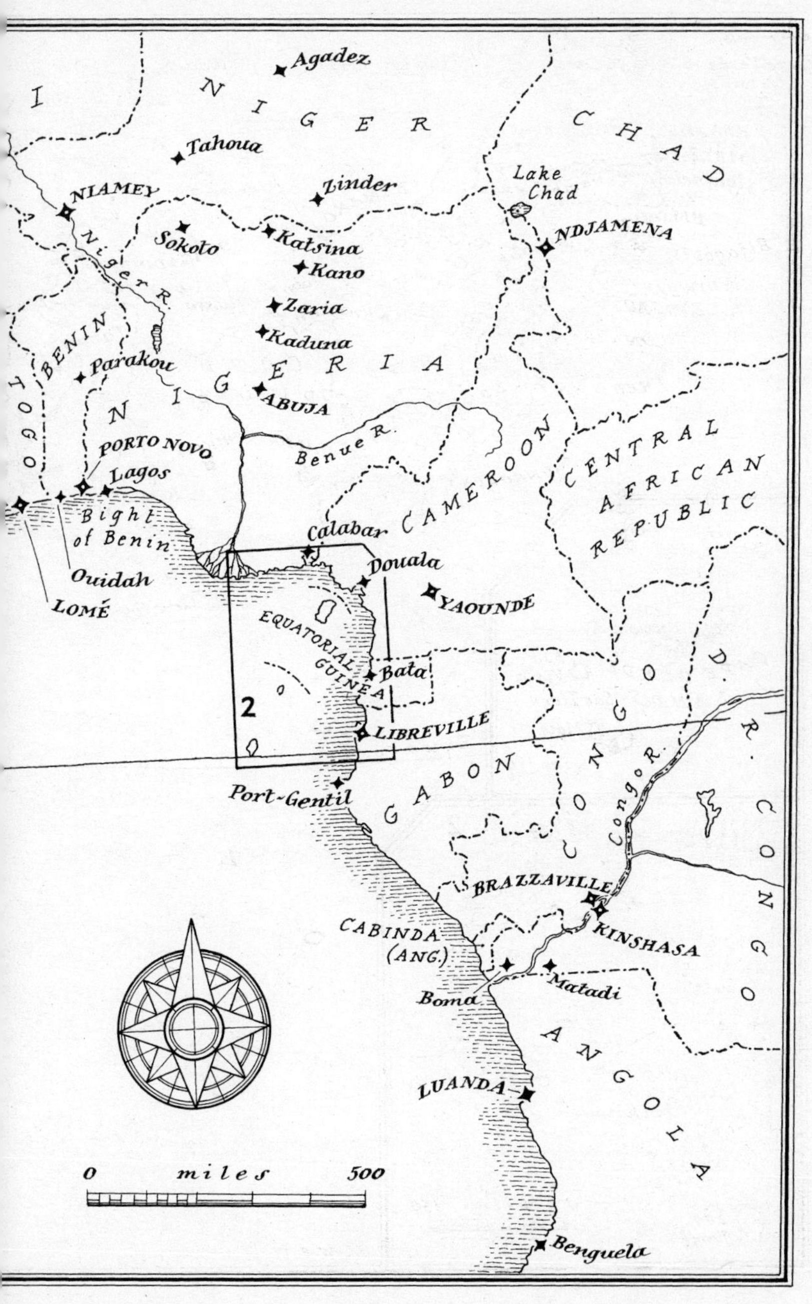

Agadez
NIGER
CHAD
Tahoua
Zinder
Lake Chad
NIAMEY
Niger R.
Sokoto
Katsina
Kano
NDJAMENA
Zaria
Kaduna
BENIN
Parakou
NIGERIA
ABUJA
TOGO
Benue R.
PORTO NOVO
Lagos
CAMEROON
CENTRAL AFRICAN REPUBLIC
Bight of Benin
Calabar
Douala
Ouidah
LOMÉ
YAOUNDE
EQUATORIAL GUINEA
Bata
2
LIBREVILLE
GABON
CONGO
D. R. CONGO
Congo R.
Port-Gentil
BRAZZAVILLE
KINSHASA
CABINDA (ANG.)
Boma
Matadi
ANGOLA
LUANDA
0 miles 500
Benguela

Foreword

On my first visit to West Africa, in 1995, I travelled to the Bijagós Islands off the coast of Guinea-Bissau. After taking a ferry from Bissau to the main Bijagó port of Bubaque, I negotiated a ride with some fishermen to the island of Canogo. We left Bubaque at night, and the sea glowed with phosphorescent algae. I can still remember that glow, and looking up in wonder at the sky salted with stars. Abibu, the Senegalese fisherman who had helped to negotiate my ride, was observing me. He saw my expression and said, 'It's beautiful to discover the world.' Over time, I learnt that that was true; but also that it was not always so beautiful.

Canogo was remote enough for there to be no ferry service nor anything resembling one. The islanders waited for fishermen like Abibu and the crew to come to the island, and then paid to travel back with them to Bubaque, where they could trade for supplies. A few days later, when we returned from Canogo, several islanders joined the boat. We made our way out into the wide channel cutting between mangroves and the neighbouring islands. After several hours' travel, we turned off into a swamp, waded ashore carrying our things, and slept on giant leaves that the fishermen had cut with their machetes from some fantastically shaped plants. The next morning, we resumed our journey, and, as we passed a creek heading off away from the main channel, one of the old women with us grimaced and spat into the water. She said something, and Abibu translated: 'Whoever goes down that creek never returns.'

At the time, although heavily educated in Britain, my knowledge was very limited. I did not understand the problematic forces that had driven Western travellers to go to Africa in the past, and that lay behind the interest in the West in what these travellers wrote. Worse, I knew little of West African history, and my ignorance made it hard to break through the carapace of exoticism. I had no idea that the Bijagó had been reputed as fearsome warriors and slave traders in the sixteenth and seventeenth centuries, launching long war canoes to the mainland. I also hadn't read the work of anthropologists such as Rosalind Shaw, who, in a later book on Sierra Leone, argued that metaphors of invisibility in West African discussions of magic had a historical meaning, referring to the disappearance of people in the slave trade. Over the years since, I have often thought back to this exchange, and the histories that may have lain beneath it. The fierce warriors who despatched their canoes from that creek or another just like it, participants in West African history, had not been forgotten on Canogo.

As I became a historian, I wondered how you could tally up these fragments of memory with the documentary evidence that is generally used to construct the historical record. Yet I soon discovered that the problem was not that there were no archives dealing with the West African past; rather, it was that they were spread all over the world, and that they were poorly systematized. In the summer of 2009, I visited the Archive of the Indies in Seville, right next door to the cathedral and royal palace. The archivists asked me what I was researching, and when I told them that it was a history of the Cape Verde Islands, one replied, 'We have no catalogue [*sección*] of documents on Cape Verde.' This was indeed the case. To research Cape Verde in this famous archive that contains many of the holdings of Colonial Spanish America, you had to read material relating to West Africa that the Spanish Council of the Indies had collated from all across South America. But the material was there all right.

This pattern repeats itself in many parts of the world. As a study of the endnotes of this book will show, my research has taken me far beyond Britain's National Archive, to archives in Brazil, Holland, Chile, Colombia, Portugal, Peru and Spain. You can find documents written centuries ago by slave traders, colonial officials and missionaries, often ill-assorted and poorly catalogued. There is detail on dates, officials, trade, warfare between African nations and African–European relations. Most, if not all, of this material was recorded because of the broader economic rationale of the trade in enslaved persons that saw these chancers (to use a polite noun) come to West Africa in the first place, and so it gives a skewed perspective. It ignores what was precisely most important to so many West Africans at the time: kinship and family, labour and production, religious practice and observance, dress and fashions, food and family, political allegiance and change. To understand these perspectives, one must spend time in West Africa recording oral histories, recovering social memories if possible (such as that of the old woman from Canogo) and consulting precious recordings of these oral histories where they already exist.

In 2010, I had a stroke of luck. The American historian Walter Hawthorne had visited The Gambia to assist in digitizing the endangered collections of the Gambian National Archive in a project funded by the British Library. While there, he had been introduced to an archive of oral histories that he thought had a lot of material on the distant past, and suggested I have a look. I arrived a few months later, the first of many rewarding research trips. I found cassette recordings made in the 1960s, 1970s and 1980s by Bakary Sidibé and a number of assistants, and these interviews with people born in the nineteenth century offered a picture of key events in the distant past. There was material here covering Guinea, Guinea-Bissau, Mali and Senegal, as well as The Gambia. Much of it had been transcribed, and some translated. As other researchers I have met in the 'mango tree' archive at Fajara can attest, this is one of the most precious archives in West Africa.

Eventually, the two approaches of oral and written documents began to match up. Visiting Peru's National Archive in May 2013, I consulted the records of the Inquisition of Lima. Here one finds the account books of Manuel Bautista Pérez, a slave trader who lived in the Guinea-Bissau region in the 1610s before moving to Peru, where he was tried and burned by the Inquisition in 1639. The auto-da-fé took place in the Plaza Mayor itself, within shouting distance of the arcade that today houses the National Archive, where the records of his brutal and sad life remain almost four centuries later. Donning the protective white gloves required for researchers, I pored over his account books, detailing among many other things his own trading activities in the same Bijagós Islands I had visited eighteen years before. Most of the material was pure numbers, 'facts and figures', a reduction of history to data alone. Yet sometimes the emotional connection to this history and the memories I had glimpsed in the Bijagós peeked through. At one point, I paused, moved, when I came upon Bautista Pérez writing in the late 1620s of his daughter Maria, who had been born to a West African mother and still lived in the town of Cacheu (today in Guinea-Bissau). Many years later, when living on the other side of the world, Bautista Pérez still wrote letters to Maria and sent her money to cover her necessities; and in time her descendants (and so his) became part of the community in West Africa that he had left, and from which he had transported captives to the Americas.

Discovering these stories on a regular basis explains how and why I have come to write this book. Here, in these dusty sheaves of paper, are regular accounts of Africa's global interactions from the very distant past; and yet the traditional Western narrative is of Africa's ahistoricity. Pretty soon, in fact, the regular visitor realizes the enormous disconnect between preconception and reality. In most Western discourse, either exclusionary language is used for 'Africa' (Africa is 'without history' or 'without modernity'); or the language implies that Africa and Africans are somehow historically predisposed to violence and savagery in a way that Europeans and those of European descent are not. Anyone with the slightest knowledge of history knows that this is an extraordinary prejudice to hold; and it is remarkable that it remains still quite widespread one fifth of the way through the twenty-first century.

Every writer approaches their subject with predispositions, and so, of course, do readers. So far as distant West African history goes, one of the deepest-rooted for some people is that there simply are not enough sources to form a coherent historical overview. Spending time in these many different archives has shown me how wrong this view is, but it has also provided its own challenge. I have written one book, but there could have been three or four produced from the sources I have consulted. Inevitably, what results here, rather than being comprehensive, is something written in the light of my own perspectives and interests: those of someone who has been travelling regularly to

West Africa for over twenty years while still, of course, remaining an outsider; someone who has spent long enough in archives around the world to feel a tickle in the throat just at the thought of all those dusty papers. There's so much more to do. Many sources in Arabic, Danish, Dutch, English, French and Portuguese are yet to be properly studied from an African perspective. One of the challenges in the writing has been to balance the sources and their importance with the reality of how historical research on the distant West African past continues to be comparatively scant: there is, therefore, a desire to say as much as possible, but this can make a book unreadable, and the historian intolerable.

What's more, to add to the danger of information overload from written sources is the remarkable oral information that is available. To the Western historical mindset, drawing on oral histories for this period is an anti-historical endeavour. But in West Africa, history is an oral genre, held and recounted by professional historians known as praisesingers, or griots, whose patrons ask them to sing important histories at key public events and commemorations. The Danish traveller Paul Erdmann Isert captured something of this practice on the Gold Coast as long ago as 1783:

> Not a day goes by but a War Council (Palaber) is held. It is not a little tedious to sit in the sun like a statue for four to five hours. Most frequently the reason for these meetings is that a newly-arrived group has to be sworn in – a process which we watch, listen to and must keep a written record of, because we Europeans cannot confidently entrust such things to memory, as can the secretaries of the Blacks, who have to keep every public trial in their heads, even 40 years after the event. We know that even though they have not learned to write and cannot read a single letter, they are accurate in recalling their traditions as well as their history.[1]

Many historians today would say that Isert was a little too credulous here. Just as literate historians shape their narratives according to the concerns of every age, so griots are likely to direct their narratives to their patrons, and to their own historical tradition of mediating between rulers and subjects according to the exigencies of the time. He who pays the piper calls the tune, whether in the twenty-first century or in West African cities, towns and villages through the ages. However, just as older written histories are not discarded because of this, neither should oral accounts be dismissed. Oral sources are important to this book not because of the 'facts' that they contain, but because of the discourses that they offer. Oral accounts offer the experience of history, the importance of the past in present memory and a sense of what may have been socially meaningful in distant times. They also offer an incomparable window on to the way that history was performed, its sounds and textures, and what it meant for ordinary men and women. Perhaps most significantly, they offer a different model of history, one that can challenge the dominance of traditional models which have misrepresented the African past.[2]

In the end, we cannot escape the reality that all 'sources' on the past represent political projects, and this is something that readers of this book should bear in mind when they encounter what follows. The oral histories I have located are shaped by their own contemporary pressures and experiences. The Arabic sources I have drawn on were written in the main by West African scholars from the sixteenth to the eighteenth centuries, trying to historicize the past within the framework of Islamic religious observance and the political world they inhabited. The European traders' narratives occupied different phases: in the seventeenth and eighteenth centuries, these slave-trading men produced books, often with a pro-slavery agenda (as is the case with William Snelgrave, for instance); by the later eighteenth century some of the books were produced by naturalists such as Michel Adanson and Adam Afzelius, participating in Enlightenment science; and, by the nineteenth, explorers such as Heinrich Barth and Mungo Park produced their own accounts, funded by European backers with an as yet dimly perceived colonial agenda that was both economic and ideological.[3]

Thus, all sources in all world regions need to be recognized as political or intellectual projects. In the African context, the best way of illustrating how these different types of sources are helpful is through examples, or what historians call 'microhistories'. In an earlier book, I compared a written external account from the 1570s that discussed how in The Gambia armies of warriors fought alongside a platoon of monkeys with an oral source that describes how some of the warriors of the Kaabu Empire of this region took monkeys as their totem. This comparison reveals the racism of the original source (believing that Africans could fight alongside monkeys), historicizes the rise of the Kaabu Empire and is revelatory of militarized secret societies* as they emerged at this time. Language, too, is extremely helpful: that the Bamana† words for 'market' and 'debt/credit' – *fèère* and *júru* – are derived from the Portuguese words (*feira* and *juro*) is very informative about processes of trade, exchange and credit in precolonial West Africa, and of the role of external trade and money in these processes.[4]

This is such a rich and complex subject. It defies generalization, yet has a universal importance. Africa was not a colonial setting until the nineteenth century, and from the thirteenth century on its peoples and rulers were active participants in shaping the modern world. Precolonial African histories are, indeed, of great relevance to modern dilemmas. Yet this precolonial history is rarely researched, even in history departments in many African universities, let alone in the West. By the time the reader finishes this book, my hope is that it will be clear why this state of affairs should not continue any longer.

The ideas that emerge in this book have been shaped by some special people. Emily, Lily and Flora gave me the generosity of spirit, time and love to take into this study. Simon Winder at Penguin conceived the idea that I should write this book in the first place, and understood at once why it might be interesting, and what were the main themes that should animate it; once I began to write, he was a model of generous and creative support and advice – a reminder of the precious importance of the editorial process. I discussed it at an early stage, too, with Priya Nelson at Chicago University Press, so it has been wonderful also to work with her as the book has neared completion. Maggie Hattersley also made many helpful suggestions, which helped me to clarify how I should approach the final draft. Richard Drayton gave

* Used rather than 'sodality' – in vogue in much anthropological literature today – to assist clarity and descriptive power.

† The language spoken by the Bamana people in the region of Bamako, Mali, and very closely related to other Mande languages such as Maninka.

me enormous encouragement and support especially at the early phase, when I was clarifying in my mind the ideas that would form the core of the book; without his unstinting friendship and belief, it would not exist.

El Hadji Mamadou Ndiaye, El Hadji Omar Ndiaye, Ablai Diallo, Ibrahima Massaly, Carmen Neto, Januário Nascimento, António Leão Correia e Silva, Zelinda Cohen, Hassoum Ceesay, Buba Saho and Ndane Faye all offered me deeply personal and humane introductions to many different parts of West Africa. My PhD students Dorothée Boulanger, Aleida Mendes Borges, Joe da Costa, Patrice Etienne, and Vince Nadeau all gave me many different questions to think about, and broadened the way I think through their own insights and experience; and all the many students I have taught at King's College London helped me to hone my knowledge and think more deeply about everything here.

As should be apparent to anyone who reads this book, I owe enormous debts to those with whom I have conducted interviews in many West African countries; I would like to thank the team managing the Ethics Review process at King's College London for helping me to develop careful formats for these interviews. I am also enormously indebted to the staff of a large number of archives in Africa, Europe and Latin America for their diligence and efficiency in dealing with my requests. My thanks to all of these patient and thoughtful people, whose hard work and dedication, often in very difficult circumstances, has helped to make this book what it is.

Once I set to work writing, my ideas emerged in dialogue with so many fellow scholars. Samuel Adu-Gyamfi, Benjamin Kye Ampadu, Mariana Candido, Hassoum Ceesay, Roquinaldo Ferreira, Vincent Hiribarren, Luis Nicolau Parés, Helen Parr, Assan Sarr and Tatiana Seijas all read drafts of the manuscript and offered me extremely helpful critiques. Many other friends and colleagues discussed ideas in the book and helped me to think through the context in which it had to be written, among others: Nwando Achebe, Gareth Austin, Manuel Barcia, Boubacar Barry, Francisco Bethencourt, Walter Bgoya, Marisa Candotti, Justin Cox, Richard Drayton, Lucy Durán, Marcela Echeverrí, Paulo Farias, Jane Guyer, Philip Havik, Walter Hawthorne, Anthony Hopkins, José da Silva Horta, Daniel

Laeomahuma Jatta, Mary Jay, Kazuo Kobayashi, Murray Last, Paul Lovejoy, Kristin Mann, Peter Mark, Joseph Miller, José Lingna Nafafé, Malyn Newitt, Linda Newson, Chibundu Onuzo, Steve Pincus, Paul Reid, Benedetta Rossi, Bala Saho, Ibrahima Seck, Carlos da Silva Junior, Hugo Ribeiro da Silva, Candido Domingues de Souza, Ibrahima Thiaw and AbdoolKarim Vakil. All these people have helped to shape the way I think about the themes that I have written about here; they have all offered vital ideas, which help to pull together the whole.

I could not have developed the perspectives in this book without the help and collaboration of colleagues in African institutions. It's been one of the great blessings and privileges in my life to have had the chance to work closely with such wonderful people, and my deep thanks go especially to the following: in Angola, Albano Ferreira, Rector of Katyavala Bwila University in Benguela, Botelho Jimbi and Elsa Rodrigues (also of UKB), and Nick Manuel, Sabino de Nascimento and José Pedro of the Universidade Agostinho Neto in Luanda; in Cape Verde, Zelinda Cohen and António Correia e Silva, of the University of Cabo Verde; in Ghana, Benjamin Kye-Ampadu of the Ghana History Teachers' Association and Samuel Adu-Gyamfi and George Bob-Milliar of Kwame Nkrumah University of Science and Technology in Kumasi; in Guinea-Bissau, Leopoldo Amado, Miguel de Barros, Carlos Cardoso and Mamadu Jao currently or formerly of the Instituto Nacional de Estudos e Pesquisa; in Mozambique, Marta Mendonça, Xavier Muianga and Adriano Uaciquete of Universidade Eduardo Mondlane, and Aldino André, Pedrito Cambrão and João Salavessa of UniLúrio University; in Senegal, Boubacar Barry and Ibrahima Thiaw of the Université Cheikh Anta Diop, Dakar; in Sierra Leone, Joe Alie, Ishmael Kamara and Stephen Ney of Fourah Bay College; in The Gambia, a particular vote of thanks to Baba Ceesay, Hassoum Ceesay, Siaka Fadera, Marcia Hall, Bakary Sanyang and Lamin Yarbo, currently or formerly of the National Centre of Arts and Culture, and to all the staff of the Research and Documentation Division at Fajara.

Beyond my work in Africa, I have also been very lucky to be supported by many people in the various countries in Europe and Latin America where I have also undertaken research. My research in Brazil in particular has been made much easier by the assistance and friendship of a number of colleagues, who helped me to locate archival material, arrange picture credits from Museums, and – equally as importantly – have a good time. I would like especially to thank Wladymyra Albuquerque, Urano Andrade, Lisa Earl Castillo, Luis Nicolau Parés and João Reis in Salvador; Alex Gebara and Mariza de Carvalho Soares in Rio de Janeiro; Thiago Mota and Vanicleia Silva Santos in Belo Horizonte; and Marina de Mello e Souza in São Paulo. But I must most especially thank Candido Domingues de Souza and Carlos da Silva Junior, who welcomed me into their lives, showed me the right places to enjoy *bobo de camarão*, *licor* and ice cream, and went far over and above the call of any duty to make sure that I felt at home in Salvador. It has nevertheless been a sadness to see at first hand the encroachment of authoritarian and thinly disguised racist governance onto Brazilian academic life, symbolized most starkly by the devastating fire at Rio's Museo Nacional on 2 September 2018, as this book went to press.

Once I took some of these ideas out into the world, I was offered generous opportunities to road-test them in various presentations: my thanks to Wladymyra Albuquerque and João Reis for coordinating along with Carlos da Silva Junior the conference we hosted in Salvador related to this topic; António de Almeida Mendes at Nantes and Christophe Giudicelli at Rennes; Emily Osborn at Chicago; Henning Schreiber and Katrin Pfeiffer at Hamburg; Karen Graubart and Pat Griffin at Notre Dame; Roquinaldo Ferreira (then at Brown); the late and missed Jan-Georg Deutsch and Jamie Belich at Oxford; Catherine Coquéry-Vidrovitch at the Université Paris Diderot and Gaëlle Beaujean at the Musée du Quai Branly; and Tiraana Bains and Russ Gasdia at Yale.

I was very lucky indeed to be formed intellectually at the University of Birmingham's old Centre of West African Studies. My PhD supervisor, Paulo de Moraes Farias, was an inspiring and wise guide, and I will forever owe a debt of gratitude to him and Karin Barber, and to all my colleagues there for countless kindnesses and a proper education. On leaving Birmingham, a fortuitous change of direction then shaped the work that led to this book. When I started working at King's College in September 2010, Ludmilla Jordanova asked me to teach economic history; and from there I found my way into many of the questions addressed in what follows.

Working at King's, I have been surrounded by people who have all helped to create an atmosphere where thinking matters. As heads of department, Federico Bonaddio, Catherine Boyle, Paul Readman, Adam Sutcliffe, Jon Wilson and Abigail Woods have always been hugely supportive both of this project and of my work in general. My colleagues Hanna-Kristin Arro, Natasha Awais-Dean, Amy Hart, Chris Machut, Alex Nightingale, Dot Pearce, Rob Templing and Lucy Thomas have provided all kinds of support, through which my many complex and often apparently impossible organizational headaches were resolved as if it were all easy. In the History Department, I have been lucky to have the generous friendship and support of Jen Altehenger, Francisco Bethencourt, the late and lamented Patrick Chabal, Chris Dillon, Richard Drayton, Serena Ferente, Laura Gowing, Alana Harris, Vincent Hiribarren, Dan Matlin, Christine Mathias, Sumita Mukherjee, Malyn Newitt, Adrian Pearce, Alex Sapoznik, Simon Sleight, Sarah Stockwell and David Todd; Anne Goldgar encouraged me to learn to read Dutch when I still had the time, and lent me her Shetter's Grammar, from which act of support and generosity this book hugely benefits. In the Spanish, Portuguese and Latin American Studies Department, I have been inspired by the comradeship, ideas and friendship of Almiro de Andrade, María-José Blanco, Italia Boliver, Nagore Calvo Mendizabal, Felipe Botelho Correa, Catarina Fouto, Alicia Kent, Daniela Doneda Mittelstadt, Antonia Moreira-Rodríguez, Daniel Muñoz Sempere, Mariví Rodríguez Quiñones, Elisa Sampson Vera Tudela, Luis Rebaza Soraluz, João Silvestre, David Treece, Alejandro Vega Franco, Jesús Villalta Loro and Julian Weiss. Beyond my home departments, Abiodun Alao, Vinicius de Carvalho, Ruth Craggs, Ekaette Ikpe, Javed Majeed, 'Funmi Olonisakin and Nayanka Perdigao have all provided friendship and collaborative inspiration.

In the end, however, it has only been possible to write this book because of the support of the funding institutions that have enabled it. A brief glance at the archives consulted, and the fieldwork notes scattered through the book, will give a sense of how costly an undertaking this has been. This book itself is thus a mark of the sort of privilege whose origins in part it addresses; it is foreign institutions with financial heft that can currently bankroll such an undertaking – another legacy of the historical inequalities considered in this book.

Some of the research on which this book draws dates back to my PhD at Birmingham, when I was funded by the old Arts and Humanities Research Board from 2003 to 2005; a little more of it then comes from the period when I was in receipt of a British Academy Postdoctoral Research Fellowship at Birmingham (2007–10). However, I first developed the ideas that emerge here in a sustained way as a Leverhulme Early Career Fellow at King's (2010–13), when I benefited from the very generous Leverhulme ECF research allowance to conduct much of the archival research for this book for the project *West Africans and Atlantic Empires, 1589–1700*. It was then as an AHRC Leadership Fellow for the project 'Money, Slavery and Political Change in Precolonial West Africa' (2016–18) that I was able to conduct further research and also have the sustained thinking time to write this book. At this stage, support from Mike Goddard and Grant Robertson at the OCR Examinations Board was also fundamental, and I am very grateful to their belief in the importance of the history of precolonial Africa, which has influenced the evolution of this book in a number of ways.

Beyond this vital funding and institutional support, I have also been surrounded by inspirational colleagues at the African Studies Association of the UK (ASAUK), working collectively on a host of important issues. The ASAUK-funded writing workshops have been especially vital in shaping aspects of my work and engagement, and I would especially like to thank for their support and comradeship Reg Cline-Cole, Carli Coetzee, Gemma Haxby, Ambreena Manji, David Maxwell, Steph Newell, Insa Nolte, Ola Oduku, George Ogola and Lizzie Orekoya, all of whom supported these workshops in one way or another.

The ASAUK funded the workshops I organized in collaboration with the Universities of Sierra Leone (2017; also co-funded by the AHRC) and The Gambia (2014, 2018; the latter also co-funded by the AHRC), and with the Universidade Agostinho Neto in Luanda and Universidade Katyavala Bwila in Benguela (2018; co-funded by the European Union). All of these were instrumental in shaping my thinking. I would also like to thank the British Academy, which funded the two workshops on Music and History which I co-organized with Lucy Durán of SOAS in 2015 and 2017, which greatly enhanced my understanding of relevant cultural universes. Without this support from many institutions and their review boards, I would never have been able to produce this work: my deepest thanks to all those individuals and funders who thereby made this possible.

I am also enormously indebted to the many colleagues who helped in putting this book together. Simon Winder marshalled both the author and the text with perfect grace and judgement, and gave me the space and the spurs to organize the book into something readable that was yet true to its original conception. Priya Nelson was always committed to the text and the idea, which has also been an inspiration in completing it. Donna Poppy provided an enormously useful and thorough copyediting of the text, saving me from many disasters, and was similarly a model of editorial judgement. Richard Duguid and Ellen Davies oversaw the editorial process and the complexity of the management of the images with great care. And I must at this point also thank Vincent Hiribarren, Daniel Laeomahuma Jatta, Anna de Mutiis, Bala Saho and Carlos da Silva Junior for helping me with the right photographs and granting me permission to reproduce their images in this book.

Finally, I wish to make due acknowledgement of publishers' permission to reproduce selected excerpts as follows:

Reproduced by permission from Fontes Historiae Africanae Series Arabica V, *Sharī'a in Songhay: The Replies of Al-Maghīlī to the Questions of Askia al-Ḥājj Muḥammad*, edited and translated by John O. Hunwick, © The British Academy 1985. From pages 70, 89 and 90.

Reproduced by permission from Cambridge University Press and Markus Wiener Publishers, 570 words from N. Levtzion and J. F. P. Hopkins (2000): *Corpus of Early Arabic Sources for West African History.*

Reproduced by permission of Brill Publishers, 307 words from John O. Hunwick (1990): *Timbuktu and the Songhay Empire: Al-Sa'dī's Ta'rīkh al-sūdān down to 1613, and Other Contemporary Documents.*

While every effort has been made to trace copyright holders, any omission drawn to the attention of the author and publishers will be rectified in any future edition of this work.

I cannot end these acknowledgements without making due recognition of the many other scholars on whose work this book often relies. Consultation of the endnotes reveals that a good proportion of the material here does come from my own archival research and fieldwork. However, much of it also comes from the written and oral sources collected by a range of scholars, without whose tireless and painstaking labour a comparative book like this would be impossible to produce. So I would like in particular to thank Jan Jansen, Adam Jones and Robin Law; and the late António Brásio, Mervyn Hiskett, John Hunwick, Nehemia Levtzion, S. P. l'Honoré Naber, H. R. Palmer and Klaas Ratelband.

Beyond this time-consuming work, this book is also indebted to fifty years of sustained research in African studies that informs my approach. The immediate post-independence era of the 1960s and 1970s saw an emphasis on precolonial history, to show that there was a long history of independent polities in Africa to which the post-colonial states were now added. The focus on histories of slavery was part of a general approach to 'world systems' and the creation of economic inequality in the world, in which Walter Rodney and Immanuel Wallerstein were very influential. Rodney's *How Europe Underdeveloped Africa* (published in 1972 in Dar es Salaam by Walter Bgoya, who it was my great privilege to be published by over forty years later) argued that Africa's economic underdevelopment had to be seen in relation to Europe's development. This coincided with the Civil Rights Era in the US, which created a different direction in historical writing, especially following Alex Haley's *Roots*, seeking to trace influences of African histories in the Americas.

While the historical writing interconnecting Africa and the Americas has grown ever since, from the late 1980s onwards there was a turn away from the economic underdevelopment models of Rodney and Wallerstein. The rise of neoliberal emphases on autonomy and personal responsibility coincided with an increasing focus from historians on showing African 'agency', with Africans as active participants in history and not as passive victims of impersonal economic forces. It is thus the aim of this book to remember the active role and creative participation of Africa and Africans in 'making history', but not to use this (as sometimes can seem the case) as an excuse to pass over rapacious forces and external agencies that eventually magnified economic inequalities between Africa and much of the world. I attempt to reconcile these two tendencies by remembering that agency is also connected intersectionally to class, examining how the agency of the enslaved both in Africa and in the Americas was instrumental in overthrowing the Atlantic slave trade system; and also through the focus on economic structures in this book, as a reminder that agency in this context is itself a response to a totalizing and unequal system.

Similarly, the emphasis on the core African roots of American cultures has also been modified in recent years to include the reciprocal influence of American transformations in Africa, through political movements (Cuba's role in the Angolan Civil War), music and religious ideas. This movement shows the complexity of African history, and belies any essentialist idea of 'authentic' Africa somehow divorced from world historical movements – another core aim of this book. To my mind, this move can also draw on the writings of the Martinican thinker Frantz Fanon, who saw the fundamental importance of reciprocity in breaking out of colonial patterns of authority. 'There is an absolute reciprocity which must be recognized,' he wrote in *Black Skin, White Masks*. 'If I close the circuit, if I prevent the accomplishment of movement in two directions, I keep the other within himself. Ultimately, I deprive him even of this being-for-itself.'[5]

However, such a rich and complex historiography may be off-putting to those new to this subject. As one of my intentions in writing this book is to engage readers beyond those who already know the importance of the topic, I have chosen in the main not to reference my fellow researchers in the text itself; those who wish to follow these strands of the discussion may do so through the endnotes. By occasionally intruding with some personal experiences, I have also chosen not to adopt the historian's fiction of a comprehensive and impartial objectivity: not to bother to pretend, in the words of the philosopher Achille Mbembe, to be 'able to know the world without being part of that world . . . by all accounts able to produce knowledge that is supposed to be universal and independent of context'.[6]

In short, as should be apparent from all of the foregoing, this book embodies the collective endeavour that is the production of knowledge. That's why it's important for me to stress that the ideas and approaches that are here have emerged through discussion with so many of the people thanked in this foreword. This is so much of a collaborative work that in some ways it makes me feel ashamed that my name is the only one to appear on the title page. Of course, however, I take full responsibility for the contents!

Note on Spellings/Names

In general, I have used the term 'enslaved person' rather than 'slave'. 'Slave' was an externalized and largely economic category developed by European plantation owners, inherited from Roman law. Its use and origins, therefore, are very different to contexts found in African institutions that are still often called 'slavery' by modern historians. By contrast, the category of an 'enslaved person', as Kwame Nimako and the late Glenn Willemsen argue, recognizes the individuality and humanity of the enslaved, and also the violent force which accompanied their captivities.

Where possible, I have tried to use the generally accepted spellings from the relevant modern nation-state; thus, 'Ouidah' for the port sometimes spelt 'Whydah' in Benin, but 'Hueda' for the precolonial kingdom. I have done my best to be accurate, and apologize for any imperfections that may result.

Glossary

Abirempon – wealthy male power-brokers in coastal towns of the Gold Coast

Abron – ward of an Akan town

Abusua – Fante term for 'lineage'

Afahene – Gold Coast traders

Ahisinon – private traders in Dahomey

Ajo – Yorùbá form of savings bank, widely developed by the nineteenth century

Akonting – stringed instrument payed by the Jola of Senegambia, probably one of the influences in the creation of the banjo

Alafin – ruler of Oyo

Almamate – Islamic state governed by the almamy, a religious and political leader

Ambasys – European term for cloths woven in Benin

Asafo – Akan paramilitary company

Asantehemaa – Queen Mother of Asante

Asantehene – Emperor of Asante

Askia – Islamized name for the Emperor of Songhay (after 1495)

Axé – Yorùbá concept of the life force in all things (also called *aché* in Brazil)

Barafula – cloths woven on the Cape Verde Islands from the late fifteenth century onwards for trade on the mainland, in a style imitating that of Fula weaves in the Sahel

Basorun – head of the council of Oyo-Mesi, influential in choosing each next alafin

Benda – measure of gold on the Gold Coast equivalent to two ounces

Beta – female religious novices in Hueda

Bixirin – name used in some sources for itinerant Islamic trader clerics in the Senegambia region
Brafo – Fante head of state
Ceddo – Wolof for 'warrior'; the warrior class of the old Jolof kingdoms of Senegambia
Cofo – currency measure of 20,000 *nzimbu* in Kongo
Cundi – Kongo woven cloth
Da – King of Segu
Dadá – King of Dahomey
Dakhlo – queen mother in Dahomey
Disongo – annual tribute in Segu
Dobra – coin issued in Portugal
Dyula – itinerant Mande traders in many parts of West Africa
Ejumba – Jola masquerade
Esusu – Yorùbá credit union, widely used by the nineteenth century
Faama – King of Segu
Farim – word used in the Mali Empire to describe a regional governor or administrative overseer
Funda – 1,000 *nzimbu* in Kongo
Griot – the praisesingers of Greater Senegambia and Mali; thought by some to derive from the Portuguese *criado*, or 'servant'
Hassānyi – warrior class of southern Mauritania
Hòrònw – the warrior freemen who fought the wars that helped Segu to expand
Ile Orí – household protective shrine using large numbers of cowries, found among Yorùbá peoples
Jamâ – rank-and-file troops in Oyo
Joliba – local name for the Niger River in Mali
Jòn – Bambara for captive or slave, used in Segu
Kabanko – taxes paid in Kaabu
Kackra – small square pieces of gold used as currency on the Gold Coast
Kanda – Kongo lineage
Kimpasi – healing society in West-Central Africa
Kindoki – sorcery in Kongo
Kola – bitter nut given as a gift widely across West and West-Central Africa, and even used as a form of currency – comes either magenta or white; also found in the Americas throughout this period

Libongo – cloth woven in Loango used as a currency in seventeenth-century Luanda

Lijwaet – Dutch-manufactured cloth, a mainstay of their African trade in the seventeenth century

Lorrendraiers – Dutch traders who had settled on the Gold Coast and had families with Fante wives; from second half of the seventeenth century onwards

Lufuku – 10,000 *nzimbu* in Kongo

Maccudo – word for slave and agricultural worker in Mâssina

Macuta – a bundle of 10 cloths, often Kongo *cundis*

Mai – name of the ruler of Borno

Mamelucos – Brazilians with mixed African and Native American ancestry

Manikongo – King of Kongo, *mani* being the Kikongo word for 'ruler'

Mansa – Manding word for 'ruler' or 'emperor'

Marabout – Islamic leader; also the word used for a diviner drawing on the Qur'ān in parts of Senegambia and Mali

Maraka – Islamic traders of increasing importance in Segu through the eighteenth century

Maravedí – the name for the gold coin in Spain from the eleventh to the fourteenth centuries, and thereafter a unit of account

Mbanza – Kongo town(s)

Migan – Prime Minister of Dahomey

Mithqāl – gold coins in circulation in West Africa by the eighteenth century

Mpu – the crown of office in Kongo, woven from raffia palms

Mwissikongo – the aristocracy of the Kingdom of Kongo

Nganga – spiritual leader in Ndongo and Palmares (Brazil)

Ngola – ruler of Ndongo

Nkisi – spiritual objects in West-Central Africa, especially Kongo and Loango

Nomoli – ancestor-spirit figures from Sierra Leone

Nsi a Bafwa – Kongo world of the dead

Nsibidi – script found in Calabar and Cross River regions of Nigeria

Nyantio – warrior aristocrat in Kaabu

Nza Yayi – Kongo world of the living

Nzimbu – the shell currency of Kongo, harvested on the island of Luanda and later imported by the Portuguese from Brazil

Ofo – staff of office necessary to gain entry to the Ékpè secret society of Calabar

Orixá – Yorùbá god(s); also used by Candomblé practitioners in Brazil and Santería practitioners in Cuba

Oyo-Mesi – ruling council of Oyo

Pano – Portuguese term for 'cloth', used in some sources (including African ones)

Pataca – silver bar mined in Mexico

Qadi – a judge in an Islamic court

Quilombo – military brigade of the Imbangala of West-Central Africa, transposed to Brazil, where, by the late seventeenth century, the institution had transformed itself into militarized communities of maroons, epecially in Palmares, superseding the earlier *mocambo*

Quintal Portuguese weight measure. A *quintal* at this time was equivalent to 128 pounds, or *arráteis* – the *arrátel* was equivalent to 16 ounces, or 1 pound

Sangamento – Kongo initiation and military display

Sarki – ruler of Kano

Secret society – also known in contemporary anthropological literature as a 'sodality'; a religious confraternity or association, often with secret languages of power and communication, and used to mobilize warfare. Secret societies control matters related to social relations, birth, marriage and death in some societies of West and West-Central Africa. This phrase has been retained, rather than using 'sodality', for the sake of clarity and descriptive power

Simboji – Dahomey's royal palace

Soba – chief in Ndongo (Angola)

Sonni – Emperor of Songhay (before 1492)

Soro – cloths woven by Fula people across West Africa

Tabanka – fortified settlement in the Guinea-Bissau region

Terreiro – temple for Candomblé practice in north-eastern Brazil

Tònjònw – military aristocracy of Segu, often former slaves

Torodbe – religiously inspired beggars for alms in Senegambia, proliferating in the eighteenth century

Tsetse – fly that passes on sleeping sickness

Ugie – state festivals in Benin

'Ulamā – scholarly Islamic class in the Sahel

Umma – global Islamic community

Vata – Kongo rural areas

Vodún – Fon word for 'god' or 'deity' (from Hueda), transferred to the New World (especially Haiti)

Wangara – diaspora traders linking up the trans-Saharan trade with cities across the Sahel

Warri – board game found throughout West and West-Central Africa involving scooping beads in a board with wooden cups

Yovogan – Governor of Dahomey at Ouidah, in charge of trade with Europeans

Introduction

On 28 July 1649, Garcia II, the manikongo, sat down to compose a letter to his counterpart, King João IV of Portugal. The Court of the Kongolese king was a luxurious affair, rich with carpets and tapestries from Flanders, cloths woven in India and silver-inlaid dining services and religious ornaments made from the ores of the New World. There were pearls fished by enslaved African divers in the Caribbean, and then sold on by Venetian traders. Beyond the high-status foreign imports, the Court was also filled with woven Kongo cloths inlaid with symbolic meanings, and the manikongo and his chief advisers wore strings of coral beads and red sashes in the Kongo style. Secretaries sat at the manikongo's side and inscribed his letters, which he then signed off with a flourish: for he wrote to the Portuguese king as someone whom he saw as an equal in the 'great game', which at that time took in Atlantic African kingdoms such as Allada, Benin, Denkyira and Kongo, as well as China and the rising European powers.[1]

Almost four centuries later, one of the best visual aides for imagining what this vanished world was like comes from across the Atlantic, from Brazil. From 1630 to 1654, half of the provinces of Brazil were under Dutch occupation. Kongo, as an ally of the Dutch, maintained diplomatic ties with the Dutch Brazilian capital of Olinda (near Recife), just as it did with the United Provinces in Amsterdam, and with the cardinals of the Vatican, and just as it had done with Portugal in the sixteenth century. When Dom Miguel de Castro arrived as the ambassador from Kongo to Olinda in 1643 to make representations to the Dutch governor, Johan Maurits of Nassau, a Dutch artist produced a remarkable portrait of two pages. The artist gives us young men of the princely caste, the *mwissikongo*, dressed in tunics embellished by white collars and fastened by gold buttons, bearing an ivory tusk and a delicate basket.[2]

Pages of the Ambassador of the King of Kongo in Brazil, Dom Miguel de Castro

If they look as if they have stepped out of a European Court, it is because this was the artist's intention. Painting at exactly the same time, Albert Eckhout produced sketches in Brazil from life of how the Kongo Ambassador and his retinue appeared that were more on their own terms. Dom Miguel de Castro and his peers were dressed with the bows and arrows, red sashes of office, and the woven *mpu* crown that symbolized power in the Kongo Court. With outsiders presenting them in different registers for different audiences, these African rulers were adept at displaying the multiple languages of power. In time, this subtle and varied performance of power would become a defining feature of political life on the continent.[3]

Just a few years later, when Garcia II sat down to compose his letter to João IV of Portugal in 1649, the context of this world of princely diplomacy and exchanges had been transformed. While both monarchs were besieged by their enemies and the long-term survival of their kingdoms was still in doubt, the Kongolese were in a far worse position. Although the Portuguese war of independence from Spain (1640–68) still had nineteen years to run, they had thrown out their main imperial rivals, the Dutch, from the slave-trading port of Luanda in Angola the year before, and had also occupied the southern Angolan town of Benguela; five years later, in 1654, Portuguese defeat of the Dutch in Brazil would follow. It was a moment that promised the consolidation of Portuguese imperialism in the South Atlantic – and, with that, the beginning of the end of the old Kongo Kingdom.[4]

Garcia II came out fighting. He was not about to capitulate to a monarch he would never see, who lived thousands of miles away from the Atlantic coast of Africa. 'In spite of our proximity to the Dutch,' he declared to João IV, 'the Catholic Portuguese have done more damage to me in a few months than I received from the Dutch in seven years.' In truth, he had been actively negotiating with the Dutch and plotting the downfall of the Portuguese. The Portuguese fleet under Salvador Correia de Sá had first defeated the Dutch at Luanda, and then his ragtag army of Luso-Brazilian and Tupinambá soldiers had killed thousands of Garcia II's men, and captured many more to sell into slavery. Yet, furious as he was at the violence and the disrespect showed to him as manikongo, Garcia managed to conclude with an olive branch: 'In spite of everything,' he wrote, 'let our sovereign Lord desire it, that the past shall be past.'[5]

There was little in Kongo–Portuguese relations that suggested that this could be possible. The Kongolese had been allies with the Dutch on and off ever since the Dutch had appeared in the 1590s, wanting to trade cloths and ivory instead of enslaved persons. By 1610, diplomatic feelers were being sent out to Amsterdam by the Kongolese. Since their first encounter with the Portuguese, 125 years had passed, and they had tired of them. For years, Portuguese traders had been destabilizing the Kongolese currency, the *nzimbu* – a shell harvested traditionally on an island offshore from Luanda – by bringing in shiploads of the stuff from Brazil to use as money for the slave trade. Meanwhile, the Portuguese colonial settlement at Luanda (founded in 1575) was being used as a springboard for mounting slaving raids against people the manikongos saw as their subjects, in the mountains of the Dembos and Matamba.[6]

By the time the Dutch had seized Luanda from the Portuguese in 1641, the Kongolese were strongly opposed to the slave trade, as Garcia II had made clear in a letter of 23 February 1641 to the Rector of the Jesuits:

> Nothing is more damaging to human beings than ambition, and this city of Luanda was full of it, and, with things going on like that, there could never be peace between us [Kongo] and them. Instead of wanting gold and silver and other things which are used as money everywhere else, the trade and currency here are slaves, who aren't made of gold or cloth but are creatures.[7]

The king articulated in the strongest words the horror of commodifying human beings, which the Portuguese had encouraged by flooding the market with *nzimbu*. It wasn't that the Kongolese themselves were blameless, of course. Far from it, for the manikongos of the sixteenth century had been happy to trade people as long as they had been dealing with those who were not born Kongos. Outsiders to the kingdom were sold at the big market at Malebo Pool on the Congo River.* They were exported by what was much the most powerful state in the forests and rivers of Loango, Cacongo, Kongo and Ndongo, the area stretching between what is now the northern bank of the Congo River and the northern part of Angola. But, as Garcia II noted in his letter to the Jesuits, with a touch of forced naivety, 'our disgrace, and that of my ancestors, is that with our lack of worldliness we allowed this trade to grow along with so many evils in our kingdoms.' The trade itself was shameful, but what was worse for Garcia was the loss of Kongo's honour, so that 'most of all, there are people who claim that we never were kings of Angola and Matamba.'[8]

For Garcia, and for people on all sides of the Atlantic ocean, slavery was connected to ideas of honour. In the new Spanish colonies in America in the sixteenth century, it was the length of a colonist's slave retinue that spoke of their position in society; prestige stood or fell according to the number of slaves that a colonist had to clear the way before them. But, as Garcia II suggests here, for Kongo the

* Between what are now the cities of Brazzaville and Kinshasa.

relationship was flipped on its head: it was the rise of slaving that had damaged Kongo's prestige, and the relentless drive to acquire slaves for Portuguese traders would decisively influence the kingdom's collapse into warring mini statelets by the end of the seventeenth century.[9]

Moreover, while forms of dependence and slavery were important in many different societies in Atlantic Africa before 1500, their practice was being transformed by the Atlantic trade. In Kongo, enslavement gradually became feared by even the highest-status families. This transformation was huge. In most parts of Africa, war captives, criminals and debtors had often become dependants of a powerful family. This condition of dependence was often related to outsider status, where those who had no kin or connections (such as war captives) were vulnerable. However, over time members of these groups could marry, have their own families, and their children (who by now had kin connections) could enter society. There was rarely at this stage the idea of 'cashing in' these relations of debt or power by selling a person to an Atlantic trader; yet these horrors had grown rapidly, as traders sought to take advantage of an economic and political whirlwind that no one really knew how to control.[10]

Garcia II's letters offer an important window on to how members of the Kongo elite had come to understand their own role in early globalization, and the changes it had wrought. They show that in Kongo, as across West and West-Central Africa in the sixteenth, seventeenth and eighteenth centuries, globalization was a fundamentally disruptive influence. But, whereas the growth of trade in this period led to decisive benefits for the 'world economy', through the accrual of capital, and the subsequent investment that triggered the Industrial Revolution, in this part of Africa a different picture emerges. Trade of all kinds certainly increased right across the region, not only in enslaved persons, but also in prestige goods such as jewellery and furniture; in cloths both manufactured locally and imported from Europe and India (the latter often via Brazil); in a number of goods such as tobacco, also imported from Brazil; in provisions; and in different types of currencies. However, instead of increasing the region's prosperity, this trade occurred alongside growing political instability and the relative global impoverishment of the region. By the eighteenth century, some West African states such as Asante and Dahomey were able to reverse this picture, to retain and even to import gold. Others in Senegambia imported large amounts of silver. Yet the picture over the long term was one of the export of 'hard currencies' that retained value over time, not imports. There was little by the way of capital accumulated through the trade of raw or finished goods. Capital accumulation became ever more heavily concentrated in other world regions, and West and West-Central Africa were by the early nineteenth century very much disadvantaged in their access to the capital needed to finance investment and economic growth.[11]

This is a finding that stands in opposition to the weight of ascendant economic theories. Curiously, despite all the evidence showing that increasing global trade does not spread wealth equally, conventional economists in the twenty-first century often hold that greater trade leads to increases in prosperity through the growth of 'the market', and that eventually such wealth trickles down. It is one of the main purposes of this book both to explore the ways in which a different path unfolded in Africa during the era of the Atlantic slave trade, and to consider what the consequences of this have been.[12]

Setting out to assess the causes and consequences of the cumulative economic disempowerment of West and West-Central Africa over a timespan of three or four centuries may seem like a hubristic undertaking. There is a danger that this book will fall into the trap laid by the griot from Naréna in Mali, Mamadou Keita:

What is troubling in the narration of the past, *Is to speak of that which you know nothing.*	*Min kè jugu kòròlenfò dò, i tèmin* *Nya lòn, i ka to k'o fò.*[13]

Grasping the cultural, social, economic and political contours of just one small part of West Africa is a huge undertaking in itself. So why embark on this enterprise, which attempts so much more? One reason is to seek to end the 'provinicializing of Africa'. Historians often write general histories of the Americas, Asia or Europe, in which they deal with anomalies by saying something along the lines of 'Meanwhile, in Portugal/Poland/Italy, it was different.' Those who research Africa have, by contrast, inherited a field developed by colonial anthropologists, who were instrumental in hardening the artificial barriers of ethnic divisions that still belabour Africa to this day. From this perspective, every society in Africa is different. This is, of course, true, for 'Africa is not a country.' But, equally, nor should Africa be exceptionalized so that it cannot be understood through more general connections both within the continent and outside it.

The Dutch portraits from north-eastern Brazil offer a powerful answer as to why the more general approach of this book may be valuable. In addition to the two pages, a remarkable portrait was painted of Dom Miguel de Castro himself, the Ambassador of King Garcia II in Brazil, testament to the diplomatic reach of the Kongo kings in the 1640s.

Dom Miguel de Castro

When we consider these portraits, it is hard not to be brought up short by the almost total failure of mainstream historians to take African kingdoms and their histories seriously when writing about the birth of the modern world. With Africa struck out of 'History' by Hegel, most historians have been painfully slow in pushing back against the stereotypes regarding the 'Africa' of the nineteenth century and before. For Kongo was far from being the only African kingdom to embark on sustained international diplomatic initiatives. In the fifteenth and sixteenth centuries, Jolof ambassadors from Senegambia lived in Portugal, alongside those from the Kingdom of Benin;* in the 1650s, the King of Allada despatched ambassadors to Spain in search of military and religious envoys; in the late eighteenth and the early nineteenth centuries, the kingdoms of Dahomey (in modern Benin) and Onim (located around Lagos) despatched ambassadors several times to the Portuguese authorities in north-eastern Brazil, and thence to Lisbon, where they regularly attended the theatre and the opera, and were patrons of Lisbon's restaurants. Looking north, Borno had regular diplomatic ties with the Ottomans; and there were annual caravans of pilgrims leaving Timbuktu for Mecca into the eighteenth century. Here were collective African diplomatic engagements and geopolitical alliances. Yet their impact has been almost entirely written out of world history.[14]

There have nevertheless been some encouraging signs. The past twenty years have seen a huge boom in studies that show the many different ways in which – even in the shadow of slavery – Africans were decisive actors in building societies in the Americas. Rice-growing technologies from West Africa contributed to the emergence of rice plantations in South Carolina and northern Brazil; livestock and herding skills from West Africa were used by African herders in many parts of the New World, from Louisiana to Argentina; and fencing techniques were imported from West Africa and used in agriculture and in defending communities of runaway slaves (known as maroons). Healing practices from Dahomey and Angola were brought to Brazil and the Spanish Caribbean, and helped to develop new treatments in the colonies; healing practices and medicines were

* Located in the south of what is now Nigeria.

also borrowed by the Portuguese in Angola in an early form of 'bio-prospecting'. Warfare techniques learnt in the Kingdom of Kongo and in the Oyo-Yorùbá Kingdom of what is now southern Nigeria were vital to the success of the Haitian revolution in 1804, as well as to the rebellions against slavery in Brazil and Cuba in the early nineteenth century. In short, just as there were shared frameworks of diplomacy through which Atlantic African kingdoms sought political influence, so the modern world emerged from a mixed cultural framework in which many different peoples from West and West-Central Africa played a significant part.[15]

Yet the specialization of academic historical writing can mean that a huge flood in one field may make very few ripples in many others. Knowledge, like most special privileges in life, and, indeed, like money, does not necessarily 'trickle down'; and knowledge of these studies remains thinly spread. The division into multiple fields and subfields means that people work in splendid isolation; and, in the intellectual silos that result, the wider ramifications of new finds and discoveries for thinking about the historical process are lost. So one key reason for attempting the more general approach envisaged here is precisely to ask what the implications are for the broader picture of both local and world historical change, when we think of the economic history of West and West-Central Africa during the period of the Atlantic slave trade. What are the historical origins of African economic 'underdevelopment'? How did African states change during this era, and how were these changes connected to early globalization? What are the implications of one of the findings of this book: that broadly analogous historical processes took place simultaneously in Africa, Europe and the Americas at this time, especially during the Age of Revolution? On my reading, one conclusion is that these histories did not somehow evolve separately until the rise of colonialism in the nineteenth century, but rather always grew together.

Offering even partial answers to these questions requires a comparative perspective. The very idea of 'Africa' emerged from shared experiences across the continent. The philosopher V. Y. Mudimbe reminds us that 'Africa' was a concept invented in the eighteenth century by Europeans through a racialized worldview. Subsequently, the appropriation of this concept in 'Africa' itself, and consciousness of being 'African' as well as a Kikongo-, Kimbundu-, Wolof- or Yorùbá-speaker, emerged alongside colonialism. The continent took shape after colonialism in the 1960s with a shared experience of the construction of inequalities and hierarchies of race, wealth and labour. That is why the economic question is so important.[16]

Yet Africa also emerged in the twentieth century as a place of amazing, myriad, almost bewilderingly creative complexity. African sculpture and masking inspired the emergence of Cubism, while the use across Africa of manufactured objects in religious shrines resonates in the readymades offered by Marcel Duchamps and Andy Warhol to the modern temples of Art. African musical traditions led to Jazz, Blues and Soul, to Samba and Salsa. African religious traditions influenced the rise of Evangelical Churches, and the nature of shrines used by the Afro-Catholic religions in the New World such as Candomblé in Brazil and Santería in Cuba and New York. In the end, therefore, the economic question cannot be separated from the cultural transformations that took place over the very same period. This is why this book also attempts to consider the cultural frameworks that reconfigured and disrupted the patterns of growing economic inequality.

This interwoven relationship of economic and cultural transformation, and the associated issue of inequality, is the broader reason to focus here on the region as a whole. Just as there was a collective experience of political relationships and of the emergence of ideas of 'Africanness' in this period, so the process of economic disempowerment is one of the things that binds together histories of the peoples of the region. To take a contemporary question, for instance, one of the things people across the continent have in common today is their economic reliance on remittances from relatives who have made it to richer places, and the desire they have to try to make it there themselves. To understand this shared perspective, it is necessary to look at the capital underpinnings of this economic relationship, and to try to grasp the economic framework that promoted an increase in trade, at the same time as it promoted an increase not in wealth but in inequality.[17]

Beyond this current resonance, a spotlight on the deeper African past belies enduring prejudices that 'Africa has no history.' This is such an old canard that it is staggering to realize that such ideas still structure no small part of public discourse. Of course some Western public institutions do increasingly cover broader themes in African history and culture, as recent exhibitions at the British Library (on West Africa), at the Metropolitan Museum of Art in New York (on Kongo) and at Paris's Musée du Quai Branly demonstrate. Henry Louis-Gates Jr's recent TV series on African civilizations also acted as a valuable corrective. Nevertheless, when much of the mainstream Western media turns to Africa, it far too often fixates on war and conflict, on famine or on Africa's 'amazing wildlife', instead of on its creative, resourceful and brilliant people. Both inside and outside the continent, professionalized historians of Africa concentrate mainly on the twentieth century, which means that the ruins of old cities, the evidence of precolonial industry and manufacturing, and the ways in which these then declined in the colonial era are all left untouched.[18]

The cultural framework and older historical questions that structure this book, especially in its second part, ensure that an alternative view of the past can be presented. By looking at cultural transformations in the context of economic inequalities, the idea of a 'static' and 'unchanging' African past can be consigned to the bin. Moreover, this focus is connected to the book's broader economic concerns; as was recognized by Amílcar Cabral, the leader of Guinea-Bissau's War of Independence against the Portuguese (1960–74), a historical view must recognize the 'complementarity existing between the cultural fact and the economic (and political) fact in the functioning of human societies'.[19]

Through this approach, the inequities produced by the slave trade are addressed, but there is also a move beyond a reductive focus on slavery alone. African history must not be reduced to that of slavery; and yet slavery must not be avoided or ignored. Indeed, slavery, of course, affected cultural change, in Europe every bit as much as in Africa. Cycles of slavery were intimately connected to the first cycles of credit and indebtedness. Modern institutional loansharks are inheritors of much earlier forms of predatory proto-capitalism from the past.

Here I am reminded of the observation of the English surgeon Alexander Falconbridge, in the 1780s, who to my eyes anticipated the future of the cycles of debt and credit of modern financial institutions in Africa. Falconbridge wrote of the River Bonny, an arm of the Niger

Delta, one of the major slave-trading zones of the later eighteenth century, that it 'abounds with sharks of a very large size, which are often seen in almost incredible numbers about the slave ships, devouring with great dispatch the dead bodies of the negroes [*sic*] as they are thrown overboard'. By the time Falconbridge wrote this, these sharks had their own history of eating captives, over countless generations.[20]

The specific origins of this book came from a research trip I made to The Gambia, Senegal and Guinea-Bissau in April and May 2011. Although I had spent long periods in these countries in the late 1990s and early 2000s, in more recent years I had been concentrating my research on the Cape Verde archipelago, and so I was looking forward to my visit. I had not been planning to research the histories of currency and inequality but, on arriving at Banjul, I found myself in the midst of a typical West African economic exchange. In return for three crisp 50-euro notes, my friend sent off for some local money exchangers, and I received so many Gambian dalasi notes in return that I needed a plastic bag to carry them. As my friend passed me the bundles of notes, and I gave him the three notes in return, I remarked fatuously to him that this was not very fair.

I had had similar experiences before, with Guinea-Bissau's peso currency in the mid 1990s, but this for me was the moment when the direct nature of unequal economic exchanges was foregrounded. The Gambia was a country with dynamic traders, full of energy and ingenuity, but without the potential to realize any capital gains at all. A pump attendant at the petrol station where my friend worked was paid the equivalent of less than 30 dollars per month; and my friend, who managed the forecourt, mini supermarket, mechanic's workshop and the restaurant, was paid less than 100 dollars per month to supervise these four outlets and the twenty-four staff who worked there. What were the historical processes that had given rise to the type of exchange that it was possible to have in West Africa in 2011, where three banknotes could be exchanged for hundreds? These were exchanges that seemed 'normal', 'the way things were'. Often, though, it is the things that seem most normal that are most worthy of attention. Why were these exchanges normal, and why was it that the access to capital in Africa and Europe was so very different?

As I proceeded with further research, I realized that there was, in fact, a huge amount of archival material related to the exchanges of currencies in the era of the Atlantic trade. The stereotyped view of Africans bartering slaves for baubles could not have been further from the truth. That assumed that money could be only coin, whereas when this trade began people around the world accepted a variety of materials as currency. Europeans brought iron bars, cloths, cowries and copper for trade, all of which were used as currencies in West Africa and were imported as part of a monetary financial exchange; in this way, they mirrored earlier imports across the Sahara of salt, which was also used as a form of currency in the Sahel. That is not to say that these imports 'invented' money in West Africa, for in almost all cases these imports from European traders added to an existing monetary base. It is worth stressing that, at the time, these types of currencies were not unheard of in Europe either: Icelandic sagas such as *Njál's Saga* make it clear that cloth was a form of currency in areas of medieval Europe, and, as the English historian Craig Muldrew has shown, many regions of England did not have much coin and resorted to credit currencies to maintain their economies well into the seventeenth century. What was happening with currency in West Africa was, then, a normal aspect of monetary exchanges in this period of history.[21]

Here alone was an interesting story. For it shows that the first economic exchanges between Africa and Europe were not through barter, but were monetized. Indeed, the idea of a 'primitive' barter economy has recently been shown to be a myth invented by economists to simplify Western theoretical models of economic growth. Like most myths, it has little grounding in reality, and many West African peoples had complex economic systems in the 1500s, in which credit and multiple currencies intersected. In other words, in the fifteenth and sixteenth centuries, West Africa had long had market economies. However, since the 1980s, the broader question of the relationship of these currency exchanges to Africa's history of economic underdevelopment has not been properly examined. As I found more material on this question in European and Latin American archives, this seemed to me to be a big mistake.[22]

Just as historians of Africa have in general passed over this question, so, too, have the new wave of 'global' historians. The much debated book by Thomas Piketty not only has no place for Africa before the late twentieth century in it, but it also defines 'capital' so as to specifically exclude 'human capital', including wealth produced by slavery ('a special case'). Meanwhile, Sven Beckert's recent history of global capitalism focuses, like Piketty's, on the period after the 1780s. Both approaches take the preceding 300 years almost for granted, as if it was inevitable that they would lead to a concentration of wealth and capital in Western countries, which were then able to invest this capital in developing new industrial technologies. By contrast, the approach of this book is to focus on this earlier period, in an attempt to understand the processes by which the capital imbalances between Africa and Western powers came about.[23]

By and by, as I conducted my research on this earlier period, an overall picture emerged. This book focuses on the era before and during the Atlantic slave trade. It looks at those parts of West and West-Central Africa that were connected both to one another and to the Atlantic economy, however distantly in some cases. The first half of this book argues that economic inequality between West and West-Central Africa and the rest of the Western hemisphere arose from inequalities in the exchange of economic value. For several centuries, Western African societies exported what we might call 'hard currencies', especially gold; these were currencies that, on a global level, retained their value over time. For the first two centuries of Atlantic trade, these societies also imported large amounts of goods that were used as currencies: cowries, copper, cloth and iron. However, these were what we might call 'soft currencies', which were losing their relative value over time, as opposed to gold and silver.[24]

By 1700, therefore, centuries of trade had been grounded in inequalities of the exchange of economic value, with the 'purchasing power' of the currencies in use in West and West-Central Africa lagging behind. The capacity for capital accumulation had grown, by contrast, outside the continent, with the rising stocks of 'hard currencies'. What this meant in practice was that a Chinese, or Mexican, or American trader with access to silver could use that silver in multiple markets, which, of course, helped that currency to retain its value. While many economies did use copper or iron currencies in the 1500s and 1600s, however, this diminished over time; and with this decline went a comparable decline in the relative purchasing power of African consumers.

A further layer to these inequalities of the exchange of value came through the slave trade – which was anything but a 'special case' in this period. As is well known, African societies exported large numbers of enslaved captives, whose labour was therefore both lost to the continent and gained by the European empires of the Atlantic world to aid their economic development. In the mid nineteenth century, it was Karl Marx who showed the connection between surplus labour and the accumulation of capital. For Marx, it was the extraction of surplus labour that allowed the production of 'surplus value', and capital accumulation. Thus, the slave trade and its production of labour outside Africa was also a key element of the growing economic differential between Africa and the European empires in the Atlantic world. The exchange value of the goods traded for captives was inevitably lower in real terms than the surplus value that could be produced through slave labour in the New World, and thus to the unequal currency exchanges were added the inequalities in economic development and capital accumulation that can be attributed to the slave trade.[25]

These transformations were especially marked in the first two centuries of the trade with European empires. During that period, the major goods traded by Europeans were not mere 'baubles', but currencies such as copper manillas, cowries, cloth and iron. Yet, while the money supply and the market increased, a huge increase in the supply of 'trade goods' failed to occur at the same time. Traditional economic theories posit that an increase in currency supply without an increase in the supply of goods for that money to be spent on causes inflation. Inflation meant that the cost of locally manufactured goods made in West Africa increased, and they were often unable to compete with foreign imports that were essentially dumped there. It was only after the 1650s, when large numbers of 'trade goods' began to be imported alongside currencies, that this pattern changed; and it was really only in the 1690s that the value of imported trade goods overtook the value of imported currencies in areas such as the Gold Coast and the Bight of Benin. However, by this time, the terms of trade had been set; and, indeed, in spite of this, inflation continued in many regions throughout the eighteenth century.[26]

Working through this core argument as I consulted the relevant material, I realized that the book needed to be divided into two parts. My hope is that the structure will allow readers to assimilate so much new material in an accessible way, while allowing the argument as a whole to take shape. The first part of the book looks at five core regions of West and West-Central Africa, between around 1300 and 1680, when the import of trade goods over currencies finally started to predominate: these are the Sahelian zones of Borno, Kano, Mali and Songhay; the Greater Senegambia region; the Gold Coast; the Bights of Benin and Biafra; and the Kingdom of Kongo in West-Central Africa. Each chapter in this part offers a case study, in which new evidence places these dynamics of unequal exchange in the context of the economic and political histories of these regions. Taken as a whole, these cases reveal many of the fundamental causes of economic inequality.

The second part of the book runs from around 1680 to the early nineteenth century. Each chapter is structured thematically, not chronologically, allowing readers to get a better sense of the connections between different regions over a broad span of time. The second part as a whole looks at the consequences of these earlier processes. These emerge through social and cultural transformations, and the rise of the revolutions from below in the eighteenth and early-nineteenth centuries. There are strong parallels found here between political changes in Africa and those in Europe. In West Africa, as in Europe, the rise of the 'fiscal-military state' grew in the seventeenth and eighteenth centuries, and, with it, powerful aristocracies. In West Africa, as in Europe, popular forces led by the trading class came to challenge these aristocracies; in both regions, the 1780s and 1790s witnessed decisive revolutionary movements. The book argues that this is not a mere 'coincidence': the transnational connections of West Africa with the Americas, Europe and the Middle East contributed to events in all these world regions, and transformed the world. Yet the unequal economic foundations of this relationship, traced in the first part of the book, meant that the consequences of these revolutions would be very different; and that these processes would pave the way for formal colonialism in the nineteenth century.

*

This book, of course, takes its title from cowrie shells. Cowries were one of the major forms of currency across West Africa, from the Niger Delta to the empires of the Sahel, and were used from the thirteenth to the nineteenth centuries. They were brought from the Maldive Islands on the dhow route to East Africa, as well as through the caravan trade across the Sahara, before the Portuguese began to bring them by sea around the Cape of Good Hope in the sixteenth century. They were an exceptionally practical form of money, because they did not degrade and because they were easily transported, first by sea, and then by porter or mule from the North or West African coasts inland. In the earlier period dealt with in this book the smaller *moneta* cowrie from the Maldive Islands predominated, but in the nineteenth century the larger *annulus* cowrie took over in increasingly large quantities.[27]

Cowrie monies remain deeply inscribed in public memory; the Akan word for 'cowrie' as a currency was *sedee*, and the cedi is the currency of Ghana today, while a cloth design widely found in Togo, Benin and Ghana called the *bceao* (the acronym for the Central Bank of Francophone West Africa) is imprinted with a series of cowries.[28] There are, too, other forms of memory. In the Ondo-Yorùbá area of southern Nigeria, the archaeologist Akinwumi Ogundiran describes one origin myth that tells how cowries were brought to the region as a form of money by vultures. As Ogundiran summarizes it, these vultures could represent both European slave traders and African slave raiders: 'vultures feed mainly on carrion and they symbolize

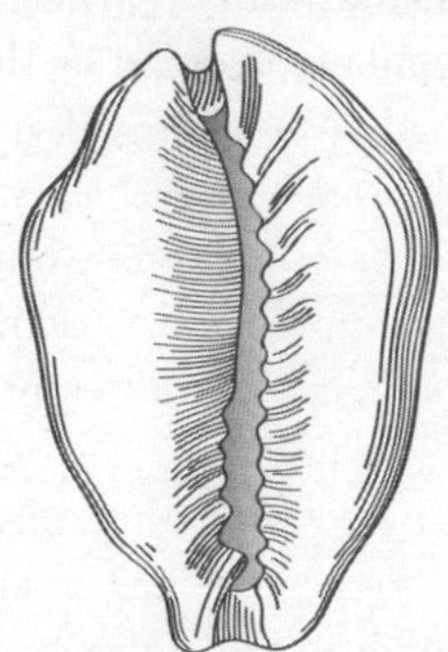

Linnaeus's drawing of the *moneta* cowrie.

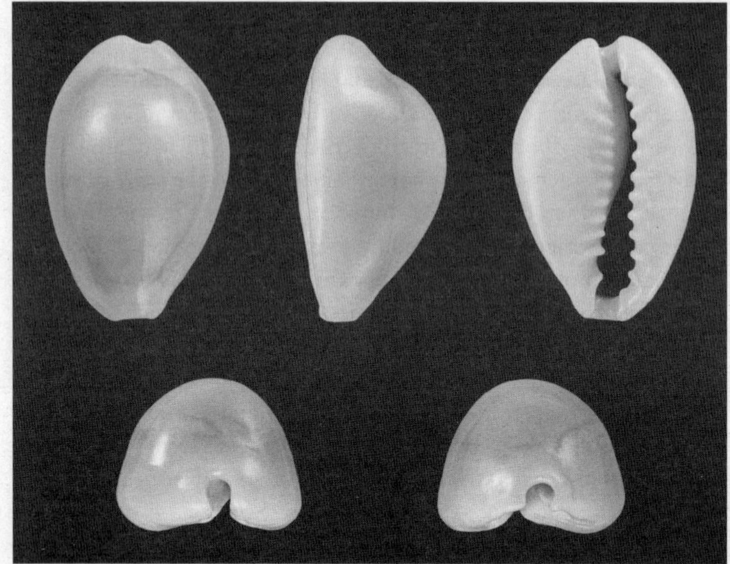

The *annulus* cowrie.

greedy and ruthless people who prey on others, but in the narrative they heralded the introduction of cowries.'[29]

Cowries became associated not just with such memories of violence but also with the ritual functions that developed around them. These are well described by the griot historian Lansiné Diabaté in his accounts of the founder of the Empire of Mali, Sunjata Keita. At one point, Diabaté discusses an 'honest merchant' of Sunjata's age, Ase Bilali, and reveals the relationship between cowrie money and religious power:

When Ase Bilali was leaving	*Ase Bilali waat əla,*
A hunter also gave him a commission:	*donsokɛ də fana y'i sar 'a la*
That if he arrived, and went to Sami	*ko n'a sera . . . a waara Sami*
And if he found cowries there	*a ko n'a da koronkisɛ sərə,*
That he should bring some back to him	*a ka n'a d'a ma,*
So that he could put them on his fetish [shrine].	*a b'a la a ya fila kan.*[30]

These histories remind us of the danger of adopting a purely capital view of money and power in West African history. Among the Igbo of the Niger Delta, the copper manillas (*armringen* in Dutch) imported through Atlantic trade were not all to be melted down and 'spent' in the local economy, but, on the contrary, had to be accumulated in order to enter the powerful Ékpè secret society. By the early twentieth century, 900 manillas were required to take the first step into the Ékpè, and further fees were required in order to be given an *ofo*, or personal staff of office. Thus, the hoarding of manillas for these purposes created a different economic dynamic in which economic accumulation and religious power were inextricable.[31]

It is also true that some of the economic surplus was used in European cultures to acquire objects of religious value, especially by ruling royal families. This was especially true in the sixteenth and seventeenth centuries, when the gold from Africa and silver from the New World found its way into the altarpieces of the Catholic world. Silver also functioned as a way of displaying status in the eighteenth century. However, over time, the growing use of money to acquire status and property through capital accumulation in European societies marked a different approach to economic value from that seen in many parts of West Africa. By the eighteenth century displaying gold in religious spaces was less and less a feature of European religious architecture, and this marked a divergence in economic and religious worldviews.

What was true of the Igbo and the Ékpè cult was true elsewhere with regard to cowries. Cowries became very important to Yorùbá religious practice by the nineteenth century, filling each household's *Ile Orí*, protective shrines hidden from public view. The importance of these shrines was described by the Yorùbá historian Samuel Johnson in the early twentieth century:

> [This is] the universal household deity worshipped by both sexes as the god of fate ... The representing image is 41 cowries strung together in the shape of a crown. This is secreted in a large coffer, the lid of which is of the same form and material. It is called 'Ile Ori' (Ori's house), and in size is as large as the owner can afford to make it. Some usually contain as much as 6 heads (12,000) of cowries.[32]

Ile Orí.

An illustration of this religious power is that 20 per cent of cowries found during one dig at Isoya were located in grave goods. Meanwhile, in The Gambia, oral histories recount the important use of cowries as forms of divination. Thus, across West Africa, examples emerge to challenge a second core tenet of economic theory: the 'rational choice model'. It is the nature of the 'rational choice' itself that must be questioned, for what is 'rational' in one society is not so in another; and, in West Africa, rational economic activities involved hoarding money and using it not for material accumulation but for the accumulation of ritual prestige. Where there was abundant gold, for instance, as in Katsina in the late eighteenth century, it was retained in people's houses as a mark of status. Where cloth currencies were used for elaborate royal burials, as in Kongo in the late eighteenth century, illustrations reveal enormous bundles around the body of the deceased member of the elite. What emerges are different worldviews, neither better nor worse than one another, but all able to reveal the potential for difference in these societies' perspectives on value.[33]

The examples above, as well as many others, show that it is simply impossible to gain an accurate and complex understanding of these distant histories without balancing written and oral materials. Over-reliance on oral accounts has its own risks, because these are not fixed and change from generation to generation. But exclusive reliance on written sources will tend to reproduce a purely European view of history, and the assumption that specific European institutional economic frameworks are 'universal', since this is what appears in 'the sources'. The drivers of historical change will then be seen in a traditional manner, as coming from outside Africa rather than emerging from an interplay of external and internal forces.[34]

By contrast, in this book I draw on both sorts of records to explore the dynamism of political change in West Africa as a response to the gathering economic and political inequalities of the slave-trade era. When, in the later eighteenth century, a series of social movements emerged to implement a revolution from below, this resulted in the overthrow of what had become predatory aristocracies grown rich through negotiating with parasitic forces from outside the continent. The reasons for this political transformation did not lie in outside factors, but in the ways in which historical change was experienced locally.

Writing African history in this period does not thus have to present insurmountable problems in terms of sources. Nor does it have to confirm prejudices, because it emerges that both in West and West-Central Africa societies were globalizing, and had complex market economies and global diplomatic links. They were also producing the cultural forms that decisively shaped modern art, religion and music – that were, in fact, key in the formation of the modern world. Nor does such a history have to be negative, concentrating only on the horrors of slavery; it must, of course, acknowledge these, but this history also shows how oppressed people rose up and overthrew their oppressors, while recognizing how the economic circumstances that accompanied these processes have dealt the inheritors of these histories a bad hand.

Histories are complex, far beyond the simplistic narratives so often presented. How did women respond to the increasing export of men in the slave trade, and did this give them greater autonomy over their lives, or rather lead to heavier workloads and demands? And what drove young men into warfare, raids and the captivity of one another during the slave-trade era? Part of the answers to these questions is economic, and part the political stranglehold of elites; but part also derives from the social consequences of all of this, and how these consequences were experienced. One hunting song of the Manding from Mali expresses the sentiment as well as any, at least insofar as it was experienced by men:

> At that time money was a lot heavier, of course! The wind didn't blow it in as quickly as it does today! No, it didn't, of course not! Ever since banknotes arrived, Yes! Their only use is in marrying women . . . That's right! You know, my friend, in the past it was difficult to marry young; ah! It was very difficult.[35]

PART ONE

Causes

Economic Divergence in West and West-Central Africa

Timelines for Part One

1 AFRICA AND ATLANTIC HISTORY, *c.* 1400–1680

1413: Portuguese 'voyages of discovery' begin along the African coast following the capture of Ceuta in Morocco

1442: Portuguese sailors arrive at the River Senegal

1444: First African captives sold in Europe, at Lagos in Portugal

1448: Diogo Gomes is the first European to travel far inland in West Africa, several hundred miles up the Gambia River

1453: Ottoman Empire seizes Constantinople; Portuguese efforts to navigate down the African coast are redoubled to seek a mythical Christian king (Prester John) to ally against the Ottomans

1471: Genoa sends traders to Saharan oases to try to gain better access to gold trade in rivalry with Portuguese; Portuguese traders first arrive on the Gold Coast

1482: Portuguese build a castle at Elmina on the Gold Coast to cement their gold trade

c. 1486: Portuguese arrive at Benin's coastal port of Gwatón

1488: Bumi Jeléen, the Jolof prince, arrives in Portugal to seek support in a conflict with a rival claimant to the Jolof crown

c. 1490: Benin sends an embassy to João II of Portugal

1500: By this date the goldfields of Ghana and Cote d'Ivoire are supplying 30,000 ounces of gold a year to Portugal

1514–16: Oba Ozolua sends an ambassador to Lisbon; Portugal then gives military assistance to Benin against Igala invaders (1515–16)

1530s: Kongo ambassadors begin to be received at the Vatican, which remains the case on and off throughout the next 150 years

1531–9: Benin refuses to trade male slaves to the Portuguese (1530); Portuguese send a failed evangelizing mission to Benin in 1539 and then start to withdraw from engaging with Benin

1571–2: Francis Drake seeks help from maroons in Panamá

1575: Foundation of the city of Luanda by the Portuguese

c. 1575–90: Traders from São Tomé begin slave trading at Allada. The slave trade from Allada grows rapidly from 1600 to 1640

1578: Moroccan forces destroy a Portuguese army at the Battle of Alcácer Quibir

1590s: Dutch begin trading for copper and textiles on the Loango coast, north of the estuary of the River Congo

1595: Major slave uprising on São Tomé sees destruction of many sugar plantations and decline of the island's sugar industry

1606: Kongo's coastal province of Nsoyo begins to send diplomatic feelers to the Dutch

c. 1607–94: Foundation and consolidation of the longest-lasting maroon society in the Americas, Palmares in Pernambuco (Brazil), which was eventually defeated by a Brazilian military force

1617: Foundation of Benguela by the Portuguese in what is now southern Angola

1622: The Kongo Army, under Pedro II, defeats the Portuguese at Mbanda Kasi

1624: Dutch seize Bahia in Brazil from the Portuguese and send a fleet to Angola, hoping to capture Luanda, but the manikongo refuses to cooperate

1630: Dutch seize northern captaincies of Brazil from the Portuguese

1637: The Dutch conquer the fort of Elmina from the Portuguese

1640–70: Mini ice age causes widespread ecological upheaval and triggers political insecurity in many parts of West and West-Central Africa

1640s: English ships start arriving along the Gold Coast and in the Bights of Benin and Biafra from London and Barbados to trade for slaves

1641: Dutch seize Luanda and São Tomé from the Portuguese

1642–3: Kongo and Nsoyo send ambassadors to the Dutch in Brazil and the United Provinces

1648: A Brazilian fleet recaptures Luanda and São Tomé from the Dutch
1654: Dutch are defeated by Brazilian troops and ejected from Brazil
1665: A Luso-Brazilian army routs the Kongo Army and destroys its aristocracy at the Battle of Mbwila, triggering a civil war that lasts until 1709
1671: Portuguese defeat the Ngola of Ndongo at Pungo Andongo

2 WEST AND WEST-CENTRAL AFRICAN POLITICAL HISTORY, *C.* 400–1680

400 CE: City of Jenne-jenò in the Middle Niger has grown to 4,000 inhabitants
900 CE: Gold from the forests of Ghana and Cote d'Ivoire found in North African mints in increasing quantities
c. 900–1000 CE: Ilé-Ifè founded, the spiritual centre of Yorùbá culture
1070–1100: The Kingdom of Kanem-Borno converts to Islam and becomes important in the trans-Saharan trade. Regular pilgrimages to Mecca via Cairo of the Borno kings begin in the 1100s
1200: Kano's city walls completed by this date; further south in Nigeria, Nupe's power grows
c. 1200–1250: Rise of the Mali Empire under Sunjata Keita; after 1250, it expands towards the Atlantic coast through Tiramakang Traoré to Kaabu
c. 1270–1300: Brass casters from Ilé-Ifè teach the practice to the Bini at Edo (Benin)
1324–5: Pilgrimage of Mansa Musa, Emperor of Mali, to Mecca via Cairo
1330s: Djinguereber Mosque built in Timbuktu with some influence from Andalusia in southern Spain
1350–90: Wangara traders bring Islam to Kano with trade
1370–1420: *Eredos* built in south-western Nigeria
c. 1400: Foundation of Mbanza Kongo and consolidation of the Kongo Kingdom
1400–1450: Rise of the Mossi Kingdom (Burkina Faso) and formation of Dogon communities in the Bandiagara escarpment (Mali)

1433–74: Emergence of Songhay to rival Mali for imperial power; with the loss of Timbuktu to Songhay in 1468 to their ruler Sonni 'Alī

*c.*1440–70: Benin's power grows under Oba Ewuare

c. 1450–1575: The Ókìpò Wars pit Igala, Nupe, Benin and other states of south-central Nigeria against one another

1470s: The capital of Borno moves south to the fortified redoubt of Ngazargamu

c. 1490–1510: Migrations of Koli Tenguella and his establishment of the Fula Kingdom of Fuuta Tòòro on north bank of the Senegal River

1492: Death of Sonni 'Alī, ruler of Songhay. He is replaced by Askia Mohammed in 1494, who inaugurates the great age of Songhay

1500–1550: Rise of Denkyira Kingdom inland from the Gold Coast, due north of Elmina

1500–1550: The Jolof Empire in Senegambia begins to fragment into five constituent provinces

1506–9: Civil wars in Kongo at the death of the first Christian king (João I) see the triumph of the Christian faction under Afonso I, who rules until 1543

1546–63: Time of famine in Borno

1565–1650: Sporadic war fought between Kano and Katsina in northern Nigeria

1568: Mbanza Kongo invaded by a force of Jaga rebels from the east of the kingdom; the manikongo is only restored with the help of Portuguese forces in 1570

1577–8: People of Elmina ally with Portuguese to defeat Fetu, until then the major power by the Gold Coast

1591: Fall of Songhay to an invasion from Morocco

1595–1630: After the fall of Songhay, a series of small statelets called the Arma form in its place

c. 1600: Oyo checks Nupe's advance in southern Nigeria and begins to grow

c. 1600: Imbangala forces begin to attack kingdoms of Ndongo and Matamba in Angola

Seventeenth century (?): Large walled cities built in Loropeni (Burkina Faso)

1644–80: Time of famine in Borno and across many parts of the Sahel to Senegambia

1665–1700: The Battle of Mbwila triggers a series of civil wars in Kongo and the collapse of the Kongo Kingdom

1673–7: Nasir al-Din, a cleric from Mauritania, leads a failed revolt against the established kingdoms on the Senegal River, connected to their engagement with Atlantic trade. He is killed in 1674, and, by 1677, the kingdoms are back in the hands of their rulers, the Fula Denyaanke

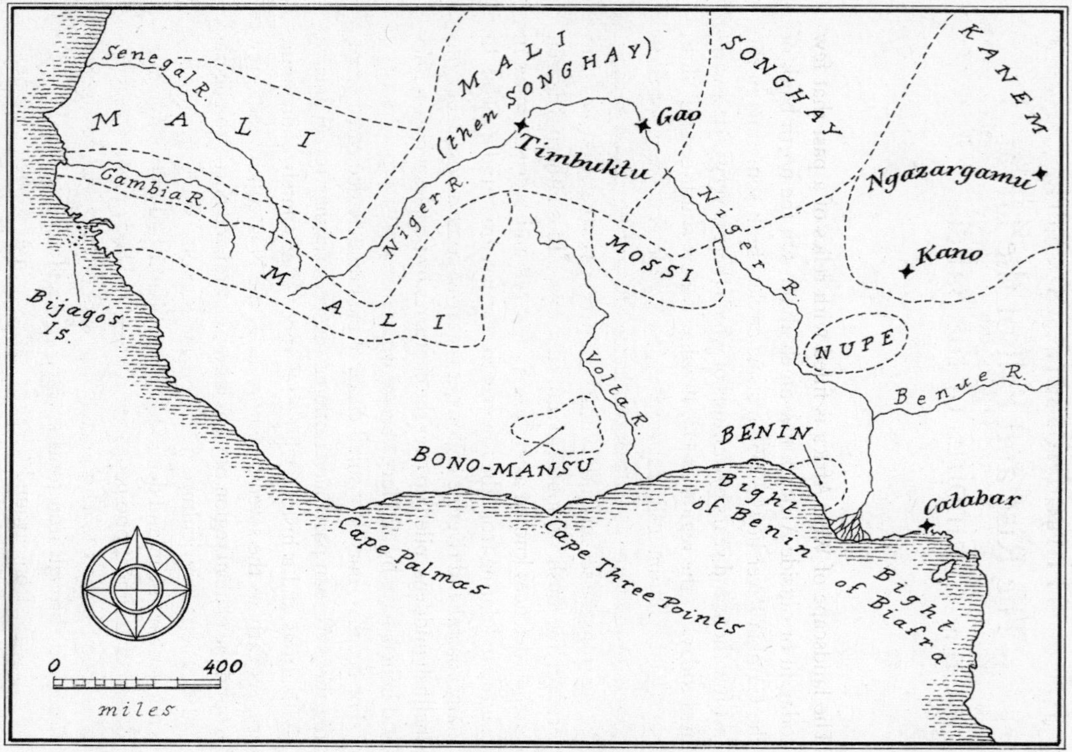

Medieval West African empires and states

I

'Three Measures of Gold': The Rise and Fall of the Great Empires of the Sahel

The landscape of West Africa is filled with relics of a past that few today in or outside Africa know much about. On the north bank of the Gambia River lie the Wassu stone circles, built sometime in the last few thousand years by cultures of which there is very little awareness today. In the region of Dô, in what is now south-central Mali, huge fields of tumuli lie scattered across a wide area, some of them 50 feet in diameter. The large walled fortress of Loropéni, perhaps dating from the seventeenth century, or perhaps earlier, now lies scattered in the bush of southern Burkina Faso. In southern Nigeria, earthen defences known as *eredos*, 33 feet tall and over 100 miles in length, and dating from the fourteenth century, are found in Ijebu. In many coastal and riverine regions, it is easy to come across enormous shellfish middens, piled up over the centuries by peoples whose names and beliefs have by and large been forgotten.[1]

For decades, outside a small circle of passionately dedicated scholars, these African pasts have suffered neglect. Yet they reveal ancient civilizations and a history whose relevance is absolutely contemporary. As early as the seventh century BCE, the Nok culture that grew around the plateau region of what is now central and northern Nigeria had developed agriculture and iron production. The settlement of Jenne-jenò in the inland delta of the Niger River had grown to a population of around 4,000 people by 400 CE, and had grown to as many as 26,000 by 800 CE. This growth was supported by rice production developed through iron tools smelted by local smiths. The iron ore was brought from around 30 miles away, while copper ornaments found in burial chambers probably came from much further afield, in the Sahara. Meanwhile, digs in the Upper Senegal River Valley have shown a similar trade in copper artefacts by around 500–700 CE, where they were traded for cloth produced on spindle-looms.[2]

Kneeling female figure (ceramic), from the Inner Niger Bend.

For most historians, though, Africa has always been 'outside history'. It is, after all, easy enough to dismiss something when you know little or nothing about it. Yet globalization came so early to many parts of Africa that one Chinese chronicle claims that ambassadors from the region of Ethiopia went to the Chinese Court around 150 BCE. It's hard to imagine the Celts or the Jutes before the time of Christ doing the same. African trade connections expanded rapidly, especially after around the year 700 CE. By around 1000, Madagascar was linked to China through the trading town of Kilwa, located on an island off the coast of southern Tanzania and founded by a Persian sultan in the eleventh century. Many artefacts of Chinese porcelain found in recent excavations of Kilwa have confirmed the very extensive long-distance connections here from an early time.[3]

In West Africa, the pattern is similar. Early cave paintings from the era of Jenne-jenò reveal chariots with wheels, suggesting that this was a technology known in West Africa, either from long-distance trade to the Mediterranean or through local use. Analysis by archaeologists of the gold coins used in Tunis and Libya suggests a major change around the ninth century CE, when gold from the forest regions of what are now Ghana and Ivory Coast was dug out in large quantities and exported through networks of local traders. By the eleventh century, there were important mints in cities from Siğilmāsa in Morocco to a variety of cities along the Mediterranean coast, and the trans-Saharan trade from the states of West Africa influenced the commercial and cultural worlds of Al-Andalus in Spain.[4]

If this surprises some readers, it is because 'History' as a subject has developed a rather selective memory over the years. There was a time when this was well known to many. One example is the Catalan Atlas, compiled by the Majorcan Jewish cartographer Abraham Cresques in around 1375. Here, the Emperor of Mali (*rey Melli*) sits enthroned with a sceptre and golden crown, dressed in elegant robes. In his right hand he extends a golden nugget to a North African trader, mounted on horseback, who emerges, his face wrapped in cloth, from the nomadic encampments of the Western Sahara. Across the Atlas Mountains, trade routes crisscross the desert towards North Africa, and some of them extend across the Mediterranean to the Iberian Peninsula. It is a powerful representation of the ways in which West African kings interacted with the Mediterranean worlds through the gold trade almost 650 years ago. It shows us how keen European rulers were to find out about Africa, and that, in fact, some of them already knew quite a bit about it.[5]

From his Majorcan home, Cresques designed the Atlas using information from travellers who knew both North Africa and the trans-Saharan trading routes. Cresques also built on the well-known pilgrimage of the Emperor of Mali, Mansa Musa, to Mecca in 1324–5; and he relied on long-standing trade routes linking Jewish communities in Saharan oases such as Tuwāt in Algeria and Siğilmāsa in Morocco with both West African kingdoms further south and Jewish

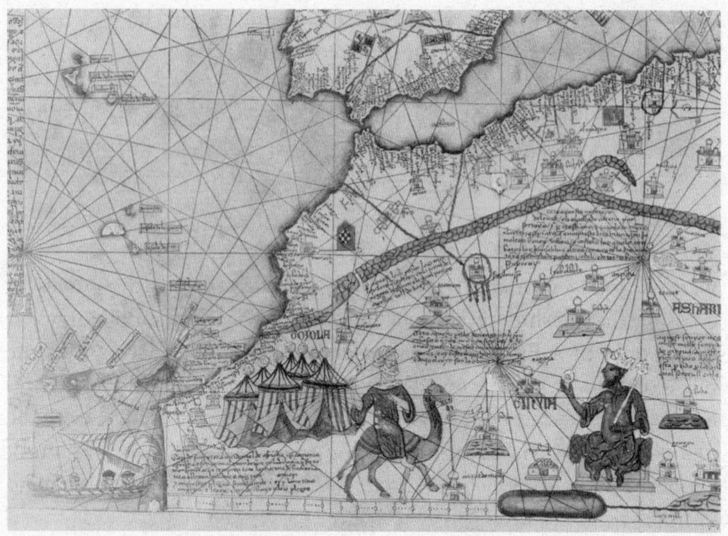

Detail from the Catalan Atlas, 1375 (vellum), by Abraham Cresques (1325–87).

communities in the Iberian worlds. Looked at like this, the Atlas is the product of centuries of cross-cultural exchange. Cities of the Mediterranean world such as Cairo, Lisbon, Seville and Tripoli did not impose themselves on West Africa and dominate their peoples; instead, West African and Mediterranean societies emerged like the Catalan Atlas, through trade and reciprocal exchanges.[6]

This chapter suggests how the histories of West African peoples and states before the rise of Atlantic trade require a rethink of embedded ideas. The Catalan Atlas speaks of networks and pathways of connection that have been covered over by the dust of time. The idea of Jewish mapmakers from the Balearic Islands having connections in distant Mali startles, just as, fifteen years ago, walking in the backyard of a house in Assomada, in the highlands of the largest Cape Verdean island of Santiago, I was startled to come across a Jewish tombstone inscribed in Hebrew – testament to a more recent movement and migration from Morocco to these African Atlantic islands in the nineteenth century. It turns out that, far from matching the Eurocentric stereotype of being static and responsive to external pressures, West African history embodies constant change, innovation and reciprocal influence with the outside world.

SAHELIAN EMPIRES AND THE GOLD TRADE

The keystone of these early connections was the gold trade. Why were so many North African traders willing to risk their lives in crossing the harsh desert, if not in search of 'the golden country'? It is not only in a European map such as the Catalan Atlas that the place of gold in such distant West African history is clear. The oral history transmitted even in the past twenty years in the Casamance region of southern Senegal describes how the King of the Bainunk people – themselves heavily connected to the Mande peoples, who founded the Mali Empire – always sat on a golden chair. Gold offered rulers masks of power, which they adopted very readily long before the era of 'European discoveries'.[7]

In West Africa, historical memories speak to the importance of gold in distant history, attributing the birth of the Empire of Mali to gold: 'three measures of gold' (*saba samun* in Maninka), as some versions of the epic oral narrative of the life of Sunjata Keita, founder of the Mali Empire (*fl.* 1235), recount it. In the version of the epic recounted by the oral historian Lansiné Diabaté of Kela in present-day Mali, it is possession of the *saba samun* that enshrines power in the hands of Sunjata:

At this moment, Sunjata was
in the bush.
He explained himself.
He said,
'Your older brother has sent me.'
Tali Mansa Konkon said,
'Mansa Dankaran Tuman has
sent me.'
He said, 'I have come to see you.
Tali Mansa Konkon

O tuma, Magan Sunjara
waaden gwonyan na
K' i dantigɛ a la
A k' i dantigɛ
k'i kɔrɔ na a bila
Tali Mansa Konkon ka
Mansa Dankaran Tuman na
a bila
Ko n ka na ka na i magwɛ,
Tali Mansa Konkon

and his younger brother are at war.	*K'a n'a dɔgɔ kɛlɛlen,*
He asks you to take these three measures of gold	*k' ika wariya saba samun nin mina*
and to cast the power on to him; and if the power stays with him,	*k'ai ka sigi fili, koni sigi tor'a la*
you kill him,	*k'i k'a faga,*
and you seize these three measures of gold.'	*ka warinya saba samun ta*[8]

This is a representative oral narrative from this part of West Africa. It is elliptical, resonant, historical storytelling at its best: Sunjata Keita is in the bush, a hunter; he does not intend to become a famous ruler known throughout the world. But, when the opportunity comes, he must seize it, and the three measures of gold with it, to accede to the throne of power. The truth of the narrative lies in its symbolism and poetry, not in the 'facts' it contains. What is really at stake here may be the transition of West African kingdoms from those led by blacksmiths and their mystical powers to cavalry-led empires of warrior aristocrats.[9]

Gold, therefore, mattered hugely both to Africans and to Europeans. But, when it comes to the gold trade, West African and European sources do not entirely match up. European expansion is often seen as the trigger for modern history. In the fifteenth century, the place of gold was central to the expansion project and the European image of Africa as the 'golden country', as, indeed, the Catalan Atlas suggests, with its depiction of the gold nugget held by Mansa Musa front and centre. In the 1490s, João II, King of Portugal, became known to Italian contemporaries as *il rei d'oro*, or 'the Golden King', because of his access to West African gold markets. The desperation of Europeans to trade in Africa was reflected in the journeys of figures such as Antonio Malfante, a Genoese trader who arrived in Tuwāt around 1471 and described a thriving commercial centre marked by pragmatic commercial protectionism. The traders of Tuwāt would perform no transaction without a commission of 100 per cent, and, when Malfante asked his North African guide where the gold came from, he received the reply that he had spent fourteen years travelling in these countries without ever finding out, which showed just how jealously the gold producers and trading middlemen protected their commercial advantage.[10]

But why assume that it is European expansion from which modern history begins? The causes of these processes should be located in an earlier period. The reason that European traders such as Malfante were so eager to locate the source of West African gold was that for several centuries West African gold producers had provided the gold that financed the expansion of Mediterranean economies. Ever since around 1000 CE, the gold of Christian Europe and the Muslim world had come largely from West Africa, and it was the growth in production there that produced the ready-cash economy. The pilgrimage of Mansa Musa to Mecca, via Cairo, triggered a boom of gold production in the forests of the Gold Coast in which technologies pioneered by Akan peoples were crucial. An expanding gold trade in the late fourteenth century (evidenced in maps such as Cresques's) led to the consolidation of important new states in West Africa in the fifteenth century, such as Kano in northern Nigeria and Mossi in Burkina Faso. The Empire of Mali was then supplanted by Songhay. Instead of European actions shaping the emergence of a globalized world, Portuguese voyages into the Atlantic were in many ways a response to processes that had already begun in West Africa.[11]

Where historical evidence from West Africa makes plain the place of long-distance trade in gold, in traditional European historical narratives it was the Portuguese 'voyages of discovery' along the Atlantic African coast in the fifteenth century that first brought West African communities into contact with global influences. Yet, as we have seen already, by the time that Mansa Musa made his pilgrimage to Mecca in the early fourteenth century, there was already a very long tradition of reciprocal influences. When the Portuguese arrived on the West African coast in the 1440s, therefore, the societies that they found had emerged from many centuries of trade and cross-cultural exchange with North African traders, scholars and craftspeople. The mixed urban cultures that had emerged in towns like Timbuktu, Kantora, Oualata and Gao were in many ways early harbingers of modernity.

Yet was it really the case that long-distance trade promoted urban growth and political complexity? There has often been a reluctance among historians of Africa to accept this, since it seems to suggest that social and material transformation came from outside – that Africans could not be builders of civilizations and their infrastructures. The archaeological evidence is, however, fairly clear that pre-contact cities such as Jenne-jenò and (further south) Mbanza Kongo appeared at the intersection of trade routes. An important context is to recall that trade was a driver for urbanization not only in Africa, but also in European cities such as Lisbon, London and Seville, all of which grew rapidly along with the rise of long-distance trade. Thus, urban growth everywhere – and not only in Africa – was dependent on influences from, and connections to, the outside world.

In fact, in West Africa itself, the narrative of how fifteenth-century kingdoms grew alongside the gold trade retains resonance. In Lansiné Diabaté's rendering of the Sunjata epic, it is through Sunjata Keita's control of the gold trade that he can then become the founder of a great kingdom, the originator, the one of whom account must be given even over seven centuries later. Sunjata Keita is:

He who gives form to the village	*Duguyoro*
He who gives form to the village chief	*Dugutigiyoro*
He who gives form to that which is inherited	*Kinyɛyoro*
He who gives form to he who inherits.	*Kinyɛtigiyoro.*[12]

These transformations are fundamental to understanding the relationship between West African history and the world economy since the rise of capitalism. But it is worth noting that, beyond West Africa, the consequences were equally profound. As Akan gold miners in the forests of the Gold Coast dug deeper into their mineral seams, and the caravans brought ever more gold across the Sahara to the north, more money was washing around in the cities of Algiers, Cairo and Tunis. This led to the transition from a credit economy to a bullion economy, which, with the growing valorization of coinage, set the terms for what would happen after the Spanish opening of silver mines in the New World. At the time, the expansion of gold production most clearly assisted the Ottoman Empire. In 1453, the Ottomans seized Constantinople, and Christendom's Eastern capital fell. Ottoman strength grew even further in the early sixteenth century, as Cairo also fell to them in 1517.[13]

The explorations of the Portuguese and Italian adventurers in West Africa in the fifteenth century thus also rose out of a realization that it was vital for European traders to gain access to West Africa's gold supplies if they were going to withstand Ottoman expansionism. Like many empires in world history, the rise of the Portuguese Empire began as a kind of lashing out in response to a growing external threat. The existing dependence of the Iberians on this earlier gold trade emerges in numerous small, telling details: especially the derivation of the Spanish word for 'gold coin' from the eleventh to the fourteenth centuries – *maravedí* – from the Sahelian Al-Murabitūn coin minted by the Almoravid kingdoms in the eleventh and twelfth centuries, and known in Iberia through this trade from West Africa.

The commercial exchange between West Africa and Europe, when it began, was thus grounded in this currency trade. And it would be the inequalities that characterized this exchange of value that would come to be integral to the larger economic relationship between West Africa and the West. Mansa Musa wasn't just rich: according to an estimate in *Time* business magazine in July 2015, he was the richest person in world history, when the relative power of his wealth is compared with that of competitors across all time periods. And yet today, Mali, like many of its neighbours, is one of the poorest countries on earth.[14]

CITY STATES OF THE SAHEL

Mansa Musa's pilgrimage to Mecca in the 1320s left many traces, and by no means only in the Catalan Atlas of Abraham Cresques. Writing in the seventeenth century, the Timbuktu scholar Al-Sa'dī described how Mansa Musa 'set off in great pomp with a large party, including sixty thousand soldiers and five hundred slaves, who ran in front of him as he rode. Each of the slaves bore in his hand a wand fashioned from 500 mq. [*mithqāls*] of gold [*c.* 5 pounds each].'[15]

How did Al-Sa'dī know about such detail of an event from three centuries before? Doubtless, people talked in reverence of this famous moment, and he had access to written chronicles that have since been lost; but also here was a scholar trying to give shape to a past that needed to be explained in the terms of a present: the great empires of

Mali and Songhay had fallen, and that earlier greatness was both disquieting and a source of pride.[16]

Enough contemporary accounts exist to put Al-Sa'dī's later chronicle in context. Gold was indeed a major source of interest for many of those with whom Mansa Musa's entourage came into contact. In the early 1330s, Ibn al-Dawādāri composed an account of the events in Cairo some ten years before – an event that still was, by Al-Dawādāri's account, the talk of the town:

> I heard the *qadi* [judge] Fakhr al-Din, inspector of the (victorious) Army say: 'I asked the king of the Takrūr [Mali: Mansa Musa]: "How is the description of the place where the gold grows with you [i.e., what is it like]?" He replied: "It is not in that part of our land which belongs to the Muslims, but in the land which belongs to the [pagans] of Takrūr. We despatch [collectors] to take from them a species of tribute due to us and obligatory upon them. These are special lands which put forth gold in this fashion: it consists of small pieces of varying sizes, some like little rings, some like carob seeds, and the like." '
>
> The *qadi* Fakhr al-Din continued: 'I said: "Why don't you take this land by conquest?" He replied: "If we conquer them and take it, it does not put forth anything. We have done this in many ways but seen nothing there; but when it returns to them it puts forth as usual." '[17]

This was clearly a well-known story in Cairo of the time. Writing a few years later, *c.* 1337–8, Al-'Umari also noted how 'the kings of this kingdom [of Mali] have learnt by experience that as soon as one of them conquers one of the gold towns and Islam spreads and the muezzin calls to prayer there the gold there begins to decrease and then disappears.'[18] But what, it might be asked, do these stories mean? How can it possibly be the case that the greater political power that came through connection to the gold trade to North Africa could go with a decreasing ability for Mansa Musa and his successors to produce gold itself?

The answer lies with the powers associated with gold production. These early West African societies enabled this commercial growth through splicing commercial exchange to a sacred geography. Religious powers were hugely important. Gold miners needed protection from malevolent spirits and occult powers, and the belief that such protection is required for gold miners in West Africa remains widespread to this day.[19]

Just as with the European philosophy of divine right, the place of religion shaping West African political structures begins to be visible in this period. An archaeological team working in Mali has recently shown how the creation of collective shrines helped to unite villages into broader political structures. Shared worship led to shared political identities. By bringing different villages together under sacred protection, collective security and collective identity could be ensured. Religious practice linked to gold production could be shared across larger communities in the same way, in the forest areas between the Sahel and the Atlantic Ocean. As the power of the gold trade grew, so did the power of those who mined it, and with this came respect for their religious practices. Thus, an Islamic ruler such as Mansa Musa interfered with this nexus at their peril.[20]

So different approaches to religion went with the expanding gold trade. Islam provided access to a wider world, and literacy in Arabic could build bureaucracies for the rulers. But those who mined the gold guarded their own beliefs jealously and refused to adopt Islam, as this, too, was a way of protecting their privileged access to the mines. Islam could not (yet) supplant the power of the smiths, who were long linked in many West African societies to holding strong occult powers. This perceived connection between smiths and the occult remains powerful to this day; for they hold powers that are literally transformative of the everyday, turning minerals into liquid, and shaping the world afresh.[21]

Yet, as trade across the Sahara Desert intensified, differences in religious practice between rulers and those who worked in their kingdoms grew. Gao – seen as 'West Africa's starting point' by Michael Gomez – was always an influential centre, given its location at the northernmost point of the Niger, which gave it access both to the Sahara and to the rest of the region; it was later the capital of Songhay. The commercial trade from Gao to North Africa had increased from the seventh century onwards. Cotton was grown to trade across the Sahara by 1300. By 1000, there were already heavy trading links with the Islamic kingdoms of southern Spain, with some marble funeral stelae in Gao made in Almería, and Andalusian glazed ceramics. Yet, all the same, formal Islam did not spread far beyond the elite, even though the eleventh-century geographer Al-Bakri described how 'only a Muslim could rule Gao.'[22]

A key state in the emergence of Islam in West Africa was much further east, in Kanem-Borno, in north-eastern Nigeria. Here, as the scrubland gives way to the deserts, ancient *mahrāms* (grants of privilege) give accounts of the Borno mais (kings) dating back to the eleventh century, where they originally founded Kanem, north of the present Nigerian state of Borno. The *mahrām* of Umme Jilmi (*c.* 1086–97) recounts how 'the first country in the Sudan which Islam entered was the land of Bornu'; an Islamic preacher, Muhammad ibn Mâni, lived in Borno for almost thirty years at the end of the eleventh century, under four different kings, and finally 'he summoned Bornu to Islam by the grace of King Umme.' In fact, Islam may have been present in some form or other for a century or more, but it was certainly in this period that it became consolidated.[23]

The mai's decision to convert was grounded in religious instruction and trading interests. Having read many Suras under Mâni's guidance, he 'gave Mâni one hundred camels, one hundred pieces of gold, one hundred pieces of silver, and one hundred slaves, all because of the reading and instruction he derived from him'. As with many ancient sources, the symbolism here is more informative than the detail, which has almost certainly been reinscribed and supplemented over the centuries by new generations of scribes. The core of this *mahrām* tells us really of the place that Arabic learning and instruction had in shaping centralized kingdoms in the Sahel from *c.* 1000 CE, and of the place of trade from West Africa in securing this learning. What mattered politically was building a bureaucratic state, and what mattered economically were the exchanges of value through a trade in currencies (gold and silver), carried by caravans north across the Sahara to Algiers, Cairo, Tripoli and Tunis, alongside the trade in captives, which was already important.[24]

The impact of these connections grew rapidly. A king list of the mais of Kanem-Borno obtained by the German scholar-explorer Heinrich Barth in the 1850s describes how Mai Umme died in 'the land of Misr [Egypt]', confirming these links. By the time of Umme's successor in the early twelfth century, Mai Dunama ibn Umme, the Borno Army was reputed to number 100,000 cavalrymen and 120,000 infantrymen, and Dunama twice made the pilgrimage to Mecca, according to Barth's sources: 'on his first pilgrimage he left in Misr [Egypt] 300 slaves, and on his second a like number.' Moreover, the rest of Kanem-Borno's connections were equally cosmopolitan, with regular trading links to Zawila in the Fezzan region of the Sahara, and merchants from Basra frequently trading in Zawila too.[25]

These sources for the very ancient history of Borno, therefore, provide an important precursor to the more famous story of Mansa Musa's pilgrimage in the 1320s. Two centuries before, the mais of Borno had also performed the *hajj*. Borno already had extensive international connections to the great cities of North Africa, and to Mecca. West Africa was globalizing. But where Mansa Musa was famous for the gold that he left in Cairo, the mais of Borno left slaves as a gift. The transition from a focus on slaves to a focus on gold in the texts that survive is resonant of the shifting importance of West Africa to the Mediterranean economies in the fourteenth and fifteenth centuries, from a provider of labour to a provider of money to lubricate growth.

As with the production of gold, the power associated with these political transformations grew out of religious frameworks. Religious power had long shaped state formation in West Africa prior to the advent of Islam. The so-called Kano Chronicle – a text probably composed in the later nineteenth century by a Kano official, the Dan Rimi Malam Barka, based on sources and traditions going back to the sixteenth or seventeenth century – describes how Borno's neighbour, Kano, rose out of a constellation of African religious leaders. Barbushe, the early leader of Kano, according to the chronicle, 'was skilled in the various pagan rites. By his wonders and sorceries and the power he gained over his brethren he became chief and lord over them . . . all the people flocked to Barbushe on the two nights of Idi – for he was all-powerful at the sacrificial rites.' From these religious origins, eleven clans arose in Kano, and the first Sarki (King) of Kano took power by *c.* 1000 CE.[26]

Muslim traders known as the Wangara brought trade to the new city-states, and the wealth associated with trade meant that Islam soon found favour among the elites. Diasporas of traders linked by shared identities were vital for linking up the extended geographies that underpinned trade: the forest zones from which the gold was mined, the savannah where the city states grew, and the desert that had to be crossed if the whole system was going to work. Only communities of traders united by shared beliefs could bridge these huge geographical divides and perilous trading networks, and in this framework Islam became ever more important. So, by the fourteenth century, the Kano Chronicle describes how, in the reign of Sarki Yaji (1349–85), 'the Wangarawa came from Melli [Mali], bringing the Muhammadan religion'; while the famous traveller from Tangiers, Ibn Battūta, described the traders of the Sudan as 'Wanjarāta'.[27]

The kings of thirteenth- and fourteenth-century West Africa needed this trade. Just as Gao urbanized by the end of the twelfth century, so the Kano Chronicle tells us that Kano's walls were completed by the end of the reign of the fifth sarki, Yusa (*c.* 1136–94). Increased trade led to more wealth, more resources, and more resources with which to defend this material power. Yet it also led to conflict and divide. Or, as the Gambian oral historian Kebba Sanneh tells us:

You know when there is prosperity	*Ye a long ning yiriwa keta*
People are separated.	*Ali ka talang talang ne.*[28]

The ways in which these divisions emerged is a rich presence within the historical discourses of modern West Africa, from Nigeria to The Gambia. In written sources, the Kano Chronicle tells us of the eleventh sarki, Kannjeji (*c.* 1390–1410):

> He hardly lived in Kano at all, but scoured the country round and conquered the towns. He lived for some time near the rock of Gija. He sent to the Kwararafa and asked why they did not pay him tribute. They gave him two hundred slaves. Then he returned to Kano and kept sending the Kwararafa horses while they continued to send him slaves.[29]

One of the most important accounts illustrating the emergence of social hierarchies and divisions is the epic of Sunjata Keita, founder of the Mali Empire. In the many surviving accounts of Sunjata, the social conflicts exacerbated by the growth of long-distance trade and wealth are symbolized by the conflict between Sunjata (a Muslim) and his vanquished predecessor, Sumanguru Kante (a follower of African religious practice). One oral account collated in recent decades describes how 'Sunjata's real name was Mohammed', while Ibn Battūta described how the grandfather of the emperor he met in *c.* 1352–3, one 'Sāriq Jāta' [Sunjata], had embraced Islam.[30] Sumanguru, by contrast, was a sorcerer steeped in the supernatural, dependent on the music of his royal balafon players to proclaim his powers. As Lansiné Diabaté, the griot and historian from Kela, tells us:

At that time, owing to his magical powers,	*O lon subaya la mara ma,*
Every fly which rested on the	*Sumaworo linɔgɔ min bar' i sigi*
Balafon of Soso [the royal musician],	*Sosobala la,*
Sumaworo was able to find it out	*a b'o mangini limɔgɔkulu rɔ k'o*
From a cloud of flies to kill it.	*faga.*[31]

There was one sorcerer who predicted that a 'lion' would defeat Sumanguru, just as Islam would supplant the magic of the sorcerers – and that lion was Sunjata (also a 'lion-thief'). The triumph of Sunjata in the oral narratives represents the gathering power of Islam, its control over trade, and also the conflict this emergence represented with existing African religious practice. In time, the two frameworks would mesh, and religious and political power remain interwoven down the centuries.[32]

GLOBALIZING EMPIRES, 'UNIVERSAL VALUES'

By the middle of the fourteenth century, the grandeur of the Court of the Emperor of Mali was becoming well known in the Mediterranean worlds. Al-'Umari provides an account of the finery of the Court, which is worth quoting at length:

> The king of this realm sits in his palace on a big dais which they call *banbí* . . . on a big seat made of ebony like a throne . . . Over the dais, on all sides, are elephant tusks one beside the other. He has with him his arms, which are all of gold – sword, javelin, quiver, bow and

> arrows. He wears big trousers cut out of about twenty pieces which no one but he wears. About 30 slaves stand beside him, Turks and others who are bought for him in Egypt. One of them carries in his hand a parasol of silk surmounted by a dome and a bird of gold in the shape of a falcon. His emirs sit around and below him in two ranks to right and left. Further away are seated the chief horsemen of the army . . . Around all these there are people with drums in their hands, which they beat. Before the king are people dancing and he is pleased with them and laughs at them. Behind him two flags are unfurled.[33]

Ibn Battūta painted a similar scene of his visit just fifteen years or so later. In the chamber where the emperor held court were three arches decked out in sheets of silver, and beneath them a further three decked out in gold. When the emperor held an audience, 300 slaves emerged from the palace gates with bows, lances and shields, and his provincial governors were preceded each by their own followers with lances, bows, drums and trumpets. This military power consisted of an army of 100,000, including 10,000 cavalry, according to Al-'Umari. The emperor imported Arab horses, alongside the slaves from Turkey and North Africa whom he described as present at the Court of Mali. The provinces extended to Kawkaw (Kukyia, near Gao) and Ghāna to the east,* while other sources tell us of Mali's hegemony in Senegambia.[34]

The Mali Empire that these writers of Arabic described was one in which Islam had grown to have a pivotal role. Ibn Battūta's account refers to a time when the impact of Mansa Musa's pilgrimage of the 1320s was still significant. On his return, Al-Sa'dī was to write in the seventeenth century, drawing on documents now lost, Mansa Musa passed through Songhay and had the mosque built at Gao. On reaching Timbuktu, he ordered the construction of the palace there, and of the Djinguereber Mosque.

The Djinguereber Mosque was designed with some assistance from the Andalusian architect Al-Sahili, born in Granada in around 1290. It was built in an urban centre of North African and Islamic Iberian architectural styles, where autochthonous West African cultural

* Ghāna was centred in present-day Mauritania.

The Djinguereber Mosque, photographed by Edmond Fortier, *c.* 1905–6.

forms were ever present. From the city streets, elaborate saddles and horses were traded across the desert, ridden by people wearing woven Fulani cloths, carrying sheathed swords and daggers wrought by the local smiths. The growth of Mali's power in the cities of Songhay, such as Gao and Timbuktu, and the employment of an architect from Andalusia were all testament to the rising power of this West African state and its global connections – connections that were certainly the equal of, or ahead of, much of Europe at that date.[35]

As its power grew, Mali depended heavily on its control of the Niger River. The Joliba (as it was known in Manding) was the vital artery for the transport of foodstuffs to the communities near by, and for trading networks to develop once products had crossed the Sahara. Meanwhile, the size of the caravans bringing these goods grew very large. Some sources suggest that caravans linking Egypt and Mali went with as many as 12,000 camels – an almost unbelievable number. These were dangerous adventures: Ibn Battūta described how 'we met a caravan on our way, and they told us that some men had become separated from them. We found one of them dead, with his clothes on him, and a whip in hand, under a little tree of the kind that grows in sand. There was water a mile or so away from him.'[36]

With the global links went the emergence of more complex state mechanisms to regulate travel and trade, to secure taxes for the running of the administration and to try to ensure Mali's regional pre-eminence. Mali was becoming bigger, stronger and richer in the fourteenth century. It had conquered its neighbours, and its power extended to the Atlantic. Preserving such wealth, however, also required the growth of what Al-Sa'dī later described as a state-sponsored apparatus of persecution: 'each [commander] had a number of officers and troops under his command. This led to tyranny, high-handedness, and the violation of people's rights in the latter days of their rule.' Mali's power was nothing if not hierarchical, and these deep inequalities fostered internal divisions that would eventually lead to a serious rebellion – in a pattern that will become increasingly familiar as this book proceeds.[37]

At the peak of this power, however, these tendencies were not yet clear. Beyond areas of formal political control, Mali's cultural influence also grew. A long way to the east lay Borno, which, by the fourteenth century, when Al-'Umari was writing, was a poor yet fertile kingdom, sufficiently rich to grow rice, wheat and sorghum, figs, lemons, grapes and aubergines: 'their king', he wrote, 'despite the feebleness of his authority and the poverty of his soil, shows an inconceivable arrogance, despite the weakness of his troops and the small resources of his country, he touches with his banner the clouds in the sky.' The royal manifestation of power was certainly acute in Borno, but nevertheless there was a strong cultural influence from Mali. By the fifteenth century, the growing number of Wangara traders in the kingdom had been followed by large numbers of scholars and preachers, bringing books and new ideas. This did not lead to formal political control, however, and Borno remained a powerful kingdom, with Kano being subordinate to it long into the fifteenth century.[38]

The thirteenth and fourteenth centuries thus saw profound political transformations in the Sahel, long before the advent of any European interest. This was an internally driven and directed process of change. State institutions and power grew with international connections, and standing armies protected the political authority of the rulers and their aristocracies. What, then, were the foundations of these ever more complex political systems and structures in the fourteenth century? Four key factors can be identified: the mixed nature of communities; the globalization of movement; expanding the labour force; and the role of the region in global trade through the place of currency use.

With the first of these, the accommodation that had to be found was between indigenous African religiosity and Islam. By the thirteenth and fourteenth centuries, Islam was widely adopted among the elites: 'they place fetters on their children if there appears on their part a failure to learn [the Qur'ān].'[39] Yet the type of Islam that emerged in many parts of West Africa was shaped by tolerant currents of Islamic philosophy. The theologian Lamin Sanneh has shown how the preaching of the cleric Al-Hajj Sālim Suware *c.* 1200 gave rise to the emergence of a Muslim clerical elite throughout West Africa who emphasized learning and pacifism. This pacifist strain of Islam was vital in a region where practitioners of African religions still outnumbered Muslims, and where creating a mixed and plural society was to be a hallmark of West African life.[40]

The emperors had to meld African beliefs and traditions with the new religion. A resonant example of this balance was the place of the musicians at Court, so clearly described above by Ibn Battūta. This derived from earlier traditions of royal authority; in Lansiné Diabaté's account of the balafon player noted above, it is when the balafon player refuses to play for Sumanguru Kante that the sorcerer-king's demise is first anticipated. At a 2015 lecture in London, the master balafon player based in Bamako, Lassana Diabaté, stressed again the royal lineage of the balafon as an instrument, as the original source of royal power. The place of music as a framework for uniting people of different backgrounds and even faiths was emphasized even more recently, in a 2017 lecture by the kora player from Guinea-Bissau, Ibrahima Galissá: kora, he told the audience, also held the meaning for Mandinka people of 'that which brings everything together'.[41]

The melding of historically grounded customs with the new religion reflected the emergence of the upcoming superpowers: Kano, Borno, Mali and then Songhay. African religious practice remained widespread, dismissed by North African travellers as 'sorcery': 'they are forever litigating before their king, saying . . . "Such-a-one has killed my brother, or son, or daughter, or sister, by sorcery."' At the end of the fifteenth century, the King of Songhay, Askia Mohammed, described how this plural outlook had been embodied by his predecessor, Sonni 'Ali, who 'used to fast Ramadān and make abundant alms of slaughtered beasts and other things at the mosques and like places. In spite of this he used to worship idols, believe in the soothsayers' [pronouncements], seek help from magicians and venerate certain trees and stones by slaughtering at them and by giving alms.' Askia Mohammed – a very orthodox follower of Islam – was saddened by the large numbers of diviners, astrologers and magicians who claimed 'they can write [talismans] to bring good fortune, such as material prosperity or love, and to ward off ill fortune by defeating enemies, prevent steel from cutting or poison from taking effect.'[42]

Kings had to be able to speak to both their Muslim and non-Muslim subjects, and this required a flexible approach. Thus, societies were still very open in 1500. In Songhay, there was a 'free mixing of men and women in the markets and streets . . . women appear . . . frequently before their husband's brother, paternal cousin, or his friend.' They developed a state founded on indigenous practice, with a warrior cavalry aristocracy, and using the traditional hunters' and blacksmiths' societies and manufactures as symbols of their kingship. However, they borrowed Islamic bureaucratic forms, religion, scholarship and legal structures to govern the new state. Beyond this, they also had to develop social structures to incorporate outside traders and preachers, those travellers whose presence symbolized the second core aspect of these kingdoms' growth: their international outlook.[43]

This growing globalism is shown through the large numbers of pilgrimages from West Africa to Mecca via Cairo and other North African cities, and the exchange of scholars. One such was Al-Kānemī, a scholar from Borno who lived and taught in Marrakesh *c.* 1200, before dying in Andalusia. The frequency of such presences of West Africans in the wider Islamic world can be illustrated by the seven pilgrimages to Mecca made by the founder of Suwerian Islam, Al-Hajj Sālim Suware, in the early thirteenth century. Even if this is (as likely) a wild exaggeration, it is symptomatic of the normality and number of these exchanges. In return, as we have seen, many craftsmen and scholars from North Africa and Andalusia came to Mali, travelling along the trade routes across which the caravans returned with gold, and enslaved persons.[44]

In terms of the third factor, expanding the labour force, by the fifteenth century, slaving had grown in West Africa. As in many other parts of the world, for instance Iberia during the same centuries and pre-Columbian America, it depended on the capture of 'outsiders' in war. We have already seen the importance it had in early Kanem-Borno, where enslaved persons were, as one historian puts it, the 'main export'. But the Kano Chronicle describes how, by the time of Sarki Abdullahi Burjo (*c.* 1438–52), Kano was also growing through slaving. One of the military leaders of this sarki, Galadima Dawdu, 'was in the south, making war on the pagans every day, conquering them and taking them as slaves'. According to the chronicle, 1,000 captives were sent every month to the sarki, who was said to have founded twenty-one towns with 1,000 captives. And this was remembered by the chronicle with a song sung about the Galadima: 'Gatherer of the axes of the south / Gatherer of the youth of the south / Drum of wealth, Galadima / Drum of land, Galadima.'[45]

Of course, these figures are symbolic; but they are also deeply indicative of the relationship between slavery and wealth. One of the fundamental relationships established in these trades was the exchange of enslaved human beings for horses. The Kano Chronicle and sources from Borno tell us this very clearly. Horses predominated in savannah areas where there was none of the sleeping sickness prevalent further south caused by the tsetse fly. They were vital for military expansion, for winning the wars that procured slaves as captives. They also could become powerful symbols of royal power, used in parades as an emblem of the king's finery. The horse came both to impose and to reflect the growing inequality between rulers and subjects. It also offered a readymade trading system that the early-European traders would copy wholesale on the West African coast, exchanging horses for captives in Senegambia from the earliest times; and breeding horses on the newly discovered Cape Verde Islands as early as the late fifteenth century, so as to increase the trade in enslaved persons.[46]

The growth of the external slave trade in Borno, Kano, Mali and Songhay also saw the growth of relations of dependence in West

Africa itself. Often these relationships provoked disputes. Askia Mohammed described how, in Songhay by 1500, 'some will sell a slavegirl and the purchaser will take possession of her without caring whether or not she is already pregnant. Then, if it becomes apparent that she is pregnant, they quarrel over the offspring. This happens very frequently.' The fundamental cause of these disputes was the growing financial value equated with enslaved persons. Money, slavery and political power were intertwined in West African kingdoms as their fame grew in the fourteenth and fifteenth centuries.[47]

This brings us to the fourth factor outlined above. As Al-'Umari put it in the 1330s, already the financial system in some of these kingdoms had conceptualized financial value in new ways. In Borno, he described a kingdom that operated multiple currencies. The standard currency was a piece of cloth that was 10 cubits long, and that was used to make purchases from ¼ cubit upwards. Cowries, copper, coined silver and beads were also used as currency, but they were 'all valued in terms of that cloth'. Money as a representation of value was becoming increasingly powerful; by the end of the fifteenth century, in Songhay, traders often adulterated gold and silver with copper dust, or did not separate all the sand out of gold dust. By the fifteenth century, 'hard' currencies, such as cloth in Borno, and gold in Mali and Songhay, were increasingly capturing some kind of pretended 'universal' value in the trade at the heart of commercial exchanges.[48]

COMMERCIAL REVOLUTIONS: GOLD, KINGDOMS AND POWER

The symbolic importance that gold and the exchange of value through currency had come to have by the fourteenth century is revealed in Al-'Umari's description of the use of gold by the military figureheads of Mali: 'Their brave cavaliers wear golden bracelets. Those whose knightly valour is greater wear gold necklets also. If it is still greater, they add gold anklets.'[49]

The importance that gold had to Mali's power is, of course, already more than apparent in Mansa Musa's pilgrimage. Historians have tended to focus on this event as the high watermark of the relationship.

However, the gold trade did not become static after the 1320s. In fact, it expanded. By the fifteenth century, the major source of Akan gold production in the Volta River Basin was connected to Borno. Borno traders brought in locally produced cloth in exchange for the gold here, which they would eventually despatch north to Tripoli. So extensive was the gold trade in the forests of the Volta River at this time that, within twenty years of the Portuguese arrival on the Gold Coast in the 1480s, it was able to supply 30,000 ounces per year. Impressive technologies had developed to expand the production, with gold apparently mined to a depth of almost 230 feet.[50]

The impact of this expanding gold trade was captured by the Andalusian traveller Hassan al-Ouazzan, better known as Leo Africanus, who provided an account in the 1520s. In Gao, he wrote:

> An infinite number of Blacks arrive here, bringing gold in large quantities so as to buy and carry off [the goods] which come from Europe and Barbary. But they tend not to find enough merchandise to spend the large quantity of money which they bring with them, so much so that they are forced to return to their own countries, bringing back a third or as much as a half of the money which they had brought with them.[51]

In other words, Al-Ouazzan described an overproduction of gold, which could not be sold for the volume of goods that the trans-Saharan trade was able to provide. The effects of this were profound in West Africa, and contributed to the setting of terms of unequal exchange. Al-Ouazzan went on to describe how the cost of the most basic manufactured goods in Gao was far higher than anything that would be paid in Europe:

> A horse which would not cost more than 10 ducats in Europe won't be found there for less than 40 or 50. The cheapest cloth from Europe is sold there for 4 ducats, an average cloth for 15, and fine cloth from Venice in scarlet, blue or violet goes for nothing less than 30 ducats . . . all ironmongery is very expensive there.[52]

A remarkable picture emerges from this early-sixteenth-century account, therefore, of overproduction of gold by West African miners and traders on the one hand, and profiteering on European trade goods on the other. At that time, the profits were mostly held by the middlemen of the trans-Saharan trade. However, as the accent of trade moved from the desert to the ocean, these profits and the subsequent capital growth would increasingly come to be held within the hands of European traders.

The thriving gold trade described here was also a key driver of the profound political transformations of the fourteenth and fifteenth centuries. The expansion of gold production meant that there were new trade routes. The Borno traders who went to buy gold in the forests of the Volta brought cloth, so cloth manufacturing grew in Borno. More traders were needed to carry this gold, expanding the foreign-trader communities in West African city-states and thereby the presence of Islam. Meanwhile, new governmental structures were needed to manage this trade: in Borno, this would lead to the movement of the capital away from the old centre of Kanem, further south to Ngazargamu in Borno *c.* 1470, and the establishment of a new system in Kano, the Sarauta system.[53]

However, what is even more remarkable than these changes in an existing kingdom – Borno – is the political transformations that took place across West Africa, from Senegambia to Nigeria. The earthworks known as *eredos*, built around Ijebu in what is now Yorùbáland, have recently been dated by the archaeologist Gérard Chouin to the period 1370–1420. These 33-feet-deep ditches have a perimeter of 110 miles, and suggest, according to Chouin, that this period saw the rise of centralized, militaristic polities, with these earthworks designed to stop cavalry. At the same time, in the fifteenth century, the Mossi Kingdom rose in what is now Burkina Faso, linked to the profits to be made from taxing the onward gold trade through the Volta forests; Al-Sa'dī described Mossi attacking the town of Mâssina. This was also when Bono-Mansu, an Akan state on the Gold Coast (and much nearer to the goldfields), rose to prominence. Meanwhile, the key gold-trading centre of Bighu, also on the Gold Coast, and which was to become very important in the seventeenth and eighteenth centuries, is mentioned by Al-Ouazzan in the 1520s, suggesting that it, too, rose to prominence in these decades.[54]

In other regions similar transformations were afoot. In Mali, the famous Dogon people of the Bandiagara escarpment probably moved there in the fifteenth century. The steep nature of the cliffs made this a much easier area to defend against attacks. Fourteen different languages are still spoken among the Dogon, making it clear that this was not one 'ethnic' population movement, but rather a common gathering of people seeking sanctuary from increasing militarization and insecurity. Many of these peoples had probably had connections to the trans-Saharan trade, since some of the textiles found here from the fourteenth and fifteenth centuries reveal Islamic-influenced designs. They also appear to have had a sophisticated astronomical system, according to some researchers.[55]

Near to Bandiagara, the city of Djenné was famous as a major marketplace for the exchange of gold and salt. Meanwhile, in Senegambia, the rise of the military leader Koli Tenguella at the end of the fifteenth century probably coincided with an attempt to control the gold trade that came from the Kingdom of Wuuli, on the north bank of the Gambia River. Tenguella, of the Fula people, would eventually lead an army south across the Gambia to the Fuuta Jaalo Mountains in what is now Guinea-Conakry and establish communities there, before returning to establish the Kingdom of Fuuta Tòòro.[56]

Dogon houses.

In other words, all across West Africa, from Borno to Fuuta Tòòro, political transformations were taking place well before trade with Europe had begun. The expanding gold trade led to the provision of much more currency for the North African and European market. It also led to the growth of trading routes, and governmental systems to control these routes. This led to the rise of new states, the transformation of others, and the migration of peoples. Armies grew, and people defended themselves. They built new fortifications, or fled to places that they could defend, such as Bandiagara. Thus, West African mining technology, economic transformation and political reorganization grew; and, as we have seen, this helped to create the framework in which European powers sought to expand their knowledge of the world, as they began to sail along the West African coast in the fifteenth century.

How can we be so sure of the way in which this took shape? The interplay of these forces is actually clear from Borno. After the sacking of Constantinople by the Ottomans in 1453, the sultans in Istanbul became considerably more involved in the Borno Kingdom, to such an extent that the later mais of Borno were able to count them as allies. In the fourteenth century, Borno had had strong diplomatic ties, both to the Mamluk sultans of Egypt and to the kings of Abysinnia (Ethiopia): the role of Borno in acting as a clearing house for the gold trade meant that figures such as the Ottoman sultans were happy to have the mais as allies, which speaks to the role of this trade in consolidating their power in the first place.[57]

The most remarkable example of these transformations came in northern Nigeria. The trans-Saharan trade was, of course, vital, but what was even more important was the regular regional trade in foods, raw materials, animals and manufactured goods (especially cloth). Kano grew very rapidly in the fifteenth century, sending out military expeditions to the south and becoming a regional hub linking trading networks from southern Nigeria to what is now Mali and beyond.[58]

The Kano Chronicle gives some details of these changes. In the reign of Kano's Sarki Dauda (*c.* 1421–38), we are told of the connections between Kano and the province of Nupe. The major power between Kano and Nupe was Zaria, and, the chronicle says, 'at this time, Zaria, under Queen Amina, conquered all the towns as far as Kwararafa and Nupe. Every town paid tribute to her. Sarki Nupe sent forty eunuchs and ten thousand kolas to her . . . in time the whole of the products of the west were brought to Hausaland [of which Kano was the capital].'[59] This is a fascinating window, too, on to little-known questions of gender and power, for here was a powerful queen in Nupe who had a major influence on what is now Nigeria. Queen Amina was mentioned in passing in some texts by the leader of the Fula *jihād* in the early nineteenth century, Uthmān dan Fodio; and was rediscovered as a historical model by the early postcolonial government of Nigeria, becoming the subject of songs sung in many Nigerian primary schools. As a concrete historical source, the Kano Chronicle is the main piece of evidence for her existence, but it offers a tantalizing view of models of governance that are very different from those that later emerged.[60]

By the 1450s, the commercial expansion of Kano meant that merchants from Gonja (in what is now northern Ghana) came there, along with large numbers of Hausa diaspora traders and North African merchants. Kano was increasingly on the map, as a clearing house for local cloth produced in Borno and Kano, the forest products from the south, the gold from the south-west and the products traded across the Sahara by the Arab merchants, some of whom 'settled in Kano and some in Katsina'.[61]

It was Kano's last sarki of the fifteenth century, Mohammed Rimfa, who was however the most powerful expression of Kano's new place in the world. This was a ruler who 'can have no equal in might from the time of the founding of Kano, until it shattered'.[62] Rimfa invited large numbers of scholars to settle in the city, and one of them – Sherif Abdu Rahman – came from Medina in Arabia, bringing his own library and many learned followers. The city walls of Kano were built, and the Kurmi Market established. Just as European power was beginning to expand along the West African coast, so Sahelian power was, too. The fifteenth century was not just the time of European expansion, but of global expansion of networks, trade, productions, and the manifestation of this power in more complex states. Crucially, such expansion required the development of ever more complex systems of finance and credit to underpin them.

An ancient Hausa poem sung long into the 1990s by the poor and destitute of Kano called 'The Song of Bagauda' captures some of these transformations in its focus on Mohammed Rimfa:

> *Muhammad Rumfa was a generous chief;*
> *The reign of Rumfa was of benefit to all.*
> *He reigned for thirty years. When he set out to give alms*
> *His malams* [priests] *shared three thousand* [bags of cowries]
> *between them.*[63]

The mention in this stanza of cowrie shells as a major form of currency ties Kano into earlier trading patterns in Mali, where Ibn Battūta described how 'these cowries are also the currency of the Sūdān in their country. I saw them sold at Mālī and Jawjawat (Gao) at the rate of 1,150 [cowries] to the gold dinar.'[64] In Gao, he wrote, cowries were the standard currency; and cowries were probably the currency used by him to buy his provisions from small communities up and down the Niger. That the use of cowries as currency to make small purchases was widely recognized across West Africa is shown by the Portuguese sailor Duarte Pacheco Pereira citing cowries as the currency in use on the Gold Coast by the early sixteenth century.[65]

However, the cowrie currency was far from the only standard money accepted in West Africa at this time. Cloth was used in Borno, as noted already, while in other areas copper and iron were imported. In Djenné, Al-Ouazzan noted in the early sixteenth century that desert merchants brought copper to trade in the famous market there.

As copper was one of the major currencies in use in many parts of West Africa through the sixteenth century, then brought as manilla arm-rings by European traders, this shows again that such trading and monetary practices were imitated by European traders, rather than having been initiated by them. The currency mostly used here was in the form, Al-Ouazzan said, of small pieces of iron, while gold dust was also used as a standard against which to measure the value of the other currencies.[66]

What emerges is the existence of a dynamic economic framework with complex trading patterns that in many cases were imitated by the first European traders arriving in the fifteenth century. Cowries had long been brought from the Maldive Islands across the Indian

The Great Mosque at Djenné, photographed in *c.* 1911 by Félix Dubois, and overlooking the market. The mosque had been substantially reconstructed in recent times.

Ocean trading routes and then over the desert; the Portuguese now began to bring them by ship from India in the early sixteenth century. Copper had been brought overland for centuries from North Africa for trade, and copper arm-rings manufactured in Europe became the basis of much of the early Atlantic trade on the Gold Coast. Meanwhile, cloth currencies had emerged in Senegambia prior to the Portuguese arrival, with textiles woven by the Fula people in high demand; and Portuguese colonists very soon started to arrange the weaving of their own equivalent on the Cape Verde Islands, where they deliberately imitated the Fula patterns, calling them *barafula*.

Gold, as we have seen, was the major export of West Africa in economic terms, so much so that there was considerable overproduction in the fourteenth and fifteenth centuries – something that actually led to the expansion of states and urban growth. In return for this 'hard' currency export, which would hold its value over time, West African kingdoms received copper, cowries and cloth, currencies whose values would all decline markedly over time.

POLITICAL TRANSFORMATIONS IN THE SAHEL: MALI AND SONGHAY

With many parts of West Africa experiencing political transformations in the fifteenth century, it is no surprise that the same was true of the empire with which this chapter began: Mali. The fifteenth century saw a crisis in Mali, and the transfer of its power to the east and the new imperial centre of Songhay. Songhay would be the great Sahelian kingdom, until their kings, the Askias, fell to a Moroccan invasion in 1591. This brought to an end many centuries of political and commercial consolidation in Sahelian West Africa.

Al-Sa'dī tells us that Mali's power began to wane around 1433–4, when it lost control of Timbuktu to the Magsharan Tuareg from the desert north. As Al-Sa'dī puts it, 'the Malians, bewildered by their many depredations, refused to make a stand against them. [The Tuareg] said: "The Sultan who does not defend his territory has no right to rule it." So the Malians abandoned Timbuktu and returned to Mali [which lay further to the south-east].' This retreat, therefore, presaged the transfer of power to Songhay, whose new young king, Sonni 'Alī, took back Timbuktu in 1468. By 1500, Al-Ouazzan tells us, 'as of today, this king [of Mali] is under such oppression that he can barely find a way to feed his family.'[67]

For Songhay, though, the late fifteenth century was the moment of its greatest expansionist power. Sonni 'Alī spent years at war, subduing the surrounding kings and provinces such as Djenné and Kebbi; or, as Al-Sa'dī puts it, 'he was a man of great strength and colossal energy, a tyrant, a miscreant, an aggressor, a despot, and a butcher . . . he passed his days campaigning and conquering territories.' Sonni 'Alī developed new administrative frameworks, putting each conquered province under a war chief who recognized his authority, and running a central administration from the Songhay heartland at Gao, where there was an imperial administration and a royal military council. Over time, Songhay's rulers would develop a complex system of titles, including the bana farma (paymaster general), fari mondoyo (overseer of royal estates), goima-koi (harbourmaster for the river ports on the Niger) and the yūbu-koi (chief of the market).[68]

This complex administration created rivalries, and where there is competition there will be conflicts. A fundamental source of dispute was the place of Islam in the empire. One of the main gripes that Al-Sa'dī had about Sonni 'Alī was that, unlike his more Islamized successors, the Askias, he gave the scholars of Timbuktu short shrift: 'he tyrannized the scholars and holymen, killing them, insulting them, and humiliating them.' However, Islam would be the glue of the new empire under his successors, and, when Sonni 'Alī died in 1492, drowned in a river after returning from a military campaign, the place of Islam as a guarantor of trade and external connections would be renewed. The hostility of Timbuktu's historians to Sonni 'Alī reflects the success of the leaders who followed him and made Timbuktu an Islamic centre of learning in the sixteenth century. As one historian has noted, Sonni 'Alī's attitude towards Islam merely reflected the fact that he ruled at a time when Islam was still not strongly rooted in the country outside of the large cities. Raised in a rural area in Sokoto, among African religionists, Sonni 'Alī viewed Islam as just another part of the plural outlook outlined earlier in this chapter.[69]

What, then, was life like in this expanding empire in the early sixteenth century? It was not all violence and conflict. Writing of his experiences, Al-Ouazzan offers a vivid picture of life in Songhay. In Timbuktu, he says, 'the inhabitants are all very pleasant by nature, and most evenings they stay out dancing in the city until one in the morning.' By the 1530s, Al-Sa'dī said, Askia Muhammed Bonkama had 'furnished the court splendidly, enlarging, adorning and embellishing it with more courtiers than ever before. He supplied it with sumptuous garments, different types of musical instruments, and male and female singers.' Music was indeed clearly at the very heart of the performance of royal power, for 'he was the first to have tambourines accompanying him when travelling by water, and it was he who introduced the *futurifu* – an instrument resembling the horn.'[70]

The causes of the rise of Songhay were various. In the first place, there was the decline of the western trans-Saharan trading route through Oualata in Mauritania, which, by 1500, was described as a wretched town. Increasingly the demand for gold and enslaved persons was centred further east, in Cairo and the Ottoman Empire, following the seizure of Constantinople in 1453. The growing diplomatic links between Constantinople and Borno reflected the desire to deflect trade in their own direction, and the shifting east from Mali to Songhay followed this pattern. Moreover, the arrival of the Portuguese in the mid fifteenth century further weakened Mali's control over western trading routes. Nevertheless, there was an important factor that would limit the potential of this new regional power: the debts incurred by Sonni 'Alī's successor, Askia Mohammed, during his pilgrimage to Mecca.[71]

The pilgrimage itself was lauded by Askia Mohammed's biographers. Setting off in the spirit of his predecessors from Borno and Mali in 1496, he took 500 cavalrymen and 1,000 infantrymen with him across the desert. He made charitable donations, and, when he reached Medina, he even bought some gardens there to be used by pilgrims from West Africa (*Takrūr*) on their own pilgrimages – testament to just how globalized a region this had become. However, Al-Ouazzan provides the key information that 'while making the pilgrimage to Mecca, he consumed all of his treasure and riches so that he ended up in debt to the amount of 50,000 ducats.' This was, indeed, a reproduction of what had happened during Mansa Musa's pilgrimage to Mecca in the 1320s, when he returned to Mali with considerable new debt caused by having used up all the gold that the caravan had brought with them to begin with.[72]

This startling information is important for numerous reasons. It shows a long-standing pattern of debt compensated for by gold production. The pattern of indebtedness would only really be resolved when Songhay collapsed at the end of the sixteenth century. One of the problems caused by the creation of these debts was that, like Mali before it, Songhay did not control the actual goldfields. With the Wangara traders increasingly taking their gold to European trading posts on the Gold Coast, Songhay could not manage production sufficiently to meet its debts. Although this trade to the coast did decline in the later sixteenth century, the new source of competition was a problem. Throughout the sixteenth century, Songhay's importance had been recognized, but, by the 1580s, the empire was riven by external and internal pressures. After a long and illustrious reign under Askia Dawūd (*c.* 1549–82), succession struggles followed and civil wars broke out in 1586–8, during the reign of Askia Mohammed IV Bani. Mohammed's successor, Ishaq II, tried hard to quash divisions that had grown in the empire between the western and eastern provinces, but this led to further divisions – authorities from Timbuktu and further west were deported to Gao and executed. Thus, the empire was weak and fractured when the overdependence that it had developed on the trans-Saharan trade began to become a major problem.[73]

Al-Sa'dī described closely the series of events that precipitated Songhay's fall, as part of his wider project of explaining, and justifying, the seventeenth-century successor states to Songhay, known as the Arma. It was from this divided political system that Mūlāy Ahmad of Morocco required 'payment to him of the tax on the [salt] mine of Taghāza'; and also, probably, to see if there were dissidents who might support an invasion. Here Songhay's economic dependence on the powerful North African kingdoms was laid bare, for the Moroccan king claimed that he had a right to the tax: he had acted as a buffer between Songhay and the Christian kingdoms. It was late in 1590, and the Moroccan kingdom was riding high: twelve years previously, the Moroccans had defeated and slaughtered a Portuguese army led by the Portuguese King Sebastião I, and this had put an end to any Portuguese territorial claims in Morocco, and, indeed, to the independence of the Portuguese monarchy from Spain for sixty years. But Askia Ishaq II of Songhay was intransigent: 'on the contrary', Al-Sa'dī tells us, 'he sent a reply couched in intemperate language, accompanied by a spear and two iron shoes' – a heavy insult and threat of war.[74]

The Moroccan Army was despatched in November 1590, and the invading troops reached the Niger at the end of February 1591. When it came to battle at Tankondibogho, near Tondibi, the Moroccans broke through at once, and the Songhay Empire collapsed in civil war: 'security turned to fear, luxury was changed into affliction and distress, and prosperity became woe and harshness.' There was widespread insecurity, attacks on households and property, and, Al-Sa'dī tells us, 'such iniquity became general, spreading, and becoming ever more serious.'[75]

How was this great loss withstood? There was much grief and

anguish at Gao, the centre of the empire. But on the battlefield itself, the essence of Songhay's strength, and of its fall from power, was embodied in the ways in which the Askia's soliders met their defeat; for they 'threw their shields on the ground and sat on them cross-legged until the [Moroccan] army came and killed them in cold blood where they were, for it was their custom not to flee when defeated. [And] Jawdar's men stripped off the gold bracelets on their wrists.'[76]

For centuries, Songhay had been the land of gold – and Mali before it. This reputation had driven the emergence of the long-distance caravan trade, and the spread of communities of Islamic priests and traders across West Africa. With these traders, West African rulers had developed a style of government that welcomed strangers, and a worldview that was plural and could accommodate different faiths. The gold trade had been the keystone in the globalization of West Africa, and had influenced events as far distant as the fall of Constantinople and the onset of the Portuguese voyages of discovery. Nevertheless, this trade had also come at an economic cost, since the rise of trade had gone with the construction of an external dependence of West African kings on their long-distance trading partners. The fall of Songhay represented the end of the first phase in the globalization of West African peoples, states and worldviews.

CONCLUSION

Sources on what might be called 'ancient' or 'medieval' West Africa are few. They allow little reconstruction of individual life stories, and offer few of the flourishes of detail that can create an approachable sort of history. They need to be triangulated together for sense to emerge. Yet, when it comes to thinking about the origins of West Africa's economic frameworks in relation to the world, they are remarkably important.

A close reading of them confirms the central importance of the trade in gold currency in the transformation of West African kingdoms, societies and worldviews from the thirteenth to the fifteenth centuries. This is the case whether we are considering oral sources developed over the centuries on Sunjata Keita, or texts written in

Arabic by travellers from North Africa. All of these may represent political projects of their creators, griots and Islamic scholars, but the focus on gold points to the wider significance this had. Over time, other texts written in Arabic emerged that confirm this view.

One such is the *Kitāb Ghanjā*, or Chronicle of Gonja, written down around 1800 and based on earlier versions in the Kingdom of Gonja (in modern Ghana), on paper that had been manufactured in Italy. This text tells of the founding of Gonja, in the sixteenth century, by Mande migrants who had come from the region of the Empire of Mali. The founding figure was called Jighi Jarā, and he sent two young sons towards Gonja, having heard reports of the goldfields at Bighu. The chronicle takes up the story:

> They conquered the town . . . and took the gold [they found] there. This gold was kept in two houses. Each year he used to take [some of it] out to bring back to his father and give it to him. Then the senior son said to his brother, 'O brother we have heard another report that the gold which we have found was previously in another town; the name of this town is Ghūna [Buna, in present-day Ivory Coast]. Therefore go there in war, quickly, in no time, then come back quickly, so that we may go back to our town.'[77]

Such written texts, produced in West Africa by West Africans, confirm the centrality of the growing gold trade in transforming political systems. And traders, too, were founders of kingdoms, as one important oral text on the founding of the Kingdom of Kong, in northern Ivory Coast, confirms:

It is through the avenue of commerce
That the Tarawele Musasi left here
And went to found the kingdoms of Kong and Sikasso . . .

[The Tarawele] *are the first to have*
Taken their bags of merchandise
To go and found the kingdom of Kong.

Tarawele Musasilu bòlen yan k'ara
jurayasen fè ka taa kòn ruwa yòmu
sigi, ka sikasso ta bèe sigi . . .

Olu fòlò le jurayaminan ta ka
mansakuńda dò sigi Kon.[78]

Thus, as the trade between West Africa and the Mediterranean worlds grew, so, too, did the number of traders, and their influence. Trade transformed politics: Borno, Kano, Mossi and Songhay all expanded in the fifteenth century along with the gold trade. And with these interconnections came the clamour of the rest of the world for West African gold. Overproduction in West Africa, as described in this chapter, created a 'gold hunger' that drove the initial expansion of the Portuguese down the Moroccan, Mauritanian and Senegalese coasts in the 1430s and 1440s.

When looked at in this way, 'history' seems somehow changed. It is no longer European actions that provoked globalization, but a complicated, reciprocal exchange linking West Africa, the Islamic worlds and Europe. At the forefront of these shared exchanges was the religion of Islam, which was the faith of the long-distance traders who plied the caravan routes linking up the Mediterranean with the markets of West Africa. Through a shared creed, those with economic investments in such long and perilous journeys across the desert could find the trust and provide the 'credit' that kept the whole thing afloat.

This was well known to European historians in the early nineteenth century. In interviews with the trans-Saharan trader Al-Hajj Abd Salam Shabinī, conducted in the 1790s and published in 1820, that commerce to Timbuktu was conducted by 'trading *shereefs*' was made clear. In a book published a year earlier, in 1819, Bowdich described how, at the Ashanti Empire's Court at Kumasi, the chief North African trader of the city was a person from whom he could find out 'much information, for at each [visit] I found strange Moors just arrived from different parts of the interior, sojourning with him'. Thus, Islamic traders had a dual role in West Africa at this time: through trade, they influenced political change, and, by bringing Islam, they prompted West African kings to develop new worldviews and ways of governing.[79]

Islam itself was a variegated faith by the time of the sixteenth century and the heyday of Songhay, with many different influences. Desert clans such as the Masūfa migrated to Timbuktu from Māsina, bringing special areas of learning in Islamic law (*fiqh*). The great Timbuktu scholar Ahmad Baba had as his main *shaykh*, or religious instructor, a scholar from Djenné on the Niger. At the same time, Jakhanke Muslims adhering more closely to Sufi teachings were very active by 1500, from the region of modern Mali to Kano. Thus, debate and dialogue – and doctrinal dispute – were entrenched across the region.[80]

So it is that some parts of the West African tradition of discussion also accelerated in this distant past. As one oral historian puts it:

The world started with discussion	*Duniyaa foloota kacoa le la,*
and it will finish with discussion.	*A be bangua kacoa le la.*[81]

These were plural kingdoms, where discussion and mediations between different parties was fundamental. This laid the foundations of cultural futures, and also of material ones. West African economies had become based on the growing export of hard currencies – gold – and human beings whose labour value was going to become ever more important, in West Africa and beyond.

2

Causeways across the Savannah: From Senegambia to Sierra Leone

This chapter moves us from the great empires of landlocked inner West Africa to events along the Atlantic coastline. It shows how processes of unequal exchange grew in one of the most geographically rich regions in West Africa, stretching southwards from the borders of the Sahara at the Senegal River Valley to Sierra Leone. In between, among the creeks and swamps between the Gambia River and Guinea-Bissau, the earliest trans-Atlantic slave trade took root in the first decades of the sixteenth century. People rapidly learnt how to defend themselves, and that memory has not been lost. As one historian puts it, the inheritors of this history today certainly do not think of themselves as victims. This was rather the era when modern Senegambian identities came into being.[1]

How did people defend their communities? They expanded food production, fortified their settlements, and moved them away from the rivers and roads. Even today, if you travel on the main road north from Bissau, you will come across few villages, as these are still located some distance off main roads. This was how you protected yourself and your community in the era of people-hunting, and – later – in the era of modern colonialism.

Almost twenty years ago, now, a young Balanta friend from Guinea-Bissau invited me to his village, 'near' the small town where I was staying. We walked for almost two hours along a path through the bush that wound in what seemed like endless circles, until we found the wooden stakes that encircled and heralded his father's house. My friend's father launched into a tirade against his son, sitting on a low stool outside his house and elaborating expansively on what a wastrel he was. I felt lost by the path. In a sense, I had been taken on a walk through history. These paths had been deliberately designed to disorientate and ward off potential attackers in the era of the Atlantic trade; they would be unable to find their way out if they arrived seeking captives. Balanta communities preserve this memory in the shape of their settlements to this day.

It is helpful to begin thinking about this region by appreciating its very diverse geography. Fly into Freetown Airport in Sierra Leone and the coast to the north fragments into islands and a seemingly unbroken stretch of low-lying swamp and estuary broken by forests and bush fires, and by wisps of rivers curling around the mangroves. To the north-east rise the dry mountains of Fuuta Jaalo, which stretch for hundreds of miles inland across Guinea-Conakry towards Mali. Due north, the coast gives way to the maze of channels around the Bijagós Islands of Guinea-Bissau. A patchwork of rivers and palm-tree-studded glades occupies the southern Senegalese Casamance region between here and the Gambia River. Further north, the situation changes. The land surrounding Dakar is unremittingly dry, punctuated only by enormous baobab trees, whose girth testifies to the age of these real watchtowers of history, which have seen everything this book can relate, and probably much that came before it.

Speaking in 2015 at a conference on history, music and identity at London's School of Oriental and African Studies, the Dakar-based historian Boubacar Barry referred to this geographical diversity as one of the key historical features of the 'Greater Senegambia' region. It was this that brought different products – gum in the desert north, and kola nuts and ivory in the forested south – into contact with the growing world demand for African produce. Of course, it is false to think of this geography as static. A prolonged dry period from *c.* 1000 to 1500 was followed by a wet period from *c.* 1500 to 1640 in which geographical boundaries shifted, and with those boundaries went movements of people; after 1640 a new dry period followed, with further migrations.[2]

This chapter looks at this region up until around 1680. Vital economic changes were also afoot, to match the new climate. Up until the 1650s, the overwhelming bulk of imports into West Africa brought by European traders were currencies. While as late as the 1680s, as much as 59.2 per cent of the value of goods imported to

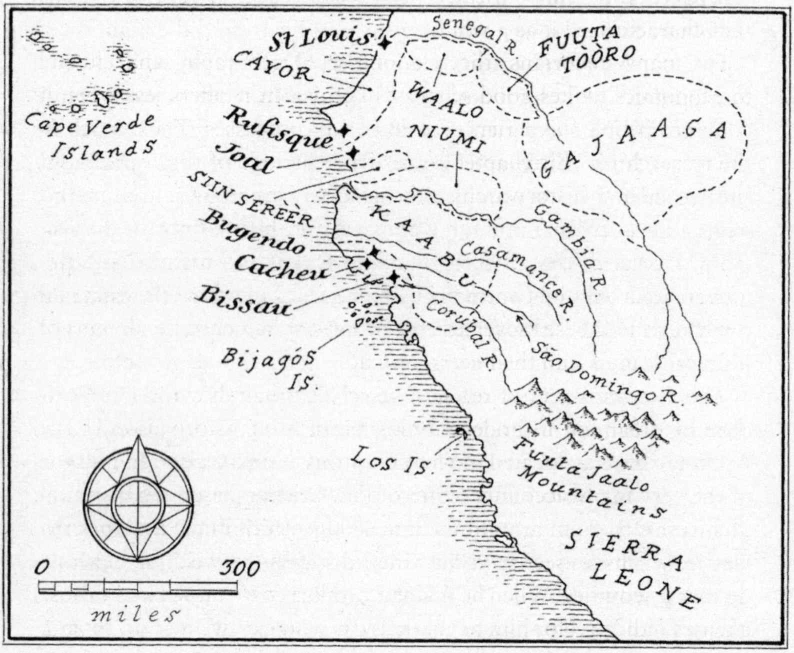

Senegambian states and trading centres

some parts of West Africa took the form of cowries, by the end of the eighteenth century, this figure would be down to 2.9 per cent. This speaks of the wider economic transformations afoot, from a setting in which an increased money supply can lubricate the long-distance trading networks and yet also stoke inflation, to one in which trade and productivity are disadvantaged. So this chapter also explores the beginnings of unequal exchange in this Greater Senegambia region. It takes the period from *c.* 1500 to 1680 all together, looking thematically at the different political, economic, and cultural transformations that characterized it as a whole.[3]

For many historians, the relationship of geography and climate to economics makes good sense of history. But it offers less when it comes to people's experiences of historical processes. Thus, much of the research for this chapter comes from periods of time spent consulting the oral-history archives held by the National Centre for Arts and Culture in Fajara, a suburb of the Gambian capital of Banjul. Here, I once discussed themes in migration and history in Senegambia with the nightwatchman, and he asked me if I knew what had really directed these movements of peoples: it had been the dreams of political leaders and their seers, he said.

This is reminiscent of recent research that has shown the importance of dreaming in understanding political transformation in the Asante Kingdom, located in what became Ghana. It also reminds me of the very many accounts of migrations held in these Gambian oral archives. One from around the late eighteenth century describes the way in which one seer travelled: '[he] was a man of wisdom, he was a diviner by cowries. When he divined with his cowries, wherever those cowries indicated for him to go, that was where he went.' But, though cowries were used for divination and as a store of ritual value in this part of West Africa, they were not the major currency in use. 'Fistfuls of shells' were important in Mali and Songhay, in the Kingdom of Kongo, and also in the Bight of Benin and in the Kingdom of Hueda; but in Senegambia other currencies were at work, especially iron bars and strips of cotton cloth.[4]

In the end, external written sources can tell us a great deal about the changes in the use of these currencies, and of the economic consequences of these transitions. However, they cannot tell us how these processes were experienced, lived and felt. For that, it is better to consult people such as Daniel Laeomahuma Jatta, a Gambian musicologist and specialist in the history of the akonting lute of his Jola people. Sitting in his compound in a suburb of Banjul, Jatta once described to me how in more distant times Jola palm-wine tappers in The Gambia used to stay by the coast, playing their akonting music and drinking palm wine late into the night. However, many of these Jola palm-wine tappers were seized at night by ghosts, which emerged with strong lights from the sea; and the akonting players were never seen again. This was a story that Jatta had been told by his father; and in this memory it is not the slave trade itself that is remembered, but rather the people who disappeared, and the culture that was theirs, symbolized by music.[5]

Instead of reproducing writing about slaving written by slavers, memories like Jatta's help to recognize how people's worlds were changing. In this transformation of subjectivity, music had a vital

Akonting lute.

part to play. The sixteenth and seventeenth centuries were, as we shall see in this chapter, a time when the trade in enslaved persons grew rapidly. Yet it would be wrong to think of this just as a time of horror and violence. As societies changed across West Africa, so did the ways in which peoples understood themselves, and music played an important part in this. As Jatta's own research has shown, the akonting lute of the Jola people was certainly one of the foundational instruments for African peoples in the New World. Many specialists agree with Jatta that the akonting was an influence behind the emergence of the banjo – 'America's African instrument', as a recent book puts it – and one illustration found by Jatta from the Caribbean of an instrument exactly like a modern akonting dates from the mid seventeenth century.[6]

Thus, as Senegambians were transported in slavery across the ocean in increasing numbers through this period, they brought with them the music and ideas that transformed their sense of themselves as they entered the New World. This would in time influence many performance styles throughout the Western hemisphere. The Jola had no griots. Indeed, there is no record of griots being sold into slavery, because they were royal praisesingers of powerful states. It would be the musical ideas and traditions of less hierarchical peoples like the Jola that would often help to transform the world's musical sensibilities, as Senegambian music morphed into American music in the New World.[7]

MALI, SONGHAY AND THE KINGDOMS OF SENEGAMBIA

Oral histories relating this 'Greater Senegambia' region to the Mali Empire are many. These accounts narrate how from the Empire of Mali, the great Sunjata Keita sent out his nephew and lieutenant, Tiramakang Traoré, into Senegambia. Like many (if not all) legendary founders of West African kingdoms, Tiramakang was the son of a hunter, Daamansa Wulaading. It was the hunters who had a virtual monopoly on bravery, testing themselves against the animals and spirits of the bush, and so it was hunters whose prowess over beasts could often be turned to strategic military ends.[8]

When Tiramakang reached Senegambia, however, he found that there were no people to rule. One oral account tells that he complained to Sunjata Keita, who provided him with 75,000 settlers, 40,000 freemen and 35,000 slaves. Tiramakang advanced until he reached the Gambia River, whereupon 'he sat down and told [his followers] to build a causeway. For three months they heaped stones in the river, until the pile of stones reached the surface of the water and extended across the river. Then the horses and pedestrians crossed to Kantora.' Kantora was probably the most important trading settlement on the Upper Gambia River, described as a major trading post linking the Gambia with the trans-Saharan routes by the first European to venture up the Gambia River, Diogo Gomes, in 1448. According to this oral account of Tiramakang Traoré's thirteenth-century expedition, once they crossed to the far side of the river and headed south towards Guinea-Bissau, they then found that 'apart from the bush and the beasts there were no habitations except those of the Baynunkoos, a very ancient people. If you departed from one village, you could walk five days before sighting another dwelling.'[9]

The many oral accounts that give versions of this foundation story are rich in symbolism. Versions reoccur in different contexts throughout Senegambian history. So, when the Fula warrior king Koli Tenguella led an army south across the Gambia River around the turn of the sixteenth century, probably *c.* 1490, his troops were also said to have built a causeway across the Gambia in this manner. What is significant in these oral accounts is not some sort of (mythical) historical 'fact', but rather the size of the armies, hence the number of new settlers to the region, and the consequent transformation of existing social and political structures.* Griots recount these histories to their own political masters, themselves often involved in changing societies. These accounts of Tiramakang's arrival also echo an important factor common to narratives of West African history: almost all of them begin with a tale of migration. Peoples were not settled, 'stuck'

* Similar symbolism is found in descriptions of the size of Oyo's army, from what is now Yorùbáland in Nigeria, where the troops were said to march over an ox hide until it wore thin.

and 'unchanging', but always moving into new moral and political communities.[10]

What was the world like into which these peoples arrived? Many of them may have been moving for a variety of reasons: spiritual reasons linked to divination, and also practical reasons related to the climatic periods of dryness in the Sahel. They arrived at an under-populated area characterized by dense forests and rice paddies, for this part of West Africa had long been a rich rice-producing region. One oral historian describes how there was a variety of smaller peoples living in the region prior to Tiramakang's migration, with no more than 120 villages across the whole of what became the large federated Kingdom of Kaabu. But when the migrations began, everything changed: 'They all came from the east. / The Mandinkas came from Manding. / They came bit by bit until their number increased. / The Fulas came from Maasina, and came to Nyoro . . . / They also came bit by bit.'[11]

The migrations from Mali to Senegambia were driven by several factors, one being the expanding influence of the long-distance trade across the Sahara. Alongside this, the changing climate was a cause of conflict. The gathering drought may explain why some oral accounts also indicate that the era prior to Tiramakang was one of disorder. According to the account cited above, Tiramakang's father, Daamansa Wulaading, grew in power after defeating a witch called Duukamisa, who had eaten 1,000 people. Militarized power was masculinized in this story, while women carried the can in the shape of the 'witch'. In many West African societies, the phenomenon of the 'cannibal witch' is invoked to represent the depredations of slavery, where cannibals are human beings who literally 'eat' others, consuming their life forces. Therefore, the rise of Tiramakang and Mali's influence, in this account, was also a way of putting an end to the discord that had increased raiding for captives. Or, as one oral historian puts it, 'These villages are where they feed on . . . / You know, all of us must have a / place to feed on?'[12]

By and by, Tiramakang Traoré and his followers founded the Manding [Mali-derived] state of Kaabu. With its capital located at Kansala in north-eastern Guinea-Bissau, by the sixteenth century Kaabu's influence extended over what are now The Gambia, the southern Senegalese region of Casamance and Guinea-Bissau. This was a federation with a fierce warrior aristocracy, the *nyantios*, who shaped Kaabu's strength and secured its power for centuries to come.

To the north of the Gambia River was the most powerful state in the fifteenth century, Jolof, ruled from a central capital near the Senegal River. 'Great Jolof' had five provinces: Jolof, Cayor, Waalo, Bawol and Siin. Jolof was also subordinate to Mali, according to fourteenth-century accounts. The size of the Jolof cavalry by the sixteenth century reveals extensive connections to trans-Saharan trade (and also, by that time, Atlantic trade). In the 1570s, the Cape Verdean André Álvares de Almada described well how horsemanship had come to influence military and social status in Jolof society:

> they are excellent horsemen . . . some among them can ride in a straight line, raising their stirrups over the horse's neck to strike one leg against the other two or three times; they often have races, or wagers as to which of them will be able to use their big arrows to cut through the girth of the saddle of the other without wounding or killing the horse.[13]

So, by the middle of the fifteenth century, from the Senegal River Valley in the north to the borders of what are now Guinea-Bissau and Guinea-Conakry in the south, important states had arisen that were connected to the trans-Saharan trade and the Mali Empire. The Jolof had a powerful cavalry, and a military apparatus that was often used to raid the neighbouring Serèèr peoples for slaves. Tiramakang Traoré had led Manding settlers from Mali into the creeks and forests south of the Gambia River, where they rapidly intermarried with the peoples there to form Kaabu. The importance of Kaabu's women in binding this new society together can be seen in one important change accepted by the Manding settlers: while Mande cultures traditionally inherited through the male line and were patrilineal, in Kaabu inheritance would pass through the woman's line and were matrilineal, allowing the region's original cultures and its women to retain importance.[14]

In the sixteenth and seventeenth centuries this framework changed. The arrival of Portuguese traders offering horses bred on the Cape Verde Islands, in exchange for captives, led to the coastal provinces of Jolof breaking away from the centre as they developed this new access to cavalry. The Serèèr peoples south of Dakar also sought alliances with the Portuguese, having hitherto been perennially raided by the Jolof for captives. Competition developed for access to the maritime long-distance trade; increased local competition placed the commercial advantage with the long-distance trader, just as it had done with the gold trade as described by Al-Ouazzan.[15]

At the same time, the potential for commercial and political power that came with this long-distance trade created new states – Niumi and Wuuli on the north bank of the Gambia River, and the Great Fula Kingdom of Fuuta Tòòro on the Senegal River inland – and consolidated Kaabu's federated system of government to the south. Fula power grew with Fuuta Tòòro, which arose after the migrating armies led by Koli Tenguella settled on the banks of the Senegal River around 1510; and Fula power was then bolstered by the increasing demand of Atlantic traders for hides. Fula peoples were traditionally cattle herders, and the first decades of the seventeenth century saw a rapid increase in demand for hides from Dutch traders in particular, who often traded them in Italy, where the leather industry was booming. In the 1670s, worried that the Atlantic trade was outcompeting them, trans-Saharan traders, led from the north by Nasir al-Din, fought back against the European traders on the coast. This saw a revival of Islamic influence, which had in fact been growing across Senegambia since the fall of Songhay in 1591.[16]

The connection of Songhay to Senegambia had always been fairly close. One of the two most important rulers of Songhay, Askia Mohammed, is thought to have belonged to the Sylla family that came from the Senegal River Valley. So it is not surprising that, after the Moroccan defeat in 1591, some of the clerics of Timbuktu dispersed towards Senegambia. By 1650, the influence of the cleric Njaay Saal in the coastal province of Cayor was said to be significant, for instance, and a clerical village called Pir was founded, probably setting in train a pattern of struggle and change. Following Nasir al-Din's uprising twenty years later, an increasingly close relationship emerged between Islam and kingship in northern Senegambia; and, by 1680, the entire Greater Senegambia region was beginning to look very different indeed.[17]

'Scene of the Army of Fouta Toro on the March'

The transformations were, of course, not just political but also economic. The aforementioned trend of importing currencies was shifting by 1680. A vital factor in this negative economic trend was the place of African labour in shaping the economy of the West. The loss of labour through the trade in enslaved captives meant that surplus-value producing young men had their economic output placed within the growing European empires. This, combined with the export of gold discussed in the last chapter, and the import of currencies that lost their relative value over time – such as iron and cloth – placed West African political systems at a distinct economic disadvantage. Indeed, these imports added value to European economies as they boosted the European manufacturing base.[18]

With a loss of economic weight went a decline in political power. In Senegambia this was apparent as early as 1488, when Bumi Jeléen, the Jolof prince, visited Portugal in the hope of gaining Portuguese military support to reclaim the title of king that he said had been wrongfully taken from him by his half-brothers. He was accompanied, said the chronicler João de Barros, by 'relatives and the nobility of [Jolof]'. Taken first to the castle of Palmela, the party were dressed in

Portuguese clothing and given horses, so that they could continue, with Bumi Jeléen 'being always served in everything not as a barbarous prince beyond the law but as if he were a European prince, used to [European] civility and customs'. And, indeed, according to Barros, this was in keeping with his dignity and presence as a prince, for he was a 'tall man with a well-fashioned [*bem-disposto*] body, of a fine aspect; aged around forty years old, he had a full beard, which was well cared for, and seemed to be a prince to whom all obeisance was owed'.[19]

Tucked away in this remarkable story are the seeds of the changes that would engulf Senegambia over the coming centuries. Bumi Jeléen had turned to the Portuguese for help because of the fratricidal civil war that augured the future fragmentation of Jolof. João de Barros had seen how the civil war had been stoked by '[the coming of] our ships which traded on that coast, the land was becoming full of horses and other trade goods which he [Bumi Jeléen] lacked'. Portuguese trade was exacerbating military build-ups on all sides, and offered an avenue for defeated princes to seek redress. Moreover, Bumi Jeléen's diplomatic mission was to end badly. In due course, João II, the Portuguese king, sent a fleet back with him to help reclaim the kingdom, but the captain-general, Pero Vaz de Cunha, then killed Bumi Jeléen at the mouth of the Senegal River, claiming to suspect treason. Although King João II did, in fact, execute many of those responsible when they returned to Portugal, the nature of this unequal political and economic relationship was becoming defined.[20]

TRADE AND POLITICAL POWER IN GREATER SENEGAMBIA

By the early seventeenth century, many of these changes were falling into place. The great empires had fragmented, replaced by smaller, centralized kingdoms in the creeks and forests of the Atlantic coastline of West Africa. The aristocracies of these kingdoms had developed a heavy dependence on the Atlantic trade to buttress their power. Thus, the local kings, and their representatives, assiduously monitored all ships that came to trade.

Asylum for Liberated Africans in Freetown.

The Dutch-based trader Willem Cunningham described arriving in Sierra Leone in June 1625. Once they had anchored, the local factor of the port came on to the ship to take payment before the ship could land. Other people soon followed him, offering 'a guesthouse for 40 or 50 pieces of red Indian cloth [*Inde Roos*]', but Cunningham found the lodgings to be 'very wretched' and slept offshore. He would have harboured at the foot of the low promontory where, two centuries later, an asylum would be built by the British Royal Navy West Africa Squadron for slaves who had been liberated from 'illegal' slaving voyages. In the seventeenth century, this was where Dutch ships came to buy water and, just a few years before Cunningham called, his Dutch colleague Dierick Ruyters scratched his name on a rock here. The etching can still be seen amid the market stalls on the shoreline, below Freetown, testament to the hapless human desire for immortality.[21]

The relationship of West African rulers to European traders was soon formalized. Europeans had to pay taxes on arrival at a kingdom's port, and in return they were offered access to local markets for trade, and provisions such as water, livestock and grain. In Senegambia, the taxes were often around a quarter of the value of the goods on each ship. In return, West African traders offered various types of hospitality to encourage the growth of their commercial networks. The English gold prospector Richard Jobson, sailing up the Gambia in 1620, described how an important *dyula* trader called Saho offered him young female captives for sale, such as other white men 'earnestly desired'. In return, Jobson plied Saho with drink, so much so that the *dyula* trader 'took more than he would, inasmuch as he fell asleepe . . . and slept soundly upon my bed by me in the boate, and in the morning complained of his head'.[22]

These trading relationships went far beyond the trade in captives and the informal exchange of (male) pleasures. Though Saho claimed to Jobson that these enslaved persons were 'the only marchandize they carried downe into the countrey', there were many trading systems at work, of which the slave trade was but one. In the early seventeenth century, the Dutch trader Pieter van den Broecke described how cloth woven near what is now Dakar was traded as far away as the Gold Coast and what is now Congo. By the 1670s, cloths woven in Gambia and the Cape Verde Islands were traded on the Gold Coast by the English.[23]

At this time, people travelled from the Dakar region three leagues down the coast by horse to the port of Rufisque,* and it was 'a very happy road, because there are many villages there and it is a very well-travelled road, and there is a lot of palm wine to drink'. Meanwhile, those bringing goods to trade to the Dakar region brought a mixture of ivory, yellow wax, gum Arabic, couscous and chickens for sale. Although accounts such as Jobson's suggested that men took the lead in trade, in fact, in Senegambia – as in many parts of Africa – traders were usually women. Women worked, and raised their own sources of funds. The wealth and dynamism of female traders are shown by their being among the richest people in the trading settlement of Cacheu in the later seventeenth century. Women there were

* Known in the sources at the time as 'Arrecife' (Portuguese for 'reef'), the forerunner of the modern Dakar suburb of Rufisque.

both 'big traders' and market hawkers, interacting with Atlantic traders on a daily basis. That many societies were matrilineal gave women a certain status, and people always felt safe if they returned to their mother's village; thus, women were often more independent and influential than Jobson's account implied.[24]

The European traders who wrote these accounts resided in Senegambian communities according to West African social models. Kings would allow strangers to settle in return for certain privileges, or if making marriage alliances into the ruling family – what historians call a model of 'landlords and strangers'. A famous example of this was someone known in the region as Ganagoga ('the man who speaks all the languages' in the Biafada language), a Portuguese man originally called João Ferreira. He had gone to the Court of Fuuta Tòòro in the middle of the sixteenth century, and once there he married the Fula king's daughter and had a child with her.[25] However, while the most successful settlers such as João Ferreira integrated into Senegambian cultures, the interests of the strangers were increasingly connected to powerful external forces: Christian and Islamic kingdoms each seeking access to West African gold and labour reserves as the process of globalization began to take shape.[26]

The kind of framework that was in place was well summarized by the Englishman William Finch, who described the trade in Sierra Leone thus in 1607: 'the Portugals get of them for Rice, Salt, Beads, Beds, Garlicke, French Bottles, Copper-Kettles; low-priced knives, Hats, Linen checkered like Barbers, Apnas, Lattin Basons, edge-tools.'[27] A further window on to the goods that West Africans received for this trade comes through the account books of Manuel Bautista Pérez, who was tried and burnt by the Inquisition of Lima, Peru, in 1639.* As a young man, Bautista Pérez had been a slave trader based in Cacheu, and his account books from Guinea-Bissau are very illuminating. On one trading trip from Cacheu to the ports of Joal, Portudal and Rufisque† in 1618, he sold taffeta, cloth, crystal and coral; however, the most valuable item traded was brandy (aguardiente), and wine was also sold. Alcohol was indeed a predominant trade good of Bautista

* Mentioned above in the Foreword.

† All along the *Petite Côte* ('Little Coast') south of modern Dakar.

Pérez: he sold ten flagons of wine in Ziguinchor and four barrels of rum in Geba in 1617.* Alongside the booze, Bautista Pérez traded large amounts of shell and coral used for ornamentation, and a variety of everyday European manufactures such as shirts, socks, strips of cloth, paper, and even cheeses from the Alentejo in Portugal. He also traded large volumes of cloth that had been manufactured in the Jolof kingdoms, and in Casamance to the north.[28]

The place of alcohol consumption in Greater Senegambian trade at this early time already shows some of the changing dynamics; and even in 1995, when I visited the King of Canogo on the Bijagós Islands in Guinea-Bissau, it was still expected that I should bring a bottle of rum as a gift. This part of West Africa is certainly not alone in this, since alcohol (most often rum) was also long a lynchpin of the trade in Angola from the seventeenth century onwards, and alcohol must also be brought as a gift to meet local chiefs, or *sobas*, in Angola to this day. Alcohol was not only for elite consumption, however, but was also used for religious purposes, often replacing palm wine as a libation at spirit shrines. For this reason, alcohol use became associated with both African kings and with African religious practice, something that, as we shall see by the end of the book, would prove very significant.[29]

A classic oral narrative to exemplify this is that of Kelefa Saane, an epic of conquest and political change set in Senegambia in the early nineteenth century. In many accounts of Kelefa, his violent actions are associated closely with alcohol consumption: one historian, Sana Kuyate, described how Kelefa went from village to village, raising hell and selling inhabitants for slaves. So it may be no accident that, alongside the sale of alcohol, Bautista Pérez also traded large numbers of knives and swords made in Portugal, stoking the sort of violence that appears in the epic of Kelefa. At one village, one oral historian says of Kelefa, 'the day they were leaving there, half the children of the village / went to gather small sticks of firewood . . . He saw those children in the woods – a hundred children. / He took all these and sold them all for alcoholic beverage.'[30]

* Ziguinchor is now the major town on the southern Senegalese region of Casamance; Geba is in north-central Guinea-Bissau.

Growing trade thereby promoted increased social hierarchies in Greater Senegambia. Those who had access to social and political capital could display this through new ornaments, through wearing imported cloths or by having a high time of it drinking imported rum; they could enforce this power, too, by buying an arsenal of guns and knives. With this increasing hierarchy came more authoritarian power structures. The political power to reorganize labour according to 'age-sets' (where field tasks were divided into groups of young people by age and gender), and to expand the agricultural production of provisions for the ships of the slave trade, was made possible by these new trading links. This meant that, initially, far from weakening West African political authority, a major consequence of this trade was the emergence of stronger centres of political power. Elites were able to charge tolls and, as mediators of the long-distance trade, develop into a powerful aristocracy.[31]

European traders knew perfectly well that they could not have lived, worked and traded there without acknowledging African power. An early-seventeenth-century account of the coast in Casamance describes how the peoples living there routinely robbed any ship that foundered and captured the crew for ransom. In nearby Cacheu, at a similar time, people would break into the houses of European traders by night, freeing slaves and stealing the ornaments from the local churches. By the 1660s, one priest described how there was no way to stop people setting Cacheu on fire, and every time that they wanted the Portuguese traders to do something, they would occupy the water sources of the town, rendering the Portuguese impotent. Further north, the dynamics were the same, and, by the 1680s, Jolof power over French traders near the estuary of the River Senegal was so clear that when one, De la Marche, stole some cotton and tobacco, he and the crew of his ship were set upon by a force of 500 sent by the Brac (King) of Waalo, killing De la Marche and three of his companions.[32]

Thus, the beginnings of global trade as it affected West Africa would not just produce greater inequalities between West African societies and other parts of the world; it also produced greater economic and political inequalities within West Africa itself. A powerful trading class did emerge, but they did so alongside the growing power of kings. European traders had to adapt to this power, and those who could not fared badly. When Capuchin missionaries refused to bury someone in 1684 because of his multiple sexual partners, they were hauled out of the house, dragged by their beards and forced by arms to carry out the burial. If wars broke out between different kingdoms, the supply line in provisions to the trading ports could be completely stopped. In these cases, only those with good local connections did well, and these could come about only when foreign traders were prepared to adapt. As two Portuguese traders accused of cheating their African associates in the 1660s discovered, failure to adapt could be very dangerous, for 'the fury of the [Africans] was so great, and so many the arrows and darts that rained down on them and on us, that we were all in danger of death . . . with the [Africans] coming to seek them out again with arms [once the traders had hidden in the house of two missionaries], shouting loudly and shrilly and promising that no one was going to leave alive.'[33]

What, then, was the fabric of life in these mixed communities? We can see well-dressed local officials in the latest cloths boarding ships such as Cunningham's at Freetown to collect taxes, and women lading buckets of water at the beachside, or holding provisions for sale. Caravans of male captives brought wax, hides and provisions along with themselves for sale to the portside. Senegambian rulers sought luxuries, smoking tobacco and drinking rum, while circumscribing access to powerful religious shrines, where they poured libations to the supernatural powers from which they sought protection.

SLAVERY AND VIOLENCE: MONETIZING THE SENEGAMBIAN ECONOMY

Writing shortly before he died of fever, in around 1616, a Portuguese missionary in Sierra Leone, Manoel Álvares, described well the growing power of the 'Emperor' of Casamance, Masatamba: 'This [title of] emperor was won by a King, called Masatamba . . . this Masatamba was the best friend which the Portuguese Nation ha[s] ever had here . . . he was very proud of being called a Brother in Arms of The King of Portugal.' Writing in the 1620s, the Cape Verdean trader

André de Donelha also described how Masatamba was 'such a good friend of the whites that neither they nor the blacks ever lost anything in his kingdom, that there were no robberies.' In order to test this out, a newcomer left a dagger by the roadside, which was brought the very next morning to the Court of Masatamba at Brucama by someone who had found it. The Portuguese saw this as evidence of Masatamba's great friendship with them and openness to trade, but things were not so clear-cut for the emperor's subjects. The fear that underpinned Masatamba's power also underlies this story: his subjects were so afraid of the consequences of going against his will that they would bring the slightest object owned by a foreigner to his Court.[34]

Other significant details show that Masatamba's power was a double-edged sword. The social transformations needed to increase production of provisions for slave-trading ships were marked, with many of the provisions coming from his kingdom. Rice-growing boomed both here and across Guinea-Bissau in the following centuries. Indeed, the idea that 'West Africa could not feed itself' was the reverse of the truth for many centuries. Social transformations in agricultural work meant that rice-growing communities produced a substantial surplus, which was bought by the slave-trade ships. It was only during Guinea-Bissau's War of Independence from Portugal (1960–74) that rice-growing went into decline, never really to recover; this cemented the country's current dependence on rice imports from China, which are bartered by farmers for the cashew nuts that constitute the country's major export.[35]

A sobering comment on these social transformations is that, in Senegambia, European traders were often assumed to be cannibals by West Africans. This notion was described by one sailor as early as 1455, and was a repeated trope long into the seventeenth century. And, indeed, across West Africa, from Cameroon and Angola to Senegambia, many different peoples believed in the cannibalism of the European slave traders; here was a mirror-image of the more famous trope, whereby Europeans discussed African 'cannibalism'. The Africans, however, had some justification, for in this case the slave trade was one that consumed people, devouring West and West-Central Africa's human resources.[36]

Rice paddy, Casamance, Senegal.

Political violence was never far away, as the growth of a monetized economy was fuelled by this trade in captives. The process of physical and psychological violence, of course, began with the initial enslavement of peoples, through warfare between West African kingdoms, banditry, judicial enslavement for crimes such as adultery or witchcraft, or sale to clear debts, as described in the 1570s by André Álvares de Almada: 'The slaves which they have [on the Gambia River] and which they sell, they capture in wars and through judicial trials and kidnappings, because they go to steal them from one part or another.' Almada also described the way in which some of this occurred, discussing a river in Guinea-Bissau where there are 'large canoes in which there are thieves called *Gampisas* in the [Biafada] language. They are like bandits . . . they are so canny that if somebody comes from the bush inland, they pretend that they want to welcome and host them, and welcome them into their homes; and, having had them there a few days, they put the idea in their heads that they have some friends by the sea, and that they'd like to take them there so that they can meet them and enjoy each other's company; and going to the ships they sell them; and in this way they trick many people.'[37]

The inscribing of violence on to the bodies of the enslaved then continued at the ports of departure, where captives were branded with the mark of their 'owners'. Such violence was further exemplified through the account books of slave traders such as Bautista Pérez, who assessed captives whom they had purchased solely on the basis of their potential economic impact, describing infirmities such as 'swollen sides', cataracts and burns as 'losses [*daños*]'. The culmination of the violence was the Middle Passage itself, when potential losses from mortality were weighed up against profits to be gained from transporting the maximum number of captives. This reduction of human life to an economic equation was made explicit in the so-called 'books of the dead': account books that listed the losses incurred through the deaths of those enslaved captives who perished on the crossing to the Americas, and in which the branding marks of the owners were written clearly in the margins, alongside the simple names of the dead.[38]

Alongside this process of physical objectification and invented hierarchies of human beings, economic values were developing their own hierarchies. There was plenty of money in Greater Senegambia, as in other parts of West Africa. Several different types of money were used in different regions, but by far the most common were cloth strips and iron bars. These currencies were not introduced by Europeans; when Europeans did trade them, again, they imitated this from an existing framework. In the early sixteenth century, Al-Ouazzan described how the kingdoms along the Senegal River used 'small pieces of iron, on which they rely for small purchases such as bread, milk or millet'. Cloth strips were also used as currencies by the Fula in the Senegal River Valley and as far south as the Fuuta Jaalo Mountains; known as the *soro*, this cloth money was the precursor of the *barafula* cloths that began to be woven on the Cape Verde Islands by the end of the fifteenth century.[39]

As trade expanded in the sixteenth century, so, too, did the currency base in the region. By the seventeenth century, iron-bar imports constituted roughly half the value of all European imports into

Senegambia. This was not thus the stereotyped trade of baubles and drink for slaves and ivory, but a monetized trade that was adding to exchanges and commercial complexity. The standard bar was 10 feet long, 2 inches wide and ⅓ of an inch thick, weighing around 29 pounds; and these bars were often notched so that they could be subdivided into smaller pieces. Once there, local smiths would melt the bars down to turn into agricultural implements, weapons and domestic tools; while some of the iron, as noted above by Al-Ouazzan, was rendered into pieces for small purchases. This vital role in shaping the tools that drove social change gave blacksmiths great power in Senegambian societies, and would also prove vital in early plantation societies in the New World, where African abilities to work with metal were vital to making the equipment without which a plantation could not have functioned.[40]

The abilities of the smiths were vividly described by the Dutch trader Pieter de Marees, around 1600: 'They make very fine ironwork, and large quantities of Iron can be sold there, especially fine long bars on which they are keener than anyone else in the world. They use them to make Tools for fishing and Agriculture, and also weapons such as Bows, Arrows, Harpoons, and Assegais.'[41]

The growth of iron bars as the standard money in Greater Senegambia is easily seen in the sources. Arriving at the port of Portudal in 1606, Pieter van den Broecke noted that the factor of the port placed a domestic help with him 'to serve me for two iron bars per month. We paid our tolls and customs together to the factor, so that we were allowed to trade here, besides other traders, which amounted to fifty-seven iron bars.' The money was also widely accepted to the south in the Guinea-Bissau region, so that, by 1617, Manuel Bautista Pérez recounted sending 40 iron bars to Geba for trade, and 250 to the Bijagós Islands. Further north, by 1640, according to Claude Jannequin, by far the most valuable items of trade on the Senegal River were iron bars and cloth imported from Rouen. By 1730, Francis Moore paid a tax of 120 bars at the mouth of the Gambia River for licence to trade – hence the name of the port located on the north bank of the Gambia today, Barra.[42]

The growth of the iron-bar economy was set by the mutual interests of Senegambian and European traders. There was ready access to iron in Europe, with many of the iron bars imported from Sweden. And, although there had been a long history of smithing and smelting in West Africa, the Atlantic iron trade without doubt increased the volumes available. More iron bars meant increased trade and currency, facilitating market exchanges. The terms were set by West African kings and their factors, so much so that Richard Jobson described how, in 1620, English traders had to take their iron bars to the local smiths on the Gambia to make sure that they were the right length for use. In Cacheu, by the end of the seventeenth century, the requirement (set by African traders) that iron bars be at least 18 palms was registered in a list of goods legally to be taken for trade in the port. It was the African peoples of Greater Senegambia who gradually pushed up the volumes of iron needed for trade, something that shows the political control of West African rulers over their territory.[43]

Yet, while this facilitated the growth of African political institutions, it also created broader economic patterns that would ultimately undermine West Africa's economic position. Key to this was the nature of this trading relationship with the Europeans. As Greater Senegambia's trade became ever more closely concentrated on enslaved captives, systems of credit were developed that would enable traders to go up and down the rivers and through the forests of the region with trade goods. As De la Courbe noted in 1685, on the Gambia, the English and French 'present them with merchandise to go and trade upriver and in the creeks, and then they return to sell them what they have brought back, making at least half of the credit back in profit'.[44]

These goods, produced in the main in Europe (though much cloth was also imported from India), became fundamental to European economies, with the bulk of the profits on the trade in enslaved persons made through the purchase and sale of European manufactured goods. Incentives were created, therefore, for the overproduction of these goods, which were 'dumped' in West Africa in the credit framework outlined by De la Courbe above; and required in consequence a greater volume of enslaved persons for sale in exchange to make up for the growing merchandise and ensure a 'balance of payments'. Thus, the credit cycle, with its growing volumes of imported currencies and other goods, went hand in hand with the expansion of the trade in captives.[45]

An example of the sheer volume of goods being imported by the 1620s comes from an extraordinary list of goods imported in a Dutch fleet of 1624. Iron remained important as the financial lubricant of Senegambian trade, with the fleet carrying 14,328 iron bars. But also on board were many different types of Indian cloths, as well as satin, silver and floral brocade, 264 pieces of English serge, and 1,039 Irish blankets (not to mention copper basins and cauldrons, and over 15,000 pounds in weight of copper bars). These goods were advanced to African traders on credit, and by and by these traders would return to port with human beings, ivory, wax and provisions for trade.[46]

By the end of the seventeenth century, therefore, an economic system had been established across Greater Senegambia that favoured the emergence of small, powerful kingdoms at the expense of larger ones such as Jolof. The economy of the region was based around trade and exchange, and depended fundamentally on credit, in common with slave-trading economies throughout the Atlantic Basin, where, as soon as a credit source dried up, so did the trade.[47]

However, the weight of these currencies as set against global currencies was in decline, and thus West African kings did not have the economic power to resist the dumping of increasing volumes of cheaply manufactured goods. Nor did they want to, for these goods facilitated greater trade, and it was through control of these trading networks that their power had grown. The authority that went with ruling was one that the new trading patterns had tended to increase, entrenching the local aristocracies. This cycle of credit from the Atlantic economy created growth – as economic credit does – but it could be cashed out only through the violence involved in the increased export of enslaved captives. The economic differential between Senegambian and Atlantic-world economies, therefore, grew throughout this period, as capital accumulation accelerated outside West Africa.

MONEY, PRESTIGE AND INEQUALITY

By the later seventeenth century, the power that went with ruling a state like Kaabu was not one that any of its rulers wanted to let go. Power was central to the identities of the new warrior aristocracies that ruled the region. Authority over trade, settlement and decision-making was concentrated in the aristocracy, and fundamental to the retention of such power was the place of aristocratic warriors, such as the *nyantios* in Kaabu. The *nyantios* were privileged; the oral accounts tell us how 'these people also, the time they became nyancho / because of their pride and how they reserved themselves, / they always feed on other people. / They do nothing.' Thus, hierarchy was everything: 'There was a well in Badora / Which was called Nyampeng Njai. / It was surrounded by pawpaw trees and by silkcotton trees with smoothish earth. / The women of the princely house used to draw water from it. / Poor women did not draw water from it.' Those who were *nyantios* had access to the best water, and they were able to 'feed' off the vital energy, and labour, of others.[48]

This increasing social division had accompanied the rise of the trade in enslaved persons and political violence. Desolation would often follow; the Dutch sailor Willem Schouten described a surprising human absence near the Magrabomba River of Sierra Leone: 'We cast anchor about a league from the coast, and went ashore, to find a desert and uninhabited land.' His colleague Jacques Le Maire sailed shortly to a nearby river, 'and saw no people, just wild Cattle, monkeys, and Birds'. The following day, on 24 August 1615, several crew members went ashore, and 'our people went in to several rivers, and touched land, to find people or some provisions . . . and they saw lots of turtles and crocodiles, but no people.'[49]

Yet, fifty years earlier, the Magrabomba River was a destination for slave-trading ships from the New World, where human captives could readily be secured. The consequence of that had been insecurity and the flight of people away from the creeks and rivers by the coast, where the ships used to arrive. North of the lion-shaped jungle-covered headland, which fell dramatically into the sea (the Leone of Sierra Leone, which can still be picked out today just south of

Freetown), the flat creeks and swamps nearby had emptied. To the south some islands rose offshore, straight out of the ocean, and, by the later eighteenth century, 'Banana Island' would become a cruel depot for captives awaiting the Atlantic crossing; here John Newton, who later composed 'Amazing Grace', himself lived in captivity for several years, and began to rethink his path in life.[50]

The fundamental dynamic at play across the whole region was of the concentration of political power, with the wealth derived from trade goods becoming a source of status and a marker of inequality. Increased trade did not, therefore, bring an equal benefit to the peoples of Greater Senegambia. It was a source of greater political violence, social insecurity and insubordination for many; whereas for the new elites, through control of trade, they were able to exercise and display their power. And resentment of the arbitrary power of the new aristocracies was beginning to emerge.

The Atlantic trade was thus highly disruptive of existing institutions. In Greater Senegambia, the Jolof 'Empire' was fragmenting, while the Empire of Kaabu was rising; in Sierra Leone, during the sixteenth century, the Kingdom of the Sapes was overcome by migrants, known as the Manes, from the collapsing Mali Empire. Everything changed: when political systems were large scale and complex, they often fell apart; when they were smaller and weaker, they became stronger. The fundamental place of the Atlantic trade in West African political life was not, therefore, universal, but depended on pre-existing conditions. The unifying theme was the disruption that it had introduced.[51]

Beyond disruption, another important unifying theme across the region was the place of long-distance trade, just as we have already seen in the Sahel. The great traders across Senegambia were the Mandinga *dyula* traders, who had dispersed here from Mali's centre, just as they had also moved to Kano and Borno. Writing in the 1620s, the Cape Verdean trader André de Donelha noted that 'the greatest traders that there are in this whole region [Guiné] are the Mandinga [from Mali], especially their *bixirins*, who are their priests . . . it would be impossible to find any port of the Jolofs, in the region of [Guinea-Bissau] and right up to Sierra Leone, in which you did not find these *bixirins*.' Or, as the oral historian Al-Hadji Ibrahima

Cissé put it, 'In stock trading, / Mandinkas did some trading. / [The Christians] gave goods to / the Mandinkas, the Mandinkas did the tradings.'[52]

The spread of the Mandinga traders throughout these regions went with the expansion of their networks and of the volume of goods traded. The inflation in currency values was also an important feature, noted by slave-trading officials, with one saying in 1616 that 'what used to be enough to buy two slaves a short time ago is now only enough for one.' As monies became more widespread, traders proliferated, and the intensity of exchanges went with them.[53]

A major characteristic of this huge expansion of trading frameworks was the place of the money that enabled the whole system to work. Greater supplies of ready cash made it much easier for markets to expand. Alongside the iron bars already discussed, the most important form of currency in Greater Senegambia consisted of strips of locally produced cloth. Almada described how, in the 1570s, 'along all this coast, from the Jolof to the Mandinga lands, there is very good cotton cloth, dark and white cloths, and many other types and styles, and the dyes are so fine that they can even blind those who see them.' This cloth was often produced in Gambia, and by the Jolof in Senegambia, and further south in Geba and the surrounding regions of what is now Guinea-Bissau.

By the time that the slave trader Manuel Bautista Pérez was living in Cacheu in the 1610s, local cloths had become a standard unit of account. By this time, Manoel Álvares tells us, the houses of the Portuguese in Cacheu '[were] mostly big and square in shape, well located, some of them with an upper storey, the walls made of adobe covered with palm fronds . . . [and] the roofs covered first with wood and then earth'.

In this prosperous slave-trading port, figures like Bautista Pérez lived 'very luxuriously . . . covered with silks and other sorts of expensive clothing . . . and various types of Damask from India and China . . . walking around with offensive and defensive weapons, daggers and swords'. They bought and sold people, wax, ivory and food provisions, but it was cloths that were the key unit of value in their account books: the price of such basic activities as renting a house, buying provisions such as couscous, and purchasing wine,

View of Cacheu, Guiné. To the right is the Portuguese fort.

shirts or jam were all accounted for in Bautista Pérez's accounts according to their value in *panos* (the Portuguese word for cloths). Thus, cloths were accounting units as well as tangible objects that people could wear, hang on their walls or place in burials.[54]

In terms of the broader theme of this book related to West Africa's economic place in the world, this use of cloth money was very important. As we have seen, the role of iron bars was a long-standing one in financial exchanges, and the terms were set by West African rulers and their smiths, who used the bars to fashion agricultural tools and weaponry. It was the West African demand for iron that established the importance of the bar as a form of currency; there had, of course, been local iron production, but the Atlantic trade expanded access to the ore and also the ability of rulers to take control of this. By the early seventeenth century, Ruyters wrote that all the way from what is now Dakar to the Gambia Estuary, and beyond, trade took place in the same way and for the same trade goods.[55]

Similarly, the growth of cloth as a form of currency reflected local demand. The increasing role of cloth as an accounting unit stemmed from its place in the display of prestige across the whole region. Like many people all over the world, people in Greater Senegambia showed off through the clothes that they wore, and through the changing of those clothes. Of what use, after all, were the cloths but to increase the variety of weaves and clothing available, which became signs of fashion and status? Manoel Álvares described well the way in which Jolof people dressed themselves to symbolize their status. 'The ordinary clothing is in white and black Moorish shirts made from their own cloths,' he wrote, 'which is also what their women dress in.' By 1670, the Dutch geographer and collator of travel accounts Olfert Dapper wrote, 'their Cloathing is onely a four-square Cotton Cloth, which they bind under their arms, and lift over one Shoulder, so that it hangs down to their Feet. The Noblemen wear a White shirt, that comes below their Knees, with wide sleeves and a Cloak over it like a Petticoat.' Meanwhile, further north, there were teams of weavers making clothes for the Jolof king near the River Senegal, and women came with some of their cloths to trade with the French at their post near the estuary.[56]

Gaining access to cloths rapidly became a core feature of European trade in the area. Slave traders did everything they could to gain access to cloth-producing areas. This included producing the cloths themselves, on the Cape Verde Islands. These were the *barafulas* discussed earlier, and Bautista Pérez was one of those to trade in them, bringing 150 of them alongside 4,400 *panos* in one shipment of 1618. Indeed, when his brother João died, he was left owing people in Cape Verde for a shipment of 1,400 *panos* and 60 *barafulas* that had been imported from there the year before.[57]

What, then, was the impact of the growing cloth-currency area in Senegambia as a whole? The pattern was for local cloth production to go hand in hand with increased cloth imports, as the use of cloths became highly specific and linked to particular events in the life-cycle, or to a particular festival. It was important that cloth was accepted as a currency throughout Senegambia. The expansion of markets led to an increase in local cloth production, in areas such as the Kingdom of Bundu, Fuuta Tòòro on the Senegal River, and Mali, and also to the intervention of European traders in the local cloth trade. Just as the Portuguese shipped cloths around the region and used them as an accounting unit, by the end of the seventeenth century, the English had to buy up to 2,000 rolls of cloth upriver on the Gambia just to use as currency elsewhere in the region, making a profit of 100 per cent on these resales.[58]

In time, cloth and its production became experienced as forms of power and control. It was not just Europeans who kept accounts through cloth monies, of course. The value of the cloth money resided partly in its transferability from one economic system to another; *barafulas* were even transported to the New World and emerged there in people's wills as valuable items bequeathed to heirs. And so in the Empire of Kaabu, the tax owed to the rulers was paid in the following way, says the oral historian S. Manneh: 'At first here, / if the king has a problem, / all the village will say, / let us give him one bull. / That was their tax. / Strips of cloths, bulls, sheep or goats.' But, as money was also inextricably linked to the slave trade, cloths were a form of money that mediated power and violence as well as status: '[The traders] sell them to each other / And dyed pagnes [*panos*]. / They will carry these dyed pagnes / and take them to other parts. / They will exchange them for slaves, / and bring them.' And they did this because '[wealth is] in a form of cloth'.[59]

The rise in significance of these different types of cloth was readily apparent in the seventeenth century. By the 1640s, *barafulas* were a standard unit of currency in the trading ports of Guinea-Bissau, and, in 1646, the new Governor of Cacheu had been expected to bring *barafulas* with him when he arrived from Cape Verde to build a fort. Why, then, were they of such importance? Again, it is Manoel Álvares who provides the telling information, stating that in Cacheu the local nobility [*fidalgos*] dressed in *barafulas*, which 'are sold to them by the Whites'. Thus, the growth in volumes of trade, and the market, had expanded forms of social differentiation, leading to the use of some of the monies as a way to represent prestige, just as money today is used as a way to represent prestige – only now the elite may purchase a private jet or, indeed, an island. This type of differentiation would soon proliferate; and oral sources from the Manjako people who live near Cacheu describe how the Manjako differentiated themselves from their neighbouring ethnicities according to the different styles of cloth that they wore.[60]

In a society where it was all too easy to be captured and sold into slavery, being able to differentiate yourself from others and claim social prestige was a vital form of power – and, no less important, a safeguard against falling victim to the power of others. This was, indeed, one of the causes of the huge variety that emerged within cultures here. The linguistic and human mosaic of the region took shape gradually, as insecurity, inequality and production changed throughout this period.[61]

CULTURAL TRANSFORMATIONS IN AN ATLANTIC ERA

As more and more people from Greater Senegambia began to be taken to the New World, they brought their cultural worlds with them. We have already seen how this may have influenced American music, but, in fact, there were other kinds of impact that began to link the region and the Americas in these centuries.

Many early Senegambians in the New World were able to retain cultural identities because they fled the slave-holding system. In the vast and rapidly depopulating continent that was sixteenth-century America, there was no shortage of territory in which maroons (escaped slaves) could take refuge. Almost as soon as Africans began to arrive in any significant quantity in the New World, these maroon communities began to form, re-creating the forms of community and economy they had known in Africa. So evident is this that, in a recent archaeological find of great importance, 12 copper manillas have been found in the maroon community of José Leta in Cuba dating to the 1540s and 1550s.[62]

Beyond the archaeological record, written records show that maroons were widespread in Cuba, and in Panamá, by the mid 1530s, with most Africans in the New World at this time being from Greater Senegambia. They roamed about with weapons, assaulting people on the roads and attacking the farms of Spanish colonists. As the sixteenth-century progressed, it was in Panamá that maroon communities became best known, most famously during the buccaneering raids of Francis Drake of 1572–3, when they gave help and orientation to Drake and his men during their raids on the Spanish.[63]

The examples from Panamá show how important these maroon communities were to the formation of new identities among Africans. In 1580, the government of Panamá wrote to the Council of the Indies in Spain, saying that there were maroons in Portobelo, Bayano and near Panamá City in the Cerro de la Cabra. The community near Cerro de la Cabra attacked and robbed on the highways and killed cattle with impunity. Some colonists accused them of stealing away enslaved Africans to become part of their new societies. Meanwhile, the maroons near Portobelo and Bayano stole clothes, merchandise and weaponry from the highway linking the port of Nombre de Dios and the colonial city of Panamá. They had killed muleteers and a Dominican friar, and lived in an area of forests and lagoons where the Spanish had been unable to capture them. Indeed, according to one report, the way in which the Bayano settlement was constructed, heavily fortified with thick stockades, had possibly been inherited from West Africa; certainly, many of these maroons came from the Guinea-Bissau region, where a similar system of stockade defences known as the *tabanka* had arisen during the sixteenth century.[64]

By this time, the maroons were becoming a serious problem for the Spanish authorities. Africans or people of African descent would constitute almost half the population of cities like Lima and Mexico City by the middle of the seventeenth century, and even by the late sixteenth century the trend was clear. They could not defeat all these communities of maroons, and so when a new settlement specifically for the maroons of Portobelo was founded by the Spanish in 1579, a visitor three years later found it settled by a whole mosaic of peoples. Most came from Greater Senegambia, but there were also some from Kongo and even one person from Mozambique. Here, new alliances were forged in building a settlement to resist external power, in continuity with practices that the maroons had already used in West Africa before becoming enslaved. New identities emerged that would come to have a lasting impact not only on the ways in which Africans conceived of identities in the New World, but, in time, on life in Africa itself.[65]

This could happen because of the flows back and forth across the Atlantic that were already developing by the early seventeenth century. The trade in enslaved persons from Senegambia was especially directed at the port of Cartagena (in what is now Colombia), and ships usually sailed directly between the two sides of the Atlantic, without bothering to go to Europe. The slavers on these ships were often Luso-Africans, with Portuguese fathers and African mothers, and so in this way ideas could move. This explains some of the things we have seen already, like the passage of musical instruments such as the akonting and of the *barafula* cloths to Africa, and also of American foods such as peanuts and maize, which were rapidly adopted in Senegambia.[66]

Indeed, just as Portuguese and Spanish cultures of the time adapted to theatrical culture in Asia and adopted music and architectural motifs from Africa, evidence shows us that Senegambians instantly began to adapt their cultures in this period, creatively reflecting the European presence and also challenging it. Among the most striking transformations are those of the masking techniques that began to take place in the seventeenth century. Changes in masks represented social changes on a major scale, not least because their wearers were always male. In Casamance, the most powerful masks were the *ejumba* of the Jola, used to accompany young men on their initiation in the sacred forests. Thus, as the wars and conflicts related to the slave trade grew, the rise of masquerades represented, and also enforced, the increase of male power in an increasingly militarized society.

Ejumba mask, Senegal.

According to the art historian Peter Mark, *ejumba* masks can be dated through the documentary record to the second half of the seventeenth century, and these first began to appear in European collections from around 1750 onwards. It was in this period that horned masks began to be made by people from different backgrounds in the Casamance region, not only by the Jola. These masks, using cattle horns, were rapidly adopted by many different peoples, with pieces from Manjako textiles being interwoven into the Jola symbolism of the cattle horns; and political power symbolized through the use of red beads. Importantly, these masks could also represent aspects of the trade in captives, since cattle were widely used to procure captives. Hence, they came to signify the performance of a new kind of power, and a new type of identity, influenced by the Atlantic dimension.[67]

Further south, Sape peoples in Sierra Leone represented in various ways the impact of the new worlds. They adapted their *nomoli* ancestor-spirit figures – made since at least 700–800 CE – and in the sixteenth century began to depict some power-figures with Portuguese armour, indicative of the force that these outsiders embodied. Another remarkable visual representaton came in their ivory carvings, created in the mid sixteenth century and at the time highly prized in Portugal. These Sape ivory carvings, of spoons, salt cellars, hunting horns and many other ornaments, are beautiful works of art, and also reflect the importance of the new trading routes, and how important it was to the peoples who lived there to find an artistic expression of the changes that had come to their world. They incorporate Sape and Christian religious symbolism, and are a complex testament to the cultural exchanges that went with the processes examined in this chapter.[68]

The demand for such products in sixteenth-century Portugal is telling. It shows how these commercial exchanges began as relatively reciprocal. However, the rise of the trade in captives produced fundamental transformations, including more militarized and masculinized societies, as shown in the *ejumba* masks. The Atlantic trade had brought conflict and violence, expressed here; but from the Americas it had also brought new foods, and new ideas of a larger community, such as emerged in the maroon communities there. All these aspects

Ivory pyx with scenes from the Passion of Christ, from Sierra Leone.

would shape new identities as the Atlantic era continued. The ability of cultures in Greater Senegambia to reflect, adapt to and adopt so many distinct new influences, and to mediate them resolutely through an existing worldview, is testament to their strength and power.

CONCLUSION: INEQUALITY AND THE SEEDS OF CHANGE IN GREATER SENEGAMBIA

One of the remarkable aspects of oral histories in the Greater Senegambia region is how enduring they are. As we have seen, the idea that the migrants from the Empire of Mali crossed the Gambia River by setting down stones until a causeway was formed was repeated in oral accounts of Fula migrations from the north of Senegambia to the south. They can still be found today. Sitting in the tiny village of Singuère in Casamance, in May 2011, I interviewed the Bainunk elder Ansumana Manga in his compound. As we sat in threadbare deckchairs in the shade of a giant mango tree, he told me that the Bainunk – reputed to be the oldest people to inhabit the Casamance – had also come to the region by building a causeway across the river.[69]

An important element of historical truth is contained in these repetitions. They speak of waves of migration of large numbers of people as a key feature of historical experience in Greater Senegambia – driven, perhaps, by warfare, drought and economic need from a materialistic perspective, but also by dreamscapes, auguries, West African political frameworks and the new cultural worlds that were emerging. The stereotype of the 'settled', 'static' and 'unchanging' village is exposed as a myth. Like the stereotype of European agency 'instigating' modernity, it is, in fact, the very opposite of a truthful representation of the past. But one of the uncomfortable realities historians must deal with in their work is precisely that some people will defend lies far more fiercely than truth.

One clear element of the historical pattern here, from both oral and written sources, is the greater hierarchies that emerged at this time. Resentment at the consequences can still be found in every small town and village from Senegal to Sierra Leone, where impoverished people mutter darkly about elites 'eating' the profits and the benefits of global trade. And it is there in the rigorous hierarchies of social life. It is rare that someone will starve in a Senegambian village, but those who have no means are the ones to make the tea for their elders, wash the dust outside the house and do everything that their elder (and richer) peers demand. This is precisely why so many young people from West Africa are prepared to risk their lives crossing the Sahara in an attempt to reach Europe, since for them the social consequences and dishonour of remaining behind in perpetual insubordination are unbearable.

Thus, even today, the consequences of this expansion of hierarchies in the sixteenth and seventeenth centuries are present. In the oral histories held at the National Centre for Arts and Culture in The

Gambia, one recalls the life of a diviner called Alieu: 'He was a seer and he had much knowledge of life. He wasn't an ordinary man . . . People inquired, "Why are you travelling about in this world? You alone travelling about with wayfarers, raiders, and foot-pads about. How is it that no one has attacked you? That is really remarkable." However, the history tells us that Alieu had special powers, and was protected by his magical abilities. This was just as well; for, when thinking of this time, it is hard to avoid recalling that those times were different from now. It was a time of war, people got together and raided others or attacked them. They captured slaves and materials, took half to the ruler and sold the other half. That was how they made money in those days.'[70]

Oral representations of these experiences of historical change run deep in Senegambia. They represent the inequalities in the access to power and wealth that grew in this era. Central to these inequalities was the new monetary basis for exchange. The currencies in use across Senegambia were losing value steadily against the gold and silver that was mined in Africa and the Americas, destined for Europe and Asia. Indeed, the iron bars imported to West Africa were enabling the growth of early manufacturing in Europe. Considerations of cost would also see cloth becoming a rival import over the course of the seventeenth century, for the cost of importing 100,000 pieces of Dutch cloth to West Africa in 1646 was only 65 per cent more than to import 7,000 iron bars. More profit could be exacted from the cloth manufacturing in the Low Countries, and thus cloth products from Europe, too, were increasingly 'dumped' in West African markets.[71]

As local manufacturers struggled to compete, inflation grew within Senegambian economies. Where copper imports once predominated in currency imports in the fifteenth century, by 1624, iron bars were more valuable than copper bars near Rufisque; consistent import of copper had undermined its value, creating a glut on the market. The value of enslaved captives measured in *panos* [cloths] in the Guinea-Bissau region also inflated at this time, from 120 to 150 over a few short years in the 1610s. Inflation meant that there were more imported currencies in circulation, but also that these local currencies struggled to compete with those in wider international circulation.[72]

By the later seventeenth century, there had been a proliferation of currencies. Iron bars and cloth strips were becoming eclipsed by other forms of money. Silver was accepted in Portudal and the Gambia River area from at least the 1620s. One Dutch source noted that there were silver plates and mugs in the Gambia region, and, by the 1660s, the King of the Jolof Kingdom of Bawol sold enslaved captives for 20 *patacas* (silver bars) – which were doubtless melted down by the Senegambian smiths to be remoulded into jewellery and ornaments. Gold, too, was mined in the Sierra Leone region and then traded to the Gambia River. But beyond gold and silver, readily accepted monies included kola nuts, used as ritual gifts across the region, and paper, used to write holy charms of protection and good luck.[73]

The existence of multiple currencies was a facilitator of more trade and deeper marketization. It was not an unusual pattern, as the existence of multiple currencies at any one time is not, in fact, a historical anomaly; many societies around the world have used multiple means of exchange at once, and to do so does not, therefore, necessarily weaken a region's economic base. Senegambian rulers, too, were keen to encourage 'free trade', much more so than their European trading partners, who usually sought to deny their European rivals access to West African markets by signing exclusive treaties. Here, historical truth again belies the historical stereotype of the role of European nations in championing free trade.[74]

However, the increasing proliferation of different types of accepted money was also testament to the different destinies of currencies. Whereas gold and silver – though used in Greater Senegambia – co-existed alongside many other currencies that were melted down, worn in clothing or used as ritual gifts, the gold and silver that ended up in the European and Chinese economies constituted a growing base for exchange – capital – which went with the accrual of political and military power. The use of currencies to be transformed into goods with a practical value meant that there was less opportunity for West Africans to accrue 'capital'. But, of course, it also revealed a different worldview, one in which not everything was given a notional value equivalence.[75]

The best example of how this worked in practice was the use of kola nuts. These nuts are still widely in use across West Africa: the red nuts are used to purify water or assuage hunger; and the 'bitter' nuts are used to stimulate sexual appetite. In this earlier period, the value of kola across West Africa was such that Dierick Ruyters could write in the 1620s that 'it is appreciated by the Africans as much as gold.' For Francisco de Lemos Coelho, writing in the 1660s, the exchange of kola nuts was one of the fundamental attributes of cultural practices in the Greater Senegambian region: 'they hold that nothing can be well done, and that there can be no marriage or legal trial, in which kola is not presented beforehand' (something that remains the case). He described how twelve ships a year sailed up the São Domingos River from Cacheu to the town of Farim, carrying nothing but kola nuts. Kolas were so valuable that a load of them cost 25 *panos* in Cacheu in 1613, or around one fifth the price of an enslaved captive, while they were used as an equivalent to the dark cloths used as monies of account.[76]

So, where gold and silver were being used to accrue 'hard' currencies in Eurasia, valuable currencies in Senegambia were being used as the glue of reciprocal giving that holds societies together, even as the hierarchies within those societies expanded. This use of these 'monies' meant that their store of capital value was lost to Senegambian societies, as individuals accumulated social power and respect by being generous with kolas at public events and ceremonies. The proliferation of currencies with practical and social value, such as cloth, iron and kola, therefore meant that Senegambian economies were not increasing their store of transferrable wealth: rather, what increased were the exchange mechanisms that saw them enter the global market.

These types of relations and uses of money can seem very distant and strange, but they have not in fact disappeared. Monetary transactions are never purely rationalized, whatever economists might pretend. A gift or a purchase in this part of West Africa usually bears more value than its purely monetary equivalent. If you buy a strip of cloth or go to a particular restaurant to eat in the markets of Serekunda, near the Gambian administrative capital of Banjul, the welcome and banter also initiates a moral exchange. If you then don't return for some time, there may be a mild silent censure the next time you return, a sense of a moral commitment somehow diluted. This plural value is part of economic life, something learnt over the years, and which expresses the multiple values inherent to exchanges in Greater Senegambia now for many centuries – values that coalesced in the sixteenth and seventeenth centuries, as cycles of credit were cashed out through the appalling violence of the slave trade.

3

Ready Money: The Gold Coast and the Gold Trade

Today, the coastline of Ghana is dotted with remnants of the history of Atlantic trade. The vast whitewashed bulk of the Elmina castle-prison sits squat upon the shoreline, with its cannons pointing at the Atlantic Ocean, its 'punishment cells', its holding pens for 150 enslaved persons at a time and its 'door of no return'. It is a reminder of a horrendous past. It was built by the Portuguese as early as 1482, and, like many a medieval European castle, was a site of torture and fear far more than of majesty. Further along the coast, there are other stone edifices: Anomabu and Cape Coast rear up from the beach, looming over neighbouring villages and towns, mnemonics of a past that is hard to overcome when, during the eighteenth century, at the height of the Atlantic slave trade and the Asante Empire in the hinterland of the Gold Coast, the trade in captives predominated. The self-styled castles of Cape Coast and Elmina are the most brooding reminders of this past, but the smaller forts such as Axim, or Anomabu – today a prison run by the Ghanaian state – are so regular that the pattern of coercion and capture from the past is impossible to escape.

Yet originally many of these European castle-prisons were built not to entrench the trade in enslaved persons, but to gain access to the gold trade. Some were not built until the eighteenth century. But many of them date from the earlier phase of trade, when gold predominated. Across Atlantic Africa, this was the region best known for its relationship with the expanding global money supply, the fabled 'Gold Coast'. Hereafter, Europeans 'named' African regions according to the commodities on offer for exchange, showing a purely utilitarian concept of land and value: the Ivory Coast, the Grain Coast (modern Liberia) and the Slave Coast (between modern Benin and south-western Nigeria) would soon follow, as Africa became seen by outsiders in the terms of the extraction and consumption of resources.[1]

In Kumasi, long the capital of the Asante Empire, artefacts of this history of gold endure. Many are located in the Manhyia Palace Museum, a restored version of the original palace of the Asantehenes. Located on a small rise above the city centre, Manhyia is still today the location of the compound of the Asantehene. During the wars between Asante and the British in the late nineteenth century, Prempeh I, the asantehene, was exiled to the Seychelles, to be followed by Yaa Asantewaa in 1900–1901, the Queen Mother of Asante, who resisted the colonial conquest. Eventually, Manhyia was rebuilt by the British colonial forces in 1925 after the destruction of the old palace, and it remains a site of Asante history, strength and resistance today.

Among the many artefacts located in Manhyia are the gold weights produced from the fifteenth century to the nineteenth. In his study of these extraordinary miniature sculptures, the artist and collector Tom Phillips offers a remarkable tribute to these works of exceptional artistry. Some reproduce the gold-buying-and-selling transaction; others animals such as beetles, the *sankofa* bird and the crocodile; others capture daily life, such as the playing of the board game *warri*;

Manhyia Palace Museum, Kumasi, Ghana.

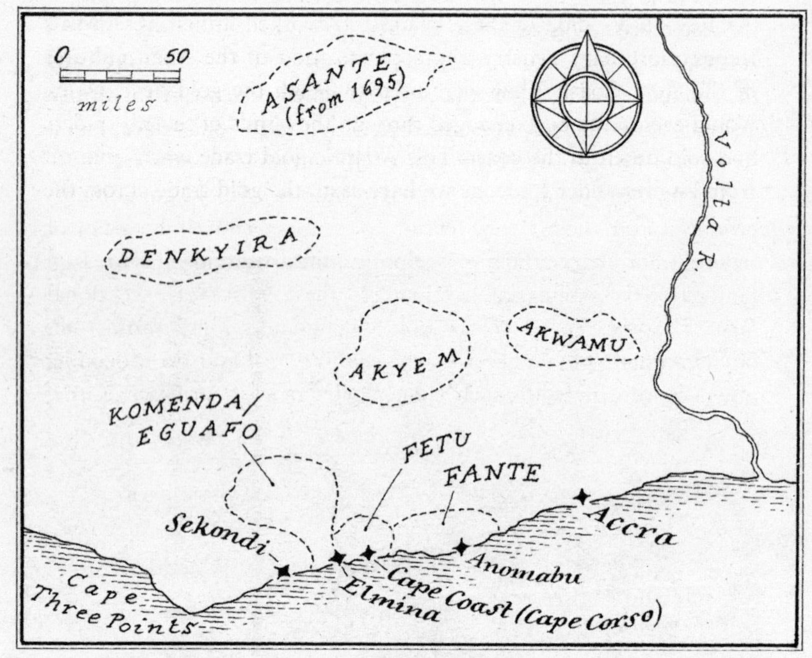

Political centres of the Gold Coast, sixteenth to seventeenth century

and others capture traditional artistic scenes, such as the mother and child. So many were made that Phillips estimates that over the course of his life in collecting he has handled more than one million. All were used as part of daily life, the weighing, exchange and purchase of gold in the markets of the Gold Coast. They offer a peerless sense of what daily life may actually have felt like, while gold still predominated; many Asante families still possess these weights, and today they have often become objects invested with spiritual powers.[2]

Close observation of these beautifully worked miniatures reveals the extraordinary artistry and sophistication of the Akan cultures of the Gold Coast. They were used to weigh the gold dust, which would eventually be exchanged through the hands of several traders and sold down to the coast. This Atlantic gold trade was a spin-off from an even older trade: as we have seen, the gold trade across the

Akan gold weight in the shape of a *sankofa* bird.

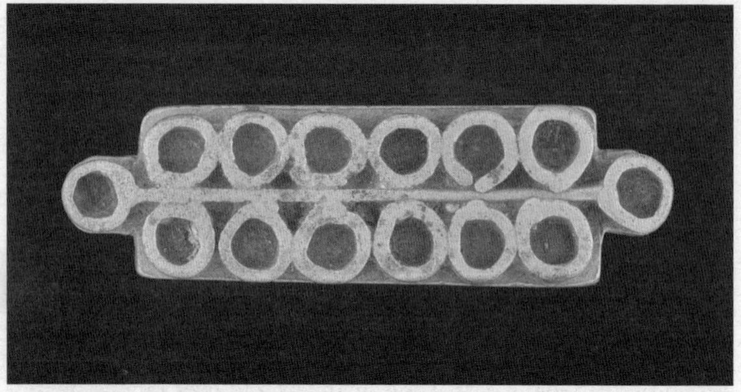

Akan gold weight in the shape of a *warri* set, showing the region's long-standing connection to Central and East Africa, where *warri* is also played.

Sahara had developed from the eleventh century onwards. Indeed, fifteenth-century Akan weights show the influence of Islamic designs, revealing the long-standing nature of this trade and how old the process of gold mining and trade was along the Gold Coast.[3]

The Portuguese immediately tried to develop this trade in favour of their own interests when they appeared along the flat, lagoon-strewn coastline of what is now Ghana. Elmina was the main base for securing access to the gold trade, but other, smaller fortresses were built at sites such as Axim and Sekondi. Until the middle part of the seventeenth century, the main aim was either to secure gold or to gain supplies of food that assisted in the overall trade. The Gold Coast region globalized very rapidly with this new direction. By the first decades of the seventeenth century, it had become a key site in European geopolitical competition.

This may seem a bold assertion. But it is precisely the global importance of the region and its gold trade that explains the preponderance of fortified European trading posts in the seventeenth century. In no other part of Atlantic Africa were there already by this date multiple castle-prisons. And the number grew, with the Danes, the Brandenburg Germans and the English all getting in on the Dutch and Portuguese act by the 1680s. By then, when this chapter draws to a close, European traders would arm African allies in an attempt to gain a mercantile advantage. Each depended on the other. It was only by this later period that the trade in captives grew, and the character of the Gold Coast region transformed.[4]

Yet, along with this increased foreign military presence, the cosmopolitan and open character that is so clear in Ghana today was being shaped. Already by the early sixteenth century, this was a place where ships from India arrived with cowries and cloths. There they met Portuguese fleets, and slave-trading ships come from the island of São Tomé. The latter had developed connections with Brazil by the 1530s, and soon American crops such as maize began to be grown and harvested on the Gold Coast. Food, manners and lives rapidly became globalized in an Atlantic dimension, long before even 1600.

By the 1640s, a trade in enslaved persons would begin, and some of the captives would find themselves in Brazil. The Dutch had taken Elmina from the Portuguese in 1637, and then some of the northern Portuguese captaincies of Brazil in 1630. In need of a labour force in their new sugar plantations in the New World, they began a slave trade from their base at Elmina. But by the mid 1640s they were facing a full-scale rebellion led by Portuguese planters in Pernambuco, north-eastern Brazil. One of the rebel generals was João Fernandes Vieira. After the Battle of Monte das Taboas, Fernandes Vieira freed many of his own slaves who had fought with him, including one Antônio 'Mina' (from the coast of Elmina). These 'Mina' slaves were part of the Dutch contingent brought from the Gold Coast. Antônio then became the captain-major of an entire company of Africans from the Mina coast, who fought alongside the Brazilian rebels as the war continued. So highly did Fernandes Vieira prize this company of Mina soldiers that, early in 1646, he sent a ship laden with sugar to Elmina 'to buy in return a cargo of cloths, those woven there as well as those made of wool, to give to his own soldiers [from Elmina]'.[5]

Thus, exports from the Gold Coast were not limited to ready cash. Textile manufactures spread to the Americas, and, indeed, also to Europe. Collections of these priceless gold weights began, as they circulated in Europe and beyond. Transnational identities were built by these early communities, some enslaved and some free, in Brazil and in other parts of the Americas. Gold Coast societies prospered for a time, and this chapter looks at this process, first in commercial, and then in political and social terms, over the period as a whole. It ends at the end of the seventeenth century, with the rise of the trade in captives. By then, the weight of political power and the possibilities of resisting the tide of capital had been decisively eroded.

AKAN STATES AND THE EUROPEANS: AN OVERVIEW

The first detailed account that exists of an Akan monarch on the Gold Coast is of Kwamena Ansa of Elmina,* called 'Caramansa' by the Portuguese, in 1482. The Portuguese had despatched a fleet from Lisbon in 1481 to build their fortress at Elmina. Ten caravels and two supply ships arrived off the coast on 19 January 1482, bringing masonry, lime and artillery. Eventually, once built, it would have 'two gates, one on the west and the other on the east side. The gate on the west side is the principal one and the strongest, and also has a draw-bridge, with a fine little Tower in which there are many Rooms,

Elmina castle's ramparts above the West Gate described here.

* As per Kwasi Konadu's approach, Elmina was known as 'Edina' – Konadu (2010: 60).

where the Lord of the Castle or the Governor has his residence. The other gate, next to the Warehouse, was made for the discharge of Ships and Barks.'[6]

Kwamena Ansa came to meet the fleet when it arrived offshore, preceded by musicians playing horns and rattles made of shells. His nobles were accompanied by pages who brought seats made of cloth for them to sit in, while Kwamena Ansa himself was covered with bracelets, necklaces and jewels made of gold on his arms, legs and neck, and had many small golden charms hanging from his hair, his beard and his head. Gold was the major product of the nearby Akan goldfields of the forests, and, as this account shows, it was symbolic of political and commercial power long before any European trade began. Indeed, Kwamena Ansa's people and the neighbouring states of Eguafo and Komenda traced their origins to the Akan gold-trading Kingdom of Bono-Mansu, which arose at least a century before this.[7]

For the Portuguese, getting permission from Kwamena Ansa to build the fortress was tough. Elmina was under the authority of Eguafo, which was such a powerful presence that between 1519 and 1524 the Portuguese sent at least seventeen gifts to its king. It may, therefore, be that Kwamena Ansa did not have the authority to make this decision alone; on the other hand, like many tributary kings in West Africa and the Americas at this time, Kwamena Ansa may have hoped that the new military power of the Portuguese would offer a route towards autonomy. The Portuguese, meanwhile, were anxious to protect their gold-trading interests from Spanish rivals, who had fought them for control of the Cape Verde Islands in a series of conflicts in 1476–7.[8]

The Portuguese had arrived to trade on the Gold Coast around 1471. They came initially in dribs and drabs, poor, feverish and desperate. Enough of them had come to settlements such as Elmina in the decade since for Kwamena Ansa to form a very poor opinion of them. As he put it through his interpreters to the captain of the 1482 Portuguese fleet, Diogo de Azambuja, 'the Christians who have come here until now have been very few, dirty, and base [*pouca*, *suça e vil*].' It's not hard to imagine them scratching the lice in their hair, their shirts torn and ragged, absolutely unimpressive compared with the carefully turned-out people they wanted to trade with.[9]

Nevertheless the two sides met here in 1482. The formalities began. The Portuguese explained their desire to build the fortress, on payment of a large sum in cloth, basins and copper manillas. At length, Kwamena Ansa agreed. However, the problems that underpinned this exchange soon became apparent. For the Portuguese, the profits of the gold trade were the overriding consideration. They would rapidly develop trading relations with a host of smaller states such as Abrem and Labadi, which traded in gold. However, for Kwamena Ansa and his people, 'the market' does not seem to have been the ultimate arbiter of value. Trade was part of a wider framework of belief and religious practice grounded in gift-giving exchanges, and in both the material and the non-material world.[10]

The Portuguese royal chronicler Rui de Pina described what happened next:

> The [Portuguese] Captain [Diogo de Azambuja] went with his craftsmen to determine the site of the fortress, which they chose to be at the top of some high cliffs, which the [Africans] worshipped and held to be Holy . . . and the Africans, seeing their holy site destroyed in this way, felt it so deeply, as if they had seen the breaking of all hope of their own salvation, that they flew into a terrible rage, [and] took up their arms.[11]

Gold Coast armies were formidable in the late fifteenth century, long before guns began to be imported. Swords were made by smiths from plain iron, and sheathed in scabbards made of animal- or fish-skins. Arrow tips were mounted with small harpoons, set in bows made from a very strong wood, and smeared with poison made from the gall of crocodiles. Soldiers took to the field protected by helmets made from pangolin- or crocodile-skin and decorated with red shells or gilt horns, and with shields woven with branches from a special tree that offered strong protection, so that they could, apparently, withstand the blows of arrows or spears. The Portuguese could not withstand them: their guns were often rendered ineffective through damp gunpowder, and their numbers were so much fewer; and, as Rui de Pina puts it, Kwamena Ansa's army 'forced our officials to take flight back to the safety of our boats, since they could not resist them'.[12]

Once again, there was never any question as to who was in political command here. Nevertheless, in the end, the inducements were such that the fortress was built; and, once established, it unleashed chains of events that could not be reversed. Within a few years, at least 170,000 *dobras* of gold were despatched annually to Portugal. Within ten years, traders were coming from every corner to Elmina. From the Gold Coast region came Abrom, Akan and Adanse traders; while Mandinga traders also came from the area near the Mali Empire, along with Susu traders from further west, towards the Greater Senegambia region. They all hoped to trade their gold for fine cloths coloured red and blue, corals and copper manillas.[13]

With the arrival of new routes for trade, therefore, the cosmopolitanism of the Gold Coast was growing all the time. There were many small kingdoms, each with its own ruler, nobility, languages and customs, and all seeking access to the valuable trade. As the pattern became entrenched, the interplay of local demand and supply became a key feature structuring lives and experiences along both the coast and in its hinterland.

A further change that came with the arrival of the Portuguese was that Gold Coast rulers entered an improved commercial position. They suddenly found themselves sandwiched between major trading networks, Atlantic and Saharan. Political leaders could play off the competing trade networks who wanted access to gold, and ensure that power remained in local hands. The sixteenth century became a time of growth and saw the formation of the powerful Akan Kingdom of Denkyira before 1550 (due north of Elmina, in the forested hills south of Kumasi); the apogee of Akan military and political power would come around 1660, according to the historian Kwasi Konadu, but thereafter Denkyira's power fell and the political situation became ever more influenced by outsiders.[14]

Thus, it was not until the later seventeenth century that European political and military pressure began to have a demonstrably negative impact. Until then, political power and decision-making remained in the hands of Gold Coast rulers. By this time, the importance of the region's gold to expanding European empires was abundantly clear. Just as the Dutch United Provinces in the seventeenth century depended entirely on gold from 'Guinea' in order to mint its currency, between 1674 and 1714 England's Royal African Company minted 548,327 guineas derived from gold mined in this region.[15]

The significance of gold was paramount, then, in the Gold Coast economy, especially as trade with the Europeans grew. There was, however, strong resistance to any trade in local enslaved persons. For almost the first two centuries of trade in Atlantic Africa, there was no export slave trade on the Gold Coast. The only people buying enslaved persons here were traders called *dyula*, who had networks spreading across West Africa. The *dyula* did, indeed, buy enslaved persons, but they usually did not come from the Gold Coast region; instead, they were brought by the Portuguese from the Kingdom of Benin in what is now southern Nigeria, and the *dyula* used these captives to carry European trade goods north, while in return the captives carried gold from the goldfields to the coast. This was a process of exchange begun by 1500, and showed the extent to which currency exchange and differing concepts of value were vital; for, in Benin, the Portuguese procured enslaved persons through trading copper manillas and cowries, currencies in widespread use there.[16]

It may be asked why, given the resistance to the export slave trade on the Gold Coast, enslaved persons were purchased at all? A key answer lies in the tsetse fly, the propagator of sleeping sickness; because of this minute insect, no beasts of burden could live in forested regions. It was for this reason that the use of forced porterage was so important. Climatic necessity and geographical boundaries forged a society where coerced labour was normal, at first forming a part of reciprocities of kin and dependence; at the same time, political leaders tried to ensure that this labour was provided by outsiders, enslaved persons brought in at first by the European traders.

A good description of this as it worked in practice was given by the German trader Samuel Brun, in around 1614, who wrote about the Akan (and who was, in fact, probably referring to Denkyira traders):

> Acanish [Akan] traders bring the best gold, about 60 or 70 pounds, all the way from Acania . . . move about very imposingly after their own fashion, with perhaps 150 or more slaves; for the [Akan] have no horses, and the goods they receive in exchange for gold, such as iron,

copper, brass basins, beads, swords, and other large knives, are heavy. The slaves must carry these articles home on their backs . . .[17]

The root of this trade lay in the West African demand for imported goods – which, as we have seen, was already creating problems of oversupply of gold in Kano by 1500 – and the demand for gold from the Portuguese to alleviate rampant inflation in their *escudo* currency. The import of copper manillas to West Africa – where copper was an important form of currency and item of ritual exchange – facilitated the growth of the market, as this was a more exchangeable currency. Meanwhile, the gold trade was a huge boon to the Portuguese, leading to profits of 500 per cent and more according to Pacheco Pereira. Both Akan and European rulers were, therefore, keen to expand trading exchanges to develop market and thereby state mechanisms. The exchange process, of gold for copper currencies, was one that could expand trade and yet, in the long term, impact on economic growth and relative economic power.[18]

Considering how essential this region was to European trading powers, it is important to recognize the early place of warfare. As one description of Fetu put it in the 1660s, 'years ago, with considerable justification, people had misgivings about trading muskets on the Guinea coast. Nowadays, however, it has become a general free trade, so that one sees with amazement what quantities of old and new muskets are sold there.'[19]

The gun trade was part of a new economic pattern, one in which the imported currencies of copper and iron were being replaced by commodities that tended to stoke disorder, such as gunpowder and alcohol. This did redress inflationary pressures in Akan states, as commodities were imported to match the rising supplies of currencies. However, political power fragmented and, with the breakdown of order into mass warfare, the export trade in enslaved persons would begin. This spelt the end of the power of Denkyira and then Akwamu, states founded on control of the gold trade, and the emergence of Asante, whose power depended on the growing trade in enslaved persons.

The connection between warfare, the gold trade and the slave trade was stated specifically in one letter from the 1610s by the Portuguese trader João Rodrigues Roxo: if only a slave trade could be instituted alongside the gold trade at Elmina, Roxo wrote, 'there will soon be war among them and that will make them have to trade more gold to finance their wars.'[20]

THE IMPACT OF THE EARLY GOLD TRADE ON GOLD COAST SOCIETY

Close to the goldfields as it was, this region was naturally the focus for the global gold trade in West Africa. Kwamena Ansa's fine gold regalia at his meeting with Diogo de Azambuja and his sidekicks made it abundantly clear that the 'Gold Coast' was already a player in a major world trade. Moreover, the large number of small kingdoms mentioned in the sources reveals a dense population and thriving commercial arena.

The region's goldfields were in the forests north of the Atlantic. As we saw earlier, growing demand from North Africa in the fourteenth and fifteenth centuries had expanded production here and trade routes across the savannah, leading to the rise of important states such as Gonja and Kong, and the growth of Kano. Archaeological evidence supports the idea of the fifteenth century as one of transformation on the Gold Coast, just as in Kano and Mossi. Excavations of the Asante region* show that this area was heavily settled prior to the 1400s. These settlements depended on iron smelted locally and then left behind in slagheaps, something that had begun as early as 800 CE. Clearly, this iron was very important in the expanding gold production, allowing the creation of equipment for miners, and the development of the gold weights, which we have seen for the fifteenth century. However, the fifteenth century also saw the abandonment of key sites and earthworks; kings like Kwamena Ansa, who had emerged by the 1480s, had done so from radical changes in the fifteenth century, which, as in Kano and Mossi, had preceded the arrival of European traders.[21]

* Around what is now Kumasi, capital of what became the Asante Empire in the eighteenth century.

The human experience of these transformations cannot be gleaned only from an economist's understanding of the role of African gold in the global money supply. The boom in demand for gold on the Atlantic coast that came with the Portuguese traders made for many social transformations. New trading towns emerged, and new routes bringing gold from the forests via Asebu. Gold developed multiple values, rather than being reduced simply to a currency equivalent. For gold was equally as important as a symbol of display, social status and ritual power as it was as a currency of export – as Kwamena Ansa showed through his display of golden regalia to the Portuguese when they arrived in 1482.

Writing around 1600, the Dutch sailor Pieter de Marees described how 'a member of the Nobility or someone who wishes to be a great Nobleman has golden Rings around his neck . . . generally they also wear a string of polished Venetian Beads mixed with golden beads and other golden ornaments around their knees'. Just a few years later, the sailor Andreas Ulsheimer confirmed this for the Kingdom of Fetu, stating that 'they also actually wear rings of solid gold around their necks.' Here were members of the nobility actually 'wearing money', to illustrate both the extent of their wealth and their proximity to the sources of power.[22]

How was it that Gold Coast peoples could afford to retain all this gold, merely for display, when it was becoming increasingly valuable in the world market? As producers of gold – 'its gold gives name to our coin', one English sailor would put it in the 1730s, referring to the guinea – the region had pole position to negotiate trade. Perhaps nothing makes something seem more valuable than another's desire for it, and so the demand for gold from traders linked to the trans-Saharan networks no doubt encouraged the use of gold in royal displays. The increased demand for gold that the European arrival created merely enhanced the perceived desirability of gold, and the alacrity with which the nobility on the Gold Coast wanted to demonstrate the access that they had to it. So the descriptions of gold ornaments by 1600 were continuities of what the Portuguese had described when they first arrived.[23]

There were two ways in which gold could be taken down to the coast: by river and by land. As Mary Kingsley noted across West and

West-Central Africa in the late nineteenth century, rivers were often the region's roads. Or, as the Nigerian novelist Ben Okri put it in his 1991 Booker-Prize-winning novel *The Famished Road*: 'In the beginning there was a river. The river became a road and the road branched out to the whole world. And because the road was once a river it was always hungry.'[24]

Away from the rivers, land routes into the great gold-producing regions from coastal towns such as Anomabu and Sekondi were different. The land rose gently from the coast and then fell into green valleys full of lilies and aloes, where gentle rises were covered in enormous silk-cotton trees. After crossing the Pra River some 50 miles north of the coast, the land rose sharply into hills in the region of Denkyira, before dropping down towards what later became the Asante heartland. It was along these routes that the convoys of captives carrying gold made their way.[25]

Once it had got under way, the rapid growth of the coastal trade to and from the goldfields would soon encourage significant changes in Akan communities. By 1503, just twenty-one years after Elmina's castle-prison was built, the association of the new faith of Christianity with this expanding prosperity was having a major impact. In August of that year, the kings of Akyem (Acomani) and Fetu (Afuto) came to Elmina to request baptism from the Catholic missionaries there. But why would some Gold Coast kings be so interested in adopting the Christian faith at all? There were, of course, political considerations; as with Bumi Jeléen in Senegambia, there was the hope that an alliance with the Portuguese would bring military and political advantages, and perhaps attenuate the growing power of the Akan kingdoms inland, where Denkyira was being formed at roughly the same time.[26]

But, beyond this instrumentalism, this willingness to adopt a new religion needs to be grasped through the West African religious lexicon, whereby the adoption of a new shrine and cult does not necessarily invalidate existing ones. Nor is it surprising that local kings were open to a range of ideas, for distant influences had long been felt in the region through the presence of the itinerant Mandinga traders linked to the Mali Empire. It was not that Mali's power somehow 'shaped' Akan society, for Mandinga traders were themselves surrounded by Akan influences and doubtless adopted many

Akan customs. Nevertheless, these links were reciprocal, and there were Manding loanwords in the Twi language by the sixteenth century, including those for canoe (*okoroo/kuru*), house (*aban/bain*), goldmine (*nkoron/kolo*) and slave (*odonko/dyonko*); not to mention the Islamic influence that could be seen in the design of gold weights at this time.[27]

Thus, the booming gold trade with the Portuguese needs to be put in the context of what had gone before. Just like Senegambia and the Sahel, the Gold Coast region was globalizing long before the arrival of Europeans. The new trading route via the Atlantic was not, therefore, some revolutionary change, but rather offered the expansion of an existing pattern. It built on the trans-Saharan demand for gold, where outsider traders linked to a major empire were already well known. Certainly, however, the Portuguese trade further increased the pluralism of the Gold Coast. By 1623, Dierick Ruyters described how the peoples living along the coast were amazingly varied, and that every five or six miles a different group was found with completely different customs. Meanwhile, the Portuguese had brought new fruits from Portugal such as lemons and oranges, figs and grapes, as well as maize from the New World.[28]

The human and physical environment was changing rapidly, and the political environment was changing, too. Akan towns had been divided into *abrons* (wards) probably since the fourteenth century, while there were already paramilitary companies called *asafos* (who had attacked the Portuguese at Elmina in 1482 under Kwamena Ansa). In the sixteenth century, as long-distance trade expanded, so did these patterns. Urban areas grew, living off the growing agricultural surplus of the countryside and the boom brought by the new maize crops; while taxes were paid to the growing political establishment in gold by 1580 at the latest. Towns and kingdoms increasingly vied for supremacy, and for access to the European trading goods. The patchwork of very small states such as Akyem and Assim that existed around 1500 gradually gave way to larger interior states that controlled the gold trade, first Denkyira and then, in the later part of the seventeenth century, Akwamu (which was located far to the east of Denkyira, north of Accra). All these states traded on the coast through Fante merchants, with Fante's power growing significantly from the second half of the seventeenth century onwards; Fante and Akan languages are related, and, indeed, some local oral histories suggest that Fante leaders settled on the coast as late as the early seventeenth century.[29]

The rise of the Atlantic gold trade was then by and large a period of growing, but unequal, prosperity. Rich men, the *abirempon*, expanded their wealth through trade and built up retinues of followers. They often had many wives and had to maintain their social position through the acquisition of luxury goods through the market trade. Meanwhile, at the ports, brokers known as the *afahene* controlled exchanges of gold with the European ships for basins, cloth, copper and cowries, which expanded the money supply and the market exchanges. Towns grew in the interior, the political heartland; coastal towns remained relatively small, and were centres for interpreters, boatmen, fishermen and the dependants of the big traders inland.[30]

By around 1602, the impact of over a century of the coastal gold trade was marked. Travelling in 1603–4, Andreas Ulsheimer described both the well-structured trade and the changes it had effected locally, where children spent long periods on the beaches scooping sand out of the rocks and shaking it back and forth from one container to the other to obtain gold dust. Meanwhile, the Akan traders came from at least 30 or 40 miles inland, and each of them often carried between 6 and 12 pounds of gold at a time, which they exchanged mainly for European linen goods, using the peoples of the coast to act as brokers for their trade with the Dutch and the Portuguese. The growing influence of European imports can be gleaned through the way in which sixteenth-century goldweights began to include copper inserts, with copper one of the major imports brought by the Portuguese at the time.[31]

Another – anonymous – account from the same period gives a similar picture of the gold trade, though, according to this Dutch author, the gold traders came from as far away as 200 miles inland. These traders brought gold with their personal slaves, often twenty or thirty of them, who were then expected to be loaded with the trade goods that had been bought from the ships, and to return with their burdens inland. By this time, the Dutch trade in gold was beginning to far surpass that of the Portuguese: the Dutch had the best industries in Europe, the fastest and biggest ships, and could therefore outcompete the Portuguese by selling better quality goods at much cheaper prices.[32]

By 1600, peoples along the coast had developed social institutions to propel their children into the lucrative trade. As just mentioned, children were encouraged to pan for gold on the beach and in the streams. They made and fished in ocean-going canoes from the ages of ten to twelve. When they had a catch, they sold it for gold, which they used to purchase linen cloth for their own needs. This way, they could soon begin trading with the *dyula* merchants who came from inland and enter the trading arena as brokers in their own right, hoping in the long term to become *abirempon*. And so, by 1600 (and probably earlier), these processes had rapidly become cornerstones of social change and daily life.[33]

Like any commodity deemed to be of great value, complex and precise mechanisms developed for the trading of gold. Towards the end of the seventeenth century, one visitor described how

> first they weigh it on the shore most precisely; then they put it in little linen cloths in amounts of 2, 3, 5 or 6 *quintchen* [1⁄16 of an ounce]. They place these little bundles in a wooden box and wrap around it a small fibre sack, which they tie up at six or seven places and then bind firmly around their neck or body like a rope. When they come aboard to trade, it takes a good three hours before the price is agreed on, and after that they still want to dispute the weight.

Nevertheless, this well-structured trading system was not proof against the typical corruption of trade when large profits are to be made; for, 'when at last the purchase is properly concluded, the gold turns out to be mixed half and half with copper or with a good portion of dust.'[34]

The complex organization of the gold trade, with both Akan traders and Fante interpreters and brokers intervening, is important. The value of gold to the trading systems at this time is shown clearly through the fact that, in Ulsheimer's 1603–4 account, gold was the major currency unit: copper (12–20 pounds per *benda** of gold),

* Each *benda* weighed two ounces.

manilla arm-rings (25 per *benda*) and measures of cloth (40–43 per *benda*) were all accounted for according to their weights in gold. Thus, this had become the standard unit of value, of greater perceived worth than the units of cloth or iron bars that, as we saw in the last chapter, were used at the same time in Senegambia, and the standard bearer of exchange linking the economies of the Gold Coast and the growing Atlantic empires.[35]

Given the centrality of this gold trade here for so many years, this is an important region in which to study the wider features examined in this book. How can such an organized system of trade founded on gold lead to political disorder and the eventual undermining of the capital base of a society, when free-trade theory suggests that trade leads to prosperity? And, indeed, is this even the case on the Gold Coast? Can, in fact, the trading relationship of gold and other currencies here go some way towards illuminating what has been described by some economists as a 'reversal of fortune', where the extent of a region's economic interaction with European trading empires, on the one hand, is linked in this model to the subsequent economic disadvantage that accrued on the other? One key factor may certainly be the ever growing dependency on the trade, beginning in the period covered in this chapter, and accelerating through the eighteenth century. This certainly made Gold Coast rulers highly vulnerable to external shocks when the terms of trade changed radically in the early nineteenth century.[36]

Located in these early descriptions of the Gold Coast is an important aspect of some of these changes. The account of the cutting of gold dust with sand and other impurities is a marker of the bad faith that quickly grew up between Akan traders, Fante intermediaries and European traders. Cheating on business transactions is, of course, a very long tradition in all societies around the world, but certainly it was quick to start here. Cheating was something that appears to have been present at the outset of these exchanges. While the Akan traders cut their gold by the 1680s, a Dutch source from around 1602 describes how the early Dutch traders deceived coastal brokers from the first, so that 'if they bought ten fathome of linen cloth, they found but eight, and by that meanes lost two fathome, and other things after the rate.' The fundamental cause of this was doubtless the high value of the trading transactions in gold, and the consequent opportunities and temptations on both sides to increase profits through chicanery: there was simply too much at stake in the gold trade.[37]

A vivid example of how this played out in practice comes from a very early period, before even the construction of the Portuguese castle at Elmina. When the French trader Eustache de la Fosse visited the Gold Coast region in 1480, he lost his trade goods in a way that made him furious. Wandering from house to house, De la Fosse sold goods from two basins he carried, hopeful of making a tidy sum. Called into one house, he listened to five or six women talking. They were probably market traders just like him. After a while he left, forgetting his basins: 'and when I had gone out into the street, and gone on past two or three compounds, I remembered what I had done with the basins and returned to the house straightaway. But when I went inside I found no one there. And then a young woman appeared and came up to me, asking if I wanted to *choque-choque* with her, and beginning to take off her dress, thinking that I wanted to make love with her. This was something I had no intention of, so angry was I at the loss of my two basins.' Doubtless it was the high value of the goods at stake, and losses like these, that prompted the Portuguese desire to build a fortress on the Gold Coast in the first place.[38]

Stories like De la Fosse's show how many interests overlapped in the formation of this gold-trading nexus. The European traders were sexually frustrated or licentious young men. They were probably desperate, for they knew that their chances of surviving the fevers and returning with profits were low, so their paramount interests were to maximize a quick profit and to leave before dropping dead. And there were huge amounts of money to be made, recalling Pacheco Pereira's view that the profits on the early trade were 500 per cent for the Portuguese. Meanwhile, the arrival of a profusion of trade goods led to an explosion in existing local currencies, the growth of the market, and changes to urban and social patterns. As we saw in Chapter 1, the arrival of European traders on the Gold Coast was of particular interest to Akan and *dyula* traders, owing to the overproduction of gold that had already saturated the market at trans-Saharan hubs such as Kano. Both sides, therefore, recognized the high value of the potential trading transactions, and sought to protect their interests. From the Portuguese side, this involved the construction of the fort at Elmina; from the perspective of the Akan, it involved consolidation of the state and the development of new mechanisms of social control.

The use of gold as the standard unit of value along the Gold Coast was important in this process of state consolidation. The presence of gold as a standard of global value led to the growth of the tax base and the currencies in use, expanding the markets and the ability of local kings to develop their political infrastructure, and to invest in imported weaponry such as muskets. One 1600 account describes how gold was used to pay for goods, not in coin but according to weight; and, if the amount owed was so small that the gold could not be weighed, then payment was done through small square pieces of gold known as *kackra*, which were kept in little purses hanging from a belt made of red, blue and yellow cloth. Kings kept their relatives as tax collectors at the ports, where they were expected to collect duties on imports, while the traders who came from inland had to pay a tax in gold in order to trade; anything weighing less than one *benda* of gold did not carry a tax, but beyond that weight they had to pay a small tax per *benda*.[39]

The expansion of these administrative frameworks and processes of control grew from the increased competition for Akan gold. The huge demand for gold by Dutch and Portuguese traders on the Gold Coast offered a ready outlet for the overproduction of gold from the Akan forests that was already apparent in the fifteenth century. However, as demand grew, it began to outstrip the supply of available gold for export – by contrast with the previous experiences of the trans-Saharan traders at Kano. As we have seen here, gold was used as a currency on the Gold Coast, and it was also used as ornamentation, with the rings of gold around people's necks. With gold used as a commodity and a store of power, as well as money, the amount available for export flattened off by 1600. Yet, at the same time, the numbers of ships coming to trade grew all the time. Samuel Brun described in 1614 how 'some years ago, no more than four ships a year came there. Nowadays a good twenty ships come, and yet no more gold comes than before; for they make the gold more expensive for each other and deprive one another of it.' Thus, prices of imported goods rose in the local currency; whereas before, in the days of fifteenth-century trans-Saharan trade, there had been an oversupply of gold and not enough trade goods to buy, the picture was now reversed. As one historian notes, this was clear in Dutch sources from the early seventeenth century, where one describes how between April and October 1608 alone, the price of a *benda* of gold rose from 60 to 70 or even 80 pieces of linen.[40]

The consequence of this rise in prices for gold was the proliferation of different currencies and of the amount of currency washing about: there were simply more linen cloths, there was more copper, and more iron, than there had been before. There were more raw materials for the smiths to fashion into ornaments, weapons and tools. The rapid expansion of materials meant that there was a growth in markets in this period, leading to more wealth for the *abirempon*, richer market towns on the coast and in the interior, and increased state capacity to grow through the extraction of a tax base. All of this was dependent on a growing currency base in the region, and, as gold was used both locally and for export, the coexistence of alternative currencies was required. A staple from an early period was copper and brass, the cornerstone of the Portuguese trade at Elmina as early as 1510, according to one source. This had developed from the existing trans-Saharan trade in copper, and by the first decade of the sixteenth century hundreds of thousands of copper manillas and bars were being traded by the Portuguese at Elmina and Axim: 287,813 at Elmina between 1504 and 1507 alone.[41]

Like gold, copper was used both as a currency for trade and as a store of ritual power, used in many offerings and burials. The same differentiation would take place later in Asante with the cowrie, for which there were two different words in Akan denoting its monetary and ritual meanings. In this way, West African economies showed similar features to those of Europe, where the altarpieces and state rooms of cathedrals and royal palaces were also dripping with the display of gold. It would only be as silver and then gold became adopted as standards of value that this relationship in Europe would change; and in countries such as Portugal, which persisted with the display rather than the monetization of gold into the eighteenth century – with the construction of the giant 'gold elephant' palace at

Mafra between 1717 and 1755, which included gold dinner services – the relative lack of economic power would develop.[42]

The relationship of the export of gold to the import of copper and brass places the social and economic changes on the Gold Coast in the broader context of a currency exchange. Indeed, in other parts of Africa, the exchange of gold for copper was also widespread, as, for instance, a similar trade appears to have linked Great Zimbabwe to the Swahili traders on the coast of what is now Mozambique between the tenth and the sixteenth centuries. Here, all archaeological finds show a preference in the value of copper over gold, where, from the tenth century, gold was being exported from the port of Sofala (now called Beira). What was fundamental was the exchange of perceived value. The imported copper had multiple values, being used both for exchange and for adornment, and in religious rituals. Meanwhile, the gold exports were storing up monetary capital beyond Africa.[43]

The impacts of the boom in the gold trade in the seventeenth century were, therefore, very varied. The new framework demanded economic transformations. The growing trade and the value attached to it by both sides meant that soon enough the imports of copper alone did not suffice. By 1600, the types of money used along the Gold Coast had diversified. Along with copper and gold, small pieces of iron 'of a finger length' were also used, and many of these had almost certainly been melted down from the large volumes of iron bars that had begun to be imported by European ships. This was in keeping with the pattern seen in the last chapter for Greater Senegambia, where, by 1600, iron bars were a standard of value across that region.[44]

The exchange of metals from the Gold Coast for those imported from Europe was accelerating; and, as this created differences in access to capital, so the increasing volumes of cloths imported would also in time undermine the weaving industries of the coast, woven from the harvests of the cotton trees that grew along the roads that led from the coast, inland towards the fields of gold. One report from 1510 from Elmina captured the competition that was taking place between local and imported cloth, with the factor at Elmina writing that 'there is among the [Africans] so much Mandinga cloth [i.e. cloth brought by the Mandinga traders] that it hinders much of [our] trade.' In time, the swamping of the Gold Coast market with cheaper linen and fine cloths from Asia and Europe would come to challenge this pattern.[45]

POLITICAL CONTEXTS OF THE EARLY EXCHANGES

In 1540, an enslaved woman known to the Portuguese as Gratia was tried by the Tribunal of the Inquisition in Lisbon. Gratia had been sent from the Portuguese fortress at Elmina on the Gold Coast because of what the Inquisitors described as her 'errors'. Though baptized into the Catholic faith in the church built by the Portuguese at Elmina, her knowledge of Christian doctrine was rudimentary, to say the least. Gratia knew neither the name of the priest who had baptized her, nor any of the core prayers of the faith such as the Pater Noster, the Ave Maria or Salve Regina. Meanwhile, her godparents who had sponsored her baptism had not even taught her the basic *credo*.[46]

Gratia's case illuminates the relationships that were evolving on the Gold Coast. For, while the rationale for Portuguese colonization in West Africa was evangelization, sanctioned by the papacy, and, while the justification of enslavement was that it was a means of saving heathen souls, sincere efforts at conversion were so lacking that neither godparents nor priests bothered to teach newly enslaved persons such as Gratia the tenets of the faith. Inevitably, the small number of newly baptized growing in cross-cultural trading centres such as Elmina, therefore, retained their existing religious beliefs and practices.

So widespread was this mixture of practices throughout West African Atlantic trading ports that this alone cannot be the reason why Gratia was deported; some personal slight to a powerful figure, or an enmity with a person who had the ear of those in charge of the Portuguese settlement, would more likely explain why she was sent all the way from Elmina for trial in Lisbon for a crime of conscience. Once in Portugal, she was accused of making idols and fetishes, and worshipping them in her home. In her oven, figures of worship were found, and also a small wooden bowl inside of which were placed four thick pieces of wood dusted with flour, each of the height of four fingers. When Gratia was asked, she confirmed that these figures represented 'her God that she worshipped'.[47]

The Inquisitors of the newly formed Tribunal of Lisbon could not permit this mixture of African religious practice with the acceptance of the Christian faith, and condemned Gratia to perpetual imprisonment, and religious instruction. What may have been most alarming to them was the evidence of the weakness of the religious power that Catholic missionaries had along the Gold Coast. The reality was that the commercial exchange which was the foundation of these evangelizing efforts depended upon the sort of mixed social and cultural framework of which Gratia was a perfect example. The Portuguese did not dominate political and economic life in the Gold Coast trading centres and thus they could not impose their religious will, even on their own slaves such as Gratia. In fact, they and their Dutch and English successors were for well over a century heavily dependent on the political power of the coastal brokers who negotiated their trade.

The extent of this willingness to accommodate to local religious and cultural practices was shown almost 150 years later by the English at their Cape Coast castle. Here, the accounts of 1673 show their factor sending money to contribute to the funeral of the King of Fetu. The receipts revealed that payments had been made in brandy for the burial, for dances and for the *feiteira* [fetishist or, rather, Fetu's religious leader] involved in the burial of the King of Fetu. As in many parts of West Africa, funerals were major celebrations with lavish expenses and participating was essential for the English to show their acceptance and assimilation of Gold Coast customs. The brandy had been used in part for ritual offerings to the religious shrines of Fetu (explaining the payment to the *feiteira*), and confirming the English acculturation to Gold Coast religious practices at the time.[48]

This assimilation was almost two centuries old by 1673. Intriguing pieces of evidence give some indications of the mixed societies that were emerging in the coastal trading hubs by the 1560s, after eighty years of institutionalized trade. In 1564, the sons of kings near Elmina were sent to the Monastery of Santíssima Trindade in Portugal for religious instruction, in the care of the Treasurer of Elmina. Nevertheless, while lip service was given to conversion and to the practice of the Catholic rites, at Elmina itself no one was in any doubt that local religious practice predominated: one 1572 account describes how, when Christians married 'gentiles' [i.e. Akan non-Catholics], they immediately began to live 'in their gentile manner', while another describes how any children that Portuguese galley troops had with local women were either aborted or lost to local ways of life.[49]

That Catholic practices were observed by Gold Coast peoples in Portugal, while Portuguese migrants to the Gold Coast quickly began to practise African religions, shows that each side was in political control of their own territory. Throughout the sixteenth century, it was abundantly clear that the Portuguese depended on Gold Coast kings for their security. When the stronghold of Axim was constructed by the Portuguese in 1503, on the western stretch of the coast, it was said that, without it, their traders would have been at the mercy of the Africans. When Duarte Pacheco Pereira was the factor at Elmina around 1520, he frequently gave out gifts of cloths to Assa and Akan kings. It was important for the Portuguese to keep these rulers on side, since, six years earlier, in 1514, the Assa king had fought with the Portuguese against the King of Fetu (Afuto), who had sought to destroy the settlement at Elmina. Thus, it was only by acknowledging African political control that the early Portuguese traders could protect their position.[50]

This evidence from the 1510s is important, since Fetu's power was constantly a thorn in the side of the Portuguese trading networks. Only by allying themselves with Fetu's enemies could the Portuguese succeed. In a major conflict of 1577–8, the Portuguese allied with the peoples around Elmina to defeat Fetu and their allies of Komenda, razing the towns and putting the people to flight; this was a significant episode, since Komenda had, over the past century, grown into one of the most important political forces on the coast. Thus, as in the New World with the defeats of the Aztecs of Tenochtitlán, it was only through military alliances with local peoples that Europeans were able to secure their own networks. As the historian Mark Meuwese notes of Dutch trade in the seventeenth century, this depended on finding local alliances, as for example in a 1642 trade agreement that was signed by the Dutch with the King of Accra. One 1624 case saw the Dutch West India Company signing a treaty with the Fante king Ambro to offer mutual military protection in case of attacks by enemies, showing both how Fante power was rising at this time, and how far both the Dutch and the Portuguese depended on local alliances to trade on the Gold Coast.[51]

In time, these alliances became of more than political significance to both sides. Cultures and ways of doing things changed, and each influenced the other. Kings of the Gold Coast adopted useful crops, expanding food production. The best example was maize, widely grown on the Gold Coast and, according to one 1572 account, imported from the Americas by the Portuguese through their settlement on the island of São Tomé. Known by the Fante as *oborowi*, or 'millet from overseas', by the early seventeenth century, it was found growing with many different colours, as, of course, had long been the case in Mexico.[52]

Meanwhile, it was not just gold that European traders brought back with them from the trading posts. Gold Coast handicrafts were widely admired in Europe, and the trader Pieter de Marees described, by the early 1600s, how they could often be found in the Netherlands:

> The girls . . . learn how to make Baskets, Hampers, Mats and straw Hats made of green Rushes, which they make with their hands. They also learn to make Caps, Purses, and cloth from the bark of trees, dyed in all sorts of colours and very artfully made, as if made with a loom, to the wonder of many people; and one can see often enough in our lands the artful work they make with their hands.[53]

With the rise of state power, and the profits from the trade so essential in maintaining it, mistrust grew between Gold Coast and European partners. The mutual-aid agreements signed in the 1620s became rarer, as Gold Coast kings played off one European against another, the Dutch against the English or the Portuguese. The reality was that, until perhaps the 1680s and 1690s, all the cards were held by the Gold Coast kingdoms.

Local kings had three huge advantages that outsiders struggled to overcome. The first was the disease environment, in which European traders fell like flies, and those who survived often wandered around yellow and sallow, or spent long periods in bed fighting off death, looking terrible. But it was also very easy to assert local priorities because Gold Coast kings controlled the water supply, without which European factors and the ships they were charged with supplying could not operate. This was a long-standing strategy, and Dierick Ruyters described, in 1623, how it was impossible even to haul an oxhide full of water without paying as much for this as beer cost in the Netherlands. Fourteen years later, when the Dutch took control of the fortress of Elmina from the Portuguese, the local king refused to allow them to build a cistern. Such strategies persisted throughout the seventeenth century in many different parts of the Gold Coast, and, writing in October 1695, the English factor at Dixcove (20 miles west of Sekondi) said that the people of the town had refused them water because of a disagreement.[54]

But, beyond European reliance on Gold Coast kings for the basic necessaries of life, the real source of control was over the trade routes that brought the gold from inland, and over information. By the seventeenth century, European trading companies were reliant on their Gold Coast servants for precious news as to what the English might be lacking, or what the Dutch might need in order to trade successfully. Even when they had made alliances, this was dependent on African acquiescence, and when the English sought to build a fort at Sekondi in 1683, it was the King of the Adoms who set the terms for their presence, with half the English payment to be made upfront and the rest on completion of the fort. Thus, as competition between European nations grew, the political advantages to Gold Coast kings grew – at first.[55]

This whip-hand was frequently shown, to make it clear where the power in the relationship lay. As we have seen, firearms were traded increasingly to Gold Coast kings by as early as 1600. It did not take long before guns were used to assert local supremacy. The logs of European factors are full of accounts of the razing of their settlements and the kidnapping of their officials by local forces; when, in 1688, the Akan kidnapped the Portuguese captain at Anomabu, they boasted that they could destroy the fort there at will. The availability of firearms and their relationship to trade would consolidate the emergence of the major Gold Coast states by the end of the century.[56]

Underpinning the differences with European traders were not just commercial rivalries, however. Trade was possible because Akan and Fante peoples had alternative views of value to European traders, and different concepts of property. In the Gold Coast, kings controlled land on behalf of their subjects. The concept of ownership as regards land was important, since the monarch's land control had customary and spiritual attributes beyond the economic ones. This meant that property was not the capital asset that it was becoming in Europe. Meanwhile, as we have seen, currencies had multiple uses not restricted to what the economic anthropologist Jane Guyer describes as 'calculative rationality'. As warfare grew along with these divergences, so did the number of captives; and this, in turn, would eventually transform the region from an exporter of gold to one of enslaved persons.[57]

IN BETWEEN THE SAHELIAN AND ATLANTIC EMPIRES

Just to the north of the Gold Coast, in what is now northern Ivory Coast's Senofo country, lay the Kingdom of Kong. Kong rose to power in the seventeenth century, helped by itinerant traders stoking the booming gold and cloth trades to and from Kano. Like its Gold Coast neighbouring states to the south, Kong sat close to the power of the Islamic trade and scholarship routes that had grown up with the empires of Mali and Songhay.

One oral text describes how the Islamic scholars, or marabouts, of Kong moved constantly from one kingdom to another. 'At this time, Ja, Timbuktu, Jenne, Kong and Bate Nafaji were the places to which the marabouts travelled. If a marabout left Walata, he went to Nema. From Nema, he came to Timbuktu. And if he left Timbuktu, it was to Ja, Jenne, Bate Nafaji or Kong that he went.'[58]

This constant migration had already been a feature of Islamic scholars in the sixteenth century. What was changing by the later seventeenth century, as this oral text makes clear, was the fragmentation of political power in many of the regions linked to the former heartlands of political power in West Africa. The state in the Sahel was becoming weaker, and there were many more political leaders than had been the case under the emperors of Mali or the sonnis and askiyas of Songhay. This fragmentation would have major repercussions, not only for the peoples who lived in the Sahel, but also for all those with whom they traded further south, such as the Akan, who had hitherto been the major purveyors of gold to the Sahel from among the Gold Coast kingdoms.

From the very early period of the Atlantic trade, the Portuguese were aware of how the Gold Coast kingdoms were already subject to the influence of Islamic trading networks. Writing in the 1540s, the chronicler João de Barros stated that João III, the Portuguese king, had halted the exchange of slaves for gold at Elmina so that those traded to the Mandinga traders did not 'make themselves into Moslems [*se faziam Mouros*]'. Meanwhile, early accounts of the kings of Akyem and Fetu described them with the Muslim title of 'cherifs' (*xerifes*), showing clearly that this was a region influenced by Islamic practices through the itinerant *dyula* traders – even though, as this letter describes it, there were already many Christians in Akyem.[59]

These accounts suggest that, by 1500, the kingdoms along the Gold Coast were already finding themselves as in-betweens, and making choices as to which of the outsider religions was more appealing. Where Islam opened up the long route across the Sahara via Bighu, Songhay and Kano, Christianity opened the door to the increase in Atlantic trade goods. The wiliest strategy was to hold the door open for both, so, while by 1600 noblemen on the Gold Coast wore Dutch and Venetian beads, they also 'wore Caps made of the Bark of trees, which they tie around their heads in the Turkish way . . .' Nevertheless, this ability to sit in between Atlantic and Saharan empires would soon change, as the Songhay Empire weakened and eventually collapsed in 1591. As the centre of political power in the Sahel moved east, to Kano and Borno, this was to have major consequences on the Gold Coast, which was no longer able to occupy a buffer zone between imperial systems as it had been throughout the sixteenth century. Indeed, Kano itself was also under pressure in these decades and could not exert as much influence over the old networks to the forest as had existed before, fighting a sporadic war against its powerful southern neighbour of Katsina from around 1565 to 1650. Hence, as the 1600s went on, the Atlantic trading system would be able to apply ever more pressure to the Gold Coast kingdoms.[60]

At the end of the sixteenth century, the changes that would see the heavy erosion of local power by 1690 were still hard to imagine. The detailed gold-trading mechanisms went with the prosperity we have seen growing through this time. People took immense pride in their appearance; Marees described the men as 'each [cutting his hair] in his own fashion and competing in style, some in the form of a Crescent, another in the shape of a Crown, a third with three or four Horns on his head', and wearing many rings around their knees and necks. Women meanwhile, wore all kinds of rings made of copper, ivory, brass and iron; while they decorated 'their heads and hair with plaits, making a bunch of their hair in the middle of their heads . . . they have small, elongated Combs with two teeth, each as long as a finger, which they stick in their hair.' The elaborate jewellery and dress went with the growth of riches in these Gold Coast kingdoms, and the rise of the new *abirempon*. However, the early 1600s would represent a high point, when treaties of mutual aid would still happily be signed with European partners. As the fallout of the political changes of the seventeenth century became clear, relations changed starkly.[61]

Central in all of this was the fall of Songhay. Following the defeat by the Moroccan Army in 1591 and the fall of the Songhay capital, Gao, the seventeenth century saw Songhay fragmenting into a small core state known as the Arma Pashlik, and then a series of Arma statelets that were beyond any central control. Songhay had developed an elaborate military infrastructure by the time of its fall, with a cavalry, fleets of war canoes and teams of smiths who created breastplates and weapons for the troops. This structure and technology was easily then called upon by the chiefs of the new Arma statelets, making it difficult to establish a strong successor state to Songhay in the Niger Bend. Without the protection of a strong state, traders moved elsewhere, and the access to commercial and political power in the Sahel moved east.[62]

Following this long struggle with Kano into the middle of the seventeenth century, it was the town of Katsina that became a major trading centre for the trans-Saharan trade by 1700. In Katsina, the reigns of Muhammadu Uban Yara (1641–71) and his son Muhammadu Jan Hazo (1671–84) saw the growth of the intelligentsia (the *'ulamā*), and the consolidation of administrative structures supervising the expansion of industries of weaving, dyeing and smithing. Yet, although Katsina grew commercially, and administratively, the area that it controlled was relatively small. Katsina was in Hausaland, which itself, like Songhay, had seen a certain weakening following the protracted conflict with Kano. In the seventeenth century, migrating invasions by the Kwarafa people from Benue, to the south, had seen the fragmentation of power into a number of small, independent kingdoms, each under a Hausa chief known as the Habe. By the end of the seventeenth century, the area of these Habe chiefdoms was huge, and occupied much of what is now northern Nigeria. The most powerful kingdom in the whole Sahel became Borno, with its trade route to Tripoli via Bilma and Murzuk soon taking over from the earlier routes from Mali and Songhay; and Borno was to remain the most important state in the Sahel throughout the eighteenth century.[63]

Looking at the seventeenth century as a whole, then, it was one of political reorientation in the Sahel. The axis of trade moved from west to east, a long way from the original centres of trans-Saharan wealth and power, which had lain in Senegambia and Mali. What was the cause of such a dramatic change? A vital factor was the worsening climate, which deteriorated across the whole of West Africa after 1640, with a series of droughts, famines and epidemics that were particularly severe in the drier Sahel. Accounts of the sultans of Borno, known as *diwans*, show the slow growth of climatic instability from the later sixteenth century onwards. The period between 1546 and 1562–3 was a time of 'the great famine'; the 57th sultan, Ali ibn Hajj 'Umar, reigning from 1644 to 1680/84, did so at the 'time of the famine called Dala Dama'; while the 59th sultan, Dunama ibn Ali (1699–1717), reigned at the time of 'the great famine of seven years' duration'. This dry period continued long into the eighteenth century, returning with particular force when a terrible drought struck across the whole of West Africa in the 1740s; inevitably, however, given its proximity to the Sahara, the area that was most severely affected was the Sahel.[64]

A variety of factors, therefore, pushed the Sahelian kingdoms into political weakness: invasion, climatic pressures and the growing competition from the Atlantic trading system. The result was that these states were placed at a disadvantage when compared with the Atlantic framework. Inevitably, those states that were closer to the Atlantic, such as those on the Gold Coast, were pushed more into their trading systems, not merely because of the strength of the European systems but also because of a complex of internal African factors linked to changing political dynamics and the impacts of drought. This was decisive in the political changes that began to take place along the Gold Coast towards the end of the seventeenth century, as the European presence became militarized through the fortress enclaves that sprang up along the whole coast after 1640.

The French official Sieur Delbée gave a good account of the different forts that he found by 1669. The Dutch had Elmina, and the English a fort very near by at Cormantin, described by Dutch rivals in 1665 as the 'chief place of the English'. Five leagues from Elmina the English had their major fort and general at Cape Corse (Cape Coast) (the Dutch had attacked Cormantin in 1665, hence the move to Cape Corse), while two leagues further to the east was the Danish castle at Frederiksborg. The European trading nations were engaged in a veritable free-for-all to strike up local alliances, rent land from kings and built fortified trading posts. By the 1680s, there were also forts being built at locations such as Accra and Sekondi (though this would be burned down in 1695 by the Fante). These fortresses were often within viewing distance of one another, meaning that the impression of the growing European trade and military presence was ever harder to escape; and today the ruins of these settlements still protrude from the headlands of the coast of Ghana, some of them better preserved than others, and all of them speaking of this contested past. Along the coast in Ghana, the sites of memory are such that history speaks with painful force and clarity.[65]

These forts were brooding reminders of the dependence of African kings and traders on European nations for the firearms so vital to their military strategies and defence. They were deliberately built to be imposing and to suggest a challenge to traditional African political control on the Gold Coast. 'The Heigth [*sic*] of the Walls is the Strength of this Fort,' John Atkins wrote of his visit to Cape Corse in 1721. 'Within the Castle is a Smith's Shop, a Cooperage, Store-houses, a Chappel, and Houses for the Officers and Servants . . .

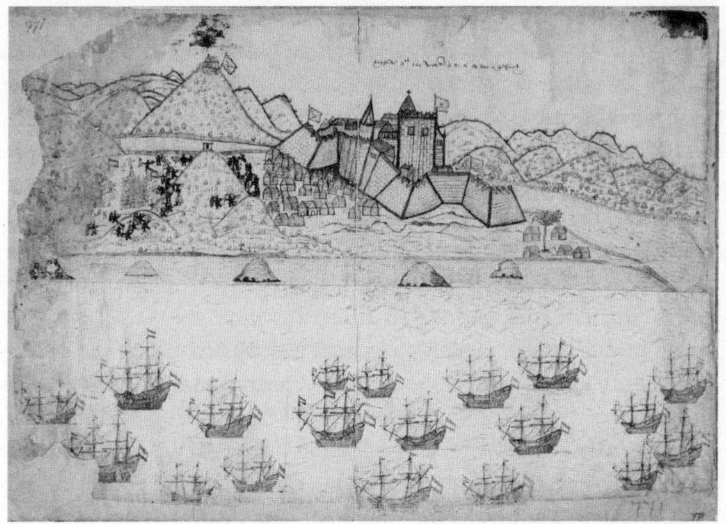

View of the fort and the roadstead at Elmina, by Hans Propheet.

A Bastion runs out from it that has a very pleasant Prospect to the sea, discerning with a Glass the Ships coming down the Coast, and very distinctly all those in the Road at *Das Minas* [Elmina].'[66]

The militarized European presence reads heavily through the documents, which talk of commercial rivalries and attacks by European powers on one another to try to secure the trading hegemony. Of course, Akan traders frequently used these rivalries to gain better terms – one in 1682 said he would only sell gold for linen sheets to the English factor if the same price was offered as by the Dutch – and yet the constant import of firearms and the rivalry of both African and European competitors stoked disorder, which the militarized presence of the forts exacerbated. By the end of 1686, there was renewed war between the Akyem and Akron kingdoms. By the end of 1687, Fetu and Fante were at war; and by 1694, Akyem and Akwamu. The large number of small kingdoms noted earlier in the century by Ruyters were breaking out into a number of nasty, short wars, which would eventually allow the larger states of Asante and an expansionist Fante Federation to emerge in the eighteenth century.[67]

There were constant attempts to manipulate these wars by European traders on one side or the other. The Dutch trader Willem Bosman gave a vivid description of how these divisions were stoked by rival European powers. At Axim – one of the oldest European trading posts, fortified by the Portuguese in 1503 – and a place where rice was grown 'in incredible abundance', the arrival of the Brandenburg trading company in the 1680s sowed divisions: 'the Arrival of the Brandenburghers divided the Inhabitants, one part of them putting themselves under the Protection of the New-comers . . . but the other part . . . staid under our Government.'[68]

Why were European traders so keen to stoke these wars? The hope was that there would be more enslaved persons for sale as captives as a result – or, as the English factor at Anomabu said of the 1686 wars between Akyem and Akron, 'we hope it will be a good time shortly for slaves.' As enslaved persons began to be substituted for gold exports, however, an eerie resemblance was occurring between these transformations in the Saharan and Atlantic trades.[69]

For in Borno, just as on the Gold Coast, a slave trade was supplementing the long-standing gold trade. One account of 1658 describes clearly the casual dependence that Borno had developed on the slave trade, with gold now nowhere mentioned; the account describes how the mai's (king's) wife Gumsu had twenty personal men at arms, each of whom commanded 1,000 slaves. Moreover, at that time the Mai wanted a thousand slaves, and he was trying to get them. 'The Mwallim prayed for the *amir* . . . Barely had he done so when the mother of the *amir* died at this very juncture and left ten thousand slaves.'[70]

That the economic relations of both the Gold Coast and the Sahel experienced similar transitions in the same period, from a gold-trading economy to a slave-trading one, gives pause for thought. The reason for this may be that the economies of coast and savannah were much more integrated than used to be thought. This shared connection in Borno and the Gold Coast in transitioning from a dependency on gold exports to one on the export of enslaved persons forged one of the links; and the shared cowrie currency used on the Niger Bend and at the coast made them even firmer.*[71]

* See also Prologue to Part Two, on how the discovery of Brazilian gold in the 1690s played a part in this.

The economic comparison can be taken further, for what was at stake was a transformation in the perception of money and value. Writing from the Gold Coast port of Anishan in late December 1687, the English factor John Bloom was explicit about how both Akan and English saw their exchange as a monetary one. Of the Akan, he wrote that they 'are gone up to the country but doe promise to be downe againe very speedily. I wish wee had some of their money before their departure.' Then less than two weeks later, he wrote that 'some [Akans] in towne have brought money, but if our goods don't come today they'll begon.'[72] Where gold and captives had always been linked on the Gold Coast, as exchanges of value, in Borno the trade in enslaved persons replaced that of gold. In each case, the trade that was in demand was that which could export the maximum surplus value; and, as political systems came under pressure in both the Gold Coast and the Sahel during the seventeenth century, external actors were in a stronger position to enforce their terms for these unequal exchanges.

THE RISE OF THE SLAVE TRADE AND THE END OF ECONOMIC BALANCE

In 1595, the island of São Tomé, which lay a long way offshore from the Gold Coast, in the Gulf of Guinea, witnessed a major uprising. An Italian missionary described what happened on 9 July of that year, when an enslaved person named Amador began to foment revolt: 'On Sunday, July 9th 1595, with the [white] people attending Church, a Black person rose up with five or six others in that Island of S. Tomé, and each of them soon led all the slaves that belonged to their Masters – which numbered around 200 each – and these began to threaten all the white and mulato men [of the island].'[73]

Amador called himself 'king', and his followers swore loyalty until death, and soon numbered over 2,000. Within three days they had destroyed thirty sugar plantations, and on 14 July they tried and failed to burn down the town of São Tomé itself. A month later, on 14 August, Amador was captured, and hanged, drawn and quartered; four years later a report from the town council reported that altogether he had burned down seventy sugar plantations, and that most of them had yet to be rebuilt because of 'the meagre assets and lack of slaves' belonging to the planter class of the island.[74]

Throughout the sixteenth century, São Tomé had been a centre of the early-Atlantic sugar trade; yet one of the earliest uprisings of Atlantic history had put paid to it within the space of a month. This was the start of a period of transformation in São Tomé and on the other Atlantic islands in the Gulf of Guinea, Bioko and Annobon (today the islands of Equatorial Guinea). Over time, maroons such as Amador and his followers fled to Bioko, which was not under colonial control, and established independent communities there. It was not until the nineteenth century that attempts would be made by Spanish and English colonial forces to bring these islands within the framework of the Scramble for Africa.

Warfare had been associated with the traffic in enslaved persons from the beginning. Many enslaved persons were war captives, and used their experience of military techniques in their struggles to free themselves – a decisive factor in the formation of maroon communities all over the New World. Warfare had long been associated with enslavement on São Tomé, home of some of the first sugar plantations in the Atlantic world, and also of communities of escaped slaves even in the early sixteenth century, where a report of 1535 describes how the bush was full of these communities who 'cause as much damage as possible and kill and rob people and destroy property . . . every day the bush is filled with runaway slaves and we are all terrified.'[75]

These upheavals on São Tomé mattered to communities on the Gold Coast. Already by 1595, São Tomé had been linked with the Gold Coast for a century through the provisions trade, which had in time brought maize and manioc from Brazil to West Africa, and as a supplier of enslaved persons who came from Benin and Kongo to work at the fortress of Elmina. The decimation of the sugar plantations by the warring, uprisen Africans was swiftly followed by the rise of a parasite that infested the cane. The sugar industry on the island collapsed, exacerbated by competition from Brazil. As a result, São Tomé slave traders began to focus more on the trade to and from the neighbouring coast; beginning in Allada, east of the Gold Coast, this trade would before long begin to have an impact in the traditional gold-exporting areas of the coast.[76]

Initially, the growth of the trade in captives at Elmina itself was limited by laws passed by the Portuguese and then the Dutch banning this 10 leagues either side of the castle. By 1620, Portuguese factors had urged the king to lift this ban, to no avail initially. Nevertheless, by the 1640s, the logs of the Dutch factors at Elmina made it clear that the trade in enslaved persons had grown rapidly in the neighbouring regions, and was beginning to affect relations on the Gold Coast itself. In January 1645, Matthew Warner arrived from London to trade for captives for Barbados, bringing tobacco, cotton and indigo for trade. This was followed by a ship loading for Barbados under Christopher Bishop, who traded in nearby Cormantin, and another under James Benton that came from St Kitts. Such mentions were simply routine over the years that followed, and were part of a major growth in English slave trading across West Africa, from Sierra Leone to Cameroon, which went with the rise of sugar plantations in the new English Caribbean colonies. Indeed, the Dutch factor at Elmina, in 1647, described the English trade in these years as almost exclusively for enslaved persons, whereas the Dutch traded for gold as well as for the labour of captives in their plantations in Brazil, where they would retain power until the Portuguese defeated them in 1654.[77]

By the later seventeenth century, these changes would have notable effects on the political conflicts in the Gold Coast region. Denkyira's decline can be seen in the way in which some of their soldiers were kept as 'pawns' (hostages) in English forts by the 1690s – some of whom could later be converted into 'capital' and sold into the transatlantic trade if debts were not repaid. Many of the pawns at this time were canoemen from the coastal regions, whose work panning for gold was perhaps no longer so profitable, since greater profits could be wrought by using them as collateral for the trade in captives. And so, gradually, the incessant demands from the New World for labour had visible political and social effects on the Gold Coast.[78]

The economic imbalances that underpinned this trading system are important. In their growing trade in enslaved persons, the English traded largely iron bars; in 1647, 1,000 and 700 bars of iron were traded in two English ships by a Captain Metcalf, with very few pieces of cloth. The Dutch, by contrast, traded huge volumes of cloth; the cloth known as *lijwaet*, made in the Low Countries, was always the highest volume import in the account books of the 1640s, with 125,000 pieces noted on one ship of 1645. Indeed, the value in florins of Dutch *lijwaet* traded to Elmina in 1645 was 929,619, with the next most valuable item worth just 31,999 florins.[79]

This is of crucial importance in understanding the accumulation of surplus value through the trade. As we have seen in this chapter, the flow of gold from this region ended up as minted gold coins in the Netherlands and England during this period. At the same time, huge profits accrued to those trading in West Africa. The Dutch West India Company's capital base grew from assets of 6.4 million guilders in 1602 to over 40 million in 1660, while distributing 62 million guilders over the same period in dividends to shareholders. Even more starkly, the Dutch textile industry – which had shrunk in the sixteenth century – boomed again after 1585, with the industrial centre being located at Leiden, where production expanded from nothing in 1580 to 100,000 pieces a year in 1630. Not a small proportion of these textiles was destined for West Africa through the Gold Coast.[80]

In other words, just as the Portuguese had reaped 500 per cent profits from their early trade on the Gold Coast, the Dutch choice to export cloth was a strategic one that boosted Dutch manufacturers and was calculated to extract maximum profits from the cloth for gold trade (where, as the Dutch factor had noted in 1647, it was the English who focused on enslaved persons). Meanwhile, the English choice to export iron (and, in the later seventeenth century, copper) was also calculated to be the most profitable form of exchange to enhance the capital base. The 1680s saw the emergence of a copper-smelting industry in Bristol that reaped large profits from increasing the export of copper bars to regions like the Gold Coast; and huge profits were available in the iron trade, even if, in fact, the English had to import much of their iron themselves, from Sweden.[81]

CONCLUSION

The argument examined in this chapter has the defect of seeming blindingly obvious. From the view of the twenty-first century, the extraction of gold in return for cloth, copper and the like must inevitably produce a capital imbalance. Yet, as noted in the Introduction to this book, what seems most obvious can be most worthy of attention. Was it obvious in the sixteenth and seventeenth centuries that this would be the consequence? Clearly not, for gold was one of many currencies then in use, and did not become adopted as the universal currency, or 'gold standard', until 1821. Almost by accident, Akan rulers on the Gold Coast participated in a trade that, in the long term, would have serious effects.

As with all economic changes, it is in the details of human life that the values exchanged become real. As European traders augmented their castle-prisons and networks of captivity and commerce, the human mosaic of the Gold Coast began to change. These lonely, greedy men married Fante women from the coast. Their mixed-race children began to people the villages surrounding the forts. Yet the economic changes were realized through African social structures, since these children could only inherit property and social position in coastal societies through their Fante mother's *abusua*, or lineage. As the material trappings of wealth became Western – imported rum, cloth, copper-made products, jewels, mirrors, and more – the cultural and social worlds remained resolutely Akan and Fante.

All the same, the economic transformations were markers for the Gold Coast's future. This was a region that had been globalizing ever since the spike in demand for gold production had begun in the later fourteenth century. The process of globalizing exchanges continued throughout the period, as Mexican maize imported via São Tomé and Brazil became commonplace in the region, alongside Dutch and Indian cloth, while, as we have seen, Gold Coast weavers exported cloth at times to diaspora communities in Brazil. Meanwhile, the arrival of Portuguese traders placed Gold Coast kingdoms in an advantageous position, between Atlantic and Saharan trading systems, which they could exploit throughout the sixteenth century as trade grew; and tax take, imports, urban infrastructure and the trading class all benefited as a result.[82]

However, the fall of Songhay diminished demand for gold from the Saharan traders as the locus for the trans-Saharan trade shifted east from Gao and Timbuktu to Kano and Borno. Meanwhile, European demand intensified, as the Dutch and English came to rival the

Portuguese. By the 1640s, both Dutch and English had become engaged in a trade that would extract maximum 'capital value': the Dutch for gold, in exchange for mass-produced cloth from their looms; the English for enslaved persons whose labour would accrue value in the sugar plantations of the Indies, in exchange for iron and homemade copper. During their crossing of the Middle Passage to the Americas, these enslaved persons would also consume large amounts of grain produced on the Gold Coast, with as many as 200,000 pounds of grain carried on some ships.[83]

At the same time, the import of copper, cloth and iron as items of exchange would extend the market for commercial trade far inland. As one 1602 report put it, 'although there are so many Basons brought thither, and no one that weareth so much as Linnen, yet you see but few old Copper things there, and therefore you must thinke, that there is great store of people inhabiting further within the land, which use so great quantitie of such things.'[84]

The cumulative impact of all these processes was large. With the growing import of firearms stoking instability, only a kingdom that could entrench its economic position in a global context of the exchange of values would prosper. Such a kingdom would rise in the eighteenth century in the Asante Empire, building on structures of previous Akan powers such as Denkyira and Bono-Mansu. Asante would prove able initially to retain, rather than export, gold, and thus develop not unfavourable currency exchanges. It consolidated its administration and army. As an intermediary between the Atlantic and Saharan trades, balancing warfare, enslavement and currency exchanges, Asante would survive long into the nineteenth century, as the 'kingdom of gold'.

4

Rivers of Cloth, Masks of Bronze: The Bights of Benin and Biafra

The upmarket suburb of Rio Vermelho lies a short way from the downtown of Salvador da Bahia, beyond the apartments and beaches of Barra. Long the colonial capital of Brazil, Salvador's history breaks out in sad, lively clusters, unexpectedly, a little like Brazil itself: dilapidated mansions selling local-made tiles in the Moorish style squat beside ice-cream parlours, while Baroque eighteenth-century churches stand high above the sea, fronting squares where hippies gather to sell each other necklaces.

In Rio Vermelho the history emerges differently. On the waterfront, as the beach curves around towards a cluster of restaurants, is the Casa das Orixás de Iemanjá, a centre for worship in the Afro-Brazilian religion of Candomblé. All day, members of Bahia's large population of Candomblé worshippers descend on the site, praying, performing ritual ablutions and staring out at the sea, at once a place of loss and memory. The ancestors of many came from what are now Benin and Nigeria, from the ports of Badagry, Ouidah and Porto-Novo, and this is why the Yorùbá term *orixá* (spirit-deity) is used in Brazil. The connections between what Bahians call the Costa da Mina and Salvador run deep, in the palm oil (*aceite dendé*) and cassava-leaf stew (*manisoba*), the *acarajé* and *bobo de camarão* that make Bahian food far and away the best in Brazil. And they are there in the Candomblé stalls that have been set up outside iconic churches in the city, selling the wherewithal for the shrines and practice of a religion that was born in the Bights of Benin and Biafra, and then transformed in Brazil.

Though most of these connections took shape in the eighteenth and nineteenth centuries, they had begun by the end of the seventeenth.

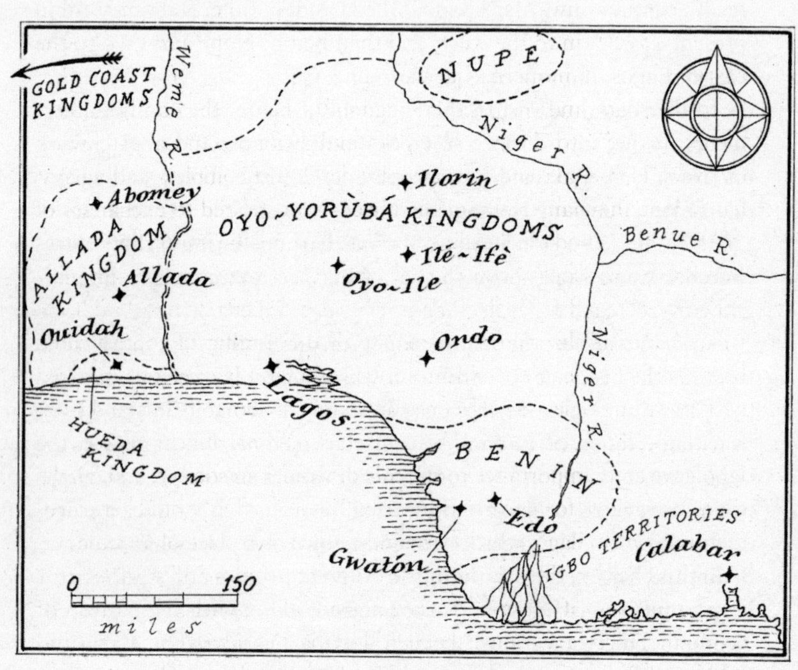

Aja, Benin, Igbo and Yorùbá polities

Bahian ships increasingly sought out the Costa da Mina from the late 1670s onwards. This coastline east of the Gold Coast fragments into long, coastal lagoons interspersed with sandbars and river estuaries, making it a good location to transport supplies and persons for the trade in captives. But, as with all the regions we have looked at so far, this part of West Africa had a long history predating the rise of the Atlantic. Inland, where the coastal lagoons and forests give way to the savannah, many important states arose from the fourteenth century onwards: Allada, Hueda and, in time, Dahomey, all in present-day Benin to the west; and then Benin, Nupe and Oyo to the east of Lagos, in modern Nigeria.[1]

To the south and east of the Kingdom of Benin, the coastline fragments further into a maze of creeks and swamps, and a patchwork of rivers. Here Igala and Igbo peoples developed complex trading systems along the many rivers of the Niger Delta, related to exchanges of forest products and the weaving of cloth. In time, the important centres of Calabar and Bonny would grow around the maze of creeks and rivers curling inland from the Atlantic coast. Further north, Igbo-Ukwu was a major civilizational centre, site of the forging of sophisticated bronzes since at least the ninth century. Igbo and Igala peoples shared various technologies and practices, including farming, fishing and iron-smelting techniques, and religious artefacts. A matrilineal people, the Igbo gave great importance to the role of women in society; and, as the times of raiding for captives increased, people often would return to their mother's village, which was (and is) seen as a place of sanctuary.[2]

In this chapter, the origins of the different peoples and states of this important part of West Africa are traced, along with the pattern of economic change we have been following. Yorùbá, Fon, Gbe and Igbo peoples in particular would make central contributions, not only in their own homelands, but also to world history and cultures. Their foods, religious beliefs, ideas and military techniques would have a major part to play in the shaping of the New World. Yet meanwhile, in their West African homelands, major changes were under way that would alter their worlds forever. The import of large amounts of copper and cowries changed economies and ideas of self-expression, reflecting transformations of identity in the era of a violent modernity.

ART, BELIEF AND POWER BEFORE THE ATLANTIC ERA

The first person to write a history of the Yorùbá, Samuel Johnson, saw Yorùbá peoples as migrants who had arrived from outside the region and founded the sacred Yorùbá centre of Ilé-Ifè. Archaeological evidence shows that this had certainly happened before 1000 CE, as glass beads existed by that time, alongside forges that melted them down and refashioned them into the insignia of high office at Ilé-Ifè. The grove of Olókun, just two miles from Ilé-Ifè, contained fired crucibles that were blended with beads in a beautiful array of colours. Beads remained core insignia of office throughout the next centuries.[3]

It is unclear whether some of these beads may have been imported through the trans-Saharan trade, but certainly the peoples who lived in the region of Ilé-Ifè developed their own technologies to fire beads. Glass beads found here have a higher lime and alumina content than those of European or Islamic production. Of 13,000 beads recently excavated by the archaeologist Abidemi Babatunde Babalola, 75 per cent are blue, while some also are red. Colour was a vital signifier of power and status with these beads, which may have been an early form of currency. Given the spiritual role that these beads held, it is again clear that currencies had more than a merely economic role in the pre-Atlantic era, but were also valued for their religious power.[4]

Manufacture and craftwork were thus deeply rooted in what was an integrated network of city states from the twelfth or the thirteenth century. To the north of Ilé-Ifè, Nupe's urban structure grew from around 1200 onwards. At Ilé-Ifè itself, potsherd pavements were laid by the late twelfth or the early thirteenth century. Some of the evidence for the shared social structure among these different states is precisely in a common pattern of urban life, where pavements in Benin, Ilé-Ifè and Osògbò were all made with potsherd.[5]

There was here a strong tradition of manufacturing for trade. Beyond the importance of iron in Nupe, and brass in Benin, there was a very old tradition of cloth-weaving. The manufacturing of loom-patterned cotton was long-standing, with archaeological evidence showing that it

Brass head with a beaded crown and plume, Ifè, Nigeria.

was widespread by the eleventh century in the savannah regions north of what became Oyo. There was also extremely skilled weaving in the northern part of Igbo country, where a strong craft base developed that endured for many centuries. Indeed, cloth from these areas was highly valued as far afield as Brazil during the seventeenth and eighteenth centuries. Igbo societies developed trade networks in the maze of rivers and creeks around the Niger Delta; the fame they developed as traders remained with them into the twentieth century, and is there to this day in postcolonial Nigeria.[6]

Igbo political structures, language and religious practice were different, therefore, from those of the peoples who lived further north, but they were not totally separated from these societies. Indeed, some Igbo origin myths suggest close connections, stating for instance that the settlements around Enugu were founded by someone from Benin. Thus, across a very wide territory, the peoples in the savannah and forest regions between the Niger Delta and Hueda were interconnected, with clear linguistic, religious and political links that cut across modern nation-state boundaries. Such commonalities then extended with migrations from the sixteenth to the eighteenth centuries, and were easier to see in the years after decolonization.[7]

Contact, where it did exist, was based on trade. In time, this led to intermarriage and other levels of mutual identification. The first Bishop of Nigeria, Samuel Crowther (himself a Yorùbá), described it thus in the mid-nineteenth century: 'This country comprises many tribes governed by their own chiefs and having their own laws. At one time they were all tributaries to one Sovereign, the King of Yorùbá [by which Crowther meant Oyo], including Benin on the East and Dahomey on the West, but are now independent.'[8]

Benin was the major kingdom in the fifteenth and sixteenth centuries. Though it remained intact until 1897, over time its power waned, and it became subject to the Yorùbá state of Oyo, which flourished from its rise in the seventeenth century to its fall in 1835. In the western part, there were small independent states in the fifteenth century, such as existed on the Gold Coast. By the early seventeenth century, Allada had arisen, most likely following migration of Aja peoples from Tado, in the north-east of what became Dahomey.* Allada was centred in what is now the Republic of Benin but with influence stretching into southern Nigeria and Togo. Allada's power would eventually be supplanted, first by Hueda, and then by Dahomey, from the 1720s onwards. Like Benin, Dahomey would remain a major political force until European colonial invasion in the late nineteenth century. Its military power would in time trigger the creation of new communities, formed by bands of refugees fleeing from its wars.[9]

In spite of the multiplicity of states that rose and fell from 1500 to 1900 west of the Niger Delta, one feature that united them was a shared spiritual practice. As new kingdoms arose, such as Benin, they retained a very close connection to the original heartland of Ilé-Ifè. One oral history recounts that in the late thirteenth century bronze casting was taught to the Bini at Edo (the capital of Benin) from a master brass caster sent from Ifè. Moreover, heads of deceased obas (kings) of Benin were sent for burial to Ilé-Ifè for centuries. With a

* In what is now the Republic of Togo.

common spiritual heritage and shared political structures, very close connections would develop right across the region, over a span of hundreds of years; and so it should be no surprise that the earliest currencies, such as the glass beads mentioned above, had a religious value above any reductive economic rate of exchange.[10]

These connections were described by the Portuguese chronicler João de Barros. Writing in the 1540s, Barros wrote of an embassy sent from Benin to João II of Portugal (1481–95), where the Bini ambassador described the relationship to Ilé-Ifè in the fifteenth century: '[250 leagues distant] there was a King, the most powerful of those parts, which they call Ogané [the Ooni of Ilé-Ifè]; who among the principal peoples of the region of Beni was held in the same esteem and veneration as the Popes are among us.'[11] Barros focused on Benin because it was where the Portuguese developed the most complex trading relations in this period. It is certainly one of the best-known states of precolonial West Africa. The Benin Bronze casts collected in the British Museum and many museums outside Africa offer a challenging face to a world which has usually doubted the complexity and potential of early-West African kingdoms. Thus, on taking possession of the Benin capital of Edo, during the colonial conquest of 1897, British troops were amazed to find exquisite ancient bronze carvings adorning the royal palace. These were looted for the benefit of European museums then developing their collections of 'primitive art'.

The bronzes were commissioned by obas to commemorate key events in their rule, and during the reigns of their predecessors. They functioned, therefore, as official histories of the kingdom and mnemonics for successive generations of the Benin Court chroniclers, the Ihogbe and Ogboka. However, while early generations of Western art historians saw the bronzes as reflecting early Portuguese influence, they embody entirely Bini aesthetics and skills. The necklaces in the bronzes are often of leopards' teeth, while symbols of royal power and status such as kings mounted on horseback and the place of royal slaves are widespread.[12]

Indeed, when describing the connection of Edo to Ilé-Ifè, João de Barros also offered a precious description of the variety of bronze manufactures of these kingdoms: 'As a sign of confirmation [of the new Oba of Benin], this Prince Ogané sends them a staff and a cap . . . all

Brass cast of the Oba of Benin with adjutants, sixteenth century.

made of shining bronze, in place of a sceptre and crown, and they also send them a cross made of the same bronze to wear around the neck.'[13]

Casters in Ilé-Ifè and Edo use a method known to Western art historians as 'lost wax', in which an intricate wax model is constructed over a clay core. Clay is then diligently layered upon the wax and heated, and the wax melts through a furrow. Molten metal is poured into the mould left behind, and the hardened clay prised away, with the image revealed now cast in the mould. These firing techniques show the sophistication of manufacturing in Benin and neighbouring areas before the fifteenth century. They were likely also related to the methods of firing beads into royal insignia that, as we have seen, date back to at least 1000 CE.[14]

This region thus shows the strength of West African kingdoms throughout the medieval period. However, the fifteenth and sixteenth centuries were a time of transition, when the strength of this network of connected states was eroded. Major wars at some point between 1450 and 1575 (known as the Ókìpò Wars) pitted the states against one another. They may be connected to the construction of the fortified ditches around Ijebu, the *eredos*, built at some point in the late-fourteenth or early-fifteenth century. The power of Benin, Ilé-Ifè, Nupe and smaller kingdoms such as Ìjèsà had begun to decline by the end of the sixteenth century. The centralized state of Oyo arose, with a powerful cavalry and far-reaching trade networks, and Oyo was to be a major force throughout this part of West Africa, until its fall in 1835.[15]

TRANSFORMATIONS IN THE FIFTEENTH CENTURY

While Benin, Nupe and Ilé-Ifè had long histories before 1500, it is important that – just as in the other parts of West Africa we have looked at – major changes were afoot in the fifteenth century. At this time Nupe and Oyo to the north were expanding; and Nupe's growth was related to the ascending power of Kano, where, as we saw in Chapter 1, the Kano Chronicle notes a link between the two at this time. The Bini oba, Ewuare (enthroned *c.* 1440), responded by strengthening political structures and expanding the road networks. The role of town chiefs was enhanced, and three associations of palace chiefs were founded. Though threatened by Nupe, Benin extended itself eastwards to the lands of the Igbo and Ijo on the right bank of the Niger, and west towards the Lagos lagoon from which today's megacity derives its name.[16]

What had led to Benin's expansion in the decades prior to the Portuguese arrival in the 1480s? Again, the way in which the whole West African subregion influenced the trans-Saharan trading system and thereby Europe offers a persuasive answer. Nupe's rise was linked to Kano, a major centre for gold exports as we have seen. Benin's flourishing trading system, and the growth of cloth production, encouraged the consolidation of political and administrative structures. It was precisely the West African 'booms' of the fifteenth century that in their turn had influenced the desire of the Portuguese to explore southwards and led to their arrival at the coastal port of Gwatón in 1486; and in this boom, Benin had its part to play, just like Mali, Songhay, Kano, Mossi and the gold-producers of Bono-Mansu alongside them.[17]

Thus, the Portuguese found a newly confident state when they arrived. Early connections were amicable. Aiming to find a route to the spice trade of India, the Portuguese were thrilled with the pepper that grew in Benin; on arriving at Gwatón, they returned with it to the spice markets of Flanders, where it was very well received. Also returning to Portugal in the fleet was a Bini ambassador, who was welcomed at Court in Portugal and presented with a gift of rich clothing. Bini ambassadors continued to attend the Court at Lisbon, and Oba Ozolua sent another embassy in 1514; one of them, known as Dom Jorge to the Portuguese, was given a velvet cape and shoes and a camlet waistcoat by King Manoel I, with the same being given to his companion, 'dom Antonio'.[18]

The main settlement of the Portuguese was at Gwatón, but relations with the Bini were good enough for them to go frequently to the capital at Edo. The best description of Benin at this time is by Duarte Pacheco Pereira, from *c.* 1506. Gwatón was a town of around 2,000 adult male residents (*vezinhos*), perhaps 10,000 people in all therefore. It was around 30 miles from Edo by a good road, and Edo itself was surrounded by a large and deep ditch, and was big enough to be about three miles across from gate to gate of the city. Benin's territory, meanwhile, was extensive, being around 250 miles wide and 125 long.[19]

However, the Portuguese soon ran into trouble. Following the 1514 embassy to Lisbon, in 1515 some Portuguese gave military assistance to Benin, in a conflict that was probably against Igala invaders, and linked to the Ókìpò Wars; after it, the oba promised to convert to Christianity and allow easy terms of trade. But this was impossible, given that the spiritual centre at Ilé-Ifè was so strongly connected to the political power of the Bini kings. In 1539, the Portuguese sent a mission to Benin, but their missionaries soon gave up, writing to

João III of Portugal that there was no 'confidence whatever nor indications to suggest that the said King [of Benin] will convert'. When the missionaries had given the oba a letter from João III, the oba had put it in a box and failed to open it for three months. Moreover, the land 'was very dangerous, full of illnesses, and not as profitable as had been hoped'. Once again, the missionaries and traders were doubtless yellow and feverish with malaria, weak, ragged and incapacitated.[20]

There was, in fact, little to tempt Benin from the Portuguese side, beyond money (as we shall see). The Portuguese brought cloths, but very fine cloths were already available locally. They offered luxury items, but these the Bini could easily do without. They could also offer military support, which was useful, but the price asked was too high; the obas could not countenance a conversion to the outsiders' religion when the basis of their political power was spiritual. The core of Benin was expanding towards Lagos, and the obas had seen off Nupe. After the victories of 1516, the Bini began to withdraw from the Portuguese, and that remained the pattern throughout the rest of the sixteenth century.

To judge from Pieter de Marees's 1600 description of the oba's Court, this was a state confident in its own power and unlikely to be deflected from this by any mere baubles offered by the new traders:

> The [king]'s Court is very big and has inside it many large, square courtyards surrounded by galleries, in which one always finds guards. I have gone so far into that Court that I have passed through four such courtyards . . . [And] when a nobleman comes to Court, he comes on horseback . . . they have as many servants walking behind them as befits their status. Some Servants have great Shields with which they protect the Nobleman against the Sun . . . the others follow behind, making some music: some play Drums, others Horns and Flutes.[21]

Such descriptions, and the huge expansion of bronze-cast-making that seems to have occurred in the sixteenth century, suggest that this was a time of great cultural flowering. This was the era of Benin's most famous obas, Ewuare, Ozolua and Esigie. Yet, while Benin's power and majesty grew, oral recollections of the arrival of the Portuguese (known as the Ikpotoki by the Bini) imply that other, longer-term changes were also at work. One oral account, taken down in the 1890s, describes very well the relationships that emerged:

> This is how the white men came to [E]do. King Esigie was very old . . . [he] sent messengers with some tusks as presents to the country by the big water [the Benin River] where the white men used to come to trade, and they told the messengers to go and salute any white men they found there and beg them to come, which they did, and ever since then white men have come to Benin. The white men stayed long, many many years they came to trade, and if a man comes to trade he must sit down and sell his things softly softly; they used to buy ivory, red-wood, oil, gum, and slaves; then there was a different white man who used to come, but he only bought slaves . . . These white men used to sit down at Gwato and there they built houses, big houses, with big doors, in which they kept their goods and slaves. We never heard of these white men bringing white women here, but the King could dash them for some girl to wife.[22]

Some of the Benin Bronzes, too, capture the Bini response to the Portuguese arrival. There are depictions of the Portuguese, often alongside some of the trappings of their trade: books, manufactured objects (such as jugs and cups) and horses. Aspects of the Portuguese language were also imported, as was also the case in Senegambia: the Edo for 'ball' is *ibolu* and the Portuguese *bola*; the Edo for 'coconut palms' is *ekoka* and the Portuguese *coqueiro*;* and the Edo for 'store' is *amagazemi* and the Portuguese *armazem*. In short, when the Portuguese presence brought useful objects, these were adopted along with the Portuguese vocabulary; but Edo culture was far too strong and connected to the long-standing spiritual practices tied to Ilé-Ifè to be overcome by Portuguese influences.[23]

There is one other aspect of this oral history of early Edo–Portuguese relations that is worth noting, in the longer term. The account makes plain – very accurately – the diverse nature of the early trade, where goods from Benin (pepper, especially) were as prized as enslaved persons. Over time, however, the account tells us, the diversity of the

* While palm trees producing nuts were native to Africa, the coconut palm was imported by the Portuguese in the sixteenth century from Asia.

Portrait of a Portuguese trader, differentiated by long hair, beard and differently shaped sword.

trade disappeared, until enslaved persons were the main demand of the solitary, feverish male Portuguese traders, who – reversing traditional gender roles in societies where usually it was the women who traded – came and expected the Bini king to 'dash them a girl for wife'. And it was these changes that would come to embody the economic and political relationships of the region with the wider world.

A COPPER RENAISSANCE: BENIN'S ARTISTIC AND POLITICAL TRANSFORMATION

A mid-sixteenth-century account from a Portuguese ship's pilot gives an interesting perspective on the ritual power at the heart of royal majesty in Benin. The pilot described how, when an oba died, a large cavity was dug out of the ground to create a royal mausoleum, in which the deceased oba was placed with his most loyal and trusted followers to keep him company. A large rock was then placed above the grave, so that none of the followers could escape, until they died one by one, keeping the king company in his journey beyond this world. Then the new oba was informed, and was able to begin his reign.[24]

Such accounts may well be more symbolic than factual. They show that much 'written history' about West Africa in this period is, in fact, based on oral history, which is why these texts need to be understood through the lens of other accounts and not seen as repositories of 'fact'. For this account and others like it were clearly recounted by African traders and go-betweens to the Europeans, who then wrote them down as they understood them. The pilot who wrote this account visited the island of São Tomé frequently, and would have heard this tale from traders there who sailed back and forth to Benin. These traders would never have been permitted by the Bini to observe these funeral rites; nor did they understand the oral cultures of Bini traders and their metaphorical framing of narratives, which meant that such stories may have been intended mainly to reflect the power and ritual importance of the oba. Certainly, these complexities mean that we cannot know if they are accurate.

Another account of this royal power was given by Andreas Ulsheimer, who became heavily involved during a visit of 1604, when the crew of the sloop in which he was travelling was called on by the oba to help quell an uprising near Lagos. After their victory, the oba offered to hold his annual festivities, 'when, for once in the year, he lets himself be seen by the people'. The festival was designed to show off the oba's majesty, religious power and political authority to the full:

> [The oba] comes riding out into the town on a horse decorated with red scarlet and draped with red corals . . . imposingly dressed after their fashion in red scarlet cloth [*ododo*] and draped not only with fine red corals but also with other strange things. In addition he hangs over his head and back, down to his heels, a white horse-tail, in such a way that anyone who see it is frightened . . . six thousand men march

> in front of him, and when he comes, all the people fall down on their knees and clap their hands.[25]

The extraordinary pomp of these festivities was confirmed by some Capuchin missionaries who were able to see them in 1651, and wrote later that 'they would never have believed that there were so many so finely dressed people' in Benin, coming across them dancing and playing musical instruments in the oba's court.[26]

The religious power inherent in these festivals evoked the spiritual strength that saw the obas spurn the Catholic missionaries. A large number of different Ugie, or state festivals, were introduced by obas from the later fifteenth century onwards. This began with Oba Ewuare's installation of the shrine his royal ancestors, known as the Ugie Erha Oba. It was followed in the sixteenth century by the fertility festival of Eko Ikhurhe (related to clearing farmland) and festivals to deities of the royal palace known as the Ugie Azama. A religious and cultural renewal was under way, prompted by Benin's political expansion, and by the confidence and power that went with this.[27]

By 1600, this growth was everywhere apparent. Arriving at Lagos, Ulsheimer found that the town 'belongs to the King of Benin', while Allada, too, was said to be subject to Benin. But Lagos itself was a frontier town, where only soldiers and four military commanders were resident. This alone would have been enough, though, to create a lively economy. Many traders went to Lagos by canoe and over land with 'their wares, which consist of beautiful cotton cloths woven in all kinds of colours and patterns'. Finally, when Ulsheimer and his crewmen went to help the oba against the rebels, the oba's army numbered 10,000, which suggests that Benin's expansion west to Lagos had been considerable. The oba had built a formidable fighting machine: when they conquered the town, 'they struck down all the men fit for military service.'[28]

This militarized expansion went with state and urban consolidation. When the Dutch geographer Olfert Dapper compiled an account of Africa from various sources (many of which he plagiarized, never having set foot on the continent himself), he described how Benin 'boasts many good towns . . . lying eight or nine days' journey beyond [Edo]'. By this time a city wall had been built, rising to a height of 10 feet; it was 'double Pallisado'd with thick Trees, with spans of five or six Foot, laid Crossways, fasten'd together, and Palister'd over with Red Clay'. Edo itself had very wide streets. The houses stood in rows, 'with slop'd roofs, covered with Palm leaves'; they were very spacious, with long galleries, and different rooms and apartments. The roofs were held together with iron nails, which were also used to weld together door panels.[29]

Just as Edo had grown and become more elaborate and impressive (from the wood-lined ditch that surrounded it in 1500 to the wall of the seventeenth century), so had Benin's administrative structure. The complex military hierarchies required to raise an army of 10,000 were replicated in the organization of the state. Each town had a council of chiefs or nobles that ran it on a day-to-day basis, with Gwatón having five chiefs by the seventeenth century and other towns seven or more. Minor civil disputes were settled in the smaller towns, while a higher court sat daily at Edo for criminal cases.[30]

In other words, what emerged in Benin by the early seventeenth century was a state whose expansion was underpinned by many of the same features of what are considered normative to political history in Europe during the same period. In Benin, as in many other African and European nations, there was a close relationship between the expansion of the state and that of the military, and a significant increase in long-distance trade. Moreover, as in Europe, these political changes went with what the historian José Lingna Nafafé has described as a 'transformation in subjectivities' (or what in Europe is seen as the Renaissance, which, of course, was under way at the same time). Whereas among the Sape of Sierra Leone this was represented in their ivory carvings, and among many peoples in Senegambia it could be seen through the transformation of existing musical and masking styles, in Benin the way in which people changed their sense of identity can be viewed today through the famous bronzes. The huge expansion in bronze casting, the choosing of new subjects such as the Portuguese traders and their trade goods, and the historicization of each succeeding oba on the palace walls – all reflected a new awareness of Bini identity. This was grounded in militarized strength, with symbols of power through the representations of horses and weaponry, and the importance of relations with outsiders through the depiction of the Portuguese.[31]

Bronze casters also had an important military function. Bini casters soon drew on Portuguese designs of helmets and armour plating, and even attempted to reproduce cannons, as the oba's army grew. Thus, the bronzes had a role both in expressing new identities and in advancing Benin's power. The significance of bronze casting to Bini identity was emphasized through the fact that it was the casters (Igun Eronmwon) who were the highest-ranking craft guild within Edo, above the ironsmiths (Igun Ematon), ivory and wood carvers (Igbesanmwan), leather workers (Iskepori) and weavers (Owina n'Ido).[32]

As in Europe, underpinning all of this was an economic transformation. In Benin, as elsewhere, the sixteenth century saw an enormous growth in the currency base, and thereby in the market and in trade. The key currency initially was copper, and imports grew rapidly. An early account described how copper was used in the first trade between the Bini and the Portuguese. The Portuguese bought enslaved persons from the Bini, Duarte Pacheco Pereira wrote around 1506, with each war captive selling for 15 manillas of copper. This, of course, was not very much, and documents from 1517 show that already the number required for the purchase of captives had risen to 57. By 1522, manillas were also being used to buy basic provisions in Benin, such as yams, wood and water, all of which were needed to feed enslaved persons on ships for the return voyage to the new sugar plantations of São Tomé. Manillas would become a currency widely used throughout this part of West Africa long into the nineteenth century.[33]

The acquisition of these manillas was important, as they increased the circulation of an object of value that had predated European trade. Archaeological digs undertaken in Benin in the 1970s showed that copper and its alloys had been used in casting and for other artistic purposes from around the thirteenth century, that's to say, for 200 years before the arrival of the Portuguese. Thus, by importing large numbers of manillas, Benin obas were adding hugely to their stock of this precious symbolic metal. However, these digs also threw up a remarkable conundrum: while all the sources show that huge amounts of copper were imported to Benin during the sixteenth and seventeenth centuries, the archaeologists found just seven manillas, most of which were not of European design. The others, tellingly, predated European arrival.[34]

Manilla currency, Bende, Niger Delta region.

So what on earth were the imported manillas used for? Beyond the melting down of copper for recasting in military hardware, as shields and helmets, Dapper's compilation of existing accounts in the seventeenth century provides a significant clue. When describing the oba's palace, he noted that it had innumerable courts and apartments, 'containing within fair and long Galleries, one larger than the other, but all supported on Pillars of Wood, cover'd from the top to the bottom with melted copper, whereon are Ingraven their Warlike Deeds and Battels, and are kept with exceeding Curiosity'. In other words, quite a large part of the manillas would appear to have been melted down to construct the famous bronzes. Thus, what distinguished this use of currency from the use of gold in Europe and silver in China to accrue surplus value at this time was that Benin appears to have employed much of the new currency base to refashion self-images and identities.[35]

Alongside the use of copper manillas as something that was highly valued came the cowrie shell. By as early as 1520, cowries were being brought annually by the Portuguese, who stockpiled them in São

Tomé; the cowries were used mainly to purchase captives in Gwatón, who were then taken to Elmina to be sold. This was easy for the Portuguese, as they simply loaded up their India ships sailing to and from Goa with cowries from the Maldives, which they brought back as ballast around the Cape of Good Hope, ready to trade with West Africa. As with copper, the trade was marked by rapid inflation. From 1522 to 1527, the price of an enslaved captive at Benin, paid for in cowries, rose by 15 per cent, while the number of cowries used to buy a standard load of yams increased from 8,000 to 89,000. As the historian Robert Garfield has noted, whereas in the 1520s cowrie imports were still described according to how many shells were carried, by the 1530s they were assessed according to weight, with 27 *quintais** of cowries carried in one ship of 1529 and as many as 400 *quintais* in one of 1540.

Sources produced in Benin also reveal the significance of cowries. An oral account from the 1890s of the first Bini–European trade noted above also captured the reality of the rising stocks of cowries, even at this very early time; this account specifically describes slave trading conducted with the cowrie currency: the white man came and 'only bought slaves . . . only paid a poor price: one to four bags [of cowries]'.[36]

Throughout the sixteenth century, the cowrie shell grew as the everyday currency of Benin, and also in Yorùbá areas to the north. Ulsheimer described, around 1600, how 'as money they use little shells . . . one can buy any thing one wants with them, too'. According to Dapper, by the later seventeenth century, judges in legal disputes could be bribed with them. Archaeological finds from the seventeenth century reveal cowries stored in jars in Yorùbá areas, just as a jar of loose change might be found in households in many countries in the twenty-first century. The hugely expanding currency base that the imports of cowries through the Portuguese had created thus had many impacts: it allowed for the collection of tolls and taxes, the expanding of Benin's state infrastructure, and also, of course, the

* The Portuguese *quintal* at this time was equivalent to 128 *arráteis*, or pounds – the *arrátel* was equivalent to 16 ounces, or 1 pound. So 400 *quintais* was equivalent to more than 50,000 pounds in weight.

financing of the growing army. It also provided the money that allowed markets to thrive, as people spent all this loose change; by the seventeenth century, there were many markets on the road between Gwatón and Edo, where all kinds of iron tools and weapons, woodwork, foods and household goods were for sale.[37]

Benin's transformations in the sixteenth century are, in the end, best described as the rapid acceleration of a pre-existing process of economic and political change. Copper was already accepted as a form of value, and cowries already existed as a form of money; they were known as *igos*, according to Pacheco Pereira, and cowrie-shaped reliefs have been found dating from the twelfth to fifteenth centuries on pottery from Ilé-Ifè to the north, suggesting that the shells were known, if not in widespread use, before 1500. Perhaps the most enduring element of the transformation of the sixteenth century would not, therefore, be in the creation of new forms of exchange but in their expansion. What emerged from this in Benin was the creation of new identities and subjectivities, reflected in the rapid increase of bronze casting. Four hundred years later, Pablo Picasso found inspiration in the newly 'discovered' bronzes, alongside other African art and masks on display in European museums, and drew on them to produce his new vision of a landscape of fractured identities and violent change – something much akin to what Benin had experienced and found ways to express since the start of the sixteenth century.[38]

Alongside these aesthetic transformations of personhood came the broader economic changes catalysed by the rapid influx of currencies brought in by the Portuguese. The currency trade drove these new changes in the sixteenth century. It provided the copper to be melted down for the bronzes in the oba's palace, and the cowries that expanded exchangeability in markets in Benin and Yorùbá land. State infrastructure and the money supply grew, along with the oba's power as his growing army was strengthened. This confidence and strength enabled the obas to reject the slave trade in the 1530s, and their refusal to sell male captives saw the official Portuguese presence decline. However, clamping down on the trade in enslaved persons was not something that Benin could do in isolation. As on the Gold Coast, the advent of rival European powers competing for trade would change the ways in which rulers related to one another, and to the outside world. As neighbouring states began to participate in the slave trade by 1600, the attitude of the obas would change.

Thus, when Ulsheimer assisted the oba in 1604 in the campaign near Lagos, he noted that, after the prisoners of war had been press-ganged into the oba's army, they 'took the women and children as captives'. At first, this was merely for use within the kingdom, but, as the seventeenth century unwound, the whole region would come to participate in the trade in enslaved persons. Indeed, for the Europeans, it became the 'Slave Coast' – thus neatly ignoring the many political, cultural and aesthetic transformations also taking place there at this time.

ALLADA AND THE RISE OF SLAVE TRADING

Once Benin had expanded west to Lagos, it bordered on to the other major kingdom along this part of the West African coast, that of Allada. Like Benin, Allada already existed as a centre of power in the 1480s, marked on a Portuguese map of 1485 as between Lagos and the Volta River on the Gold Coast. In time, its extent ran from Lagos in the east to Great Popo in the west, in what is now the Republic of Benin.[39]

The peoples of the region around Allada were the Aja. By the sixteenth century, they had already been heavily influenced by the Yorùbá migrations that had led to the foundation of Ilé-Ifè and the network of city-states near there. Yorùbá was the lingua franca of Allada and the surrounding areas by the 1600s, and the Aja had adopted Yorùbá customs and some Yorùbá political organization: there were hereditary chiefs with specific duties, a kingdom with one principal town and subject towns and markets, and a monarch with tax-raising and judicial powers. Many religious shrines of the Aja had clear Yorùbá origins, such as the Fá divination (from Ifa) and the Sakpata shrine of Dahomey, in the eighteenth century, which still today uses an archaic form of Yorùbá as a liturgical language. It's probable that many of the Aja had originally lived in the region of what is now central and southern Nigeria, before being pushed westwards by the Yorùbá migrations.[40]

Visiting the Candomblé *terreiros* (meeting places) of the north-east of Brazil, or the shrines to the Lucumí *orixás* (spirit-deities) of the Afro-Cuban religion of Santería, the wide power and spread of this religious idiom makes more sense in the light of the early history of this region of West Africa. The spiritual centre of Ilé-Ifè had already developed a strong power, taken by waves of migrations beyond southern Nigeria into Benin and Togo. Religious shrines such as Sakpata and the Fá divination had been shared, and the power of this influence as an interpreting force of life had already bound together new communities. When in time peoples from this area came to the New World, this historical experience would offer a powerful example of how to remake a world, and a life, again.

The peoples who lived in the region of Allada and what was later Dahomey became known as Fon. Fon identities were fairly defined by the seventeenth century. Important traces of the language spoken in Allada exist in a catechism produced by Capuchin missionaries in 1660. When the King of Allada, Tojonu, sent a mission to Madrid in 1658 with a servant from his palace known in documents as 'Bans', the Allada ambassador returned in 1660 with some missionaries who developed a catechism for use in the Kingdom of Allada. The language used in this catechism is heavily related to Fon: the word for God (*Vodu*) and that for power (*popo*) are both clearly connected to Fon counterparts, which shows the emergence of a strong Fon identity in Allada by this time.[41]

Like Benin, Allada grew in power during the sixteenth and seventeenth centuries. With a good port at Offra, where all the Europeans lived while they traded, it offered major advantages for European traders. Once the obas had turned away from the trade in captives, the attention of slavers from the island of São Tomé shifted from Benin to Allada, with significant consequences for the whole region by 1600. But why was it that Allada saw the Portuguese slave traders as useful commercial allies? Like Grand Jolof's coastal province of Cayor in Senegambia, and (as we shall see) Kongo's coastal province of Nsoyo, Allada's rulers may have hoped that, through trade with the Portuguese, they would achieve greater independence in their relationship with the Yorùbá. The arrival of new routes for trade created an opportunity, at the expense of rising tensions with those who had been overlords.[42]

By the second half of the sixteenth century, the trade in enslaved persons was taking root. By the 1570s at the latest, a trans-Atlantic dimension had begun: an enslaved person from 'Arda' was recorded in Bogotá in 1579, and another in nearby Tunja in 1582. The push towards this influence grew all the time. The first contract permitting enslaved persons to be shipped direct from São Tomé to Brazil was signed in 1582. And so many factors pushed slave traders to open up new slaving markets such as that of Allada.[43]

Though in the sources produced in Latin America such enslaved persons are said to have come from 'Allada' or 'Arda', it is not certain that they were taken from this state itself. There is little evidence at this time of Allada fighting aggressive wars against its neighbours, such as might have produced captives. Thus, some may, indeed, have been criminals or perceived enemies of the rulers, who sold them into captivity; but others most likely came from smaller and more decentralized areas such as Great Popo, which had yet to rise to prominence as a centre for the trade in enslaved persons.[44]

By 1600 at the latest, Allada had grown out of this loose Aja federation and turned into a more centralized state. At the time of the visit from the Capuchin missionaries in 1660, Allada had already seen impressive growth. The missionaries said that the Court at the capital had 30,000 adult male residents (*vecinos*), which could indicate a total population of 100,000 people or more. Another visitor ten years later said that, while the kingdom did not have a large coastline, 'it penetrated deep into the hinterland, and spread out greatly there.' As in Benin, this political expansion went with a heavy militarization, with an army that was reputed to be able to reach 40,000 when the king demanded it. Political centralization had brought a standing army and urban growth to Allada. In this state, as in so many, West Africa exemplified the standard models of state formation in many parts of the world.[45]

There was, however, a very important difference between Benin's political growth in the sixteenth century and that of Allada. Benin's political infrastructure had grown before the Portuguese arrival, and the use of Edo titles had been maintained, while Portuguese influence was confined to a vocabulary of imported luxuries; but the same was not true of Allada. Officers who negotiated with European traders at

Offra were required to speak Portuguese, and even the son of the King of Allada conversed with visitors in Portuguese in the 1670s – something conceivable in Benin only during the first years of exchanges. Nobles in Allada bore the Portuguese name of *fidalgos*; while it may also have been through the influence of people from Allada that maize-flour bread known as *kenkey* grew as a staple dish as far away as the Gold Coast, with maize originally imported by the Portuguese through São Tomé. Thus, the opportunity offered by the Portuguese traders from São Tomé to create some independence from the Yorùbá came at a price: adaptation to external economic and political demands.[46]

All the same, while Portuguese (and in time other European) influences were significant, Aja worldviews remained paramount. The significance of Aja spiritual beliefs in a deity, or *vodún*, would be crucial in the development of African religious practice in the New World, among the *vodunun* shrines of Haiti and alongside the Candomblé *terreiros* of north-eastern Brazil. Cultural memories were not inscribed through writing: the French official Sieur Delbée wrote in 1671 that, in order to 'communicate certain things that they wish to make known, [the Aja of Allada] use little knotted ropes, in which each knot has a meaning, such as the time of a meeting or the place where one is to meet, or the price of a piece of merchandise'. As Delbée noted, this was like the much better-known *quipus*, or 'talking knots', of the Incas, since 'this usage is not only common along the coast of Africa, but is also practised by all the Indians [*sic*] of the mainland of the Americas.'[47]

But, although Allada retained key aspects of its indigenous Aja culture, its adoption of products from the Atlantic was important. It was, as one anonymous 1602 account noted, just 10 miles from the entry into the Lagos lagoon to the waterway that led to Allada. Cross-cultural influences spread from Portugal to Africa and then back out into the Atlantic world. Indeed, many of the traders Ulsheimer found at Lagos in 1604 probably came from Allada, since markets often spring up at border areas.[48]

These commercial influences meant not only the spread of new crops such as maize, but also a growing demand for enslaved persons coming from the slavers from São Tomé. For by around this time, Allada itself was becoming a major market for the trading of captives, as the 1602 account made clear:

> This River is much used to be entered into by the Portugals, and is well knowne, not because of any great commoditie that is there to be had; but because of the great number of slaves that are bought there, to carry to other places, as Saint Thomas, and to Brasilia, to labour there and refine Sugar: for they are very strong men, and can labour stoutly . . . There the Portugals Traffique much with Barkes [boats] to buy slaves . . . no other Nations come to buy slaves there, but the Portugals onely. And there are some Portugals dwelling there, which buy much wares and Merchandizes, such as there are to be had.[49]

Certainly, by the seventeenth century, there were large numbers of enslaved persons being taken from Allada to the Americas. This source mentions that the slaves were shipped to São Tomé and Brazil, and in Spanish America, too, the Allada influence grew. While a roster of forty-five ships arriving in Cartagena and the Mexican port of San Juan de Ulúa* in 1600 and 1601 did not include any from Allada, the three ships noted as originating from São Tomé probably traded there. Meanwhile, two Allada slaves were included in the inventory of goods belonging to the prisoner Jorge Fernandez Gramajo in Cartagena in 1611, and throughout this decade many enslaved persons from Allada were appearing in what was then the biggest slave-trading port of the Americas. By the 1620s, there was an active trade here, with Damião Ramires shipping two vessels for Cartagena from Allada annually between 1619 and 1625, trading heavily for slaves in return for cowries.[50]

Thus, the 'globalization' of Allada emerged alongside the rise of a trade in enslaved persons. By the 1640s, enslaved Africans named as 'Alladas' were regularly mentioned in Brazil. At Offra, meanwhile, Dutch and Portuguese ships were joined by English ships set for Barbados. Those persons called 'Allada' in the Americas did not represent any particular 'ethnic' designation; rather, the term simply indicated where they had been procured. According to Delbée, captives in Allada were prisoners of war, foreigners, those who had been judicially enslaved or those who had inherited the status of the enslaved by birth.[51]

* Near the modern city of Veracruz, on the Atlantic coast of central Mexico.

Ifa divination tray, early seventeenth century, Aja-Fon region.

All the same, while the growth of European economic demand for labour had important economic and political consequences along the coast, the traffic between Allada and the European empires of the Atlantic world was not one-way. Cotton cloths were also exported from Allada in the seventeenth century, both to Brazil and also south to Luanda in Angola. Some of these Aja products found their way out into the Atlantic communities, like the woven handicrafts of Fetu before them, and even today give tantalizing glimpses of the complex world-views and industries that had arisen here by the seventeenth century.[52]

What was it, then, that drove the political transformation of Allada? In the early sixteenth century, this had been a small decentralized federation nestled between the lagoons and the savannah, with sacred forests and a variety of shrines to *vodunun*. How did this small polity become a centralized slave-trading kingdom in the seventeenth century, able to send embassies to Spain and to export its cloths as far afield as Brazil and Angola? External demand for enslaved persons and the growth of a political infrastructure were, of course, important, but two other key factors must be considered.

First is the place of the cloth trade. While Allada's cloth was originally in demand, by the 1660s the local trade was becoming undermined by cloth imports. Writing in 1660, the Capuchin missionaries noted that when they reached Offra, they spent four days on board ship, 'waiting for the captain of the ship to land his cargo of cloth, which was what they [the people of Allada] anticipated most keenly, and was their principal concern'. As on the Gold Coast, the import of cloth began to pose a challenge to local production. It was true that Allada cloths were traded by the English to the Gold Coast into the 1670s and 1680s, but the volumes mentioned were very small, which suggests that they were increasingly challenged by the imports. Yet why were the kings of Allada so ready to import local cloth at the expense of their own production? This may relate to the markets at Lagos, where cloth was the main item traded among the market vendors; by moving to import from Europe, as well as from their neighbours and rivals in Benin at Lagos, Allada was further able to advance its interests ahead of its neighbour, keeping purchases from their potential rivals to a minimum. Rulers could also control the import of cloth through diplomatic exchanges and official tallies in a way that local production may have been harder to micromanage. Thus, to increase the value of imported cloth was also a means of increasing the ruler's own power. But, in doing so, they would begin to undermine local industry.[53]

A second crucial catalyst was a changing climate. When the Capuchin missionaries returned from Spain to Allada in 1660 with the Allada ambassador known as 'Bans', and proposed conversion to the king, they were met with a response that they had not been expecting:

> He took some time to answer and at length told the missionaries that he was very grateful for the favourable offer which his brother the King of Spain had made him, but that the embassy which he had sent with Bans, a gateman of his palace, was not so that he should change beliefs and adopt a different faith to that which he professed and which had been that of his ancestors; but rather so that they should send him some Christian priests who would be able to conjure away

> the thick clouds, which were causing great damage in that land, with innumerable bolts of lightning and thunderstorms falling with which many people and animals were dying, and crops and houses were being destroyed.[54]

This was during the period known more widely as the mini ice age, whose peak cold years began around 1640, at the time of the collapse of the Ming Dynasty in China, the English Civil War, and the war of independence between Portugal and Spain, which saw the restoration of the Portuguese monarchy. As we have seen, these were also years of rapid climatic change in Senegambia and in the Sahel. In Allada, too, this evidence shows that the changing temperature had led to variations in the rainy seasons, and uncertainties with regard to harvests and the security of people's homes. This was an important driver of accelerating conflicts, and contributed to the growth in the supply of enslaved persons into the Middle Passage by the end of the seventeenth century.

Climatic insecurity was indeed a vital feature of changes in West and West-Central Africa at this time. It was apparent everywhere, in the alternation of droughts and floods, in plagues of locusts and in the destruction of crops. Food insecurity grew in spite of the new crops of maize and manioc imported from Mexico and Brazil. In São Tomé, there was a famine around 1660 as a result of irregular rains. Climatic insecurity was also widespread in Kongo and Angola: a drought around 1640 caused a crisis in provisions from Kongo, and, from 1646 onwards, a series of locust swarms devastated the province of Nsundi. Epidemics spread, noted around the rivers of what is now Gabon, in Loango and in Angola; they reportedly decimated Kongo in 1655. Evidence of the impact of this instability is retained in oral traditions, as the archaeologist Akinwumi Ogundiran notes for the formation of Osògbò in the period around 1600: oral accounts say that at that time the 'rain refused to fall and yam refused to grow; and . . . rivers, brooks and streams dried up.' Thus, climatic change and associated disease were major causes of the instability that provoked conflict, warfare and an increase in captives.[55]

Yet were these changes natural or induced by human conflict? Most environmental historians have pointed to sun-spot movements rather than human activity as the key to the mini ice age. This consensus has been challenged in recent years by a team of archaeologists, who have noted how the collapse in temperatures coincides precisely with the decline in the Native American population of the sixteenth century, which is widely recognized as having fallen by 90 per cent, allowing for extensive reforestation. While this is generally agreed, the controversial ideas of this team suggest that the population fall led to a large decline in the burning of woods for fuel. With both reforestation and reduced CO_2 emissions, this surprisingly modern account of the distant past suggests that carbon capture was the result. Whether this or the sun-spot shift caused the climatic shifts we have seen remains debated; both may have been relevant, certainly with a huge impact on human experiences right around the world.[56]

By the 1650s, this had led the King of Allada to seek outside intervention from the Capuchin missionaries with the forces of nature. This was symptomatic not only of the growing climatic instability, but of the relationship with the outside world in Allada. As the number of competing European ships began to grow in the region, the nature of political rivalries, power and majesty also began to change. Benin's position on slave trading had become less and less tenable; at the same time, slave-trading states like Allada became ever more powerful, and yet also ever more dependent on their European allies, as this mission to Spain shows. An economic shift began to take hold that turned states such as Benin and Allada away from exporting their fine cloths and towards the slave trade.

THE RISE OF OYO AND THE DECLINE OF BENIN IN THE SEVENTEENTH CENTURY

By the early seventeenth century, Benin's capital at Edo was a town that impressed visitors, such as the Dutch traveller Dierick Ruyters, who described it in 1623:

> At first the town seems very large; when one enters it one comes into a great broad street, which seems to be seven or eight times broader than

> the Warme Street in Amsterdam; this extends straight out, and when one has walked a quarter of an hour along it he still does not see the end of the street, but he sees a big tall tree as far from him as the eyes can reach, and some Netherlanders say that the street stretches still so much further, that if one had been as far as that tree he would still see no end to the street . . . Houses in which well-to-do people such as gentlemen dwell, have two or three steps to go up, and in front have an ante-court where one may sit dry, which court or gallery is closed every morning by their slaves, with straw mats for sitting on . . . the houses are all alike red, and were surrounded by walls . . . they make the walls about two feet thick, so that these are not easily upset [by a heavy rain].[57]

The nobility of Benin wore fine clothes, as befitted their status. Towards the end of the seventeenth century, the rich men wore 'a white Calico or Cotton Cloth about one Yard long and half so broad . . . over that they wear a finer white cotton dress, that is commonly about fifteen or twenty Yards long, which they ornamentally pleat in the middle, casting over it a Scarf of about a Yard long and two Spans broad, the End of which is adorn'd with Fringe or lace'. Women wore cloths woven in Benin, which were 'very fine and beautifully Chequered with several Colours'.[58]

Yet Benin was in decline in the seventeenth century. By the 1690s, though there were daily markets in Edo selling ivory, cloth and European trade goods, there were also the 'ruins of half-remaining Houses . . . at present the Houses stand like poor men's corn, widely distant from each other'; whereas in the 1620s Ruyters had said that 'the houses in this town stand in good order, one close to the other, like houses in Holland.' By the end of the seventeenth century, Benin's population was said to be low compared to Allada, while Gwatón, though 'formerly a considerable trading place . . . hath suffer'd so much by the Wars, that it lies in a manner waste at present'.[59]

Why was it that Benin's power had declined? The answer lay in a combination of internal political competition and the impact of European trade. Benin in the seventeenth century was eclipsed by the rise of the great Yorùbá Kingdom of Oyo, with its capital at Oyo-Ile. Though Oyo had risen as early as the fourteenth century, and, like Benin, had a strong spiritual dependence on Ilé-Ifè, during the sixteenth century it had been immerṣed in the Ókìpò Wars with Nupe to the north. Nupe invaders crossed the Niger River in the early sixteenth century and sacked the Oyo capital at Oyo-Ile, founding many towns in the northern part of what would become the Kingdom of Oyo. However, by 1600, Oyo had checked the Nupe advance and begun to become the regional powerhouse.[60]

Oyo's growing power in the seventeenth century can be deduced especially from archaeological evidence, as Aribidesi Usman has shown. Excavating the area of Igbominaland, on the northern fringe of Oyo, Usman found that the Oyo centre there was probably founded around 1600. During the seventeenth century, defensive walls were constructed around towns and villages, many of them very high and built with deep ditches; by the end of the century, some stone embankments were used, all suggestive of a centralized state and the ongoing threat from Nupe to the north. Settlements grew bigger throughout this time, and there is increased evidence of ironworking, through furnaces, slagheaps and quarries. There was growing industry, and the migration of specialized craftspeople to work in these areas, all of which followed Oyo's defeat of Nupe and its emergence as the most powerful state in this region.[61]

Written sources produced by outsiders from the later seventeenth century confirm this picture. One described the use of cavalry by Oyo in 1698 in a conflict with Allada, and Oyo's military power was, indeed, grounded in the use of cavalry. The importance of Oyo's cavalry is beautifully expressed in the following Yorùbá proverb:

One cannot beat a warrior who is a swimmer in the river,	*A ki. i ba onwe jagun odo*
Who shall beat a warrior who is a horseman in the plain?	*Tana i ba ẹlẹ sin jagun papa?*[62]

The Alafin (King) of Oyo who reconquered Oyo-Ile from Nupe in the early seventeenth century was Abipa. In his authoritative written history, constructed drawing exclusively on oral accounts, the Yorùbá historian Samuel Johnson wrote that it was Abipa who moved the capital of Oyo from Gboho to Oyo-Ile, and introduced new taxes. During the time of Benin's decline in the seventeenth century, Oyo was developing a complex administration: provincial rulers had a coronet of office, the *akoro*, and were invested with their titles by the alafin at Oyo-Ile. At the capital, a royal guard of Esos with seventy military captains protected the alafin and his council, the Oyo-Mesi, which was headed by the basorun. The political stability went with social stability for those who lived there; archaeological finds indicate a great deal of care taken with food, which suggests stability and meals as a focus for social life, as Oyo grew.[63]

The rising strength of Oyo as a savannah state certainly would have acted as a pressure on Benin, contributing to its relative political and economic decline. Willem Bosman's mention of the wars that laid waste to Gwatón by the 1690s implies that there may well have been a fierce military battle for political supremacy between the two. However, beyond this strong internal factor in Benin's political decline, the economic impact of the European trading presence along the coast from Allada to Calabar must be considered.

As we have seen in this chapter, the early relationship between Benin and the Portuguese had soon foundered on disputes over the trade in enslaved persons. The Portuguese wanted to be able to export male slaves to Elmina for use in the gold trade, but Benin refused to export male slaves. This had prompted withdrawal, though towards 1700 a series of obas emerged who sought to strengthen the kingdom: rulers such as Akengboi (1669–75), Ahenkpaye (1675–84), Akengbedu (1684–89) and Oreoghene (1689–1700) found a place in Benin history. Indeed, under them, the refusal to export male slaves remained Benin's royal policy right until the end of the seventeenth century, according to Bosman, who wrote that, 'all Male Slaves here are Foreigners; for the Natives cannot be sold for Slaves . . . nor is it allow'd to export any Male Slaves that are sold in this Country, for they must stay there.'[64]

Benin's refusal to sell male slaves and thereby participate in the Atlantic slave trade nevertheless placed it at a disadvantage with its neighbouring states. By the 1640s if not earlier, a slave trade had resumed from the ports closest to Gwatón in the neighbouring Bight. Dutch accounts from their factory at Elmina show that by this time the English were sending ships into the Bight of Benin to purchase captives. Further south and east, among the Kalabari Igbo of the Niger Delta, a trade in captives was also growing: English ships went there frequently and returned laden with as many as 400 enslaved persons at a time. By the 1650s, missionaries noted that neighbouring towns that were traditionally subject to Benin had set up independent settlements for European traders from which to sell captives. But, while surrounding states grew their stocks of currencies, weapons and manufactured goods, throughout this period Benin persisted in its policy of exporting only its very fine woven cloths (known as *ambasys*) into the Atlantic trade.[65]

The production of *ambasys* and their sale at Lagos was already apparent in Ulsheimer's account of 1604. A French report from 1671 said of Benin that 'the only trade there is in small cloths of Benin, for local consumption . . . a yacht is sent two or three times a year, to go and get these cloths, then taking them to trade along the [coast of the Gulf] as far as the Equator.' However, this export trade in cloths was becoming less and less economically viable, as the gathering profits from the trade in captives grew everywhere else. One serious problem was that, as we have seen in Chapter 3, the Dutch trade in this period was overwhelmingly in imported cloths from Flanders and Gujarat: the sturdy Flanders cloths and the satin, silk and damask alongside the finely woven cloths known as *kannekins* from India provided exotic and cheap competition to the locally made cloth of Benin; indeed, even the oba preferred to have his throne as an 'Ivory Couch, under a Canopy of Indian Silk' by 1700. The demand for foreign fashions and styles was such that, by this time, Bini weavers had to use imported cotton and dyes brought by European traders to make cloth. But how could they compete against Dutch ships, which, by as early as 1645, might transport 300,000 ells of cloth annually to Elmina alone? The competition thus undermined the profitability of cloth production and therefore Benin's power against the rising strength of Oyo in the hinterland.[66]

The key decade for this transformation was the 1680s. Until this time the *ambasys* had still been traded to Elmina and the surrounding area, but in 1684 the Dutch director-general at Elmina wrote that 'the trade in [Benin] cloths is nowadays of little importance, as they are not much in demand . . . also there is still a considerable stock of them here, and that several thousands are still expected from Benyn.' By January 1685 the Dutch West India Company was considering withdrawing its factor from Benin altogether, 'in view of the fact that the Company has in stock over 12,000 [Benin] cloths, and that the boat

De Liefde has added to this number another 5,000 on its arrival [last month], leaving 4,000 more in the Rio de Benyn'. In truth, it was no surprise that the Dutch took this decision, for where the cloths were supposed to be sold at 40 per *benda* of gold, 'there [were] no buyers.' Though there were still Benin cloths traded by the English to the Gold Coast in 1687, it was clear that this was a trade under threat.[67]

What had caused this sudden collapse in the stock of Benin cloth on the Gold Coast? Again, it does not take much to work out that this was largely due to the huge imports of cloth with which the Dutch had flooded the market since the 1640s. By the 1680s, the English had joined in, and the country was 'extraordinarily full of merchandise'. The availability of luxury Indian cloths, and the rich variety of European cloths imported, meant that the human taste for variety and novelty made it very hard for Benin to compete. As we have seen, weavers tried to innovate through using imported cotton and dyes, but already by this time Benin was in decline, faced with the rising success of those kingdoms such as Oyo and Allada that grew in power as their dependence on warfare and the trade in enslaved persons correspondingly increased.[68]

CONCLUSION: MONEY, POWER AND POLITICAL CHANGE TO THE LATE SEVENTEENTH CENTURY

Benin is rightly one of the most famous precolonial West African states. Its bronzes are testament to sophisticated craftsmanship, evolving identities, and a powerful aesthetic of majesty that evolved in the sixteenth and seventeenth centuries. The obas of Benin were wary of trade with Europeans. They were only rarely seen by them. According to one account of the 1650s, they refused to see European visitors face to face because of an augury saying that one of the obas would die at the hands of the Europeans – as indeed would happen when the kingdom was finally conquered by the British in 1897.[69]

Partly through careful management of its relationship with European traders, Benin grew its institutions as well as the interdependence of Edo and its surrounding settlements. A large tax base developed, in the principal Benin currency of cowries, which had existed before the

Portuguese arrival. The armchair geographer Olfert Dapper wrote in the 1660s that one third of all goods traded to Arda, Benin and Lagos had to take the form of cowries. By 1700, Bosman noted the efficiency with which this system of tax and government worked, which was testament to its longevity, having endured since the fifteenth century: '[Benin's] Territories are very large and full of Governors, and each knows how many Bags of Boesies [cowries] (the Money of this Country) he must annually raise to the King, which amounts to a vast Sum.'[70]

The existence of ready coin in the form of the cowries imported by the Portuguese had greatly grown the markets of Benin. Government institutions grew along with the ability to tax. It was an analogous process to the way in which a powerful bureaucratic state had arisen in Spain in the sixteenth century, bolstered by the massive expansion of coinage facilitated by the mines of the New World. For a long period this was all to Benin's advantage as the state grew. But, in the later seventeenth century, the cumulative effect of various pressures had significant effects on the cowrie currency in the kingdom, and serious inflation set in. As the 'sugar revolution' took off in the Dutch and English Caribbean, captive labour was in very high demand, and between 1685 and 1703 the price of captive persons rose by as much as 200 per cent across Atlantic Africa, from Hueda and Offra to Angola. As the number of enslaved persons exported increased, so, too, did the amount charged per person: at Offra one captive cost 35 guilders in 1685, but 100 guilders and more by 1703.[71]

As Dapper had rightly noted, the use of cowries as a currency had spread along the coast to Hueda, which by this time was supplanting Allada as the major slave-trading state to the west of Lagos. Just as the Portuguese had imported their cowries from the Maldives as part of their East India trade, so, too, did the Dutch once they had supplanted the Portuguese in the Indian Ocean.[72]

One account of 1705 gave a vivid picture of the volumes of cowries required by the Dutch now to trade there: 'Before one is allowed to start trade, one is compelled to pay the King 720 lbs cowries customary duties, 200 lbs to the Captain, and 30 to the town-crier . . . furthermore one has to pay 120 lbs cowries for the [slave camp] with which they guarantee that the slaves will not run away . . . [and] 400 lbs cowries [also] for the carrying of the goods to the ship.'[73] The dependence on external trade for the money supply was thus a key factor in the transition of political power from east to west. When Benin was the major regional power, it accrued large supplies of cowries, and was able to build governmental and fiscal institutions. But once the interest of European traders passed from the cloth to the slave trade, the supplies of cowries dried up, as the Dutch lost interest in the Benin cloth trade. Indeed, it is notable that Benin oral histories suggest that the kingdom at length began to participate in the slave trade by the 1730s: the realities of accessing the money supply to keep institutions viable could not, by this time, be avoided.[74]

Hueda's power, therefore, grew at this time, along with its stocks of money and the access it offered to European traders. It was then beautifully verdant country, with the villages said to be as populous as whole kingdoms on the Gold Coast. European travel narratives written for an increasingly racist public at home focused on trade, slavery and war, but that is surely not what was at the centre of everyone's concerns all the time. People were interested in what they would wear, new fashions coming in by sea and the attempts of local weavers to innovate to compete. They wondered whether their neighbours had a good catch of fish; what the unstable rainfall patterns were doing to the cycle of harvests; and what were the demands and auguries of the keepers of the major shrines. However, since none of this was of interest to the slave traders whose journals have shaped much historical discourse, these are not aspects of the region's history that are often discussed. Yet it is also true enough that alongside these social changes which came with the Atlantic trade, European ships flocked and the trade in captives boomed. By 1693 the palace of Hueda was built partly of stone, and the king's throne was draped with red silk cloths, while behind it was a scene of elephant hunting such as would not have been out of place in a European imperial drawing room.[75]

Hueda's rise ahead of Allada, and Benin's decline alongside Oyo's rise, spoke to wider truths about economic and political change. Though cowries had been a global currency, in use in parts of China and in Arabia and the Indian Ocean, its perceived value was declining to European traders, who equated these shells with ballast and the trade in African captives. The relationship that cowries had to the gold exports from the Gold Coast (exchanged for captives and cloths, which were resold at Elmina for gold) tied the cowrie currency to the relative decline in value of monies in use in Africa, just as 'hard' currencies that held value over time developed in Europe and Asia. The increasing volume of cowries imported as part of the exchange, in fact, merely exacerbated the tendency. Meanwhile, the dumping of cheap cloth from Asia and Europe was part of the process that saw the growth of manufacturing industries in those continents at the expense of manufacturers in Allada, Benin and elsewhere in Atlantic Africa, who could not compete.[76]

Cowries were part of a global currency, of course, while the other currencies imported helped to shape new and strong identities. Both sides in these exchanges knew that they were engaged in a form of exchange of value. When the English slave ship *The Arthur* arrived at Calabar in February 1677, the first thing its crew did was to negotiate a price with the King of New Calabar, who came aboard with some of his nobles, 'and after a long discourse came to Agreemtt for Current for negro [*sic*] man 36 copper Barrs for one negro woman 30'. Copper and iron bars and manillas remained the currencies of choice here: copper was used to add to existing stocks, which might then be used to fashion art, or in war, while iron could add to the growing industries at work across the region, including the manufacture of weapons and agricultural tools.[77]

In economic terms, West African states lost out in the accrual of surplus value. Yet they also acquired currencies that would help to deepen identities and cultural force, later so important in shaping modern cultures in West Africa, the Americas and Europe. The members of the Igun Eronmwon guild of Bini bronze casters were part of the process of exchanging cultural for economic capital, working their art from the copper manillas that were exchanged by those such as the crew of the *Morning Star* in 1677 for captive persons. As manufactured items and material accumulation characterized the shrines of the powerful, so the religious traditions of this and surrounding kingdoms shaped ideas in the Americas. Thus, those Bahians worshipping today in the Casa de Iemanjá in Rio Vermelho are the direct inheritors of the renewed idioms of belief and identity acquired in the 'Costa da Mina', at the same time as the region's economic heft began to be undermined.

5
The Kingdom of Kongo: From Majesty to Revolt

Spending any length of time in Angola and Mozambique today involves more than a passing acquaintance with cassava. This long tuber covered with a flaky brown skin is a core staple, one of the items that will be found at all markets, boiled up or mashed in eateries and mixed with whatever protein is available. A visit to Brazil involves the same culinary experience, as it is hard to escape cassava. At its best the cassava leaf will be boiled and flavoured with spices and oils into a tasty dish often mixed with peanuts or fish, found in north-eastern Brazil, as well as in Yorùbá areas of what are now Nigeria and Benin, and in Guinea-Conakry. But cassava can more easily be found in Brazil in most workaday restaurants, ground up into powder and stored in shakers that can be sprinkled like parmesan on to a dish. This shared food grew up alongside other movements in this first phase of globalization; with its stodgy pulp and bland flavour, cassava root was the taste accompanying the peoples in West-Central Africa alongside the growing violence of the Atlantic trade.

Cassava was originally a Brazilian crop, used by the Tupinambá both as a staple and as something to take with them on their military campaigns against their enemies. Ground into a powder and stored as flour, easily portable and nutritious enough to ward off hunger, cassava was something that the Portuguese rapidly borrowed as a means of feeding troops in the sixteenth century. As with most world changes at that time, the Portuguese did not innovate; rather, they copied and intensified existing practices. Cassava was first cultivated by their planters and indigenous American slaves in north-eastern Brazil, and despatched in the slaving ships that began to trade in Angola in the later sixteenth century. Their armies fed themselves with this imported cassava flour in the slaving wars waged by Portuguese troops and their African Imbangala allies in the first half of the seventeenth century. Soon enough the Jesuits of Luanda were overseeing slaves who planted cassava in their plantations on the Bengo River north of Luanda. Over time, cassava grew to become an African staple, often produced by unfree labour.[1]

Cassava stands in many ways as a symbol of the ways in which the kingdoms of West-Central Africa changed in the sixteenth and seventeenth centuries. Imported techniques, flavours and people from the Americas interacted with BaKongo and Umbundu peoples, who brought their own skills in healing, weaving and manufacturing. The cassava imported to Angola was used by the armies fighting to undermine the power of the Kingdom of Kongo, the unquestioned political power here at the time. Although it became ubiquitous, this was not a food that somehow sustained a continent that could not feed itself – as some older ideas would have had it – but one that helped to undermine a system.

At the same time, cultural mixes flowed not only in West-Central Africa, but across the South Atlantic Basin. The way in which this may have happened was described by the Capuchin missionary Antonio Cavazzi, writing of his experiences of the 1650s and 1660s. Cavazzi claimed that the practice of excising two teeth from the upper gum, common among the Imbangala, was introduced via those who had served with the Inca Army in Peru, led by Tupuco-incay-Timpanqui. Many of those there, according to Cavazzi, also took to excising teeth, and then, 'with the practice of traders taking slaves to the Spanish mines in America, many of the very same Blacks, after a certain time, returned to Africa, and transported the custom to their own countrymen'.[2]

It's impossible to be sure if this is accurate, but it speaks to wider exchanges of peoples and ideas that took hold of the South Atlantic in the sixteenth and seventeenth centuries. Even if this rite did not flow from Peru to West-Central Africa, other ideas, skills and tastes moved in each direction. West-Central African rulers sought to globalize their kingdoms, as we have seen already with the discussion of the Kongolese ambassadors in Brazil in the 1640s. This was an era

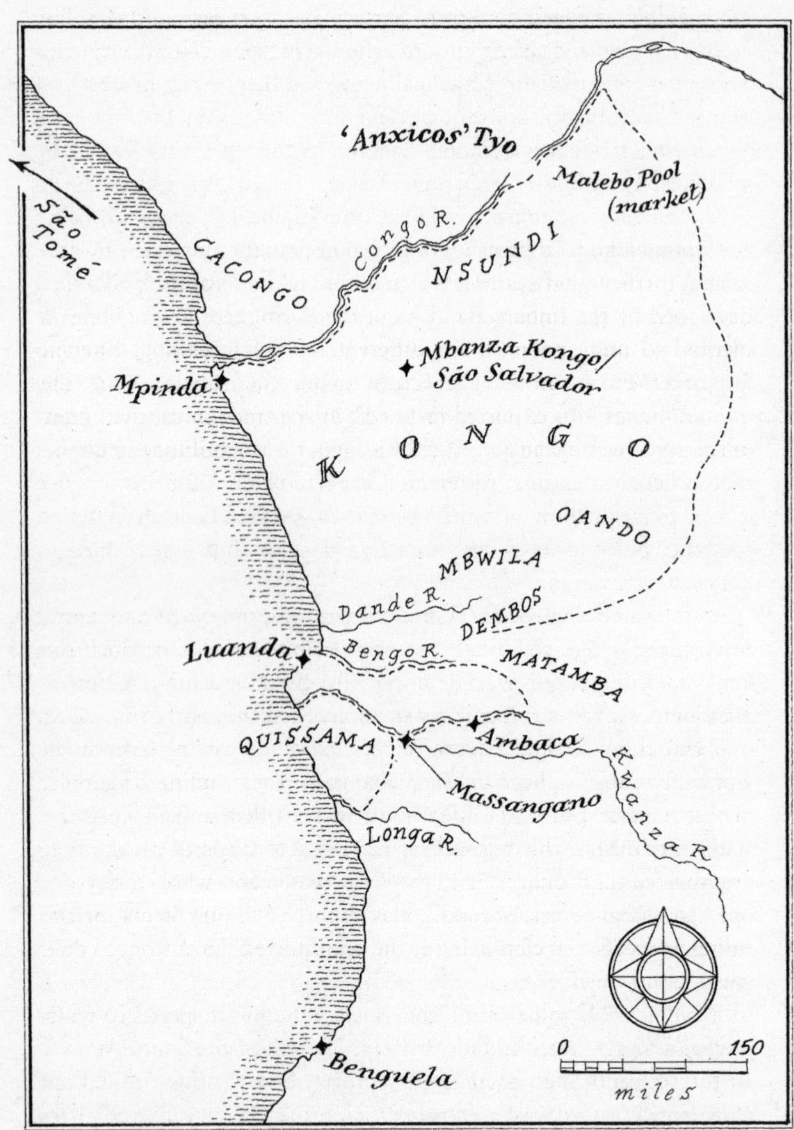

West-Central Africa, *c.* 1400–1700

when Kongo ambassadors were frequent visitors, negotiating in an attempt to shore up their power against the encroachments of the Portuguese and their Imbangala allies. Royal letters were despatched along with them to the Vatican, Lisbon and Amsterdam alongside Brazil, and it was as yet impossible to imagine the sorry state into which Kongo would fall by 1700.[3]

Beyond these attempts to seek political influence, there was also the strong cultural dimension to global exchanges illustrated by cassava. A further good example is an institution known as the *quilombo*, developed by the Imbangala allies of the Portuguese in Angola as a method to unite people from different lineages speaking different languages. From a military structure used in the Angolan Wars, the *quilombo* was also exported to Brazil, as the trade in captives grew in the seventeenth century. As the *quilombo* was a military structure that brought strangers together, it became vital in integrating the Africans from different backgrounds who reached the Americas, as they formed new communities in enslavement, and fought against this institution in maroon communities.*

All of these changes occurred as the majesty of Kongo grew, resplendent in the portraits we have seen. Yet, as this chapter also explores, Kongo's power had come at two great prices. The globalization of foods, ideas and military structures here was part of a process of eventual political decline. In the first place, a growing resentment was felt by subjects, both in Kongo and in the surrounding kingdoms, of the violence and trade in enslaved persons that underpinned the state's expansion; this resentment prompted a series of revolts that destabilized the monarchy and made the region as a whole ever more open to global forces. Secondly, the import of luxury items for the ruling *mwissikongo* clan living at the capital of Mbanza Kongo came at the price of wider economic imbalances. As copper and enslaved persons and the 'value' of their surplus labour were exported from Kongo and Angola, Atlantic traders flooded West-Central Africa with the main Kongo currency of *nzimbu* shells. Imports rose, currencies proliferated, and the value of the *nzimbu* went into freefall in the seventeenth century. The combination of this and a revolt 'from

* See below, Coda to Part One, for a more detailed discussion of the *quilombo*.

below' contributed decisively to the implosion of the kingdom by the end of the seventeenth century.

Kongo was, thus, a kingdom in a vice between internal and external forces. To understand the eventual erosion of Kongo's power, it is important to grasp the origins of the complex global networks that it had developed by the seventeenth century. Kongo had had these connections since the early sixteenth century, where already young *mwissikongo* were despatched as ambassadors to Lisbon and for religious training in Portuguese monasteries. By the seventeenth century, though, Kongo's relations with Portugal had soured, owing to the constant incursions of slave raiders from Luanda, founded in 1575 in what would become Angola. As the Governor of Luanda described it in 1631, Kongo's copper mines were very difficult to secure 'owing to the mistrust with which they [the Kongo peoples] view the Portuguese'. By 1652, the situation would be even worse, as all the peoples of Kongo and Angola came to 'despise the Portuguese with mortal hatred'.[4]

Where did this mutual distrust spring from? How had Kongo's own complex worldview and ideologies clashed with those from outside to create such enmity? What were the changes that large-scale global trade had brought to Kongo, and how had they been experienced locally? To answer these questions, we must reconstruct, as closely as possible, early Kongo and its worldview, and look at the ways in which its rulers dealt with the Atlantic powers. This chapter, therefore, looks in detail at early Kongo culture, early interactions with the Atlantic, and the misunderstandings and greed that led to the wars of the 1640s.

As we shall see, the stakes were too high for human ambition not to sow hatreds: where there is great wealth to be had, there will so often be sorrow. There was a huge amount to fight for in this region of West-Central Africa: mineral wealth in the form of copper mines to the north of the Congo River, and rumours of silver and gold mines besides; and a centralized power in Kongo that ambitious European powers thought offered similar prospects of a colonial takeover as had the great Native American empires of the Aztecs and Incas. But, of course, in all of this immensity of historical change, there was far more at stake for Kongo itself.

KONGO: DIPLOMACY AND GEOPOLITICS IN THE DEFENCE OF MAJESTY

On 3 September 1645, Garcia II Ncana a Luquini nzenze atumba, the manikongo, granted an audience to the Capuchin missionary Joseph Pellicer de Tovar. The wars fought by the Kongo Kingdom and their Dutch allies against the Portuguese were entering a decisive phase, which would lead in the end to the collapse of the Dutch presence and their withdrawal from Luanda in 1648.* This defeat and the harsh peace treaty forced on Kongo by the Portuguese afterwards would pave the way for Kongo's defeat by Luso-Brazilian troops at the Battle of Mbwila in 1665, and the unravelling of the kingdom into decades of civil war.[5]

However, twenty years earlier, little of this could be glimpsed in

Dutch ambassadors at the Court of Garcia II, King of Kongo.

* See above, Introduction, for an elucidation of these wars.

Tovar's description of Garcia II's majesty at his Court in Mbanza Kongo, the capital of the kingdom:

> The King was in his Chapel, having heard Mass, dressed in all his Finery, with golden Brocade sewn with Pearls, and other extremely expensive jewels. On his head was a Hat, in which the Royal Crown was formed, all embossed with the thickest Pearls, and Jewels of extraordinary value. His Throne was a Seat, made in the style of the [Kongo] Country, of crimson velvet; and at its feet a very wide Cloth with some Cushions made of the same crimson, with golden Fringes and Tassels.[6]

Garcia's pomp had many sources. The *mpu* crown woven into a conical shape in the illustration above was a Kongo symbol of power, and the red colour used was a symbol of royal power that was also expressed in the red sashes with which Kongo nobles fastened their clothes, and that was found richly on their royal coat of arms as early as the first half of the sixteenth century.

Coat of arms of the Kingdom of Kongo, issued to King Afonso I.

Tovar also described imported cloths, which blended with the Kongo textiles and clothing. This brocade and crimson drew from 160 years of long-distance trade linking Kongo to Portugal, Brazil and the Netherlands. In this chapter the local context of the growth of such majesty is made clear, as this wealth arose out of what was already a strong kingdom in the fifteenth century, and the complex state infrastructure that this kingdom then developed to manage its expanding trade. Yet, at the same time as global trade brought opportunities, it also brought enormous pressures that it was beyond any ruler or kingdom entirely to withstand.

When Pellicer de Tovar wrote this description of the manikongo, the kingdom was fighting for its life in the face of these pressures. Nonetheless, this unravelling was yet to be imagined. Cloths, jewels and flamboyant manufactured goods had by then long become hallmarks of royal majesty in Kongo. This was, indeed, one of the reasons why there was often a vicious fight to inherit the crown on the death of each incumbent manikongo. As the Spanish missionary Antonio de Teruel described it, the Kongo crown was elective, not hereditary, and, as Kongo inheritance was passed through maternal uncles, not to the firstborn down the male line, there were many who could stake a claim to the throne. Such disputes, as Teruel noted, had characterized Garcia II's own accession: '[He inherited the crown] with violence and against the will of his vassals . . . he knew that they had no love for him, and so he was wary of them, never eating with his nobles as was the tradition of the [Kongo] kings . . . he feared everyone, and if he suspected anyone of treachery he would find an excuse to send them to another Province, and order them to be executed when they least suspected it.'[7]

Like his predecessors, Garcia II had attempted to navigate the minefield of seventeenth-century world politics by moving into the camp of the Dutch. It's useful to begin an understanding of Kongo in this period by looking at this diplomacy, for it presents the kingdom in a distinctive light, and shows how far it had changed since its origins in the early fifteenth century. The reality was that, like the rulers of many a major power before and since, the manikongos were well able to swap camps when a more promising partner appeared on the scene. Garcia had comprehensively ditched the Portuguese, allying with the Dutch in the 1641–8 wars that attempted to expel the Portuguese from Angola. But this was a move that had begun twenty years earlier, and had been building ever since.

The Dutch were attractive because they brought better-quality and lower-priced goods, and they were not yet involved in the trade in enslaved persons (and would not be until they conquered some of Brazil in 1630). Kongo's coastal province of Nsoyo began to send out diplomatic feelers to the Dutch as early as 1606, and, by 1612, Nsoyo's troops defended the Dutch when they were attacked by Portuguese forces from Luanda. A series of violent slave-trading governors in Luanda during the 1610s then made Kongo ever more opposed to the Portuguese. A Kongo force defeated the Portuguese in a battle near Mbanda Kasi in 1622, leading the manikongo, Pedro II Mkanga Mbemba, to propose an alliance with the Dutch to drive the Portuguese from the region entirely.[8]

This was when it seemed like victory and a different sort of relationship between a West-Central African and a European state might be possible. The Dutch did not yet even trade in captives in the 1620s, as they had no plantations in the Americas. For them, the 'imperative' of the trade in enslaved persons for the colonization of America was not yet apparent, while Kongo kings hoped that the Dutch would retain their broader interests in trading cloth, copper and ivory. With things looking good after the 1622 defeat of the Portuguese, Kongo tried to press its military advantage. In 1624, the maninsoyo (Governor of Nsoyo Province) wrote to the United Provinces seeking military support, and the Dutch West India Company asked the fleet led by Piet Heyn, which had just seized Brazil's colonial capital of Salvador from the Portuguese, to sail to assist in the defeat of the Portuguese in Angola as well. Heyn set sail with three large ships, two boats and two sloops, and arrived in Luanda on 30 October 1624. But there he found the Portuguese newly bolstered with twenty-four ships and 1,800 troops in the city. When he sailed north to Nsoyo, the maninsoyo informed him that they had renewed the alliance with the Portuguese and no longer wished to fight; and he palmed Heyn off by claiming that the letters he had written to the Dutch West India Company asking for assistance were written on behalf of his lord the manikongo, for whom he was just a lowly assistant.[9]

Heyn was understandably frustrated by Kongo's volte-face. But why had Kongo had this sudden change of heart? As we have seen was generally the case, this was due to African political dynamics far more than to any European influence. The manikongo that had suggested the alliance, Mkanga Mbemba (Pedro II), had died in 1624, and his death had been followed by infighting. Perhaps as a result of these events, Mkanga Mbemba's successor, Mbemba Nkanga (Garcia I), was more open to the Portuguese. At the same time, the new Governor of Luanda had been more conciliatory towards Kongo, reining in the excesses of the Portuguese slavers and their Imbangala allies; and this, combined with the political changes in Kongo, brought peace between the two sides for a while.[10]

Yet these events were creating an unstoppable momentum that would lead to the wars and diplomatic jockeying of the 1640s. Already in 1625, the Portuguese governor of Luanda said that Kongo could no longer be considered an ally. Kongo manoeuvred continually in these years. Tensions with the Portuguese mushroomed through the 1630s, as the trade in captives for the Americas grew again, and the power of the Dutch continued to expand as they took the north-eastern states of Brazil around Pernambuco in 1630. By 1638, the maninsoyo had told the Dutch that his troops would support them overland if they attacked the Portuguese in Luanda by sea, and he invited them to build a fort at their port of Mpinda. Everything was ready for Kongo to ally with the Dutch when they seized Luanda in 1641, for, as the Portuguese wrote in Luanda in 1660, nineteen years later, 'the main cause of the Dutch taking this fortress was having been asked three times to do so by ambassadors of [the manikongo].'[11]

The importance of Kongo as a major diplomatic player in the early history of modern empires is rarely stressed. The role of Kongo ambassadors, Kongo's trade and the economic transformations that followed it are rarely emphasized. Yet this was all well enough known at the time, and the 'struggle for Brazil and Angola' was a defining moment in world history. Portugal's defeat of the Dutch in Angola (1648) and Brazil (1654) allowed for the rise of English power and, over time, helped England to become the dominant European imperial power. Portugal's victory in Brazil depended on English finance in the development of the Brazilian fleet. Even after these victories, Portugal's independence war with Spain would not be concluded until 1668, and so it required an alliance with a strengthening England, confirmed by Charles II's marriage to Catherine of Braganza in 1662. In all of these European ups and downs, Kongo was a diplomatic player in global affairs, and the major kingdom in a world region of great importance to the supply of captive labour to the plantations and mines of the New World. As the Portuguese often put it in these years, 'without Angola there is no Brazil.'[12]

Why did Kongo come to hold this key role in global affairs, securing its majesty on the world stage through its diplomacy and manoeuvring? Central to this was the place of the literate class, which, as in most parts of the world in the seventeenth century, was an extension of the aristocracy. In Kongo, as across the world, this class was very adept at seeking its own advantage. The missionary Antonio de Teruel described how the manikongo, Garcia II, had many enemies at Court and in Nsoyo, and they wrote often to the maninsoyo to try to sow discord. Garcia II and Nzinga, the famous Queen of Ndongo and Matamba in these years, wrote frequent letters to one another to discuss their wars against the Portuguese. This elite literacy was used by the state to seek its own diplomatic benefit, to arrange the despatch of ambassadors and to negotiate attacks; but it was also employed beyond the Court of the manikongo, in the key provinces of Mbamba and Nsoyo by governors seeking their own advantage. During the wars of the 1640s, the manikongo sent two ambassadors to the United Provinces in 1643; early in 1642, Nsoyo itself sent ambassadors to the Dutch government in Brazil at Recife, asking them not to provide military support to Kongo; and, by the middle of that year, nobles from Kongo itself were sent to Brazil with letters from their king, and from the Duke of Mbamba, seeking further alliances.[13]

Beyond the portraits we have of some of these embassies, the traveller Nieuhoff's account from Brazil makes it clear that these embassies made a considerable impression. This widespread literacy among the ruling *mwissikongo* was important to the perception of Kongo and its role in world affairs. The ambassadors of Nsoyo, Nieuhoff wrote, 'understood *Latin* very well, and made several learned harangues in the same'. This was a curiosity for the Calvinist Dutch, with Latin so deeply connected to the Catholic faith against which they had rebelled. But, as Garcia II noted in his treaty of alliance with the Dutch in 1642, while he would allow the Dutch to build forts wherever they wished along his coastline, the 'wickedness of the Portuguese, founded in their own ambitions, is not sufficient for me to abandon the Catholic faith'.[14]

Thus, a second key aspect of Kongo's diplomatic manoeuvrings in this era was its profession of Catholicism. As a Christian African kingdom, Kongo was in some ways testament to the original purported justification of European colonization and their trade in enslaved persons. Kongo's Christianity was heavily interlaced with Kongo religious beliefs, and when Capuchin missionaries were at length sent there in the 1640s after repeated requests from Kongo, many of them complained that the kingdom was completely devoid of actual Christian practice. These fevered emissaries of the Church spent their time burning 'idols' and haranguing 'infidels' before – generally – dying of malaria. But their dogmatism was not the whole story: Kongo peoples had produced an autonomous form of Christianity, where shared symbols, such as the cross, and beliefs in divine powers melded into a new form of religious practice.[15]

All the same, despite the fact that the Dutch were Protestant and the Kongos autonomously Catholic, religious difference was not allowed to intervene as it might have done between two European powers. During the 1640s, the Dutch and the Kongo state pursued their war against their common enemy, the Portuguese. The Dutch fought alongside Kongo troops, and the manikongo encouraged chiefs who had sworn loyalty to the Portuguese in the region of Luanda to rise up against them. But, in the end, a fleet of Brazilian troops came to the rescue of the Portuguese in 1648. Kongo and the Dutch were vanquished, and Kongo was forced to submit to a harsh peace. The troops occupying the region from Brazil were immune to many of the diseases found there – many of them were Tupinambá – and all this contributed to the defeat of Kongo at Mbwila seventeen years later.[16]

How different this West-Central African kingdom looks in this light from Hegel's infamous idea that 'Africa has no history'! Its diplomatic manoeuvrings to protect its power and sumptuous Court are striking. It is useful to start with these in this chapter to see just how adept and influential Kongo had become by the middle of the seventeenth century – to understand the extent to which its trajectory became interdependent with global forces over the preceding century and a half, and how far it had to fall when these alliances then disintegrated apart.

In Kongo, there is a huge variety of written sources for this resonant and important history. Not a little of it is written by Kongo peoples. But oral history, too, can encapsulate the transformations of the kingdom in this key phase of world history. The oral history of the western Bapende, as reported by a Belgian anthropologist in the 1930s and 1940s, described well the trajectory that followed this phase of Kongo history, when Kongo collapsed and the slave trade became impossible to root out. It described how the Bapende had originally lived near the coast at Luanda, in Angola. However, on the arrival of the Portuguese, they fled into the interior in several waves, moving further and further inland, until they reached the region of Tshikapa, in Kasai, around 1700. On the arrival of the Europeans, the Bapende's oral traditions stated:

> All of a sudden they saw a large boat appear on the sea. This boat had completely white wings, shining like knives. White men came out of the water and spoke words which no one understood. Our ancestors became afraid, and said that they were *Vumbi*, returning spirits. They forced them back into the water with volleys of arrows. But the *Vumbi* sparked fire with the sound of thunder. Lots of men were killed. Our ancestors fled. The nobles and the priests said that these *Vumbi* were the ancient owners of the land [into which the Bapende themselves had migrated, moving across Southern Africa from the Zambezi area]. Our ancestors left the plain of Luabala, fearing the return of the boat Ulungu. They retreated along the Lukala River. Others stayed near the great sea. The boat returned and more white men appeared. They demanded chickens and eggs; they gave cloth and pearls. The Whites came back again. They brought maize and cassava, knives and hoes, peanuts and tobacco. From that time to our days, the Whites never brought anything more, except wars and misery.[17]

UNDERSTANDING TRANSFORMATIONS IN THE KINGDOM OF KONGO: ORIGINS, PEOPLES, FRAGILITIES

What kind of kingdom was Kongo, then, when the Atlantic trade began in the late fifteenth century? Professional historians of Africa mark an important difference between the region of West-Central Africa in which Kongo lies and the regions of West Africa that this book has considered so far. In the first place, in West Africa the influence of long-distance trade to North Africa and pilgrimage to Arabia was felt as a distant but significant presence on the Gold Coast and in the kingdoms of Oyo and Benin. Geographically, the thick forests and sharp mountains in which the Kingdom of Kongo abounded were very different from the savannahs and semi-deserts in which most of the great kingdoms of West Africa arose. Moreover, the Bantu languages of Southern and Central Africa are not found in West Africa. Yet Kongo, too, was probably distantly connected to long-distance trades taking in the Arab world prior to European arrival. In fact, similar patterns concerning long-distance trade, state-building and economic growth emerge here, as in West Africa.[18]

These connections between West and West-Central Africa to the world are anathema to historical traditions in which 'Africa''s isolation from the rest of the world, before contact began with Europeans, is assumed. But they emerge from a number of factors. As the historian Jan Vansina showed, similar techniques in wood-carving found from Yorùbá regions as far south as Loango suggest shared techniques and exchanges. Seventeenth- and eighteenth-century carvings from the Kuba kingdoms* depict the playing of *warri*, a game found widely further north in West Africa, as well as in East Africa. Other evidence suggests that these exchanges then interconnected with the long-distance routes linked to the Sahara – and these patterns may in turn have influenced how the Kongolese reacted when the Portuguese first arrived in the 1480s.[19]

Kongo's connection to long-distance trade routes is the only logical

* South-west of the present-day Democratic Republic of Kongo.

explanation for how sugarcane – long cultivated in the eastern Mediterranean and in the Arab worlds – grew in Kongo before the Portuguese arrival. Long-distance trade can also help to explain the use of a shell currency in Kongo (the *nzimbu*), for the use of the *nzimbu* surely was not unrelated to the experience of the use of the cowrie-shell currency in West Africa and the Sahel; the Kalahari regions to the south were connected to the Indian Ocean trade by perhaps the ninth or tenth century, and cowries may have been involved in this trade – which offered a route for this influence to spread to Kongo. In addition, there seems to have been an important spiritual dimension that connected the forest Kingdom of Kongo with that of Benin to the north, for it is noteworthy that both Edo and Kongo peoples (and, indeed, peoples of the Kingdom of Ndongo in northern Angola) used diamond-shaped crosses as a religious symbol prior to the arrival of the Portuguese. In Kongo, the 'cosmogram' connected the worlds of the living and the dead, and was used widely on textiles and bowls used for daily life, as well as later in Christian art. The use of the cross as a religious symbol among the Edo also suggests some cultural and perhaps commercial connection between Edo and Kongo peoples, as does the shared use of shell currencies, similar wood-carving techniques and the presence of sugarcane in Kongo, since all had likewise existed in Benin prior to the Portuguese arrival.[20]

Yet how did these connections develop, in a region famous for its thick forests and swamps? As we have seen in other parts of the continent, rivers and seaways were roads. Many peoples along the coasts of West-Central Africa were good boat-builders, with the Vili of Loango remarked upon as such by the Portuguese in the sixteenth century. There were fishing groups to be found everywhere, and their skill in making seagoing ships is shown by the presence of Bubi peoples on the Island of Bioko by the time the Portuguese arrived in the fifteenth century. The idea that Europeans 'brought' seafaring to Africa must also, therefore, be challenged. Thus, it was most likely through African navigators that related religious and aesthetic practices grew up; and when the manikongo Afonso I wrote in 1526 of a number of traders from Benin resident in the Kongolese port

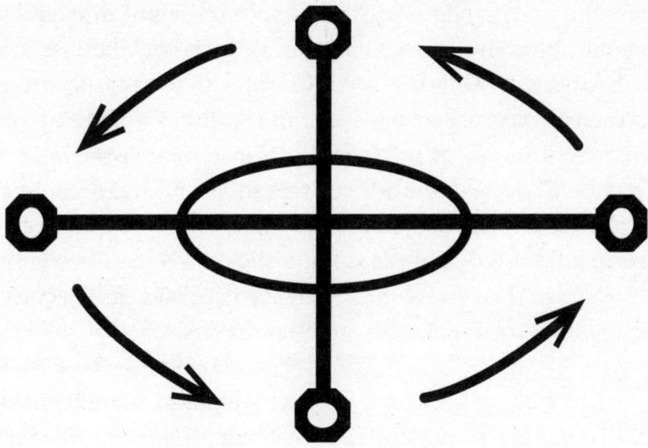

The Kongo 'cosmogram'

of Mpinda, it is possible that they found their way there in local embarkations rather than through Portuguese networks.[21]

Kongo may not, therefore, have been as isolated from other parts of West Africa as has hitherto been supposed. The pre-existence in Kongo of long-distance trade routes and a shell currency helped a strong power to emerge by the fifteenth century, as had been the case in West Africa in Benin and Mali. In fact, the similarities between what happened to the *nzimbu* in Kongo and to the cowrie in West Africa offer a vital comparison: each saw growth in the fifteenth century, once Atlantic trade began; increased currency imports without increased imports of products for trade then created inflationary pressures; and negative economic consequences followed in the loss of political control over the volumes of currency imported.[22]

At the time of the Portuguese arrival, Kongo was growing in strength, probably having been founded towards the end of the fourteenth century. Its process of growth and urbanization grew from within the society, not from outside. The political power of Kongo's *manis* derived from the capital at Mbanza Kongo (known to the Portuguese as São Salvador), seen as a sacred city. Markets were dotted around the countryside, and would often take place at many different neighbouring locations over the course of a week (as was the case in many parts of Africa). Cloth was traded widely, with fabrics surviving from the seventeenth century giving a hint of the diversity and skill of Kongo's weavers. Iron mines in Nsundi province were also vital, and the iron was used to make the agricultural tools and weapons that were also traded at market. With numerous markets, the idea of a universalized currency existed, and the *nzimbu* shell, fished in Luanda, was in widespread use. The established currency base must have contributed to the founding of the Kongo state by the first part of the fifteenth century.[23]

Linked to trading networks were geographical boundaries within Kongo. To the north, the province of Nsundi's border with the Tyo* was impassable because of the mountains; to the south, one of the things that differentiated Nsoyo was that it was the site of salt. Such boundaries helped in making trading networks across Kongo: forest products came from the north, and salt from the south. It was no accident that the most famous market in Kongo, at Malebo Pool on the Congo River, was sited at a major boundary, which still serves as the border between the two Congo republics in the twenty-first century, or that Mbanza Kongo itself was sited at a junction of trading routes. Indeed, as Antonio Cavazzi put it, drawing on Kongo oral histories, the first manikongo, Lukeni, chose the site because it was 'the only and most necessary point of transit for the whole of the population'.[24]

South of Kongo lay the Kingdom of Ndongo, inland from Luanda, its heart in the Kwanza River Valley. In Ndongo, a more precarious balance existed between human beings and their environment. The land of this state was drier, with four seasons as opposed to Kongo's six, only one of which – Kitombi – was especially wet. Dutch colonists of the 1640s described Ndongo as dry for the most part, but with very fertile valleys where many crops could be cultivated. This was also good terrain on which to raise cattle and oxen, which were traded north to Kongo. As in Kongo, trade in Ndongo linked up different ecological settings, so that cattle and hides from the plateau were exchanged for salt and fish from the coast.[25]

* Known as the 'Anxicos' in early Portuguese documents.

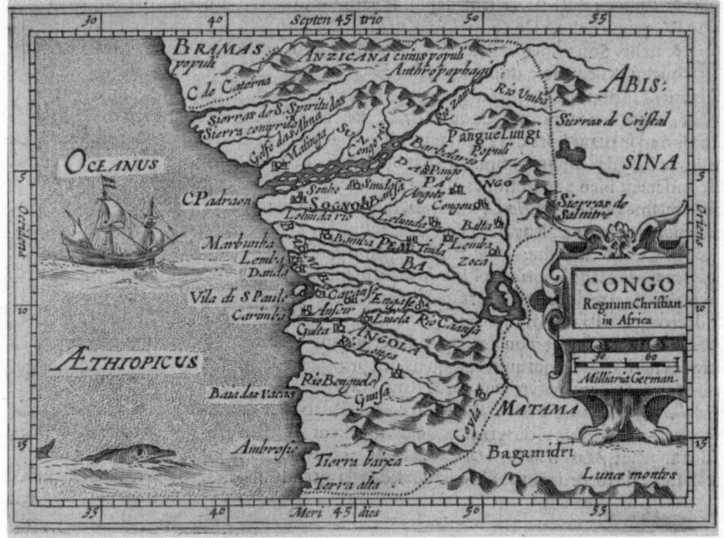

Map of Kongo, by Bertius.

Networks of traders and a growing political power base meant that Kongo's influence spread across West-Central Africa. Some early Portuguese observers described the original Kongo cultures as incorporating the polities of Caconda, Loango and Tyo to the north of the Congo River, and Matamba and Ndongo to the south of Mbanza Kongo. One source claimed that when Ndongo had been reached by the Portuguese, 'the King of Angola was a friend and almost a subject of the King of Congo and sent him tribute each year.' In the sixteenth century, it was suggested that Loango had at some point broken away from Kongo, while, as early as 1516, the manikongo, Afonso I, wrote to Manoel I of Portugal that it had been 'necessary for me to go and make war on the Ambundos [Mbundu of Ndongo] as they have rebelled against me'.[26]

It is worth considering of what this 'rebellion' consisted. The pattern was, in fact, similar to that of Jolof in Senegambia, and Allada with the Yorùbá states. What Loango and Ndongo became in the sixteenth and seventeenth centuries were smaller, centralized states that broke away from any distant obligation to Kongo, and that created structures whose wider economic function was to extract surplus value from the hinterland and export it into the Atlantic world. By being located on the coast, local *manis* had better access to Atlantic trade goods and could develop strong military defences and advantageous trade terms; but they could only do so through meeting the demand for 'value', first, as we shall see, in the form of copper, and then in the form of enslaved persons.

In spite of this fragmentation, this was a region of deeply interlinked cultures. All the same, where there are people, there will be divisions, and so it was in West-Central Africa. In spite of the connections, and the affinities of language, culture and belief, there were three core faultlines within Kongo that external pressures could exploit. These were between the ruling *mwissikongo* and the commoners, between town (*mbanza*) and country (*vata*), and between men and women – divisions that in many ways emphasize just how modern Kongo's concerns were so very long ago.

The *manis* of Kongo were always chosen from among the lineage group (*kanda*) called the *mwissikongo*, who occupied Mbanza Kongo; and the *manis* themselves always chose from among this lineage when it came to appointing governors, councillors and ambassadors. The *mwissikongo* caste was based on heredity, and they made alliances through marriage that expanded their *kanda*. The origins of the power of Kongo's nobility are obscure, but may lie in their association with iron: oral traditions credit the kingdom's founder, Ntinu Wene, with inventing the forge, and, writing in 1704, the missionary Laurent de Lucques noted that all the blacksmiths in Kongo remained nobles. The caste nature of political power in Kongo was one that divisive forces could exploit: where inferiors had to fall to their knees and clap to greet superiors, and where power was restricted to such a small coterie that it was impossible to access, resentments grew.[27]

The division between *mbanza* and *vata* was also very deep rooted. Archaeological finds north of the Congo River from 2,000 years ago suggest that even then there existed networks of large central towns surrounded by smaller settlements. Many oral traditions hold that the *mwissikongo* migrated across the Congo River from these regions, which suggests a connection. By the 1490s, there was a corollary between urban status and nobility: it was the *mwissikongo* urban classes that consumed the surplus produced in the rural areas, with villages being forced to transfer some of their agricultural surpluses to the towns; meanwhile, the class and caste divide between *mbanza* and *vata* was also rooted in belief, with Mbanza Kongo not just the economic heart of the kingdom, but its spiritual centre also. This division increasingly came to represent ideas of civility and barbarism for urban elites; and so they were thus more willing to allow for the disposal of some of those in the *vata* as captives.[28]

Relations between the sexes were, in turn, based around strictly gendered divisions of labour, inheritance and spirituality. All agricultural labour was done by women. Since inheritance passed through the female line, elder males sought to control this labour, and the lives of their nieces and sisters. Inheritance through the mother's line meant that men could succeed their uncles, and this also allowed for new alliances to be formed and new settlements made as *kandas* expanded their kinship ties. While property and inheritance went through the female line, however, spiritual identities and markers of personality went from father to son. Hence, given the importance of labour, property and spiritual belief in all societies, the overall structure was one that fostered gender segregation, yet created a social realm in which each gender held roles of great importance to society as a whole.[29]

Thus, by the late fifteenth century, a Kongo state had emerged that was growing powerful through trade links to north and south, and had some connection to longer-distance trade routes that brought cowries and sugar, and an established currency. These connections had helped Kongo to grow. However, there were also some markers of inequality that would in time threaten the long-term survival of the state.[30]

SPIRITUALITY AND CATHOLIC CONVERSION IN KONGO

This presentation of the history of Kongo so far seems to match expectations. As a kingdom, it grew along with wider trade networks and consequent political power. Long-distance routes supplemented its power, as did access to a currency through the shells fished at Luanda. But a difficult question then arises: if Kongo's power was growing in the fifteenth century, why then did its *manis* adopt the new faith of Christianity brought by the Portuguese?

This is a subject that has drawn much attention from anthropologists. It shows why the place of religion is fundamental in understanding changes in Kongo society in this era. Kongo's cosmology was one that saw the universe as separated into connected worlds of the living (*nza yayi*) and the dead (*nsi a bafwa*), with an overarching spiritual force, *Nzambi a Mpungu*, overseeing these relations. Only by seeing how these ideas linked with the great economic and political changes that occurred in Kongo in the sixteenth century does this period begin to make sense.[31]

As the oral histories of the Bapende cited above noted, there was an important spiritual dimension in the ways in which the Portuguese were initially welcomed: they were seen in that account as ancestors, and the original possessors of the land. According to Kongo cosmologies in the north of the kingdom, albinos (*ndundu*) were viewed as ancestors, whereas in the south they were seen as incarnations of spirits of the water (*nkita u simbi*). There is, therefore, every reason to believe the accounts that suggest that the spiritual dimension was the one through which the arrival of the 'white' Portuguese was initially seen. Yet very soon this spiritual dimension would be allied to a material one, as Catholicism became the key glue between Kongo and the outside world. The perception of the spiritual powers of albinos became allied with maleficence, and by 1602, in Loango, they were raised as 'the king's witches', able to enter markets and take what they wanted at will – symptomatic of the selfishness that witchcraft, and the trade brought by those we might call the 'European albinos', came to symbolize there.[32]

One further strong reason to credit the early spiritual power that linked Kongo to Portugal was the shared symbol of the cross. The cross had symbolic power for the BaKongo, representing a transition point between the worlds of *nza yayi* and *nsi a bafwa*. Kongo peoples took the symbol of the cross to the Americas, where it was frequently found in the design of stringed musical instruments, on bowls used as kitchenware, and as popular symbols in plantation societies. Thus, the Kongo cross found an enduring place in Atlantic African identities. When, in the nineteenth century, some Kongo peoples ended up in Freetown, Sierra Leone, freed from slaving ships, they brought it with them: they formed a neighbourhood that is still today in Freetown called Kongo Cross, sitting between the old centre of Freetown and the steep mountains rising up towards Leicester Peak, and marked by a small roundabout with a sculpture bearing the name and figures to recall that past.[33]

The arrival of a new religion with this potent religious symbol of the cross was surely, therefore, a key factor both in the spiritual prism through which Kongo peoples saw the Portuguese, and also in the apparently earnest desire of many of them to adopt the new faith. Historians have tended to seek the reason for the conversion of manikongos to Catholicism in self-seeking political advantage, and, of course, this may have been a factor. Yet to limit understanding to this is to reproduce a materialist paradigm that does scant justice to fifteenth-century Kongo worldviews. There was no reason why the needs of state alone should have driven *manis* to convert to Catholicism any more than they should have pressed the obas of Benin, the kings of Allada or the buurs of Cayor: all sought political and military advantage from alliance with Europeans, but, when it came to doing so at the price of full conversion, negotiations in those kingdoms went no further. What may have been different in Kongo was the spiritual resonance of the Portuguese, these albinos who worshipped crosses. It was this, and not some reductive economic factor alone, that offered the Portuguese a 'comparative advantage'.[34]

The first manikongo to convert to Catholicism was Nzika Nkuwu, who took the name João I in keeping with the name of the then king of Portugal, João II, in 1491. Rui de Pina described in great detail the arrival of the Portuguese ambassadors at Mbanza Kongo. Disembarking at the port of Mpinda in the coastal province of Nsoyo, the Portuguese were met by a member of the *mwissikongo*, who guided them on the journey of almost 200 miles to Mbanza Kongo, which took twenty-three days. The trip was undertaken with a retinue of 200 black troops.[35]

The ceremonies that greeted the Portuguese, including the role of the standing army, are clear testament to the fact that Kongo was already a significant state. When the Portuguese eventually reached the city, they were met with extraordinary pomp and ceremony:

> On the day that the Christians entered the Court, they were received by innumerable people, and with great clamour and acclaim. They were soon housed in some new and select houses, provided with everything . . . the King sent some noble courtiers to the Captain and the friars, dressed up in a huge range of masks and costumes, and after them an infinite number of archers, and then the lancers, and then other infantrymen with weapons of war, and also women all divided up into divisions, with many ivory trumpets and kettle drums, singing great praises of the King of Portugal. And in this way they reached the King.[36]

The great popular feeling that accompanied the arrival of the Portuguese was matched by the sense of occasion of Nzika Nkuwu's conversion to Catholicism. However, already in the 1490s the new religion sowed divisions, and on his death in 1506 a civil war broke out between rival factions: one that wanted to adhere to the new faith and one that opposed it. According to some sources, a principal objection of those who opposed the new faith was its prohibition of polygamy. This was not – as the missionaries assumed – due to 'loose morals'. Rather, in a society where *kandas* saw inheritance passed through the female line, marriages were important ways of expanding each *kanda*'s alliances. Owing to matrilinearity, sons of the manikongo's principal wife could not succeed him, and thus the new religion's challenge to this posed a serious threat to the interests of many, and, by extension, to Kongo's entire political structure: naturally, this was resisted tooth and nail.[37]

The Catholic faction won the civil war, and the new king, Afonso I, was installed. It was not an accident that, as the historian Anne Hilton noted, he was, in fact, the son of Nzika Nkuwu's principal wife, and could not, according to the traditional *kanda* structure, have inherited the throne. Only the new faith could legitimize his succession and supersede the rights of his cousins, and Afonso I became, over the next thirty-four years, the longest-serving and most orthodox of the Catholic manikongos. Nevertheless, instrumentality alone does not account for his remarkable adhesion to the faith, which was, as we have seen, also grounded in wider dimensions of Kongo spirituality, and in the cultural framework that the Portuguese met with among the BaKongo.[38]

One letter written by Rui de Aguiar in May 1516 described Afonso's remarkable fidelity to the Church in almost lyrical terms:

> His [devotion to] Christianity is such that he seems to me not to be a man but rather an Angel that God has sent to this Kingdom so as to convert it . . . because I can relate to Your Highness that he himself knows more about the Prophets and the Gospel of Our Lord Jesus Christ, and of all the lives of the Saints, and all the rites of the Holy Mother Church, than do we ourselves, and teaches us about them . . . he speaks so well and correctly, that it seems to me that it is always the Holy Spirit who speaks through him: because, my Lord, he does nothing other than study, and many times he falls asleep on his Books, and he often forgets to eat or drink because he is [lost in] speaking of the things of Our Lord . . . [and after hearing Mass] he goes to preach to the People with great love and charity, urging them for the love of Our Lord that they should convert . . . and he does this every day . . . punishing those who worship Idols and ordering that they should be burnt . . . and he has already spread many Christian [Kongo people] throughout his Kingdom, who run schools and teach our Holy Faith to the People; and there are also Girls' Schools, run by one of his sisters, who must be all of sixty years old, and can read very well.[39]

The widespread adoption of Catholicism suggested here is also apparent in the earliest account of conversion in the kingdom, by Rui de Pina. According to Pina, when Nzika Nkuwu was baptized in 1491, he chose six leading *kanda* heads from the *mwissikongo* to accompany him. At this, many other leading figures of the *mwissikongo* came to him and asked, 'what lack of service or treachery you found in us, not to remember us alongside those who you saw fit to become Christian with you . . . and so we ask you to instruct that we too should be baptized.' Following this mass baptism, the first church was constructed within two months, completed by July 1491 with the help of 1,000 labourers who carried the stone on their backs for almost 10 miles.[40]

From this point on, the new religion added to the potential for division in the kingdom, alongside the factors discussed in the previous section. The Portuguese very quickly did not meet the missionary needs of the kingdom, in spite of the popular fervour, and Christianity soon became principally a royal cult. Many BaKongo lived largely oblivious to it, while, for the *mwissikongo*, it was seen as a way to access luxuries through trade with outsiders. By 1704, Laurent de Lucques had described how, while the nobility of Nsoyo chose those who would be trained as priests, to sing at Mass and hear confession, 'there are very few who attend lessons on the catechism . . . and hardly anyone pays attention when the bell sounds for Mass or some other religious act.' However, the maninsoyo attended Mass, 'sumptuously dressed in silk clothes acquired in exchange for slaves and ivory'.[41]

By this time, even the *mwissikongo*'s original fidelity to the strictures of the new religion had been replaced by a hybrid, 'Creole' Christianity. The orthodoxy of the *mwissikongo* was certainly discouraged by the venality and greed of the first waves of missionaries who came in the sixteenth century. A report from 1539 to King João III of Portugal advised him to get rid of all the 'white men' in the kingdom, secular as well as ecclesiastical, for 'if envy, greed and ambition reign in the world, in [Kongo] they have made their home and permanent base.' A complaint from King Diogo I in 1549 of the behaviour of Portuguese priests and missionaries went unheeded, and so the attraction of the new faith waned. When the Spanish priest Diogo de Santíssimo Sacramento went to Kongo in 1583, he told the manikongo, Álvaro I Nimi a Lukeni, that they had come to spread the gospel, to which the answer came 'that other friars had come there, and said that they were going to spread Christianity, and that then they had accumulated property and turned to vice'.[42]

The greed and cruelty of those priests prepared to go to Kongo had spoilt the fruits of the first mission. The devotion and popular enthusiasm of the early decades captured in Rui de Aguiar's letter of 1516 had dissipated so much by the end of the century that one Jesuit wrote in 1603 that Kongo was 'completely finished with good customs, and the people are only Christian in name'. By the 1640s, the Governor of Luanda wrote that 'if anyone informs your Majesty that there is Christianity in [Kongo], it's a blatant fraud.' A later seventeenth-century account said that, even in the colonial capital of Luanda, both whites and Africans blended Christianity with Mbundu religious practice.[43]

It is important to read against the grain of these narrow criticisms, written by colonial missionaries and slave traders for whom the only orthodox practice of Christianity was one imposed by them. The alacrity of the initial conversions, the devotion of Afonso I in the first half of the sixteenth century and the subsequent disenchantment should not be taken as meaning that the *mwissikongo* rulers first followed and then abandoned Catholicism as an elite cult. The intermixture of Kongo religious culture and symbolism with Christianity was in keeping with the pluralism of shrines in Kongo worship, even if it did not meet with the demands of Catholic orthodoxy in the era of the European Wars of Religion. Indeed, the type of mixture described for late-seventeenth-century Luanda was a very typical form of worship, promoting an inclusive approach to the otherworldly, rather than exclusion and conformity. It would prove very useful and enduring as peoples from Kongo and Ndongo were then taken enslaved to the New World.[44]

This sort of pluralism had even been tacitly accepted by the missionaries who sought to promote Christianity in the kingdom. The rite most eagerly sought after in Kongo was baptism, which, it was believed, protected against sorcery and witches. Christian priests in Kongo adapted the rite to include a piece of salt, seen by the BaKongo as a strong protection against witches. By the middle of the 1640s, a Dutch official wrote from Kongo in March 1642 that 'the country is full of wooden crosses that they greet with great devotion and prostrate themselves before. Each noble has a personal church and crosses in his village. What's more, they all have a rosary or chaplet around their neck . . . holding them in their hands as if they were praying, even though they do not know a word of Portuguese.' Yet, as we have seen, these crosses had a multidimensional symbolism, both Kongo and Catholic; other accounts of this era described how, while many were voluntarily baptized, they retained at the same time all of their customary shrines and beliefs – and this was because baptism had been incorporated by the missionaries themselves into these beliefs.[45]

By this stage, therefore, the initial fervour of Catholic belief described

Sixteenth-century Kongo cross.

in 1516 had changed. While the original conversion of Nzika Nkuwu and Afonso I's triumph had represented episodes of religious renewal and spiritual broadening, these were now being systematically replaced by a hybrid elite Catholicism and a return to Kongo religious idioms elsewhere. This change would prompt a further renewal movement in the early eighteenth century, an Antonine movement led in 1704 by a Kongo noblewoman called Beatriz Kimpa Vita, widely seen by the Portuguese as heresy – but, in fact, confirming the *mwissikongo*'s renewal of the Kongo religious institutions through the vehicle of a Catholicism, which had, by now, taken on a thoroughly BaKongo strain. Beatriz's movement fought against *all* witchcraft, and the unjust use of power in the now growing trade in enslaved persons.[46]

Why, then, did orthodox Christianity collapse in Kongo even among the ruling class, being but a shadow of its former self by the end of the eighteenth century? The central reason relates to the strength and resilience of Kongo culture on the one hand, and the impotence of the Christian religion to protect Kongo peoples from the worst evils of the trade in enslaved persons on the other. From Kongo's side, the ability of Kongo artisans to create crosses and art that met a Kongo aesthetic ensured the longevity of Kongo worldviews; while the development by Kongo manis of mixed ceremonies such as the *sangamento* initiation and military display equally ensured the incorporation of outside symbols within Kongo cosmology. The cross as a symbol of the bridge between the living and the dead allowed for spiritual renewal; and, as the trade in enslaved persons grew, this also incorporated beliefs about the dead residing in a realm beyond an ocean – the *nlangu* – to which the souls of the living departed year by year. Thus, Kongo culture grew stronger and found resilience, renewed itself, and made meaning of the violence and transformation associated with the rising trade in captives. This strength meant that, even as the economic and social pressures grew, people were able and willing to resist the growing power of the Kongo state.[47]

And, on the other hand, for all the overt adherence of its rulers to Catholicism, Kongo gained few benefits. Insecurity, warfare and violence grew exponentially, driven remorselessly by the Portuguese from Luanda. But Kongo was widely recognized as a Christian kingdom. It had kept ambassadors at the Vatican ever since the 1530s, and persisted with this into the 1620s and beyond. By the 1630s, Kongo's kings recognized that their Catholic faith could be an advantage, and began to use their diplomatic networks to lobby the Vatican to despatch more missionaries. They clearly hoped that the Vatican could act as a bulwark between them and the depredations of the Portuguese. When the Capuchins arrived in 1645, Garcia II greeted them with a very valuable gift, much as Nzika Nkuwu had greeted the Portuguese when they had first arrived, 154 years before. And, after the defeat of 1648, Garcia II complained bitterly to the Vatican about the peace terms and urged it to intercede on Kongo's behalf.[48]

Yet none of it worked, and the symbols of hypocrisy came to infuriate the manikongos. By the 1650s, the Jesuits in Luanda had the most luxurious houses in the city. Just to the north, they had more than fifty substantial plantations in prime fertile land, worked by over 10,000 enslaved persons. In the face of this, and the increasing disorder, disillusion with the Church naturally grew as the impact of the violence and inequalities of commercial relations became ever more apparent.[49]

THE SLAVE TRADE IN KONGO: STATE EXPANSION AND POPULAR REVOLT

In July 1526, the manikongo, Afonso I, composed a letter to João III of Portugal in which he expressed serious reservations as to the direction in which Kongo–Portuguese relations were headed. He was frustrated by the failure of Portuguese priests to respond to the popular turn towards Christianity. But even more damaging were the negative consequences of the huge growth in trade. These resulted from the great freedom that Portuguese officials gave to the merchants who came to Kongo with prohibited goods, which were distributed throughout the kingdom 'in such abundance that many vassals who were obedient to us, have rebelled against us since they have greater abundance of these goods than do we'.[50]

In this letter, Afonso complained about the way in which the traders stole away natural-born Kongos, 'and the children of our nobles and vassals'. He understood how the trade spread political weakness, as vassals such as the maniloango and the Ngola of Ndongo declared independence from his influence. However, he made his feelings felt even more plainly in a second letter, dated 15 October 1526:

> many of our people, for the avid desire which they have for the merchandise and objects of [your] Kingdoms which your people bring here, and so as to satisfy their rampant appetites, steal many of our free and protected people. And it has happened many times that they have stolen nobles and the sons of nobles, and our own relatives, and have taken them to sell to the white men who are in our Kingdoms; and they take them hidden and others go by night, so as not to be discovered. And as soon as they are in the power of these white men they are at once branded with fire and clapped in irons.[51]

Initially, Portuguese interests had been directed towards the copper mines beyond the River Congo, but, with the emergence of sugar plantations on São Tomé in the early 1500s, there was an increasing demand for enslaved persons. While Western historians have usually seen this as a function of European commercial demand, the requirements of Kongo were equally if not more important. Copper was a key product with high ritual and commercial value, and the Portuguese were unable to get hold of it because the Kongolese would not let them: when a metalsmith was sent in 1536 to try to work on the copper mines, the manikongo was said to respond 'as if the Kingdom was already stolen from him, with its mines and everything', underlining the ritual and commercial power that the metal had.[52]

With the copper trade baulked, the new sugar plantations on São Tomé offered a good commercial outlet for the Portuguese. The colony had to be made to pay its way. Traders from the islands came to Kongo's port at Mpinda, in Nsoyo, wanting to meet the demand for labour from the planters, and from the Portuguese ships coming from Lisbon and Elmina in the hope of obtaining captives. Initially this demand was met through the sale of Tyo people, who were strangers to Kongo, from north of Malebo Pool. However, this letter shows that, by 1526, things were changing: people were already stealing freeborn Kongos, even noble members of the *mwissikongo* caste and their children, and selling them to the European slave traders.[53]

The island of São Tomé would often prove a potent disruptive force in Kongo. To the Portuguese, slave trading had always been the major economic interest of this island, and one of the very first grants of privileges to the Portuguese residents, from 1500, said that they could trade freely 'for [enslaved persons] as for anything else'. By 1510, many Portuguese ships went straight to São Tomé and bought enslaved persons there directly. It was pressure from São Tome traders to increase the number of enslaved captives that led to the expansion of this trade in Kongo, as described by the manikongo in his letter of 1526.[54]

The trade in captives in the first half of the sixteenth century was large, abetted systematically by Portuguese interests. Already, in 1516, over 4,000 enslaved persons were despatched that year into the Atlantic from the port of Mpinda, and similar numbers were traded through the 1530s. By 1548, the numbers had grown to at least 6,000, and there were more captives available had there been enough ships to load them. While most of these were captives taken by Kongo in wars against the Tyo, or were traded to São Tomé traders from further south in Ndongo, there were still significant numbers of Kongos who were vulnerable. In view of this, the manikongo, Diogo I, who succeeded Pedro I in 1546, protested to the Portuguese and began to prevent traders from going inland and sowing disruption.[55]

It is important to read beyond a twenty-first-century economic worldview in understanding this growing trade in enslaved persons. It was a trade that in itself transformed worldviews, concepts and ideas, in Kongo as in Europe. European-written records present this trade through the lens of profit and loss: when a captive died on a voyage, the death was annotated by a scribe in the official log of the ship, and a certificate was drawn up by the captain and his scribe for their 'legal owner', with death and the body of the enslaved viewed only through the lens of (Portuguese) property and law. However, from the Kongo side, with the ocean seen to separate the worlds of the living (*nza yayi*) and the dead (*nsi a bafwa*), there was a strong spiritual dimension to what, from a Western view, seem to be just economic and social changes. As the trade and its impact grew, it would be this dimension that would have much the most resonant meaning in Kongo. It was the 'selfishness' of witches who stole souls that made the daily realities of the trade comprehensible. It was also the spiritual dimension that made the trade subject to sanctions such as did not seem to exist in the world of *nza yayi*. The growth of this trade allowed the idiom of witchcraft, and belief in its powers, to gain much greater strength: far from being an 'age-old superstition', witchcraft, as we now know it, was a modern invention in Kongo that helped in understanding the violence, selfishness and greed associated with the trade in enslaved persons.[56]

Of course, beyond the multiple levels of meaning, a core part of the day-to-day reality was a growing trade in captives, and of the wars to maintain this fought by the Kongo Army. In December 1515, when a Portuguese ship arrived at Mpinda on Christmas Day, Afonso I wrote swiftly, urging the captain to come to Mbanza Kongo to accompany him to war. In the seventeenth century, it was well known how Portuguese adventurers had sailed from Mpinda to Kongo, 'to help those Kings in their conquests and to defend them from [hostile] armies'. By this time, a market for captives had evolved at Malebo Pool, and Portuguese traders resided there, assisting the manikongo's armies in raiding wars and purchasing the Tyo captives that resulted. This allowed Kongo to become a middleman in the trade, taxing the passage of enslaved persons, who had to pass through its territory, while trying as far as possible to prevent enslavement of Kongo subjects, as Afonso I's letter of 1526 showed.[57]

Nevertheless, Kongo peoples were becoming increasingly restive as the dangers of enslavement grew. While there was resistance within Kongo, manikongos also found resistance from outsiders. By the 1550s, as we have seen, Pedro I's successor, Diogo I, was seen as an obstacle by the Portuguese, who sought various ways to destabilize him. By 1552, the Jesuits were plotting alongside the Portuguese traders in Mbanza Kongo to depose Diogo. This was an alliance of faith and profit in the raw: Diogo was increasingly opting for a hybrid version of Catholicism that did not please the Jesuits, while he had also sought to impose greater taxes on Portuguese traders making for Malebo Pool's slave markets. As a Jesuit who wrote to Ignatius Loyola described it, 'you will already know how the King of Kongo is to be deposed from his kingdom, for hidden reasons, with another introduced in his place . . . which cannot be achieved without wars and much difficulty, which although they have to pass, will then leave a certain profit among those souls, so that everything is ordained to this end. And the king who is due to succeed through divine grace, is all ours.' A pattern was developing of resistance to the growing autocratic power of the manikongo from inside the kingdom, and of pressurizing force from the outside, all related to the trade in enslaved persons: and this was to break out decisively in 1568 in the 'Jaga' Wars.[58]

In that year, the gathering resentments at the inequalities and insecurities erupted. A group of people whom the Portuguese sources call 'Jagas' invaded Mbanza Kongo and terrified the kingdom. The first-hand account of Duarte Lopes, written ten years later after discussions in Kongo with those who had witnessed it, described what happened: 'These people have no king, and live in huts in the forest, after the manner of shepherds. They went wandering up and down, putting to fire and sword, and spoiling and robbing every part of the country through which they passed, till they reached Congo, which they entered through the province of [Mbata].'[59]

In response to this invasion, the manikongo, Álvaro I Nimi a Lukeni, fled from Mbanza Kongo with some Portuguese priests and the *mwissikongo*. This was no easy journey, and must have been well organized to be effective as a retreat; for the roads in Kongo rose continually up and down sharply inclined mountains and crossed many rivers, while they were so narrow that people could travel only in single file. Probably the destination of those who were evacuated from the city would have been near to the estuary of the river and the port of Mpinda, where the river broke down into numerous islets, which, as a seventeenth-century description put it, 'make so many straight and beautiful waterways [between them] that they are beautiful to see. On each island grows a sort of tree which looks like a laurel, very close to the bank . . . and from the top of which springs a root which falls straight to earth, like a skein of cotton from a finger, until a flower blooms when it reaches the earth or the water.'[60]

Meanwhile, Mbanza Kongo was put to the sword by the 'Jaga'. Famine struck, and 'the price of a small quantity of food rose to that paid for a slave.' Many were forced to ransom family members, who were despatched by slave traders to work on the sugar plantations of São Tomé, where by this time there were seventy of them, each worked by over 300 enslaved persons. The islanders of São Tomé collaborated, and sent an army with the Portuguese that eventually drove out the 'Jaga' from Mbanza Kongo and restored the manikongo – but at a considerable price.[61]

Who were the 'Jaga' and what were they rebelling against? Specialists on Kongo history engaged in a protracted dispute about this over thirty years ago, with some claiming that they were a faction from within Kongo and that this was a civil war, and others that they came from the Kwango River Basin to the east of Kongo, and were rising up against the depredations provoked by the slaving wars. The likelihood is the former, but, whichever is right, the key point was that this represented a popular revolt, led by those who had nothing to gain from the changes that had come to Kongo. This was a revolt from below at the growing violence and inequality that went with the expansion of a trade in captives: as we shall see in the second part of this book, this was a pattern that was to be repeated widely across West and West-Central Africa.[62]

The likelihood is that the 'Jaga' did come from beyond the eastern frontier region of Kongo, in the forests near the border of the kingdom around the Kwango River. A 1610 account of Kongo by the Frenchman Pierre du Jarric suggests this strongly in its description of Kongo's easternmost province of Mbata:

> The capital city of this Province is also called Mbata, where the Governor usually resides, who is permitted before all others to have at his side some of the kingdom's troops; which is not even granted to the son of the [manikongo]. Because if he is in need, the [manikongo] grants him some foreigners to help him, usually the Portuguese. The reason why the [Governor of Mbata] has this privilege is that there are certain peoples on the Eastern side, beyond the mountains of the Sun and Saltpetre, which the Kongos call [Jágas], and who call themselves Agag, who live ordinarily through theft and crime, frequently giving strong annoyance to this Province. This is why they must always be for this reason armed, and ready to defend themselves against these peoples.[63]

This account gives a strong indication both of the origins of the 'Jaga' and of the consequences of the 1568 invasion. In order to supply Mbata with arms, Kongo had to redouble their dependence on external trade to ensure a ready supply. The political price of having been rescued from the 'Jaga' by the Portuguese in 1570 was, therefore, very high. Not only did trade increase, but after this point Portuguese advisers – usually priests – held a seat on the electoral council of Kongo, and could therefore shape elections to favour the growing external influences. What would prove equally if not even more important was the agreement of the manikongo after 1570 to the Portuguese colonization of Luanda, which, as we shall now see, was effectively the bank of Kongo; this would add economic deterioration to the other symptoms of the kingdom's rise, and fall.[64]

CURRENCY WARS AND THE CRISIS OF KONGO AND NDONGO

Writing of his experience of the kingdoms of Kongo, Matamba and Ndongo in the 1650s and 1660s, Antonio Cavazzi wrote eloquently of the fears held by enslaved dependants in the Kingdom of Kongo. What they dreaded most was 'being sold, and conducted to America and New Spain [Mexico]'; once there, they believed that they would be killed, their bones burned as coal and their flesh transformed into oil. This belief in the physical consumption of their bodies was widespread among the enslaved: others believed that, once in the Americas, they would be killed and their remains turned into the flags of the ships, with the red colours of these flags coming from their own blood.[65]

This belief held no less power for the BaKongo because of its symbolism, which, as we have seen, saw the *nsi a bafwa* as lying across a large expanse of water; thus, the belief in death waiting across the Atlantic held multiple foundations. To the south of Kongo, in Ndongo, similar symbolic meanings grew all the time in this era. Around 1600, following the attacks on Kongo by the 'Jaga', new groups of marauding invaders coalesced in Ndongo and to the south along the coast towards Benguela. These people were known as the Imbangala (and, to the Portuguese, also as 'Jaga'). They were first described by the Englishman Andrew Batell, who came upon them near Benguela, some way south of Luanda, around 1602. Batell described how the Imbangala would move from region to region, attacking their enemies and enslaving them, and in the meantime enjoying 'plenty of cattle, corn, wine, oil, and great triumphing, drinking, dancing and banqueting'. Their custom was to settle themselves somewhere and to 'cut down as many palms as will serve them wine for a month, and then as many more so that in a little time they spoil the country. They stay no longer in a place than it will afford them maintenance. And then in harvest-time they do arise, and settle themselves in the fruitfullest place they can find, and do reap their enemy's corn, and take their cattle.'[66]

Certainly, the Imbangala were fearsome warriors who laid waste to large areas of the interior of Ndongo and Matamba in the first decades of the seventeenth century. They were said to practise infanticide and to renew the stock of their warriors by incorporating the adolescent males of the regions they ravaged. They were widely rumoured to be cannibals. Like the 'Jaga' of Kongo, the Imbangala were most likely formed of groups of those who had come under political or economic pressure following the rise of slave trading. The violence with which they laid waste to huge swathes of country before forming a new kingdom, Kassanje, speaks of hatreds at the depredations of political overlords. By the 1570s, the ngolas of Ndongo had been conducting slave raids on neighbours for several decades, with one account of 1576 saying 12,000 captive persons were sold annually. There had been widespread disruption, and the displacement and discord that led to the Imbangala movement arose as a result.[67]

Once established in Kassanje, Cavazzi wrote, the favourite drink of many Imbangala military leaders was European red wine, symbolizing the blood of those killed in their campaigns. This wine also shows their identification with witches, who 'ate people', as Umbundu beliefs claimed. For the Imbangala were deemed to be 'cannibals' in European eyes; their foes in West-Central Africa held them to be cannibal witches who ate people and sold them into enslavement. Indeed, one account from the 1620s, in what is now Colombia, claimed that enslaved peoples believed that their voyage was a kind of witchcraft, at the end of which they would be eaten.[68]

By the first decade of the seventeenth century, therefore, there was widespread ideological and political upheaval in West-Central Africa. The slave trading of Kongo had provoked an uprising to the east and the sacking of Mbanza Kongo, while Ndongo's slave raiding had had a similar effect and produced the rise of the Imbangala. Meanwhile, the concept of malevolent witchcraft was gaining ground in response to these changes. In each case, this was symptomatic of the refusal of peoples of West-Central Africa to accept the depredations of Atlantic economic forces without a fight: these were revolutions from below, and they forced existing political leaders into a closer relationship with Portuguese traders than they had had before. As fighting continued, people preferred to flee to the deserted forests and mountains of the kingdoms, rather than to remain subject to capricious political leaders increasingly involved in the trade in captives.

One account by Antonio de Teruel from the mid 1640s describes the sort of thing that went on in Kongo by that date in vivid terms:

> On our first day, I stopped at a large *libata* [village] which had been inhabited two months before when I passed by, with a large number of people, but which I now found deserted; for it had been abandoned by everyone, leaving a few crops which they had harvested lying on the

ground. The cause of this was (as I was told by those who were accompanying me) the coming of the [manimbamba (Duke of Mbamba)], fearing the extortions of his companions and slaves . . . this is indeed one of the great misfortunes of that wretched people, that they have nothing safe: because the powerful rob them of everything: and they would rather live banished among the forests, than subject themselves to the capriciousness of [such] tyranny.[69]

A little while later, Teruel was travelling through a region of Kongo when there were Imbangala invasions. In one town he found the men with all the weapons at the ready, and, continuing on, he came to a large plain and found 'the women, children, and old people of all those places . . . They had made their huts with sticks and canes covered with straw, and some were cooking some herbs on a fire, others roasted some roots, and all of them were very poor.'[70]

By this period, then, which as we saw in the previous chapter was one of intense climatic instability and epidemic, the human costs of the prolonged cycle of warfare, drought and political transformation was deepening. The fear was nowhere more potently symbolized than in the Portuguese view of the Imbangala as cannibals, while all the enslaved who were sold into the Americas believed that they would be eaten. Villages were reduced to bands of refugees roaming the hinterland's forests and mountains, inhabiting impromptu dwellings that read like a seventeenth-century version of camps for internally displaced persons. The global diplomacy of the Kongo state did not prevent the fraying of the social fabric, and this was rapidly becoming evidenced most clearly in Kongo's long-term economic decline.

In a pattern that is by now becoming familiar in this book, one of the key indicators of the region's continual economic decline was the relative loss in value of its *nzimbu* shell currency, and the relationship this had to wider world economic patterns. Inequality had characterized the economic exchange between Kongo and the Atlantic world from the beginning. From the economist's perspective, this relates to different access to technology (ships, mining materials) and consequent advantages in trade. However, from the Kongo perspective, this economic divergence sprang also from the two cultures – Kongo and Portuguese – attaching different symbolic meanings to exchange. Whereas in Kongo, spiritual meanings were attached to objects of economic value such as copper, and not all currencies were used for capital accumulation, in Portugal economic ideas would become increasingly related to the accumulation of capital value. Thus, for Kongo, giving more than receiving was a symbol of spiritual and political power, and privilege; in Atlantic economies, accumulating more capital than was given was to be a means of acquiring power, something that would become ever more potent to ideological formations by the end of the seventeenth century.[71]

These different worldviews are very easy to see in records of early exchanges between the manikongo and the kings of Portugal. As early as 1511, Manoel I of Portugal gave instructions to his official Simão de Silveira with regard to his behaviour in Kongo. Manoel seemed to show concern about the pressures faced by the manikongo, so Silveira should not allow 'any demands [to be] made to the [manikongo], nor [should there be] any importuning made with them; because we are informed that those who go from here are always asking for things, and that he receive[s] a lot of bother with this, and gives from his own hand much more than he reasonably ought to'. Nevertheless, Manoel was not averse to making his own pressurizing demands, for in the same letter he gave an idea to Silveira of how to proceed, should Afonso I be reluctant to trade as much as the Portuguese desired:

> [You should] remind him of the great expense that we make here through sending these ships, friars and clerics, and the things which we send him; and that this has been going on since before your mission, as also in the expense which we have here in the teaching and maintenance of his sons; as a result of which he ought to load the said ships as fully as he can, and in a way which gives us even greater reason to carry out his requests, as we [already] do.[72]

There was a remorseless logic, therefore, to the encounter of these two different philosophies in the sixteenth century. Kongo's *manis* had always attracted power and status through gift-giving, and sought to do the same with the arrival of those seen initially as incarnations of ancestors from *nsi a bafwa*; while Portugal's traders also sought to accumulate as much as possible through their own worldview of the accumulation of surplus material as embodying actual power. The consequence was an imbalance in exchange whose roots were both material and spiritual, ideological and philosophical; and that continued in this vein for many centuries.

Perhaps the best example of this multiple meaning of currency is the place of copper. The copper mines to the north of the Congo River may have helped in the emergence of the Kongo Kingdom in the first place. Copper was certainly the prestige metal in both Kongo and Ndongo before the sixteenth century, as elsewhere in Central Africa. We have already seen how a letter of 1536 from Afonso I makes it plain that copper still held a very important ritual and economic place in the kingdom at that time. But what was the place of this copper in Kongo and Ndongo, and how did it compete with the *nzimbu* shell currency? An important answer is offered by Andrew Batell's account in the early years of the seventeenth century: he attended the funeral of the uncle of the Ngola of Ndongo in around 1604–5 and saw that a 'great store of copper, cloth, and many other things [were] laid upon his grave, which is the order of that country'.[73]

The Portuguese recognized this spiritual place of copper in the societies of West-Central Africa and tried to gain access to reserves, while at the same time paying lip service to the beliefs of their commercial partners. Governors of Angola sent gifts of copper manillas to *sobas* (Umbundu chiefs) inland in the hope that this would open access to local mines. In the sixteenth and seventeenth centuries, in fact, it was as much if not more the region's place as an imagined Eldorado as a desire for enslaved persons that fired Portuguese interventions. All sides were well aware of the monetary aspects of the exchanges as they developed, and, as in the Americas, the lack of minerals and the inability to open these mines would soon direct the interest of these economic brokers to the next best 'thing', which in their eyes were captive persons.[74]

Portuguese interest in Kongo's mines was almost as old as their presence in the kingdom itself. Rumours of silver mines in Ndongo began in the 1520s, and, by 1536, smiths were despatched to Kongo in an attempt to gain access to the copper there. Repeated mention of silver and copper mines were made in the 1550s and 1560s, but it was after the 'Jaga' invasion of Mbanza Kongo in 1568 that the emphasis on minerals became even more pronounced. The foundation of Luanda in 1575 was motivated, according to a letter written in 1607, by the information received in Lisbon 'of the big silver mines which there were there'. Throughout the first thirty years of the seventeenth century, the Portuguese crown would continue to pressurize the manikongo in an effort to get the copper mines opened. They tried to investigate copper mines in Benguela and wrote repeated summaries of where the best mineral deposits might be. They sent miners with experience from the New World on military expeditions and made frequent diplomatic attempts backed up by force to find the mines. For Portugal, Spain's silver riches in Mexico and Potosí (in modern Bolivia) were tantalizing, and they kept on thinking that something similar awaited them around the corner. It was a desire for monetary riches that drove their pressure on the region; yet, in the end, it was the trade in captive persons that ensued.[75]

The upshot was never what the Portuguese had hoped. While the Portuguese governor of Luanda, Fernão de Sousa, made strenuous efforts in the 1620s, sending experienced miners to *sobas* who were said to have silver, investigating copper and lead, hearing rumours of iron and more, it was always what miners most feared: a flash in the pan. In 1633, he wrote from Luanda that the attempt to conquer Benguela should be abandoned: there were no rich mines there. It was all so different from the heady days of the 1590s, where the 'conquest' of riches in Angola seemed within touching distance, and even the Jesuits had written in glowing terms of Angola's richness in copper, iron, tin and silver.[76]

It is important to step back and consider the wider uses of these minerals that the Portuguese hungered after. As we have seen, in Kongo and Ndongo, copper had ritual uses, as did iron, through the religious and political power of smiths in both states. However, in Portugal, copper had growing monetary, military and industrial uses. While silver was used for export to China, where it was the royal currency of the Ming Dynasty and could be used by European traders to balance payments against imports of cloth, porcelain and manufactured goods, copper was an important form of coinage in Lisbon itself. In 1550, it was the coin that 'the people use most to buy ordinary things'. But there was not enough of it, and shortages led to problems by 1568, not least the attempt of people to pass off fake copper coins as genuine, which led to further devaluation of the currency. The access to copper in Kongo and Benguela could, therefore, have a clear monetary benefit, increasing imports and stabilizing the currency there.[77]

Beyond this monetary use, there were important military and industrial applications for copper. In the 1620s, it was hoped that the fabled copper of Benguela might help to make artillery to defend Pernambuco in Brazil from the Dutch – who seized it in 1630. In Lima in Peru, in the late 1630s, around about the time when the slave trader Manuel Bautista Pérez was being burned to death by the Inquisition in Lima's Plaza de Armas, a Dutch observer wrote that the best artillery in the world was made there because of the access to good supplies of copper. Meanwhile, most of the equipment used on sugar plantations was made of copper: the vats for boiling the sugarcane, the ladles for scooping it out and the tins in which it was placed to cool.[78]

Thus, while the Portuguese access to copper was often frustrated in West-Central Africa, it speaks to a larger truth about the nature of the exchanges taking place there. These were grounded in the enhancement of economic inequalities, and the desire from the outside to develop greater surpluses in the Americas, by military force, economic power and the industrialization of the sugar economy. The value of currencies in the Atlantic world was increasingly shifting from a shared view both of economic and of religious functions – as revealed by the use of gold in altarpieces and religious reliquaries in the sixteenth and seventeenth centuries – to one in which, for European mercantilist nations, the power of currency as a way to accumulate material value (through capital or industrial growth) predominated.

In both historical documents and historical memory, the place of currency thus became a key pivot on which the interactions of rulers and outsiders in West-Central Africa turned. That this is an important reality emerges in an oral account from Angola that was first noted down in the nineteenth century. On an expedition to Kassanje, the kingdom founded by the 'Jaga' migrants in the seventeenth century, António Rodrigues Neves was the first outsider to hear and describe the oral histories of Kassanje's foundation. This vital oral historical record shows that when, in the 1620s and 1630s, the new Kingdom of Kassanje became an ally of the Portuguese, they did so to drive back the fabled Queen of Matamba, Nzinga. Two of the settlements they passed through were called Quifa-ngondo (meaning 'She lost copper here') and Mujo-aprata (meaning 'She lost silver here'). Many historians have debated the truth of these nineteenth-century oral histories, but the key point is that they show that there was a strong connection in the minds of the rulers of Kassanje between the Portuguese thirst for metals and the wars of the seventeenth century: for it was, indeed, through these wars that the trade in enslaved captives had grown so fast, and Kassanje's power had been cemented.[79]

CONCLUSION: DEVALUATION AND ECONOMIC DECLINE IN KONGO

When the Spanish Capuchin missionary Teruel reached the Court of the manikongo, Garcia II, in 1645, he was greeted with an elaborate gift that included 'around two hundred ducats in the currency of that Kingdom, fifty for each friar, called *cofos* in the language of that country, which are certain measurements of small shells, which are harvested on an Island off the shore of Angola, near the port of Luanda'. However, the leader of the Capuchin mission responded to this gift by saying that they were forbidden from accepting money, and so could not take the *nzimbu*.[80]

While modern economists have sometimes accounted for shell currencies and the like as 'primitive monies', the account of Teruel makes it clear that this was not how outsiders saw it at the time. *Nzimbu* were money for the Portuguese as for the Kongo peoples, so much so that there were exchange rates linking them to the Portuguese *milreis* throughout the early seventeenth century. In 1642, for instance, each captive in Luanda cost 15,000 *milreis*, or 30 *cofos* of *nzimbu*. As this account implies, there were regular measurements of shells: a *funda* was 1,000 shells, a *lufuku* was 10,000 and a *cofo* was 20,000. The shells were fished for by women in Luanda. They were the standard currency in Kongo, in use in the many markets as a heart-shaped means of exchange. Thus, when the Portuguese founded the colonial city of Luanda in 1575, they also did something of crucial importance to the relative economic power of Portugal and West-Central Africa's kingdoms: they seized the source of the money supply.[81]

The importance of this aspect of the Portuguese establishment at Luanda was seen at once. Manikongos kept two governors there to control the *nzimbu* trade and its supply, which the Portuguese wanted to disrupt. Already in the 1550s, the presence of Portuguese traders in Ndongo had led to their trading for *nzimbu* at Luanda as a cheap means of accessing money directly. After the 'Jaga' invasion of Mbanza Kongo in 1568, Portuguese traders were easily able to establish themselves at Luanda, and the access to the money supply quickly made them rich. One of the reasons why Paulo Dias de Novais suggested making his base there in 1575 was precisely the combination of its proximity to the border with Kongo (only 10 miles to the north), and the fact that it was 'the biggest treasury in [Africa] because it is where [*nzimbu*] are fished'. Although Kongo retained a token administrative presence in Luanda for some years after 1575, its power was gone.[82]

The seizure of Luanda was a disaster for Kongo, as the manikongos soon realized. An account of the kingdom under Álvaro II, in 1604, made it abundantly clear that the economic cost was enormous. It describes the basic economic process that was unfolding: on the one hand, the control of the money supply being taken from the manikongos, and, on the other, the economic base of the country being undermined through the flooding of the country with cheap imports in exchange. It was a process that subsequent colonists of Africa would repeat ad nauseam:

> [The Portuguese] have made themselves masters [of Luanda] . . . the fisheries for the *nzimbu* of Congo are located near the town of S. Pablo de Loanda. There, against the [manikongo's] wishes, they sell whatever they like. When his governors, the chiefs of the island, protest, they are beaten and wounded in such a manner that these mines and fisheries are destroyed and unproductive. They take hold of all the money, and give foreign articles in exchange.[83]

Of course, the manikongos were well aware that in order to rectify this state of affairs, they needed somehow to recapture the impetus in Luanda. The Dutch incursions in the 1640s gave them just that opportunity. *Nzimbu* were marked with royal seals, with each *funda* bearing one. And, by 1648, when the Portuguese recaptured Luanda, Kongo had reinstalled royal governors on the island. Kongo remained wedded to the use of *nzimbu*, which was the major currency long into the eighteenth century, but the loss of Luanda heralded the economic decline of the kingdom.[84]

The inflationary pressures following the loss of Luanda were made even worse by the large numbers of the shells now imported by the Portuguese from the Americas. The *nzimbu* came from all over, not only from the Brazilian colonial capital of Salvador, but from the Brazilian province of Ilhéus and from the River Plate in what is now Argentina. And the shells were destined not only for Luanda but also for Benguela to the south, such that by the 1640s it was the most profitable part of the trade there. But, while it was profitable for the European traders, who essentially were able to load up 'free money' in the Americas for West-Central Africa, it was a disaster for the value of the Kongo currency. The inevitable process of inflation followed an oversupply of currency without enough goods to purchase: in 1619, one *cofo* of *nzimbu* fetched only one fifth of the value raised just four years earlier, and the manikongo estimated that the value of his stock of *nzimbu* had been eroded by two thirds.[85]

In the face of this economic assault on Kongo, the diplomatic manoeuvring of successive manikongos makes more sense. As their wealth lost value, Kongo's rulers fought hard to preserve their elite advantages, as elites always do, and switched sides to the Dutch in an effort to maintain them. As he tried to negotiate an alliance with the Dutch in 1623, Pedro II Mkanga Mbemba, the manikongo, wrote to his ambassador in Lisbon to urge lobbying on the kingdom's behalf, describing how the previous Governor of Luanda, João Correia de Sousa, had allied with the Imbangala and with them 'destroyed and ravaged many provinces and killed an infinite number of Christians . . . with many reduced to slavery'. Pedro's successors manoeuvred with the Dutch, and, even after their defeat in 1648, Garcia II continued to welcome enslaved persons who fled to their side in the 1650s in an attempt to reverse the growing power of Luanda. Yet the economic rug had been whipped from under Kongo, and it was powerless to prevent the mass import of currencies, which continued even under its Dutch allies in the 1640s. As the value of the *nzimbu* fell in relation to other currencies, this created further cycles of debt, which could only be paid off through a trade in enslaved persons.[86]

The final economic attack came with the undermining of Kongo's cloth exports. These beautiful woven cloths (known at the time as *cundis*) had long been admired outside Kongo, and constituted Kongo's major export in the first decades of the seventeenth century. Many visitors noted that Kongo did not trade in captives but rather in cloths, 'well woven, and of fine colours', as had been the case long before the Portuguese arrival. The trade in captives was concentrated in Angola, and, as one writer put it in 1620, 'in this kingdom of Congo there is no trade for people, but for cloth', and, by the seventeenth century, many of the *cundis* were woven in Momboares, the richest province in the kingdom.[87]

The move from a trade in enslaved Tyo captives to a trade in cloths

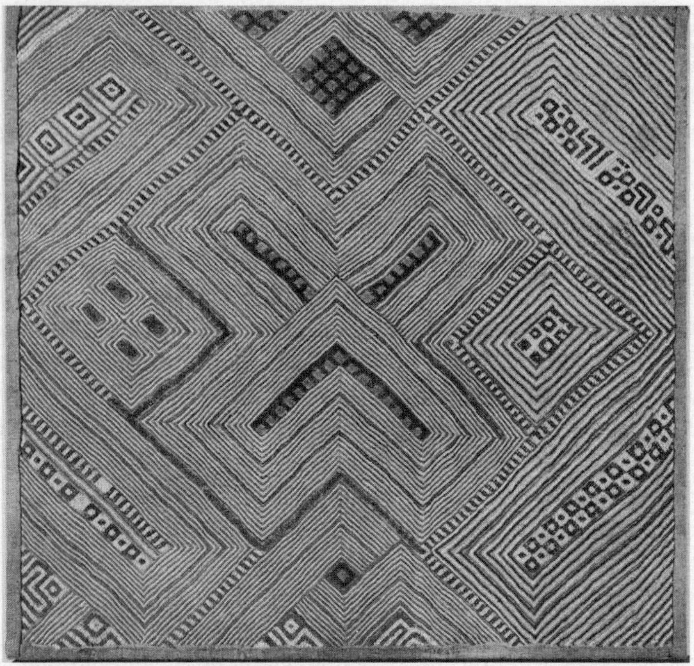

Palm-leaf fibre (raffia) panel, early twentieth century.

suggests that Kongo's rulers had deliberately decided against the former. Indeed, all the evidence points in this direction: the alliance with the Dutch, who at first did not trade for people; the letters of the manikongos, who lamented their predecessors' early trade in people; and the concentration on the cloth trade. All the same, Kongo could not escape the connection to this trade completely, for the Portuguese bought *cundis* only to trade them at Luanda into the slave-trading economy: in the 1610s, more than 90,000 pieces of cloth were being traded annually there. This trade was so important that, by the 1630s, *cundis* had become a form of currency in Ndongo. According to Antonio de Cadornega, writing fifty years later, *cundis* had even been sealed with the royal stamp of Luanda's Municipal Council.[88]

Nevertheless, the arrival of the Dutch trade changed things. The Dutch began to trade in Loango in around 1595, and soon established a trading post to sell Loango cloths known as *libongos* to Luanda, alongside the Portuguese trade in *cundis*. By 1610, the Portuguese were also busily sailing here from Luanda to buy these cloths, which were the common currency in use in Loango. The *libongos* rapidly came to act as a parallel currency in Luanda, adding to the proliferation of cloths that marked the rise of the Dutch trade in the seventeenth century, linking Dutch and Indian cloth producers to West and West-Central Africa.[89]

The result was spiralling devaluation. The supplies of *cundi* dried up, and the value of both *cundis* and *libongos* fell into a decline that was well described by one contemporary account: 'time saw a depreciation in this currency [of *cundis*], since they were not sent as much from Kongo as they used to be (the cloths of Kongo were in short supply and they became less valuable than the *libongos* of Loango) so that they fell into continual attenuation, so much so that the *macuta* of *libongos* was only worth fifty *reais*.'[90] Yet this economic decline in some ways affected the elites most of all. In Kongo, as in so many kingdoms in West Africa, the proliferation of currency which had come with the increase of trade had, indeed, led to economic destabilization. Yet the systemic violence and economic decline produced by the demand for captive persons and minerals to create surplus value also led to the strengthening of new idioms of power and spirituality to comprehend and fight against these processes. As the impacts grew, Kongo cultures asserted themselves in an indigenization of Christianity, and sustained waves of revolt against the *mwissikongo* who had benefited from the new dispensation. The pushback began, and the overthrowing of the old elites in the Kongo Civil War begins the second part of this book. Against economic pressures from outside, BaKongo responded with internal strategies of resistance, in a prefiguring of many of the transformations that West and West-Central Africa would experience in the eighteenth century.

Coda to Part One

The flight from Praia to Sal was full, and I was seated next to a man whose face was lined with the passing of time. Both of us were travelling en route to Europe. It was 2008, and in those days, before the international airport at Praia was completed, flying long distance usually required a change of planes in this smallest and most windswept and desert-like of all the nine inhabited Cape Verde Islands. Sal, like the 'Gold Coast', the 'Ivory Coast', 'Cameroon' and the 'Slave Coast', had been named by the Portuguese according to the resource that it produced, and that was desired: salt. The vast salt pan of Pedra de Lume still scoops out a cavernous mile-wide hollow along the eastern side of the island, where no one lives now.

We flew over the glittering Atlantic, which, I remember, seemed especially beautiful in the afternoon sunlight, azure and gold. As we talked of the reason for my visit, the interviews I had conducted, and of the differences of our lives in Europe, some of the difficulties that come with studying this history surfaced. I was studying history, and this was good, the man said, for it was a reminder of the roots of Cape Verdean identity. Then he said, repeating it for emphasis: what you must understand is that 'We were born in the traffic' (*Nascemos no tráfico*).

Indeed, many of the processes examined in the first part of this book were born in these desert islands. Cape Verde was the first entrepôt for the Atlantic slave trade. Its first city, Ribeira Grande, was the first urban colonial settlement of Europe, the site of the first church in the tropics, and also prompted the first maroons to escape this cruel system. As a report card for historical significance, this seems hard to beat. But, as we have also seen so far, the consequences of these processes did not just relate to the devastations of the institution of slavery itself, but also to the wider framework of economic inequality that was developing between Africa and other parts of the world, of which this Cape Verdean's comments reminded me.

We have by now seen mapped out the seeds of these changes to around the 1680s. The complexity of the different factors driving change in Africa at this time has emerged. There was the importance of long-standing trading networks, grounded in currencies such as cowries in the Sahel, iron and cloth in Senegambia, copper on the Gold Coast and in the Bight of Benin, and *nzimbu* shells in Kongo. These networks brought in outside ideas and religious practices. Islam and cosmological symbols such as the cross travelled between different states, indicating new ideas and plural beliefs. Social and political frameworks grounded in these exchanges placed significant value on the stranger. The stranger was a purveyor of trade goods and riches, and thus to be valued; but the stranger was also a potential source of wealth simply as prey, since enslaved persons were those who tended to be outsiders.

One Mandinga proverb exemplifies this perfectly, with the invocation 'Luntaŋo mu buñaa ta le ti' ('The stranger should be honoured'). The injunction 'they should be' is revealing, for in practice as purveyors of wealth, they not always are. The reality was closer to one of the epigraphs of this book, from Lansiné Diabaté:

The stranger is like a dish, that the host can blow on.	*A ko kolan siman gwɛlidi, jatigil'i fɛla.*[1]

With the rise of Atlantic trade, a complex new set of pressures had emerged in the western part of Africa. There was the pressure to provide captives. The trade in enslaved persons required more surplus food supplies to feed enslaved persons on the Atlantic crossing, which led to new modes of production and also new methods of control over the population. Ecological changes associated with the global mini ice age would bring disease and droughts, exacerbating the pressures on food supplies and the incentive to sell the poor or outsiders. And, at the same time, economic inequalities were augmented, because of the growing imbalances in capital accumulation produced by exchange.

We have seen this pattern of capital inequalities repeatedly through the first half of this book. This repetition is not just the work of a tedious historian (or this tedious historian) bludgeoning the reader with the blunt instrument of 'fact'; nor have I wanted to make economic change seem like a catch-all, somehow separated from the human experiences of change (new patterns and styles of clothing, of adornment, of the taste of food), of war, of artistry and of trauma. But what the repeated finding of capital accumulation can do is suggest a paradigm for examining how the global inequalities with which everyone today is familiar were constructed.

It is worth concluding this first half of the book with a comparison to the kingdoms of Angola, which we have not looked at in depth. For this comparison reveals how generalized this pattern had become across a broad swathe of Africa by the 1680s. Though connected historically and politically to Kongo, these kingdoms were probably beyond the direct influence of the trans-Saharan trading zone before the Atlantic trade. In Ndongo, Libolo and Quissama, any outside contact before 1500 was probably more via the Indian Ocean. Moreover, after the wars of the seventeenth century, the region around Luanda, along with the Cape, would become the only proto-colonial European imperial space in Africa, and remained so until the nineteenth century. Angola, therefore, lies outside the broad scope of this book; but it is much too important to be excluded altogether.[2]

By 1650, the ecological situation in Angola was stark, following the same triggers noted for Allada.* As the population declined and fled owing to the wars of the seventeenth century, the impact of growing numbers of wild animals grew immensely – in striking parallel to what had happened in the New World following the ecological collapse of the Native Americans. Lions roamed the main road linking Luanda with the major Kongo province of Mbamba, and, when the Capuchin Girolamo da Montesarchio made the journey in the late 1650s, he heard that lions had recently eaten ten people. Antonio Cavazzi had an even worse story, claiming that fifty people had been eaten near where he lived in Ndongo in the space of a few days. The Court of Nzinga, Queen of Matamba, was surrounded by a palisade

* See above, Chapter 4.

woven together with palm leaves, and whose trunks were high enough to keep out wild animals; such defences were inadequate in the Kongo province of Pemba to stop wild lions entering the central town of the province and attacking people. The novelty of these happenings is revealed through the astonishment with which they were recounted, suggesting that the balance between people and the environment had changed.[3]

The ecological pressures on Angola were mirrored in the economic pressures. In the seventeenth century, the main currency in use in Luanda were cloths imported from Kongo and Loango. These cloths had various social and practical uses in Luanda, as sails, clothes and sacks, and were widely recognized as the principal currency throughout the first half of the seventeenth century. There were fixed currency rates linking the different cloths, with forty Loango *libongo* cloths being equivalent to 500 Portuguese *reais*, which shows the way in which currency exchange and convertibility existed. However, over the seventeenth century, competing pressures saw huge inflationary pressures on the value of these cloths, which became virtually worthless, and were removed as a currency in 1679.[4]

There were many different causes of this decline in value. One was that both Kongo and Loango cloths stood as parallel currencies in Angola, and the competing values meant that each lost its commercial edge; many different types of Kongo cloth circulated in Luanda, alongside the red cloth traded from Loango, the raffia cloth and the *libongos*. By the 1650s, people had learnt how to falsify them, as they usually will with anything of value. These cloths were less well made, which meant that they frayed easily and lost their value. Inflation followed as surely as it had done in the other parts of West and West-Central Africa, we have already examined. The value of the *macuta* (a bundle of 10 cloths) fell from 500 *reais* in the 1640s to 350, and then to 150 under the governorship of João Fernandes Vieira in the 1650s. By 1673, it was said to be worth no less than 40 *reais* on the street, even though 150 remained the 'official' exchange rate. Demands began to be made by royal officials for the minting of a copper coin, and the value of the *libongo* went into permanent freefall.[5]

The rise and fall of the cloth currency of Luanda in the seventeenth century mirrors much of the historical framework that we have seen in the first half of this book. The *libongo* was an African form of currency, which, as one Portuguese writer noted, originally 'had the value of money' in Loango. It was then taken up by Atlantic traders as a general-use currency, and rose as a parallel currency to Kongo cloth in Luanda, initially owing to Dutch and Portuguese trading, for European traders reaped more profits on the *libongo* than on Kongo cloth. Thus, European economic interest deriving from the accumulation of capital drove competition between Kongo and Loango cloths, which saw the erosion in value and quality of both, as an account of *libongos* disintegrating in three days by the 1670s attests.[6]

Into this situation came the mass imports of cloths from Europe and India. By 1699, when an English ship arrived in Luanda from India with six bundles of cloth consisting of a total of 1,072 pieces of clothing, these were categorized by the Portuguese officials into twenty-four different groups, showing how well known Indian cloth was in Angola by this time. As on the Gold Coast, the Dutch had played an important role here, and, during their occupation of Luanda in the 1640s, they found that the biggest demand in Kongo was for all different types of cloths from Europe and India. They thus imported huge amounts of textiles, including cloth from Rouen and Silesia, and many different types of Indian silk. Whereas cloth manufacture was the major industry in Loango in the 1640s, it thereafter entered a rapid decline, and, by the eighteenth century, trade had shifted to enslaved persons, with Loango becoming one of the major centres on the coast of West-Central Africa.[7]

Yet, at the same time, these changes did not occur for want of skilled manufactures. Just as Sape people in Sierra Leone adapted their *nomolis* and made salt cellars, candlesticks and swords that were traded in Europe, and the Igun Eronmwon casters of Benin made beautiful works of bronze admired to this day, in Kongo there was a candle-making industry, swordsmiths, and people who made pots, jugs and beautiful dark-clay glasses in the 1640s. Yet such local industry was being swamped by the mass import of cheap goods from Asia and Europe. Manufacturing for export declined, along with economic power, and the values of local currencies did not hold their own on a global scale. The combination of the dumping of cheap commodities such as cloth and copper-made basins and pans, and the declining value of currencies, as capital was accumulated elsewhere, led to gathering capital disparities between Africa and the world economy.[8]

Why, then, did the values of local currencies not hold their own in the world economy? One reason was the rise to global power of a worldview that privileged accumulation of surplus value, and the way in which the export both of 'hard' currencies that held their value – gold and copper – and of people whose labour helped to produce it contributed to this growing divergence. As we have seen in the first half of this book, this was a worldview whose predominance in the West gathered pace over time between the middle of the fifteenth century and the end of the seventeenth. But the other side of this picture was the alternative view of value that persisted in many different places. Again, the case of societies from West-Central Africa offer a useful perspective: here, cloth currencies were used beyond their practical descriptions as sails and sacks, in order to wrap bodies for burial, while shells were key symbols of the sacred in Kongo, beyond their monetary use as *nzimbu*; iron and copper manillas were worn by people as symbols of status and social power, and not always melted down into a convertible 'money'; and, meanwhile, one of the currencies that circulated in Angola, the dye known as *takula*, which came from Loango, was used for a variety of ritual purposes, including at weddings and in religious ceremonies.[9]

There was thus a worldview that did not view numerical surplus as a privileged economic value isolated from other forms of social and moral value. But the era of the sixteenth and seventeenth centuries was one in which this outlook was eroded by the gathering winds of globalization. Far from their being 'cut off' and 'isolated' from the world, it was its integration into global systems that triggered the comparative economic decline of Africa. It turned out that free trade did not promote universal economic growth and development; unequal trade hampered production and manufacturing, and triggered economic decline.

Yet these pressures did not somehow destroy or weaken the cultures and peoples who faced them, as the case of Angola shows. It was also during the increasing pressures of the seventeenth century that Angolan captives taken to Brazil drew on their cultural frameworks to embark on the longest and most successful rebellion against slavery until the late eighteenth century, known as the *quilombo* of Palmares. Located inland from Olinda in Pernambuco, the *quilombo* of Palmares lasted throughout the seventeenth century until it was finally put down by a military force in 1694. Palmares drew specifically on a variety of West-Central African social and religious idioms, such as the palm tree and the role of the *nganga*, or spiritual leader. As we saw previously, what may have been most important was the Imbangala practice of welcoming people from different lineages into the community, helping to shape a new Afro-Brazilian world that was created from among so many different peoples and languages.[10]

The *quilombo* offered an intellectual and social model for forging a plural Afro-Brazilian identity in the New World, strengthening and transforming institutions that had emerged originally in Africa. It also offered an institution that could resist the appalling abuses of power enshrined in the imperial systems of the Americas. It would be this nexus, between the increasing centralization and abuse of power on the one hand and uprisings driven from African institutions on the other, that would characterize much of the next century in West and West-Central Africa, and, indeed, beyond.

PART TWO

Consequences

Politics, Belief and Revolutions from Below

Timeline for Part Two: West African Political History, *c.* 1680–1850

1680–1700: A series of wars between the different statelets of the Gold Coast before the Asante Empire rises in the early 1700s

1685–1703: The price of captives rises by as much as 200 per cent across Atlantic Africa, because of increased demand

1690s: Discovery of gold in Minas Gerais (Brazil) changes the emphasis on gold demands on the Gold Coast

1690s: Wars lay waste to Gwatón, Benin's main Atlantic trading post

1690s: Bundu founded by the cleric Malik Sy in the wake of the wars led by Nasir al-Din in the Senegal River Valley

c. 1695: Rise to power of Asante Empire based in Kumasi

1704: Beatriz Kimpa Vita leads the Antonine movement of religious renewal in Kongo

1709: A weaker Kongo is reunited under Pedro IV

c. 1712: Rise of the Kingdom of Segu under Biton Kulubali

1724–7: Dahomey defeats Hueda on the coast and becomes the major political force in the region of 'the Slave Coast'

1727–8: Fula migrants from Fuuta Tòòro found the Almamate of Fuuta Jaalo in what is now Guinea-Conakry under Karamoko Alfa

1730: Oyo begins to attack Dahomey

1730s: Katsina overtakes Kano as commercial hub of Hausaland (northern Nigeria); muskets begin to be imported to Hausa states from the south

1740s: Terrible drought in West Africa

1740s: Rise of communities of escaped slaves in Angola, known as *quilombos*

1740s–1770s: Rise and expansion of the Salafiya reform movement in Arabia

1747: Peace signed between Dahomey and Oyo in which Dahomey agrees to be tributary

1747–71: Reign of Babba Zaki in Kano, which sees expansion of cavalry and state power

1750: Dahomey sends an ambassador to the port of Salvador in Brazil

1754: Seizure of power in Oyo by the basorun (leader of the Oyo-Mesi), Gaha

1758, 1771: Tuareg raids on Timbuktu

1766: Rise of the Jara-Ngolosi Dynasty in Segu, after ten years of civil war following the demise of the Kulubalis; they retain power until 1861

1774: Civil war in Oyo as Gaha refuses to cede power; he is eventually replaced by a new alafin, Abiodun

1776: Fall of the Denyaanke Dynasty of Fuuta Tòòro (Senegal River Valley), which has ruled since the 1510s; it is replaced by a theocracy led by the scholar Ceerno Suleyman Baal, and then by his successor, Abdul Qader

1780s: Maria Theresa silver *thaler* begins to flood into West Africa

1785: Attempted rebellion of slaves against the Fula theocracy of Fuuta Jaalo

1788: Following the establishment and growth of a large scholarly community at Degel in Hausaland, the King of Gobir attempts to assassinate its leader, Uthmān dan Fodio, known as the shehu; the failure of the Gobir King presages the rise of the Fulani *jihād*

1790: The civil wars of Oyo have weakened it to such an extent that it has to pay tribute to Nupe

1791–1804: Haitian Revolution, concluding with the declaration of Haiti's independence on 1 January 1804

1792: Freetown founded

1795: Rise of maroon community outside Freetown, consisting of escaped captives from Freetown and escaped failed rebels from Timbo, capital of Fuuta Jaalo

1795: Substitution of *annulus* cowrie for old *moneta* cowrie on the Niger Bend

1795–1818: Dahomey engages in concerted diplomacy with Brazil and Portugal, sending four embassies; Allada sends an embassy in 1809; and Onim (Lagos) three, through to 1823

1801: Danish abolition of trans-Atlantic slave trade

1801: Ascension to the throne of Gobir of a new king, Yunfa, who drives confrontation with the followers of Uthmān dan Fodio

1804–8: War between Gobir and the followers of the shehu sees the rise of the Fulani *jihād* in northern Nigeria. Kano falls in 1807, and the rebels have subdued the Hausa kingdoms by 1808

1807: Act for the Abolition of the Slave Trade passed by the British Parliament

1808: Free maroons from Jamaica found the St John's Maroon Church in Freetown, Sierra Leone

1808–12: Wars fought between Sokoto and Borno, following the success of the Fulani *jihād*

1817: Death of the shehu in Sokoto

1817: Insurgent rebellion led by an Oyo military leader, Afonja, precipitates collapse of the Oyo Empire

1820: Rise of theocratic rule in Borno under Al-Kanemi, eclipsing the mais

1830s–50s: Soninké–Marabout Wars north and south of the Gambia River see the overthrow of existing kingdoms by the marabout class and their followers

1835: Malé rebellion in Salvador, Brazil, inspired by the revolutions in West Africa

1835: Fall of the Oyo Empire

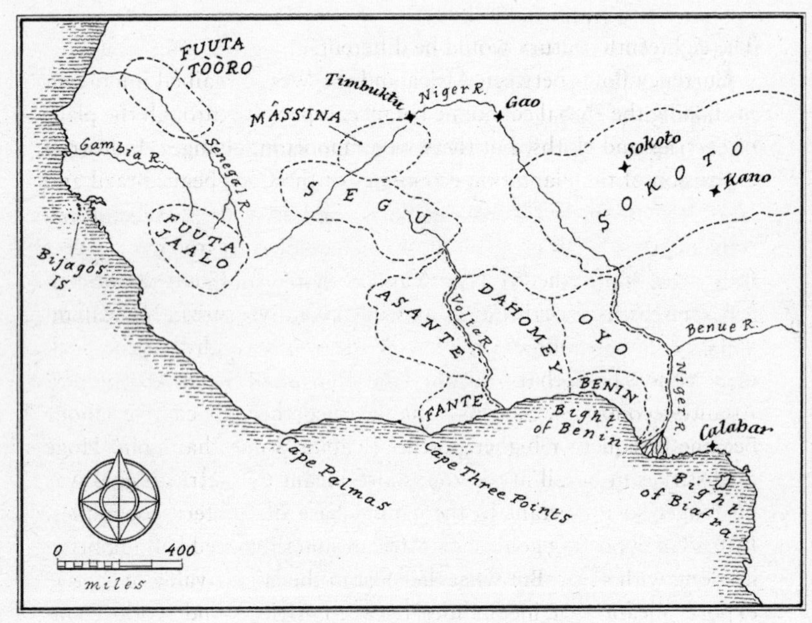

West African kingdoms, *c.* 1600–1900

Prologue to Part Two

The eighteenth century would be different.

Currency flows between Africa and the West remained important in shaping the global economic balance, especially through the place of cowries and cloths, but there were important changes. Industrial expansion of the plantation economies of the Caribbean, Brazil and North America saw the peak of the trans-Atlantic trade in captives, transported both by chartered European companies (the Dutch West Indian Company, the Royal African Company, the Compagnie Française des Indes Occidentales) and by private ventures. The capital value of slave labour in the New World was so high that the peak of demand saw a change in the relationships between African and Atlantic economies. Surplus value accrued through captive labour became of equal or higher potential capital value than coin. Huge gold strikes in Brazil in the 1690s also meant that African gold was no longer so important to the capital base of Western economies. Instead of exporting gold, some African states retained and imported it, along with silver. But what they lost in the labour value of captive exports meant that inequalities between African and world economies still grew.[1]

The switch in currency transactions was marked. Akan kingdoms on the Gold Coast switched to the sale of captives through Asante, which retained gold. Dahomey imported gold smuggled from Brazil, while Senegambian kingdoms brought in Mexican silver. Other currency imports (iron bars, copper) were substituted in many parts of Africa by the import of manufactured goods, alcohol and weapons. However, cowrie imports grew, with their exchange value inextricably tied to the worth of exported captives.

Thus, in Africa, exchanges of capital value by the eighteenth century were largely reduced to the value of the captive. They had become predicated upon the programmatic cruelty of the plantation, the subterranean mine and the logic of the market.

Power in both Africa and beyond became loaded with paradox. For European empires, the extraction of surplus value depended on dehumanizing captives, 'branding them' into marks of commercial value – and yet relying on their humanity and intelligence to bring skills in farming, smithing and healing to the plantation and make them successful. In Africa, power was ever more centralized in the hands of the ruler – but with this centralized power came new social structures that soon critiqued abuses of authority. The division between rulers and subjects, state and society, grew in a manner that hindsight makes seem irrevocable. In his seminal 1972 book *How Europe Underdeveloped Africa*, Walter Rodney saw the move to decolonization in the 1950s as spawned by the contradictions of the colonial system in Africa; two centuries earlier, analogous paradoxes and contradictions would spearhead the overthrow of the warrior aristocracies that had grown up in Africa with the Atlantic and Saharan slave trades.[2]

The example of the Gold Coast can best introduce these changes. The unforgiving surf of the beaches between Axim in the West and the Volta River in the east saw the focus shift from the gold trade to captives, who had to be rowed out to the prison-ships across the perilous breakers. Boats often overturned in the process.

Inland, the craftsmanship behind the Akan gold weights remained as powerful in the eighteenth as in the sixteenth and seventeenth centuries. Gold was a currency in Asante, and gold-dust transactions were a powerful part of daily life in the eighteenth century. But the castle-prisons built along the Atlantic coast had become sites of misery. They were the termini for the coffles of captives marching coastwards, and for the shiploads of captives purchased at Ouidah by local agents awaiting transport. Here people lay in chains enslaved for debts or crimes, or as war captives of military expeditions sent by Asante and Dahomey to crush their neighbours.

The most important English castle on the coast was at Cape Coast, just a few miles from Elmina.

Cape Coast castle. The cannons to the left sit on top of the dungeon walkway along which captives marched to the lighters that carried them to sea. The mid-sized building with tiled roof to the centre right is the chapel, which was sited above the dungeon for enslaved persons.

The Dutchman Bosman described in *c.* 1700 how Cape Coast was sited at the town of Ooegwa. It was 'furnished with fine and well-built Dwelling-places; before it they have also built a high Turret . . . The Fort is strengthened with four very large Batteries, besides a fifth; on which are planted thirteen Pieces of heavy Cannon.' The cannon could protect English interests from foreign interlopers arriving by sea, and attacks by rival Akan and Fante groups on shore. Slaves were responsible for the daily running of the castle, as they were for the houses of the English allies, such as some mixed-race agents like Edward Barter, who had their own private militias.[3]

English visitors to Cape Coast through the eighteenth century, such as William Smith, who visited in 1726, admired its 'beautiful spacious neat Apartments and Offices, particularly on the Southside a large well built Chapple'. There were verdant gardens 'being near Eight Miles in Circumference . . . They are very fertile, and produce every Thing that grows within the *Torrid Zone*: Such as, Oranges, Lemons, Limes, Citrons, Guavas, Papaws, Plantanse, Bonanas, Cocoa-Nuts, Cinnamon, Tamarinds, Pine-Apples.' The castle was well defended, and could protect English interests. It enshrined a sense of power, which may have been why English visitors saw it as beautiful.[4]

Yet, beyond the flowery prose, the realities were grim; reproducing these external accounts alone is to reproduce a fantasy that was deliberately designed to conceal the truth. This is one of the reasons why the style and structure of this second part of the book are different from those of the first.

Cape Coast was not beautiful. It was the ultimate site for the acting out of the ugliest side of human nature – a place for the brutal exercise of male power. The English officers had multiple mistresses, taken from among their slaves, throwing those who refused into the 'punishment cell'. They were routinely 'punch-drunk' on imported Brazilian rum, sugar, water and limes (an early form of the Brazilian *caipirinha* and Cuban *mojito* cocktails). They presided over a regime of violence, their chapel and beautiful apartments sited above the foetid and grim realities of the slave dungeons, which housed 200 people at a time on a floor awash with their own excrement, vomit and death. Those who survived their imprisonment were marched along a tenebrous basement corridor lit by torches, counted through by spyholes to make sure that no money was lost, despatched through the 'door of no return' and taken in lighters over the dangerous surf to the ships resting in the road of the castle, which would carry people chained to the New World – the lights of the ships bobbing by night, just as today the oil tankers do along the coast by Lomé, in Togo.

These realities of the many European slave-forts were not for 'public consumption' in the colonial capitals of London, Lisbon, Amsterdam and Paris. They appear not to have been discussed in 'polite society'. They were rarely written about in the many travel books on the region, which, of course, were calculated to appeal to the market, such as it was, in eighteenth-century sensibility. The violence that underwrote the expansion and accumulation of capital was hidden from European public view; but, in West Africa, it was in plain sight and remains so in view of the castle-prisons, and the memorial at the small town of Assin Manso, around 30 miles from the coast, which was the last stopping point for captives on their march to the coast.

The English regime at Cape Coast castle was one of power and

The site of Assin Manso and the memorial to the last bath taken by captives marched to the coast.

fear. Yet the English were also dependent on the people of the town of Ooegwa. English agents would travel by sea with their interpreters from Ooegwa to Ouidah, where they bought captives from the kings of Hueda – and, after the 1720s, from Dahomey. The captives were then brought back to Cape Coast, where they were kept in the castle dungeons, piled on top of one another, a thousand at a time, alongside those who had been sold by intermediaries from Asante and marched down to the coast. They were branded with the mark of their owners, after the commodification of their bodies had been completed. After some time in the dungeons, these enslaved persons were taken through the 'door of no return'.[5]

The industrialization of this calculated programme to dehumanize human beings in the eighteenth century is one of the more significant episodes in human history. Its consequences in the Americas and Europe are, perhaps, well known; but its consequences in Africa are less so, and that is the focus of the second part of this book. As Africa globalized into the world, the world globalized into Africa. As increasingly authoritarian West African leaders profited from the Atlantic trade, they became ever more distant from their subjects in social and political terms. At the same time, their religious shrines became associated by some with the cruelty and corruption of the existing system, opening the door to the greater influence of, first, Islam, and then – in the nineteenth century – Christianity.

The eighteenth century in Africa reveals one long period of struggle against the new political and religious power associated with the slave trade, which, in many places, was eventually overthrown. Yet successful revolutions do not always succeed in implementing restorative justice. In nineteenth-century West and West-Central Africa, one type of inequality was replaced by another, as gender imbalances grew and new systems of captive labour were introduced to meet the needs of the 'legitimate' trade in tropical produce for European factories: palm oil, groundnuts and the like.

This part of the book looks at the cumulative nature of this process. So complex was it, across so many different states and kingdoms, that it does not proceed chronologically. Instead the chapters examine each of the different themes – the commercialization of people (Chapter 6); the centralization of power (Chapter 7); the impact on society and religious belief (Chapter 8); and the transnational forces (Chapter 9) – that, combined, drove the revolutions that are examined in the last two chapters of the book. In fact, this cumulative process was something that had already been foreshadowed in West-Central Africa at the end of the seventeenth century. Here, the forces of the slave trade and global power had shaped resentment and resistance from such an early time that they coalesced by the 1680s in a period of revolutionary change. The collapse of the Kingdom of Kongo after the Battle of Mbwila in 1665 had offered a foretaste of things to come in West Africa.

PRELUDE TO THE EIGHTEENTH CENTURY: INEQUALITIES, RESISTANCE AND THE COLLAPSE OF OLD KONGO

Throughout the first half of the seventeenth century, the Kingdom of Kongo held a little known but pivotal place in the relationship of economic value and global inequality that was traced in the first part of this book. The wars fought there by the Dutch, the Portuguese and their West-Central African allies in the 1640s were not only over access to the slave trade. They also related to the region's role in providing surplus: surplus agricultural production, which fed value growth outside Africa, and the surplus value provided by the global currency trade.

European slave traders continually relied on African agriculture. Without African provisions, it was impossible to sail across the Atlantic. After seizing São Tomé in 1641, the Dutch outpost there always took inventories of provisions on ships, to make sure there was enough food before despatching them across the Atlantic. But often there wasn't. In 1648, their captain in São Tomé spoke of the difficulties of provisioning the ship the *Noorthollandt*, which spent at least two months trying to procure flour; with 270 captives, there was not enough food for them to make the crossing, in spite of carrying 9,800 pieces of ship's biscuit, 600 *alqueires** of flour, 6,300 pounds of meat, 3 vats of butter and over 3,000 pipes of wine.[6]

For the Dutch, the inability to procure enough food influenced their failure to take over the slave trade between West-Central Africa and Brazil. Their officers repeatedly complained of the lack of provisions, and, by 1642, war and drought meant that no provisions were to be had within 50 leagues (about 150 miles) of Luanda. The Dutch lacked the means and labour to start their own manioc plantations, they did not have the necessary local contacts to gain access to food supplies and their ships frequently had to wait for months to find enough food to cross the Atlantic. By 1643, there was a real fear of famine. Repeated complaints about the failure to gain access to provisions continued until the Portuguese retook the city in 1648.[7]

The role of provisions produced in West-Central Africa confirms the place that the Atlantic trade had in relations of value (as surplus agricultural products were exported), and its impact in Kongo. Moreover, relations of value were compounded, since in West-Central Africa the rise in the trade in enslaved persons went with a silver trade from the Americas to China. While large numbers of captives were shipped to the Americas, this was 'paid for' illegally by contraband

* At this time, each *alqueire* was equivalent to the volume of approximately 13 litres of grain.

silver. The silver came from Potosí in what is now Bolivia, via Buenos Aires, and was then shipped via Luanda as ballast on the slave ships, thence to Asia to enter the Chinese economy. The relationship between silver and the trade in enslaved persons is vital: the resentments created by the latter were tied umbilically to the profits generated by the former.[8]

By 1600, slave ships already sailed regularly from Luanda to Buenos Aires. Spanish officials protested that this was a means of hiving off silver into the Portuguese Empire. Silver was continually moving from the Portuguese trading posts in Angola around the colony at this time, said one report; and the Portuguese governor of 1625 mentioned using silver to trade with the Dutch at Loango. The place of silver in 'cashing out' the profits of the trade in captives was clear in one 1623 document, which show taxes on the trade from Angola being paid by ships from Buenos Aires in bars of silver. At the height of silver production, in the early 1600s, the volume of silver that left via Angola in this way can be gauged by the eighteen ships that came under the contract to Buenos Aires in 1603, of which fifteen were registered in Angola.[9]

This trade was important to the wider process described in this book in several respects. Silver remained the principal item traded from Europe to Asia until the collapse of the Ming Empire in 1640. Up to this point, silver had been worth considerably more in China than it had in Europe, and by shipping it there European traders were able to extract surplus value through arbitrage (i.e. buying something cheaply in one place and selling it for a big mark-up somewhere else). Moreover, the exchange of silver for enslaved persons constituted a drain on the economic potential of West and West-Central African economies. Thus, this trade accelerated global inequalities in capital, and increased the political instability that ate away at the power of the Kongo Kingdom.[10]

This delicate balance was then decisively worsened after the Dutch lost Luanda and São Tomé to the Portuguese in 1648. At the same time, the profits generated by the silver trade had collapsed, as the profits gained in China all but disappeared as the price of silver there fell. The governors of Luanda who followed its recapture, João Fernandes Vieira and André Vidal de Negreiros, had both been leaders in the wars against the Dutch in Brazil. They brought a violent militarism to the relationship with Kongo. It was this that triggered the final confrontation between Kongo forces under António I, the manikongo, and the Portuguese at the Battle of Mbwila in 1665. The aftermath of António's death (and that of many of his key courtiers) in this conflict precipitated a revolt of Kongo peoples against their ruling elite.[11]

As is becoming familiar in this book, this conflict was not simply mobilized through access to European weapons and military strategies. Crucial to it was the spread of a healing society called the Kimpasi, whose growth had already been concerning to the Kongo elite before Mbwila. The Kimpasi was a secret society that exemplified the changes that had come to Kongo. It aimed to help a community or a group of communities that had been afflicted by devastating problems. Those entering the Kimpasi were reborn with a new identity after passing through a process of ritual death, symbolic of the death throes of old Kongo society. The Kongo elite had tried to stall its growth, but, in the aftermath of Mbwila, its significance grew again, channelling the destructive energies unleashed by decades of warfare, slavery and predation by the Kongo elite.[12]

Six years after the Battle of Mbwila, Francisco de Távora, the Portuguese governor of Angola, wrote a long description of the consequences. 'The state of Kongo is such,' he wrote, 'that if help is not offered swiftly, so many new Kings will be introduced into it, that they will be as many as the quantity of subjects which live there.' Following the defeat at Mbwila, the maninsoyo had invaded Mbanza Kongo from Mpinda, in an attempt to install his own candidate as manikongo. This led to the destruction of churches, the profaning of images and widespread attacks on Portuguese settlers and on priests.[13]

The context was stark. As Távora described it: 'With these disruptions, and wars which are less than civil, roads are blocked, business is dwindling, the *pombeiro* traders are becoming desperate, and I have such little news of the white men who live in those provinces, that I almost consider them to be limbs which have broken away from this body.'[14] The civil wars that followed signalled the unravelling of the old Kongo Kingdom, and Portugal's definitive early colonial settlement in Angola. The Portuguese overthrew the maninsoyo who had invaded Mbanza Kongo and installed a puppet; in 1671 they also defeated the army of Aidi, the Ngola of Ndongo, at Pungo Andongo (a redoubt known as 'the 'Stones'). After this, they were in command of the Kwanza River Valley. In spite of Portuguese power in Ndongo, the invaders had no power whatsoever in Kongo itself, where Mbanza Kongo was said to be 'totally ruined and depopulated' by 1684.[15]

What caused these civil wars, and how were they related to the overthrow of elites driven by resentments brought on by the Atlantic trade? On one hand, these civil disputes were between the two major lineages that ruled Kongo: the Kimpanzu and the Kinlaza. In 1704, a Kongo princess, Beatriz 'Kimpa Vita', would lead a movement against the relentless greed characterizing the trade in captives. This religious uprising paved the way for the eventual return of peace to Kongo, with Pedro IV (*c.* 1696–1718) brokering a truce between the Kimpanzu and the Kinlaza in 1709 that would see their lineages alternate the title of *manikongo*, and the reoccupation of Mbanza Kongo, which had been almost in ruins for several decades. The second half of the eighteenth century would be a time of relatively long and stable reigns by the manikongos.

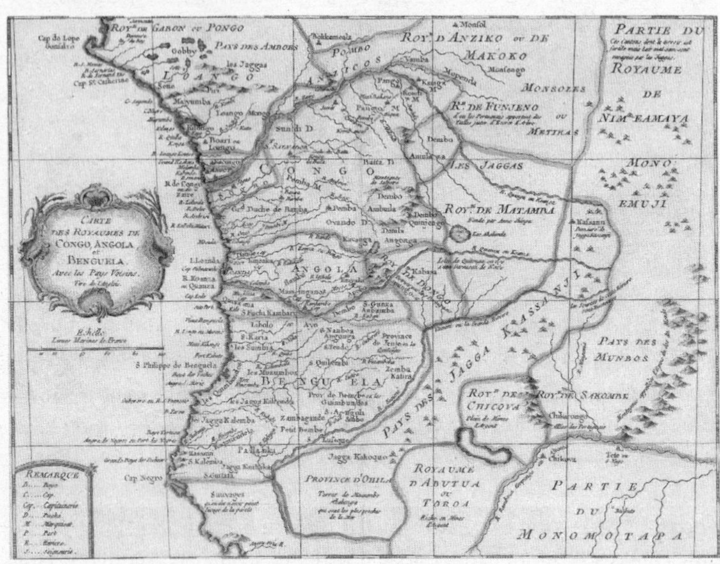

Map of Congo, Angola and Benguela by Jacques Bellin, 1754.

Yet, by then, the kingdom was a shadow of its former self, and many of the provinces had seceded or were de facto independent.[16]

Yet why did this civil war gain ground in the first place? Here, the resentment caused by the corruption of ruling elites takes centre stage, allied to the collapse of the nobility at Mbwila and the place of international forces in disrupting Kongo. This is the first of many cases we will see in this second half of the book in which people overthrew unpopular rulers, whose unpopularity stemmed exactly from their role in the Atlantic trade.

There was in the first place an irreconcilable structural tension in the kingdom, well described by one historian as being that of the 'lineage against the state'. On the one hand lay the old Kongo lineage system of inheritance and kinship, used to build alliances and family structures; and on the other stood the centralized administration that had arisen in Mbanza Kongo since the onset of the Atlantic trade, which was at odds with this. It was impossible for the old system to retain its strength in the face of state power, and yet the lineage system offered opportunities for alliance building and rebellion that could be used against the state. There was an inherent tendency for division. Tensions had, therefore, been simmering in Kongo for many years. Before Mbwila, the previous manikongo, Garcia II, had arrested important members of the nobility in 1657, including several relatives of the *mani* of Pemba. Many claimed that these lords were the rightful heirs to the throne, and thus tensions were high, as the manipemba and his allies withdrew to Nsoyo and plotted Garcia's overthrow.[17]

With this internal contradiction eating away at the power of the Kongo nobility, the flower of the *mwissikongo* nobility was then destroyed at Mbwila. An account by the Portuguese military commanders who had marched from Angola described how the manikongo, António I, had arrived at Mbwila with an impressive retinue, carrying many trunks filled with precious cloths woven in Kongo, as well as Indian silk and damask, and two cases filled with jewels. He was also accompanied, they noted, by 'his leading nobles, of whom 98 [lineage heads] died . . . along with another 400 lords of the minor nobility'.[18]

In other words, the fierce battles between rival lineages that followed Mbwila were the result of an enormous power vacuum created by the decimation of the Kongo nobility. It should be remembered that people in Kongo already inhabited a kingdom in which revolution against predatory aristocrats had become the norm. As we saw in Chapter 5, the invasion of Mbanza Kongo in 1568 and the rise of the Imbangala warriors by 1600 can both be seen as popular movements against the aristocracy. The lineage structure of Kongo favoured these movements of resistance. After Mbwila, angered by decades of civil conflict and slaving wars on the one hand, and by an elite that gathered chests of fine clothes and jewels such as those described here on the other, rival kinship groups turned inwards.

Into this conflict were pitched the transnational influences and tensions that were also at play, and stemmed from the military build-up in Kongo. The defeat of the Dutch allies of Kongo in 1648 had shown how Kongo's fate had become inextricably bound up with colonial projects in Brazil. Further geopolitical tensions followed. Between 1640 and 1668 Portugal fought a long independence war from Spain, and as a result barred Spanish ships from many of its ports. The exception, however, was Luanda, since the Portuguese remained keen to access Spanish silver and they continued to allow payments for enslaved persons in Luanda with silver from Buenos Aires throughout the 1650s. The Spanish Empire in the Americas, meanwhile, faced a crisis of African labour during its war with the Portuguese, and was desperate to secure supplies of enslaved persons. Hearing a rumour that this was going to lead to a Spanish invasion of Luanda, in May 1664, the Portuguese governor of Bahia in Brazil sent three platoons of infantry to Luanda as a defence; and, when the invasion never took place, the governors of Angola used these troops to launch their offensive against Kongo at Mbwila.[19]

Thus, the intersection of global geopolitical rivalries linked to the silver trade and the crushing of the Kongo nobility triggered the rise of the civil wars, which destroyed the old kingdom because of the resentments that this had generated. Many more soldiers were mobilized, and warfare became a generalized condition. Different lineages seized control of different *mbanzas*, and the central power of Kongo fractured. It took until 1690 for a truce to be signed between Nsoyo and Portugal, and it was not until 1709 that Kongo was re-united again under Pedro IV.[20]

What emerged in the eighteenth century from the collapse of Old

Kongo into fragmented provinces? Instead of stemming the injustices of the trade, the consequent discord meant that in the intervening years a series of minor conflicts between different lineage heads saw an ever greater number of captives seized for sale into the Atlantic trade. Over 2 million persons from West-Central Africa were enslaved and shipped across the Atlantic in the eighteenth century, almost twice the number taken from any comparable region, and a good proportion of them emerged from the conflicts in Kongo. A process of social fragmentation was triggered that continued for many centuries, as the number of core clans in the old kingdom proliferated.[21]

It would be wrong to suggest that the consequences in Kongo were universally negative. Kongo art blossomed in the eighteenth century, and it was during this period that Jesus began to be represented as an African in Kongo crucifixes and religious art. Nevertheless, a difficult pattern had set in. The impact of Kongo's fragmentation was widespread. North of the Congo River, Loango went from having been a major producer of cloths and an exporter of copper in the seventeenth century to one of the most important traders in captives in the eighteenth. As one observer put it in the 1770s of Loango, 'many small kingdoms or sovereign states share today [this part of Africa] and were originally dependent provinces of other kingdoms. Local governors then usurped sovereignty. It is not long past since Nsoyo ceased to be a province of the Kingdom of Congo.' With the fragmentation into many smaller states, warfare for captives was a constant risk, so towns were built to make a quick escape very difficult, as occurred in many parts of the continent: each town 'is a real labyrinth, from which a stranger will not manage to find their way out'.[22]

Beyond Kongo's southern border, the impacts were also many. Some distance south of Luanda, the port of Benguela became important in the trade in captives to Brazil. In the nearby region, small states such as Kakonda and Viye rose and then collapsed completely. Near Kakonda, to the north of Benguela, the local ruler, or *soba*, was powerful, and defeated a Portuguese force in 1687, slitting the throat of the Portuguese captain-general. A larger army was sent in 1688, and found the *soba* in a well-defended spot, with three stone stockades and deep ditches; the Portuguese defeated him largely by seizing his cattle, and the *soba* then died in Luanda in 1690. A Portuguese fortress was built in Kakonda, and, by the eighteenth century, the old kingdom had disappeared from the historical record.[23] Yet while Kakonda and other kingdoms like it were destroyed, in Benguela today the ruins of the pier from which countless slave ships departed for the Americas still poke out eerily above the sea.

What followed the fragmentation of the old Kongo Kingdom was not, therefore, some form of static structure, in which Africa was 'outside history', or in which identities were ossified into unchanging 'tribes'. The only unchanging element was the external perception of Africa. Instead, new identities were created following the overthrow of the old aristocracies. In Kongo, the number of clans proliferated, as Kimpasi societies grew in importance as a way of responding to the enormity of the social changes. In the region around Benguela, meanwhile, a changing identity coalesced around the idea of an Ovimbundu 'ethnicity'.[24]

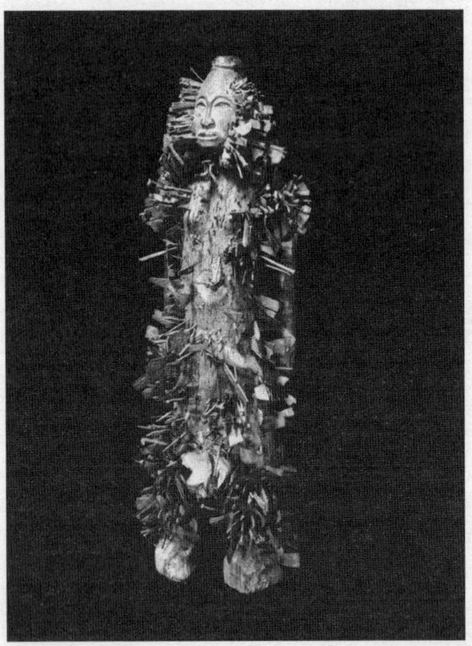

Nkisi power figure from nineteenth-century Kongo.

Thus, the overthrow of the old aristocracies led to radical transformations in identities, and in alliances. The power of the transformative changes accumulated through the eighteenth century, to burst out in the extraordinary Kongo 'power sculptures' of the nineteenth, which reproduced the violence and frenetic social reconstruction of this era as powerfully as any historical text could ever do.

In these multiple contexts, Kongo stands as an early example of a frequent pattern we shall now see in the histories of West and West-Central Africa. By the 1670s, the overreaching of an aristocracy had fomented revolt. When the dust settled by the eighteenth century, the consequences of the overthrow would have been impossible to imagine when the process began.

6

'With Boots Worth 3 Slaves': Slavery and Value in the Eighteenth Century

In 1731, Ayuba Suleiman Diallo, a minor noble from the small state of Bundu in the Upper Senegal Valley, was captured on a visit to the Gambia River and sold into the Atlantic slave trade. However, Diallo was not a member of the growing Senegambian underclass. Once enslaved in the English colony of Maryland, his owner befriended him and began to see a different side to the captive. Diallo wrote a letter back to his family in Senegambia, and in an amazing find in the British Library in 2015 this letter was located. Written by Diallo to his father and addressed in English, French and Arabic, it named thirty-two individuals of status in Senegambia to confirm his identity. These impressive connections were all to Diallo's advantage, and he was returned to his homeland; after arriving, he became an agent for the Royal African Company in Senegambia, where he tried to promote the gum trade until his death in 1773, forty-two years after his initial enslavement.[1]

Known to the English as 'Job Ben Solomon', Diallo was presented at the Court in London in 1733. An account of his return to Senegambia was later published by the English trader Francis Moore, and the case has since become famous to historians. During the return voyage to Senegambia, Moore got to know Diallo well, and learnt from him the details of his capture. Diallo had gone from Bundu to one of the trading posts on the Gambia River in order to sell two captives and buy some paper. Paper was an important commodity among the Islamic communities of Senegambia, for knowledge of the Qur'ān protected against enslavement. Indeed, as Diallo described it to Moore, 'Among other institutions [there], one was, that no person who flies thither for protection shall be made a slave. This privilege is

Portrait of Ayuba Suleiman Diallo, called Job ben Solomon (1701–73).

in force there to this day, and is extended to all in general, that can read and know God, as they express it; and it has contributed much to the peopling of the place, which is now very large and flourishing.'[2]

Thus, knowledge of Islam was becoming a form of self-defence against the trade in enslaved persons. The protection that it was seen to offer was encouraging people to move to Bundu, helping it to grow. For those who were Muslim or were prepared to convert, as Islamic kingdoms grew across West Africa, they offered something of a haven, at least as far as the trans-Atlantic trade was concerned. By the end of the eighteenth century, Islamic states sold fewer captives to European traders than kingdoms such as Dahomey and Loango, where African religions were practised. Yet this, too, reveals the paradox of power in West Africa by this time, for Islam and slavery were by no means incompatible. Religious dogma of all stripes often justifies oppression of others; Islamic states in West Africa raided their neighbours on the justification of their being infidels, and large numbers of slaves would work plantations of cotton and dyeing pits in the Caliphate of Sokoto in northern Nigeria in the nineteenth century.[3]

On arriving at the Gambia River in 1731, Diallo had concluded his trade and begun to return home. Moore picks up the story:

> As he was returning home, he stopped for some refreshment at the house of an old acquaintance; and the weather being hot, he hung up his arms in the house, while he refreshed himself. Those arms were very valuable; consisting of a gold-hilted sword, a gold knife, which they wear by their side, and a rich quiver of arrows . . . It happened that a company of Mandingos, who live by plunder, passing by at that time, and observing him unarmed, rushed in, to the number of seven or eight at once, at a back door, and pinioned [Diallo], before he could get to his arms, together with his interpreter, who is a slave in Maryland still.[4]

Diallo, of course, was one of the very few lucky ones, someone who was freed early from captivity and was able to return from America to his homeland. There are very few such accounts of the actual reality of capture for the trade in enslaved persons. But those accounts such as Diallo's as do exist clarify a number of key factors of what had occurred by the eighteenth century: that the slave trade was absolutely integrated into daily life and commercial exchange across West Africa; that it was accompanied by serial violence; and that this was a world of migration and insecurity, as evidenced here by the account of roving bands of marauding 'Mandingo' raiders, and by the number of people who, Diallo said, were moving to Bundu for protection.

Moreover, the value of the trade in enslaved persons was such that, as this chapter discusses, they had become the ultimate store of monetized 'value' in a system where people had themselves become currency. Since this process began at the very inception of the trade, this chapter offers a bridge between the time periods of the two parts of the book, looking first at these early developments and then considering their consequences in the eighteenth century. With several periods of prolonged drought in the mid eighteenth century, and the cycle of economic demand growing year on year, incentives to capture people were not in short supply. As people were taken in wars between neighbouring states, taken hostage for debts, kidnapped in raids or legally enslaved for crimes against increasingly authoritarian states, captives in West Africa became part of the world economic system that led to the accrual of capital beyond. This was how enslaved persons became money.

This shows the importance of understanding the relationship between slavery and the accumulation of capital in the West. Lasting revolutions require coherent ideologies to see through change, and the financial revolution of the eighteenth century was no different. Enormous ideological reconfigurations were required both in Africa and in the West by the dehumanization on which the trans-Atlantic trade depended, reconfigurations that today are taken as read. Yet, before looking at this in detail, it is important to understand at least some of the contexts involved in the study of Atlantic slavery.

THE PROBLEM OF SLAVERY IN AFRICAN HISTORY

Ever since the Abolition debates around 1800, there has been a strong tendency in Western nations to associate African history reductively with slavery. These debates began at the height of the trade in African captives, as the industrialization of plantations in Brazil and the Caribbean meant that the late eighteenth century saw the most intensive slave trade from Africa. The debates saw pro-slavery activists argue that this intensive slave trade 'rescued' Africans from the wars and discord of their home countries and set them on the path to civilization; and against them were the Abolitionists, who argued that it was this accelerating slave trade that had set West African societies on the path to the political turmoil that they faced in the 1780s and 1790s.

The colonial era saw the continuation of this reductive association between Africa and slavery. The 1884–5 Berlin Conference is famous as the meeting in which the partition of Africa began. However, it was at the 1890 Brussels Conference that the moral justification for the colonial project was laid down as being the determination to 'end slavery', just as it had been publicized by missionaries such as David

Livingstone in his campaigning texts of the 1860s. Slavery, it was argued, without any apparent sense of irony, could be ended in Africa only with the trusteeship of the different territories being passed over to European powers.

Thus, ever since the 1780s, the history of Africa in Western discourse either has been dismissed as non-existent ('Africa has no history') or has been associated more or less exclusively with slavery. There is little scope in this frame to allow for sustained discussions of art, music or poetry; or to consider, for instance, the changes in religious lives and practice through which all these historical convulsions were experienced. The focus on slavery has, therefore, contributed to a narrow view of African history. Beyond this, these debates surrounding Abolition have also contributed to humanitarian ideals, and the impulse of political interventionists of more recent times seeking to 'save' Africa. Yet, just as this impulse in the late nineteenth century led to colonialism, so the impulse to 'save' Africa usually has been accompanied, even to quite recent times, by concerted forms of exploitation, be it diamond-mine concessions in Sierra Leone or a cocoa plantation on the Gold Coast.[5]

Focusing overwhelmingly on slavery in African history is thus problematic, and this book does not seek to do so. Nor does it try, however, to pretend that slavery is not of enormous significance to precolonial African history. The physical and emotional violence of captivity, dislocation and forced labour must be recognized. At the same time, it is also a mistake to study these as somehow separated from the broader economic system to which they belonged, which related to the accumulation of capital outside Africa. Nor can they be considered in isolation from other vital social and cultural changes afoot on the continent.

Two core misapprehensions need to be addressed before going any further. First, slavery did not just exist in an Atlantic context, and is not just an Atlantic story. The trans-Saharan trade to North Africa and Egypt probably involved the forced migration of six million persons between around 800 CE and 1900; a further four million were sold into the Middle East and Indian markets via the Red Sea and the Indian Ocean. The trans-Atlantic slave trade database of slave-ship voyages* estimates that, between 1492 and 1866, 12,521,337 persons crossed the Atlantic Ocean as captives.[6]

The second core misapprehension is that slavery is exceptional to Africa. When talking of enslaved persons being a 'form of currency' in West Africa, the word 'slavery' can be problematic, for it carries a different meaning in different historical settings. Far from being the norm, the New World chattel slavery that enabled this to take place was the exception. Among the Aztecs, for instance, slavery was important for religious rituals of sacrifice; and among the Maya, while people could be enslaved for debts or could sell themselves into slavery to avoid starvation, chattel slavery did not exist, and – as among the Aztecs – war captives were usually sacrificed for religious reasons. In other words, the institution of slavery has not always been related to labour and economic value. In fact, economic value as it related to enslaved persons was largely a construct of the system of Atlantic slavery.[7]

The key to understanding slavery as it emerged in West and West-Central Africa from the fifteenth to the nineteenth centuries is not just its economic function, but its relationship to warfare, kinship and honour. Just as among Native American peoples, warfare often shaped how slavery was seen in many parts of Africa. Successful wars helped a society grow in size and strength. War captives could be incorporated as new members of an expanding society, with dependent status. By the seventeenth century in Angola, for instance, slaves were frequently described as 'captives' – just as they were among the Bambara of Segu† (the *jòn*). In the mid 1680s, the French colonist Michel Jajolet de La Courbe described a trade on the Senegal River in 'captifs' and did not use the word 'slave'. The use of the word 'captive' shows that the concept of 'slave' was, in fact, a rather different one, derived from Roman and then New World contexts and later imported to Africa.[8]

* www.slavevoyages.org. A thorough collation of data from historians on four continents, compiled over many years from notarial and other records, that aims to give as complete a view of the statistics of the slave trade as possible, alongside other information.

† A powerful state on the Niger River downstream from Bamako, in modern Mali.

This fundamental relationship of dependence and warfare did, however, change over time. As the slave trade expanded hugely in the eighteenth century, so, too, did the capture of enslaved persons by warfare. Since slavery in West Africa created a class of dependent foreign aliens, it encouraged an expansion of warfare in order to create an ever larger servile class and greater social differentiation. From the Western viewpoint, thus, economic cycles of demand provoked the increase of enslavement in the eighteenth century; yet, from the West African viewpoint, this increase had more to do with the place of foreign dependants in society, and the ways in which these societies were transforming themselves as social hierarchies grew.[9]

That enslaved persons were most often outsiders is important, as it shows up the fallacy in the idea often put forward that it was 'Africans' who sold 'Africans' into the slave trade. This argument is usually developed as a way of alleviating discourses of Euro-American guilt, discourses that themselves emerge from the history of abolitionism. But it completely misunderstands identities in the seventeenth and eighteenth centuries, when, as noted in the Introduction, people did not see themselves as 'African' but rather as belonging to a specific lineage, kingdom and ritual community – just as people did not see themselves as 'Europeans' at the outset of this time, but rather defined themselves according to the style of Christian belief and nation.

An interesting piece of evidence of this comes from the Gold Coast in 1682, where the factor at Anomabu, Richard Thelwall, wrote that 'as concerning slaves, though the [Aboms] panyarrd [kidnapped] the Cormanteen people, yet they dare not sell them for they are all of one country.' Clearly, identity was not based on some common sense of belonging to an abstract continent, but on local and regional ties, ties that also determined who could and could not become enslaved.[10]

In sum, whether a person had uncles, aunts, brothers, fathers, mothers, sisters or cousins with inheritance and lineage rights shaped the social rights that they held. One anthropologist described well how it was those who were 'not integrated into the domestic community . . . who, having no relations of kinship, affinity or vicinity, were most vulnerable to capture'. It was not always the case that enslaved persons had no kin in the region where they lived, but it often was; and certainly the concept of 'slavery' cannot be separated from other forms of personal dependence that defined the claims that people might make on each other.[11]

Finally, it would be a great mistake to consider the place of slavery in African societies without considering the question of honour. There has always been a strong relationship between warfare and honour. As we saw in the narratives of the fall of the Songhay Empire, defeated warriors waited on the battlefield to be cut down as a matter of honour.* It is certainly, in part, owing to questions of honour that so many enslaved persons sought to take their own lives, as this narrative from the Gold Coast, on 25 May 1687, illustrates:

> Yesterday I bought one of the lustiest men slaves I have sene a longe time. He had not been ½ an houre in irons, when Mr Elwes's slaves came for watter, and whiles drawing of an anchor the slave of his owne will sprang into the tank, and Henry Underhill standing by cryd out for help, which immediately got downe a ladder and John Pound and Will Goff boath went in and failed and after some tyme brought him up but dead, though endeavord what we could to get life in him, by rowling him on a caske and hanging him by the heckles, but all in vaine.[12]

One sociologist described how, as archetypal outsiders, 'slaves were always persons who had been dishonoured in a generalized way'; and thus slave-owning was also in part a form of giving honour to the slave-owners. In the history of the trans-Atlantic slave trade, this also took the form of accruing honour through material accumulation rather than merely through the maintenance of a large slave retinue. The loss of honour felt by many enslaved persons in Africa explains both why there were so many accounts such as these of suicide, and the fierce attempts to secure freedom, be it through shipboard revolts or escape from the plantation once in the New World. Inversely, the way in which the holding of slaves came to betoken honour among planter societies reveals one of the moral pillars of modern capitalism, where financial honour is achieved through the dishonouring of

* See above, Chapter 1.

'others'. Only when ideals of honour change is it possible to envisage a change in ideology, and with it, in this case, the collapse in the system of Atlantic slavery.[13]

The relationship of honour to warfare, enslavement and freedom can help us to understand the enduring role of African warfare in slave revolutions in the New World. But it also puts the terrible fears that accompanied the process of enslavement into a different light. When we hear that slaves in the Kingdom of Kongo in the late seventeenth century believed that they would be eaten by their buyers and that their bones would be turned into coal, we can see that this was a reflection not just of terror at the literal 'eating' of Africa's human capital by this trade, but also of the worst debasing of honour that could be imagined.[14]

In the end, these ideas help us to see that the growth of slavery in West and West-Central African societies between the fifteenth and the nineteenth centuries went with the growth of social inequalities. As we have seen, enslaved persons gave honour to their 'owners', and the growth of this ideology across society stimulated increasing warfare and capture of enemies who could be enslaved. In Segu, the strength of these relationships is abundantly clear in the oral narratives: here, we are told, 'three are worth more than three': that is, there is no equality, and one group of people can have a higher value than a different group of the same number.[15]

In Segu, then, it was the elites who depended on others, on warfare and on violence:[16]

Because he who does not rest on anyone cannot sleep:	*sábu lá nyɛ jìgintan té sùnəgə*
In the bush, the birds rest on one another,	*kənəw jìgi yé nyəgən yé kúngokolo rə*
With them, the sons of Adam rest on one another,	*búnahadamadenw jìgi yé nyəgən yé só*
As for power, it rests on gunpowder:	*ə fànga jìgi yé múgu yé.*
Without gunpowder, power is never certain!	*fànga tɛ sùnəgə hábada mí múgutɛ àbólo*

SLAVERY AND MONEY IN THE ATLANTIC: FOUNDATIONAL CONNECTIONS

The transformation in the ideal of honour and its relationship to slavery was fundamentally connected to the core economic processes studied in the first half of this book. The expansion of credit and market institutions in West Africa saw an economic revolution; but this also represented a moral transformation, since 'credit' had a moral meaning. Whereas until the sixteenth century, credit in Europe and Africa was closely associated with religious value, it now developed an ostensibly economic meaning. It thus moved from being a moral concept to one associated with material value; and this was how material value itself became a moral instrument.[17]

This conceptual connection matters, as it helps us to understand how enslaved persons could be seen as money. Relations between people always involve moral values and judgements. As these relations became instrumentalized for material ends through the slave trade, so the value of captive people changed from one depending on moral claims to one in which economic claims were paramount. This was 'how' moral relations of interdependence became economic ones of dependence, with a pseudo-moral value judgement attached: dependence now bore with it the cast of moral opprobrium.

Understanding how this took place requires us to go back to the early period of trade, to see how these connections evolved from the beginning. With the entire Atlantic economic system dependent on credit, as credit expanded, and currencies with it, the relationship with slavery became ever closer. The first clear example comes from West-Central Africa. Here, the use of enslaved persons as forms of payment was apparent as early as 1500. In one will from the island of São Tomé from 1499, the judge Diogo Diaz was to be paid '8 slaves, out of the salary of the judge [*ouvidor*]'. The key value of enslaved persons at this time was that they were a form of value accepted outside the kingdoms of Kongo and Ndongo, as several examples show. Already by 1516, Afonso I, the manikongo, was giving people *nzimbu* money so that it could be exchanged for captives to be carried out of Kongo. In 1577, a document relating to the property of Portuguese men who had died in Angola stated that this should be stored in *nzimbu* and then converted into slaves, who were to be shipped to Brazil, with all profits then converted into goods and returned to Lisbon. From earliest times, therefore, captives were seen as a form of 'convertible currency'.[18]

These relationships became entrenched in the seventeenth century. One judge in Angola, André Velho da Fonseca, described in 1610 'charging debts in slaves, which are the currency of this country', while three years later one Portuguese official noted that 'the men have to be paid in [slaves].' The Portuguese governor of Luanda, Fernão de Sousa, stated in 1628 that there were many different types of currency there and that the 'best' was 'slaves which are embarked for the Spanish Indies'. In 1635, receipts in Luanda were taken in slaves, with financial equivalents in Portuguese *reais* given.[19]

This clear view of enslaved persons as currency was equally as stark in Greater Senegambia. In Guinea-Bissau, we have already seen that the enslaved person was a unit of account for the slave trader Manoel Bautista Pérez in the early seventeenth century.* The enslaved body was the ultimate arbiter of value. These books refer to 'debts [held] in slaves' and to slaves taken as 'trade goods [*fato*]'. And when, in 1632, Bautista Pérez's business associate João Rodrigues Duarte part-financed a trading mission to Sierra Leone, the goods sent were all accounted for according to their value in enslaved persons. The way in which concepts of money and slavery were interchangeable in this worldview was summed up by another business associate, Diogo Rodrigues de Lisboa, who wrote in November 1617, 'I will be delighted if we end up owing not a penny to anyone, especially [in] slaves.'[20]

This material equivalence of their captives was fundamental in the minds of everyone who participated in this trade, wily slaver or Jesuit missionary (and slaver). But how was it possible for people to be money? This view of captives as currency is best explained through the place of credit as both a moral and an economic category. In a 1632 account book from Lima, Peru, Bautista Pérez listed forty-five

* See above, Chapter 2.

creditors owing him a total of over 60,000 pesos; as with the creditors for 1631, none of these slave buyers had paid anything down at all, and thus the entire transaction, dependent on Bautista Pérez's excellent contacts in Guinea-Bissau, was based on credit. Even once sold in Peru, Bautista Perez tended to sell enslaved persons for as much as five times credit as cash, and even sometimes for credit only. Meanwhile, slave traders working between Salvador in Brazil and Luanda in Angola would usually obtain credit from five or six different people, who paid half up front and the rest later once the trader had returned to Brazil with enslaved persons, who thus acted as the 'collateral' for credit.[21]

In Angola, obtaining credit was a costly business, since Luanda had become the most expensive city in the Iberian imperial world, according to several sources – in an eerie forerunning of the situation in oil-rich Luanda in the early twenty-first century, also then the most expensive city in the world. In 1595, Lorenzo Garcés noted that, while his personal expenses and hiring a house for five months in Rio de Janeiro cost 35 pesos, seven months' rental and personal expenses in Luanda cost 75 pesos, almost twice as expensive. One commercial agent wrote in 1609 of Luanda that 'this land is very expensive, six times more than Madrid for housing and food.' Meanwhile, the slave-trade contract holder Antonio Fernández d'Elvas wrote in 1617 that he did not want taxes to be paid in Angola, since 'the money of Angola is not worth the same as that in [Brazil and the Spanish Indies].'[22]

What was it, then, that made Angola so costly? In part, it was that almost all the daily necessaries had to be imported (again, in striking similarity to the twenty-first century). In a complaint from Luanda's municipal council from the early 1630s, they noted that the foreign sailors who came and 'sold them goods on credit for one, two and three years ... all the necessaries for their life and sustenance, sell them for very high and excessive prices as they all come from overseas'. As one 1653 letter, from the royal judge of Luanda, noted, 'everything is bought on credit.' This financial credit was for long periods of time, but, more importantly, from the Angolan perspective, it could only be 'cashed out' through the violence associated with enslavement. How this worked in practice was made clear in the will of Sebastião Pinheiro, who died in Luanda in 1665, and was owed thirteen slaves by Cosme Carvalho, a resident of the Portuguese fortress in the interior called Massangano, 'on whose account I gave two boxes of goods from the sea, and a barrel of soap, which he took on account'; these goods on credit could be paid back by Carvalho only with the thirteen slaves, which meant that enslaved persons had become a form of currency that could be transferred out into the Atlantic economy.[23]

What can be observed here is the fundamental interconnection of the development of modern systems of financial credit and the violence involved in the enslavement of human beings. While credit as a means of financing maritime trade was a long-standing procedure, dating from the fourteenth century and the Hanseatic League, what was different here were the complications stemming from the longer distances, and the violence involved in repayment.[24]

Additionally, what can also be observed in these foundational centuries is the accumulation of credit and capital outside the African continent. One very important document from the National Archive in the Netherlands provides an account of the Dutch seizure of three Portuguese ships in October 1636, during the Dutch–Portuguese War. One ship held 215 enslaved persons, which were owned by 51 different slavers, 23 of whom had shipped just one person on their own account, evidence of low access to credit and small capital accumulation. However, a second ship held 498 enslaved persons, 483 of whom were shipped by one person alone; and the third ship held 368 enslaved persons, shipped by just 7 slavers, one holding 118, another 116 and another 80.[25]

Thus, some traders had very little capital, and could trade only small numbers of enslaved persons on credit. But other Atlantic traders were, by the mid-seventeenth century, developing significant capital and credit frameworks. Their access to credit networks allowed them to increase demand, which had its own consequences in many African societies; and the fact that financial credit always flowed from the imperial centres of Europe to the African coast, and thence from the coast inland, reflected the growth of the capital market in Europe, and how African societies were becoming locked into a cycle of indebtedness and political violence, which has since continued.[26]

Finally, once the proffered credit had been 'cashed out' through the violence exacted on human beings, enslaved persons could then be 'converted' into capital in the Americas following the Middle Passage. The stored value of their future labour meant that they more than repaid the economic credit that had been 'paid down' for them, and this was why the capital value of the captive grew in the eighteenth century. This was a process that, in its turn, increased external demand to accelerate the processes of violent enslavement and capital extraction from the African continent. Yet, in Africa itself, the transformation of credit and the relationship of slavery to money had a quite different aspect.

SLAVERY AND CREDIT IN AFRICA

The oral chronicler of Songhay societies, Fatimata Mounkaila, attributes to Songhay the following proverb:

It is he who carries out a commerce of children	*Atakurma neerako*
Who knows the cost of a short man.	*no ga Gazeere Hay Bay.*[27]

As Mounkaila's Songhay proverb shows, the relationship between warfare and human capture was also an economic one: it is the trader in children who 'knows the cost of a short man'. This fundamental relationship of money and value on the one hand to warfare, and to African identities on the other, had emerged alongside the new global credit dynamics.

In West Africa, there was a key difference to the context of credit to that which is understood by modern economists, and to the one we have just seen in the Atlantic. Credit was widely associated with the institution of pawnship, where elders would place young men in one another's care for apprenticeship and as an indication of a mutual bond of trust. As has been widely noted by historians, this institution was gradually eroded in the era of Atlantic slavery into one that was also a means of providing economic credit. When European traders arrived on the coast with goods to give to traders, the traders would take them to markets where they would be able to buy slaves; and in order to provide a bond against the goods advanced on credit, they would place a member of extended kin or a dependant as a pawn against the loan. Some of these pawns were eventually themselves sold as captives, when the debt was not repaid for some reason or other, and pawnship thus tied local (moral) credit arrangements to the slave trade.[28]

Something of the transformation of this institution is captured in a remarkable Arabic chronicle written down in the early twentieth century by Siré-Abbâs-Soh. Soh's account provides much detail of the life of Koli Tenguella, the famous Fula founder of the Kingdom of Fuuta Tòòro, and describes Koli's conflicts with the Farim (King) of Jaara, called Mahmadu in the chronicle. In this section, Soh recounts how Koli Tenguella's troops arrived at Jaara to begin negotiations:

> Farim Mahmadu answered him that, if [Koli] was sincere, he should give him as a sign of his word 100 young men from among the chief families of his country. Koli passed them over to him all on the battlefield to confirm his promise to renounce war. Farim Mahmadu passed them over to his brother Dyambere, so that they should constitute the peace agreed between him and Koli. But his brother Dyambere killed them all at once during the night. At daybreak when Koli asked for the 100 young men back from Farim Mahmadu, he asked for them from his brother Dyambere and Dyambere said to him: 'I ate them all last night for supper.'[29]

As noted before, discourse in Senegambia sees a fundamental connection between the idea of 'eating' people and capturing them for slavery.* This was a widespread concept across West and West-Central Africa. In Kongo culture, *kindoki* (sorcery) signifies a power through which 'the person who possesses it can "eat" (suppress or make die) another person'. This 'eating' is not literal, but conveys the life force of the eaten consumed by the practitioner of *kindoki*. Beliefs identifying slavery with cannibalism and witchcraft were many; and there is a clear connection in Kongo ideas between greed and the sorcery associated with cannibalism and slavery, since the word *kindoki* derives from the root *loka*, meaning 'greed' in Kikongo.[30]

The reference in Soh's account to Dyambere's 'eating' of the pawns is symbolic of his consuming vital energies, and despatching them

* See above, Chapter 2.

into slavery. This Senegambian account thus suggests how the passing of dependants as pawns was transformed into the passing of enslaved persons as a form of economic credit – how the credit economy began to transform into a money economy. In this case, the captives themselves represented the new currency and started to hold monetary and not just human or moral value.[31]

According to Soh, the result in this case was continued warfare: 'And so Koli fought both of them, until Dyambere and his brother Farim Mahmadu had perished.' The institution of pawnship was adjusting an indigenous credit system based on trust into a material one connected to economic value and chattel slavery. But trust was frequently broken (as in this case by Dyambere), and warfare often resulted. This underlines the economic framework of Atlantic slavery as an institution, and the importance, therefore, of considering the economic impact that it had in West and West-Central Africa: the transformation of credit from a moral into an economic model was something that worked alongside the rising economic value of enslaved persons, and the rise in warfare in Africa.[32]

In many African societies this new economic instrumentality is memorialized through the relationship perceived between witchcraft on the one hand, and selfishness, slavery and death on the other. Yet the associated moral judgement is ambiguous. Among the BaKongo, *kindoki* is seen to provide relative success, and the terms for those who lack it are belittling. It may be that witchcraft is a cannibalistic act that consumes the flesh of the victim, and whose relatives release their souls as 'fees', an idea that reproduces the realities in which legal cases leading to slavery could see all of the accused's relatives also enslaved as a consequence. But this does not mean that BaKongo automatically decry such actions; as one observer puts it, 'BaKongo . . . accept the reality of witchcraft because it is a way of representing the real competitiveness of their society and the covert, self-seeking maneuvers in which most people feel they must indulge from time to time.'[33]

Over time, the economic and moral functions of credit systems merged. Importantly, this was not only a feature of West and West-Central Africa. In England, too, credit had a similar vital moral significance in the sixteenth and seventeenth centuries, and was related to a person's perceived religious bearing and standing, the extent of their practice of belief ('crediting the supernatural'). Credit developed its economic dimension, but would never lose its moral basis, so that a credit crisis could also very much be a moral one, and lead to crises in the authority of power. The shared blurring between these features of credit in European and African societies is very important, for the concealment of the moral value of credit beneath its economic carapace would have vital consequences. As we shall see, far from evolving in isolation from one another during these centuries, transnational connections made transformations within Africa and Europe ever more closely intertwined and parallel.[34]

As in England, from the perspective of Africa, the economic and supernatural models were also perfect allies. Each of them envisaged the consumption of people, the one through the selfishness required for enslavement and trade, and the other through the selfishness required to consume the flesh of others through occult destructiveness. Thus, to consider the economic place of slavery in African societies is impossible without considering the transformations of belief and practice that this required. To take contemporary discourse for a moment, African societies do not still practise 'witchcraft' in the twenty-first century because they are 'backward' and 'lacking progress'; they practise 'witchcraft' because their experience of the violence of modernity makes 'witchcraft' the most powerful social institution that can still make sense of the destructiveness of the new economic model.[35]

Beyond Kongo, the most famous example of how the economic and supernatural models worked together in forming credit institutions was in the Ékpè society of Efik traders such as Antera Duke, at the port of Calabar (in what is now south-eastern Nigeria). As recent commentators note, there is a fine description of the Ékpè figure by the English sailor Silas Told from 1729: 'a native, in a fine silk grass meshed net, so curiously made to fit him, that nothing but his hands and feet appeared; the [net] ended with a fringe, not unlike ruffles. This man is looked upon as both God and devil, and all stand in the most profound awe of him.'[36] However, this description does not grasp the economic significance of Ékpè. In one way, indeed, and also as Antera Duke described it, by the 1780s Ékpè was a cult with major social and political power in Calabar, so that if a son flouted the authority of Ékpè, the father 'blows [unleashes the power of] Ékpè' on him. In January 1786, Duke described how 'the Bush Ékpè was being blown to keep anyone from coming to the house all day. After 5 o'clock we saw one King Tom Salt coming from Duke Ephraim with 2 canoes to stay here to settle an Ékpè dispute'; and once the dispute was settled, Duke and his fellow Ékpè men performed masquerades and 'plays' long into the night.

And yet, beyond this function of resolving disputes and staging performances of the type described by Silas Told, Ékpè was also fundamentally connected to credit and the slave trade. Duke described how he and his associates 'began carrying the Ékpè money to Duke Ephraim's palaver house to share among all the old Ékpè men. I put in money for 3 men, Esien Duke put in money for 3 men, Egbo Young for 2 men, Ephraim Aqua for 1 man, Hogan Antera for 1 man.' Ékpè was thus a means of securing payment for debts, and this was usually cashed out through the slave trade.[37]

This relationship of Ékpè to credit and the trade in captives was a marker of the transformation of social relations. Whereas Ékpè had originally been purely a religious cult, the emergence of problems of bad debt saw Ékpè expand and develop an economic function. In fact, by 1800, the key relationship between Ékpè and the trade in enslaved persons came through money, representative of how moral relationships had acquired economic weight. Accounts began to be annotated in the old *nsibidi* script of 500 characters, and this script spread from Calabar along the Cross River and east into Cameroon. Heavier entrance fees came to be required for entrance to the Ékpè cult, and this money could be acquired only through some relationship with the trade for captives. But what mattered to Igbo adherents of Ékpè was by no means just money; money was a means of accessing the spiritual power inherent in Ékpè.[38]

These examples from a variety of different societies show just how important it is to grasp the transformations of these societies through more than an economic lens. From the Western perspective, the transformation of economic frameworks is crucial, but, in African societies, these transformations were experienced also as religious and social changes; they cannot be understood through computing the lists of trade goods, the sheets, shirts, mirrors, pans and fine cloth, that are meticulously annotated in the logs of European slave traders, representing largely how they perceived the slave trade.

Bowl and lid from Calabar with *nsibidi* script.

As more credit was required with the expanding volume of purchases of enslaved persons into the eighteenth century, more complex credit instruments and banking frameworks were required – something that contributed to the rise of England's banking sector in the eighteenth century. Meanwhile, in West Africa, credit retained its fundamental importance to trade, with the King of Dahomey, Agaja, able to demand as many goods on credit as he desired in 1733.[39]

Antera Duke's diary tells us in detail how vital credit remained at the end of the eighteenth century:

> April 21, 1785
>
> . . . At 12 o'clock noon we 3 went on board Burrows's ship. We begged him to 'trust' for slaves but he would not. After that we came back . . .
>
> July? 15, 1785
>
> . . . Then we 3 went aboard . . . Cooper's ship. I got goods [i.e. through credit] for 50 slaves for the 3 of us.[40]

It is important to understand what had changed in this context of credit and slavery. After all, credit had long been related to dependence in West Africa as a form of moral indebtedness, and probably this relationship had arisen before the Atlantic trade. Nevertheless, something new was afoot here: the relationship between the actual inciting of enslavement and credit. Whereas the previous relations in many parts of West Africa had included slave-owners being responsible for the debts of their slaves, with the economic autonomy for some enslaved persons that implied, the new system saw the stripping away of such autonomy, as enslaved persons became chattels, convertible 'currency' for the Atlantic system.

CONSEQUENCES OF THE SLAVE AS CURRENCY IN AFRICA

So far, we have seen how slaves became a convertible currency and source of credit for Atlantic traders, both Africans such as Antera Duke and Europeans such as Manoel Bautista Pérez. Yet this was also the case for African rulers and traders in many societies away from the Atlantic coast. The monetization of slaves changed the moral ties binding rulers and subjects, and would have lasting consequences. The place of credit offers a way in to considering this more profound human question, which remains of such fundamental importance to this day.

Few accounts exist to supplement Diallo's of his own capture and enslavement, but those that do bear out the broader picture to be found there. Another important record of the moment of his captivity is that of Sālih Bilāli of Mâssina (in modern Mali), who was interviewed as an enslaved person in the American state of Georgia in the 1820s, having been captured in the kingdom of Segu at sometime around 1785. He described how, 'when about twelve years, as he was returning from Jenne to Kinnah, alone, on horseback, he was seized by a predatory party and carried to the capital of Segu, and was transferred from master to master for hundreds of miles until he reached the coast, at Anomabu [a major slave-trading port on the Gold Coast].'[41]

Bilāli's account echoes many oral narratives from Segu and the surrounding regions that can be found to this day. These confirm how groups of marauding warriors would raid for slaves in the eighteenth century. The Bamana word for prisoner – *jòn* – is the same as that for slave, which shows how interconnected raiding and slavery were, as the following account shows:

He destroyed this village and seized prisoners	*A ye o dugu o cèn, ka o jòn bò*
The next village was also destroyed	*A nòfè dugu, ka o fana cèn*
And he seized prisoners there	*k'o jòn bò.*[42]

Sālih Bilāli's account also confirms the impression of the more famous narrative of Olaudah Equiano. Equiano was a prominent Black Abolitionist at work in England in the 1780s, who described his capture in the Igbo societies north of the Niger Delta. He also wrote how he was passed from owner to owner until eventually he reached the coast. The impression is of the integral function of the institution of human credit in many different West African societies at this time, and how 'dependants' were transferred from one person to another as part of the political and social fabric.[43]

A vast and significant literature exists on the agonizing pain of the Middle Passage, and the creative fortitude and resilience of Africans who reconstituted communities and lives once in the New World. This literature movingly emphasizes the bravery and skill of these individuals in the face of the institutional violence of New World slavery. But these works do not always reconstruct the journey of enslaved persons in Africa itself, nor the experience of capture there. Because of the very nature of the institutionalized inequalities of colonial societies, very few accounts exist that can offer a window on to this process, for they were simply not written down. Yet, as we now see, these accounts are crucial because they speak of the human worlds that these processes opened up, far beyond any economic or political consequences.[44]

One of the best examples of how these microhistories can reconstruct the human experience is the narrative of Samuel Ajayi Crowther. Captured in southern Yorùbá country in 1821 by a raiding army from the north, Crowther was sold into slavery but freed by a British Naval Squadron ship and brought up in Freetown, Sierra Leone. Eventually, he returned as the first Bishop of Nigeria, and gave this moving account of the morning of a slave raid in his home community, in the heartland of Old Oyo:

> We were preparing breakfast without any apprehension; when about 9 o'clock a.m., a rumour was spread in the town, that the enemies had approached with intentions of hostility . . . [they] entered the town after three or four hours' resistance . . . Here a most sorrowful scene imaginable was to be witnessed! – women, some with two, three, four, or six children clinging to their arms, with the infants on their backs, and such baggage as they could carry on their heads, running as fast as they could through prickly shrubs . . . while they were endeavouring to disentangle themselves from the ropy shrubs, they were overtaken and caught by the enemies with a noose of rope thrown over the neck of every individual, to be led in the manner of goats tied together, under the drove of one man. In many cases, a family was violently divided between three or four enemies, who each led his away, to see one another no more.[45]

Bishop Samuel Ajayi Crowther

As a devout Christian, Crowther was well able to impart the significance of the process of captivity in his life story. But this did not just relate to warfare and the instrumentalization of human relations, and the cruelty that he described here. Finally, it is the way in which human bodies became forms of currency that helps to explore the multiple meanings of credit, value and money most deeply. Just as enslaved persons were valued in the Atlantic context for their economic worth, as we have seen, so economic worth also became a marker of 'value' for a human being in African contexts connected to global slave trades.

There are many examples of this, for which just a few will have to do. Oral histories from Mandinka villages in Senegambia describe how trading caravans paid taxes in slaves to the local rulers of each state they passed through; each captive was worth sixty rolls of cloth, which was sometimes paid as a substitute, with the final 'monetary worth' computed through the value of the captive. Nor was this an isolated instance. Interviewed in the north of Senegal in 1969, the Fula elder Mamadu Ndiari Mbengue described the ways in which this process had played out during the eighteenth century in the states of Bundu and Fuuta Tòòro that Ayuba Suleiman Diallo knew so well: 'One day an old *ceddo* [warrior] from the village of Satigi mounted a horse costing 20 slaves, carrying a rifle worth 7 slaves, and with boots worth 3 slaves.'[46]

It is clear from these accounts that, by the eighteenth century, the enslaved person had become a unit of economic worth in these parts of Senegambia. This is a very significant but little discussed aspect of the realities of slavery in West and West-Central Africa. Enslaved persons were, in fact, a form of credit, and a currency, here for African as for Atlantic traders connected to the global flows of human 'capital'. Oral sources from many different societies confirm the idea of enslaved persons as holding exchange value. Oral sources from Kongo show that slaves represented 'human capital' and could be used as a 'currency of exchange or method of payment', becoming in time 'the highest "denomination" in a system of exchangeable "prestige" goods'. The oral histories of Senegambia confirm this very clearly, with one account of the early-nineteenth-century warrior chief Kelefa Saane describing how he used slaves to buy gunpowder: 'He went and found the young / girls and boys of Bijini in the / outskirts of the village, / he took them and went and / exchanged them for gunpowder at Bajeba.' Thus, as has been noted for the eighteenth-century Kingdom of Segu, when a person became a captive-slave (*jòn*), 'They were at once units of value and units of labour.'[47]

Slaves thus became 'units of account'. In the 1820s, Theophilus Conneau wrote that 'in Africa, where coin is not known, the slave is made a substitute for this commodity, and in each district a positive value is given him which is passed for currency and legal tender . . . fields of cassava, rice, or yams, are paid in slaves.' Meanwhile, what was true on the Atlantic coast was also the case in the Sahel: enslaved persons were widely used as a currency in the trans-Saharan trade, and Islamic scholars in the Hausa states of northern Nigeria were often paid for their skills in literacy with captives by the late eighteenth century. Connection to long-distance trades in captives brought with it into African societies the financial equivalence of bodies and currency at play in the Atlantic and Sahara.[48]

The ubiquity of these relations by 1800 across many different regions of West and West-Central Africa forces us to pause for thought. They show that moral and economic equivalences had become more or less universalized. The consequences were vast. The terms of the social and moral contract had been changed. Not only did African leaders feel less moral obligation towards their subjects, but the tie of dependence that subjects felt towards their rulers was loosened.

CONSEQUENCES OF SLAVING: TRADERS, WARFARE AND NEW IDENTITIES

The current estimate of the trans-Atlantic slave trade database (www.slavevoyages.org) is that 6,494,619 Africans were taken in slavery across the Atlantic between 1701 and 1800, over half the total estimate between 1492 and 1866 and therefore the trade's peak. While, until the 1680s, the impact of this trade tended to be on specific regions, such as Allada, Angola and Senegambia, after this time, they became generalized. The trade for cloths, ivory and other manufactures declined, and that for captives grew. Areas affected expanded to include the Gold Coast and Loango, while the raiding of states such as Borno, Kaarta, the Lunda Empire and Segu grew. By 1750, almost every area in West and West-Central Africa was affected by trans-Atlantic and/or trans-Saharan slave trades.[49]

It is worth taking a moment to take stock of the shifting dynamics over these centuries as a whole. In the sixteenth century, it was captives from the Greater Senegambia region who predominated, alongside the so-called 'Anxicos', or Tyo people, from north of Malebo Pool near the modern city of Kinshasa. Already in the Americas, however, there were enslaved persons from Mozambique, brought through the Indian Ocean trade to Manila and thence across the Pacific Ocean to Acapulco. By the late sixteenth century, there was also a growth in the numbers of enslaved persons coming from Allada, with their number beginning to be recorded in Colombia by 1582.[50]

The first half of the seventeenth century saw the great expansion of the impacts of the slave trade. In Allada, a letter written in 1617 described how, while just twenty years before there was no active slave trade, 'it would now be possible to supply the [Spanish] Indies just from these rivers.' By the time of the Dutch–Portuguese War, in Brazil in 1644, the Portuguese missionary Manuel Calado described how many of the slave troops used by the Brazilian resistance against the Dutch came from Allada. The seventeenth century saw the Dutch exponentially expanding their hold on the slave trade – and, after 1675, relying increasingly on *lorrendraiers*, Dutch traders who had settled in the Gold Coast region and intermarried according to Fante custom. Meanwhile, in Kongo and Angola, during the second half of the seventeenth century, the focus of the trade moved south to the Benguela region and north to Loango, a process that continued long into the eighteenth century.[51]

By 1700, then, several cycles of the rise and fall of states associated with the slave trade had already passed. In West-Central Africa, Kongo had fragmented after the 1665 defeat to the Portuguese at Mbwila. In Senegambia, Jolof in the north and Kasamansa in the south had been overtaken by Fuuta Tòoro, Waalo, Niumi and Kaabu. The Akwamu state that had controlled the gold trade to the European forts on the Gold Coast was in the process of being supplanted by slave-trading Asante. In the region known to the Europeans as the 'Slave Coast', this led to the conquest of Allada by Hueda, which, in its turn, was superseded in 1724 by Dahomey.

By 1700, these political convulsions had had major impacts on the volume of the slave trade. Ships landing at the Hueda port of Offra in 1694 were able to load 600 enslaved persons in between eighteen and twenty-four days and then depart, a speed that showed just how efficient the trade had become there. The Dutch slave trader Bosman estimated that between twenty-five and fifty ships called at Ouidah annually by 1700. This was something that would continue throughout the eighteenth century, so that Ouidah became the African port from which more enslaved persons departed into the Atlantic trade than from any other.[52]

Three immediate effects of this expansion can be identified in the first place: the formation of new classes of long-distance traders; the impact of the trade in forming a demographic crisis, especially among the young men who were most often killed in warfare, or captured to be sold into the trade; and the way in which the warfare associated with the trade shaped new identities.

The lifestyle and beliefs of the new trading classes are vividly described by the Efik trader Antera Duke. A typical day in Duke's diary was 27 July 1785, in which he recounts how a friend 'and one of his boys put pawns [captives] on board the ship, and I went on board Cooper's ship to deliver pawns and I gave him some goods. We drank all day. Before night Captain Tatem went away with 395 slaves.' Indeed, much of Duke's time was spent getting together parties of men and accumulating credit for which enslaved persons could be purchased. Six months earlier, on 18 January, for instance, he noted 'Egbo Young paid 1 goat and 4 [copper] rods and Little Otto paid 4 [copper] rods. All the Ékpè [secret society] men came down to Duke Ephraim's palaver house and joined together to put in money for 20 men.' However, alongside the close attention to detail and the complications of pooling resources to exchange for captives, the minutiae of the organization of the trade emerges, as Duke procured provisions and water for slave ships, and occasionally suffered serious losses: on 11 April 1785, he noted, 'at 7 o'clock at night I saw two of my people come that I had sent to find Ephraim Aqua Bakassey, and they said that the canoe overturned in water and everything was lost, including the canoe.'[53]

The matter-of-factness speaks as volubly as Duke here, with traders drinking rum all day as captives are stowed away for the horrific voyage across the ocean. These Atlantic West African trading communities formed a crucial nexus with European traders. Each was dependent on the other, something that Duke acknowledged when he described how he and his associates dressed in European clothes in order to trade with the Europeans – 'then we 3 dressed as white men and went down in [Captain Comberbach]'s boat with one big canoe to bring up his ship.' But, at the same time, European traders were very much dependent on their African intermediaries, for provisions such as yams, and for the water supplies without which it would have been impossible for their slave ships to cross the Atlantic Ocean. Writing in 1788, Paul Erdmann Isert noted that a ship with 500 captives needed to load up to '600 barrels of water, each of which holds . . . [roughly 100 gallons]'.[54]

The emergence of these African trading communities was a feature of coastal communities. They were classic 'go-betweens', able to dress as Europeans and speak creolized languages comprehensible to European traders, but, of course, they were thoroughly 'African'. Where the slave trade was especially intense, the role of these brokers in violence, and of their European partners, was neither forgiven nor forgotten. In the late seventeenth century, one judicial report on Angola held it certain that the reason the Portuguese had lost Angola to the Dutch in the 1640s through the rebellion of Kongo and Matamba was because of their cruelty. Such was the enduring memory of this that, when one Belgian anthropologist was conducting interviews among the Mukongo in the second decade of the twentieth century, he wrote, 'A Mukongo said to me one day: "There are four species of human being [*hommes*]: Whites, Blacks, Ngandu [*crocodile-sorcerers*], and the Portuguese" . . . which is testament to the intensity of the hatred accumulated for centuries by this entire race [*sic*] towards the "brothers" of the slave traders.'[55]

Violence was, of course, practised by all associated with the trade in enslaved persons. The core relationship between the trade in enslaved persons, violence and warfare meant that areas where the trade was concentrated suffered severe demographic consequences. In Dahomey, the English trader Robert Norris described in the 1770s how those found guilty of crime were condemned to death or slavery, while their 'domestics, relations, and friends are all seized; some of them perhaps suffer death; the remainder are always sold for slaves . . . and together with the carnage of war, [this] has contributed greatly to depopulate this unhappy country.' Bosman, meanwhile, discussed how, on the Gold Coast, war between the Fante and Adom 'hath reduced it to a miserable condition and stript it of most of its Inhabitants'.[56]

In the case of Angola, the demographic result of the early 'boom' in the trade was abundantly clear by 1700. Those threatened with capture fled to sanctuary in isolated villages. By 1657, the route from Luanda to Matamba had been 'deserted and the *pombeiro* traders do not have anywhere to seek provisions'. By 1684, the effect of depopulation was such that, according to one official, 'the fortresses are so helpless with the lack of people in the neighbourhood, that you can walk three and four days without finding a village.' As one late-seventeenth-century account put it, 'in the past, when Angola did not have a span of land which was not populated, there was much confusion in the trading markets . . . but today they are reduced to such penury [that] you have to travel three months along deserted paths to reach the markets.'[57]

Warfare had played a major role in creating this desolation. As we have seen, the idiom through which many West and West-Central African societies understood the production of enslaved persons was as war captives. Just as warfare produced captives, it also reshaped societies through the development of new militarized secret societies, and new understandings of the place of combat and war in rituals of coming-of-age and social power. And, when it came to the landscape of desolation described in these accounts of Angola, warfare was also key. The army of the Governor of Luanda, Bernardino de Távora, was described as 'not leaving anything behind, not even any provision that they did not eat, as they seized things and burnt [everything]'. A late-seventeenth-century account describes how there were no people to sow and harvest crops, as they were all seized to be porters on slave-trading missions. Portuguese armies in Angola in this era often burned all the palm trees as soon as they could – a key source of nutrition through palm oil and palm wine.[58]

Warfare and rituals of war had a major impact on young men who sought a place in a society that increasingly saw their value as residing in their potential as enslaved persons. Thus, the oral historian Fodé Bereté recounts:

At the time when people submitted themselves	*O a sòdò mògòyi ye kèlèmansayi*
To the war chiefs so as to join their war brigades	*magwèla k'wa don sofayi dò, i bè*
They made a fortune . . .	*fèn sòdò . . .*
When a young man heard of a war chief	*N'i ye kèlèmansa dò komèn,*
He went and put himself at his service	*i bè taa don o fè n'i kèda kè fadin di*
Or he took to brigandage on his own account	*ubinyè i kè taa tegereya kè.*[59]

In other words, it was vital for young men to take proactive steps either to enter under the protection of famous war chiefs, or to seek renown and fear through their own actions in the capture of enslaved persons. The consequent relationship between warfare and trade was laid bare in one 1767 account, which said of the Jolof King near the island of Gorée, in Senegambia, that 'When the King is at peace with his neighbour, he produces few captives for the trade; [but] when he is at war, he produces a considerable number of them.'[60]

Abbé Proyart described in Loango, in 1776, how victors in battle 'pursue the vanquished, and busy themselves only in making prisoners, which they sell as slaves to the Europeans'. As late as the 1820s, the slave trader Theophilus Conneau stated how, in the region of the Fula theocratic kingdom in the Fuuta Jaalo Mountains of what is now Guinea-Conakry, 'suffice it to say that three quarters of slaves shipped are the product of native wars.'[61]

These were relationships that cut deep to the heart of identities as they were in the process of transforming themselves in West and West-Central Africa. The cycles of warfare and slavery shaped militarized secret societies, agricultural practices and the architecture of the built environment. The English trader Richard Jobson's description of a village at the mouth of the Gambia makes this clear:

> It is seated upon the Riverside and inclosed round nearer to the houses, with hurdles, such as our shepheards use, but they are above ten foot high, and fastned to strong and able poles, the toppes whereof remaine

> above the hurdle; on the inside in divers places, they have rooms, and buildings, made up like Turrets, from whence they within may shoot their arrows, and throw their darts over the wall, against their approaching enemies; on the out-side, likewise, round the wall, they have cast a ditch or trench, of a great breadth, & beyond that againe a pretty distance, the whole Towne is circled with posts and peeces of trees, set close and fast into the ground, some five foot high, so thicke, that except in stiles, or places made of purpose, a single man cannot get through.[62]

Only a highly militarized society, in which warfare was an integral part of daily life, would have constructed such elaborate defences. Sometimes in Senegambia communities grew around semi-fortified Portuguese trading positions, which were established along various tributaries of the Gambia River. In Bintang, for instance, there was a prosperous community of Portuguese traders and their African wives,

The ruins of the Luso-African settlement at Bintang, The Gambia.

in a small fortified settlement built on a mound overlooking the wide river, where wax, hides and captives were traded.

People sought this kind of protection because, in many parts of West Africa, warfare and capture made for an increasingly insecure world. Far from being static, as traditional Western historiography posited, these were societies undergoing a constant process of violent transformation throughout this period. It was this transformation that would later see them challenging and overturning the power of the elites whose reliance on warfare had been one of the cornerstones of their power, as they had come to participate in the Atlantic commodification of captives as money.

CONCLUSION: HUMAN BEINGS AND ECONOMIC VALUE IN AFRICA AND BEYOND

The interrelationship between human beings as money and the ways in which West African economies themselves were monetized is hauntingly captured in a remarkable oral account from Togo, of the relationship of the coming of cowrie shells to both money and slavery. It recounts how one person discussed how their ancestors had no money, and began to employ cowries. But where, in turn, could one get hold of cowries, except from the sea? 'Hunters used to travel in the forest. To scare everyone, they began to hunt human beings. Helped by fishermen on the coast, the hunters brought the captives by boat into the middle of the sea. They bound the slaves' hands and feet. They attached big stones around their neck and then let them drop into the water. After some hours, the hunters recovered the bodies, which were completely covered by cowries.'[63] Recalled here in this pithy oral history is the way in which different types of money interacted through the violence and massive death associated with slavery. Yet, once money had proliferated, the relationship became stronger still: there were no banks, and so people had to buy more captives with their cowries, and the credit that this afforded, since these were the only available 'commodities'.

The relationship between enslaved persons and currencies here in

Togo is very important. It reveals the process by which captives were exported, in return for forms of currency such as cowries. Another account from Senegambia makes the relationship even more explicit. One oral informant described how slave traders would 'sell [slaves] to each other / and dyed cloths. / They will carry these dyed cloths / and take them to other parts. / They will exchange them for slaves and bring them.' Cloth was, as we have seen, an important form of currency in Senegambia; so what is described here is the exchange of one form of currency for another, the enslaved person, whose value rose as capital accumulated beyond the African continent. This oral source also shows the explicit relationship between the value of a human being and the emergence of wealth. It describes wealth as 'a form of cloth', and notes that the cotton used to make the cloth was produced by slaves. Thus, only those with access to enslaved persons could produce wealth, and so acquire political power.[64]

Language captures well the social hierarchies that these relationships produced. In Segu, three types of *jòn* were recognized: those sold as slaves (close to chattel slaves); those appropriated and kept as dependants; and *foroba-jòn*, enslaved persons kept by the community for agricultural work. Meanwhile, enslaved persons were usually shaved, in Segu, Songhay and Senegambia; slaves were not allowed to grow beards, and this was a mark of their servitude, dishonour and subordination, as well as being an identifier. Thus, the Songhay proverb puts it: 'Everyone knows that the beard is a royal attribute, / That a slave cannot permit himself to grow one.'[65]

The fundamental psychological and economic relationship that was emerging was one of property on the one hand, and (dis)honour on the other. Human property could be 'branded', in the way cattle long had been in Europe, marked with the brand of ownership. Just as enslaved persons were 'branded' for sale into the Middle Passage, so were the iron bars that were used as currency up and down the coast from Greater Senegambia to the Gold Coast. As one English trader noted in Komenda, on the Gold Coast, in 1686, iron bars had to be 'marked' – or branded – with the Royal Africa Company seal, to ensure a swift sale. The connection between commerce, capital and the importance of the brand was instituted through slavery, before becoming universalized in global consumer culture.[66]

Of course, currencies used locally, such as cloths, shells, iron bars and copper rods, were vital for material comfort and the acquisition of status. However, for traders in West Africa, cashing out this status with capital accumulation required the transfer of enslaved persons to the Americas. In terms of money, it was especially the enslaved person's body that linked the economies of West Africa with those of the world.[67]

The rise of enslaved persons as currency shows the extent to which globalization was a key factor in shaping precolonial West African societies. The first part of this book has already shown the depth of social and economic complexity in many parts of the continent, and the ways in which societies transformed themselves during the early phase of globalization, to the later part of the seventeenth century. The growth of the export trade in enslaved persons, of course, also meant what modern economists might call the emergence of a growing 'balance of payments deficit'. Enslaved persons had become the ultimate unit of account in many areas; and thus, as the volume of exports of captives increased massively in the eighteenth century, this deficit had the tendency to increase.

Moreover, the monetization of captives and the reliance on external credit created a structural imbalance in the world economy. As credit lines came from Europe, the economic dependence of Africa on European economies developed. This added not only to imbalance but to African economic vulnerability. External shocks could have a major impact on conditions, as would happen in the nineteenth century with the abolition of the slave trade by the European powers.[68]

Beyond this imbalance, the dependence on external credit also tended to drive down prices in new African markets, while leading to inflation in established ones. Clear evidence of this comes from Ouidah in 1704, where one Dutch account noted that the cost of an enslaved person on the Gold Coast (where the trade had only recently begun) was 30 per cent lower than in Angola; and where it was also said that the huge trade growing in Ouidah had seen prices rise by more than half in the previous four years. The same process was always at work: when most of the enslaved persons going to the New World came from the Greater Senegambia region, prices were higher, so that, as a letter from the 1610s notes, 'the slaves from Cape Verde and the rivers of Guinea[-Bissau] are so expensive, that the profits that can be made with them in the Indies [are] very limited.' At this time, in fact, almost a century before the Dutch assessment from Ouidah, it was in Angola where the greatest profits were to be had; in 1622, an official noted that, where the profits on 500 enslaved persons from Greater Senegambia would be 49,500 *reais*, they would be 79,558 *reais* for 600 from Angola.[69]

What was the relationship between profit and the trade cycle that is revealed here? The European demand for captives pushed up African demand for currencies circulating locally, and therefore the cost of purchase to European traders. Lowering profits would make this region unattractive to European traders, and the trade moved on to prey on a different region. This added to the negative relative economic position of African societies, where the unequal exchange of 'hard' for 'soft' currencies was a key element of the process of globalization.

How did people experience these exchanges of value, and the monetization of human beings? One sinister hint comes from a recent suggestion by the historians Tatiana Seijas and Jake Fredericks that the dollar symbol $, in use in Mexico and the United States, derives from slavery. Although this is disputed, according to this line of thought the Spanish word for slave, *esclavo*, contains the sound for *s* and the word for 'nail', *clavo*, and so slave traders might brand their captives in an abbreviated form, with an *s* and a line through it to represent the nail, $. Account books of the slave trade often place the branding mark of the owner alongside their slave 'property', revealing just how fundamental this perception of property and ownership was. By the 1820s, much Anglo-American capital was held as slave property, and this drove the tensions that resulted in the American Civil War: along these lines, a fistful of $ was based on the ownership of slaves.[70]

7

On a War Footing: The 'Fiscal-Military State' in West African Politics

The growth of mass enslavement discussed in the last chapter, from the late seventeenth century onwards, required the expansion of organized warfare. As with the case in Europe, political power was militarized in West Africa. Armies grew, especially in savannah areas, and with them state power. The result in the eighteenth century was the emergence in many parts of West Africa of what historians of Europe have called the 'fiscal-military state'. Like most historical concepts, this terse phrase conceals many layers. The 'fiscal-military state' saw the convergence of the interests that led to the modern state, and permanently connected its reason for being to the prosecution of wars. The state offered a monopoly of violence – which was good if it protected the interests of subjects, but not if its interests opposed theirs.[1]

In West Africa and Europe in the eighteenth century, these military and state interests converged, to create an early form of the 'military-industrial complex'. More taxes were required to pay for expanding armies. As taxes grew, so did the requirement for an administration to oversee it. And as the administration grew, so did the power of the state. Local forces were overcome, and the centralization of power and administration became institutionalized.

The rise of the 'fiscal-military state' had enormous consequences for Africa and Europe. Historians researching this topic think this kind of governing system entered a major crisis in Europe towards the end of the eighteenth century, during the Age of Revolution. As we shall see in the following chapters, an exactly analogous crisis occurred in West Africa at the same time. While traditional historical approaches posit fundamental differences between Western and non-Western trajectories, the nature of state development and the resistance to it in the eighteenth century shows a historical interdependence between Africa and Europe. This may be a controversial finding, when a good number of historians have tended to emphasize the distinctiveness of the Western experience, as well as Africa's disconnection from 'history'.[2]

It is not just Western historians who link taxation, rising military power and the new states. The Asante Empire was founded in 1695 at Kumasi by Akan peoples uniting under a banner of militarized expansion – the name 'Asante' deriving from the Twi for 'war', *esah*, and *esantefor*, meaning 'because of war'. The internal wars on the Gold Coast of the 1680s and 1690s had led to increasing disorder and a need to find unity in combined military strength. Subsequently, like many an eighteenth-century fiscal-military empire, as Asante grew, it incorporated customs from subject states. The Mossi state that bordered Segu to the north was subdued in the mid eighteenth century, and, in the Manhyia Palace Museum of Asante history in Kumasi today, there is a Mossi bronze carving of the last King of Mossi mounted on a horse, together with his drum. Drums from other peoples, including the Dagomba and Ga, were also incorporated into Asante military and political life – hence the meaning of one of

Okomfo Anokye sword site, legendary site of the foundation of the Asante Empire in Kumasi, Ghana.

the *adinkra* symbols used by Asante elders of two crocodiles joined in the middle: 'unity in diversity'.[3]

Oral historians across West Africa know well the significance of the 'fiscal-military' state. According to Bambara griots, this was how the *tònjònw* (nobility) addressed the Da (King) of Segu after that state had arisen in the first half of the eighteenth century, showing how money brought weapons, and power:

Diara, Master of the Waters!	*à kóji tìgi Jara*
Diara, Master of Power!	*fànga tigi Jara*
Diara, Master of Gunpowder!	*múgu tigi Jara*
Diara, Master of Cowries!	*kòlon tigi Jara*
Diara, Master of Men!	*mɔgɔw tigi Jara.*[4]

Historians of Europe have entirely ignored this development in West Africa, unaware of how the parallels help to grasp the role of the state in world history. They have not seen the money accumulated there as a fiscal base with which West African rulers could finance their expanding armies. Understanding that this was fundamentally a monetary trade, and that plural monies have often existed, allows us to look at these changes in a new light.[5]

Historians of West Africa, meanwhile, have generally passed over these interconnections. Many early historians conceived the idea of a 'predatory state', in which militarized polities preyed on weaker peoples, in a conflict between 'centralized' and 'decentralized' societies. The difference in political organization between states is certainly important. Nevertheless, the reductive focus on the trade in enslaved persons has obscured the reality that warfare ever was the handmaiden of hard state power, in Africa and beyond. States require armies, and few rulers enjoy the power of having an army for long if they don't then use it.[6]

This chapter explores these convergences, looking at how the rise of the state was related to money and military power. A fundamental comparator is that, as in Europe, access to capital in Africa could make the difference to a state's long-term survival. Those kingdoms that did use gold as a hard currency were among the longest lasting, relatively immune from the revolutions sweeping much of the region in the nineteenth century. This holds for Asante, Dahomey and

Gajaaga on the Upper Senegal River: access to gold seems to have allowed these states to protect themselves in a way that many other rulers could not.

West African rulers were well aware of how vital this was. During the eighteenth century, a gold coin called the Nikky *mithqāl* began to be minted in what is now Benin,* and was in widespread circulation. This was minted with the gold that was retained by Asante. The Nikky *mithqāl* was in circulation around the Niger Bend into the nineteenth century, connecting West African economies to the trans-Saharan trades. The minting of this coin reveals the renewed strength of some states in West Africa at this time, and the way they were able to fiscalize their military growth. Even though captives were becoming in many ways the ultimate store of financial capital during the eighteenth century, the ability both to produce and to retain gold was an important factor in state-building and political longevity.[7]

A brief description of the case in Dahomey can serve to introduce this topic, and show its importance to the broader theme of money and state power explored in this chapter. In the 1720s, Dahomey supplanted the kingdoms of Allada and Hueda discussed in Chapter 4, and rapidly became an importer of gold from Brazil. Vast strikes in the Minas Gerais region in the 1690s had seen the rise of smuggled gold carried by Brazilian slave ships. The import of this gold as a prestige currency (cowries were the day-to-day currency in Dahomey) seems to have allowed a greater fiscalization of the state. Gold imports declined after the 1750s, but by this time the power of the dadá was such that his troops frequently attacked the Brazilian commercial agents at Ouidah.[8]

But was gold really so important in Dahomey, which was, after all, an upstart kingdom in the 1720s? When the English merchant Bullfinch Lambe was captured in 1726 and sent to Abomey – the capital of Dahomey – he wrote that the dadá 'abounded in plate, wrought gold'. English traders at Hueda hungered after this Brazilian gold. In 1720, their commercial agent, William Baillie, travelled to Brazil to try to increase the gold trade. He wrote in August 1721 from Bahia, 'I have endeavoured to have the Portuguese trade with you for their

* Nikky remains a small town in northern-central Benin.

Gold.' He was successful, for the gold ledger at Ouidah in the years 1724–6 is filled with large amounts traded by Brazilian merchants: 147 ounces from Joseph Pereira in May 1724, 60 ounces by Francisco Nunez in May 1725, 142 ounces from Senhor Gregorio in July 1725, and so on. Much of this was traded directly to Dahomey, but some was purloined by the small English merchant class, and so, for instance, when Joseph Adcock weakened and died at Ouidah in September 1727, his will included various bequests of gold dust.[9]

The craven attempts of the English to access Brazilian gold was motivated first by the Kingdom of Hueda and then by Dahomey's demand for it: as Baillie wrote in a fawning letter of November 1718 to his backers, 'I am sorry I could not send any more money . . . the reason was as was last advised, that I was forced to buy slaves with gold . . . I am likewise Intended to send some slaves to Brazil but I have not opportunity of getting gold enough for my despatch here.' The cursory report of the log of the Royal African Company Factory at Ouidah in March 1731 gives a sense of just how large this trade was: 'March 6th: Anchored in this Road a Portuguese Ship Captain Custodio Gomez with Tobacco & Gold from Parnambucca for 600 slaves, the Capt advizes of more Portuguese coming down soon.'[10]

Another important state in West Africa that used gold as a monetary standard in this period was Asante, in the hinterland of the Gold Coast. Here, all relative values were measured against the standard of gold by the early eighteenth century. By the 1750s, Asante controlled virtually all the production of gold, where the goldfields of Wassa, Twifo, Denkyira and Akyem Abuakwa in the south were worked by royal slaves. As in Dahomey, gold was occasionally paid *to* Asante by the Europeans, having also been sneaked away from Brazil; and so when, in January 1730, the Royal African Company factor at Dixcove, Mr Cruickshanks, sent 'a present to ye King of Asshantee to encourage trade', this included a gift of gold.[11]

Some readers may feel there is a paradox, for we see how, in the eighteenth century, some gold and silver imports appeared alongside the pre-existing 'soft' currencies. The minting of the Nikky *mithqāl* by the end of the century confirms the trend. This seems to reverse the picture of the export of monetary value away from Africa. However, the import or retention of these 'hard' currencies in some areas came at the price of a huge increase in the export of captives, whose labour accrued further surplus value beyond Africa. The external dependence discussed in the last chapter meant that once the picture reversed in the nineteenth century with the abolition of the slave trade, and gold was exported again by Asante, inequality in access to capital grew exponentially.[12]

This chapter thus looks in detail at the militarization of the African state in the eighteenth century. It moves from the importance of spirituality to the relationship of warfare and the state, the financing of this through currency, and, finally, how the experience of state power through money and warfare created a legacy of suspicion of the state. Journalists, political scientists and other outside observers may ponder over 'state failure' in Africa; but, as this chapter suggests, from the perspective of the historian, this is an entirely explicable outcome of ordinary subjects quickly having had a poor experience of hard state power.

FROM SECRET SOCIETIES TO STATE ARMIES: SPIRITUAL BELIEFS AND MILITARY STRUCTURES

Traditional historical analysis relates militarization purely to material questions of state and national advantage. This is curious, since historically in most societies warfare is fundamentally connected to spirituality. The Christian use of the concept of 'just war' and the Muslim reformulations of the concept of *jihād* (spiritual struggle) show how warfare and conceptions of spiritual strength (and legitimacy) have ever been connected. Thus, it is no surprise that the same was true in the operation of warfare in West Africa in the eighteenth century: in accounts of the secret societies that emerged in the forest regions, and of the armies of the savannah states, it becomes clear how far spirituality underpinned the new relationship of warfare and the state.

We can begin by looking at the secret societies. Writing near the end of the nineteenth century, the English traveller Mary Kingsley provided a detailed description of the role that secret societies had come to hold in many West African societies:

> I cannot close this brief notice of native ideas without mentioning the secret societies; but to go fully into this branch of the subject would require volumes . . . The Poorah of Sierra Leone, the Oru of Lagos, the Egbo of Calabar, the Yasi of Igalwa, the Ukuku of the M'pongwe, the Ikun of the Bakele, and the Lukuku of the Bachilangi, Baluba, are some of the most powerful secret societies on the West African coast.[13]

Kingsley described well the way in which secret societies were strictly segregated by gender, and had an overriding judicial function. Two of the best known were the Poro and Sandé secret societies, found in a large region encompassing parts of Guinea-Conakry, Ivory Coast, Liberia and Sierra Leone, where the Poro initiated men and the Sandé women. The spirit embodied by each society was often represented through masquerades, which appeared at specific religious festivals and moments in the social calendar. Initiation often required participating in a successful raid. According to Kingsley, among the Yorùbá, those young men who had yet to perform a military incursion remained dressed in white, wearing only a piece of grass cloth, under the control of their initiators. Painting the body in white as part of the initiation rite was common in many regions of West Africa, and is still practised to this day among the Balanta of Guinea-Bissau; Islamic practice here adapted this rite, so that children awaiting initiation in Muslim areas of the country are dressed in white robes, much as Kingsley described for the Yorùbá.[14]

Kingsley's account of the secret societies of such a wide range of West African people seems somewhat generic, but there is a reason for this. Writing of Cameroon, she tells how a guide informed her that one of the shrines of a local secret society had been brought from Sierra Leone. There, secret societies had existed since at least the seventeenth century. By the late nineteenth century, the establishment of the Royal Naval Squadron base at Freetown in Sierra Leone had led to a great intra-African migration. Royal Naval ships that captured slave-trading ships took the liberated Africans with them to Freetown, where they were taught English and evangelized. Many then moved to other parts of West Africa, including Yorùbá land in Nigeria and the island of Fernando Pó (Equatorial Guinea). From both of these areas, the Cameroons were easily accessible, and thus ideas and practices could coalesce.

Thus, militarized secret societies in West Africa were not somehow 'authentic', static as if frozen in time, and isolated from one another. They were deeply connected to world-historical changes, and transformed along with them. And it was not just societies from Sierra Leone that moved to the Bight of Biafra, as some moved the other way. The Ékpè secret society of Calabar had itself spread to Sierra Leone in the nineteenth century, along with liberated Africans who had been freed there; it had also spread to Cuba, where it formed the kernel of the Abakuá society, which endures to this day. Meanwhile, as we have seen, Kongo religious ideas also moved to Freetown at this time with the formation of the Kongo Cross community, showing the kind of reciprocal religious and social influences at work by this time across Africa and the diaspora.[15]

The connection between initiation into these societies and military activity related to the trade in captives is important. Until a potential initiate had captured someone, they were not a full member of the secret society. Ultimately, the importance of secret societies grew, as they could support established political authorities, by restraining the tendency of societies formed through lineage alliances to fragment. They could help societies to expand by creating shared frameworks of belief that neighbouring peoples could adopt, as was the case with the Ékpè masquerade in Calabar and the Cross River. They strengthened the power of political authority in non-Islamic societies, ostracizing those who lacked the bravery to be initiated, but welcoming those who had proven themselves by capturing others for sale. They also could act as a cohesive social factor by unifying people spiritually and politically across a wide geographical region, as occurred with the Poro and Sandé societies.[16]

The place of secret societies adds to the understanding of warfare in Africa during the Atlantic slave-trade era. Whereas standing armies based on large cavalry forces were the norm in many parts of the Sahel and the savannah, in the forested regions nearer the coast these military structures did not work. Instead, warfare and these secret societies grew out of the power often held by hunters. In one of the epic oral accounts of the formation of Segu, in the eighteenth century, the power of the kingdom's founder, Biton Kulubali, is located in his prowess as a hunter, for '[he] was a hunter. / The love of hunting was in him.' Hunters had access to iron, and traditional hunting songs among the Manding peoples have a strong emphasis on blacksmiths, since 'whoever is not an ingrate must give thanks to the blacksmith / who made wood usable.' Beyond the power given by iron, it was only the hunter who was brave enough to confront the spirits of the forest (and the many wild animals who lived there). From this bravery in defeating the spirits and the animals stemmed the totems of animals often invoked by these societies, in the shape of the leopard, crocodile and monkey cults.[17]

The importance of these cults and this connection is apparent in the oral histories of Kaabu, the great Senegambian federation that endured from the fourteenth into the nineteenth century. The founder of Kaabu, Tiramakang Traoré, was – like Biton Kulubali – said to be the son of a hunter, Damaansa Wulaading. The name of the founder of the Empire of Mali to which Kaabu was tributary, Sunjata Keita himself, derived from 'lion' (*jara* in Manding). And the warrior caste of Kaabu, the *nyantios*, were said in oral histories to be 'like monkeys', with certain types of *nyantio* being equivalent to certain types of monkeys. Thus, in Kaabu, the defeat of the spirits of the bush was embodied in the vanquished animals being appropriated as totems, and this became a key emblem of the power of the new militarized secret societies.[18]

Beyond Segu and Senegambia, the role of the hunter in state formation is also evident in oral histories of the Akan and Yorùbá. It is not that precolonial African states 'evolved' from hunting, but rather that the spiritual powers associated with hunting lent themselves to wider political power. This was an approach grounded in a fear and respect of the world shared by people and creatures, and enshrined in the sacred importance of the secret societies to which the brave gained entry. These societies became sites for proving the potential to enter adulthood, in an increasingly violent world that was mirrored by the ways in which these societies took shape. One could say that the violence of the new secret societies reproduced and represented the violence of the Atlantic slave trade: they embodied and memorialized the human experience of warfare and violence related to the trade.[19]

Benin soldier with leaf-shaped sword.

Away from the secret societies, there are many ways in which the spiritual place of warfare can be grasped in West African states and their armies. It is striking to observe the swords of Benin warriors as depicted in some of the famous bronzes, still easily accessible in many museums in Nigeria and in the West, which take the shape of a leaf. Here there appear to be connections to the neighbouring Yorùbá spiritual concept of *axé*, the life force that is in all things and that is manipulated by the *orixás*, who live in the other world. *Axé* is closely related, therefore, to nature and to religious power, and the shape of these swords speaks strongly of the way in which warfare was seen by the soldiers of Benin.[20]

Sacred forests were at the heart of many important states, including the ancient Empire of Ghana and at Ifè. The importance of sacred forests and nature to spiritual (and military) power is also shown by the description of the way in which the Borno Army of the Grand Imam of Borno, Ahmad B. Furtū, attacked the Sau-Gafata:

> The Sultan cared nothing for their assembling but advanced towards them with his army, horse and foot, until he reached their trees and their strongholds. This was in the summer-time. He then drew up the shieldsmen and bucklersmen in front of the people in ranks; behind them stood the horsemen dressed in coats of mail, with quilted armour on their horses, not separated but also in ranks. Then, behind the horsemen the axe-men lined up so that they might cut down the trees, feeling themselves secure from any damage or mischief on the part of the pagans.[21]

What is described here is clearly the attack on the sacred forests of the Sau-Gafata, and their attempt to resist, 'attacking the Muslims with arrows and spears'. But the cavalry of the Borno Army won out, in the dry savannah, and those who survived were dispersed as captives. The description sets up well the contrast between Islam and African religions, between scriptural and mystical power, militarized secret societies and cavalry-led armies, and the different approaches to warfare that each had.

The place of religious power in state warfare is also abundantly clear on the Gold Coast. At the port of Anomabu, the English factor described in February 1687 how 'yesterday they sent from [Fante] to command all able men to bear arms up thither and hang a fittish [charm] at the gate that no man should come to trade to sell any corn or any other thing, but immediately repare with arms to [Fante].' A few years later, at nearby Dixcove, in 1694, the factor described how 'all the people under this Fort have taken fetishes and several Caboseers [headmen] of great force in the country that they will fight for the English to the last man.'[22]

These relationships were thus central on the Gold Coast, too. Bosman described how, in Fante, there could be no warfare without the 'suffrage' of the priests. One oral account collected from Asante deals with its rise to power in the eighteenth century, when, from 1695 onwards, it expanded enormously at the expense of neighbouring kingdoms, conquering and subduing them, and then often incorporating some of their customs and bringing in military leaders from the conquered to help retain order. At the conquest of Takyiman, in *c.* 1722, the King of Takyiman had been warned by an oracle that his kingdom might fall if he slept with an especially beautiful woman with evil designs. The king ignored this, and the High Priest predicted the kingdom would fall within forty days. When a short time later some Asante nobles visited for a funeral, and started attacking, the king's headmen were furious that he had ignored the priest, and everyone fled, leaving the field for Asante.[23]

The place of religious belief and practice was at the core of West African societies and their military structures, whether through Islamic or African belief, and whether involving large-scale armies or secret societies. It should, therefore, not be a surprise that these beliefs also shaped the ways in which armies initially formed. The state functioned alongside these social and religious structures, and worked with them; as state power grew with the increasing monetization of the economy, so, too, did the power of these structures. This was important, since, in time, these structures could themselves mobilize power against the state.

WARFARE AND STATE FORMATION: THE EXAMPLE OF DAHOMEY

A good example for a clearer understanding of the relationship between warfare, fiscalization and state formation in West and West-Central Africa is Dahomey. In the Western imagination, Dahomey epitomized everything that was 'wrong' with Africa in the nineteenth century and in much of the twentieth. Said to be a cruel slaving state ruled over by a despotic king, lurid descriptions of its brutality make it hard today to understand exactly what it was like. Certainly, it was much more complex than these accounts suggested. By the end of the eighteenth century, Dahomey was able to incorporate a wide range of influences and act as the fulcrum of Fon culture and belief. A letter written in Portuguese by a scribe for Dadá Agonglo, in 1791, kept time according to the Christian calendar, and he was answered by the Portuguese regent, Dona Maria, as 'The Honourable King of Dagome'.[24]

This trade with the Portuguese and Brazilians, and with other Atlantic trading nations, coexisted with a familiarity with trans-Saharan trade. Writing in 1793, the first European historian of Dahomey, the pro-slavery writer Archibald Dalzel, noted that the most popular amulets were written in Arabic by the Muslim traders who visited the capital at Abomey. The balancing act performed by the dadás of Dahomey between Atlantic and trans-Saharan traders was confirmed in the account of another British trader, Robert Norris, from the 1770s:

> At a little distance from me sat a dozen swarthy men with turbans on their heads, they wore loose cotton shirts made like surplices, long loose drawers or trousers of the same, and Morocco leather slippers . . . They speak, and write Arabic, and are supposed to come from the northern part of Africa, from the confines of Morocco, and the States of Barbary . . .they buy hides, and skins, which they tan and work into horse furniture, tobacco pouches, and other useful articles; and carry some small bales of skins back with them.[25]

Not only were there people at Dahomey's Court presumably able at the very least to communicate, if not write, in Arabic, so as to deal with these traders, but there were also many who could do the same in Portuguese. Those who knew how to write and read in European languages were called *yovo*, and were often either of mixed African-European descent, or occasionally of Fon background themselves. One document composed in 1804 for Dadá Adandozan was written by a Portuguese scribe who concluded the long letter with his own personal plea to the authorities in Brazil for assistance: he had been at the Court in Abomey for twenty-three years, he wrote, with no company from his Portuguese compatriots, and was desperate to leave, even though he could only write a very brief note, since 'as all those who are looking at this message know how to read I cannot say more for fear of causing distrust.'[26]

In other words, by 1800, Dahomey had become a transnational state with a sufficiently large Court administration to house functionaries bilingual between Fon and Arabic or Portuguese. Although few scholars think that Adandozan wrote these letters personally, but rather that these were dictated to Court officials, the implications of the transnational influences are significant. In 1810, Adandozan signed a letter to Portuguese royal officials in Salvador, Brazil, regretting the departure of the Portuguese Court from Lisbon to Rio de Janeiro in 1807 to escape Napoleon's troops. Indeed, Dahomey was the first nation to recognize the new Brazilian Empire, in 1822; and its neighbour Onim* followed in 1823, sending an embassy to Brazil to recognize the independence of Brazil from Portugal. Thus, these states had strong international connections and a multilingual Court by the end of the eighteenth century: the process of state-building, and its connection to warfare, had clearly progressed rapidly since Dahomey had first come to prominence in the 1720s.[27]

The role of warfare in Dahomey has long been recognized. It was Dahomey's dependence on military conquest for authority that distinguished it from predecessors such as Allada. Yet warfare was not just a means to procure political power; as we have seen, spiritual power was also very important to it. When Dahomey finally conquered Hueda in 1727, the soldiers of Dahomey killed and ate the

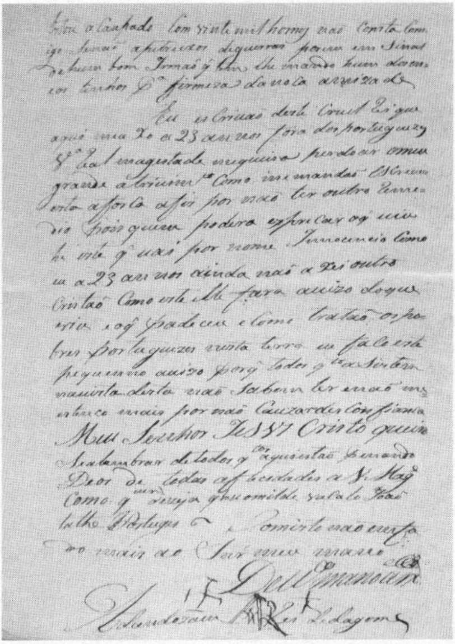

Adandozan's signature (*bottom left*) on a letter to the Portuguese Overseas Council, 20 November 1804.

* Which became Lagos – a small kingdom then tributary to Oyo.

pythons that were revered as deities in the shrine of Dangbé at Hueda (and, indeed, where pythons are revered to this day). Just as the Borno Army cut down the sacred forests of their enemies the Sau-Gafata, so the eating of the python symbolized the consumption of the enemy's *actual* power in this case. This waning spiritual power of Hueda can be seen prior to this defeat, by the ever fewer references to the Dangbé shrine between 1704 and 1727.[28]

This renewal of spiritual power offers an important explanation for the extraordinarily rapid rise of Dahomeyan power in the 1720s; perhaps Dahomey's emergence cannot be grasped without it. Between 1724 and 1727, under Dadá Agaja, Dahomey conquered all the neighbouring states and became the pre-eminent force in the region, having hitherto not been in the least bit significant. Agaja was without question the most important ruler in Dahomey's history. He had acceded the throne from his brother Akaba in 1708, and was described by a French observer in 1728 as middling in height, full-bodied, 'slightly bigger and having wider shoulders than Molière'. Writing around the

Temple of Pythons, Ouidah.

same time, the English slave trader William Snelgrave described him as having a face pitted with smallpox, but nevertheless as having a majestic bearing. His name, Agaja, came from a Fon proverb, 'No one throws into fire, a green tree which is still standing.'[29]

The importance that Agaja placed upon keeping control of religious practice in Dahomey can be seen in his purge of members of the Sakpata religious movement, some of whom he appears to have deported to Brazil. By sweeping out forces from rival shrines, Agaja was able to harness strength in his kingship. But this also showed that Dahomey's power grew through a transformation of religious power into something public, and not as it was previously practised in household shrines and sacred forests. The centralization of political power in Dahomey was deeply dependent on the use of, and subversion of, existing religious practice, and on the concentration of these cults in new royal shrines, embodied in the leopard cult, Agassu.[30]

This control of religion and warfare made the kings of Dahomey analogous to those of Spain or the Aztec Empire. European monarchs also saw a strong interconnection between their power and divinity, as the concept of 'divine right' makes clear. The vicious warfare involved in the Spanish conquest of the Americas was justified through the 'divine imperative' of religious conversion, just as *jihād* justified wars fought by Islamic peoples. Temporal power could be granted only by some higher force, with the connection between rulers and the supernatural a factor in many places around the world over time – usually as a justificatory element of the wars that so many rulers fought, and fight.[31]

In Dahomey, the royal Court was at Abomey, where the palace – the only building permitted to have more than one storey – was called the *simboji* (or 'big house'). The *simboji* was surrounded by a mud wall about twenty feet high, protecting a large square of land each side of which was just under a mile in length. There were many inner apartments, connected to each other by long corridors, while large houses were placed at the middle of each of the walls, in which armed guards of women and eunuchs were posted.[32]

Certainly, power in Dahomey was radically centralized during the eighteenth century. The longest-serving monarch was Tegbesu

(1740–74), who ruthlessly disposed of potential rivals and created complex administrative machinery to process wider trade. Many of his brothers and other members of the nobility were either killed or sold into slavery, as was the case with his brother Truku – also known as Dom Jerónimo – who spent twenty-four years in Brazil before being brought back under Tegbesu's successor, Kpengla. Meanwhile, Tegbesu personally got to know the directors of the European company forts at Ouidah, and acted as a middleman for many of the enslaved persons sold on by Oyo. This negotiation was easy for Tegbesu, who had spent several years as a hostage at Oyo in the 1730s, before a peace was finally signed in which Dahomey recognized itself as a tributary of the Yorùbá Kingdom.[33]

Tegbesu's wealth was well described by Robert Norris, when he visited him at Court in Abomey in 1772: 'The king was seated on a handsome chair of crimson velvet, ornamented with gold fringe, placed on a carpet, in a spacious cool piazza, which occupied one side of the court. He was smoking tobacco and had on a gold laced hat, with a plume of ostrich feathers; he wore a rich crimson damask robe, wrapped loosely around him; yellow slippers, and no stockings.'[34]

Royal authority and power grew year on year in this era, bolstered by trade. By the 1760s, there were some private traders, the *ahisinon*, who traded on behalf of Tegbesu and nobles at Ouidah. These traders could not act without a royal licence, and the dadá – a real believer in 'free trade' – encouraged all who wished to trade to come to the port. There they would be taken to the governor's palace at Ouidah, in the centre of which was 'an assembly room to which the Europeans are brought when they have business with the governor. The assembly room is open on one side, like a gallery, and is decorated with columns. There is nothing inside but Black Stools [the token of political authority] and, at times, a European chair.'[35]

Agaja, Tegbesu and Kpengla did not only develop the administrative apparatus for international trade in these decades; according to the Brazilian priest Vicente Pires, who visited in 1797–8, the entire domestic infrastructure of Dahomey grew rapidly. Markets were held every day, selling cloths and food; the location rotated day by day, and the markets were administered by an official called the migan, and his armed guard of a hundred men. Meanwhile, Pires cited a range of laws regarding curfews (9 p.m.), theft, the prohibition of drawing blood from another, poisoning, adultery and trade, and a legal framework prescribing respect for established authority: 'All children show great obedience and respect towards kings, parents, and other superiors.' Property, meanwhile, reverted always to the dadá, who inherited from his vassals, and who was the legal owner of the goods of all ships that might founder on the sand bars between Ouidah and the Atlantic.[36]

This infrastructure speaks of a kingdom at full throttle, where, just a hundred years before Tegbesu came to power, it barely existed as a political entity. The state apparatus arranged the infrastructure, and also attended to the need to grow enough produce to feed the population. By the later eighteenth century, there were royal roads, and Robert Norris described crossing a river 'over a tolerably good bridge, formed by wooden piles placed at proper distances, and covered with faggots and hurdles'. The road on to Allada was very good, and at Allada itself (now part of Dahomey) there were plantations of palm trees harvested for palm oil, which was traded at Ouidah, while near other towns were plantations of yams, potatoes and maize.[37]

Thus, while European visitors and traders generally sought to barbarize Dahomey in their writings, the reality that emerges from their texts is complex. European traders lived absolutely under the power of the dadá, and were not even able to leave their trading posts without royal permission. At every turn, they were greeted with imposing demonstrations of Dahomey's power. When the yovogan (governor) visited the European governors, he was accompanied by four or five hundred armed men, and if European parties did venture inland, they would be greeted as Pires was in 1797, by 'Africans armed with rifles and swords . . . with shouts and rifle shots they circled us three times, and each time they passed by us they bowed to us, and we responded in kind'. Attached to this military force were reminders of the strength and dignity of Dahomey, the yovogan travelling with 'musicians, flag-bearers, umbrella-carriers, and several employed immediately about his person'.[38]

What was it that allowed this expansion of the military and administrative infrastructure in Dahomey? Spiritual transformations offer part of the answer, but the economic framework has to be considered, and the place of the expansion of the revenue and money supply. In the late seventeenth and early eighteenth centuries, Dahomey's predecessor state at Hueda had already developed its power in close relationship to the expansion of the cowrie money supply. The cowries were transported in sacks by the English and the Dutch, while at Ouidah people were 'continually endeavouring after work to get Money'; men wove cloth, made calabashes and ironcraft, while the women traded, 'so that both Men and Women here are employed in getting of Money, and each zealously strives to outdo the other'.[39]

Prior to the rise of Dahomey, Hueda's wealth depended on this trade. The King of Hueda, in fact, charged a mark-up on the import of currency, as opposed to trade goods, since enslaved persons bought in cowries cost 50 per cent more than other captives. By 1700, Hueda was, said Bosman, an extremely populous and impressive place:

> the great number of these Villages composed of Houses, which are round at the top, and encompassed with mud Walls or Hedges, together with the great numbers of all sorts of beautiful and lofty Trees, which seem designedly planted in exact order; afford the most beautiful Prospect in the World . . . nor can I believe that any Country in the World can show the Like. Besides which this Land is covered with a beautiful verdure, composed either of Grass or Trees, and plentifully provided with three sorts of Corn, Beans, Potatoes, and other Fruits.[40]

The importance of cowries in this era in the Kingdom of Hueda has already been noted, and the increasing volume imported by the Dutch into the region as prices of captives rose at the end of the seventeenth century.* This was matched by English interest, with 150 pounds of cowries kept in store at the Royal African Company trading post at Ouidah in 1698. The consequence was naturally further to extend the fiscal base, and the area in which cowries were used as currency in local markets. One source claimed that prices had tripled at the end of the seventeenth century, and this meant a huge increase

* See above, Chapter 4.

in the volume of cowries brought to Hueda, with as many as 30,000 enslaved persons a year being exported. A bigger slave trade meant much larger stores of cowries were in circulation. Money became more widespread, and rulers were able to fiscalize their administrations and expand the state apparatus.[41]

However, the rapid increase in cowrie stocks was a destabilizing factor in the local economy. Cowrie imports reached unprecedented levels in the 1720s, stoking inflation in Hueda, which may well have influenced its decline in perceived spiritual power, and popular unwillingness to defend the kingdom when Dahomey attacked it in 1727. At Allada, in 1725, the inflation meant that taxes in cowries were increased for European traders. This may also explain why both Hueda and Dahomey were also so keen to access Brazilian gold, and why this gold helped to stabilize Dahomey's rulers after the 1720s.[42]

Once in charge, the Dahomeyan state's growth was financed throughout the eighteenth century by the import of cowries. Much of the gold procured by the English at Ouidah in the 1730s was used to purchase cowries for trade. Costs of running the Portuguese fort at São João de Ajudá had to be paid for through the purchase of cowries, 'which is the money which is used among these Peoples'. It is important to stress that, as Bosman's account above suggests, all saw cowries as money, not as a 'primitive' item of exchange, either for Dahomeyans or Europeans. When, in 1791, one slave-trading ship from Salvador in Brazil found itself without money, it sought to draw cowries against credit letters, as might have been done with any form of currency at that time. Thus, the massive increase in slave trading in the eighteenth century, and the consequent increase in available currency, was a vital factor in the consolidation of the state in Dahomey; that Dahomey had grown through military and fiscal expansion shows an analogous mode of state formation in West Africa to that of Europe through these centuries.[43]

In all of this, warfare (and its fiscalization) was a fundamental attribute of Dahomey's rise to power over Allada and Hueda. However, after 1730, Oyo armies forced Dahomey to acknowledge itself as tributary. Oyo's army assembled, and the Fon were in great fear, as the logs of the English factor at Ouidah noted. By 9 January 1730 the rumours of an invasion were imminent, and huge numbers of Fon gathered at Ouidah, apparently for protection; on 21 February, Agaja sent notice that the Oyo Army was advancing, and by April he was in retreat from Abomey to Allada. Throughout the 1730s, annual armies were sent from Oyo, at which point Dahomey's forces would withdraw into wildernesses to hide, until a final submissive treaty was signed under Tegbesu in 1747.[44]

Given Dahomey's tributary relationship to Oyo, it is worth noting that a very similar process linking cowrie imports to state formation was at work in that Yorùbá state. As in Dahomey, all the available evidence suggests that cowrie imports increased there exponentially from the sixteenth century onwards. The value of a cowrie was never fixed, being worth more the greater the distance from the coast; cowries were strung in 5 strings of 40 (200), with 50 strings equalling a head (10,000), and 10 heads (100,000) a bag of cowries for major purchases. These denominations and the different uses of the cowries grew over time, as the import of cowries grew and their use in the kingdom with it.[45]

As with Dahomey, the increasing import of cowries is central to understanding the growth of the Oyo state in these centuries. What was occurring was the rapid expansion of the money supply, and the power of the state with it. At least 30 billion cowries went to the Bight of Benin between 1500 and 1875, accounting for 44 per cent of the total value of merchandise shipped. The increase was marked in this period, for, although cowrie-shaped reliefs are found on pottery and terracotta sculptures at Ilé-Ifè in the period between 1200 and 1500, cowries themselves are scarce in the archaeological record until the sixteenth century. The archaeologist Akinwumi Ogundiran's excavations at Ede-Ilè, a turnpike at the borders of Oyo, are even more revealing. It was said that a toll of five cowries was paid here, and Ogundiran describes the settlement as 'awash' with cowries. That they were used as money is shown by the find of cowries in a broken jar.[46]

Thus, this period of the monetization of the economy in Oyo also saw – as in Dahomey – an increase both in militarization and in state apparatus. A royal council in Oyo – the Oyo-Mesi – chose each new alafin on the death of the incumbent; the head of this council was the basorun, who came from a hereditary lineage. Guardians of the kingdom, the Esos, held a military title that came through achievement in war. There were seventy captains of the guard among the Eso, led by the kakanfo. Meanwhile, government was devolved to each village, and provincial governors ruled each district, sending taxes in cowries back to the centre at Oyo-Ile. Money, military success and government were, therefore, all interconnected in the growth of the Oyo state.[47]

This parallel account of Dahomey and Oyo shows in detail how spiritual powers were co-opted by a nascent state whose military power grew with growing monetization. But, whereas writers in the eighteenth century saw this as an 'African barbarism', what they were in fact describing was a projection of, and mirror to, similar processes of state formation in Europe, where militarization, appeals to divine power, appalling wars, rising tax revenues and fiscal control had also been deeply interconnected. The parallel political trajectories are instructive; in Europe, as well as in Africa, the growth of the use of 'hard' currency, rather than credit currency, from the fifteenth century onwards, went with rising state power and the ability to monopolize violence beyond private militias. The endemic violence and warfare described by European observers in West Africa in the late eighteenth century as a by-product of the trade in captives was, equally as much, a by-product of the state-formation process, in West Africa as anywhere else. It was this process of state formation in kingdoms such as Dahomey and Oyo that would then be interrupted by encroaching colonialism in the nineteenth century.[48]

WARFARE AND FEDERAL STATES: THE CENTRALIZATION OF POWER IN KAABU AND FUUTA JAALO

The rise of powerful states in West Africa in the eighteenth century was linked to the potential to fiscalize the government through tax revenues and – often – access to gold. Yet there were many regions of West Africa that did not have such good access to the 'hard' currencies, and that also preferred other forms of money in cloth, iron pieces, copper manillas and the like. Moreover, geographies often did not facilitate hierarchical states covering a large terrain. Regions such as the creeks and swamps of Guinea-Bissau and the Niger Delta did not lend themselves to this sort of control; to this day, they do not.

One oral account from Senegambia gives a good window on to how these more federal societies worked. Among the Mankanhes from the Guinea-Bissau region who preceded the formation of the federation of Kaabu, 'everybody was on his own. / But they don't fight, don't steal from each other, / and don't harm each other. / They settled on their own. / But their villages were not more than one hundred and twenty.'[49] This may offer a romanticized view, but it's pretty clear that decentralized societies favoured autonomy of communities; in these small-scale societies there was no 'surplus' population to trade as captives, and little incentive for military competition.

These communities privileged both age and a certain form of equality. Social organizations were grouped around the household. Speaking of the Manjaco people, who were related to the Mankanhes, another oral historian, John Mendy, described how, over time, young people were segregated by gender and divided into age grades for agricultural labour. By around the middle of the eighteenth century, Manjaco labour itself was strictly gendered: men did the weaving, collected palm oil and left the relative security of home communities to trade at markets. Yet these societies were also more egalitarian than those in the hierarchized states. Although specialized crafts such as smiths were the preserve of specific castes in many places, among the Manjaco, Mendy said, 'There is no smith family . . . / To say that this person is a smith by birth, / no that does not exist there / If you want to be a smith you can learn it.' The caste divisions that often followed – who could or couldn't marry smiths, griots, warriors – were less entrenched as well.[50]

In practice there was often an overlap between strong states and these smaller states with a less vertical hierarchy. In the Niger Delta, while the Aro traders formed a dispersed state, they often traded captives who had been secured by the armies of Oyo. Among the Bassar of what is now Togo, iron production increased at least fivefold between 1550 and 1750, allowing this small community to trade with larger states such as Gonja. Thus, in many regions of West Africa, smaller political units in practice interacted with larger centralized states. Learning how this interaction occurred is a useful way of seeing how the currents of warfare and state formation had taken shape by the end of the eighteenth century, driving a centralization of power.[51]

The Greater Senegambian region saw many such interactions. It was home to the Kaabu Federation, as well as to centralized states such as Bundu, Fuuta Jaalo, Gajaaga and Fuuta Tòòro.* Kaabu's federal structure was itself centred around its capital at Kansala. As the informant Saajo Mane described it in 1979, 'the real leadership / came from Kansala. / That Kansala, / any matter that arises, / it is finally decided there.' Kansala's fort, as another put it, was 'the most senior', though there were at least thirteen other forts in the federation by the early nineteenth century. Yet, although ultimate authority clearly rested at Kansala, Kaabu did operate a federal, decentralized system – or, as Bakary Sane, Nyanco Mane and Malang Kamara put it in 1979, 'Kaabu was not that big. / Because it was just districts.' There were many smaller kingdoms, such as Pachesi, Pachana, Puropana, Konyaji and Tumana Basari, all of which in practice became, in one form or another, client states of Kaabu by the eighteenth century.[52]

Defiantly a non-Islamic state, the religious frameworks of the Soninké who ruled Kaabu were vital. Religious power came from what became the central shrine, of the idol snake Tamba Dibi, worshipped in a grove of sacred trees: the fruits of these tabo trees were said to protect warriors from knife wounds (a belief later transferred to Islam, where verses from the Qur'ān are now said to offer the same protection). In this religious practice, Kaabu offered continuities from many long-standing religious traditions. The role of snake shrines was established as early as in the Empire of Ghana (if not before), where there was a royal snake, while, as we have seen, the python temple in Hueda was very important.[53]

In Kaabu, there were many other shrines to which valuable

* Both Bundu and Gajaaga were located in the Upper Senegal Valley, while Fuuta Tòòro was in the Middle Senegal and Fuuta Jaalo lay in the mountains of what is now northern Guinea-Conakry.

sacrifices were made, including bulls, which prevented wealthy people from being 'eaten' (exploited/sold into slavery). Spiritual concerns also meant that the borders of the federation were marked by empty bush ('nobody was in this bush/forest here . . . between here and [the border] at Bansang'), and when Kaabu warriors founded a new settlement, their first act was to burn the surrounding bush. This was a religious gesture as well as an act of conquest. Just as cutting down an enemy's sacred forests could destroy its spiritual protection in the case of Borno, so burning the bush could dispense with the enemy's spirits, establishing Kaabu's spiritual pre-eminence – and also the material conditions for settlement.[54]

From this starting point, Kaabu grew its institutions. Taxes (known as *kabanko*) were paid from each village in cloth currencies (pagnes). Wealth was 'in a form of pagne'. Sometimes these cloths were woven by slaves in Kaabu, as slavery grew through the seventeenth and eighteenth centuries. Cotton, too, was harvested by slaves on organized plantations. As in centralized states such as Asante or Dahomey, taxation and circulating currencies (in this case cloth) were important for Kaabu's power; and, as cotton production grew with the increase in numbers of slaves in Kaabu, so, too, did the amount of cloth currency that could circulate.[55]

Associated with these changes was the militarized state. The *nyantio* warriors of Kaabu formed an aristocracy. The warrior line was matrilineal, passing from mother to son. The importance of warfare to Kaabu was underlined by the oral historian Saajo Maane when he said that in 'Kaabu's old generations, by then there was only war. The Soninkés [pagans] feed on that.' *Nyantios* had a privileged place in the society, greeted as victorious heroes when they returned from raids, and often marrying women from societies who became client-states of Kaabu. The growing tax base thus allowed Kaabu to support these raids, which were grounded in the state, military power, and the propitiation of the apposite shrines and bush spirits.[56]

Warfare's social position is emphasized by the connections between the *nyantios* and other forms of daily life. One prescription for a woman's overcoming childlessness was that, 'When the warriors are returning from their tours, / and the horses come, / you must be the first

A Kanyeleng group at Foni Kalagi, in The Gambia.

to run to them / and give them water to drink.' Childlessness was seen as the fault of the woman, and, to this day in The Gambia, it is female Kanyeleng societies who celebrate the end of a prolonged bout of barrenness (and the men who pay for the festivities); but, at the same time, in this older view, it was the military power of successful *nyantios* that gave the power to overcome it.[57]

However, the constant warfare waged by Kaabu *nyantios* would exact its price, eroding the federal structure. In the early eighteenth century, Fula migrants from what is now northern Senegal came to the Fuuta Jaalo Mountains of what is now Guinea-Conakry and established an almamate in *c.* 1727. The Fula came in successive waves from the north; they 'came from Massina, and came to Nyooro, they left Nyooro and entered a place called Bundu. / They came to Bundu and then to Tanda. / They entered and came all the way to Kaabu. They also came bit by bit.' At first, they settled as the guests of Kaabu, and the Kaabu rulers forced Fula villages to cultivate farms for the government and pay tribute. However, as the Fula communities grew, they enslaved the local population in Fuuta Jaalo and created a centralized state that traded in captives with the Europeans: for the 'cause of the friendship / between the White / Men and the Fulas / [was] that the Fulas / and the white men / united and fought / these other nations'. In time, Fula power grew, and they challenged Kaabu.[58]

Political power, therefore, had many different faces here over this long period of time in Greater Senegambia. It resided in control over specific religious shrines, in the growth of a tax base and the power of the itinerant warrior aristocrats, the *nyantios*. Smaller communities such as the Manjacos and their neighbours, the Balantas and Felupes, had various geographical advantages they could use in defending themselves against raids by Kaabu or Fuuta Jaalo. They could flee into the creeks, and devise circuitous paths through the bush to and from their villages. They were certainly not passive victims. And yet, over time, the power of a centralized slave-trading state such as Fuuta Jaalo grew significantly, overtaking these smaller communities and the Federation of Kaabu.[59]

Why did the power of Fuuta Jaalo grow? Again, religion was not disconnected from state power. The Muslim state's religious scholars claimed to have secret religious powers that could dispel the spirits of the bush. In clearing land, more food could be produced, feeding the growing army. Eventually, religious power, state power, and the ability to harness the tax base and expand production would all contribute to the fall of Kaabu to Fuuta Jaalo in 1866, and the rise of centralized state power in a region where smaller political units had previously prevailed.[60]

CURRENCIES AND THE STATE IN THE EIGHTEENTH CENTURY

The eighteenth century was one of endemic warfare in West Africa. 'Those times were different from now,' says one oral historian from the Kaabu region. 'It was a time of war, people got together and raided others or attacked them. They captured slaves and materials, took half to the ruler and sold the other half. That was how they made money in those days': this is the 'fiscal-military state' in West African experience and memory.[61]

Also remembered here is the interplay of state and private power. The vital role of funding the warfare state through cowrie tax receipts has already been shown in detail in this chapter for the cases of Dahomey and Oyo. Indeed, Oyo's expansion towards the Atlantic from the late seventeenth century onwards occurred, according to some, because of the desire to control access to cowrie monies. At his *simboji* in Abomey, the King of Dahomey kept storehouses of cowries and iron bars – the bank of the kingdom – and the cowrie was the single largest import to the kingdom – even in a period when the availability of alcohol, gunpowder and clothing from the Atlantic trade had increased. The import and securing of the money supply was, therefore, all-important to the fiscalization of the state, and the expansion of the army.[62]

This relationship between money and state power had been growing for some time. As early as 1686, the Dutch complained that the English were giving huge numbers of cowries for enslaved persons at Allada, 82 pounds for one person, and as a result had at least four times as much trade as the Dutch. By 1720, around 450 tons of cowries were exported to the Bight of Benin per year, and this was a third of the value of all goods exported there. By the 1730s, the Portuguese, too, carried cowries from India and Mozambique via Brazil, and cowries were also being shipped between the Gold Coast at Accra and Hueda. Meanwhile, as we saw in the introduction to this chapter, the place of Brazilian gold grew throughout these decades. Thus, the continuous role of the money imports in state growth and the expanding military apparatus in West Africa shaped many things: the experience of power, the financing of expanding armies, the growth of enslavement, and the divisions between aristocratic warriors, traders and the rest of the population.[63]

Moreover, Dahomey was far from being the only state with a close relationship between the strength of state institutions and access to the cowrie currency. Another was Segu, where the oral narratives suggest that it was in the reign of Ngolo Jara (*c.* 1766–87) that the cowrie money economy grew into its own; as the griot Tayiru Banbera put it,

In those days we lived in the time of cowries.
Rows of granaries full of cowries were the legacy of Ngolo.
At that time there was a granary full of nothing but cowries.
It was so full that if a lizard hit it with its tail, cowries would come pouring out.[64]

This represented a big change, since, in the early days of the kingdom, according to Banbera, 'there was no currency. / In those days there were no cowries.' Indeed, according to many oral narratives, polities in this region of what is now Mali charged no taxes, and it was Segu that brought about this innovation. Very early on, Biton Kulubali (*c.* 1712–55) had seen the importance of growing power through access to taxes. As one oral narrative puts it:

People collected the tax and took it to Biton	*Segu disɔngɔ dè tùnbé bɔ kà tága dí Biton*
Kulibali at Old Segu.	*Kulibali mà Segu kɔrɔ.*
Each year it was to this Biton Kulibali	*Ò Biton Kulibali sàa mána yɛlema mí dísɔngɔ álájɛra*
That you had to bring the tax which had been raised.	*ù bé tága kà tága à dí Biton Kulibali mà.*[65]

Thus, in Segu as in Dahomey, cowrie taxes grew, and with them government power and authority. By the time of Ngolo Jara's successor, Da Monzon (1787–1808), the palace of Segu had seven halls, and was guarded over by special military chiefs. Segu had an imposing army: the cavalry was powerful, and each captain and each lieutenant had a thousand troops under his command. The military expeditions of the kingdom were often related to tax- and tribute-raising. Here is a now-familiar pattern, in which tax receipts in cowries and the growth of the warrior state were deeply connected; the arrival of more currency expanded the potential market, and the potential for political control of the market.[66]

Nevertheless, it is important to understand that the use of money in these West African kingdoms had a varied purpose and was not limited to accumulation according to some paradigm of a supposedly rational (and male) *Homo economicus*. As noted previously in Senegambia, in Segu, cowries were used for divination; as Tayiru Banbera put it, 'the cowrie throwers scattered cowries on the floor of a room and sat down to study them.' But what is also important is that these divination practices with cowries were connected to the *mithqāl* gold coin that also circulated as a form of currency in the Niger Bend region at this time. Diviners placed a *mithqāl* at the bottom of a special drink called *dègè*, and whichever child found the *mithqāl* would, said the diviners, inherit the power of the household when the owner had died. Gold brought power, and that was, indeed, the diviners' message.[67]

In Segu, as in Dahomey in the eighteenth century, the gold coin and cowries coexisted – emphasizing the importance of access to gold to military success, since Segu was also a state that endured long into the nineteenth century. The Nikky *mithqāl* was a standard currency weight in a very wide region of the Niger Bend. Carried by traders connected to the trans-Saharan trade, this was a gold coin minted in the town of Nikky, in the northern part of today's Republic of Benin, with characteristics similar to coins circulating in Morocco. Its interchangeability with trans-Saharan trade is shown through its name (*mithqāl*, very closely connected to *mistqal* in Morocco). Its worth was tied closely to a hundred wheat grains, which was useful for traders who by now used a decimal system for the cowries. Its minting and circulation show the awareness in many West African rulers of the importance of retaining gold to retain power: gold's wider global capital value was a vital source of strength in the eighteenth century.[68]

That cowries and the *mithqāl* are connected in oral narratives is therefore important, and here the account of how Ngolo Jara found his *mithqāl* himself is quite revealing. According to Banbera, 'On that day Ngolo was wearing his loincloth. / He wore a loincloth, and a small net bag for cowries hung at his side.' Once he found the *mithqāl*, he put it in the net bag with the cowries. That is, cowries were carried in a purse much like coins, but political power was also closely related to the use of the *mithqāl* and to control over it (explaining how and why gold mattered for the success of the state).[69]

As the eighteenth century unwound, the relationship between warfare, money supply and the trade in enslaved persons became ever more acute. States that had access to gold, such as Asante, Dahomey,

Gajaaga and Segu, were stronger economically and thus better able to finance their expanding armies and resist growing movements of popular unrest. If a kingdom lost its access to gold, as happened to Dahomey after the 1760s, when the rate of Brazilian exports declined, it had to pursue alternative means to access capital. This meant that Dahomey sought to redouble its trading activities, because this was the only way of accessing the cowries that underpinned the state money supply. By becoming perhaps the major African exporter of captives in the eighteenth century, Dahomey was able to substitute 'captive money' for gold and retain access to capital for military defence. Warfare and the capture of enslaved persons had become a core means of political and social power, and of access to money, in an environment in which, as we saw in the previous chapter, captives were often viewed as stores of value and a form of currency.[70]

Looking at the history of the state, therefore, offers vistas that may seem surprising to some. For, as we have seen, the development of the state in West Africa occurred in a very similar paradigm to that of Europe at this time. In Asante, Dahomey, Kaabu and Segu, as in England, France and Spain, monarchical power was enshrined by spiritual power, and state power grew alongside the spread of currencies and the growth of the tax base that was needed to fight wars. Moreover, while historians have often implied that state institutions in West Africa were static, this was no more true here than elsewhere. As the money supply grew, so did new administrative offices in Dahomey and other states, and so there was a direct connection between the globalization of West Africa in the era of the slave trade and changes to the structures of political power. And yet the interconnection of gold and cowries was also significant in broader global relationships. These vast cowrie imports in the eighteenth century saw the relative value of cowries against gold decline, and played their part in the relative economic decline of West Africa's access to capital and surplus value. Where states had no access to gold, as in Kaabu, their power might collapse.[71]

There is a major irony in these findings. As we saw in the previous chapter, slave traders often claimed that they were 'saving' Africans by enslaving them and transporting them to a Christian life across the Atlantic Ocean; meanwhile, Abolitionists often decried the political disorder in West Africa as 'caused' by the trade in captives. But the political violence that both pro-slavery and Abolitionist activists noted in West Africa was not any the less related to state formation there than European political violence had been in Europe. Denunciations of 'barbarous' polities were, as much as anything, projections of the experience of state formation in Europe, which, during such periods as the Thirty Years War (1618–48), had also been one of extraordinary violence.

THE EXPERIENCE OF STATE POWER: THE EXAMPLE OF KANO

The relationship between money and power has never been limited to politics. As we have seen, in West Africa (and in Europe, too), it was deeply connected to religious practice and authority. Of course, some of the gold that arrived in Spain from the New World found its way into magnificent altarpieces and ornate decorative art that spoke of Spain's religious power in the sixteenth century, its golden age. Gold was similarly used for royal display on the Gold Coast and in Dahomey, as were coral beads and cowries. Money's new power in Africa was experienced in various ways: through the expansion of armies and the state, but also through royal symbols of power.

Further east from Dahomey, Benin also offers a good example of how imported currencies were seen as an opportunity for the display of political power, beyond any simple monetary value. 'The Wives of the Great Lords [of Benin],' wrote Bosman around 1700, '[have] their Necks adorned with Neck-laces of Coral . . . their Arms are dressed up with bright Copper or Iron Arm-rings; as are also the legs of some of them, and their Fingers are as thick crowded with copper-rings as they can possibly wear them.' Coral beads had been imported from the start by the Portuguese, supplementing existing locally manufactured glass beads as a symbol of religious and political power.[72]

Benin symbolizes well the changing face and use of money in West Africa. Some of the military helmets depicted on the Benin Bronzes were garlanded with cowrie shells. The use of cowries as symbolic of money and power probably derived from the place of coral beads in designating the aristocracy; and the Ugi Evie coral-bead festival, dating from the sixteenth century, shows how important this had already become in the performance of royal power in Benin. The place of the cowries on helmets in Benin reveals that, symbolically, money and military power were interlinked. The idea of the 'fiscal-military state' is not, therefore, simply a Western concept, but one that also makes sense of the experience of power and money in different parts of West Africa over this period of time.[73]

Beyond the rising symbolic importance of money and commerce, how was this growth of militarized state power experienced by subjects? What was it like to be on the receiving end of military raids, or increasingly remote and authoritarian kings? This matters enormously, for it is in this experience of power that the relationship between African subjects and the modern centralized state was first established. Questions of postcolonial statehood may have much to do with the historical forms through which people first experienced the state in Africa – whether as a sort of 'protection racket' broadly protecting people from arbitrary violence, as in Europe, or as a potential source of danger and predation.

The memories of capture narrated in the last chapter give some sense of the nature of this experience. As so often, oral narratives supplement these with some of the richest accounts of the human experience in West Africa. In the Sahel, the case of Kano exemplifies this. In 1960, a historian managed to interview a woman named Hawwa, aged around a hundred years old, who had been taught the 'Song of Bagauda' in Kano as a child, *c.* 1870.* Bagauda was a 'mighty hunter' who, the song had it, was the first to clear the bush around Kano and set the ground for the great city-state that emerged there. However, once the bush was cleared and the people came,

> There came a killing famine
> And there was no corn to be had; only by coming to them
> Could it be had, and they doled it out in small quantities.
> They became well off in slaves and horses too;
> They were the great traders.[74]

* For a discussion of the 'Song of Bagauda', see above, Chapter 1.

Although after 1730 Kano's power was eroded by its neighbour and rival Katsina, it remained strong. Kano's indigo-dyed, deep-blue cloths were fashion accessories across the desert, in Timbuktu, and as far north as the Mediterranean cities of Fez and Tripoli. Moreover, Hausa traders from Kano connected up the two trading systems, Atlantic and Saharan. The Atlantic dimension grew in the eighteenth century, as Kano merchants developed a heavy trade in textiles, leather goods and enslaved persons with the Volta River Basin and Oyo. As in the Atlantic kingdoms, credit was a fundamental part of the expanding trade system, retaining its dual moral and financial meaning. Thus, the economic models of the northern and southern systems became intertwined.[75]

Indeed, it was in the later eighteenth century, according to the 'Song of Bagauda', that this commercial influence became experienced in formal military terms. Under the rule of Babba Zaki (1747–71 according to the Kano Chronicle):

> It was his sovereignty that set the standard for Kano.
> It was in his time that horses were amassed.
> He had a strong force of cavalry with protective quilting, and of
> body-guards.
> It was he who introduced remoteness into kingship,
> Setting body-guards to rebuke the people.[76]

Remoteness, violence, and the growing strength of the army and cavalry: this was the experience of state power, of the 'fiscal-military state', as expressed in the 'Song of Bagauda'. Other sources also suggest the terror that these well-armed cavalries created across the savannah regions, among those preyed on by the states of Borno and Kano. 'The Sultan of Borno is continually at war,' one English traveller in Tunis learnt in the 1780s, 'tak[ing] prisoners [who] are sold to the Arabs, and this traffic constitutes the principal commerce of the country'. His military force 'consist[ed] in the multitude of his horsemen: for his foot soldiers are few in number, and are scarcely considered as contributing to the strength of the battle'.[77]

Thus, the picture in the Sahel of expanding exports of captives across the Sahara in the eighteenth century mirrors that across the Atlantic. The experience of organized warfare was fundamental, and the place of the cavalry in this expansion is marked in these accounts. Further west, the importance of horses is underlined by the Tuareg attack on Timbuktu in 1771, in which the guardian of the royal stables was killed. Though it was not the first time that the Tuareg had sacked Timbuktu, the attack on the royal stables seems significant: controlling access to horses and seizing them with force had by this time become a vital aspect of success in warfare in Timbuktu, Kano and Borno.[78]

When we consider the experience of warfare and state power, then, the memories of the centralization of power and the fear and struggle which that provoked are clear. The rise of statehood was associated with violence, predation and an ultimate refusal to accept it. Those who hungered after power for its own sake, for pseudo-religious exaltation and acclaim, are not remembered kindly in the oral sources. The 'Song of Bagauda' captured vividly the emptiness of power and its demise, once the great Kano aristocracies and families had been overthrown in the early nineteenth century: 'You will not find another who talks as vainly as the world does / In your longest memory and searching / . . . The master's compound in which the great ones lived / Has become empty, and there are none in it.'[79]

This suspicion of the emptiness of state power had grown with the violence that it had meted out. In the end, in both the Atlantic and the Sahelian cases, the expanding trade in enslaved persons prompted the militarization of the African state. These states could fight wars and supply captives, to meet African religious and political needs and external economic demand. Economic growth in the West was thus directly dependent on military build-ups in Africa. There was little better way to destabilize a political environment than through engaging in an active arms trade, and the weaponizing of these conflicts through the export of cheap arms manufactured in Europe. As a consequence, state power in Africa became suspicious to African subjects, connected to extractive economic cycles and the experience so many in the region came to have of predatory warfare.

CONCLUSION: MONEY, STATE POWER AND POPULAR REFUSAL TO 1800

This chapter has shown how the expansion of the trade in captives in the eighteenth century required the militarization of African state power. In the Sahel, this was provided by cavalry, since there were no tsetse flies to kill off the horses with sleeping sickness. In the Atlantic areas, where horses could not be involved in military campaigns, warfare was organized differently, with the rise in imported firearms and militarized secret societies. Here, centralized states did not arise, and smaller societies and federations emerged, often with a similar approach to revenue-raising, but with an alternative approach to statecraft that was frequently modelled on the household unit. In all cases, warfare and the state required more money, and the growth of tax to support them.[80]

The fundamental relationship between warfare, a monetized state and the trade in captives can finally be put into a full context by Benin's history. By the eighteenth century, Benin's flourishing output of bronzes declined significantly, having been cut out of the Atlantic trade owing to its refusal to trade in male captives. Into the late seventeenth century, Benin had traded in cloth, but then external demand had lapsed. As late as 1682, English factors described how Benin produced 'all sorts of clothes', and, in 1687, the English factor at Komenda on the Gold Coast received 400 Benin cloths for trade. But already the writing was on the wall, for these cloths were 'sold cheap for any sorts of goods'.[81]

The economic decline had begun, reminding us of the oral narrative of how at a certain point a 'different white man' arrived who would buy only slaves.* This key change took place around the start of the eighteenth century. By then, while cowries were still the currency, and taxes were paid by regional governors to the capital at Edo, the weaving industry was in steep decline. The markets at Edo still operated, but the city was full of 'Ruins of half remaining Houses . . . at present the Houses stand like poor Mens Corn, widely

* See above, Chapter 4.

distant from each other.' The glory days of the powerful military, the expanding royal festivals and the complexity of a powerful administration were gone. Benin's 'fiscal-military state' had beaten a retreat.[82]

Yet, later in the eighteenth century, Benin's fortunes underwent a revival. By belatedly entering the trade in enslaved persons, obas were able to gain access to the cowries that could recapitalize the state. The army grew, and with it the ability of the obas to defend Edo. By 1799, Dahomey's king would write to propose a joint military alliance against some mutual foes near Elmina, testament to Benin's revival.[83] Through the trade in captives, the imports in cowries stemmed the decline, and a visitor in 1786 gave a rich description of the oba's council:

> Four fiadors conducted us to the council chamber, which was at least sixty feet long, and at the other end we saw the king in an arm-chair raised three steps up. He was dressed in a very fine white pagne ... sixty old men about seventy years of age, known as the 'big men', dressed in superb pagnes, surrounded their master. Every one of them wore around his neck, ankles, and wrists two rows of very large coral, which is the distinctive mark of the highest office of the state ... the above number of old men is divided into three sections; twenty of them have charge of receipts and expenses, and are called the council of the finance minister, twenty others make up the council of the minister for war, and occupy themselves with all that concerns peace and war; and the last twenty have control of trade.[84]

This account offers a neat summary of the fiscal-military state by the late eighteenth century: trade brought money, which was accounted for by some officials of the state, and spent on warfare to procure captives, to be exchanged for more money by others. As the trade in captives had grown in the eighteenth century, so Benin's power had recovered; that re-engaging with the trade in enslaved persons was a means of recapitalizing shows how far these persons had become stores of value – currencies – by this time. The display of the currency of state – the cowrie – on military helmets symbolized the power of this relationship.

In the end, as we saw at the start of this chapter, those West African states best able to access the capital needed to build a military infrastructure were the ones best able to endure. Beneath this state consolidation lay deep tensions. The administrative apparatuses of the larger states developed strong military power, but alongside them in many non-Islamic West African states were the secret societies. Popular discourses of warfare, religious practice and belonging here created powerful vehicles to resist state power. By the end of the eighteenth century, when the link between warfare and enslavement had become industrialized, the social institutions that would then resist this convergence had been born. Struggle against state power would characterize much African history from this point on, as it still does today.

8

Feeding Power: New Societies, New Worldviews

By the early eighteenth century, rituals surrounding the installation of kings had become highly elaborate in many parts of West Africa. In Dahomey, Robert Norris provided a fair description. On the last day of the annual customs at the capital of Abomey, 'a large stage is erected near one of the palace gates, adorned with flags and umbrellas, and surrounded with a fence of thorns, to keep off the rabble; on this are piled heaps of silesias, checks, callicoes, and a variety of other European and Indian goods; a great many fine cotton cloths that are manufactured in the *Eyo* [Oyo] country; and a prodigious quantity of cowries.' The dadá distributed the cloths to the European military captains and Dahomeyan nobility who had come to Abomey for the ceremony, while the cowries were flung into the crowds.[1]

The installation of kings was lavish in many places. One oral account from Senegambia described what happened when a new mansa took the throne in Kaabu:

> You know the Mandinkas, when they were installing a ruler,
> they took palm leaves and tied them on the person's head.
> Next they made it into a chair-like form, just like a chair . . .
> They made the chair and decorated it nicely.
> They then set him on it.
> The mansa (ruler) then sat on that chair.
> Next, there were a number of eight people.
> The other was then on poles, long poles.
> Then these people raise up those poles with him.
> At that moment, they would say, 'Say, what you have seen?'
> The person then says his desires.

That was how the Mandinkas did it, earlier on.
They put him down.
They raised him up again and say to him
'What do you say?'
He would talk.
His desires, he says them.
He says them.
They paid greater attention to his utterances.
Then they put him down.
That was what they did for seven times.
Then they fired guns.
That was twelve gun salutes.
The griots then extolled him,
they put him down.
When they put him down, they spread mats
from where they installed him right up to his bed . . .
Bulls were slaughtered continuously, the griots [musicians] were playing.
There was a feast,
Night and day, only feast.[2]

The growth of royal majesty was testament to the power of the new fiscal-military states. It also accentuated the gathering divide between rulers and subjects. As this description from Kaabu shows, along with the militarized violence discussed at the end of the last chapter, it was through these new hierarchies that transformations in power were experienced by a ruler's subjects, female traders, farmers and servants, the warriors, weavers, fishermen, hunters and craftspeople, who together made up society. In fact, the social changes that went with the economic transformations of this era ran very deep; the new social institutions that emerged would be galvanizing forces in the revolutions of the late eighteenth century.

What were the major factors at play in the growing gulf between rulers and subjects in West Africa, one that in many ways continues to the present day? As we have seen, the increasing currency imports allowed the fiscalization of the state and the concentration of military power. By controlling currency imports and production, rulers enhanced their control of society. Growing state power both arose with the imports of currency, and fomented the place of 'real' money in society. Newly powerful states such as Asante and Dahomey, with their treasuries of cowries and pouches of gold dust, were underwriters of the new social and economic dispensations.[3]

These transformations prompted fierce struggles against them. A core dynamic to emerge was the struggle between civil society and state power. While warrior elites and their chosen rulers benefited from the rise of the fiscal-military state, it was commoners who became expendable as troops and potential captives. Pushback followed. By the middle of the seventeenth century, rulers recognized that in order to consolidate power in the hands of the king and local elites, they would need to develop systems to control people's time and labour. Correspondingly, religious practice itself changed to reflect the new priorities and experiences that had come to be normal.[4]

This chapter studies the enormous transformations in West African societies in this era, belying the Western stereotype of a static and unchanging world. Labour, gender relations, religious belief and the perception of slavery as an institution were all radically transformed in this period. Understanding this is essential to understanding the movements of reform and revolution that then arose at the end of the eighteenth century.

CONTRADICTIONS IN THE NEW ROYAL POWER

For the newly powerful monarchs in West Africa, controlling the population was vital to cementing the authority invested in rulership. Fiscal-military states required authoritarian power, and so allowed for the disposal of potential young rivals as captives or in warfare. Yet these powers also produced the social structures and imbalances that helped West African subjects to fight back. The mechanisms of power increased coercion, while also producing contradictions of power. It was these paradoxes that would eat away at the power of the new states by 1800.

It's important to recognize that these paradoxes were part of global ideological tensions in the eighteenth century. The economic revolution sweeping Africa, Europe, the Americas and the Middle East required a new worldview. In Europe and North America, this depended on the sublimation of material value. In the West, this would find its ideological expression best in the emergence of the discipline of economics, and the Adam Smith School, in the late eighteenth century; and yet the sublimation of material value had stemmed from treating people as commodities, from the paradox of denying their humanity while requiring their intelligence as planters, coopers and smiths to keep the plantation working. In the Islamic world of West Africa, somewhat analogous paradoxes emerged in the tension between Islam as a religion that protected people from enslavement, and the enormous increase of the institution of slavery itself in Islamic states such as Sokoto in the nineteenth century.

Beyond these elements, the contradictions of power in West Africa included some of these trends, but had also their own qualities. The core tension was between the respect the newly powerful kings demanded, and the structures they created that had the potential to undermine this. These ideological tensions connected with those in the West and in the Islamic world, catalysing between them the Age of Revolution. This chain reaction saw the consummation of this disruptive drive, which had been born through the emergence of capitalism.[5]

For West African rulers, controlling the population often depended on an interplay of new systems of production and transformed religious worldviews. Along the Gambia River, this was apparent by the eighteenth century. The agricultural transformations of the previous centuries already were clear. An illustration in the 1738 book of Francis Moore of a village in the region depicts a carefully structured enclosure, with crops cultivated and stored in defined sectors of the village.

One French account written in the 1750s describes manioc, yams and potatoes grown in these villages, while rice was virtually the only grain grown. Small dykes were cut through the floodplain, holding in the waters and flooding the ricefields, meaning that 'the Country look'd beautiful, being for the most Part woody, but between the Woods pleasant green Rice Grounds, which after the Rice is cut are stocked with Cattle.' Meanwhile, village houses had thick mud walls, which became very solid as they dried: the thatched roofs descended out at even angles to a low wall around the perimeter of the house, which formed a small gallery where people were sheltered from the sun in the hottest part of

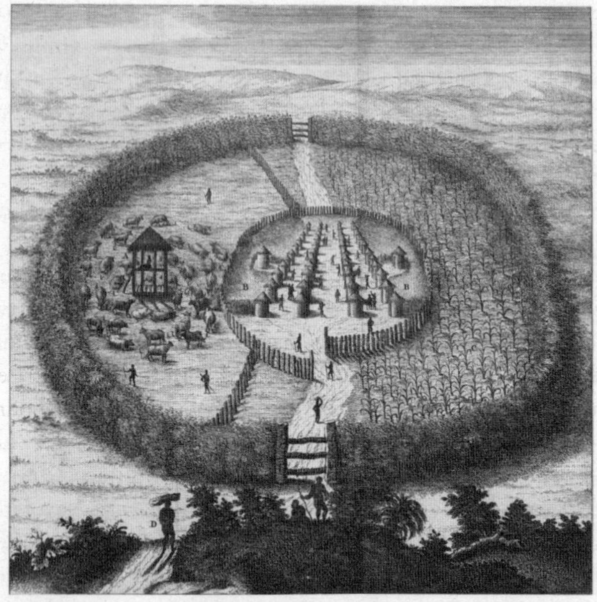

Francis Moore's depiction of a village in Gambia, with cattle pastures to the left, houses in the centre and crops to the right.

the day (as, indeed, still occurs in some parts of Greater Senegambia, especially the Fuuta Jaalo Mountains of Guinea-Conakry).[6]

Carefully organized systems of production to intersperse rice planting and cattle-raising, and to allocate certain portions of villages for cultivation and grain storage, all required stronger political hierarchies. No wonder the ceremonies accompanying the installation of the mansas of Kaabu became so elaborate. However, for these new structures to be effective, people needed to internalize them in transformed systems of belief. Multiple secret societies emerged, and the masquerades associated with them (such as the Ékpè in Calabar examined in the last chapter). Far from somehow being 'unchanging' and ossified in a 'primitive past', West African religious beliefs and social structures transformed themselves in this era. They were new and as specific to the eighteenth century as, say, Christian Methodism and the Salafiya reform movement of Islam; they were the West African response to modernity, just as Methodism and Salafism embodied Christian and Muslim responses.

The new shrines and religious societies represented the growing materialism and violence of the Atlantic era. They embodied this through their masquerades and the offerings presented to freshly created shrines – for it was impossible to make these offerings and so gain religious access without participating in the extractive trades that could finance this participation. In this way, the peoples of West and West-Central Africa performed truth to power; yet, at the same time, by embedding religious worship in the structures of the slave trade, some of the paradoxes and contradictions of these new beliefs were exposed.

One of the best examples of how production and belief intertwined comes from Senegambia. Here, a masquerade known as Mama-Jori emerged some time before 1700, associated with the tasks of rice production and the power that was required to distribute labour and resources. This masquerade made the trans-Atlantic crossing to Louisiana alongside enslaved captives from this region, where it became known as Mama-Jombo, still represented during masquerades in New Orleans' Mardi Gras parades. Many of the enslaved Africans working in the rice-fields of South Carolina in the eighteenth century also came from the Senegambian region, traded by the French from their posts in Senegal.[7]

The Mama-Jori masquerade was often associated with rites of passage, especially circumcision ceremonies. Travelling in Bambuk, in the Upper Senegal Valley, in 1729, Claude Boucard recounted how, during these ceremonies, 'there are some men who are reputed for sorcerers, who are called *mama yambaux* [Jombo], who paint their bodies with clay, cover themselves in branches and [pieces of] trees.' When the young gathered for the circumcision ritual, the *mama yambaux* charged after them, cutlass in hand.[8]

A famous account of the masquerade is found in Francis Moore's travel book, providing an account of the 'Mumbo-Jumbo' masquerade of Senegambia:

> It is dressed in a long coat made of the Bark of Trees, with a Tuft or fine Straw on the Top, and when the person wears it is about eight or nine foot High. This is a thing invented by Men to keep their Wives in awe, who are so ignorant (or at least obliged to pretend to be so) as to take it for a Wild-Man . . . It never comes abroad but in the Night-time, which makes it have the better Effect. Whenever the Men have

> any dispute with the Women, this Mumbo-Jumbo is sent for to determine it; which is, I may say always in favour of the Men.[9]

Roughly seventy years later, the French traveller Jean-Baptiste Durand offered a similar portrait. The Mumbo-Jumbo was created 'to contain the women ... when a husband thinks they have reason to complain about the conduct of his wife, he disguises himself or calls on one of his friends to disguise himself with this mask'; making for the meeting point, or *bentaba* (also known as the *bentang*), the Mumbo-Jumbo 'terrifies all the women ... each of them thinks that his visit concerns her alone'.[10]

Durand and Moore offer a window on to a vital aspect of social change in this period, but one so difficult to access. Religious transformations brought with them gendered divisions. Just as secret societies were segregated by gender, so, too, these masquerades reproduced this experience. Thus, gendered experiences of power were among the main features of social transformations at this time. Increasing male casualties in warfare and through the trade in enslaved persons (where men were in far greater demand than women from European slavers) led to frequent gender imbalances. In some places, such as among the Igbo of the Niger Delta, this was dealt with through women being allowed to marry other women and adopt a masculine role in terms of childrearing and household life. For others, as in many Mandinga societies of Senegambia and among the Anlo of the Gold Coast, it meant that elder male political leaders determined there should be a greater onus on controlling women's labour and marriage choices.[11]

It's important to consider this transformation in relative terms, especially since the catch-all of 'Mumbo-Jumbo' later became a racist trope used in a variety of obnoxious cartoon strips and pseudo-scientific publications in twentieth-century Europe. For, of course, West Africa was hardly alone in seeing a picture of increasing male power alongside the rise of the fiscal-military state. This was also a feature of European societies; in Britain, for example, the Reform Act of 1832 enshrined the suffrage as male, and was the first specifically to bar female voting. In Africa, as we will see, there were nevertheless alternatives for women seeking more autonomy, through trade or at Court.

The paradoxes underpinning these social transformations are important. On one hand, the growth of currency and the spread of the market saw centralizing power in the hands of rulers such as the asantehenes of Asante, the alafins of Oyo and the obas of Benin. And yet this centralizing power came to be in great tension with the new frameworks of societies, as trade, religious practice and gender interacted in new ways everywhere. Respect for royal power, as manifested in masquerade, royal investitures and performances, was also fear when this power grew, propped up by royal control of religion and the supernatural. If that control ebbed, and the mask of power slipped, the wave of unrest would be hard to hold back.

GENDER AND POLITICAL STRUCTURES

On 25 March 1684, the Portuguese captain-general in the Atlantic trading port of Cacheu, Joseph Gonçalves de Oliveira, was captured and imprisoned in a conspiracy led by the most powerful trader in the port, a woman named Bibiana Vaz. A major slave-trading port throughout the seventeenth century, Cacheu was often a site of power struggles and ill temper, and gambling was a frequent pastime to while away the time. Vaz and her trading partners had become angered by Oliveira's attempt to prevent the entrance of all non-Portuguese ships into the port, since they traded freely with the English. Eventually her ally, the factor, Manuel de Souza, seized Oliveira, held a show trial and sent him in irons to Vaz's house in the town of Farim, more than 50 miles upriver on the borders of Kaabu. Oliveira remained chained in abject isolation here for fourteen months, in a dark corridor of Vaz's provincial trading house.[12]

Vaz's power had grown with that of her brother, Ambrósio Gomes. In the late 1650s, Gomes had been among those fomenting a conspiracy against another powerful woman in Cacheu, Crispina Peres, who was then the richest trader in the port. Peres was arrested on trumped-up charges of 'fetishism' and deported for trial by the Inquisition in Lisbon. The seizure of her goods and the ill health of her husband meant that Gomes and Vaz were able to take control of trading networks between the port and the surrounding kingdoms. By 1684, Gomes had died and his sister, Vaz, was widely cited as the ringleader of the uprising against Oliveira.[13]

Vaz had come to dominate in Cacheu using many of the same stratagems that Crispina Peres had used before her. When officials tried to seize Vaz's goods in 1687, they found none in Cacheu, as they had all been moved to the homes of her allies outside the city, 'in the land of the gentiles'. They could not seize her nephew, either, since he was trading in Sierra Leone, while Vaz herself had taken refuge in the house of a local king. Clearly, her alliances with local rulers had become close, and long-distance trade was vital in building her power. Of mixed African and European ancestry, people like Vaz and her relatives were ideally placed to trade between African and European kingdoms and networks, and to become the richest members of the community.[14]

Across West and West-Central Africa, many coastal ports saw similar patterns. On the Gold Coast, Fante women often became important traders. Any children that they might have with Dutch traders at the fort could inherit property and goods only through the *abusua* (mother's lineage), which meant that women were able to exert considerable autonomy in their relationships both with European men and in local trading ties. An important study of Benguela in Angola shows a similar pattern, where women could become upwardly mobile by marrying foreign traders, and then dominate the trade in Atlantic goods inland through their personal networks. These 'Donas' modelled themselves on colonial women in Brazil, walking the streets of

The ruined fortress of Cacheu, with a severed statue of an early Portuguese governor.

this small colonial town surrounded by their slaves, dressed in foreign fashions, heavy jewellery adorning their ears, arms and necks.[15]

Thus, in trading centres along the coast of Atlantic Africa, a clear pattern emerges. With men preoccupied by warfare, hunting and the growing structures of political administration, trade could become the preserve of women. Moreover, some women could gain preferential access to prestige goods through marriage to the Atlantic traders, who were all men. Local kings often encouraged them to do this: if a male spouse died, the property would remain in the kingdom, sometimes with the king himself or else with the children of the marriage. When one Portuguese trader died in Bissau in 1699, for instance, the King of the Pepels announced that all the man's property belonged to him.[16]

In these Atlantic settlements, women became an important class of traders. This was not merely because they gained power through marrying outsiders, since this was also true in areas without an influential European trader presence, and women's trading prowess remains the norm in many West African markets to this day. Women were the main traders of the Fula in Senegambia in the seventeenth century. Meanwhile, writing of Benin in the early seventeenth century, the Dutch sailor-trader Dierick Ruyters noted that many of the market sellers were women, who 'brought all sorts of things to sell, such as live dogs, of which they eat many, roasted monkies, catfish, rats, parrots, fowls, yams, manigette pepper in pods or ears, dried lizards, palm oil, large beans, as well as various sorts of fruits, vegetables, and animals fit for food'. There was also woodwork, fine thread and cloths, and a large variety of ironwork for sale, and ample opportunity for women to make sales and accrue cowries.[17]

Such evidence suggests the need to rethink traditional stereotypes regarding female power in West and West-Central African societies. Prior to the arrival of Christian missionaries and the Islamic reform movements, in many African societies women had substantial autonomy, which was by no means limited to trade. Women were active warriors in states as distant from each other as Dahomey and Ndongo, where women held positions of military command in the armies led by Nzinga in the 1640s and 1650s against the Portuguese in Luanda. In both Dahomey and Ndongo, too, women possessed religious power and could act as priests. Women rulers existed as well, in Ndongo, and also in some smaller decentralized states in Senegambia and in the

Niger Delta. Power was becoming masculinized in many parts of West Africa, as we shall see, but this process was in some places overturning earlier structures that could be more equitable.[18]

Beyond trade, the other major arena in which women had the chance to gain autonomy was within the royal palaces. As more and more men either died in warfare or were exported as captives into the trans-Atlantic trade, gender imbalances grew. This increased polygamy; and in royal palaces such as Dahomey's this offered royal wives the opportunity for substantial influence. Even the Yovogan of Ouidah had several hundred wives in the 1730s, despite being a eunuch, showing that the huge number of royal wives did not always have sexual connotations. The extent of this female power is expressed well by the account of the Brazilian priest Vicente Pires, who described, of his 1797 to Dahomey visit, how the migan (or prime minister) was the most powerful of all the king's councillors – except for the Council of Wives, who could overrule him on all affairs. According to Pires, the king's wives all had different jobs, with some being barbers, others key bearers and others supplicating the deities in the shrines.[19]

This pattern is well documented at Dahomey. All residents of the palace were called *ahosi*, or royal wives, and they were often titled officers of the state. Princesses, the *ahovi*, also lived in the palace, and had a central role in selecting dadás. The *ahosi* farmed selected lands, and could trade and sell goods in their own right. No man was allowed within twenty feet of the dadá, not even the most senior military commander, and instead had to communicate through the dakhlo, or queen mother. Meanwhile, in Oyo (to which Dahomey was subject), when the alafin was no longer popular with his subjects, it was his wives who strangled him.[20]

Wherein lay the power of women in the Court of the Dadá of Dahomey? Various factors were at play: in addition to the loss of males through warfare and enslavement already mentioned, there was also the fear of palace coups by potential male heirs/rivals. Above all, the religious role of women in the royal cults was vital. The cult of the python of Hueda, Dangbé, existed with the help of thousands of female novices, the *beta*. They held significant power, and, when they were possessed by the spirit of Dangbé, their husbands had to prostrate themselves before them and do whatever they commanded.

By the later eighteenth century, many of the warriors of Dahomey were women, and the religious power accrued by women may have contributed to their military prowess, since, as we saw in the previous chapter, warfare and spirituality were deeply connected.[21]

One text written in the late 1790s, probably by the leader of the Sokoto revolution, Uthmān dan Fodio, described well these gendered parameters of royal power: 'One of the ways of their government is to place many women in their houses, until the number of women of some of them amounts to one thousand or more. One of the ways of their government is that [a man] puts the affairs of his women into the hands of the oldest one.'[22] However, this text was written not about Dahomey, but about the Hausa kingdoms of what is now northern Nigeria. Indeed, the place of women in political rule in the Sahel is clear from a number of sources. In Borno, a similar pattern of the political power of women in royal palaces existed in the middle of the seventeenth century (and probably long before): one account of 1658 describes the mai's mother as having twenty personal retainers-at-arms, each of whom commanded a thousand slaves. This is striking evidence from a part of West Africa that is not today known for its gender equality, and shows how huge were the transformations that began to take place in the eighteenth century.[23]

Thus, the centrality of royal women described above for Dahomey and Oyo was widespread in diverse regions of West Africa by the end of the eighteenth century. An early nineteenth-century description of the Kumasi Court of the asantehene offers a similar impression: when the asantehene at length emerged for an audience with the English emissary, 'he was followed by his aunts, sisters, and others of his family, with rows of fine gold chains around their necks.' As in Borno and Dahomey, at the Asante Court, the queen mother (asantehemaa) held a large amount of actual authority over decisions that were taken; in around 1800, for instance, the asantehene, Osei Kwame, feared that the asantehemaa was engineering a palace coup against him, and even removed the Court from its capital at Kumasi; however, this was all in vain, since he was deposed, in part because of the fear that he had secretly adopted Islam as his religion.[24]

This potential for female power within the royal Court seems remarkable; yet, at the same time, it was a part of the growing contradictions of power in West Africa. For, while royal female power grew, for many women the situation was all to the contrary. The balance of gender and power was connected fundamentally to class, and so an overview of gender relations requires also an awareness of this intersectional relationship. There was a very harsh divide between the lives of noblewomen at royal courts and the lives of other women beyond. Those in Atlantic ports could do well as traders, but away from there many others were compelled to a greater share of agricultural work because of the loss of men through warfare and slavery.

The division is perfectly expressed by one oral account of the way in which the wife of a powerful warrior rose and breakfasted in Kaabu, probably in the late eighteenth century:

> When she rose from her bed,
> her slaves helped her to rise,
> and brought her to bathe.
> When they got there,
> they put a chair there
> so that she could sit down
> while they washed her.
> After she had bathed
> they put on her clean clothes
> they helped her to rise
> without her feet touching the ground,
> and put her back on to her bed.
> When breakfast was ready
> they brought it to her room.
> The nyantio's wife took her breakfast
> until she was finished,
> the slaves brought her water
> to wash her hands with,
> and then they left her
> to take their own breakfasts.[25]

It is striking to read this account when, in many of the smaller-scale states that became clients of Kaabu at this time, women had themselves been rulers. In the small state of Pachesi – to the north of Kaabu's capital at Kansala – there were at least three female rulers in the earlier phase of the kingdom (probably before 1750). However, eventually, as

Pachesi became a client state of Kaabu, a different form of inheritance was adopted, in which power went to the nephew of the ruler. As power centralized and organized warfare became more important to state growth, women's power became more circumscribed and limited. Thus, oral accounts such as this describe the divisions that grew up, since, as in many societies in world history, this kind of domestic slavery was always performed by women in West Africa.[26]

In sum, the growing impact of social transformations had made for an increasing division between and within the sexes. Men ruled, and in some places their wives governed, while at the same time the labour demands on poorer women became ever harsher. One of the driving features of this nascent process was, indeed, the growing burden of the export agricultural trade, and the increasing shortage of men. This heavy agricultural burden – 'it is women who do the agriculture', one 1770s account of Cacongo, north of Kongo, put it – made the lot of many women hard. Though women could gain power and better their lot, this was often through masculine structures of kingship or trade.[27]

In the nineteenth century, these patterns would then be exacerbated by the appearance of Christian missionaries from a Victorian Britain regressing in terms of gender roles, and of Islamic scholars fresh from the reaction to the Salafiya revival movement, which advocated a return to patriarchal values of early Islam. The rise of global capitalism, it becomes clear, was also a conservative male retrenchment to bolster patriarchy: that this was the case in Africa, Europe and the Islamic world shows again how interconnected the rising global value systems were, and how closely the emergence of capitalism relied on squeezing female power.

There were exceptions, such as among the Igbo of the Niger Delta, where women could hold political power. In Dahomey, too, women remained key traders of textiles and ceramics, and retained their military functions. But, by the later eighteenth century, it was often hard for women to gain political power on their own account, as the role of a masquerade such as Mama-Jori in enforcing male choices shows. And today, in southern Senegal, when the Kankurang masquerade, seen by many as a descendant of Mama-Jori appears, it is women who wait up all night, playing percussive rhythms on sharp sticks, in anticipation and fear of the morning.[28]

A life-sized model of the Kankurang, outside the National Museum, Banjul, The Gambia.

POWER, PROFIT AND PRODUCTION

When trade began from the area around Hueda into the Atlantic, one of the first products was the malaguetta pepper. Malaguetta peppers remained an important item of trade until 1700, with 43,336 pounds bought by the English at Cape Coast castle in 1687. Yet, while from the European perspective this was a welcome and cheaper alternative to Indian spices, in West Africa this trade would adopt a different symbolism. In the *vodún* religious practice in the Republic of Benin today, the malaguetta pepper is renowned for its magical properties. After spending decades studying the role of plants in the super-natural medicinal practices of Benin, one ethnographer concluded that

Aframomum melegueta was 'the most important of all ingredients in the pharmacopeia [of supernatural medicine]'. Other scholars have also found a wide variety of uses for this plant: in medicines to combat curses, to bring victory over an enemy and to make the body powerful, among many others. In Benin today, malaguetta peppers are present in all magical concoctions, where their role is to reinforce the power of the active verb invoked. For example, a malicious sorcerer wishing to throw a curse on to someone must mix certain ingredients, while then chewing two malaguetta peppers and pronouncing the name of the targeted person.[29]

It is impossible to know if this magical property of the malaguetta pepper was always experienced by Fon and Yorùbá peoples. However, it seems unlikely. Why would people in the fifteenth century have eagerly exported surplus of this product if it was perceived as capable of producing great harm in the wrong hands? As we saw in the previous chapter, religious ideas changed markedly in the succeeding centuries, as the dadás of Dahomey centralized religious cults. These changes involved other plants beyond *melegueta*; among the Fon of what is now Benin, and the Yorùbá, some incantations require the use of maize, which did not exist in West Africa before the sixteenth century.[30]

This perception of the spiritual power of the malaguetta pepper is, therefore, likely associated with the rise of the Atlantic trade through which the presence of maize began and grew. One way of conceiving this is that the malaguetta pepper magnifies effects for the sorcerers and herbalists of modern Benin, perhaps because the Atlantic trade itself was such a huge magnifier of effects within their societies. In spiritual terms, the meaning of this humble plant changed, as it came to represent the material forces at work in a changing society. Thus, it is also no surprise that cowries, too, are often used in Benin today in magical spells to ensure desired effects.[31]

It is not just the religious symbolism of the malaguetta pepper that is important: political power went with it, and was also associated with agricultural production for the Atlantic trade in malaguetta peppers and maize. This was because people often experienced the transformations of power in these centuries through changes to their patterns of work, alongside the religious changes. Just as trade in these products magnified effects in a way that could be interpreted as giving them supernatural properties, so it was reinforced by power.

The new and growing political hierarchies built different labour systems. At the port of Bonny, east of the Niger Delta, for example, tilling fields was seen as an entirely dishonourable activity by the late eighteenth century. When the surgeon Alexander Falconbridge discussed the movement to abolish the slave trade with a trader at Bonny in the 1780s, he wrote, 'One of these black merchants being informed, that a particular set of people, called Quakers, were for abolishing the trade, he said, *it was a very bad thing, as they should then be reduced to the same state they were in during the war, when, through poverty, they were obliged to dig the ground and plant yams*.'[32]

By the later eighteenth century, working in the fields was closely equated with slavery in many societies across West Africa. As the slave trader Joseph Corry put it in 1807, agriculture was performed along the Windward Coast of Liberia and Sierra Leone 'by women and slaves'. Along the Gold Coast, noblemen had gardens tended by slaves, and increased the traditional tithe that independent farmers had to provide to them; they also appropriated the labour of others to clear lands and so increase production. Meanwhile, in Fuuta Tòòro in northern Senegambia, all forms of manual labour became linked to slavery in the seventeenth and eighteenth centuries. In part this was because of the crucial role that warfare had had in forming the new kingdoms, and the lack of time available for production to the warrior aristocracies. But this disdaining of labour also related to the widespread association of slavery with dishonour in many societies.[33]

There were many societies with these connections between dishonour and working the fields. When Segu arose in the first half of the eighteenth century, it was founded by hunters-turned-warriors who were averse to farming; farming was done by the *faraba-jòn*, or the slaves who worked the state fields. Female captives often did the agricultural work, and the raids that the Segu warrior aristocracy carried out were increasingly aimed at maintaining the supply of female slave labour and male captives who could be sold or inducted as soldiers into the army. All menial labour was carried out by captives, as this oral account makes clear:[34]

So, the next morning	*ə jàa dùgu mána jɛ*
beside the river	*bá dá lá*
twelve women captives of *Bakari Dim*	*Bakari jan fána kú jɔnmuso* *tán á fìla bé biri*
on one side of the path	*síra fàn dɔ fɛ*
facing the east,	*kà tága kɔrɔnyanfan fɛ*
twelve of his women captives *were there, bent over, washing* *the laundry.*	*ù bé fìniko lá.*
Twelve of Da's female captives *were also there*	*Da fáma ká jɔnmuso tán ní* *fìla bé bín*
on the west side,	*síra fàn tìlebin fɛ*
also washing the laundry, bent over *by the river.*	*ù bé fìniko lá bá dá lá.*[35]

A further cause of the close association of coerced labour with agricultural production was the place that agricultural exports had in the trade in enslaved persons. The increase in this trade across the Atlantic and the Sahara meant that there was a growing demand for agricultural supplies. As we have seen, in both the Atlantic and Saharan trades, long-distance traders relied on African agricultural production to feed their captives. Far from being unproductive, or somehow dependent on European technologies, African farmers innovated with new crops and production techniques to meet the requirements for surplus exports. In the first era of the trade, such innovations were often directed at local consumption, but, as the firearms trade and the power of states grew after this time, coercion increasingly came to play a part.[36]

Procuring food supplies was, therefore, a key aspect of Atlantic trade. As English trade grew after 1650, this became an important part of the Royal Africa Company's considerations. When the *Arthur* sailed to Calabar to trade in 1677, its accounts noted almost daily the difficulty of procuring provisions, and the crew often held off buying captives if there was not enough food; on 22 February of that year they sent a boat inland to a market, which returned with '1000 yams which they had purchased from severall persons there: finding yams very scarce this day we bought 7 men & 4 women'. In the same period, trading posts along the Gold Coast, such as Egya and Wyamba, usually bought over 200 chests of corn a month. By the 1680s, factors here frequently wrote about how their trade for food was going. James Nightingale often discussed this at Komenda in January and February 1682, writing on 19 January, 'as to the corne [I] have bought and paid for 129 chests, whereof is remaining above 40 odd'; the amount he bought was clearly large, since, by 15 February, he had more than 80 chests again. Factors at neighbouring forts had the same concerns. Some posts, such as Anishan, existed solely so as to provide provisions to slave ships; as the factor there wrote in February 1681, 'Captain Coates hath now 135 chests of corne aboard.'[37]

Thus, without an increase in agricultural production in West and West-Central Africa, the entire enterprise of Atlantic trade was unviable. The huge expansion of the trade in captives from the late seventeenth century onwards was only possible because of an expansion in West African agricultural production to feed the enslaved persons on the crossing. This, in turn, depended on the political reorientations of the rise of the fiscal-military states in West Africa, and the role that coercion could have in increasing farm outputs. Selling enslaved persons and the food they could eat on the Atlantic crossing became two threads in the same economy. With this growing state power also linked to rising volumes of money supply, the currency revolutions examined in this book were deeply connected to these transformations that were taking place.

This was the context for the growth of new crops, often having come from the Americas. Portuguese ships moving back and forth between Africa and the New World brought crops such as maize and manioc with them, which were rapidly adopted by coastal farmers, as a variety of languages show us. The Akan of the Gold Coast describe overseas countries as *aburokyire* ('countries where maize comes from') and their Fante neighbours called maize *oborowi* ('millet from overseas'), while it is called 'white man's grain' both in the Mande spoken in Senegambia (*tuba-nyo*) and in Kikongo (*maza mamputo*).[38]

Much was at stake in this increase in food production. Farming techniques had to change, and new tools were developed. Moreover, this growing agricultural export from West Africa was to have an important place in the link between the region and the world economy. There was a close relationship between provisions and money in Atlantic trading ports. Writing in the 1760s of Serèèr kingdoms in Senegambia, Abbé Demanet singled out the cattle there as costing only '2 bars [the trade currency] at the most', while it was possible to sell goods for 8 pounds to the Serèèr that cost no more than 6 or 7 in France.[39]

The agricultural trade was, therefore, another way in which surplus value could be accrued in the Atlantic economy. It was an important facet of commercial relations. As one diary entry for Calabar from Antera Duke in 1785 suggests: 'March 23, 1785: At 5 a.m. at Aqua landing, a fine morning. I went to see Duke Ephraim in his yard. We carried all our yams and rods [copper-rod pieces, a currency] for the Guinea Company people to share.' Food, of course, cost a lot of money to traders, but it also sucked potential surplus value out of the West African economy, feeding instead human beings who would produce surplus for the European economies in the plantations of the New World.[40]

How much food was necessary for this trade? The quantities were vast. Dutch officials at Allada in 1687 complained of the cost of spending a long time in the port there, where four and a half chests of millet were needed daily to feed 300 captives on one ship. For the one month that was really the minimum length of time during which these captives might be kept ashore or on board ship as they waited to leave port and then cross the Atlantic, at least 175 chests of grain were needed. English ships often laded 600 chests of corn at this time, while the English factory at Cape Coast alone bought 5,430 chests of corn in 1679. By the 1750s, it was estimated in Fuuta Tòòro on the banks of the Senegal River that each captive consumed approximately 200 pounds of millet annually.[41]

The powerful sense that emerges from these fragile paper records is not of economies somehow immobilized in time and space, but actually of a hugely dynamic increase in food production to satisfy the market. As the editors of Antera Duke's diary note, in a six-month period in late 1769, one English ship captain purchased 82,935 yams at Calabar alone. A powerful sense is created of the increased volumes of farm production that this booming trade required. And once the dynamic of powerful rulers and forced labour had begun in the eighteenth century, it could easily be transferred to the plantation production of palm oil and groundnuts during the era of 'legitimate trade' in the nineteenth century, to cocoa beans and cotton during the age of European colonialism in the twentieth century, and to other 'cash crops' in the postcolonial age.[42]

In terms of the wider argument of this book, this process is important. As we have seen, the trade across the Atlantic in enslaved persons reached its height in the eighteenth century, with the current estimate of the trans-Atlantic slave trade database being that 6,494,619 human beings were shipped in these years, over half of the total involved in the trade. This also means that it was during the eighteenth century that production of surplus food for the trade reached its peak, and this production could not be used to lower food prices within the West African market itself. A sense of the surplus agricultural value that was lost to West African economies, and could not be reinvested, is palpable. The growing use of agricultural surpluses from Africa to underpin and finance the extraction of surplus labour from the continent exacerbated the process of gathering inequality discussed in previous chapters.[43]

The many descriptions of growing trade and increasing production do not contradict a picture of economic divergence. In fact, they were an important part of it. Trade in provisions was, indeed, everywhere, and this was not concentrated merely in areas with large exports of captives. Production boomed, so that ships arriving in Liberia in the 1790s were greeted by canoes with traders offering yams, coconuts and plantains for sale. One visitor to Sierra Leone in the same decade described how people had 'wonderfully huge baskets standing at the doors of their houses and containing rice from [300- to 800-weight] each – They are mostly whitewashed and used to stand there all the year round. All the rice in the town amounted certainly to 30 or 40 tons.'[44]

Throughout West Africa in the eighteenth century, therefore, workers expanded food production. They reorientated their labour practices, often developing new systems that depended on 'age grades' (young people of the same age working together on similar tasks), in which labour was not coerced, or becoming part of the growing force of enslaved labour at work in West Africa. Some of the large imports of iron from the Atlantic helped in developing agricultural implements that could be used to increase the yield of farmlands. In some cases these tools could clear lands. Alternatively, people adopted new higher-yielding crops, expanding food security and allowing them to trade supplies to Atlantic ports.[45]

Freetown, Sierra Leone, early nineteenth century.

Social and farming innovations were thus needed to achieve this growth in production. And yet West African societies did not achieve the sort of economic growth that traditional theories of economics would usually see as a companion to an increase in productive output. Indeed, as we saw in the first half of this book with relation to the cloth production of Senegambia and Benin, the evidence is that exports of manufactured goods not related to the slave, ivory and gold trades actually declined in this period of increased output. One description of the famous Mbundu Queen Nzinga related how, in the 1650s, she loved to dress herself in elaborate cloths imported from Bombay, and also those new ones made by the islanders who lived on São Tomé. From this point on, however, the money needed to invest in such productive innovations was increasingly lost to the economies of West and West-Central Africa, as the surplus food that could have helped to finance it was leached away instead into feeding the trade in enslaved persons. It is small wonder, then, that crops related to this trade, such as the malaguetta pepper, became invested with enormous meaning and power.[46]

SLAVERY AND THE TRADING CLASS

By 1700, trade had become so important to so many different societies along the coast of West and West-Central Africa that rich trading classes had emerged. While many powerful merchants were women, men were also important, drawing on their connections and credit both with European factors and with local rulers to develop their influence.

One such was Bonashee, described in detail by the English factor at Anomabu in 1686, Ralph Haskell. Bonashee was one of Haskell's major suppliers of food and pawns, young dependent persons left as a form of credit or surety against advances of goods given by Haskell to West African traders.* By the 1680s, many of the 'pawns' who were left as surety with traders like Haskell were young canoemen, who had initially plied their trade transporting provisions and persons to and from ships and the factories of European companies before becoming pawns. In 1679, fifty-one canoemen 'pawned themselves' to the English at Cape Coast. Anomabu, meanwhile, was one of the major centres of the English for procuring enslaved persons along the Gold Coast, equalled only by Accra and Wyamba at this time, while other 'factories' exported gold and supplied food. Thus had human beings become a form of credit value, to go alongside their sometime role as currency units.[47]

Bonashee came regularly to trade at Anomabu with a group of caboceers (headmen, leading traders), leaving such youngsters as credit and then taking these trade goods inland to the markets of Akwamu, and returning with captives, gold and provisions. Usually this process worked well; in 1686, Bonashee sent a woman slave on 9 December, 'according as he promised', and another pawn followed later, and these were eventually returned to Bonashee 'as per the inclosed receipt'. But where there is profit there will always be greed and double-crossing, and such a trade was not without its tensions and disputes. In 1686, a row blew up over a pawn that can be taken as fairly typical. Bonashee had left two pawns with Haskell, which he then sought to repay with one captive and a sum of gold. A long discussion had to be held at Haskell's factory: Bonashee swore an oath ('t[ook] a fittish') and the negotiation took up most of the morning, with Bonashee threatening to withdraw the captive and gold if his pawns were not returned. He noted as part of the discussion that the brafo of Fante, the head of state, was a kinsman of his, alluding to the

* See above, Chapter 6.

possible loss that might fall on the English and Haskell if they did not comply; and, indeed, the English at Cape Coast were paying annual 'customs', or charges, to the brafo. Clearly Haskell took the message on board, for Bonashee was soon back trading at Anomabu.[48]

This trading class was growing all the time. In some circumstances this allowed for the rise of women such as Bibiana Vaz and Crispina Peres. In others, those with close ties to ruling elites such as Bonashee prospered. As the long-distance trade became ever more profitable, political control over it required hierarchical systems of governance, and this, too, was a factor pushing political centralization. At the same time, this system placed influence in the hands of the trader, witnessing the emergence of something like a bourgeoisie characterized by conspicuous displays of consumption – as happened in Europe during the same period.

In order for trade networks to prosper, and the market to expand, it was essential that West African political rulers were in control. European traders lived as clients of African rulers, and they were not able to move about with any ease or freedom, and rarely ventured more than 30 miles from the coast. The type of trouble they could run into was powerfully described in the will of Charles Testefolle, taken at the English fort at Ouidah on 30 April 1731 shortly before he died a miserable death, after he had fallen foul of the King of Dahomey. 'It is impossible to express the torments I have undergone since being here, they stripd me naked, put me in irons, both my leggs and my hands behind me and Cords all round both my arms in an open yard which treatment makes me believe the king will finish me there.' As African political power grew, so, too, did the risks for European traders and the power of the African merchant class, exemplified by the confidence with which someone like Bibiana Vaz could imprison a bothersome Portuguese official, or with which Bonashee could hold forth in the office of the English factor Haskell and get his own way.[49]

A second vital aspect of the success of this economic class of trader in West Africa was the freedom to move about in search of the best deal. Often, convoys of captives were marched to the ports, as happened at Ouidah and as Mungo Park would describe of Senegambia at the end of the eighteenth century. But waterways also played a part. Rivers were the roads of West Africa – a leach of human and material resources, as Ben Okri so memorably puts it – because it was along rivers that everything moved: captives, food supplies, and the gum, cloth and ivory that were also to be traded in return for knives, mirrors, weapons and other assorted goods. The ability of traders to mobilize people or crops around a particular area was central to the place of that area in the trade: if traders could not bring enslaved persons or surplus agricultural produce along riverways to the ports, an area would rapidly cease to be an attractive destination for Atlantic traders.[50]

These river journeys were carefully curated by the traders. In the Guinea-Bissau region, sunblinds were placed on small trading boats, and sacrifices were often made as a propitious offering to the success of the venture. Once the boats or canoes set out, there was often entertainment; in 1796, Adam Afzelius described in Sierra Leone a clear example of the 'call and response' style of singing that remains popular in many parts of West Africa and beyond, writing how the rowers 'were almost continually singing, and they kept in time with the rowing – There was one very like a fiddler from Gambia and sung in the same tune, which he always raised. The sung [*sic*] was wild, loud, sharp and melancholy. One who began sung always half . . . before the others or chorus began.'[51]

European traders were utterly dependent on the provision of these supply boats and canoes, as their diaries make clear. Factors at the Gold Coast had to pay every time they hired a canoe, and this was their excuse for not writing back to their headquarters more frequently. Another complained from Ouidah that 'within two months I hired 30 canoemen [to go to Cape Coast] . . . and on a sudden for noe reason that I know the most of them ran away, and dispersed themselves among the [Elmina] canoes. Therefore unless you can [hire] and oblige a gang of canoe men to come down and returne immediately, it will be almost impossible to persuade them to goe up.' The exchange of goods by Atlantic traders with one another – English cowries for Brazilian gold, Dutch cloth for Brazilian tobacco – meant that these boats were essential, and any loss of mobility was a serious problem for the trading classes, African and European.[52]

The importance of trade and the market by the eighteenth century, therefore, had a number of related social effects. Pressures grew on producers, who were increasingly likely to be women as men were drawn into warfare and enslavement. The power of the trading class grew, and with it their relationship with rulers of the newly powerful states; it was, after all, the traders who often mobilized the currency on which the power of the centralizing states depended. Underlying all of these transformations were gathering divisions, underscoring the contradictions of power. While traditional economic theory links increase in trade and output with an increase in wealth, this can often tend towards an increase in inequality: in West Africa, during the eighteenth century, these increases in output went with the growth of disparities in wealth, even as the pressures to produce grew year on year.[53]

MONEY AND PRODUCTIVITY

As far as capital investors were concerned, the most important role of Royal African Company officials posted in West Africa was to log their expenses. Leafing through the account books of the late seventeenth century, it becomes clear that they did this in a peculiar way, according to each item of trade. Profits and loss were recorded carefully in the crabbed hand of the time for each item of trade: receipts for copper, iron and lead bars, for cloths of various types and for cowries on one page, and expenses on the other – 'customs' (taxes) paid to the kings of Egya, Fetu and Hueda, expenses for trade of various ships, the cost of the deaths of enslaved persons awaiting transport.[54]

As we saw in the first half of this book, copper had been one of the first major currency items traded to the Gold Coast, Allada and Calabar, in the form of manillas. By the seventeenth century, manillas were accompanied by copper bars, and yet, by 1700, the use of copper bars was changing rapidly. The 1670s show more iron bars being laded than copper bars, both in Calabar and on the Gold Coast. By the late 1680s, hardly any copper bars were laded for use on the Gold Coast, where iron bars were still traded regularly up to 1700. Copper bars that were traded to the region were generally given to ships heading to ports in Gabon and Cameroon, trading for enslaved persons.[55]

This process changed even further in the first decades of the eighteenth century. By 1730, the value of copper and iron bars laded to the English forts along the Gold Coast at Ouidah had become insignificant compared with other goods. While Dixcove on the Gold Coast received almost £130 worth of the woollen cloths known as *perpetuanoes* in 1730, the combined value of iron and copper bars was less than £9. At Sekondi, there were cloths worth over £150 (again, mainly *perpetuanoes*), and less than £20 of iron and copper bars; and at Komenda the picture was very similar. The place of imported bars that could be melted down for local currencies was being transformed, and replaced, by that of manufactures; these *perpetuanoes* had been manufactured in England since at least the early seventeenth century, and were helping industrial production to grow there, while industrial production in areas such as the Gold Coast declined in relative terms.[56]

These account books provide a good perspective on the way in which the use of money was related to the social transformations in the West African societies considered so far in this chapter. Copper had a variety of artistic, economic and ritual uses. Iron was altogether different, and its major use was in the creation of new forms of weaponry and agricultural tools. The way in which iron bars continued to be imported where copper declined pinpoints this period from around the 1670s to 1700 as a moment when the transformations described in this chapter gathered speed. Iron was still in demand because societies needed to expand their food production, and because rulers sought to expand their military hardware. Rulers controlled money imports, and therefore could fiscalize the growth of a political administration and central power; copper was losing its relevance, as the previous social structures to which it had been related were superseded.

There is, however, also the question of why iron had been imported at all. Lengthy debates have taken place on this question, since iron production expanded in many regions of West Africa during this period. Why, then, was imported European iron of any value at all?

One answer may lie in its use as currency and the relationship of currency to royal power. Kings could control the import of foreign iron, and, by branding it as currency, could, therefore, control the circulation of money. The decline of iron bars in the eighteenth century in this region at least was probably due to the wider transformations and instabilities that we have seen unfolding.[57]

Fundamentally, both sides saw this trade as connected to exchanges of value. For African traders, value was perceived in the economic transactions within their kingdoms and in the status that gaining and holding power through warfare allowed. The iron bars speak to the latter, used for economic exchanges in the same way as cowries. For European traders, however, value lay in the ability to accumulate surplus capital; this was why houses were rented out by their value in gold, and why factors often complained if the price of the goods they imported for trade rose.[58]

Both sides saw this trade not as barter but as a transaction for money. The English described the trade with Akan middlemen on the Gold Coast as one for 'money' – as one factor put it in 1686, 'I wrote your worship this morning that the Acanians had been with me for powder and that they would bring money this afternoon.' At the same time, iron bars were said to hold their value on the coast only if they bore the stamp of the Royal Africa Company; poor or rusting ones could not be sold, whereas those that were marked were rapidly picked up, with the stamp of the RAC acting rather like the stamp or signature on a banknote, a guarantee of value.[59]

The trading classes in West African societies set the prices at which these currencies would go for in many parts of the region. The evidence for this power over market rates is abundant, and European traders repeatedly stated how dependent they were on the economic demands of their African trading partners. At Komenda, in 1683, the chief trader, known to the English as Captain Bracon, refused to accept sheets of cloth at 28 per *benda* of gold, and would take only 32, since this was the price the Dutch would offer him; or, as Mark Whiting, the English factor at Sekondi, wrote in 1683, 'I have sent your Worship a sample of what beades is most vendible here. Pray faile not to send us word wheither your Worship pleases to alter the prices, for they will not sell at those rates before mentioned.'[60]

The control of traders over market rates is significant. Formal monetization was at work across the region, with set prices for iron bars and cloths in Senegambia, and (by the 1770s) in Cacongo for cloths produced in India (known as Guinea cloth), where one captive was sold for fifteen pieces of the designated cloth. The ability to set such rates underlines the political control of West African rulers, and how European traders were tributary; it is also a reminder of how important currency control had become to political power. The setting of exchange rates was their prerogative, given the political control of African rulers, just as, under formal colonialism in the twentieth century, it was European colonists in Africa who set market rates for African exports and European imports.[61]

Why, then, did this increasing monetization and expanding trade and productivity not yield economic growth? The answer lies with competing ideas of value, and with the growing inequalities that resulted. As we have seen in this book, the imported currencies were used for a variety of reasons beyond accumulation (to enter secret societies, in acts of worship and in display). This was because social status and worth were not reductively associated with the accumulation of financial capital. And yet, as the relative value of these currencies declined over the seventeenth and eighteenth centuries, imbalances grew economically between West Africa and the world economy, and also within the societies of the region. The multiple social revolutions at play – in work, belief and daily life – promoted differences between peoples, rather than unity. They created the contradictions that would undermine the strength of the new states.

CONCLUSION: NEW WORLDVIEWS AND PUSHBACK

In Greater Senegambia, the Gambia River acts as a watershed. To the south, the land stretches away into Casamance and Guinea-Bissau in lush swamps, interspersed with glades where long-horned cattle graze. To the north lies the *jeeri*, the flat savannah that becomes as dry as a crisp in the weeks before the rains finally arrive in June or July. When I drove through the *jeeri* one year with a friend, he remarked how different the landscape had become: there used to be many more trees, he said, sacred forests that people were afraid to cut down, but in time people lost their fear and more and land was given over to farming groundnuts.

Looking out at the hard plains in the last days of the dry season, the loss of the sacred forests seemed to have had a profound effect on the land itself. In the last chapter, we saw how the rise of military power in West and West-Central Africa was intimately linked to conceptions of the sacred and the supernatural. Important as this relationship was to military revolutions, however, it is equally matched by the relationship of religious ideas to the social changes we have looked at in this chapter: it is by looking at this question of land that these different ideas can come into focus.

Changes in agricultural productivity and in the organization of labour and the trade all required a new understanding of land use. But this was difficult, since, as the historian Assan Sarr has brilliantly shown, land was itself seen as sacred, much of it occupied by spirits. These beliefs meant that large tracts of land were seen by outside observers as 'unoccupied', though to the people who lived there they were fully occupied by potentially malevolent forces; and, indeed, this system of belief allowed often delicate ecologies to be strengthened, since 'empty land' produced wildlife havens, so that here was a sort of ecophilosophy long before such ideas had been considered by Western thinkers. With the erosion of these ideas in the nineteenth century, the land was put to more utilitarian and productive economic uses, and the *jeeri* became drier.[62]

A glimpse of what happened when people used the land without considering these forces was offered by the French traveller Michel Adanson, on the Upper Senegal River in the 1750s: 'Podor used to be covered in woodland; but the amounts which the French have cut in the last ten years, since they established themselves [at a trading post] there, means that the forest has retreated by as much as half a league [almost two miles] around it.'[63] The peoples who lived near to such spaces that were taken over by outsiders would often say that such land was in any case worthless, as inhabited by malign spirits, but this kind of impact was significant all the same. In order to transform land from 'economically unproductive' spaces and increase production, therefore, either materialistic political outsiders or internal religious transformations were required. As traders became more powerful, and societies more unequal, religious ideas changed.[64]

The spiritual significance of land may now be deemed economic illiteracy, but it was well understood by those traders who spent long periods in West Africa. 'Last night I received yours with a mould for to cutt some timber,' the factor of the Royal African Company at Anomabu on the Gold Coast wrote on 1 February 1682. 'It will bee difficult to get, and if should find any if itt be their fetish trees they will not suffer any body to cutt them.'[65]

The spiritual value of land was thus fundamental to national identities. In Segu, the oral epics of the kingdom's foundation by Biton Kulubali lay great importance on the place of the *balansa* (acacia) trees:

> Segu of the *balansa* trees . . .
> Four thousand *balansa*,
> And four hundred *balansa*,
> And four *balansa*
> And one small humpbacked *balansa*.
> Not every native understands their significance,
> To say nothing of a stranger.[66]

Regarding worship to the *vodunun* in Hueda and Dahomey, public shrines were usually found in sacred forests. Further south, in West-Central Africa, land was considered the property of the ancestors among the BaKongo, whose priests, or *nganga*, took as their name that of the place whose shrine they served; in Loango, territorial shrines known as *nkisi* were common, stressing the connection of spirits to the land.[67]

This spiritual power of land is essential to understanding the political and cultural transformations we have examined in this chapter. As material value and currency equivalence became ever more important, land, too, adopted its own monetary power. Indeed, English traders on the Gold Coast were so well aware of the priceless nature of these beliefs that they were prepared to accept religious objects (which they called fetishes) as pawns, with one factor writing in 1693 that he had been brought one such weighing more than nine ounces, 'which I have taken in pawne for 35 English carpets'. For these

Former palace of Biton Kulubali in Ségoukoro, Mali.

European traders, the relative nature of economic value was a given in the decisions they took when it came to trade. Through such eyes it is the idea of universal value, rationally calculated according to numerical equivalence, that seems like a myth.[68]

This different approach to land must also be seen as a cause of the economic divergence that opened up between West Africa and the world in this era. In the worldview of Western economics, land was a material good to be used as a basis for capital accumulation. This was an approach deriving from the land security that came with the ruthless process of land enclosures, something that its advocates always called an 'improvement' – a teleological herald of 'progress'. Some modern economists still see lack of titled access to land as a core driver of poverty in the Global South. That in West and West-Central Africa land had a spiritual value above its material use meant that societies there would always be at a 'competitive disadvantage' in a global economic system in which 'rational' exploitation of land was essential for economic growth.[69]

The importance of this relationship of spiritual and political power to land is, then, hard to overstate. In the previous chapter, we saw how the ability of hunters to vanquish spirits in the bush was associated with their hold over power in new states; and this spiritual power was something that the rulers who followed them retained, and, with it, their control over the land. In time, though, spiritual practices altered to accommodate the new parallel worldviews. Though land retained its spiritual meaning, new shrines and secret societies emerged in which trade goods associated with the Atlantic world became valuable, and, indeed, in which trade goods could become part of the offerings to the deities of a shrine – 'commodity fetishes' a century before Marx invented the term. In order to gain entry to the Ékpè masquerade of Calabar, or the Hupila Hudjenk shrine of the Diola of Casamance in Senegambia, it was necessary to 'pay' material goods that it was possible to obtain only through the Atlantic trade, such as copper rods or slave fetters. Yorùbá proverbs describe how slaves could not wear masks and pawns were banned from parading in the Otomporo masquerade. Thus, new religious traditions enforced growing hierarchies, representing the power of the new worldview that had intruded into West and West-Central Africa.[70]

This perspective is not somehow to barbarize or primitivize such a complex history, but rather to take seriously the perspectives of the actors themselves. The idea that taking African spiritual beliefs seriously is to 'exoticize' and 'primitivize' them begins in the long history of ridiculing African spiritual beliefs and denying the religious practice of Africans, which are instead seen as 'rituals', a perspective that goes back to European travel accounts of the sixteenth and seventeenth centuries. It starts from the view that Western economic rationality is some kind of universal given to which all societies ought to aspire, and that Judaeo-Christian monotheism offers universalism, whereas everything else is a particularistic 'cult'. Yet the reality that 'rational' exploitation of land is not some sort of universal value is becoming more and more apparent in the light of ecological degradation. Alternative perspectives are of potential significance in themselves. Certainly, it is impossible to understand the history of West Africa without acknowledging the place of spiritual beliefs in shaping social realities.[71]

How did these social and spiritual transformations finally take hold, then, in West and West-Central Africa? Rulers were increasingly becoming ideological go-betweens, bridging the Atlantic and their home societies. This position seemed to offer solidity, but it also eroded the connection between land stewardship and spiritual power. There was an enormous tension between the extractive requirements of the new global economic paradigms and the meshing of African spiritual and political outlooks. In trying to be all things to all people, the contradictions underpinning the rulers' power became clear, paving the way for new revolutionary ideologies. When these emerged in the late eighteenth century, they would be wrought by the same transnational forces that had helped to transform social relations over the preceding centuries.

9
Transnational Africas, Struggle and the Rising of Modernity

When in 1793 Archibald Dalzel published his history of Dahomey, he did so at the height of the Abolitionist arguments then convulsing the British body politic. Did the slave trade barbarize Africans, so that they needed to be 'saved' from it; or did it 'save' them from a barbarous reality? With perhaps some subtle shifts of emphasis or tone, such have been the discourses acted out in Western nations regarding Africa ever since. Thus, in the classic analysis of the philosopher V. Y. Mudimbe, an external framework of knowledge about 'Africa' and 'Africanness' has been constructed that is foreign to the continent and its lived experience.[1]

Indeed, lurking in Dalzel's pro-slavery account was a description revealing that the realities were far more complex than most of these debates on Abolition ever would allow:

> Antonio Vaz Coelho was . . . born in Brazil, where he had been taught to read, write, and keep accounts. He had inherited some property from his parents; and being of an enterprising disposition, he had made several voyages to Ardrah [Allada], where he at last settled, and became a very respectable trader . . . He had an uncommon share of vanity, and was excessively fond of military enterprises . . . he generally armed his dependants with blunderbusses, which he purchased from the Europeans. [2]

Vaz embodied some of the complex realities of the late eighteenth century. He had enough money to set up business, and had decided on West Africa (the Costa da Mina, as it was known in Brazil), whence his ancestors had come. In the nineteenth century, a steady stream of fellow Brazilians of African heritage would follow. Many, like Vaz, became agents for the continuing trade in enslaved persons. How could ex-slaves participate in this? It has to be remembered that, in a society such as colonial Brazil, or the stratified world of many West African kingdoms by the nineteenth century, there was little alternative: those who did not own slaves were potentially enslaveable.[3]

This chapter tries to gain a sense of the importance of the identities embodied by someone like Vaz. It looks at the transnational dimensions of African ruling classes, religious frameworks, ethnic identities, and also of the seeds of resistance that this created to what were increasingly authoritarian states. It shows how the impetus for the political revolutions that overturned West African aristocracies came not only from internal unrest at rising inequalities, but also from the transnational awareness of the late eighteenth century. Societies of West and West-Central Africa had close diplomatic and commercial ties with North Africa and the Arab world, with the Americas and Europe. By the eighteenth century, global factors influenced movements of struggle, identities and the cultural framework.

The transnational focus of this chapter is vital to this book as a whole. It nails once and for all the canard that African societies were somehow divorced from wider patterns of modernity. But it also invites us to look anew at patterns of influence in shaping that modernity. Here, language shapes discourse, as well as perceptions of power: if modernity and humanism are 'Western', they become the child of Europe. Yet more than three out of every four migrants to the New World before 1800 was African. These men and women were captured and enslaved not only for their labour but also for their skills. African cattle herders were valued from the Argentine pampas to the Venezuelan Llanos and the deserts of northern Mexico. The rice-growing skills of West Africans from Sierra Leone and the Guinea-Bissau region were valued in the Carolinas and northern Brazil. The cultivation of foods that became staples of the American South – such as peanuts – was the preserve of African slaves until the nineteenth century. And, as we have already seen, African institutions like the *quilombo* were vital in allowing new integrated societies to emerge in the New World.* As so often there is a disconnect between the patterns of influence that shaped history, and the way in which historical discourse about the past is shaped.[4]

In the eighteenth century, influence came to reflect not only the ways in which new societies were formed, but also how they were challenged. Warfare techniques learnt in Kongo led to major rebellions, such as the Stono Rebellion in South Carolina in 1739. These challenges were painfully slow to have lasting effects, because of the institutional enormity of the tyranny of New World slavery. However, when the insurrectionary movements gathered pace in the late eighteenth and early nineteenth centuries, they were decisively influenced by events in Africa. Kongo techniques again influenced military strategies of the Haitian revolutionaries in the 1790s – with enduring success.† Military experiences of the wars in northern Nigeria in the late eighteenth and early nineteenth centuries then drove risings in Brazil and Cuba, stoking the tensions which saw the abolition of slavery in both countries in the second half of the nineteenth century.[5]

Yet these influences did not just travel from Africa and Europe to the Americas. They also returned to Africa, alongside figures such as Vaz. This direction of influence grew, especially in the nineteenth century, when whole communities of maroons arrived in Freetown with the new Sierra Leone colony. To consider how the transnational forces of slavery and resistance generated one another and collided, we can turn to St John's Maroon Church, Freetown. Visiting in May 2017, I was shown around by a church elder. Outside, I could not help noticing that he was wearing a red baseball cap, and when I remarked on this he laughed. Red remained a symbol of military power, the colour of the maroon flag and of the rafters in the church.

The colour red retains this meaning also in The Gambia – where, in 1998, the red cap was reinstated for soldiers – and among the Jola of Casamance, where it remains the badge of rulership for village heads. The red hat's voyage from Senegambia to the Americas, and the voyage of that colour back again, speaks loudly of the way in

* See above, Chapter 5, and Coda to Part One.

† For more detail on the Haitian Revolution (1791–1804), see below, pp. 390–92.

Maroon flag outside St John's Church, Freetown.

which political rulers despatched people to the Americas – only for the same idioms of power and warfare to return to challenge them in the nineteenth century, and to help overthrow what had become tyrannical warrior aristocracies.[6]

TRANSNATIONAL CULTURES AND AFRICAN RULING CLASSES

In an upmarket restaurant in Dakar's *plateau* (downtown), the menu will include food better known elsewhere for being found in Paris: profiteroles, *pain perdu*, even well-known French wines in this overwhelmingly Islamic country. In Luanda, until the recent arrival of Chinese-funded skyscrapers and shopping centres by the bay, it was Portuguese-style cuisine that was upmarket, with grilled fish and *vinho branco*, just as you might find in Lisbon's *baixa*. This adoption of foreign luxuries as a sign of status has a long history; in his seminal book *Black Skin, White Masks*, the psychiatrist Frantz Fanon described in detail the ways in which members of African and Caribbean elites sought to perform this class- or status-signalling once in Europe. But this process reflects a far older history of African elites and their responses to transnational forces.[7]

As we have seen, these transnational influences entering and leaving Africa are as old as the globalization of the world (and Africa) from the fifteenth century and before. What changed in the late seventeenth and eighteenth centuries was the way in which political elites in Africa took advantage of these growing influences to harness personal and family wealth, developing patterns that did not disappear with postcolonialism. In the eighteenth century, by manifesting their difference through importing outside clothing, education and religious practice, the African ruling classes created a growing distance between themselves and their subjects.[8]

Ruling classes have always distinguished themselves through symbols of power. Sceptres and crowns are neither unique nor unusual symbols of rulership. In Ndongo, Angola, regal power lay in the horse's tail and the iron arm-ring. In Benin, the aristocracy adorned themselves with coral; while on the Gold Coast, umbrellas shaded the ruling class (and still do), and the throne of power was symbolized by the royal stool. These trappings of royal majesty all preceded the rise of European trade.

What changed with the rise of transnational influences was the dependence of African ruling classes on access to foreign luxury goods. It was not that old symbols of power were discarded, but that they were supplemented with a kind of double symbolic meaning, directed both at African subjects and at European traders. In Kongo, for instance, the crown of office known as the *mpu* – in which loops of raffia fibre were intertwined into a tall spiral growing out of textiles – remained important into the eighteenth century. Kongo ambassadors and kings usually wore both local cloth and coral beads, but they merged these with the insignia of Christian nobility to demonstrate their access to this external power. Meanwhile, Kongo religious and initiation ceremonies such as the *sangamento* often merged Kongo and European forms, with Kongo dresses and weaponry mixing with European hats and golden crosses.[9]

The old, therefore, was not discarded but rather melded with foreign symbolisms to represent the new bases of power. From the perspective of the kingly families, this symbolic transformation cut to the heart of their authority to rule over subjects. Moreover, as the West African trading classes grew, and ruling families lost control over the Atlantic trade in the eighteenth century, more people were able to gain access to

Mpu hat, late 1800s–early 1900s (palm-leaf fibre (raffia), leopard claws).

these symbols of power. This, too, may be an important explanation for the collapse of the aristocracies, and the ongoing civil conflicts that affected so many societies. As in Europe, the spread of consumption challenged the ritualized performances of consumption and status as aristocratic power; and with this came challenges to the aristocratic classes themselves that could not be held back.[10]

It is useful to see that these symbols of distinctiveness were cultivated from the very beginning. They appeared at once in the ways in which the ruling classes of West and West-Central Africa engaged with European trading nations. This trend was apparent even in the very first audience granted to the Portuguese in 1491 by the manikongo, Nzika Nkuwu: 'The [manikongo] was in a courtyard of one of his Palaces, accompanied by innumerable people, and sitting on a platform richly decorated in their style. He was naked from the waist upwards, with a cap woven of palm cloth raised very high on his head, and a silver-embossed horse's tail on his shoulder, and from the waist down dressed with some damask cloths, which the King of Portugal had sent to him.'[11]

Thus, as soon as the Portuguese arrived, the manikongo had dressed himself in luxury imported cloths, which were matched by his own symbols of power in the horse's tail and palm-woven *mpu*. The process of social differentiation through access to the imported luxuries had begun. Very rapidly, ambassadors from places as distant from each other as Benin, Jolof and Kongo appeared in Europe. With so many rulers from West and West-Central Africa seeking political representation, and making political claims on European trading partners, this kind of interchange could only grow. And with it grew the gifts of luxury goods to the ruling classes from whom the African ambassadors were sent.[12]

A good illustration of the way this happened in practice comes with the embassies sent by Dahomey to Brazil and Portugal in the late eighteenth and early nineteenth centuries. In 1750, Dahomey had sent an embassy to Salvador in Brazil. Such embassies were quite frequent from this region through the eighteenth and early nineteenth centuries: in 1783, the King of Badagry in what is now south-western Nigeria was seized by his subjects and sent to Salvador with twenty slaves to attend him, with a letter explaining the situation to the governor there and hoping for increased trade, while Allada also sent an embassy to Salvador in 1809.[13]

In the 1780s and 1790s, then, the recurrence of these embassies became more intense. As the Age of Revolution swept the Atlantic world, Dahomey embarked on a series of diplomatic forays, sending several embassies. In that of 1795–6, the main costs for the prince and his ambassador were in the purchase of fine cloths, capes, hats, jackets, coats and shoes; these perhaps seemed necessary to the royal status that they enjoyed once they were in Portugal, but certainly also helped to create a strong differentiation in clothing with Fon subjects in Dahomey.[14]

Dahomey sent at least five embassies to Brazil and Portugal – in 1750, 1795, 1805, 1811 and 1818 – as did its neighbour Onim (which became Lagos, and was subject to Oyo), sending three up to 1823. The ambassadors were lodged in colonial official buildings, and the entire cost of their visit was defrayed by the Portuguese state (the voluminous documentation on the costs of these visits survives). This could be quite a large sum, since Dahomeyan ambassadors generally travelled first to Salvador in Brazil, for discussions with the Portuguese governor who administered the Portuguese fort at Ouidah, and thence to the royal Court at Lisbon.[15]

As the political pressures of the Age of Revolution and the Abolition campaign mounted, so, too, did the transnational dimensions of these Dahomeyan embassies. By 1811, when Dadá Adandozan despatched an embassy to Salvador, the British had abolished their slave trade and political pressure was mounting on the Portuguese to do the same. As the commercial consequences of this seemed disastrous for Dahomey, the need for diplomacy was strong. By the time that the embassy arrived, the Portuguese royal Court was also in Brazil, having fled to Rio de Janeiro from Napoleon's troops in 1807–8; and, in a long letter of October 1810, Adandozan lamented that he could not assist the Portuguese royal family in their trouble with the French.[16]

War standard sent by Adandozan, King of Dahomey, to João, King of Portugal, when exiled in Rio de Janeiro, in 1810, representing Dahomey's defeat of the army of Porto Novo in 1805. Tragically, this standard was destroyed in the 2018 fire at Rio de Janeiro's Museu Nacional.

One of the conventions of this sort of embassy was the reciprocal exchange of gifts. Ambassadors from Dahomey brought thrones, cloth and ivory, and enslaved persons, and returned with gifts such as pieces of fine silk. As in the earliest periods, such diplomatic exchanges accentuated material differences in clothing and access to luxury goods between African rulers, the new trading classes discussed in the last chapter, and their subjects.[17]

Good examples of this differentiation by the late eighteenth century come from the diary of Antera Duke of Calabar. The diary suggests that he owned either a clock or a watch, as he frequently notes in it precise times (such as '6am'). Duke also writes how he and his fellow trader Esien Duke 'dressed as white men', that is, in European clothes, to go down to a ship that had recently arrived near Calabar at Parrot Island, 20 miles downstream from the port and named after the huge flocks of parrots seen daily near by. The idea of dressing in European clothes for a European audience does not in itself suggest that the display of luxury clothes was a sign of status. However, often public events in Calabar required the display of both Ékpè and European clothing styles. As Duke noted in one entry of 11 November 1786, 'about 4 o'clock we went to the town palaver house, and we dressed again in town style in long cloth and Ékpè cloth [tie-dyed with blue and white triangles] and hat and jacket and every fine thing.' For wealthy traders such as Duke, therefore, it was important to show access to luxuries such as imported hats and jackets at major social events of the Ékpè society.[18]

This sort of symbolic pluralism, incorporating African and European styles, was widely found among traders in many areas of West and West-Central Africa by the eighteenth century. Bosman described along the Gold Coast, in around 1700, how the rich traders and members of royal families were very keen to display their access to European clothing: 'They are very fond of our Hats, never thinking they pay too much for them . . . Their common Habit is made of three or four Ells of either Velvet, Silk, Cloath, *Perpetuana*, or some sort of Stuff; and several have this sort of Habit or Paan, as they call it, made of fifty sorts of Stuff.'[19] But the desire to display power through access to these luxury clothes was itself related to the royal classes and their interest in acquiring foreign goods. This element to the performance of royal power remained very potent throughout the eighteenth century. The Englishman Robert Norris described how, in the 1780s, the Dadá of Dahomey's bedroom consisted of a bedstead and mattress made in Europe, with check curtains, and how the floor was covered by a carpet that Norris himself had sold to him a few months before. In the 1770s, one of the most important *manis* of Cacongo had an apartment furnished in a European style, with beds, commodes, and dressers covered with silver ornaments, and chairs with which to receive European visitors, while the *mani* himself sat on the floor.[20]

The importance of such displays of power was very well described when Paul Erdmann Isert visited the ruler of Great Popo, in 1788: 'His outfit consisted of a very costly Black *pantjes* reaching from his hips all the way to the ground. Over this he wore a loose silken dressing gown, and on his head, a coachman's cap, on top of which was a European hat worked all over with large silver flowers . . . in his hand he also carried a Spanish manilla cane with a silver knob.'[21]

Of course, African monarchs were not alone in their use of 'exotica' as a means to demonstrate their political power. Just as symbols of royal power were universal, so many monarchs across the world sought to show their power (and modernity) by displaying their access to previously undreamt-of beings or objects. Following Vasco da Gama's return from India to Portugal in 1499, for instance, King Manoel I had five elephants brought back, too, which went before him whenever he rode through Lisbon, preceded by a rhinoceros. All rulers found the new forces bringing peoples together astonishing, and a display of the novelties that came from these exchanges was important. What was emerging by the early eighteenth century was, in fact, a shared culture of elite consumption and power, spanning Africa, the Americas and Europe.[22]

One of the best examples of how this shared language developed is the visit of the ambassadors of Dahomey to Portugal in late 1795 and early 1796. As soon as the Dahomey royal party reached Europe, they began to enjoy the delights of Lisbon. In January and early February of 1796, they made twenty-four visits to the Opera House on the Rua dos Condes, and nineteen to the Theatre of São Carlos. Meanwhile, among the bills sent to the Portuguese crown for payment in February was one from the restaurant run by Isidro Barreiro in the Mouraria district. On 17 December, the Dahomeyan royal party had tucked into soup, roast chicken, veal, puddings, three bottles of port and three of table wine, and similar outlays followed. By adopting luxury foreign clothes, food and entertainments, therefore, the royal lineages made a clear distinction between themselves and those they ruled, as well as a connection to the royal families of their transnational trading partners.[23]

African ruling families had multiple strategies to help to build this sort of mutual understanding. Beyond the adoption of European styles of clothing and furnishings, they also knew it was important to be able to switch languages easily. By the very late seventeenth century, it was becoming widespread for African kings to send their senior children for schooling in Europe. The ruler of Bissau sent his son to Portugal as an envoy and for instruction in 1694, noting that he had had no instruction or knowledge of the Portuguese language as yet. By the eighteenth century, the sons of some trading families from Calabar were sent to Britain to be educated, as was also the case among some of the princes of Fante ruling families in Anomabu on the Gold Coast. A prominent African trading family at St Louis on the Senegal River in the 1780s was run by three sons, according to the traveller Saugnier: one, Thévenot, had spent a lot of money in Paris in his youth and taken the title of 'the African prince'; another, known as 'Saint-Jean', was the son of a former English governor of Senegal, and had been in London; and a third, Lejugê, had travelled as far as India and in all of Europe.[24]

One of the key skills that African traders and rulers hoped their children would learn through this education was proficiency in the European languages needed to trade successfully. Like elites in all societies, they hoped that by expanding their skillset they would enable their children to reap greater profits in business and political negotiations with the outside world. In a pattern that strikes us as enormously familiar in the twenty-first century, they recognized that it was by understanding and living with Europeans in their societies that they would develop the cultural flexibility and knowledge necessary to 'do business' in Atlantic Africa. By the 1780s, Lathe – the most successful trader at Great Popo* – had one son studying in England and another in Portugal, where, as one observer put it, 'they are learning to write and calculate.' And, while around 1700 the ruler of Hueda understood some Portuguese, by the 1780s, the yovogan could speak English, French and Portuguese; the Court of Dahomey, in 1797, had people who could read Portuguese well enough to discuss the tenets of the Catholic faith, while the new regent of the kingdom mentioned that his own uncle had died in Portugal.[25]

These strategies were, therefore, fairly widespread in many different societies of West and West-Central Africa. It was far from unknown for African diplomats or princes and merchants to study in Europe and the Americas. European city-dwellers were thus fairly well accustomed to the presence of members of African ruling families among them from at least the eighteenth century. So this makes it all the harder to fathom the incredulity with which evidence of this broad transnational awareness was sometimes greeted by outsiders. When an English emissary, Bowdich, reached the Ashanti Court at Kumasi, in 1817, he found that one member of the nobility could 'astonish us by offering to lend us some books to read; he showed us two French volumes on geography, a Dutch bible, a volume of the Spectator, and a Dissuasion from Popery, 1620'. Yet really this should not have been astonishing in itself: what was astonishing was Bowdich's ignorance of the strategies of African elites, as they had grown over the preceding centuries, in tandem with those of their European trading partners.[26]

The growing differentiation of African ruling classes from their population was in some ways one of the more significant political changes on the continent during the slave-trade era. It anticipated many subsequent political upheavals. When, in the 1970s, the historian and Black Power activist Walter Rodney wrote that this era saw the alliance of African and European elites at the expense of the African poor, he recognized that these transformations also paved the way for the continuing inequalities in postcolonial African societies. The construction of economic exploitation thus had a long, painful,

* In what is now the Republic of Benin.

history. A complex interplay of elite agencies was involved, in which no one came out of it with much credit.[27]

From an African perspective, it was in the elite incorporation of transnational influences that the new idioms of power were most visible – today's *pains perdus* and imported wines are the elaborate cloths and furniture of yesteryear. But, although this appeared to buttress the authority of African monarchs, it also unleashed forces that could not be controlled. More people might gain access to the symbols of power, and challenge ruling families. Finally, it was in the emergence of new forms of syncretic religious belief, and strategies of flight and conflict, that a powerful vehicle would develop to threaten the aristocracies.[28]

TRANSNATIONAL RELIGIOUS PRACTICE AND THE RESISTANCE TO POWER

Towards the end of the dry season of 2011, I spent some weeks in a small town some way north of Bissau. Electricity did not work in the streets, but the town was bright at night because of the waxing moon, which rose every evening. One evening, a friend suggested I follow him through some back alleys off the main road, as there was a visiting marabout, or Islamic seer. The marabout was renting a room in a compound behind the one where I was staying, it turned out. After dark, we went into his room, which was empty except for his bed and an impressive collection of exegeses on the Qur'ān. My friend was excited, for this seer had trained widely: born in Guinea-Bissau, he had studied with *shaykhs* in Mauritania, in Mali and as far away as Egypt.

This transnational religious element from the Sahel brings with it today its own political connections. Mosques in small villages carry their characteristic signs, which announce that they have been built with funds generated elsewhere in the Umma. Meanwhile, instrumental connections with the Islamic world rise and fall with regularity. Today, it is the people-smuggling route through Libya, but it was not so long ago that Muammar Qaddafi himself used to try to act as a bridge, attempting to build his own secular empire. For many years, one of the most famous landmarks in Bissau was the crumbling whitewash of the Libya Hotel, said to be owned by Qaddafi himself, who would drive down on occasion with caseloads of dollars that he used to give to his clients, in Guinea-Bissau and elsewhere.

For the Sahel and its hinterland, this interconnection of transnational religious and political power is very old. Plural symbolic dimensions to royal power are as old as the trade that linked Mali, Kano and Borno with Morocco, Tripoli and Cairo. In the early times, while Mansa Musa's pilgrimage is the most famous reminder of this, these exchanges had affected all the major Sahelian kingdoms; already by the early fourteenth century, while Mansa Musa was passing through Cairo, there was a madrassa for the people of Borno in the Cairo district of Fusṭāṭ, where Borno travellers lodged when they visited the city. Sahelian kings rapidly adopted Islam, as did many of their rulers; and yet their control over the ideas that followed the religion to Africa was weak.[29]

These transnational influences on Sahelian cities grew ever stronger through the period from the fifteenth to the eighteenth centuries. Katsina overtook Kano as the commercial hub of Hausaland from the 1730s, but Kano's administrative base remained very powerful, with separate military and civil administrations and influential throne slaves. The regional economy worked through locally produced cloth currencies and imported cowries. Gradually, social structures emerged in the Sahel that ensured integration with transnational connections. By the 1790s, any foreign merchant settling in Timbuktu married a local woman. In the early nineteenth century, Al-Hajj Abd Salam Shabinī described how merchants came to Kano from India, and that Indian manufactured goods were found in local markets, in continuity of long-standing practices of globalization.[30]

Yet the adoption of Islam by the kings of Borno and Hausa created religious tensions. Religion was fundamentally political – just as it always is. As change swept across schools of Islam in the eighteenth century, there were some who claimed that the 'Muslim kings' of the Sahel were not sufficiently pious and strict in their faith – just as had been said of Sonni 'Alī of Songhay as early as in the 1490s. And it was true that practices were mixed. The installation of a new Sarki of

Katsina was one that involved many aspects of the pre-Islamic rituals of kingship. Meanwhile, it would be the alleged 'hybrid Islam' of the mais of Borno, and of the King of Gobir in Hausaland, that would be used as a justification for the attack on them by the soldiers of the Sokoto Caliphate in the early nineteenth century.[31]

The incorporation of distant religious ideas and external trappings of power had a longer history in the Sahel than it did in the Atlantic kingdoms of West Africa. Yet, as we shall now see, the consequences were not entirely dissimilar. As in the Atlantic kingdoms, the transnational influences brought with them the danger that monarchies would lose control over the levers of political power. In the same way that kings of Atlantic states could not control the flow of trade, so the ideas that crossed the Sahara could not be controlled, and nor could the ways in which they were dispersed through the community. Itinerant *shaykhs*, forerunners of the one I met over two centuries later in Guinea-Bissau, could 'stir the pot' with new discussions. It became harder and harder for political rulers in the Sahel to control this, and so transnational religious forces would come to challenge their power.

While these transnational influences in the Sahel seem far away from the Atlantic kingdoms, the economic pressures on Africa from both north and west meant that there were areas that saw a crossover. By the late seventeenth century in Allada, the word for Christ in a catechism created by Spanish missionaries was 'Lisá', clearly linked to the name given to Jesus in Islam, 'Issa'. Meanwhile, a century later in Kumasi, the capital of the Asante Empire, there were North African as well as Atlantic influences (just as there were in Dahomey), which culminated in the late eighteenth century, when Osei Kwame, the asantehene, was said to have secretly adopted Islam. Bowdich's description of the palace at Kumasi ('Coomassie') can stand as a telling indication of the integration of different architectural and ideological frameworks that characterized many savannah states such as Asante, caught between the Atlantic and Sahelian systems in the early nineteenth century: '[The palace] is an immense building of a variety of oblong courts and regular squares, the former with arcades along the one side, some of round arches symmetrically turned, having a skeleton of bamboo; the entablatures exuberantly adorned with bold fan and trellis work of Egyptian character.'[32]

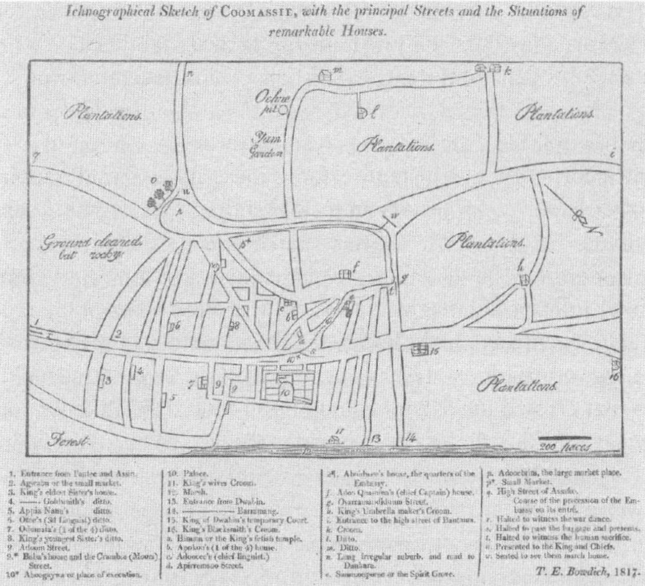

Map of Kumasi (spelt 'Coomassie' by Bowdich).

And so it should be no surprise that in areas touched by the Atlantic, ruling elites incorporated external religious idioms and ideas, just as they had done in the Sahel with Islam. Further west, in the coastal regions of Guinea-Bissau, by the end of the seventeenth century, Bacampolo, the ruler of Bissau, had adopted aspects of Catholic ritual that were having an effect locally. One report declared that there were 400 Christians in the trading centre of Bissau by 1694, and that 'when a Christian dies, if the illness struck them in the house of a non-believer, the said [gentile] goes to call the Vicar to administer the last rites, and when the said Christian is buried their [gentile] relatives accompany the funeral procession to the doors of the Church.'[33]

There had always been a strong religious element to the trading and cultural relationships linking the peoples of Greater Senegambia with the Portuguese. Much of the wax exported from the region accompanied enslaved persons to the South American port of Cartagena: once there, it was often traded to be made into the candles that adorned the churches of the New World, from Cartagena to Lima and Santiago in Chile. This relationship between long-distance trade and religious belief did not dissipate over the eighteenth century. At times of political need, West African monarchs often flirted with Catholicism, as had their predecessors in the sixteenth century. This rarely led to much, as the frustrated letters of Brazilian missionaries to Dahomey in 1797 attest, and kings and their successors would often row back on early expressions of interest. Nevertheless, the frequent presence of missionaries had its own slow influence, and the impact of the Catholic missions on religious ideas in Sierra Leone can be gauged by the Temne word for 'Hell' in 1796 being 'Satanas'.[34]

What emerges is the transformation of local ideas about religion and power. These were not somehow 'authentic'. They drew on transnational connections, and shaped that wider world, too. In this light, the very idea of authenticity reveals a worldview that requires Africa and Africans to have been separated from the rest of the world, isolated from world-historical processes. For the adoption of external ideas on the one hand was a mirror to the way in which, as we have seen, Africans also shaped the development of new ideas in the Americas on the other. It was a process of reciprocal influence.

The hybrid nature of some religious ideas both in the Sahel and in the Atlantic in the eighteenth century offers an intriguing mirror to the experience of Africans in the New World. As early as the late sixteenth century, a movement emerged in north-eastern Brazil known as *santidade* that was seen as a real threat to colonial power in Salvador. Adepts of *santidade* installed their own 'pope' and melded Tupinambá religious practices with the beliefs of African maroons into a new religious movement. Africans and mixed-race African-Native American *mamelucos* flocked to the community, until it was crushed. Relevant African religious symbols may have included the palm tree, while the religious leaders were Tupinambá. Syncretism with Christianity emerged in the reappropriation of the myth of Noah, and of the place of baptism.[35]

This blend of religious transformation and struggle against colonial power became a strong feature of the experience of enslaved communities in the New World, especially as this grew in the eighteenth and nineteenth centuries. In Jamaica, in the 1730s, the leader

Eighteenth-century panorama of Salvador da Bahia.

of the maroon communities was known as 'Nanny' of the Maroons, who was also a leader of the Obeah cults of Jamaica, which were derived from religious shrines in Great Popo and Dahomey. When the religion of Candomblé emerged in late-eighteenth-century Bahia, it interwove Yorùbá religiosity and Catholic form; here, the use of African plants and healing techniques allowed the creation of religious cults that rejected the prevailing colonial culture. In the nineteenth century, direct resistance to slavery was mobilized through Islam in Bahia in the 1835 Malé Uprising.[36]

The early emergence of religious practice as a channel to contest power in the Americas was significant. The passage of Africans back and forth between the two continents was not restricted to enslaved persons, and African travellers brought this way of looking at religion as a way of speaking back to power. As early as the seventeenth century, free Africans in the New World returned to Angola and set up as commercial agents and traders. By the later eighteenth century, free Africans from north-eastern Brazil were returning to Dahomey and Great Popo. Many of them seem to have settled in the region of Lagos, before 1800. Since religious transformation was a key aspect of the experience of Africans in the New World, this meant that these persons brought back with them a new understanding of religion and its potential to challenge power.[37]

Enslaved persons also travelled between Brazil and Africa. Some were exiled to Angola from Bahia for misdemeanours and overtly challenging Portuguese colonial power in Brazil. Meanwhile, slave-trading ships sent from Brazil were usually manned by a large number of African sailors, many themselves enslaved. Many of the sailors used on small ships to transport sugar and provisions within the state of Bahia itself were African: 426 enslaved sailors have been recorded as working these ships in just four towns in Bahia between 1776 and 1800. This pattern was also true of the trans-Atlantic trade. Ship captains used African crew from Yorùbá- and Gbe-speaking areas* in the trade to West Africa, as they could act as interpreters when they landed at African ports in present-day Togo, Benin and Nigeria. Many of these crew appear to have also been employed for their knowledge of African medicine, listed as *sangradores* (bleeders) in the ship's roster; and, since medicine was inserted in a metaphysical and religious worldview, these crew members also brought with them insights into the new religious framework emerging in the New World.[38]

By the later eighteenth century, there were thus two channels for the incorporation of transnational religious power in West and West-Central Africa. Ruling elites sought to offer a hybrid face to their religious practice, incorporating Islam in many parts of the Sahel, and Christianity in some Atlantic kingdoms (especially in Kongo and parts of Greater Senegambia), but at the same time holding fast to existing religious shrines and practice. However, by the eighteenth century, the same transnational forces that brought these faiths also brought with them new models of religious struggle against power. From the Muslim world, this took the form of the Salafiya revival movement of the late eighteenth century, and from the Atlantic the use of religion as a challenge to colonial power in the Americas. As new forms of ethnic identity began to emerge, people in different parts of Atlantic Africa were able to harness them and these models of religious struggle to challenge the aristocracy's monopoly of power.

TRANSNATIONAL CULTURES AND THE 'INVENTION' OF ETHNICITY

Whenever the issue of political conflict in Africa emerges in the news, it is often ascribed to 'ethnic' discord. The implication, stated or not,

* Known in Salvador as 'Jeje'.

is that such ethnic conflict is age-old. The model that is thereby conveyed is the familiar one, of static peoples and histories. It reminds us how old historical discourses still feed into preconceptions, and shape contemporary debates; and why many African thinkers insist on the historicity of the problems of 'development' in the twenty-first century.[39]

When it comes to the question of age-old 'ethnic' discord, there is one overriding problem with this analysis. This is that most modern ethnic categories did not emerge in Africa until the nineteenth century. Ethnicity is resoundingly modern; and, as a category of use in Africa, it emerged in response to the transnational pressures, and the need to mobilize identities in the struggle to overturn the authoritarian power of the slave-trade era. Nevertheless, veritable mini armies of political scientists, think tanks and their institutional political backers discuss the significance of the topic, and how outside intervention can resolve the ethnic discord that this discussion is itself helping to create through its classifications. And, indeed, however problematic the concept may be, like all strategic actions conceived by empires, the invention of ethnicity has created 'facts on the ground'.

This sort of intellectual sleight of hand goes right back to the early centuries of Atlantic trade, and the strategies developed then by European outsiders. While ethnicities themselves are new, the attempt by outsiders to categorize Africans through ethnic labels is very old. In the seventeenth century, for example, the Jesuit Alonso de Sandoval composed an early ethnographic study of the different African peoples of the port of Cartagena. From Cartagena, ships sailed to the Cape Verde Islands and Guinea-Bissau, and to Angola and the ports of Allada for captives. The mix of peoples arriving in the port made Cartagena one of the most cosmopolitan cities on earth. Some Africans were enslaved in the mines of what is now Colombia, while others were transported across the Panamá Isthmus, to be shipped on to the Viceroyalty of Peru. Captives were auctioned by the Cartagena town crier by the gates of the main square, and all colonists had a stake in the trade in one way or another: Sandoval himself acted for the Jesuits in the trade for enslaved persons to the Cape Verde Islands during the period in which he wrote this work.[40]

Sandoval's 1627 book sought to describe all the 'nations' of Africans in the New World, but, in so doing, he revealed some of the problems with this project. Of the peoples of Greater Senegambia, the Bainunk 'Bootes' who lived at the mouth of the Casamance River shared a language with the people known as 'Floups', but could not understand those who were just 'Bainunk'. Meanwhile, the Balanta people included 'many different castes of this nation, some of whom do not understand each other'. To make things more complicated, though, many Balanta spoke other languages, such as Brame or Mandinka, while many Brames could speak Bainunk, Floup, Balanta and Mandinka.[41]

If Sandoval's picture of different categories sounds somewhat confused and contradictory, that is because it is. The emerging 'ethnicities' that were being drawn up in the New World were categories that, again, simplified hugely complex affiliations of kinship, belief and language such as existed in different parts of West and West-Central Africa. Often, some peoples of the same 'ethnicity' could not understand one another, something that remains the case today among the Serèèr of Senegal, and the Jola of Gambia, Senegal and Guinea-Bissau. Further south, in the region of Benguela in Angola, the 'Ndombe' category first noted by the Portuguese in the late seventeenth century incorporated different peoples with different rulers. A better-known example would be among the Yorùbá of south-western Nigeria. There are large numbers of 'Yoruboid' variants, on a spectrum of mutual intelligibility, of which Yorùbá is by far the most widely spoken (standardized following the translation of the Bible into Yorùbá in 1884).[42]

Ethnic designators had locally ascribed meanings, and are best seen as an extension of political identity. These political identities were far from being reducible to any one component, but incorporated many different aspects of identities in West and West-Central Africa: kinship, lineage and religious beliefs, and affiliation to a particular area of land. Indeed, for this reason, 'ethnicities' might appear to have some sort of continuity, as they were used continuously to refer to these constellations of different factors. It became strategically valuable for people to use these terms themselves in Africa, to create distinctions between themselves and other potentially hostile groups, thereby allowing them to stake claims to land and other resources.[43]

That ethnic categories were retrospective is also suggested by the archaeological record, which shows common origins, whereas today nations are divided into different 'ethnicities'. By and by, the construction of these categories had an effect in Africa as to how identities were conceived. The migration of Africans back and forth across the Atlantic, and the importance of these categories in defining affiliations and boundaries, meant that African peoples used their own frameworks and priorities to define what they were to mean. This led to the construction of new forms of ethnic identity, which were mobilized in the eighteenth and nineteenth centuries to very important effect.[44]

Why was ethnicity important in the first place? There was a mutual interest in the concept of 'ethnicity', as some early examples from the diaspora can show. It mattered greatly to the fight for freedom for Africans, and to the securing of economic status for colonists in the New World. For Africans, too, knowledge of these new labels was important. Seeking freedom through legal channels of redress in the New World meant that understanding these ethnic markers was vital. This emerges in the evidence of a ship arriving in Hispaniola in 1575 under Captain Cristóbal Cayado with captives from Greater Senegambia. Among the passengers on the ship were a number of free Africans who identified themselves to the colonial authorities on arrival in port. These individuals ascribed their own 'ethnic' origins to themselves and successfully asserted their free status. One was 'a black called Manuel who said he was a Creole and free', another 'a Black called Hernando from Çape lands who was bearded and said that he was free', another 'Amador Lopez who said he was raised in the island of Santiago [Cape Verde] and was free'. Ethnicity was, therefore, a category that helped navigate the new territory, and thus formed another new strand in the ideas of belonging that Africans developed in their new communities in America.[45]

Beyond any mere usefulness of ethnicity, however, was the reality of the emotional pull of the discovery of a shared background with people so far from home. Africans in the New World often sought out people from the same shared cultural region. They married one another and stood sponsor to one another at baptism, in sixteenth-century Colombia and Cuba as in eighteenth-century northern Brazil. The children of people of the same 'ethnicity' born from these marriages would be called Serèèr, Nalú or Mandinka 'Creoles', showing that they had been born out of this new love discovered in the Americas. Who can fail to be moved by the story of the Bijogó Francisco, a barber, who described how, in 1632, another Bijogó called Gaspar had been sold in Lima's market? Francisco had gone a few days later to the house of the buyer and had found Gaspar there, 'and had spoken to the said Gaspar Bioho as someone from his land and who understood his language, and Gaspar Bioho was delighted by this as was he'. Francisco agreed to become Gaspar's godfather when he was baptized into the Catholic faith, and so the strength of the community, and of the 'Creole Bioho' identity, grew.[46]

What, then, was the source of this growing imperative to ethnicize African identities from the sixteenth to the eighteenth centuries? The evidence shows a variety of pressures: the economic realities of the 'value' of human labour in the New World, the attempt to 'order reality' by missionaries and traders, and the growing military conflicts in West and West-Central Africa that made it a strategic advantage to claim one identity over another, and to create clear differences from other ethnicities, who might then become legitimate targets for capture as enslaved persons. In other words, what emerges is a vital tension between African imperatives and strands of identity (kin, religion, language, land) and transnational forces linked to economic profit and a categorial worldview.

Maybe the best example of how this interaction worked is in the emergence of the Yorùbá ethnicity in southern Nigeria. As many historians have pointed out, 'Yorùbá' ethnicity did not exist until the nineteenth century, when it emerged probably initially among communities of liberated Africans in Freetown, Sierra Leone, and also among communities of free and enslaved Yorùbá speakers in Salvador. In Salvador, only 3 per cent of enslaved Africans arriving in the nineteenth century came from outside of Yorùbá regions, and, by the middle of the nineteenth century, sources describe the emergence of a general language spoken by these people. With the passage of many of these liberated Africans from Brazil and Sierra Leone back to

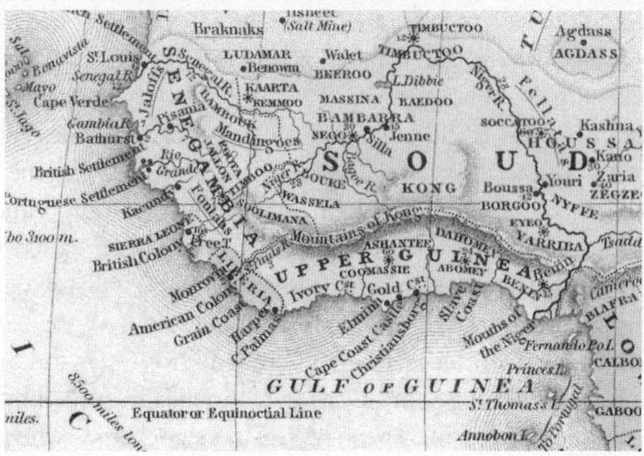

West Africa, 1839. Mitchell map, drawn from an 1839 atlas. 'Yarriba' peoples at centre-right, below Eyeo [Oyo].

southern Nigeria, the construction of a shared identity emerged, and, as this 1839 map shows, it was already becoming a 'hard' identity by the middle of the nineteenth century. This was then more or less standardized into modern Yorùbá following the translation of the Bible into the language in the 1880s.[47]

However, as in many other parts of West Africa, this did not imply in practice a shared ethnic or linguistic identity; indeed, in regions such as Ekiti in southern Nigeria, to this day, neighbouring villages speak mutually incomprehensible forms of the 'Yorùbá' language. It was well known that there were many different branches to the Yorùbás, and that they did not all share one common ethnic origin.[48]

The transnational process was at work in the construction of a Yorùbá ethnicity. Not only did the liberated Africans from Sierra Leone play a part, but so, too, did transformations of Yorùbá identities in the New World. In Cuba, many different lineages of Yorùbá speakers – Oyo, Egba, Ijebu and Ijesha – were all subsumed into one ethnic designator, that of 'Lucumí'. In time, other peoples from the same region, such as Arada and Igbo, were also called 'Lucumí', and this identity became the cornerstone of the new Afro-Catholic religion of Santería. Similar changes and streamlining of complex identities took place in Brazil, where those who worshipped Yorùbá *orixás* collectively worshipped in Candomblé shrines. The nineteenth century saw some free Africans in Brazil returning to settle in what are now Ghana, Togo, Benin and Nigeria, bringing with them this new sense of collective identity and helping, as we have seen, in the construction of the new ethnicity.[49]

Writing of the Jahanké people of Senegambia, the religious historian Lamin Sanneh notes that 'they are not an ethnic group as such and possess no language of their own.' The evidence is that this holds true for very many different peoples across West and West-Central Africa. Ethnic categories emerged, as we have seen here, as much in the Americas as in Africa itself. They were, in the end, of use both for Africans and for imperialists. For imperialists, they helped to categorize a reality that escaped them; and, in Africa, the construction of hard ethnic boundaries helped to define who was and was not a friend or an enemy, a potential threat or a potential ally in times of warfare, insecurity and political destabilization. Finally, the struggles of the eighteenth century would become a contest for power, and the new categories would help to mobilize identities and communities in the fight against an unequal economic and political system.[50]

MAROON COMMUNITIES AND THE GATHERING FIGHT FOR FREEDOM

Influential historians of the American Revolution in the late eighteenth century have shown how the American value of freedom was deeply marked by the presence of slavery. Yet already, for two centuries and more, this connection had been deeply imprinted on the consciousness of enslaved Africans in the New World.[51]

One poignant speech shows how African warfare in the New World was shaped by the struggle for freedom from the start. In Venezuela, in 1552, Miguel, the leader of one group of maroons, was said to have declared: 'That the reason that had moved them to withdraw from the Spanish, was well known to have been in order to gain their freedom, which only in such a difficult and unjust manner was open to them; since God had created them free just like all other peoples in the world, and yet the Spanish kept them subjected and tyrannically held them in perpetual and wretched servitude.'[52]

Struggle against enslavement offers perhaps the best way of grasping the significance of this early African globalization, and the impact of liberation struggles in the Americas on Africa in the late eighteenth century. Conflicts led by Africans against their warrior aristocracies were not somehow isolated from the revolutionary fervour of the rest of the world. As we have seen in this chapter, many connections had grown up between Africa and the rest of the Western hemisphere. When the Age of Revolution struck the United States and then Haiti in the 1780s and 1790s, the pattern of reciprocal influences continued with transnational impacts in Africa.

Maroon communities had been growing in Africa through the eighteenth century, too, partly in response to the slave trade. People appear to have escaped from the plantation island prison of São Tomé to the island of Fernando Pó (Equatorial Guinea) throughout this century. And on the continent, communities of escaped captives were growing. They formed in present-day Benin as people escaped the armies of Dahomey. And when Adam Afzelius visited Sierra Leone in 1795, for instance, he found that enslaved persons had escaped their captors. Some had come from a failed slave rebellion against the Fuuta Jaalo Almamate, which had begun in 1785; others had set off over the jungle-covered hills that rise sheer behind Freetown. Here they had formed maroon communities in inaccessible regions, much as their counterparts had done in the New World. The parallels with the Americas are striking. Afzelius described how a group of captives awaiting sale into the Atlantic trade had escaped to land held by the Susus, and then made military attacks on their neighbours – much as maroon communities had long done in Brazil, Jamaica and many parts of the Caribbean. The Susus had tried to put the maroons down, but with no success, so they had had to call on Mandinga allies 'for assistance, which being granted, there are now assembled nearly 4,000 men to exterminate the villains'.[53]

Afzelius himself visited the maroon community, to see conditions there. The name of the settlement was Yanghia Cori, and by the time of Afzelius's visit it had a population of five or six hundred. At first, the community had been joined by some free people, and there had been fields of cotton and rice. However, as the Susu and Mandinga united against the maroons, these lands and the water used to irrigate them were taken. The main military strategy was to starve out the maroons. The besiegers surrounded the mud walls of the town and camped there in temporary huts; they had cut down all the trees and bushes surrounding the settlement to make it impossible to escape out of sight. The community did not survive much longer.[54]

The patterns of influence from the Americas were soon striking. It would not be so very long before a new and powerful channel of that freedom returned to Sierra Leone. In 1808, free maroons who had come from Jamaica to Sierra Leone founded the maroon church, St John's, in central Freetown, a little way uphill from the asylum where liberated African slaves would be housed when they first were freed from 'illegal' slave ships later in the nineteenth century. They built the rafters of the church with planks taken from the slave ships, and, as we saw at the start of this chapter, outside the church would in time stand the maroon-coloured flag that was their emblem, embossed with a ship. Beyond Senegambia, other societies in West and West-Central Africa also saw red as the privilege of royal power, as was the case in Dahomey and Kongo. Symbolic power coalesced and then returned from the Americas to influence ideas and struggle in both the New World and the Old.[55]

It is notable that the struggle of this maroon community near Freetown occurred in the very same years as the Haitian Revolution unfolded in the French colony of St Domingue. Here, enslaved persons had risen up in 1791 against the planter class in France's richest New World colony, ultimately overthrowing it in 1804 in an event that would prove as significant for the nineteenth century as the abolition of the slave trade. Indeed, in the Sierra Leone case, the escape of these maroons was itself connected to French policies, as Afzelius noted. The disruption of the trade in captives caused by the Haitian Revolution was widely discussed in African Atlantic ports, and thus the move by these maroons in Sierra Leone to join escapees from Fuuta Jaalo connected revolutions in the Americas with struggles in Africa. Awareness of the diaspora in the Americas was, by the end of the eighteenth century, becoming a relevant factor in movements to overthrow the dominant slave-holding aristocracies in some parts of West Africa.[56]

Rafters of St John's Maroon Church, Freetown.

Such techniques of flight were not unusual. In Senegambia, among the Serèèr peoples of the Saluum Delta north of the Gambia River, villages were in a condition of permanent armed defence against slave-raiding parties. Some villagers, the Safèn, lived in areas that could be better defended from slave raiders because of the terrain of forests and hills. They welcomed refugees from other communities, and fiercely defended an autonomy free of the hierarchy of both monarchy and slavery. Serèèr 'ethnicity' thus in time came to incorporate many different peoples, as a group characterized not necessarily by linguistic use or physical heredity, but by its struggle against both unbridled Jolof state power and also Islam. In the nineteenth century, the Serèèr retained their hostility to Islam, while speaking different languages, many of which are mutually unintelligible.[57]

While the Serèèr example does not illustrate transnational connections for African maroons, there were other regions that did so, especially Angola. As noted earlier, the *quilombo* of Palmares in Brazil was perhaps the most important maroon movement in the

Americas until the Haitian Revolution. The very term *quilombo* derived from the Imbangala military platoons of Angola, and came to be used to describe the maroon settlements in Brazil in the early eighteenth century. By the 1740s, the many communities of escaped slaves in Angola also began to be called *quilombos* by outsiders; and, by the nineteenth century, members of these maroon communities called themselves *quilombos*, showing the incorporation of a term from the Americas into a description of a situation in Africa. As in Sierra Leone, defeating these communities of maroons required outside African military assistance in Angola.[58]

By 1795, and with the rise of the community described by Afzelius in Sierra Leone, the roots of connection and influence become blurred. The rise of enslavement in Africa had clearly led to the development of multiple maroon communities who adopted strategies of geographical isolation and militarized defence in self-protection. Beyond the communities of Serèèr and Angola runaways, settlements in Igbominaland in southern Nigeria were always sited on hilltops, as an echo of these maroon settlements. When these strategies failed, some among their communities might be captured and transported to the New World, where they would bring this strategic awareness of defensive isolation into new maroon communities. News of the success of some of these communities then returned to Africa, along with figures like Antonio Vaz, who, as we saw in the introduction to this chapter, increasingly established themselves during the eighteenth century. Meantime, the strategies of African maroon communities were intensified as the forces of the Atlantic world became more constraining. Transnational cultures of political struggle were emerging that connected communities in a large part of West and West-Central Africa to the cruel empires of the New World.[59]

CONCLUSION: THE SOUNDS OF STRUGGLE

At a meeting of musicians and historians from West Africa in London, in June 2015, the Bissau-Guinean *gumbe* musician Manecas Costa performed one of his signature tracks, 'Ermons di Terra' ('Brothers of the Land'), before discussing the music itself. *Gumbe*, Manecas Costa said, had been a vital form of resistance during the independence war fought against the Portuguese dictatorship in the 1960s and 1970s. Other *gumbe* musicians describe how it was a key way of communicating information across the *mato* (bush), which the Portuguese could not understand, and also a way of asserting a national identity in the Kriolu language that was used, and that the Portuguese often could not understand. Yet *gumbe* music itself is not indigenous to Guinea-Bissau, for when, in the early nineteenth century, some maroons and freed slaves from Jamaica went with the British anti-slave trade squadron to the settlement at Freetown, in Sierra Leone, they brought their 'gumbay' drums with them. The *gumbay* was performed loudly and heedlessly in the street, to the annoyance of the British colonists; and *gumbay* drums remain popular in Sierra Leone to this day, and can be found in the maroon church of St John, while gumbay music plays raucously from loudspeakers on the beaches near Freetown.[60]

So *gumbay* was a music developed to communicate among maroon communities in Jamaica during the eighteenth century, which was then used in the same way in Guinea-Bissau during the successful 1960s War of Independence. Music followed routes and movement, and allowed people to share new identities that could challenge power. As Paul Gilroy showed in his foundational book *The Black Atlantic*, music was an intellectual production that embodied many of the pathways – human and other – crisscrossing the ocean.[61]

Like the thirst for freedom, this connection was also something that had developed very early, and had developed globally. In the first decades of the seventeenth century, Jesuit missionaries going to establish their missions in Paraguay sought special licence to take with them 'eight Black slaves, musicians from Angola', who would be brought for their skill at singing and playing the flute and cornet, so as to accompany Mass. African musical style itself provided the soundtrack to many historical experiences in the New World from a very early time.[62]

It is not surprising that musical styles emerged along the routes of the trade in captives. This, too, was a transnational trade bridging worlds. Ironically, just as patterns of maroon settlement were linked to flows across the Atlantic, the same was the case with the institution from which they were escaping, that of slavery. Servants crisscrossed the Atlantic, bringing with them the imprint of the institution of slavery in both directions. Some went from the Americas back to West Africa. 'Castle slaves' were well known at Elmina on the Gold Coast, and came to influence local forms of dependence and slavery at the Elmina settlement. Meanwhile, by the later seventeenth century, there were many domestic slaves in Cacheu, in Guinea-Bissau, and some enslaved persons were known to have travelled between there and Cartagena. In this way, some ideas of dependence and enslavement also became transnational, like the practices of escape from them by maroons – and the music that accompanied them.[63]

Thus, the musical interchange bridging African communities and those of Europe and the New World was established alongside the transnational institution of slavery. Iberia was a perfect theatre for this sort of cultural transformation, being already a product of exchanges between Catholic, Jewish and Muslim cultures going back several centuries. African musical influence was then embodied in a variety of dances and popular cultures that spread quickly in Iberia and the Americas. In Portugal, stories and dances from Guinea-Bissau became embodied in dances such as the *guineu*, as well as in folk tales that spread across the Alentejo region and were still recounted in the twentieth century.[64]

Yet how could music really accompany the consolidation and expansion of such an institution as slavery? Microhistories from Senegambia and West-Central Africa offer the best way of reflecting on this unexpected aspect of African history. In Senegambia, the rise of the slave trade linking French 'factories' at St Louis and Gorée with Louisiana in the eighteenth century saw the removal of many peoples to the American South – indeed, 'Senegal' remains a common surname in Louisiana to this day. These Senegambian captives brought with them the structure of the xalam or ngoni tradition, these being lutes of four or five strings, similar to the Jola akonting.* The musical structure employed in Senegambia of the fodet had a remarkable similarity to the '12-Bar Blues'. In this way, the American Blues

* See above, Chapter 2.

emerged from the fusion of different instruments and styles from Senegambia in a New World setting.[65]

Also remarkable was the reciprocal influence that this would in time have in Africa, far beyond the *gumbay* drum. Following the independence of Haiti in 1804, there was an increasing interconnection of formerly French New Orleans with Santo Domingo and Cuba. The trade in enslaved persons continued to Cuba until 1866, and, as many of the crew on these ships were freed Cubano-Africans (just as Afro-Brazilians had manned the ships to West Africa in the eighteenth century), they brought with them strains of these new musical styles on the return voyages to Africa. When, in the 1940s and 1950s, modern Senegalese music began to emerge, it was heavily influenced by Cuban music played on the radio, just as was Congolese *rumba* in the 1950s. Here was the echo of an earlier struggle again, this time to a different yet familiar soundtrack, formal European colonialism in Africa.[66]

As the flow of music shows, experiences of the diaspora in the New World would influence cultural expression in many different parts of West and West-Central Africa. The reciprocal transnational influence did not rest only with music but was also, as we have seen, central to the maroon communities and the strategies needed for survival in a society with slave-holding, and to the way in which religious practice could be used to develop an ideology of militarized resistance. As these changes took hold in America, ongoing struggles against overreaches of power linked up the Age of Revolution in the Americas with movements in Africa.

And yet this relationship of transnational influence from and to Africa cannot be left, finally, at the moment of a rising against power. The context for that rising, the depths of the need that it answered, has its own sound. The whip, brute signal of the animalization of the slave-owning class (which they projected on to slaves), was the other core soundtrack to the Atlantic. It was embedded in fantasy and coercion, and sublimated in psychotic racial and sexual neuroses, as Frantz Fanon so excoriatingly analysed. It was as brutally enduring an instrument as the akonting or the banjo, flogging the dead horse of colonial consumption and desire for so many centuries; and it was resurrected from the Americas in twentieth-century colonial Africa, like this music itself, in the hands of Belgian rubber tappers, Portuguese *cipaios* (military police), French *corvées* and British conscripts panicked by Mau Mau, in the era of European imperialisms in twentieth-century Africa.[67]

How to take account of these parallel sounds, of music and brutalism? Many Africans formed their own vehicles of struggle, and individual cases explore this best. There is the experience of Manuel Bran, hauled before the Inquisition in Cartagena in 1650. Born in the Cape Verde Islands, he had been taken as a captive with his mother to the Azores as an infant, where eventually he had grown up and married a Spanish woman, Leonor de Sosa, who was a servant to the same owner as he was. He had then been taken off by his owner to Brazil, for four months, and thence to Cartagena, where they sold him to his current owner, Rodrigo de Lobo. Stripped multiple times of his family by the institution of slavery, it was not surprising that Manuel Bran was accused of spitting on crosses and denying the existence of God, when in the midst of being whipped by his owner; in Cape Verde, whipping crucifixes was a common accusation before the Inquisition, and, where cruelty and abuses of power were so universal, so was the disbelief in the master's God.[68]

The whip, like the banjo and the drum, was a transnational instrument. It was the instrument of the Atlantic slave-owning class, as base as the rhythms and melodies of the African experience were moving. Yet music, too, memorializes the place of the whip. The infamous nursery rhyme 'Eenie Meenie Maine Mo' is given its fullest and ugliest context in one study of the Creole language Papiamentu, from the Dutch West Indian island of Curaçäo. Here, it is suggested, that, 'Reconstructed to its original Creole form, this song would read (in an English orthography): "Eene meene maine mo / K'e cha ting ke bai deto / I fi! / Ole es latigo", which, when properly translated, reveals its slave origins: 'Children / Boys / Girls calm down / For you have to go to bed / It is finished! / Here's the whip.'[69]

10

Warrior Aristocracies and Pushback from Below

In the nineteenth century, the famous French historian and political thinker Alexis de Tocqueville argued that the American Revolution grew out of a conflict between aristocratic and democratic forms of government. Democratic forces had convulsed against the power of European aristocracies. The rise, and rise, of commerce overthrew the landed aristocracies. It was this crisis in elite power that was a key element in the 'Age of Revolution'. In America, Tocqueville wrote, 'the aristocratic element, always feeble since its birth is, if not destroyed, at least weakened further.'[1]

Tocqueville's vision has been hugely influential in the writing of Western history. Generations of historians have debated his ideas since, emending but never really surpassing his analysis of democracy and aristocracy. Some examples may be useful. In his analysis of the First World War, Arno Mayer suggested that, in fact, the aristocratic classes had managed to retain much of their power and influence in Europe in the nineteenth century in the face of the bourgeois revolutions of the late eighteenth century, and that the First World War was in part the conclusion of this struggle. Another influential American historian, R. R. Palmer, took Tocqueville's view further in suggesting that both aristocratic and democratic forces were gaining in strength throughout the period after 1760, and that the Age of Revolution was the logical consequence of this.[2]

These discussions of aristocratic and democratic forces in this vital period of world history have never included Africa. Yet this chapter shows that such convulsions were also an important part of the political revolutions in West Africa in the late eighteenth and early nineteenth centuries. Moreover, the parallels do not end there. As in Europe and America, these revolutions against the aristocracy were led by the merchant class (or bourgeoisie as called in Europe), the Islamic traders who dominated commerce in many parts of the region. As in Europe and America, the revolution was against aristocracies that in many cases were relatively new. And, indeed, the year regarded by some as the high-water mark of the Age of Revolution, 1798, also coincides with the last years before the onset of these revolutions in what is now northern Nigeria.[3]

This is all vital evidence for incorporating West Africa into the Age of Revolution. Why, for instance, did the revolution against the Chinese and Russian aristocracies not take place until the first decades of the twentieth century, whereas in Europe, Africa and the Americas it happened more than a century earlier? There are many answers to this question, but part of the answer certainly lies in the intertwined histories of those continents. It is not only that West African ideas and military movements influenced unrest in the Americas; the very structure of these movements against aristocratic elites, driven by the merchant class, was held in common. To put it bluntly, African revolutionary movements were not dependent on those in the Americas and Europe; each revolt depended on the other, and they emerged together.[4]

To be sure, the discussion of the merchant role in the Islamic revolutions in West Africa in the eighteenth and early nineteenth centuries is complex. As with most questions in which historians can divide, there is plenty of debate. The place of Islam is emphasized by some scholars and roundly critiqued by others. Yet commerce certainly was a vital part of Islamic religious identity in West Africa in the eighteenth century. Describing the Senegambian Kingdom of Gajaaga in 1744, Pierre David noted that it was 'the marabouts who are charged with trade. They make journeys every year, either to buy captives themselves, or to bring with them Bambara merchants.' Or, as Pierre Labarthe put it in 1802 of Manding merchants: 'They form caravans, and traverse all of the interior of Africa; they carry merchandise there which they have bought from the Europeans, and return with captives; as well as with gold and ivory; they are . . . all marabouts or scholars of the law.' These same scholars would drive many of the revolutionary changes in West Africa in these decades – just as the merchant class drove the revolutions in Europe and America.[5]

As we saw in the previous chapter, by this time the transnational orientation of West African aristocratic elites had crystallized differences between them and many of their subjects. These transnational relations and influences had become intertwined in West Africa, coming both from the Americas and from North Africa. It was, for instance, West African elite demand that saw planters in northeastern Brazil switch to tobacco planting in the second half of the seventeenth century, so that ship captains from Salvador could bring this tobacco to trade for captives sold from Ouidah; and, in 1794, the Dadá of Dahomey would give detailed demands for good-quality tobacco in large rolls when writing to Brazil, 'because they are very small now where in the past many of them came in larger volumes.' On the trans-Saharan side, products from North Africa were found widely in West Africa by 1800, traded across the desert in return for captives: in Katsina, new *unguwoyi** had risen for markets selling textiles from across the desert, where silversmiths, tanners, tailors and leather workers had settled.[6]

The experiences of these revolts against untrammelled elite power were not uniform, and it's important to recognize the differences. Those kingdoms such as Asante, Dahomey and Gajaaga that had either retained gold (in Asante's case) or acquired it (in Dahomey's) during the eighteenth century appear to have been in a stronger position to retain power. In other states, African leaders refused to participate in trade. States where large elites had not emerged were less affected, especially in the forest regions.

Nevertheless, popular movements against elites form a distinctive and widespread pattern by the late eighteenth century. This is why it helps to look at this period of West African history comparatively. As we saw in the Prologue to this second part of the book, this pattern can even be traced from the civil wars in Kongo in the late seventeenth century. As we shall see in this chapter, the pattern continues from the rise of Segu in the eighteenth century, to revolutions in

* Quarters.

Senegambia, to the fall of Oyo and the Hausa kingdoms in the nineteenth century.

One oral tradition from what is now Mali captures very well the anger and injustice that this experience of history provoked: 'three people have power over three, three and three do not get on.' Not only was there no equality, but it was this that provoked resentment, and the collapse of so many aristocracies by the early 1800s.[7]

EXACERBATING INEQUALITIES: SILVER, GOLD AND BOOZE

Grasping the power of popular resentments by 1800 requires in the first place an understanding of how inequalities had continued to expand in West Africa throughout the previous century. In economic terms, these were driven by the rise of new currencies and by the continuing gulf that was developing between the production of economic value in West Africa and the rest of the world. The uprisings that grew by the century's close emerged in close parallel to these developments; driven both by these inequalities and, as we saw in the last chapter, by a growing transnational awareness of movements of revolt led by Africans in the diaspora.

In terms of currency exchange, one of the leading global patterns in the eighteenth century was in the relationship between silver and gold. Gold's global power was gathering strength. As we have seen in this book, during the sixteenth and seventeenth centuries, economic imbalances characterized the trade in currencies between West Africa and the world. In the eighteenth century, there appeared to be something of a rebalancing, however. Silver became an important currency in some places, especially in Senegambia, where it was traded for gold in Bambuk by the 1720s, and had become a standard unit of currency on the Upper Senegal River by 1785. Mexican silver dollars were in demand in Senegambia, as they were still in China and India.[8]

Yet this is not on a closer view evidence of the levelling off of the imbalances of economic exchanges between Africa and the world. For, on a global level, the emphasis in the eighteenth century was on a gradual depreciation of silver's relative value. Silver's value had stalled in the late seventeenth century, as the profits to be made through arbitrage of silver trading in China were wiped out by the relative decrease there in silver's value. The move towards a gold standard began as early as 1717, when the British Royal Mint under Isaac Newton established a new ratio between silver and gold. The eighteenth century then saw a tripling of American silver production, with a special focus on Mexico. The world market was flooded with silver, which led to its depreciation relative to gold. A good example was in Bengal in the 1750s, where an oversupply of silver led to its devaluation.[9]

Thus, even though there were imports of silver into Africa in the eighteenth century, they were still not of high relative global value. It was largely those states that could retain or import gold that were strengthened, and even here, as we have seen, this was in a context in which it was captives themselves who could now produce the highest 'capital value'. For example, Asante retained its gold in the eighteenth century (before losing it in the nineteenth), and so was well fiscalized as a state. It developed a powerful army and a very effective administration that could resist the forces of revolt, trading captives with the Atlantic system and kola nuts with the Islamic Hausa states of northern Nigeria; when there was a threat of Islam superseding Asante religions, as with Osei Kwame, the asantehene *c.* 1797, the ruler was deposed. However, where – as in Senegambia – American silver was traded for African gold, the process of capital value extraction continued. Moreover, as in Europe, the silver was often melted down for use in jewellery; and silver jewellery can still often be readily bought in the markets of Gambia, Mali and Guinea-Bissau, perhaps from metal that has been repeatedly reshaped over generations.[10]

The relationship of silver to gold thus illuminates the way in which the process of value extraction continued in many areas. It was only a very few kingdoms, such as Asante and Dahomey, that were able either to retain or to import gold. Here, political power grew, and this is why these states were able to strengthen themselves in the eighteenth century, and become widely known beyond Africa. But, in general, the access to and ability to produce surplus value declined, through the loss of capital (gold) and value-producing labour, as well as the export of agricultural surplus into this economic system.

Inequalities between Africa and the rest of the Western hemisphere thus continued to grow.

In these circumstances, it is illuminating to consider the way in which money and value were being constructed by the end of the eighteenth century. A good illustration comes from the account books kept by the British trading post at Accra. In 1791, the year in which the Haitian Revolution began, far and away the most expensive and valued item kept in the store of the British at Accra was computed in 'gallons of liquor'. By November 1791, £764 had been spent on this for the expenses of the fort, while only £99.8*s.* had been spent on cowries. In 1792, accounts were kept using gallons of liquor as a unit of value. In January, 3,001 gallons of the stuff were received (including 2,152 from 'an American'), and the staff at Accra logged expenses of 183 gallons spent on captives, 159 and a half on gold, 96 on ivory, and 258 on purchasing cowries. In February, the pattern was similar, with 377 gallons accounted as spent on captives, 52 and a half on gold, 94 on ivory, 154 on cowries, 6 on stock, and 102 and a half on 'house expenses'.[11]

The rise of liquor as the most valuable trading good in Accra by the 1790s speaks volumes as to the transformations of these centuries. The Gold Coast, as we have seen, had been an area in which European traders were desperate to find a toehold in the sixteenth and seventeenth centuries, and where they resided at that time entirely at the mercy of the Gold Coast kingdoms in their quest for the gold trade. The transition to the trade in enslaved persons in the late seventeenth century had emerged from the growing power of the Atlantic trade routes following the collapse of Songhay. As we have seen, European intervention in wars at this time on the Gold Coast was normal, with the Danes, Dutch and English all arming one side or the other and fomenting conflict to produce captives, thus kick-starting the trade in them from this region.* As late as the 1780s, European officers commanded armies of Gold Coast troops in various wars, with the Danes fighting alongside Ofari Thosu, son of the King of Accra, in 1788. And, at Accra, liquor became the unit of account – not

* For discussion of this involvement in the wars of the Gold Coast, see above, Chapter 3.

copper, cowries or cloth, as in the sixteenth and seventeenth centuries, the currencies that might have helped to grow the market and finance the industrial base of the region.[12]

Thus, the dependence on alcohol in Accra also symbolizes the growing gulf between the coast – where alcohol was consumed – and the interior societies, where it was increasingly avoided. By now, the alcohol trade did not just indicate the economic inequalities in the region. Alcohol was valued by rulers in places from Accra to the Senegal River, where the trading partners of Europeans were frequently offered it by the gallon. As the inequalities of the trade became ever more manifest, to many peoples in West Africa the consumption of alcohol symbolized the corruption of their rulers.

Oral histories of warrior aristocrats who were offered children as pawns and then sold them for alcohol represents just how deep these relationships were, and how much ordinary people came to resent them. We shall see by the end of this chapter how this contributed to the growing popularity of a religion like Islam, which spurned alcohol. As the eighteenth century gathered pace, a series of movements began to show how these resentments could be harnessed and overthrow the established order.

EIGHTEENTH-CENTURY SLAVE REVOLUTIONS: THE TÒNJÒNW OF SEGU

The Jesuit missionary Manoel Álvares gave a striking portrait of the role of the griots, or praisesingers, who accompanied the Jolof rulers of Senegambia. Álvares saw the griots as dextrous musicians. They could play their stringed instruments while riding a horse, but they were not popular. No one would receive them in their homes, neither the king nor the ordinary people, though they were happy to give them money to sing the histories of the power-brokers of the kingdom. Even into recent times, griots were not buried like other people in Senegambian societies but taken to be interred in the hollows of cavernous baobab trees. Thus, the life of the traditional historian: lackeys of established power, liked and trusted by few.[13]

Nevertheless, rulers depended on their griots. In Gajaaga, the *sakko* were the official holders of the genealogies of the *dambe*, or dynastic ruling class of the kingdom. Learning the genealogies was a public duty for members of the *sakko* caste, and boys of this caste would gather each night after dinner in front of a fire, which was lit in the compound of the member of the *dambe* who was the protector of the griots; here they would recite the genealogies in public, as they learnt them.[14]

While these griots were praisesingers, however, they also had a far more critical role than might be imagined. The griots of the seventeenth century were not afraid to confront power, as the Jesuit observer Manoel Álvares disparagingly described it:

> According to popular tradition, these [griots] are the oldest inhabitants of these Provinces . . . and the whites have no better bailiffs than them of the debts owed to them by the Kings. This is so much the case that where the King himself is the debtor these frauds are the ways of getting paid by them. They speak to one, recounting what has happened, and with this comes the real paid work, which consists in the Singer coming to the House where the debtor King lives, where they speak so much and make so many mentions of the debt, speaking strongly to him: saying that it is does not meet your honour not to pay what you owe. So pressurised is the poor King, that sometimes these buffoons return themselves with the debts to the hands of the creditors.[15]

Interestingly, this reliance of European traders on griots to argue their case with the nobility of Senegambia was to be long-standing. In the 1760s, a regular item of expense at the British Fort Lewis, at the mouth of the Senegal River, was for payments of brandy to the town griots: three gallons of the stuff in April 1764, with more wine and brandy following in May 1765. But why were griots so influential, when they were also despised? Part of the answer lies in their enormous power of speech, the versatility of their language and the power of their voice: as anyone who has heard the high pitch of a griot harangue can attest, this is a hard combination to resist.

However, the power of the griots also lay in the fact that their histories explained and legitimated each successive dynasty. Like the chronicles of Songhay and Mali history written by Al-Sa'dī in the seventeenth century, griots were mediators between the ruling class and the people. The histories they recounted explained the legitimacy of each dynasty's rule. Just like modern historians, the ruling class could not, therefore, dispense with them, and they were able at times to shape policy – especially, it seems, if a keg of brandy was in the offing. But, as no monarch likes to be dependent, this also explains why griots were also shunned and publicly disdained by the ruling class.[16]

Where the ruling class were newcomers, their dependence on griots was all the stronger. A very good example of this is in Segu. Here, and in the Kingdom of Bamako,* there emerged the famous musical style practised today by kora players, in which singing praise (and not criticism) to the patron was paramount. Whereas the Jolof kingdoms and the Bacili Dynasty of Gajaaga were very old, the rulers of Segu and Bamako were both newly powerful. These kingdoms had been founded recently by rebellious slaves, and they needed griots to sing praises and invent the legitimacy of their power for all who would listen. For the reality was that the rulers of Segu were upstarts who had overthrown their masters.[17]

Segu was a kingdom that, in its heyday, in the late eighteenth century, was one of the biggest in West Africa. Its kings came from two dynasties, the Kulubalis (*c.* 1712–56) and the Jara-Ngolosis (1766–1861). After founding the dynasty in the early eighteenth century, the Kulubalis failed to cope with the severe droughts of the 1740s and 1750s, which restricted the power of the military. However, once the Jara-Ngolosis took over in the 1760s, the state grew, and with it the administration. Segu would, in time, stretch all the way from the north of what is now the Côte d'Ivoire to Timbuktu, and from Wahiguya in Burkina Faso to the modern borders of Senegal and Mali. There were as many as sixty provinces, and by the end of the eighteenth century provincial representatives lived at the capital.[18]

In 1796, when Mungo Park visited the capital of Segu on the banks of the Niger, the kingdom had clearly risen to be a major power, as his description makes clear:

* An offshoot of Segu from the late eighteenth century – now the capital of Mali. Cf. discussion of Segu in Chapter 7.

> Seg[u] . . . at which I had now arrived, consists, properly speaking, of four distinct towns; two on the northern bank of the Niger, called Seg[u] Korro and Seg[u] Boo; and two on the southern bank, called Seg[u] Soo Korro and Seg[u] See Korro. They are all surrounded with high mud walls; the houses are built of clay, of a square form, with flat roofs; some of them have two storeys, and many of them are white-washed. Besides these buildings Moorish mosques are seen in every quarter . . . I have reason to believe that Seg[u] contains altogether about thirty thousand inhabitants.[19]

The city had grown very fast from its rise in the first half of the eighteenth century. There were several ferries across the Niger, in one of which Park saw four horses being carried. The fare was ten cowries, which went to the royal treasury. The importance of money to the expansion of the state and the city is clear, and oral sources show that the cowrie reserves of Segu had grown rapidly under Ngolo Jara, the predecessor of Da Monzon (*c.* 1797–1817), and Da Monzon himself gave Park a gift of 5,000 cowries to help him on his way. As Park himself put it: 'The view of this extensive city; the numerous canoes upon the river; the crowded population, and the cultivated state of the surrounding country, formed altogether a prospect of civilisation and magnificence.' It is somewhat ironic that at the height of the age of Abolition, when the public debate revolved around the relationship of the slave trade to the 'barbarism' and discord of African societies, Park's somewhat different account of Segu was almost entirely ignored, even while the author himself was fêted.[20]

The emergence of Segu arose through what is becoming a familiar pattern. It should be remembered that this state lay within what had once been the Songhay Empire, standing roughly 400 miles upstream of Timbuktu. As we saw earlier, Songhay's power was linked to its expanding military organization. The growth of aristocratic warriors whose power depended on violence produced a substantial class of commoners, where resentment seethed. The power of this force in Songhay still bursts from proverbs in the Songhay language. So:

He who has no men	*zama boro kan sinda boro*
Cannot stop fighting.	*Si goro ya yanje.*

And:

Enmity is born with the neighbour	*Basankonne gama jiri ma-taaku*
Enmity is born with the bedroom companion	*Basankonne gama jiri makunkalemmu*
Enmity is born with the confidante.	*Basankonne gama jiri a safe kooru.*[21]

Life was hard, and many were destined for short and difficult passages through this world. As one ballad traditionally sung to a young married man in Songhay put it, one does not wish a long life to all children: some must be left to their fate, to the mercy of the fine grains of millet that soon will cover them over, along with the passing of time.[22]

But as for war, it was everywhere:

When a town has thirty princes from the royal line	*Kog-ize si to waranza*
No war can ever come to an end.	*Wangu ma i kwaara mwa.*[23]

After the fall of Songhay in 1591, the territory of the former Sahelian empires had been overtaken by a series of smaller states, the Arma Pashlik. In these statelets the intersection of aristocratic military strength and predatoriness inherited from Songhay endured, and it was against this that the Kulubalis rebelled when they formed Segu at the start of the eighteenth century. This overthrow of what had become an aristocratic warrior class prefigured the revolutions that transformed other parts of West Africa from the late eighteenth century onwards.

Segu's power grew initially out of the intersection of hunting and statecraft. As we saw in Chapter 7, Biton Kulubali's strength was always linked to his prowess as a hunter, in keeping with the strength of hunting associations among Manding peoples. 'Biton Kulubali and his people were six in number, / They ruled for forty years. / Biton Kulubali the man-killing hunter and his people . . . / He was a master hunter because he loved to hunt. / His work was to hunt.' Hunters accumulated power not only because of the mystical powers associated with vanquishing the 'empty lands' filled with spirits, but also because of the speed that went with success. To be a hunter relied on a swift pounce and kill, something that went also with the ability to transform a military manoeuvre from failure into success.[24]

Hunting's importance to power in Segu also reveals the growing tension with the rise of Islam. Islam posed a threat, for here was a religion that paid no attention to caste divisions, to nobility and heredity, but embraced all, regardless of descent or kinship; or, as one French observer put it in 1791, 'All the Moors [*sic*] are equal by birth.' The oral literatures see Biton Kulubali as a vanquisher of Islamic power; and when one Faama (king) of Segu, Ali, tried to impose Islam as the state religion in *c.* 1757, he was deposed. This conflict in Segu with Islam is preserved in the oral sources. One tradition tells how Biton's power first emerged when he was hunting an antelope in the bush; when he killed the antelope, it transformed into a djinn, over which in West Africa the marabouts are said to hold secret powers. By then vanquishing the djinn/antelope, Biton Kulubali showed there was no need for Islam to overthrow rulers. Local West African institutions such as hunters' associations could do this just as well.[25]

The rise of Segu, when it came, was mobilized by these Manding structures of hunting and mystical power. In the early eighteenth century, a dispute formed between Kulubali and Bambara elders after he had been elected *tòntigi*, head of a bachelors' association. Very quickly, Kulubali's *tòn* challenged traditional Bambara power structures, as some slaves joined in order to escape excessive labour demands and the *tòn* became a fighting unit. Some of these slaves became military leaders, *tònjònw*, leading fighting regiments, and thus the nucleus of the new state offered an avenue of escape to slaves in the region of Segu. Captives from Segu's wars could be incorporated into the warrior class and rise to be *tònjònw* commanders if they showed sufficient military derring-do.[26]

By around 1800, oral accounts give a striking sense of the power that these *tònjònw* had in Segu's society. One describes how the Court of the faama, Da Monzon, had a palace of seven halls, in each of which stood an armed *tònjònw* armed with a hatchet. 'The hatchets were for breaking people's heads. / The *gendarmes* and police have replaced the hatchetmen today. / Those hatchetmen were slave chiefs, each with a special name.' Segu thus offered a genuine route for advancement for those who came from the lowest rungs of society, for every slave in Segu had the chance to fight and thereby grow in status.[27]

Several of the most important chiefs of Segu's history came from slave origins, including Ngolo Jara himself, who had originally been handed over as *disongo* (annual tribute) to the Kulubalis by his village. As one account has it, his villagers claimed that they could not pay the full amount of the annual *disongo*, and so they added in Ngolo as a pawn. From being a pawn, Ngolo became a *tònjònw*, and from there grew to power. Though Ngolo was an exceptional leader, the origins of the *tònjònw* as a whole in slavery and warfare are obvious from some accounts. One describes a party attacking the village of Fabugu: 'They shaved the men's heads, / leaving only a big tuft of hair. / The women were shaved in the ordinary way, / but the men were left with a big tuft. / So they were recognized as slaves among the other people. / This was the origin of *tònjònw*, council slaves . . . / These *tònjònw* were in the house of every warrior.'[28]

But, in spite of the opportunities that Segu offered underclasses, there was also great sadness in the way that young men were stripped from their communities to become part of the *tònjònw*. Mungo Park described a moving encounter in 1796, as he was on his way to Segu's capital: 'In the course of the day, several women, hearing that I was going to Seg[u], came and begged me to inquire of Mansong [Da Monzon], the [faama], what was become of their children. One woman in particular told me that her son's name was Mamad[ou] . . . and had been taken about three years ago, by Mansong's army: since which she had never heard of him. She said she often dreamed of him.'[29]

The rise of Segu was like a match lighting a powder keg. Bachelors such as Kulubali were ready to fight, frustrated at their elders' control over marriage. The inability of many young men to accrue wealth through the new trading patterns and so to find a wife surely lay at the heart of these disputes. Beyond this, the gathering anger and resentment of the *jòn* slaves could now be effectively mobilized through Segu as a military state. Ngolo Jara himself epitomized this anger, for, after he had risen to be faama, he returned to the village that had handed him over as *disongo* and destroyed it. Kulubali thus established a precedent where slave chiefs could rise to actual power, and, when the dynasty fell in the 1750s, several *tònjònw* held power until the Ngolosi Dynasty emerged in the 1760s.[30]

While Segu's strength was driven forward by former *jòn* who sought revenge against the aristocracy, this did not mean that slavery itself vanished from Segu. On the contrary, the institution was a lynchpin of Segu's society. The *tònjònw* did no agricultural labour, but instead produced slaves. The communities that they invaded and that became tributary provided food in the form of *disongo*, while Segu's power grew. Captives in Segu's wars were divided into two categories: the *jònfin* could be marketed by the faama as enslaved persons, whereas the *jònba* were put to use for the state, either as members of the elite guard, as *tònjònw*, or as the *faraba-jòn* who worked on the state farms.[31]

Segu's growth in the first half of the eighteenth century does not just emerge in the oral narratives. The rise of the volume of Bambara captives found for sale on the Senegambian coast in the eighteenth century was directly related to it. The French traveller Adanson wrote of the 'Banbarena Empire', in 1757, that 'it is known to be very extensive . . . [although] not enough is known to determine its borders. It is from this country that the Mandingas bring to Ga[jaaga] and to Gambia the Bambara slaves.' By 1763, English traders at Fort Lewis on the mouth of the Senegal River were buying Bambara captives for service in the fort. They were routinely paying for the service of Bambara interpreters, who would have been needed to act as linguists for the Bambara captives. Nor was this traffic directed only towards the Atlantic coast, since one 1790 account for the Royal African Association of the trade from Timbuktu to Morocco said that of the 3,000 to 4,000 captives taken every year on this route, most seemed to be Bambara.[32]

There were strong ironies in the rise of Segu. For in many ways this new state reproduced the categories of the old system against which its founders had rebelled. The power of the new state, praised to the skies by the griots with their elaborate homilies and accompanying kora melodies, depended on a huge underclass of *jòn*, castes of craftsmen such as blacksmiths and carpenters (the *nyamakalaw*), and the aristocratic warrior freemen, or *hòrònw*, who fought the wars that allowed the state to keep expanding. The Kulubalis had initiated the revolt using the structures of lineage and hunting, the familiar building blocks of Manding states; and thus, just as postcolonial nation states found it hard to overthrow the structures of the colonial state that they had inherited, so in the end the state that emerged in Segu tended to reproduce that which the people had first risen up against.

Yet, though rising in part against Islamic structures and systems, Segu depended heavily on Islamic traders, the *maraka*, who linked them to global markets through the trades to the Sahara and the Atlantic. The *maraka* lived in separate towns. Sālih Bilāli, a Fula who was captured by Segu slave traders around 1785, and ended his days as an enslaved person on a plantation in Georgia, gave the following description of them in an interview in the 1820s:

> Arab traders, who are nearly white, Mahometans in religion, and who speak the languages both of the Koran and the country, trade between Timbuktu, Kuna, Jenne and Segu. They travel in large boats, covered with awnings, and propelled by poles. They are armed, wear turbans, and travel in large parties, having frequently thirty or forty boats together. They bring for sale, salt in large thick slabs, blankets, guns, pistols, cotton cloth, beads, shell money [cowries], and sometimes horses.[33]

This description makes sense of some later oral accounts that describe Segu's largest towns of Markadougoba and Bussen as big, and of the *maraka* themselves as influential. Sālih Bilāli's account makes it clear that they brought with them the necessaries for the maintenance of the power of the faama and the *tònjònw*: the firearms, money and salt without which the growth of Segu could not go on. It was the *maraka* who provided the wherewithal for the fiscal-military state in Segu to expand, and for this to become one of the most important West African states in the eighteenth century. So essential had they become that, in the later eighteenth century, Ngolo Jara placed the *maraka* towns under direct state protection. At the same time, it was this merchant class that would later sow the seeds of the wider revolutions that would overtake West Africa in the nineteenth century.[34]

Segu's rise shows clearly the irreconcilable tensions that gathering inequalities were creating in many parts of West Africa. Where long-distance trade had the deepest roots – as in Kongo, dating from *c.* 1500, and here in Segu with the previous connection to Songhay – the revolutionary movements appeared earliest. The long-distance trade favoured the formation of narrowly composed elites and gathering inequality between them and the rest of the population. As the patterns of long-distance trade grew, so, too, would the pattern of aristocratic formation and popular resistance.

It is striking that a key element of a successful resistance movement was the ability to unite people from different backgrounds under one ideological framework. In West-Central Africa, this already had begun in the early seventeenth century prior to the Kongo revolutions, when the Imbangala armies of Angola rejected previous patterns of kinship and incorporated all captives into their army.* In Calabar and Sierra Leone, new secret societies and shrines helped to serve the same function of incorporation, offering a point of inclusion for newcomers and those who had been outsiders. In Segu, meanwhile, old kinship structures were rejected, since it was the newly incorporated *tònjònw* who could rise to power, so long as they could prove their valour in warfare and in capturing others. In all these cases, corrupt elites could be overthrown by expanding a state structure and allowing others into it who did not have to demonstrate their heredity or nobility.

There are striking parallels elsewhere in West Africa as well as beyond. Numerous kingdoms at this time arose with rulers from what had previously been the 'slave class'. There was an attempted revolt of the many slaves in Fuuta Jaalo in 1785, the remnants of which found their way to the mountains inland from Freetown in the 1790s. Meanwhile, writing in the early nineteenth century, the Sultan of Sokoto, Mohammed Bello, described how the Hausa Kingdom of Kebbi had arisen with a slave named Kanta, who had rebelled against the king whom he had served, but then 'rose up and conquered the towns and ruled countries far and near'. Often, these new rulers then worked with the griots to construct a 'magnificent' past. In Dahomey, for example, the griots became very important to

* See above, Chapter 5.

the dadá's grip on power. The influence of the griot who could invent a noble past grew. It was no wonder that in West Africa these wordsmiths produced such elaborate epic texts, or sang with such a piercing tone; the griots needed all the vocal and linguistic power at their disposal to forestall any interruptions to their elaboration of a fiction of hereditary power for those who may well have come from the 'slave class'.[35]

INSTITUTIONALIZING RESISTANCE: THE CASE OF OYO

By the eighteenth century, many parts of West and West-Central Africa saw prolonged struggles and civil wars at the death of the ruler. This was the case between the different ruling lineages in Kongo, during the civil wars in Segu in the mid eighteenth century, and also perhaps especially in the Yorùbá Kingdom of Oyo. The power of the rulers was increasingly absolute, and so was the fear under which their relatives lived. Newly installed kings often persecuted their brothers as potential rivals, as Tegbesu had in Dahomey, and then depended on the persuasiveness of their praisesingers to be sure of their rule.* The power of the ruler's wives in many kingdoms was also in part a reflection of the ruler's mistrust of his male relatives. In this environment, the struggle over succession became a major feature of West African history in the eighteenth century.

There were various ways of overcoming corrupt warrior aristocracies, who became unpopular as they distanced themselves from the population through extravagant foreign imports and changes to religious shrines. It was possible to follow Segu's lead, and for slaves to overthrow rulers. Another alternative was to decapitate the royal power by changing religion, as we shall see. But a third option was the one followed in Oyo. Here, the kingdom remained relatively stable into the early nineteenth century, but with one major anomaly: no alafin was allowed to reach the end of his reign, and it was his wives who strangled him when the time had been signalled that his

* On Tegbesu, see above, Chapter 7.

power was at an end. Thus, becoming Alafin of Oyo was also, in its way, a death sentence, for not a single alafin lived out his natural lifespan in the eighteenth century. Indeed, overthrowing the alafin had become almost institutionalized in the kingdom by 1800.

The first historian of the Yorùbá, Samuel Johnson, put it like this: 'The feeling had gained ground by this time that Kings should not be allowed to die a natural death. Unchecked despotism, unrestrained licence, insatiable greed, and wanton voluptuousness should not be allowed to flourish through the full term of a natural lifetime.'[36] The people of Oyo had a special way of indicating when the time had come for an alafin to go. Archibald Dalzel, writing in 1793, described it in detail:

> When the people have conceived an opinion of [the alafin's] ill government, which is sometimes insidiously infused into them, by the artifice of his discontented ministers, they send a deputation to him, with a present of parrots eggs, as a mark of its authenticity, to represent to him that the burden of government must have so far fatigued him, that they consider it full time for him to repose from his cares, and indulge himself with a little sleep. He thanks his subjects for their attention to his ease; retires to his apartment, as if to sleep; and there gives directions to his women to strangle him.[37]

Although Oyo was a powerful centre, overlord to Dahomey, and importing increasing numbers of the cowries that enabled it to fiscalize its state, the struggle over power was also at the heart of the strife there in the eighteenth century. As we have seen, the balance of powers was enshrined into Oyo's structure. The alafin had a council, the Oyo-Mesi, who both selected a successor and held the alafin to account; the alafin appointed representatives, the *ajele*, in provincial towns, who were also answerable to the council. And yet, in spite of the development of this increasingly complex administrative machinery, the tendency of the eighteenth century was for growing centralization of power. In 1754, the leader of the Oyo-Mesi, Basorun Gaha, seized power and ruled as alafin; and when, in 1774, according to Dalzel, ministers sent the parrots' eggs to him to seek his removal, he 'peremptorily refused [them] . . . telling his ministers that he had as yet no inclination to take a nap'. This precipitated a crisis in Oyo, until Gaha was in turn overthrown by Alafin Abiodun in 1774.[38]

The conflict over rulership and the extent of the alafin's power would eventually weaken Oyo. By 1790, Oyo was paying tribute to Nupe, to the north, a reversal of almost two centuries of pre-eminence over its northern neighbour. The balance of power was shifting in what is now Nigeria, from south towards the north, and with it went the emergence of powerful strands of popular action to challenge the aristocratic elites such as those that had ruled Oyo for centuries.[39]

Of what did this centralization of power consist? There was the growth of the fiscal-military states, the administration, the rafts of taxes that kept the whole edifice standing. But beyond this, too, was the religious centralization, which we have already seen with the leopard cult of Agassu in Dahomey in the eighteenth century, with the response of the manikongos to Christianity, and with the creation of Poro and Sandé secret societies in a large area of West Africa. The changed religious practice became associated in some places with autocratic forms of government, and so people would be more willing to cast off these cults when new and powerful forms of religious practice spread in the nineteenth century, in the shape of Christianity and Islam. The spread of monotheism in Africa was a reflection of a political as well as a religious crisis – a crisis of the authority held by the guardians of the old cults in the face of their co-option and manipulation by the political elites.

Oyo saw the intersection of different forces, of different resentments: religious, class-based, and against the authoritarian powers of the state that had emerged. For some time, this was channelled through the figure of the alafin, and the eventual determination that it was time for his wives to strangle him. This was sufficient for much of the eighteenth century. However, when Oyo finally collapsed in the first decades of the nineteenth century, the kingdom's unravelling was prompted by a new level of rebellion.

The war was prompted by a rebellion by a military commander called Afonja. As in Segu, Afonja drew on those who had plenty to fight about. Again, Samuel Johnson provides the best description. Rank-and-file troops – the *jamâ* – were often, in fact, escaped slaves who used the mobilization of Afonja to rebel against their former owners and seize their property. Revenge against the rampant inequalities was at the heart of the movement, as Johnson explains:

> The *Jamâs* were increasing in number [in Afonja's time] and in rapacity, to the utter distress and ruin of the country. When there was no war in hand they usually scattered themselves all over the land plundering the people and committing outrages. They would enter any house, make it their headquarters, from which they would pillage the neighbourhood and surrounding districts. They fed upon the cattle of the house and led the rest away at their leisure and pleasure . . . slaves who had deserted their masters often returned to the same town, and even to the very house as a Jamâ, making their former master's house their headquarters for their rapine: masters who were kind to them formerly were now repaid by protection against the rapacity of their comrades; unkind ones were now treated with heartless revenge.[40]

Johnson's account makes clear that a large motive force in the success of the revolution that began to overthrow Oyo *c.* 1823 was the desire to remove the aristocracy. As we begin to see, this was a common feature in many parts of West and West-Central Africa. The rise of long-distance trade fomented a centralizing state power in many parts of West and West-Central Africa, which was, in turn, overthrown by a revolution driven by popular resentment, by the lack of attachment that many in the underclass felt towards the new elite and the public cults that they had enshrined.

How does this fit within the broader pattern traced in this book of currencies and global inequalities? It is striking that this trend is especially apparent in areas where the long-distance trade was important, and powerful states of the fiscal-military type had grown up. It was exactly in areas with strong states, slave castes, long-distance trade and a growing merchant class that the move to overthrow established authority grew most powerful – in places like Oyo. Yet the same pattern of overthrowing rulers does not seem to have occurred in smaller-scale societies. Thus, unequal dynamics of trade, and political and religious centralization, had shaped the unrest that now began to topple the aristocracies of West Africa in a domino-style effect.

MOBILIZING AGAINST INEQUALITIES: TRADING IRON FOR CLOTH IN EIGHTEENTH-CENTURY SENEGAMBIA

By the late eighteenth century, as we have seen, Segu had established its power through an aggressive expansionist policy, bankrolled by a state with growing stocks of money, as griot narratives attest. Some accounts describe gold stores, but, though there were gold *mithqāls* circulating with the trans-Saharan trade, cowries clearly predominated.* The power of the *tònjònw* showed how slaves could rise up against their masters and seize power, as happened in Oyo some decades later. Here were lessons as to how mobilizations were beginning to take place in different ways across West Africa.

Elsewhere, however, it was often gold rather than cowries that represented power. By the mid nineteenth century, the goldfields of Asante were increasingly exporting their gold rather than keeping it, since European traders on the coast would no longer buy captives. It was only the Islamic trading networks that could give access to gold to those states without it, through the strong links they had at Asante, and because of their role in transporting goods between the Asante capital at Kumasi and the Sokoto Caliphate. The power of the Islamic merchant class, therefore, grew in a state like Segu, along with the value of gold. This was also to be significant, since, as the power of Islam increased, it slowly came to offer an alternative way of challenging the aristocratic title-holders of West African states.[41]

In Senegambia, the opportunity offered by Islam to challenge established power can be read through the lens of the changes to currency imports that took place in the eighteenth century. For whereas in the sixteenth and seventeenth centuries iron bars were the major currency in Senegambia, with cloth a smaller element, by the eighteenth century, the role of iron bars became equalled by those of Indian cloths (bafts, the so-called *pièces de guinée*).† Iron remained important, and the bars were scrupulously measured so that each one

* On the *mithqāl*, see above, Chapter 7.

† On iron bars in the sixteenth and seventeenth centuries, see Chapter 2.

weighed between 15 and 16 pounds. These bars were used especially for the trade in provisions; however, *pièces de guinée* had nevertheless become the standard currency on much of the upper Senegal River by the middle of the eighteenth century.[42]

Some context is needed. There were by this time four major kingdoms in the Senegal River Valley. The nearest to the Atlantic was Waalo, which stretched along the valley some distance inland and was the most immediate trading partner of the European posts at St Louis on the coast. Waalo's brac (king) often sent ambassadors and members of his households to St Louis, where gifts of brandy, cloth and iron were received. Further inland was the Fula Kingdom of Fuuta Tòòro, a centre of Islamic scholarship and connected to the Fula populations who lived further east, in Segu and as far east as the Hausa states of Kano and Katsina. A smaller Fula-majority state between the Senegal and Gambia rivers was Bundu, while possibly the strongest state of all historically was Gajaaga, whose ruling dynasty, the Bacili Sempera, date back in some accounts to before 1000

Guillaume Delisle's 1707 map of North-West Africa. Nearest to the coast is Waalo ('Oualle'), then Fuuta Tòòro (the 'Royaume des Foules'), followed by Gajaaga ('Galam'); just below here, 'Bonda' is the as yet small Kingdom of Bundu.

CE. However, in the eighteenth century, Bundu grew, and colonized many of the lands that had originally belonged to Gajaaga.[43]

By the 1760s, the sway of *pièces de guinée* in these states had become huge. At the British trading post in Podor, sixty leagues beyond Waalo in Fuuta Tòoro, the annual custom paid to the king in 1764 was due entirely in bafts of cloth; while the annual custom to the King of Gajaaga in 1765 again predominated in cloth, alongside military hardware and a small quantity of Mexican silver dollars. Similarly, Mungo Park described, in 1795, how the custom payable to the king in the capital of Bundu consisted of one Indian baft and six bottles of gunpowder.[44]

Keeping a steady flow of currencies was vital to a successful trade in these kingdoms, as European traders all recognized. The goods kept by the English to pay the garrison at Fort Lewis in 1763 consisted of 1,278 iron bars valued at £297.10*s*.; and 507 bafts of cloth of Indian dye and 433 of English dye, the total value of these being £1,713.2*s*. These were not mere 'trade goods', as the account suggested, but real money; as Major Mason, governor of the British post, put it in July 1758, 'the bringing money here to pay the Men, is to no manner of purpose, as it is not known in the Country. Dutch Dollars is almost of as much value [as] good Blue [Indian] Bafts, and Beads of the best sort is much better.' Though, as in the seventeenth century, cloth and iron were parallel currencies, cloth had become much the more important, and, by early January 1764, the value of trading goods sold for the bafts was at £63.15*s*., whereas for iron bars it was only £10.5*s*.4*d*.[45]

Yet why were these Indian cloths so attractive? Local cloth manufacture was hardly small. One 1729 description emphasized the Fula production of deep-blue indigo-dyed cloth, and went into great detail as to the different types of richly decorated and embellished cloths woven by the Fula of Bundu – with the fame of Fulani weaving dating back to the fifteenth century and before, and influencing strongly decorative patterns and styles found on Asante cloth and beyond. Another account of 1802 extolled the weaving prowess of the Jolof. The argument that cloth production declined for ecological reasons put forward by some may not be a sufficient explanation of the attractiveness of the *guinée* cloth.[46]

But the Indian cloth was in demand for other reasons. In the first place, the deep indigo-blue dye mirrored the styles of the indigo-dyed cloths being made in Kano, where production was beginning to grow rapidly; so local demand in Senegambia accentuated this industry and its growth in India. It was, moreover, a sign of status to wear indigo-dyed cloths, when farmers wore white cloth in the eighteenth century. Yet a major attractive feature of the Indian-made cloths may also have been that their import could be controlled by the local ruling class. Controlling the import of currencies was always attractive to kings, from silver flowing into China and gold into Spain, to cowries being imported into West Africa. This preference of ruling elites can thus also explain the importance of Indian cloths as currency in Senegambia, just as the import of foreign-produced iron bars in preference to local iron also favoured the West African ruling elites.[47]*

These economic changes reflected the growing extraction of value from Senegambia and the relative economic imbalance emerging between the accumulation of value in West Africa and beyond. Though as we have seen some Mexican silver dollars were traded to Senegambia by the seventeenth and eighteenth centuries, the relative global value of silver was falling. Imported cloth from India was far and away the most important currency. The major goldfields were near Bambuk and Buré in Gajaaga, where French trading posts were established, and gold was siphoned off, even though some of it was retained. The disproportionate accumulation of value outside West Africa continued apace.[48]

Beyond the economic changes, though, the rise of the *pièce de guinée* over iron reflected important political transformations, and it is here that the place of cloth helps us to understand the way in which Islam was beginning to challenge existing religious and political frameworks. Ironsmiths and their power to manipulate metal and create tools and weapons had long been endowed with magical powers and related to kingship in Senegambia. The decline of imported iron suggests that the power of these ideas, and of the indigenous African religious and political world that went with them, was also in decline. It was important, too, that decentness of dress, and the style

* For this discussion, see above, Chapter 8.

for long flowing robes for men and women, was something prized by many Islamic societies of the Sahel. The growing economic significance of the imported indigo-dyed cloths from India reflected the power of Islamic ideas and political organization in Senegambia. As these grew, existing frameworks of the warrior aristocracies began to come under threat.[49]

How was this growing power experienced? One important aspect was the decline of Gajaaga, as the Fula Kingdom of Bundu grew in power. While Bundu originally grew on lands lent to the Islamic scholar Malik Sy by the kings of Gajaaga, during the eighteenth century Bundu's power grew significantly, and it occupied much of what had been Gajaaga. The two were frequently at war, and there was a large no-man's land between the two by the eighteenth century, occupied by wild animals and fearful to all who crossed it.[50]

> As soon as the people of the village had gone to sleep, we set out [Mungo Park wrote of his crossing of the border in 1796]. The stillness of the air, the howling of the wild beasts, and the deep solitude of the forest, made the scene solemn and impressive. Not a word was uttered by any of us but in a whisper; all were attentive and everyone anxious to show his sagacity, by pointing out to me the wolves and hyaenas as they glide like shadows from one thicket to another.[51]

Gajaaga's decline and Bundu's rise symbolized that kingdoms that practised original African religions were in decline. Much of this conflict involved large-scale instability. Settlements rose and vanished frequently: in Gajaaga and Bundu, of forty-three sites excavated by one archaeological team, only thirty had very slight cultural artefacts, representing 'short-term occupation campsites'. Among the Serèèr of Siin, on the Atlantic coast north of the Gambia, meanwhile, settlements from 1500 to 1700 were on average larger, more densely populated and occupied for longer time stretches; after 1700, settlements were smaller and dispersed.[52]

So in Senegambia, a pattern of political instability and the accumulating power of Islam rose up during the eighteenth century. The most devout Muslims were the Fula, who themselves often seemed to wander at will, simply 'break[ing] up their Towns, and remov[ing] to another' if they felt themselves badly treated, as Francis Moore described it in the 1730s. Bundu was a Fula state, and the devoted practice and knowledge of Islam attracted outsiders to it, growing its power. According to Moore, most Fulas spoke Arabic, 'being to them as *Latin* is in *Europe*; for it is taught in Schools, and their Law, the *Alcoran*, is in that language. They are more generally learned in the *Arabick*, than the People of *Europe* are in *Latin*, for they can most of them speak it.'[53]

In time, migration became a necessity driven by wars and flight from enslavement as well as a spiritual duty. One Fula cleric, Sālih al-Fullānī, was born in present-day Mauritania, visited the Fuuta Jaalo (modern Guinea-Conakry) and eventually became a revered teacher in the holy Islamic city of Medina in Arabia. The life of another Fula cleric, Karamoko Ba (*c.* 1730–1829), is emblematic of how deeply this sort of movement affected lives in Senegambia in the eighteenth century. Ba left his home in Bundu in around 1770 to study first by the Gambia River with a student of his father, and from there he went to Goundiouro in what is now eastern Mali. He would spend time there, and then twenty years in Djenné, learning the science of magic squares, visiting various *shaykhs* in nearby towns. One of them then moved him to travel to Fairo, in what is now southern Sierra Leone, where he married and went on to Kankan on the Upper Niger River around 1800. In 1805, he moved to Timbo, capital of Fuuta Jaalo,* where he established a new town in around 1812, with many followers moving to join him.[54]

What might these movements of people have been like? They were not simply flights of panic-stricken refugees, but experienced as rich with spiritual meaning. Dreams may often have been an important aspect that moved people to leave; and the ways in which people followed leaders believed to be blessed with great spiritual power is epitomized in one description of the warrior-cleric Omar Tal in the nineteenth century.[55] According to this account, after travelling from Mecca and making peace between Borno and Hausa, Tal moved to the Fuuta Jaalo, where he was pursued by thousands of adepts who left everything to follow him: 'He dwelt at Jugunko, and many Fulah people moved from Fu[u]ta on account of him; and from Libbe and

* For a more detailed discussion, see below, Chapter 11.

from Timbo [the capital of Fuuta Jaalo] and from Kakunde Maji, and from Kollade and from Boji; from Timbi Tini, from Koyin, from Kebu, from Kolle; from these nine principal towns many people moved on account of him and lived with him. At that time some of the F[u]uta T[òò]ro people also lived with him.'[56]

In the end, making meaning from history depends on the audience, as griots and chronicle writers of the West African past were well aware. Thinking about this in the twenty-first century, when economic forces underwrite appreciations of morality, we find that the economic imbalances that grew throughout this period between capital accumulation in a region like Senegambia and in the West seem like the most important aspect of this past. Yet spiritual power mattered much more to most of those in West Africa who lived through this time. Kingdoms rose and fell according not only to local patterns of allegiance and religious power, but also to the impact of the globalizing economic forces at work. With capture for enslavement a real threat, Islam was a religion of great appeal, since no Muslim could legally be enslaved. Moreover, Islam offered a unifying identity, pretending to eschew former differentiations of caste and class. The import of Indian cloths as a currency was a sign of changing times, which would challenge and overhaul the hierarchies that had grown along with the trade in captives.

CONCLUSION: PATTERNS OF DISSENT

In the first part of this book, we saw how in the sixteenth century African kingdoms often fragmented from their previously federated imperial structures. In Greater Senegambia, Greater Jolof broke into five different provinces, as coastal areas gained better access to cavalry and firearms. In Kongo, Loango and even Nsoyo became de facto independent by the first part of the seventeenth century because of their easier access to Atlantic trade. Now, in the second part of this book, we see how what began as the fragmentation of larger states became outright revolt: revolt by slaves in Segu and Oyo, revolt against the aristocracy's religion, revolt against the alafin by deciding when his wives should strangle him.

This pattern of revolt is, on a close look, related very heavily to the patterns of rising inequality. It is no accident that these processes of revolt began first of all in the areas with the longest connection to the long-distance trades. This was the case in Segu, which grew up from within what had been the Songhay Empire, connected to the trans-Saharan trade; in Kongo, with its long-held Atlantic connections; and in Greater Senegambia, where several of the states that were strong in 1500 had disappeared within a little over a century, such as Greater Jolof, Kasamansa and Brasso.

This pattern of revolution and inequality is not only important from an African perspective. It helps us to think more deeply about the connections that had grown up between Africa and the rest of the Western hemisphere by 1800. The traditional Western historical narrative of the revolutions of the late eighteenth century sees a smooth transition from America to France, and the Napoleonic Wars. However, recent work by those focusing on the history of the peoples of West Africa and the African diaspora has shown how these communities were also vital parts of this movement. The Haitian Revolution (1791–1804) was directly connected to the revolutions both of America and of France, with some of the ideas from France and military experience of fighting in America contributing to the initial revolt of 1791.[57]

As we have seen in this chapter, these movements in the diaspora themselves did not grow out of nothing. They followed a growing pattern in Africa of revolt from below against elites whose wealth had grown disproportionately through the rise of the trade in enslaved persons across the Atlantic and the Sahara. In a striking echo of events in Europe and America, in many places these revolts would be led by the merchant class, the Islamic traders, as we shall now see.

In the end, kingdoms like Asante and Dahomey were exceptions, surviving into the nineteenth century, when many of their peers collapsed through successful movements of revolt. Just as Segu had risen with an ideology that bound people together regardless of their lineage or background, so the growth of Islamic scholars and their followers offered a similar avenue for resistance. Transnational forces spreading these ideas from the Islamic world, and news of the slave revolutions across the Atlantic, coalesced in movements of great power.

In Gonja, one of the tributary kingdoms of Asante, a mid-eighteenth-century chronicle gives an idea of how human experience triggered these transformations. In the first place, there were the episodes of climatic instability that fostered social instability, wars and inequalities. The chronicle describes a haunting scene in 1745:

> In that year prices rose excessively in the land of Ghānja to the point that people were about to run away; a measure of millet . . . cost one hundred and fifty cowries. In that year hosts of locusts came, and people were afraid that these would ruin the sown farms . . . In that year there were heavy rains that destroyed many houses. There had not been rains like that for many years, and rains had never destroyed houses like these did.[58]

At the same time, traditions were alive equating warfare and religious idealism. As the traditions in Gonja put it, 'if you want to wage war and you don't find a mallam [religious leader], then it is impossible for you to do so.' The place of religion as a means of struggle and overthrowing the elites was becoming embedded. The uncontainable desire in West Africa to overthrow the corruption of great power would soon come to a head.

11

Let Them Drink Rum! Islam, Revolution and the Aristocracy

While Islam had long remained the most significant external religious force in the Sahel, in the Atlantic zones African religions and their shrines and secret societies predominated still in the last decades of the eighteenth century. As the ruling elites of kingdoms such as Asante, Dahomey and Oyo, who retained religious power, differentiated themselves ever further from the people who suffered the consequences of Atlantic trade, these religions became tarnished for many. The adoption of the new, centralized royal cults made the chasm from 'traditional' religious practice seem bigger still. By 1800, Islam had become a religious and ideological force that could challenge a ruling elite who in many cases had made an unacceptable pact with the outsider cannibals: the European slave traders.

One Manding hunters' song from northern Ivory Coast, captures this process very well:

But all at once I was certain of Allah,	*Cúca wé á kà lò ní Ala yé,*
So I lit the powder in my rifle,	*Àwasa tá blá mésia má,*
And the elephant turned into a devil.	*Àwasa sàma dènna fùrunyan á,*
And the devil killed the elephant,	*Wa fùrunyan mán nyí sàma mà,*
And the devil killed the elephant.	*Fùrunyan mán nyì sàma mà.*[1]

In this song, the animal totem of a secret society (the elephant) is killed by the military power of the growing Islamic presence. That secret-society totem is transformed into something that can be vanquished through Islam; devils can be overcome through faith in Allah and the proper observance of the Holy Qur'ān. At the same time, one of the emblems referring to the pre-Islamic past is killed off through certainty in Allah, just as Islamic *shaykhs* claimed that they could exterminate the spirits of the bush.[2]

Secret societies were, and are, strongly associated with the religions and power of precolonial and non-Islamic rulers. New research conducted by a remarkable team of linguists at Ernest Bai Koroma University in Makeni, Sierra Leone, reveals how the languages of secret societies remained hidden. The use of these private-language codes was a way of excluding outsiders from power. In the Rågbenle Society of the Temne people of northern Sierra Leone, different linguistic registers were used by the ruler and their closed circle of supporters to communicate secret messages. These meanings were hidden even from those who were fluent speakers of the language, and thus a secret discourse of power was constructed. This was also the case among the more widespread Poro secret society, present in various parts of Ivory Coast, Sierra Leone, Liberia and Guinea-Conakry, where an esoteric language was developed to communicate concealed information. Moreover, we know that this was the case with some religious shrines, such as the cult of Dangbé in Dahomey, where the female novices learnt a new language during their three months of initiation. Islam, by contrast, offered in principle equal access to the levers of influence, as knowledge of the Qur'ān was open to outsiders prepared to learn Arabic. Thus, the desire to break the stranglehold of the old aristocracy saw increasing numbers gravitate to the religion.[3]

Through the chapters of this book, multiple reasons have emerged for the widespread desire in West Africa to overthrow these aristocracies. As we shall see in this final chapter, the first seeds of the discontent grew in Senegambia, but it would be in northern Nigeria that a civil conflict erupted that would have major consequences not only for West Africa but for the entire Western hemisphere. The African societies that Europeans colonized in the late nineteenth century had emerged from the social and political revolutions that grew over the previous century, grounded in the experience of economic inequalities. These related to global patterns, and were finally 'cashed out' in the spiral of depreciation that hit the continent at the same time as the waves of revolt.

THE PANORAMA OF INEQUALITY: CURRENCIES AND ENSLAVEMENT IN 1800

By 1800, the monetary framework across West African societies was increasingly shared. Along the coastline, there were three major currency zones by 1805. One ran from the Senegal River to Cape Mesurado (Liberia), where the medium was a 'bar' of currency. From Cape Mesurado to Cape Las Palmas at the border of the Ivory Coast, the measure was in 'rounds'. On the Gold Coast, it was in ackies of gold, which were valued in relation to pounds sterling. Official and unofficial exchange rates had been invented long before the modern era, since the trade value of the ackie was only half that of the notional value of the ackie against the pound.[4]

The trading system thus established was described well by Joseph Corry in a book published in 1807: 'The annual return from this commerce in colonial productions [*sic*], has been from *two* to *three million sterling*, for although large remittances have been made in bills to the African merchants, yet these bills have been provided for in produce by the planters.'[5] In other words, what was going on here was a complex and unequal exchange of produce for capital-added labour and currencies. A good example is in Senegambia, where Jahanké traders produced cloth that entered the currency markets of the region. They converted this into gold at the Bambuk goldfields, and then exported much of this gold through the European factories on the coast. They imported, in turn, silver, which was often melted down to make silver jewellery, and which was in any case, as we have seen, losing value against gold.[6]

Beyond the Atlantic region, Sahelian societies, too, saw analogous processes. By the 1780s, the Maria Theresa silver dollar began to flood into the Sahel to act as a medium of exchange. This was an intermediate currency that could connect the silver mines of Mexico and the specie-using markets in Europe and Asia with the economies of West Africa. Meanwhile, the competitive advantage of trans-Saharan traders was ensured in some major commercial centres, such as Kano, where, by 1790, they paid no taxes, probably in an attempt to lure traders away from the rival centre of Katsina. Where Muslim traders did have to pay taxes to unbelievers, as in the Hausa kingdoms near Kano, this was widely resented.[7]

As had long been the case along the West African coast, the consequences of these dynamics were inflationary in the Sahel. A chronicle of Timbuktu, written by Mawlāy al-Qāsim b. Mawlāy Sulaymān, captures the economic transformations taking place. The old *moneta*, or koronī cowrie, was replaced by the *annulus* cowrie on 19 September 1795, Sulaymān wrote, since the 'exchange rate of the koronī had reached 100,000 for the *mithqāl*, the same for the bar of salt, for the piece of cloth, and 1,500 for a measure (*nāfqā*) of grain'. The new exchange rates were 3,000 for a *mithqāl*, 4,000 for a bar of salt or piece of cloth, and 100 for a *nāfqā* of grain. And yet rampant inflation of the *annulus* cowrie in turn would accelerate, too, in the nineteenth century, when the value of the cowrie plummeted in relative terms. In Yorùbá areas, a bag of cowries was said to be enough to start a new business venture, and was equivalent to 20,000 shells, known to the Yorùbás as an *egbawa*. Yet an *egbawa* was worth only approximately 5 shillings on the global market.[8]

The early nineteenth century also saw the emergence of modern economic theory, grounded in the idea of an evolution of economies from barter to trade, from primitive to specie currencies – from the perception of a backward Africa to the reality of an expansionist Europe. At this time, economists began to consider the rise of capital as linked to the flows between Europe and the Americas, in which the place of Africa was entirely excluded (little has changed). Yet multiple currencies were, indeed, still in use in many parts of West Africa, from cloths in Senegambia and Sierra Leone to copper and brass in Borno, from cowries in Yorùbá lands and the Niger Bend, to the gold *mithqāl* and the silver dollar, and the kola nut on the Gold Coast. All of these currencies were part of a complex system that made these currencies fully exchangeable with European and Asian monetary systems, via the silver dollar, gold dust and the cowrie. This interchangeability was amply described by European travellers, and so this material was readily available to economic theorists of the new Adam Smith School.[9]

But evidence did not have to get in the way of the formation of the modern 'science' of economics, a theory that would confirm the superiority of European economic mechanisms. Such evidence would build a theory of the market that has since doggedly prevailed, holding sway even now against the tide of the growing number of counterexamples that could suggest alternative readings of the history of money and value. In sum, the evidence from Africa shows that the abstract concept of the 'market' and growth do not take account of what really occurs when human societies with different conceptions of value enter into relationships of exchange. There was no 'barter' in Africa, for many of the products being traded were used as currencies; what occurred was an exchange of value, and the hollowing out of capital value from African economies. Yet, in spite of the clear evidence for this, in this book as elsewhere, the 'logic' of the market prevails in modern economic discourse.

All the while that these theories of barter and primitive economies were developing in the nineteenth century, West African peoples continued to develop economic mechanisms and stratagems that in practice used money. Yorùbá communities developed the *ajo*, a sort of savings bank where people could deposit money with a savings collector and withdraw it at a time of their choosing, and also the *esusu*, a sort of credit union where money was pooled by a group of creditors, then paid out to each creditor in turn. These were capital-market structures that emerged with monies that were certainly not 'primitive', but rather were currencies that the structure of the capital market had emptied of relative global value by the nineteenth century.[10]

In the end, the relationship of currencies to enslavement meant that, as in European economies, these capital structures were deeply tied to the trade in enslaved persons – the monetization of human beings discussed in Chapter 6. When Ali Eisami Gazirmabe of Kano was a slave in Oyo in 1817, he would much later recount, 'the friend of the man who had bought me said to him, "If you do not sell this slave of yours, he will run away, and go to the war, so that your cowries will be lost." ' The Islamic armies of the advancing Fula state of Sokoto were at that time freeing all slaves who went to the war. Thus, the appeal of Islam grew as a means of overcoming oppression. Value, money and enslavement had by this time become linked not only in the Americas and Europe, but also in Africa.[11]

The way in which Islam became the catalyst to resist and overthrow these channels of overreaching power speaks loudly of some of the core priorities in West African societies. As anyone who knows the place can attest, societies place strong importance on religious belief, the connection to the dead and the living, and the ritual symbolism of hidden powers. In some places, of course, the old power structures were able to resist. Secret societies remained especially powerful in Liberia and Sierra Leone, where British and American colonial power insulated rulers from the Islamic revolutions further inland. In Freetown, the British established the headquarters of their Royal Naval Squadron. After the Abolition of the Slave Trade Act of 1807, it was in Freetown that they based their efforts to free captives from 'illegal' American, Portuguese and Spanish slave ships. Once the liberated Africans had been rehabilitated in the asylum beside the port where for centuries slave ships had called to draw water, they formed their own communities of Kongo, Efik and Yorùbá peoples beyond the new colonial town, and brought these influences to bear

Name tags of liberated Africans affixed to the railings outside the Asylum for Liberated Africans in Freetown.

on Sierra Leone's own secret societies. Thus, African societies and worldviews remained resolutely transnational long into the nineteenth century, engaged in a process of constant self-transformation.

SENEGAMBIA AND THE SEEDS OF REVOLT

One of the classic oral epics of the Senegambia region tells of Kelefa Saane, a warrior *nyantio* from Kaabu. This is a story that probably dates to the early nineteenth century. According to Sana Kuyate, Kelefa came from Badora, to the east of the capital of Kaabu at Kansala. After an argument with his cousin, he killed him because his cousin had insulted him by offering him a bone to eat. Kelefa moved from Badora to Biyama, where he became a leader. From Biyama, he went to Mali Kondara, and then fought again at Naliduu. Kelefa fought there for a whole year until the land was destroyed. He was always sending slaves: at every village, Sana Kuyate's narrative says, he fought, killed and caught slaves: he put to death all those rulers who honoured him with meat, praising only those who brought slaves.[12]

In the style of these oral epics, it becomes clear that Kelefa is not one of the converts to the new religion of Islam. In the north of present-day Guinea-Bissau, Kelefa sells children from Bijini – a renowned village of Islamic clerics – for rum. He demands slaves, not meat. In the religious lexicon of people of Senegambia, the religions of the aristocracy were becoming inextricably tainted by the trade in captives. Alcohol remained a major import for ruling elites in Senegambia long into the eighteenth century, in kingdoms such as Waalo and Kaabu. The fetish shrines of these rulers 'ate people', as one 103-year-old from near Bafatá, in Guinea-Bissau, put it in 1979. Certainly, it was often the shrine that condemned people into slavery for crimes for which they were charged.[13]

In other words, these shrines were seen to be part of the cannibalizing process that saw the eroding of West Africa's human capital. The injustice could be overturned only with an alternative, cohesive and religious ideal. This was one reason why people turned increasingly to Islam. Though that religion itself was not free of divisions, it promised a modicum of egalitarianism, for all who became Muslims were equal before the law, and none could be enslaved.[14]

Moreover, while Islam did facilitate the enslavement of non-Muslim populations, much of this was for use in local production. Islam's relationship with the Atlantic trade was complex. The historian Paul Lovejoy holds that Muslim-led states deliberately held back from trading captives to Christian Atlantic slave traders, which is why after 1760 or so 80 per cent of the enslaved population in Atlantic ships came from non-Muslim areas (West-Central Africa and the Bight of Biafra). And where Muslims themselves kept slaves the type of relationship was different from that of the plantations in the New World. One account of the 1820s, written by an English Abolitionist activist, describes how 'I have known instances of a slave being liberated after a few years of servitude; and his master's confidence has been such that he has advanced him money to trade with, and has allowed him to cross the desert to Timbuctoo, waiting for the repayment of his money till his return. This is often the treatment of the Mohamedans to slaves! how different from that practised by the planters in the West Indian Islands!!!'[15]

The frameworks of African religions and Islam in relation to these external forces soon became sharply defined. Alcohol (generally, rum) was to become the touchstone symbolizing these irreconcilable factors. Already by the 1760s strong differences were growing in Senegambia as to the use of alcohol. Whereas Waalo and Kaabu imported rum, for use in libations at religious shrines as well as for recreation, several kingdoms no longer did. The British trade to the Wolof Kingdom of Cayor (between St Louis and Dakar) and Gajaaga in 1765 included cloths and iron but no alcohol. The same was true for the trade with Cidi Hamet, religious leader and ruler of Fuuta Tòòro at the same time, where Indian cloth and gunpowder were offered but alcohol was forsworn. Was it not after all the European (and Christian) Atlantic traders who brought alcohol, an anathema to the Muslim faith?[16]

To understand the power that a figure such as Cidi Hamet developed by the late eighteenth century, it is important to see the roots of these movements. These differences between African religions and Islam had grown since the late seventeenth century. The beginnings lay in the war led by Nasir al-Din along the Senegal River (1673–7).* Al-Din was a member of the *zwāya* clerical class in what is now southern Mauritania during the early 1670s. Drawing on their new distinct identity and the divisions growing up between them and the warrior *hassānyi* class, Al-Din led a group of *zwāya* in seeking both religious and political reform along the Senegal River. He sought an end to the preying by aristocratic elites on their people through the slave trade, and greater purity in the practice of Islam. Swiftly the movement swept through Waalo, Fuuta Tòoro and Cayor. But Nasir al-Din was killed in 1674 and eventually the reform movements were overturned. By 1677, Fuuta Tòoro was back in the hands of its original rulers, the Fula Denyaanke.[17]

Though Nasir al-Din's movement failed, the triggers that had caused it still existed. There was huge resentment of the violence associated with the slave trade among the population, and the rising influence of the *zwāya* remained. In this context, Islam was not a cover for slaving wars led under the flag of *jihād*. It was seen as a form of popular resistance against arbitrary abuses of power by the ruling aristocracies, something initially catalysed by the 1673–7 wars. Somewhat paradoxically, given that it was also a cover for many slaving wars led against non-Muslim populations, it gained the reputation as the religion best able to act as a form of self-defence for threatened communities. This was a core part of the contradictions in the exercise of power emerging throughout the Atlantic world in the eighteenth century.† And, in this context, a new and negative undertone grew around African religions.[18]

After the initial uprisings of the 1670s, it did not take long for the influence of the reform movement to spread. Madrassas had been noted in Cayor by the 1650s, and had spread to the north bank of the Gambia by 1686. Here children were sent to study by night; they could be heard reciting prayers and singing prayers in Arabic in Barra, the port on the north bank of the river, where today ferries still travel to and fro across the Gambia River from Banjul. The

* For a discussion, see Chapter 2.

† On the paradox of political power in the eighteenth-century Atlantic world, see above, Prologue to Part 2.

prayers were written out on small wooden tablets (as, indeed, they are to this day).

Meanwhile, in the Upper Senegal Valley, Bundu was founded by the mystic Malik Sy in the 1690s. Sy had migrated from Fuuta Tòòro and was renowned as holding a special power to make protective amulets. Though Sy had no direct connection to Nasir al-Din, the climate of religious reform and the rising appeal of Islam as a mode of resistance against ruling elites made his claim for land to the King of Gajaaga hard to resist. Sy was followed by more Fula migrants from Fuuta Tòòro, and used the same title as Nasir al-Din, to suggest a continuity.[19]

Why was someone like Sy so appealing? Clerics, amulet-writers, those with close connection to the scriptures and to God – all of them possessed a special value in the religious universe of West Africa. So the role of clerics in founding towns and settlements became an important motor for historical transformations in this era. Many chronicles (*ta'rīkhs*) describe other clerics founding settlements. A Jahanké *ta'rīkh* tells of Su'aybu ibn Yusuf, who founded villages in Wuuli (on the north bank of the Gambia), and whose sons then founded several villages more in the Fuuta Jaalo Mountains. It is hard to understand the attraction of these clerics without paying heed to the instability of the eighteenth century, and the spiritual meaning that West African peoples sought from life. People resented the aristocratic warrior elites, and the growing insecurity of their livelihoods and families, as they had to move from one place to another, send armed guards with those who worked the rice and millet fields, and lost friends and family as captives. They were quite willing to follow wandering mystics such as Sy, who offered both protection from the slave trade and a more meaningful path through life – especially in a context in which no Muslim could be legally enslaved.[20]

This appeal grew from the Senegal River in the north to the Fuuta Jaalo Mountains of what is now Guinea-Conakry in the south, and with it the authority of the Fula clerics who spearheaded it. Connections crisscrossed with the wandering clerics and their followers. In the first quarter of the eighteenth century, Fula clerics would take control of the mountains of Guinea-Conakry from their Jalonke and Mandinka neighbours, forming the Almamate of Fuuta Jaalo in 1727–8 under their leader Karamoko Alfa, with its capital at Timbo.

This was not an isolated power grab, since from around 1700 there had been growing links between the large Fula communities in the Fuuta Jaalo and Bundu. Malik Sy's son Bubu Malik Sy studied in Fuuta Jaalo with the same scholar who taught Karamoko Alfa. When Bubu Malik Sy returned to Bundu from Fuuta Jaalo, around 1700, he came with an idea of refounding the kingdom, and further family and scholarly ties followed.[21]

Further north, the Fula Kingdom of Fuuta Tòòro, on the banks of the Senegal River, remained at the centre of these changes. The Denyaanke Dynasty there remained in power until 1776, and Islamic learning among Fula communities grew. Writing in 1767, Abbé Demanet said that 'there are, along the whole length of the [Senegal River] . . . many villages who are only inhabited by marabouts.' The religious power of the *zwāya* meant that the purpose of the Fula was not to sell slaves but to convert them, as Saugnier put it in 1791: they 'never or only rarely come to sell their captives'. Whereas Bambuk, Gajaaga and Kaarta were all 'favourable for the trade in captives' in the 1760s, Fuuta Tòòro sold only cotton and indigo. Thus grew the reputation of Islam in the region as a religion of sanctuary, and with this the population of the Fula kingdoms.[22]

Fuuta Tòòro was a kingdom in the throes of great religious renewal throughout the first half of the eighteenth century. As *zwāya* went from village to village preaching, they produced a large number of followers, the *torodbe* (or beggars for alms) – a practice that continues among the marabouts of Senegal, who send out young children to beg in this manner to this day. The *torodbe* shunned material wealth and trade goods. The West African equivalent of Franciscans, they were thus beyond the reach of the lures of the Atlantic trade. Many different peoples joined their number, making them a powerful force as the century unwound.[23]

Linguistic evidence supports this way of viewing historical transformations in West Africa. It is important to see this kingdom as a combined effort of Fula and other peoples. As noted by the preeminent historian of Fuuta Tòòro, Oumar Kane, many Wolof surnames are found among warrior groups (*sebbe*) and fishermen (*subalbe*) living among the Futanke. Many Serèèr surnames are also found among the farmers and fishermen. This was not an 'ethnically pure' Fula kingdom, but one that was composite and multi-ethnic, to which any person wishing to convert could come.[24]

This was, moreover, a foundational characteristic, since Fuuta Tòòro was also recognized as an Islamic kingdom almost from the beginning, as a very early account of the kingdom's founder, Koli Tenguella, shows. In this account compiled by Siré-Abbâs-Soh in 1913 from oral sources and other chronicles now lost, Soh recounts how Koli Tenguella heard about the Kingdom of Dyāra and sent twelve companions to find out more. On arrival at this Manding kingdom, the ruler (*farim*), called Mahmūdu, invited the twelve to stay and gave them a servant to attend to all their needs. They stayed for two years, 'and then Mahmūdu sent them back to Koli, having put them in chains of gold around their neck, around their hands, and around their feet. When they arrived . . . and they had told Koli all the marvels that they had seen at Dyāra, he thanked God that the people there were polytheists, which would allow him to attack the town of Dyāra himself.'[25]

Once established, the Denyaanke Dynasty ruled uninterrupted until 1776, and it would only be the transformations of the eighteenth century that brought about lasting change, as the *torodbe* grew in strength. Though long insulated from the Atlantic trade, over time some Fuuta satigi (kings) became embroiled in the trade in captives, bringing discord. In 1776, taking its cue from the changes in Fuuta Jaalo, the scholar Ceerno Suleyman Baal declared an Almamate. Having studied in Fuuta Jaalo, he was well aware of the transformations there, and declared a manifesto that included equality of all before justice, all taxes to be used for the public good, and protection of the weak such as women, orphans and the elderly. It was a programme that had a strong appeal, especially among the *torodbe*; and when Baal was killed in a revolt later that year, the mantle was taken up by the almamy and scholar Abdul Qader.[26]

Abdul Qader's policies showed the complex relationship that Islamic traders and preachers had come to have with the Atlantic trade by the eighteenth century. On the one hand, Fuuta Tòòro depended on European traders for the weaponry and gunpowder needed for self-defence and holy struggle, trading captives and gum for weapons and powder. And yet on the other hand religious expansion was also Abdul Qader's overarching priority, as he founded thirty to forty new mosques, installed many new imams, and furthered clerical connections as far as Bundu, Cayor, Kaarta and the Saluum Delta north of the Gambia River. In short, the almamy needed imported military hardware to safeguard religious and political gains.[27]

By 1800, Fuuta Tòòro had become one of the most powerful states in West Africa. A large number of nearby kingdoms had pledged allegiance, and it had strong connections almost 600 miles to the south in Fuuta Jaalo. The inequalities of the Atlantic trade had driven resentment, and fear. Conversion to Islam offered protection against enslavement and the depredations of the Atlantic trade. The inequalities in the exchange of value showed no sign of slowing, as the French traders exported large volumes of gold from Bambuk and Gajaaga. Even the gum trade brought huge profits. The gum came from a spiny acacia tree with little white flowers, and produced two harvests, one

Harvesting acacia gum.

in December and the other in March. Demanet described the profits as large in 1767, since it was bought for a very low price in Africa, and was sold for a very high one once outside the continent.[28]

As the empty wine bottles piled up around the French trading posts, alcohol came to symbolize everything that was corrupt about the old regime. The purity and lack of intoxication associated with Islam became ever more appealing and intense. The clerical class were about to take control, and when Joseph Corry went ashore at Dakar in 1805, he found that the local 'chief or king' was named 'maraboo'. As in many places across Senegambia, he had been the Islamic priest of the Damel of Cayor, and had then led a rebellion against his king. He was still at war with him when Corry visited, and this was a pattern that was repeating itself in many distant places across West Africa.[29]

SOCIETIES OF DIVISION ON THE EVE OF REVOLUTION

Writing in 1812 in his *Infaq al-Maisuri*, the first Sultan of Sokoto, Muhammed Bello, wrote clearly of the connections between the Fula of Fuuta Tòòro and those who had just led a successful *jihād* in the Hausa kingdoms around Kano:

> The [Tukulor] made war on the Fula, till the latter split into three divisions. One stayed among the Tukulor and followed them, another returned to Falefa and Fu[u]ta Jaalo and dwelt there, a third went east to meet the tribes of their father, the Arabs. They went thither until some reached the tribes of the Arabs. They left the weak behind them in this land [of Hausa] ... our Sokoto clan of Toronke came from Fu[u]ta to this land a little after the dispersion of the Fula. Among them, the number of them who made the pilgrimage was greater than the number of those who had not done so.[30]

In his own words, Muhammed Bello described the migrations of the Fula from Fuuta Tòòro to what became northern Nigeria. Some of his ancestors came as far back as around 1500, while others followed with the wars of 1670s. Many of them travelled on pilgrimage to Mecca, and they formed the nucleus of the new Fula theocracy who would seize power at the end of the eighteenth century. Fula migrations opened up a new diaspora across West Africa from the sixteenth century onwards, a diaspora that would be crucial to the revolutions of the eighteenth century. In northern Nigeria, these were led by Bello's father, Shaykh Uthmān dan Fodio – known popularly as the 'shehu' – and crystallized an era of transformation across West Africa.[31]

Once the ancestors of the Dan Fodio clan had migrated from Fuuta Tòòro to Sokoto, the connections among the Fula community continued during the seventeenth and eighteenth centuries with the wanderings of the scholarly *'ulamā* class. From as far back as the reign of Sonni 'Alī in late fifteenth century Songhay, the *'ulamā* had long come from across the Sahel. During the sixteenth-century apogee of Songhay, they wandered throughout the empire and began sustained literary production. Books arrived along with the caravan trade, and were widely available in Kano in the sixteenth century. Following the fall of Songhay, the migrations of the *'ulamā* continued. They were not limited by geography, but were instead inspired by mysticism and the desire to learn the esoteric knowledge of the Qur'ān. Many of them left Timbuktu in the eighteenth century, while what is now Mauritania became the heartland of scholarly production in West Africa. Meanwhile, the community of Fula preachers grew also in the Hausa kingdoms.[32]

One 1658 account of the scholar 'Umr ibn Othman, from the capital of Borno at Ngazargamu, gives a good impression of the type of *'ulamā* class that was emerging by this time. According to one chronicle, Othman

> lived in the country of Bornu for about fifteen years. He afterwards journeyed east and went to the mosque of Al-Azhar and stayed there to learn and instruct the people. Thence he went to Mecca and duly performed the pilgrimage . . . He went to Medina and visited the tomb of the Prophet, and remained at Medina for two months. From Medina he went to Baghdad, where he remained six months . . . finally he returned to N'gazargamu.[33]

Such migrations were very common throughout this era; as Bello put it in *Infaq al-Maisuri*, more Fula made the pilgrimage to Mecca from

Hausa lands than did not. Thus, the connections between the Dan Fodios in Sokoto and the transformations in Fuuta Tòòro were important, because they connected to the global network of this class of preachers, many of whom were in contact with new currents of Islamic ideas in North Africa and Arabia. This was why the leaders of the *jihād* in Sokoto had deep intellectual and family ties with the leaders of the wave of Islamic reform sweeping through Senegambia in the eighteenth century, and also why they influenced that reform through their own connections to the wider Muslim Umma.

Gradually an ethnic Fula diaspora grounded in a religious framework and mutual commercial ties emerged. Like many diasporas, the Fula had begun as outsiders and guests in the land of their hosts, and this experience of marginalization had constructed a shared cultural framework beyond religion. Interesting evidence suggests more than intellectual contacts, with a common culture across the space from Senegambia to Nigeria. Weaving was at the heart of it, with Fula weavers famous and influential across West Africa. One source of the 1730s for Senegambia describes how 'all round their Towns they open for cotton', for use in the important weaving industry that the Fula were developing; while an account from the 1780s from someone who was captured and enslaved in what is now central Mali by warriors from Segu describes there a strong Fula weaving industry of deep-blue indigo-dyed cloths and blankets. Meanwhile, the weaving industry of indigo-dyed cloths would be the economic mainstay of the Sokoto Caliphate.[34]

By the late eighteenth century, therefore, the Fula *'ulamā* were a small and highly educated minority in the Hausa kingdoms. They had retained religious knowledge for over two centuries, and their influence and authority among Muslim communities was high. Their knowledge was based on voracious reading, and also on extended periods of mystical wandering through the desert spaces of West Africa, as they apprenticed at the hands of famous scholars. They were also influenced by experiences of the pilgrimage to Mecca, and of contacts with scholars from the Middle East; by the 1750s there was an annual caravan from Timbuktu to Mecca, which travelled either through Kano itself or north through the oasis of Touāt.[35]

The level of learning and intellectual discussion among the Fula *'ulamā* by the late eighteenth century is well illustrated by the writings of the leaders of the *jihād* that took hold in the late eighteenth century. One of their intellectual seers, Abdullah ibn Muhammad, was both a prolific and erudite writer in Arabic, with a rich vocabulary and a complex literary style that can have come about only through careful study. This was a knowledge that had been gained by wandering through the desert spaces and living with elder scholars, and through the trade in books.[36]

The existence of the *'ulamā* class makes clear that Islam was becoming a vehicle for political transformation in Senegambia and beyond. Waves of new ideas crossed the Sahara with the caravans of trade, re-energizing scholarly discussions. One great-grandson of the shehu (Uthmān dan Fodio) wrote of a *shaykh* who had been brought to Sokoto from across the Arab world, 'I learnt from him the knowledge of mysticism which belongs to the forming of good character in oneself, and that which belongs to perfecting oneself in science.' With such global connections and new ideas, the Fula preachers had come to form a key class in what became northern Nigeria.[37]

These connections mattered, for, by the late eighteenth century, the Hausa kingdoms around Kano had become ripe for conflict. On the one hand, the political power of Kano was becoming impressive. The account of Al Hadji Abd Salam Shabīni, who knew Kano in the 1770s, confirms its strength. According to Shabīni, the Sarki of Kano had to confirm the appointment of a new ruler in Timbuktu. Timbuktu was dependent on Kano for troops and the garrison that protected the city from Tuareg raiders, whose attacks were worrisome. Kano's overlordship was not surprising, since it was much larger than Timbuktu, 'and nearly as large as London' – which, as Shabīni had visited London, gives pause for thought. Kano was a thriving city, full of cowries and gold dust, which were the currencies for trade, with imported cotton cloths and towels from India, merchants from all across West Africa and even from India, and slaves brought from as far afield as Fez in Morocco.[38]

It is also interesting to consider the manufacturing base that Kano had developed by this time. Shabīni tells us that muskets and gunpowder were manufactured in the Hausa kingdoms, while arrows were forged using steel made in Timbuktu. Crafts boomed in Kano,

Kano from Mount Dala.

with quarters for smiths, carpenters, cobblers, tailors and masons, while those of Arab descent tended to predominate as weavers. Saddlers made peaked saddles for the 600 horses in the royal stables, manipulating the leather that was harvested from the herds of cattle tended by the Fula herders. Medicine, too, was advanced, since, as Shabīni described, 'they inoculate for the smallpox; the pus is put into a dried raisin and eaten', much in the manner of modern vaccines. The streets of Kano were full of life: 'they play at chess and draughts, and are very expert at those games; they have no cards; but they have tumblers, jugglers and ventriloquists.'[39]

Every indication suggests a thriving city, but if there were a shadow it was in the divisions that grew at all levels between Hausa rulers and the people. It was in the reign of Babba Zaki (1747–71) that, according to the 'Song of Bagauda', the cavalry grew and the retinue of body-guards surrounding the sarki became strong: 'One could not see him – the Great one – except through an intermediary.' Deep-set hierarchies were entrenched across the Sahel, from Timbuktu to Kano. When the Tuareg attacked Timbuktu in December 1758, the chronicler Mawlāy Sulaymān described the victims in strictly hierarchical order, from the qadi and the sharif to the pasha (governor), followed by 'a large number of inhabitants of Timbuktu, soldiers, peasants [*harratin*], slaves and others'. In Katsina, there were divisions between Muslims and non-Muslims, Hausa ruling clans in the urban settings and Fula herders in the countryside. All the great centres of urban life and political power in the central and western Sahel had grown up alongside divisions.[40]

One of the clearest boundaries that established these divisions was the place of slavery. Just as slavery was a fundamental institution in the Fula Kingdom of Fuuta Tòòro by the eighteenth century, so it was in the Fula diaspora in the Hausa kingdoms and Timbuktu. Islamic leaders in West Africa might not capture people for sale into the Atlantic trade so regularly, but they certainly became ever more dependent on slave labour. Just as along the Atlantic coast and in Segu, agricultural labour had become reductively associated with captivity and slavery, so the Fula word for 'slave' or 'captive' in Mâssina (in what is now central Mali) was the same as that for a cultivator or worker of the earth, *maccudo* – as we saw earlier was the case in Segu. In Timbuktu, by the 1770s, travelling merchants would arrive and find porters who 'assisted them and procured every thing they wanted; but when they were settled they hired a man and a woman slave to cook and to clean their rooms, and to do every menial office. Slaves are to be bought at all hours.'[41]

Slavery was, in fact, becoming a contradictory institution by the later eighteenth century, owing to the tension between its origins as a form of moral and kin dependence in West African societies, and the new forces that were shaping a different institution. The indigenous West African tradition of powerful palace slaves continued. Known also in Asante, Dahomey and Oyo as well as in the Hausa kingdoms, this was a way of limiting the possibility for palace revolts, since the theory was that no kingdom would accept the revolt and rule of a slave (even if, in practice, as we have seen in the case of Kebbi, by the eighteenth century this was not the case). This meant that, according to the Kano Chronicle, in the mid eighteenth century under Sarki Baba Zaki, 'the great men in his time were forty-two . . . these were all slaves.'[42]

And yet slavery was rapidly outgrowing its traditional frameworks in West Africa, and creating a vast underclass of resentful dependants that was mushrooming year on year. The growth of the Atlantic trade was changing the dynamics at play. In the 1730s, muskets had been imported from Nupe to Kano, from the Atlantic traders. By the 1770s, as we have seen, these were now manufactured in Kano. Cowries, too, were imported through Dahomey, bolstering the currency supply in Kano. All of this rapidly enhanced the potential for raising funds and fighting slaving wars. As the export slave trade increased, so, too, did the number of local slaves; so that, by the eighteenth century, in Fuuta Tòòro there were entire villages of slaves, and agricultural labour was the domain of the dishonoured captive, who was forbidden from growing a beard.[43]

Political infighting became entrenched. The tension was irreconcilable between the old institution of slavery as dependence, and the new framework of slaving wars and captives designed to enhance the status of the warrior aristocrats. Timbuktu saw the emigration of its scholarly class in the eighteenth century, because of continual instability provoked by Tuareg attacks, and internal wrangles and political assassinations from the 1750s onwards. In Kano, meanwhile, the value of captives meant that insecurity had grown rapidly. By the 1770s, slave stealers were operating: they '[take] children by night out of the town, and sell them to some peasant, who sells them to a third, and so from hand to hand, too they are carried out of the country'. It was not surprising that the Hausa disliked camels, for '*they are the beasts that carry us into slavery*.'[44]

In short, the area encompassing the Fula diaspora, spreading from Fuuta Tòòro to Kano via Timbuktu, was one of ideological and political ferment in the eighteenth century. Military technologies changed with the import of muskets, and their local manufacture. Slaving wars increased, and, with them, the position of the slave changed, away from the old system of patronage and dependence, to one where their value increased insecurity as well as the resentment of the slave class. While the Sahelian cities were far from the Atlantic coast, they were connected to it through complex chains of middlemen traders who brought firearms and cowries, and contributed to the forces that were catalysing resentment and the desire to overthrow the ruling class.

By the late eighteenth century, therefore, an unsustainable coexistence had grown up. Hausa rulers claimed adherence to Islam. But their traditions of rulership remained heavily mixed with African cultural forms, through the use of palace slaves and the importance of musical performances of history. In practice, there was a syncretism with African religions and cultural practices, and this was something that allowed the Fula preachers to claim that there was a need for purist reform. A central area of discord was that the relationship between men and women did not conform to religious gender norms but rather to West African traditions, which saw women having power in the royal palaces, as traders and, indeed, as wives. This was alluded to by the shehu himself in a text in which he criticized the Hausa kings for forbidding 'the worshippers of God part of that which is legal for them, such as the veiling of women, which is incumbent upon them, and turbans for men'. As Shabīni noted in the 1770s, 'men and women [in Kano] mix in society, and visit together with the same freedom as in Europe'; the women 'walk out or visit [alone] . . . with the same freedom as in Europe'.[45]

By 1800, Islam had emerged as a vehicle that could challenge other types of hierarchy in Kano and elsewhere. In doing do, however, aspects of West African traditions that allowed more gendered equality would be overturned. Fula women were active traders in Senegambia, certainly in the seventeenth century. Meanwhile, where women in Fula society and in the agrarian societies of Borno and the Hausa kingdoms had been free to work and play outside the house, their activities were now restricted to the compounds. Just as some new masquerades in Senegambia such as Mama-Jombo enforced new gender norms, so, too, did the ideas shaping political revolt in the Sahel, influenced as we shall see by the Salafiya revival of a more patriarchal strain of Islam in Arabia. One of the greatest inequalities to grow as a result of the globalization of West African economies and societies in the slave-trade era appears to have been that between men and women.[46]

Where one injustice is righted, another can often follow. Certainly, the existing corruption in the Hausa kingdoms was a source of all the anger that poured out with the revolts. This was poignantly expressed in a poem by Abdullah ibn Muhammad, composed in the 1820s and describing the pomp of Kano before its fall to the Fula *jihād*:

> I was left behind among the remainder, the liars
> Who say that which they do not do, and follow their desires,
> And follow avarice in everything incumbent upon them,

And who have no knowledge and do not ask for it . . .
Whose purpose is the ruling of the countries and their people
In order to obtain delights and acquire rank,
According to the customs of the unbelievers and the titles
of their sovereignty.
And the appointing of ignorant persons to the highest offices,
And the collecting of concubines, and fine clothes
And horses that gallop in the towns, not on the battlefields,
And the devouring of gifts of sanctity, and booty and bribery,
And lutes, and flutes, and the beating of drums . . .
They were many, but their righteous men were few;
They showed the dissimulation of wicked people, the people
of the squadrons
And of the sellers of free men in the market.
Some of them are posing as *qādīs*, in the clothing of foxes![47]

JIHĀD IN THE HAUSA KINGDOMS OF NIGERIA

After the *jihād* that he led had been successful, the shehu composed a text called the *Kitāb al-Farq*, in which he described the Hausa kingdoms around Kano that his troops had just overcome. Here, the resentments of the Fula population ring through clearly across the centuries. The Hausa rulers and administrators were quite happy to impose taxes, drink, decorate their palaces with carpets and eat foods, 'all whether religiously permitted or forbidden'. They were 'occupied with doing vain things (continuously) by night or by day, without legal purpose, such as beating drums, lutes, and kettle-drums, and the giving of gifts to one who conducts them before the ruler'. They had compulsory military conscription on penalty of a fine, charged taxes on Islamic merchants and seized the property of those who died in their country.[48]

By the end of the eighteenth century, this sort of halfway house between Islam and African religions was no longer acceptable to Fula mystics and preachers such as the shehu, who were in touch with the religious reform movements sweeping through the rest of the Muslim world. The eighteenth century saw the rise of the Unitarian reform movement, now known as Salafism, which would ultimately lead to the uniting of much of Arabia under the Ibn Saud family. There were, indeed, striking parallels between the leader of the Salafist movement, Muhammad ibn Abd al-Wahhāb, and the shehu. Al-Wahhāb (1703/4–92) began his reformist movement as a response to what he saw as the practice of pagan rituals in Arabia, such as the veneration of trees and stones, animal sacrifices and the leaving of food offerings for djinns (spirits). Once the movement had got under way in the 1740s, it brought in increasing numbers of followers attracted to the desire to renew Islam through a return to the tenets of the faith, and, by the 1770s, its influence was very strong, and new leaders and followers were joining all the time. With the migration of scholars from Borno to cities in Arabia, there is no doubt that the growing sense of a renewal of Islam influenced the emergence of the reform movement in Sokoto.[49]

Salafism would have an important though indirect effect on West Africa. West African Muslims tended to belong to Sufi movements, from Borno to Senegambia, and some scholars now see Sufism as having been an important aspect of the political philosophy of the shehu's movement. Sufi theologians preached distance between administration and religion, holding that there was an irreconcilable gulf between faith and statecraft. Sufi scholars had thus always refused to assist in political life in West Africa, and had concentrated instead on mystical practice and on the refinement of their knowledge of the law. Salafism was, by definition, hostile to Sufi movements, and, during the 1780s and 1790s, many of them began to respond to the movements taking hold of Arabia with their own renewal. The shehu and his followers were not Salafis themselves; in fact, they adhered to the Qadiriya strain of Sufism, which had been revitalized during the second half of the eighteenth century. But these movements of reform and renewal themselves were responses to the rise of Salafism, and the Fula preachers were certainly in touch with the reform movement in Arabia through the time they had spent there. In the text of the shehu criticizing the Hausa restriction on veiling women noted above, the influence of Salafi patriarchal ideals can be seen.[50]

Salafism had arisen in part as a response to the decline of the Ottoman Empire, the weakness of its hold over Arabia and the increasing power of Christian Europe, particularly along coastal areas around the southern Mediterranean. Followers of Al-Wahhābi sought a complete reform of Islamic society, taking as their ideal the early Islamic patriarchal community, and holding that it was a divergence from this that had prompted the empire's decline. The place of these new religious ideas sweeping the Fula reform movement is suggested in several texts by the shehu on relations between the sexes. Though in some texts the shehu claimed that women were not obliged to be tied to the kitchen and domestic tasks, his main concern here was to encourage women towards a more mystical way of life. Yet, during the eighteenth century, there *had* been female Fula scholars in what is now northern Nigeria. While Fula women were restricted in many ways in their communities, they were allowed to study. Some became scholars and mystics who were renowned as much as their male peers. Indeed, according to the shehu's son Muhammed Bello, the coming of the shehu was itself foretold by a female Fula mystic: 'There is also the prophecy which was made by Uma Hani, a holy woman, a Saint, a Fulata. She says, "A holy man shall appear in the country of the Soudan, he shall renew the faith, he shall revive religion and establish the service of God." '[51]

So who was this Uthmān dan Fodio, the shehu, whose reform movement was to have such profound effects not only in northern Nigeria but across West Africa? He had been born around 1754 in the north-west of what is now Nigeria, in a settled Fula community in Sokoto. Though in the fifteenth century this had been a stronghold of African religions, by the middle of the eighteenth century, the Fula preaching community was important. The shehu grew into a slender man of medium height. He apprenticed himself to a scholar called Abd al-Rahmān ibn Hammat, accompanying him for two years. Ibn Hammat embarked afterwards on pilgrimage to Arabia, where he certainly came into contact with the currents of Salafism and the reaction of Sufi movements to this. When the shehu came into contact with him again on his return, he was already embarking on his own career of preaching and contemplation.[52]

The character of the shehu may perhaps also be glimpsed through the moral qualities admired by Fula communities. Much Fula poetry treats of the ceaseless quest of the cattle herds for pasturage and water. Fula communities in West Africa were traditionally cattle herders as well as preachers, and, indeed, the rising demand for leather in African and European crafts had strengthened their economic hand. All of these Fula verses, one specialist writes, 'praise without cease the qualities of soberness, endurance and pride' of their cattle; virtues that 'are precisely those of the human ideal of the Fula'. Wandering through the deserts of the Sahara and Arabia, studying without cease in the quest of God, the shehu and other members of the *'ulāma* class in many ways embodied the migratory quests of the cattle herded by their Fula brethren. Such quests certainly made them tough as well as learned in Islam – a quality that would prove important when the war against the Hausa kingdoms finally broke out at the end of the eighteenth century.[53]

By the late 1780s, the shehu had acquired quite a following in the Hausa kingdoms of Gobir and Zanfara. Commoners and nobles alike came to follow him and hear him preach, and the Hausa kings developed a fear of his power. He established a community at Degel, which was a refuge for slaves who had escaped masters who practised African religions. As Muhammed Bello put it, 'he was loved and honoured by men to a degree that is not often seen . . . men came to him in such crowds that they jostled each other. He showed them a smiling face and kindly nature and was glad with them.' The shehu was becoming a source of power to rival the Gobir kings – not something that could long be tolerated.[54]

In *c.* 1788, Bawa Jangwarzo, King of Gobir, summoned the shehu and other Islamic scholars on the pretext of celebrating the festival of Id-al-adha. In fact, he intended to kill them. Yet, once they were all there, he realized their power had grown too strong. He hesitated and then desisted, and thereafter the shehu became a powerful leader in the 1790s. One of the shehu's biographers, Abdullah ibn Muhammad, described well the hatreds that were brewing between the Hausa and the Fula by this stage:

> Now when the kings and their helpers saw the *Shaikh*'s community making ready their weapons, they feared that. Moreover, before that

> the numerousness of the community, and its cutting itself off from their jurisdiction, had enraged them. They made their enmity known with their tongues, threatening the community with *razzias* and extermination, and what their breasts hid was worse than that. They began to forbid what they had heard concerning the dress of the community, such as turbans, and the order that women should wear the veil.[55]

In other words, the conflict over dress and women's place in society came to be at the forefront of the symbolic struggle between the Hausa kings and their Fula subjects. The Fula community had expanded, and the teachings of the shehu and his growing real power meant that the Hausa kings had every day less real authority over a large number of people in their kingdom. In 1801, a new king came to power in Gobir. Yunfa did not want to tolerate this situation any longer. War came closer. The shehu and his followers retreated to Gudu, where they built a fortress and the shehu kept his library. In February 1804, the shehu summoned an act of allegiance at Gudu. Yunfa interpreted this as a threatening move, and, by June of that year, Gobirawa troops were marching against the shehu and his followers.[56]

The key battle took place on 21 June 1804, at Tabkin Kwotto. The Gobirawa troops outnumbered the Fula army of the shehu, who had only twenty horses. The Gobirawa 'had quilted armour and tall caps and soft clothing which gave them comfort; they had ambling horses with flowing manes'. Although severely pressed on both flanks, the Fula held out, and then pushed forward:

> They fell back. They retreated, they ran and scattered. The Mohammedans pursued at their heels and killed them and took their property. Of those that were killed, God alone knows their number. Their King fled. His friend Baidu was killed and Magaji and some others ... many were the horsemen slain by our arrows and our swords. The vultures and the hyenas devoured them. Many were there in quilted armour whom our hands slew, whose heads our axes broke, and cut in pieces ... the whole army of Yunfa was scattered; each company had gone its own way, and they did not assemble again.[57]

News of the defeat of the King of Gobir spread among the Hausa kingdoms. The Hausa kings were alarmed, and began to persecute the Muslims among them, who rallied in groups. A month after Tabkin Kwotto, the shehu's followers attacked Kebbi and Alkalawa, the capital of Gobir. They spread throughout the country, conquering twenty fortresses, and, in 1807, took Kano: throughout these wars there was bloodshed, although the numbers who died may, in fact, have been quite low, since the capture and enslavement of defeated enemies was appealing to many who fought. After Kano, Katsina was attacked, and then their attention turned towards Borno in the east. Though Borno was a Muslim kingdom, its standards did not match the purity and renewal that was preached by the shehu, and so war began here as well.[58]

Once again, it was Borno's declaration of adherence to Islam while holding to many African traditions that most offended the shehu and his followers. As Muhammed Bello described it:

> It is stated that [Borno] remained steadfast up to the time that our Jihād began, but we have heard that their Chiefs used to ride out to certain places and make sacrifices there and that they used to pour the blood of sacrifice upon the gates of their cities. It is said that they had houses with snakes and other reptiles in them and that they used to sacrifice to the snakes . . . They used to allege that it was the custom of their country . . . they said that if they did not observe their customs, their crops would spoil and their prosperity be diminished and their strength become weakness . . . they were heathen. For these idols of wood and water that they made sacrifices to were the idols of their forefathers who were not Moslem.[59]

Just as transnational influences had had a major impact in coastal areas of West Africa, and had helped to drive a wedge between the rulers and their subjects, so they became of fundamental importance to the movements aimed at overthrowing the ruling class in the Sahelian states. Given the strong links between scholars in the Sahel and Arabia, it may, for instance, be no coincidence that the years of the Sokoto *jihād* correspond almost exactly with the apogee of the Salafiya reformist movement in Arabia, which, between 1803 and 1806, took control of Mecca and Medina. Yet what was at stake through these multiple influences was the long-standing practice of cultural flexibility, in which African religious practices intermingled with the Islamic religion. The rise of Salafism and the reaction of Sufi movements to this created a fertile ground to overturn the status quo, and the aristocracy that had been sustained for many centuries in Borno, Kano and beyond.

One verse written in Borno in 1799 gives a sense of the atmosphere of change and reform, the sense that the world was poised on the cusp, and of the hostility that had grown, and that would only be resolved in the war of 1808–12:

> Verily a cloud has settled upon God's earth,
> A cloud so dense that escape from it is impossible.
> Everywhere between Kordofan and Gobir
> And the cities of the Kindin [Tuareg]
> Are settlements of the dogs of Fellata [Fula]
> Serving God in all their dwelling places
> (I swear by the life of the Prophet and his overflowing grace)
> In reforming all districts and provinces
> Ready for future bliss.
> So in this year of 1214 AH [1799 CE] they are following their beneficent theories
> As though it were a time to set the world in order by preaching.
> Alas! that I know all about the tongue of the fox.[60]

THE *JIHĀD*'S CONSEQUENCES: BORNO, OYO AND BEYOND

The years after the rise of the Fula *jihād* in 1804 were full of omens in Borno. In 1807, there was a solar eclipse. Then, a year later, according to Ali Eisami Gazirmabe, who was the son of a *shaykh* from Kano: 'In the weeding time, in the rainy season, at about two o'clock in the afternoon, we looked to the west, the Kaman-locusts were coming from the west, forming a straight line across the sky, as if one of God's thunderstorms were coming, so that day was turned into night.'[61] The locusts were followed by a famine, and then an epidemic that created huge mortality, 'completely destroying all the Ful[a]', according to Eisami. It was then that the armies of the shehu advanced as part of their struggle against perceived impurities in Islamic practice, putting to flight the Mai of Borno and part of his family, and unsettling the country still further. Eisami gives a moving account of how a religious person tried to face down the violence and chaos with equanimity: 'As they were coming to our town, my father said to me, "My son, times will be hard for you: this year you are nineteen years of age, and though I said that when you are twenty, I will seek a girl for you, and let you marry, yet now the Fula have unsettled the land, and we do not know what to do: but what God has ordained for you, that shall we experience." '[62]

In fact, Borno had for several decades been weakened. The mais had never entirely recovered from the severe drought of the 1740s and 1750s, which had led to increasing Fula migration into Borno, and a decline in cotton production and textile industries. The trans-Saharan trade in captives had grown as a result, and, with it, the influence of the Ottoman Empire in Borno. One important account of 1790, written by the Englishman Beaufoy on the basis of interviews with two interpreters in Tunis, describes how many captives came from the east of Lake Chad and were sold to Borno by intermediaries, the Baguirmi. Meanwhile, the 'sultan of Borno is continually at war with the various idolatrous tribes of blacks who border on his dominions. Those who are taken prisoners are sold to the Arabs, and this traffic constitutes the principal commerce of the country.'[63]

As in the Atlantic kingdoms, Borno's slave trade created a well-to-do leisured class, who played chess and draughts, and wore fine clothes. This went with the cultivation of a substantial scholarly *'ulamā*, which was still very active in 1800. The militarization of Borno, meanwhile, appears to have been geared largely to sustaining this elite through slaving wars. Though the mais had cavalry, they had very few infantry. Thus, though the capital at Ngazargamu was fortified by a wall around fourteen feet high, with a wide ditch around the whole and seven gates that were shut at night, the lack of foot soldiers was a problem. The lack of infantry and the increasing depredations of the slave trade meant that Borno would not be readily defended when a well-organized and cocksure army such as that led by the shehu's followers arrived in 1808.[64]

The battle was waged between 1808 and 1812, and was a sore

matter of controversy in Borno. The mais of Borno rejected the right of the shehu and his followers to attack them, on the basis that they were Muslims every bit as much as were the Fula. There was a large literate class in Borno, and, by the late eighteenth century, the school of scholars there was known as the 'Group of Ten', who were strongly connected to a wider group of scholars in the Dar al-Islam. These links went back as far as the twelfth century, when scholars from Kanem (Borno's predecessor kingdom) were noted as far away as Marrakesh. This was why Bello and, before him, his father, the shehu, insisted on pointing out in their texts the African religious practices that the mais melded with Islam; indeed, the shehu went as far back as the doctrinal disputes regarding the Islamic practice of Sonni 'Alī, Emperor of Songhay in the late fifteenth century, who was again said to have melded African religious practice with observance of the Qur'ān.[65]

In the end, Borno was not going to prove as easy to overturn as some of the Hausa kingdoms. However, as in Sokoto, a religious figure – in this case Al-Amin al-Kanemi – would become the most powerful person in the kingdom. The shehu died in Sokoto in 1817, to be succeeded by his son Muhammed Bello, who took forward the development of the Sokoto Caliphate. In Borno, however, the authority of Al-Kanemi only became established by 1820, following his role in defending Borno against the armies of Sokoto.

Though Borno's capital at Ngazargamu was attacked by the Fula armies in 1808, they were driven out in 1809. Repeated attacks from the Sokoto troops saw the capital move around the kingdom. In the defence of Borno and the marshalling of troops, Al-Kanemi's leadership and influence among Arab and Kanembi followers became crucial, and when the mai, Dunama, sought to eliminate him in 1820, he was no longer powerful enough to do so. Al-Kanemi and his descendants would rule Borno through most of the nineteenth century. As in Sokoto, the power of Islam as a religion to harness popular movements in a time of instability and political upheaval was in the ascendant.[66]

Over the first half of the nineteenth century, this pattern would spread throughout West Africa. Though beginning with the Fula preachers, Islam became a banner under which people from many different ethnicities sought identity and power. The wars became a matter of belief, and revenge against the abuse of power and entrenched hierarchy. Slaves had sought sanctuary with the shehu in Degel, converting to Islam and being freed, and the same pattern would emerge in many parts of West Africa. The political instability associated with slaving wars, the relationship of capital and inequality that had hampered West African kingdoms in global geopolitics, and the rise of transnational ideas coming from North Africa and Arabia as well as from the maroon communities in the New World – all combined to create an irresistible force that overthrew the status quo.

As we saw in the previous chapter, the first signs were felt in the Yorùbá state of Oyo, when, in 1817, the local military commander Afonja led an uprising in Ilorin, drawing on support from many who were ex-slaves. Eisami, the slave who had witnessed the 1808 invasion in Borno, had by this time been sold from person to person, until he reached the area of Oyo. Here, he witnessed the outbreak of the 1817 revolt led by Afonja: 'all of the slaves who went to war, became free', he noted; 'so when slaves learned these good news, they all ran there, and the Yorùbá saw it.' Samuel Ajayi Crowther, who was captured by the Fula Army in 1821, described how 'the army was composed of Foollahs, Yorriba Mahommedans and slaves of every description who had run away from their masters. These collected into an army of about 20,000 having strong swift horses.' The ex-slaves wanted to break down the old order. In 1835, Oyo would eventually fall, and the Yorùbá refugees from Old Oyo would found new settlements at Abeokuta and elsewhere, which became the kernel of Yorùbá societies in colonial and postcolonial Nigeria.[67]

Across West Africa, the class of literate Fula scholars held power in many places. In Mâssina, a small kingdom on the Niger between Djenné and Timbuktu, a new almamate was founded in 1817 after a *jihād* led by Ahmad Lobbo. This had long been an area of Fula chiefdoms, but, during the eighteenth century, they had been subordinate to Segu. Now, with the reform movement sweeping through West Africa, Mâssina declared independence and Segu's boundaries shrank. Lobbo deliberately sought the shehu's blessing before beginning his campaign, and, after Mâssina had broken from Segu, sent out annual expeditions to ensure independence was maintained.[68]

Literacy in these communities was widespread among both men and women. Far to the west of Oyo, in the Fuuta Jaalo Mountains, Fula (Fulfulde) was becoming a vernacular written language using Arabic script, with epic poems composed in the middle of the nineteenth century about faith, law and proper behaviour. Theophilus Conneau, visiting Fuuta Jaalo in 1826, wrote that many women there could read the Qur'ān. The interconnections with events in Sokoto were clear (as in Senegambia), for the son of the Almamy of Fuuta Jaalo, whom Conneau met on the Pongo River, was called Ahmadu Bello.[69]

To the north of the Pongo, in the Gambia River region, the same pattern also developed. As we have seen, the oral literatures make it clear that by this time there a strong division between rum-drinking practitioners of African religions and Muslims. As one 1790–91 account of the Kingdom of Wuuli, on the Upper North Bank of the Gambia, puts it: 'Two different sects of religion [exist] . . . the one is composed of the professors of the Mahomedan faith . . . the other, and it is said, the most numerous, consists of those who, denying the mission of the Prophet, avow themselves deists, and from the custom of drinking with freedom the liquors of which he prohibited the use, are denominated Soninkees, or drinking men.'[70]

The first decades of the nineteenth century saw the decay of the old ruling elites here and the growing power and number of Muslims. By the 1830s, Wuuli was under attack from the theocracies that had grown in Fuuta Tòòro and Bundu. By the 1850s, kingdoms on the south bank of the Gambia were paying tribute to the Fula theocracy in Fuuta Jaalo, and its capital at Timbo. There were Muslim clerics in nearly all the states of the Senegambia, and all of them were in touch with the new leaders of Mâssina, Sokoto and Fuuta Jaalo. In the 1840s, Muslims living in the Casamance called for Fula assistance from Fuuta Jaalo to overthrow the Soninké, and, by 1850, the marabout class controlled the area. The Soninké state near the estuary of the Gambia River in the Kombo region was in collapse; Fodé Kaba in the south and Omar Tal in the north led large armies and overthrew what remained.[71]

Just as was the case in Mâssina, and in Fuuta Jaalo, there were strong links between the revolutions in Sokoto and these transformations in Senegambia. Omar Tal made a pilgrimage to Mecca in the 1820s, and spent time in Borno, Hausaland, Mâssina and the Fuuta Jaalo Mountains on his return home towards Senegambia. He visited Gambia in 1850 and met with powerful local leaders, including Maba Diakhou of the north bank state of Badibu. The principle of religious revival was being taught by clerics in many Wolof states in the north of the region, where many of the same social and religious conditions pertained as elsewhere: a large slave class, a desire for renewal and hatred of the corrupt aristocratic class that had subsisted off inequalities for so long.[72]

Thus, in a huge region spreading from what are now Nigeria and Mali to Guinea-Conakry, Gambia and Senegal, the first half of the nineteenth century saw a comprehensive overturning of the established order through the vehicle of Islamic theological renewal. The enormous popularity of this reform movement captures the yearning that many people had for a new beginning, and the sloughing off of the old habits of elite corruption and predation on the weaker classes of society. If this meant the killing off of the old shrines and religious practices, it was a price that many were now willing to pay, associating these as they did with the excesses of their old rulers.

The rise of the slave trade, and the material frameworks that sustained it, had enhanced the power of this aristocratic elite. The resentment that rose against it was all the more bitter because of it. But this did not mean that the society that emerged in the nineteenth century would necessarily be any the fairer.

CONCLUSION: REFORMING THE SYSTEM OR REPRODUCING IT?

In January 2000, I walked with a friend from one village in the Fuuta Jaalo Mountains of Guinea-Conakry to another. I had stayed several days in his village, and was now planning to walk for a day to a town in the valley. When we reached the neighbouring village, my friend told me in a low voice that the people in this village were the slaves of those who lived in his own village.

In most parts of West Africa to this day, it is well known who comes from the background of a slave family and who does not.

Marriages can easily be broken off if those from a noble family decide that it would be too great a stain on their honour if a child marries into a slave family. Thus, the movements that drove forward the triumph of the Islamic reformers did not bring about the real change that many of those who took part in them had hoped for. Instead, the old models of dependence and coerced agricultural labour persisted, and were then renewed with the rise of colonialism; and the memory of them endures to this day.

Slavery and injustice did not somehow disappear following the movements of revolution that we have seen in this chapter. In fact, slavery as an institution increased in West Africa during the nineteenth-century era of what has been called 'the crisis of adaptation'. With the shutting down of Atlantic trade, captives were no longer exportable from the ports of West Africa, but the processes that had created them did not vanish overnight. Instead, coerced labour was used to increase agricultural output and the supply of produce to the European traders in the era of what is called 'legitimate trade'. According to a recent estimate, the slave population in West Africa became comparable to that of the Americas by 1850, with between a quarter and a half of the population of Sokoto enslaved by that time. Islamic reform movements were great vehicles for producing slaves working in Africa, as previous warrior movements had produced captives for the Atlantic and Saharan trades.[73]

How this worked in practice is shown in many accounts. The trader Theophilus Conneau provides a detailed portrait of the way in which the new Fula theocracy of Fuuta Jaalo worked with the slave trade. Walking up towards the capital at Timbo in 1827, Conneau wrote how 'our caravan marched in single file. The branded slaves formed the vanguard; two men escorted them, cutlass in hand and each armed with a well-loaded gun.' Near Timbo, there were numerous slave towns, which were abandoned completely when a caravan appeared with European traders, owing to the fears of the slaves that they would be sold into the Atlantic trade – an infinitely worse fate, as was widely known. As in so many parts of West Africa by the nineteenth century, all the agricultural work was done by these slaves, whose villages 'were surrounded by plantations and patches of gardens'.[74]

In Sokoto, large numbers of plantations worked by slaves were needed to harvest the cotton used in the textile industry. Kano's textile industry expanded hugely in the nineteenth century, with a centrally planned economy from the caliphate's leadership beginning under Muhammed Bello, and an abundant supply of slave labour. Meanwhile, Kano's demand for stimulants that were lawful in Islam saw a rising kola-nut trade from the forests controlled by Asante, and stabilized the power both of Asante and of the merchant class in linking the two regions.[75]

One of the major entrepôts of this trade was Salaga, which was close to the Asante capital at Kumasi. Salaga was, like most trading towns in West Africa from the sixteenth through to the nineteenth century, a place where peoples speaking many different languages and of many different backgrounds converged. Salaga was long a slave-trading centre, and remnants of the trade can still easily be found in the town today, including fetters and wells for water for the captives. However, in the nineteenth century, a different trade took over. As one *ta'rīkh* from Gonja put it, 'Salaga became a big town with a population of different races.' The Hausa came for kola nuts, their Beriberi traders asked for land, and there they met people from Borgu (on the borderlands of modern Burkina Faso and Nigeria), Borno, Nupe and Yorùbá. As in many parts of West Africa, a unifying feature for these people was the shared practice of the Islamic faith. Mixed religious practices followed, but the region would never be quite the same again.[76]

It is interesting to conclude by asking which areas rejected Islam. Two main features characterized this trend. In the first place, these communities tended to be close to the coast, and closer to Atlantic ties. In coastal communities, power still remained decentralized in some places (as in, for example, the Niger Delta and the Guinea-Bissau region), and thus a sweeping movement of reform and conquest found it difficult to succeed. On top of this, the close proximity of a proto-colonial presence in areas such as Freetown, Luanda, Monrovia and Lagos made it hard for the reform movement to gain traction. In Kongo and Angola, of course, Islam had never been a powerful presence, even though this area was probably connected to early-medieval trade routes. In new towns such as Freetown, Monrovia and St Louis, meanwhile, the increasingly militarized presence of European traders, backed up by the Royal Naval Squadron in the case of the British, and by the military exploits of Faidherbe and others in the case of the French, ensured that Christian missionaries gained ground. In some of these areas, African religious movements such as secret societies and spirit shrines remained.

Alternatively, in the second place, those areas that did not fall to Islamic reform tended to be in powerful states such as Asante and Dahomey. These states had grown as fiscal-military entities through the eighteenth century, partly as a result of their ability to retain gold and pay for a powerful standing army. While they could no longer act like this in the nineteenth century, they still remained strong, at first. Gradually, however, the mass import of the new *annulus* cowrie combined with the export of gold, saw a progressive inflation and a deteriorating economic situation. The development of the breech-loading rifle in the 1860s and the new balance of economic power meant that none of these states would be able to resist the rise of formal colonial control when it got under way in the 1880s.

Conclusion

At the height of the Abolitionist controversy in Britain, in the 1790s, the Scottish surgeon and slave trader Archibald Dalzel wrote *The History of Dahomy*, one of the first histories of an African state written by a European. Dalzel was in favour of the slave trade and wanted to halt the Abolitionist engine in its tracks. He alighted on the ruse of inventing a speech that he attributed to the Dadá of Dahomey, Kpengla, and said had been made to the English governor, Abson, at Ouidah. Having been shown some of the Abolitionist pamphlets then circulating, Kpengla ridiculed the Abolitionist movement. It was an absurdity, he said (through the rather less than trustworthy mouth of Dalzel), to suppose that ending the trade would prevent wars, since he had never embarked on a war just to get trade goods. Dalzel continued this 'speech':

> What hurts me most is that some of your people have maliciously represented us in books, which never die, alledging, that we sell our wives and children, for the sake of procuring a few kegs of brandy. No, we are shamefully belied; and I hope you will contradict from my mouth, the scandalous stories that have been propagated; and tell posterity that we have been abused. We do, indeed, sell to the white man a part of our prisoners, and we have a right so to do. And are we to blame, if we send delinquents to a far country? I have been told, you do the same . . . for a parcel of men with long heads, to sit down in England, and forme laws for us, and pretend to dictate how we are to live, of whom they know nothing, never having been in a black man's country in the whole course of their lives, is to me somewhat extraordinary.[1]

Modern historians view Kpengla's 'speech' with the jaundiced eyes of people who have read rather too many justifications for what cannot be justified. Yet the content is revealing. Certainly, many African kings were opposed to Abolition, and when Bowdich visited Kumasi and met the asantehene in 1817, the asantehene proposed a treaty in which the slave trade would be renewed. In this case, even though Dalzel probably invented the tenor of this discussion to promote his own aims, it is clear that, for the audience of a pro-slavery activist, it was entirely plausible that an African king would make such a speech. And, moreover, some caustic phrases and home truths stick, as if Dalzel had heard them from Fon interpreters in Dahomey; for the 'parcel of men with long heads' would, in due course, indeed, during the Scramble for Africa, sit down and devise laws and borders for countries they had never visited, a process that in many ways continued the paternalistic zeal of the Abolitionist movement.[2]

As the struggle in Britain over the abolition of the slave trade was being waged to its conclusion, in 1807, the new science of economics was gaining traction. The disciples of Adam Smith cited the approach of enlightened self-interest as the rational ground for economic activity, a progression from the 'barter' economy whence all commerce had begun. The notion of a barter economy was surely influenced by the perception of economic exchanges in Africa, that baubles and 'stuff' were 'swapped' for enslaved persons and gold. The huge profits that could be made from this trade certainly made rational self-interest seem the most logical explanation of economic activity, to scholars sitting in armchairs by warm fires in Great Britain, rationally promoting the self-interest of their own careers. Similarly, the philosophy that suggests that free trade promotes wealth, and that more trade promotes more wealth, made perfect sense from such comfy perches.

The intervening two centuries, however, have made several planks in these foundational premises of economics seem very shaky. In the first place, the idea of a 'barter economy' is a gross simplification of the types of exchanges that actually went on in pre-industrial economies. In West and West-Central Africa, there was no such thing as barter during the entire era of the Atlantic slave trade. As we have seen, there were monetized economies that used a variety of different currencies. There were complex credit frameworks, and set rates of exchange for various currencies at various times and in various places. Meanwhile, from the sixteenth to the eighteenth centuries, it was usually the African rulers who were the most active proponents of free trade, wanting all European nations to trade in their ports, while individual European merchant companies resisted this and sought preferential access. And yet such belief in free trade did nothing to secure African states a greater share of wealth in this period, even if oftentimes their leaders could ally with the outsiders to make rich pickings at the expense of their subjects, in a striking anticipation of the economics of neo-colonialism.

But, secondly, the twenty-first century has made it quite plain that people in general do not always take decisions in their own 'rational economic self-interest'. They will vote for options that economic rationality suggests will make them poorer. The fact is that economic choices are also ineluctably connected to perceptions of value, and that concepts of value retain moral as well as material economic meanings – which is what explains electoral choices. This can be seen especially when it comes to the issue of credit and capital. As this book has shown, understanding the moral coding of 'credit' is vital to making sense of economic transitions in the slave-trade era, in Africa and Europe. Rebalancing a credit/capital cycle that began through 'cashing out' the violence involved in enslaving African captives may, therefore, involve more than 'pragmatic' decisions grounded in the political economy. It may involve something more fundamental: namely, questioning the moral value attributed to the credit system that underpins modern economics, which, as we have seen, was initially associated with the violence required to 'cash out' credit in the trade in captives.[3]

The place of contrasting ideas of value in making sense of economic exchanges has turned out to be fundamental in this book. Why did Africans export gold in exchange for cloths, copper manillas and cowries? Because cloths, copper manillas and cowries had multiple economic and religious uses, and developed over time greater value in many African societies. Why did Europeans, on the other hand, export the many manufactures that they invested so much effort in procuring and making? Because the creation of capital and surplus value through the circuits of long-distance trade came to hold greater value than these material objects themselves, as the capital structure of the Atlantic system took hold in the sixteenth and seventeenth centuries. Money became a 'universal' value, a process that began in the sixteenth century, alongside the development of universal grammars such as Antonio de Nebrija's of Spanish, objective maps such as Mercator's projection and the emergence of the universal 'natural sciences'. Objective equivalences could circulate, through the equivalence provided by an expansion of the importance of number. This was the particular type of value that came to produce capital, and saw economic capital's importance grow through the sixteenth and seventeenth centuries.[4]

This conclusion elucidates one of the core paradoxes of economic theory as it relates to African history. We have seen how trade boomed, and all kinds of things were traded in precolonial West and West-Central Africa; 'for hundreds of years, the people of this country have had the honour of trading with the Noble and Polite Nations,' as the ruler of Allada wrote to the Portuguese king in 1810. Yet how can it be the case that an expansion of trade on the one hand provoked less access to the wealth of capital on the other? Indeed, since it is so impossible to square this conclusion with much conventional economic theory, economic historians have not tried to do so. The dynamism of precolonial African economies is stressed by these 'formalists', who argue that the dynamism is proof of market economies long before European colonialism, that economic self-interest dictated African economic choices every bit as much as was the case in Europe, and that to freight cultural frameworks into economic choices is to 'primitivize' African cultures and their decisions.[5]

However, economic and cultural frameworks are inextricably connected. This argument that African economies were 'rational' and market-orientated was developed in the 1970s, when the rationality of Western economic models to which all should aspire was unquestioned. At that time, it seemed important to show how African economic actors had partaken in the rationality of economic activities, like those Europeans with whom they traded. Yet, in the intervening decades, such universalism has come to look rather less assured. Rational economics seems to lead to some rather irrational ends, such as galloping climate change and resource depletion, which will make any future 'growth' impossible. Moreover, it has become clear that people don't make 'rational economic choices' all the time, but rather make choices that depend on their values, beliefs and also – why not? – their material interests. In this light, demanding that African economic histories match up to formalist economic rationality looks rather dated. It is to expect them to adhere to a conceptual standard that, it has become clear, needs rethinking. Indeed, the most far-sighted economists, such as 2017 Nobel prize-winning economist Richard Thaler, have begun to do exactly that, recognizing the myth of *Homo economicus* that yet underpins most economic modelling.[6]

In fact, understanding the moral as well as the economic import of value is vital to understanding what happened in precolonial Africa. Just as credit has always involved moral as well as economic dimensions, the same is true of value, and whatever betokens it. Currencies are tokens of value, and this is why they can hold different types of meaning – economic, religious and practical. That is why cloths can be traded, cowries stored in treasuries as well as used in divination and *Ile Orís*, and gold minted as coins or displayed in altarpieces. The continuing multiple uses of currencies in Africa meant that the reductive economic value increasingly attributed to currencies by European empires produced growing capital differentials. This was exacerbated by the trade of currencies that were losing economic value globally – such as cowries and cloths – for those that were either gaining or producing surplus value, such as gold and human beings.

From a purely economic perspective, therefore, the gathering divergence between African and Western economies also makes sense. When currency imports to Africa were not matched by trade goods, there was inflation of currencies used in Africa and their relative depreciation. When trade goods were also imported, these competed with local production and reduced extensive exports of African manufactures. This declining export deterred investment in those societies that did retain capital, such as the gold hoarded in Katsina, and the silver used to make necklaces in Senegambia. Thus, where there were stores of capital, these were not invested in manufacturing for economic reasons to do with the trade balance, since there was a reduced incentive compared with other types of value.

In spite of all of this, manufacturing still existed widely in different parts of West Africa by 1800. As we have seen, many different peoples produced beautiful cloths, and this continued long into the nineteenth century. In Sierra Leone in the 1790s, Mandinkas produced ink and Fulas soap, while there were also bricks made locally. Remarkable swords were manufactured on the Gold Coast in the 1780s, and, moreover, only these swords could be used in warfare 'because those that come from Europe are not considered worth using for any other purpose than to chop wood'. Beautiful swords were also manufactured in Benin, Kongo and many other regions. We have already seen, too, how muskets were being made in Kano in the late eighteenth century. Where capital was invested, manufacturing moved ahead, but it could not compete with the growing industrialization of Europe because of the capital differentials that had already grown up.[7]

Thus, in this book we have seen the dynamism of precolonial African economies, which did manufacture, trade and innovate in terms of production. But we have also seen the growing gulf between these economies and those of the European empires, which would move on to take formal colonial control as the nineteenth century dragged itself out. In many parts of West and West-Central Africa, these dynamics produced resentment and anger, and drove the revolutions that overtook the region, as people sloughed off the aristocracies that had emerged to prey on them in the preceding centuries.

The consequences of these transformations were huge, and not only in Africa. The fall of the Oyo Empire at the hands of the Sokoto *jihād* led to many Muslims being transported as captives to the New World, and especially to Brazil and Cuba, where the slave trade persisted long into the nineteenth century. Texts written in Arabic and in Ajami (Hausa or Manding written in Arabic) script in the nineteenth century by slaves are not infrequently found in Brazil, and at least eighteen books in Arabic were confiscated during the 1835 Malé Uprising in Salvador da Bahia, with many more Arabic papers confiscated in Porto Alegre, in southern Brazil, in 1838. When Abd al-Rahmān al-Baghdādī, an imam from the Ottoman Empire, visited Rio de Janeiro in 1866, he said there were at least 500 people in the city who knew part of the Qur'ān.[8]

In Brazil, Islam came to be associated with struggle against slavery. Many of the rebels from Salvador were deported back to Lagos after the 1835 revolt. With the collapse of Oyo, Lagos was becoming the most important market in Yorùbá areas, ready to become one of Africa's super-cities. Meanwhile, Islam was being adopted by the dispossessed as a religion of struggle to resist inequality and the rising power of capitalism. As inequalities had grown, so had more and more people converted, drawing on this religion to fight back. This relationship is not something that seems to have become any the less prevalent over the years, and offers pause for thought as both inequalities and military ideologies of *jihād* grow again in the twenty-first century: the history of West Africa suggests that weakening the latter requires addressing the former.[9]

States that resisted these transformations in West Africa in the nineteenth century were those that had had the strongest capital and military base. Asante and Dahomey shifted from retaining gold to exporting it, and from exporting slaves to using slave labour to develop plantation economies. It was not difficult for European colonialism to impose cash crops in the twentieth century, since this had already begun in the nineteenth century with the export of cotton, palm oil and peanuts, continuations in effect from the export of food that had begun with the Atlantic slave trade. These states were able to resist because of their tax and fiscal base. With a long history of tax collection for the development of the army and the state, they were able to prevent the rise of local militias. A strong state funded by tax was the best way of preventing disorder and revolution. The creation of stable, taxing states had a long precolonial history, something that is not irrelevant to the importance of creating stable, well-fiscalized states in the postcolonial era.

Yet, at the same time, although models for these states and for political stability exist, the precolonial state was often one that developed on a predatory model. As we have seen, enormous divisions grew up between rulers and subjects, a model that was further entrenched in the era of formal colonialism. Thus, what contemporary political scientists of Africa analyse as 'problems of the state' – 'state failure', 'narco-states', 'safe havens for terrorists' – have deep historical roots. African peoples learnt to have a deep distrust for the state owing to its historical role in creating predatory economic and political patterns. They did not want to hand over to the state the monopoly of violence that is a prerequisite for state success, when that violence had often been used against them. Overcoming this pattern requires deeper thought and activity than a merely immediate analysis of 'proximate' causes, effects and 'solutions'. For, in Africa, suspicion of the state is steeped in centuries of inequality, predation, and the construction of systems of governance that reproduce those structures.

There is so much to learn, therefore, from precolonial West and West-Central Africa. Yet, in Africa itself, the subject has fallen off the syllabi of many universities and schools. In Nigeria, from 2009 to 2016, History was removed as a subject from the secondary-school syllabus, while in many famous universities, such as the Université Cheikh Anta Diop in Dakar, Fourah Bay College in Freetown and Ibadan in Nigeria, there are few specialists researching this more distant past. The focus is on the present, and on the problems of the present, as it is in the overwhelming number of universities where African history is taught, from the UK and the US to Brazil. Where older African history is taught in the West, it is almost always as this relates to slavery, repeating an old trope of primitivism and oppression. Yet African history is much more complex than this allows; and the root causes of many of the problems of the present lie precisely in this more distant past.

How can meaning be made of this difficult, painful, complex and yet also inspiring history today? In his moving study of the art and ritual of the Afro-Cuban religion of Santería, David H. Brown describes how he first began to explore his subject:

> In the early 1980s, I began exploring the botánicas of Hudson County, New Jersey, and the boroughs of New York for Yorùbá religious iconography. The botánica is the principal retail outlet for Afro-Cuban religious images and ingredients . . . I was trying to identify which iconography was 'African' amid a welter of mass-produced objects and homemade assemblages including candles, flowers, oils, gourds, good-luck sprays, incense, little metal tools, cow horns, beaded baseball bats, dried flying bats, hunting traps, rococo soup tureens, rosaries, tourist machetes from Puerto Rico and maracas from

> Mexico, black plastic dolls in colourful skirts, iron cauldrons, conch shells . . .[10]

Why so much manufactured junk for religious worship? The answer may be that using local values to build new meanings for objects was central to West African religious transformations. As Western trade goods were dumped in Africa, they were invested with symbolic religious meaning. As they acquired religious power, their heaping up in these piles in *botánicas* acquired spiritual value.[11]

This piling up of objects in the 'religious fetishes' was a mirror of truth to the commodity fetishism developing in the West. The inversion of values meant that, while African peoples imbued with religious meaning the new objects of value, in Western economies they were associated with economic values, and cashed out as surplus. Fetishism was objectified in the new commodities. Exchange of currency values mirrored transformations of moral values. Each side in the trade derived new forms of meaning, which were nonetheless deeply connected to one another, and would shape value systems long into the twentieth and the twenty-first centuries.

As Brown's story shows, by the twentieth century, just as from the eleventh to the nineteenth centuries, transformations in Africa were deeply globalized. It is, of course, inviting ridicule to try to construct one African narrative for such a long period, when there are so many. It has been one of the aims of this book to try to give a sense of these multiple histories, and yet at the same time show how they fit within a broader picture of world historical change through the economic dimension. It is this economic transformation and relationship to the world that can give a coherence to this picture, and speak to many ongoing debates of wide interest to this day.

Africa's place in 'connected histories' speaks loudly of the way in which similar processes unfolded in Africa, the Americas and Europe at key moments in world history. In this book we have seen how the rise of the 'fiscal-military' state in the seventeenth century, the overthrow of aristocracies in revolutions led by a trader class in the eighteenth century, the rise of gendered imbalances, and the connection to movements of Islamic reform in the eighteenth and nineteenth centuries occurred simultaneously in Africa and in other parts of the world, alongside the birth of global capitalism. People moved, connections crossed continents, and these links were forged. Africa has been so global for so long that its continued exclusion from 'world history' speaks volumes about misconceptions that have arisen outside the continent over so many centuries.

Such resonances and connections can seem to have come very late to the historical narrative when, as the griot Tayiru Banbera puts it, 'If the world were a human being / All its hair would now be grey.'[12]

But, like a politician or *mansa* seeking the history that suits them best, I find it better to take courage from a different griot, in the hope of fighting for another day and another view.

As Lansiné Diabaté of Kela in Mali put it:

The end of the day is not the end of the world.	*Ko lon ban ye jamanabanni ko tɛ.*[13]

Bibliography

ABBREVIATIONS

ACV, *A Collection of Voyages and Travels . . .*, 4 vols. (London, 1704)
AGI, Archivo General de las Indias, Seville
AGNB, Archivo General de la Nación, Bogotá
AGNL, Archivo General de la Nación, Lima
AGNSCL, Archivo General de la Nación, Santiago de Chile
AHN, Archivo Histórico Nacional, Madrid
AHU, Arquivo Histórico Ultramarino, Lisbon
APEB, Arquivo Público do Estado da Bahia, Salvador
ASM, Arquivo da Santa Casa de Misericórdia da Bahia, Salvador
BA, Biblioteca da Ajuda, Lisbon
BNM, Biblioteca Nacional de España, Madrid
CEA, N. Levtzion and J. F. P. Hopkins (eds.), *Corpus of Early Arabic Sources for West African History* (Princeton: Markus Wiener Publishers, 2000)
CU, Conselho Ultramarino (section of AHU)
DHA, *Documentos para a história do Açúcar*, 3 vols. (Rio de Janeiro: Serviço Especial de Documentação Histórica, 1954)
DHRJ, *Documentos históricos [de Rio de Janeiro]*, 110 vols. (Rio de Janeiro: Braggio & Reis, 1928–55)
GAA, Gemeentearchief, Amsterdam
IAN/TT, Instituto dos Arquivos Nacionais/Torre do Tombo, Lisbon
IHGB, Instituto de Histórico e Geográfico Brasileiro, Rio de Janeiro
KH, Koninklijk Huisarchief, The Hague
MMAI, António Brásio (ed.), *Monumenta missionaria africana. África ocidental*, 15 vols. (Lisbon: Agência Geral do Ultramar, 1952–88)
MMAII, António Brásio (ed.), *Monumenta missionaria africana. África ocidental: segunda série*, 7 vols. (Lisbon: Agência Geral do Ultramar, 1958–2004)
NA, Nationaal Archief, The Hague
NAA, Notarial Archive of the Gemeentearchief in Amsterdam

NCAC, National Centre for Arts and Culture, The Gambia
NT, Notaría Primera de Tunja, section of AGNB
OWIC, Oude West-Indische Compagnie, section of NA
PV, *Primeira visitação do Santo Officio ás partes do Brasil. Denunciações da Bahia, 1591–1593* (São Paulo: Homenagem de Paulo Prado, 1925)
SG, Sociedade de Geografia, Lisbon
SO-CO, Santo Ofício Contencioso (section of AGNL)
TNA, The National Archive, London, UK

FILMS

Identities in Greater Senegambia and Beyond: Interdisciplinary Approaches through History and Music in Dialogue, directed by Anna de Mutiis (2015): https://www.youtube.com/watch?v=DMytlZcXRwA.

Puigserver, Xavier, and Tomàs, Jordi (2014): *Kásuumaay: una experiència de pau a Casamance*. Production: GESA (Grup d'Estudi de les Societats Africanes) and ICIP (Institut Català Internacional per la Pau).

PUBLISHED PRIMARY SOURCES

A Collection of Voyages and Travels . . . (1704). London: Awnsham and John Churchill; 4 vols. (abbreviated as *ACV*).

Abitbol, Michel (ed. and trans.) (1982): *Tombouctou au milieu du XVIIIe siècle d'après la chronique de Mawlāy al-Qāsim B. Mawlāy Sulaymān*. Paris: G.-P. Maisonneuve et Larose.

Adanson, M. (1757): *Histoire naturelle du Sénégal* . . . Paris: Claude-Jean-Baptiste Bauche.

Africain, Jean Léon (1896–8): *Description de l'Afrique: tierce partie du monde* . . . Paris: Ernest Leroux; 3 vols.

Anguiano, Mateo de (1957): *Misiones capuchinas en África. Vol. 2: Misiones al reino de la Zinga, Benín, Arda, Guinea y Sierra Leona*. Madrid: Consejo Superior de Investigaciones Científicas.

Anonymous (1665): *The Golden Coast, or a Description of Guinney* . . . London: S. Speed.

Arnett, E. J. (ed. and trans.) (1922): *The Rise of the Sokoto Fulani, being a Paraphrase and in Some Parts a Translation of the* Infaku'l Maisuri *of Sultan Mohammed Bello*. Kano: Kano Emirate Printing Department.

Atkins, John (1970; first published 1735): *A Voyage to Guinea, Brazil, and the West Indies in His Majesty's Ships, the* Swallow *and* Weymouth . . . London: Frank Cass & Co.

Axelrod Winsnes, Selena (ed. and trans.) (1992): *Letters on West Africa and the Slave Trade: Paul Erdmann Isert's Journey to Guinea and the Caribbean Islands in Columbia (1788)*. Oxford: Oxford University Press for the British Academy.

Barros, João de (1945): *Ásia de João de Barros: primeira década*. Lisbon: Agência Geral das Colónias.

Behrendt, Stephen, Latham, A. J. H., and Northrup, David (eds.) (2010): *The Diary of Antera Duke, an Eighteenth-Century African Slave Trader*. Oxford: Oxford University Press.

Bellagamba, Alice, Greene, Sandra E., and Klein, Martin A. (eds.) (2013): *African Voices on Slavery and the Slave Trade. Vol. 1: The Sources*. Cambridge: Cambridge University Press.

Blake, John William (ed. and trans.) (1942): *Europeans in West Africa, 1450–1560: Documents to Illustrate the Nature and Scope of Portuguese Enterprise in West Africa, the Abortive Attempt of Castilians to Create an Empire There, and the Early English Voyages to Barbary and Guinea*. London: Hakluyt Society; 2 vols.

Bontinck, François (ed. and trans.) (1970): *Diaire congolais (1690–1701) de Fra Luca da Caltanisetta*. Louvain and Paris: Éditions Nauwelaerts.

——— (1964): *Brève relation de la fondation de la mission des Frères Mineurs capucins, du séraphique Père Saint François au Royaume de Congo, et des particularités, coutumes, et façons de vivre des habitants de ce royaume*. Louvain and Paris: Éditions Nauwelaerts.

Bosman, Willem (1967; first published 1705): *A New and Accurate Description of the Coast of Guinea: Divided into the Gold, the Slave, and the Ivory Coasts*. London: Frank Cass & Co.

Bowdich, T. Edward (1966; first published 1819): *Mission from Cape Coast Castle to Ashantee*. London: Frank Cass & Co.

Brásio, António (ed.) (1969): *História do reino do Congo (MS 8080 da Biblioteca Nacional de Lisboa)*. Lisbon: Centro de Estudos Históricos Ultramarinos.

——— ed. (1958–2004): *Monumenta missionaria africana. África ocidental: segunda série* (abbreviated as *MMAII*). Lisbon: Agência Geral do Ultramar; 7 vols.

——— ed. (1952–88): *Monumenta missionaria africana: África ocidental* (abbreviated as *MMAI*). Lisbon: Agência Geral do Ultramar; 15 vols.

Cadornega, António de Oliveira de (1972): *História geral das guerras angolanas, 1680*. José Matías Delgado (ed.). Lisbon: Agência Geral do Ultramar; 3 vols.

Calado, Manoel (1648): *O valeroso Lucideno e triumpho da liberdade*. Lisbon: Paulo Craesbeeck.

Camara, Seydou, and Jansen, Jan (eds.) (1999): *La Geste de Nankoman: textes sur la fondation de Naréna (Mali).* Leiden: Research School CNWS.

Carretta, Vincent (ed.) (2003): *Olaudah Equiano: The Interesting Narrative and Other Writings.* London: Penguin.

Cavazzi da Montecuccolo, Giovanni Antonio (1687): *Istorica descrizione de' tre' regni Congo, Matamba, et Angola, situati nell' Etiopia inferiore occidentale e delle missioni apostoliche esercitatevi da religiosi capuccini.* Bologna: Giacomo Monti.

Conneau, Theophilus (1977; first published 1854): *A Slaver's Log Book, or 20 Years' Residence in Africa.* London: Robert Hale Ltd.

Conrad, David C. (ed.) (1990): *A State of Intrigue: The Epic of Bamana Segu, according to Tayiru Banbera.* Oxford: Oxford University Press for the British Academy.

Coppier, Guillaume (1645): *Histoire et voyage des Indes occidentales.* Lyon: Jean Hugueton.

Cordeiro, Luciano (ed.) (1881): *Viagens, explorações e conquistas dos portuguezes: collecção de documentos.* Lisbon: Imprensa Nacional.

Corry, Joseph (1968; first published 1807): *Observations upon the Windward Coast of Africa . . .* London: Frank Cass & Co.

Cultru, P. (ed.) (1913): *Premier voyage du sieur de La Courbe fait à la coste d'Afrique en 1685.* Paris: Édouard Champion et Émile Larose.

Curtin, Philip D. (ed.) (1967): *Africa Remembered: Narratives by West Africans from the Era of the Slave Trade.* Madison: University of Wisconsin Press.

———, and Boulègue, Jean (eds.) (1974): 'Relation de Bambouc (1729) par Claude Boucard', *Bulletin de l'IFAN*, Série B, 36/2, 246–75.

Cuvelier, J. (ed. and trans.) (1953): *Relations sur le Congo du Père Laurent de Lucques (1700–1717).* Brussels: Institut Royal Colonial Belge, Section des Sciences Morales et Politiques.

———, and Jadin, L. (eds. and trans.) (1954): *L'Ancien Congo d'après les archives romaines (1518–1640).* Brussels: Académie Royale des Sciences Coloniales.

Dalzel, Archibald (1967; first published 1793): *The History of Dahomy, an Inland Kingdom of Africa.* London: Frank Cass & Co.

Dantzig, Albert van (ed. and trans.) (1978): *The Dutch and the Guinea Coast, 1674–1742: A Collection of Documents from the General State Archive at The Hague.* Accra: Ghana Academy of Arts and Sciences.

———, and Jones, Adam (eds. and trans.) (1987): *Pieter de Marees: Description and Historical Account of the Gold Kingdom of Guinea (1602).* Oxford: Oxford University Press for the British Academy.

Dapper, Olfert (1686): *Description de l'Afrique.* Amsterdam: Wolfgang, Waesberge, Boom & van Someren.

David, Pierre-Félix-Barthélemy (1974): *Journal d'un voiage fait en Bambouc en 1744*. Paris: Société Française d'Histoire d'Outre-Mer.

Delbée, Sieur de (1671): 'Journal du voyage du sieur Delbée . . .', in Vol. 2, 347–473, of *Relation de ce qui s'est passé, dans les isles & terre-ferme de l'Amérique, pendant la derniere guerre avec l'Angleterre, & depuis en execution du Traitté de Breda*. Paris: Gervais Clouzier; 2 vols.

Demanet, Abbé (1767): *Nouvelle histoire de l'Afrique françoise . . .* Paris: Duchesne and Lacombe.

Derive, Jean, and Dumestre, Gérard (eds.) (1999): *Des hommes et des bêtes: chants de chasseurs mandingues*. Paris: Association Classiques Africains.

Documentos históricos [de Rio de Janeiro] (1928–55): Rio de Janeiro: Braggio & Reis; 110 vols. (abbreviated as *DHRJ*).

Documentos para a história do Açúcar (1954): Rio de Janeiro: Serviço Especial de Documentação Histórica; 3 vols. (abbreviated as *DHA*).

Dumestre, Gérard (ed. and trans.) (1979): *La Geste de Ségou, racontée par des griots Bambara*. Paris: Armand Colin.

Durand, Jean-Baptiste-Léonard (1802): *Voyage au Sénégal . . .* Paris: Henri Agasse; 2 vols.

El-Wakkad, Mahmoud (ed. and trans.) (1961): 'Qissatu Salga tarīkhu Gonja: The Story of Salaga and the History of Gonja [1]', *Ghana Notes and Queries*, 3, 8–31.

Falconbridge, Alexander (1788): *An Account of the Slave Trade on the Coast of Africa*. London: J. Phillips.

Felner, Alfredo de Albuquerque (1933): *Angola: Apontamentos sôbre a ocupação e início do estabelecimento dos portugueses no Congo, Angola e Benguela, extraídos de documentos históricos*. Coimbra: Imprensa da Universidade.

Gaeta, Antonio da (1669): *La Maravigliosa Conversione alla santa fede di Cristo della Regina Singa, e del suo Regno di Matamba nell'Africa meridionale . . .* Naples: Giacinto Passaro.

Gamble, David P., and Hair, P. E. H. (eds.) (1999): *The Discovery of the River Gambra (1623), by Richard Jobson*. London: The Hakluyt Society.

Giesing, Cornelia, and Vydrine, Valentin (eds.) (2007): *Ta:rikh Mandinka de Bijini (Guinée-Bissau)*. Leiden: Brill.

Góis, Damião de (1949–55; first published 1566): *Crónica do Felicíssimo Rei D. Manuel*. Coimbra: Por Ordem da Universidade; 4 vols.

Hallett, Robin (ed.) (1964): *Records of the African Association, 1788–1831*. Edinburgh: Thomas Nelson & Sons.

Haynes, John (1706): *A View of the Present State of the Clothing Trade in England . . .* London: Printed for the Author.

Heintze, Beatrix (Vol. 1 (1985); Vol. 2 (1988)): *Fontes para a história de Angola do século XVII*. Stuttgart: Franz Steiner Verlag Wiesbaden GmbH; 2 vols.

Hiskett, Mervyn (1965): 'The "Song of Bagauda": A Hausa King List and Homily in Verse – II', *SOAS Bulletin*, 28/1, 112–35.

——— (1964): 'The "Song of Bagauda": A Hausa King List and Homily in Verse – I', *SOAS Bulletin*, 27/3, 540–67.

——— (ed. and trans.) (1963): *Tazyīn al-Waraqāt, by 'Abdullāh ibn Muḥammad*. Ibadan: Ibadan University Press.

——— (1960): '*Kitab al-farq*: A Work on the Habe Kingdoms Attributed to 'Uthmān dan Fodio', *SOAS Bulletin*, 23/3, 558–79.

——— (1957): 'Material Relating to the State of Learning among the Fulani before Their Jihād', *SOAS Bulletin*, 19/3, 550–78.

Hunwick, John O. (ed.) (2003): *The Writings of Western Sudanic Africa*. Leiden: Brill.

——— (ed. and trans.) (1999): *Timbuktu and the Songhay Empire: Al-Sa'dī's* Ta'rīkh al-sūdān *down to 1613 and Other Contemporary Documents*. Leiden: Brill.

——— (ed.) (1995): *The Writings of Central Sudanic Africa*. Leiden: Brill.

——— (ed. and trans.) (1985): *Sharī'a in Songhay: The Replies of Al-Maghīlī to the Questions of Askia al-Ḥājj Muḥammad*. Oxford: Oxford University Press for the British Academy.

Innes, Gordon (ed. and trans.) (1976): *Kaabu and Fuladu: Historical Narratives of the Gambian Mandinka*. London: School of Oriental and African Studies.

Jackson, James Grey (ed.) (1967; first published 1820): *An Account of Timbuctoo and Housa Territories in the Interior of Africa by El Hage Abd Salam Shabeeny*. London: Frank Cass & Co.

Jadin, Louis (1975): *L'Ancien Congo et l'Angola, 1639–1655, d'après les archives romaines, portugaises, néerlandaises et espagnoles*. Brussels and Rome: Institut Historique Belge de Rome.

——— (1966): *Rivalités luso-néerlandaises au Sohio, Congo, 1600–1675: tentatives missionnaires des récollets flamands et tribulations des Capuchins italiens, 1670–1675*. Excerpt from the *Bulletin de l'Institut Historique Belge de Rome*, 37, 137–361. Brussels and Rome: Academia Belgica

Jannequin, Claude (1643): *Voyage de Lybie au Royaume de Senega, le long du Niger, avec la description des habitans qui sont le lon [sic] de ce fleuve, leurs coûtumes & façons de vivre: les particularités les plus remarquables de ces pays*. Paris: Charles Rouillard.

Jansen, Jan, Duintjer, Esger, Tamboura, Boubacar (eds.) (1995): *L'Épopée de Sunjara d'après Lansine Diabate de Kela*. Leiden: Research School CNWS.

Jarric, Pierre du (1610–14): *Histoire des choses plus memorables advenues tant en Indes orientales, que autres païs de la descouverte des Portugais*. Bordeaux: Simon Millanges; 3 vols.

Johnson, Samuel (1937): *The History of the Yorubas: From the Earliest Times to the Beginning of the British Protectorate*. Lagos: CMS Bookshop.

Jones, Adam (ed. and trans.) (1985): *Brandenburg Sources for West African History, 1680–1700*. Stuttgart: Franz Steiner Verlag Wiesbaden GmbH.

——— (ed. and trans.) (1983): *German Sources for West African History, 1599–1669*. Wiesbaden: Franz Steiner Verlag GmbH.

Kingsley, Mary (2015; first published 1897): *Travels in West Africa: Congo Français, Corisco and Cameroons*. London and New York: Penguin Books.

Konadu, Kwasi (forthcoming): *Africa's Gold Coast through Portuguese Sources, 1471–1671*. Oxford: Oxford University Press for the British Academy.

Kup, Alexander Peter (ed.) (1967): *Adam Afzelius: Sierra Leone Journal, 1795–1796*. Uppsala: Studia Ethographica Upsaliensia.

La Fleur, James D. (ed.) (2000): *Pieter van den Broecke's Journal of Voyages to Cape Verde, Guinea and Angola (1605–1612)*. London: The Hakluyt Society.

La Roncière, Charles de (1924–7): *La Découverte de l'Afrique au moyen âge: cartographes et explorateurs*. Cairo: Société Royale de Géographie D'Égypte; 3 vols.

Labarthe, P. (1802): *Voyage au Sénégal, pendant les années 1784 et 1785 . . .* Paris: Dentu.

Lange, Dierk (ed. and trans.) (1987): *A Sudanic Chronicle: The Borno Expeditions of Idrīs Alauma (1564–1576) . . .* Stuttgart: Franz Steiner Verlag Wisebaden GmbH.

Law, Robin (ed.) (1997–2006): *The Local Correspondence of the Royal African Company of England, 1681–1699*. Oxford: Oxford University Press for the British Academy; 3 vols.

Lessa, Clado Ribeiro de (ed.) (1957): *Crônica de uma Embaixada Luso-Brasileira à Costa d'África em fins do século XVIII, incluindo o texto da Viagem de África em o Reino de Dahomé, escrita pelo Padre Vicente Ferreira Pires no ano de 1800 e até o presente inédita*. São Paulo: Companhia Editora Nacional.

Levtzion, N., and Hopkins, J. F. P. (eds.) (2000): *Corpus of Early Arabic Sources for West African History* (abbreviated as *CEA*). Princeton: Markus Wiener Publishers.

Mauny, Raymond (ed.) (1956): *Esmeraldo de situ orbis: côte occidentale d'Afrique du Sud Marocain au Gabon, par Duarte Pacheco Pereira (vers 1506–1508)*. Bissau: Centro de Estudos da Guiné Portuguesa.

Moore, Francis (1738): *Travels into the Inland Parts of Africa . . .* London: D. Henry & R. Cave; second edition.

Naber, S. P. L'Honoré (1931): *Het laerlyck verhael van Johannes de Laet 1624–1636. Vol. 1: 1624–1626*. 's-Gravenhage: Martinus Nijhoff; 4 vols.

——— (1913): *Toortse der zee-vaart, door Dierick Ruiters 1623.* 's-Gravenhage: Martinus Nijhoff.

Neves, António Rodrigues (1854): *Memoria da expedição a Cassange commandada pelo Major Graduado Francisco de Salles Ferreira em 1850.* Lisbon: Imprensa Silviana.

Norris, Robert (1968; first published 1789): *Memoirs of the Reign of Bossa Ahádee, King of Dahomy, an Inland Country of Guiney, to which are Added the Author's Journey to Abomey, the Capital, and a Short Account of the African Slave Trade.* London: Frank Cass & Co.

'Nota van Pieter Mortamer over het gewest Angola', *Bijdragen en Mededeelingen van het Historisch Genootschap*, 54 (1933).

Ogilby, John (ed. and trans.) (1670): *Olfert Dapper: Africa, being an Accurate Description of . . .* London: Tho. Johnson.

Palmer, H. R. (ed. and trans.) (1931): *The Carthaginian Voyage to West Africa in 500 BC, together with Sultan Mohammed Bello's Account of the Origin of the Fulbe.* Bathurst [Banjul]: Government Printer.

——— (ed. and trans.) (1928): 'The Kano Chronicle', in his *Sudanese Memoirs*, Vol. 3, pp. 97–132. Lagos: Government Printer.

Palmer, Richmond (1936): *The Bornu Sahara and Sudan.* London: John Murray.

Park, Mungo (1983; first published 1799): *Travels into the Interior of Africa.* London: Eland.

Peres, Damião (ed.) (1990; first published 1953): *Duas descrições seiscentistas da Guiné de Francisco de Lemos Coelho.* Lisbon: Academia Portuguesa da História.

Piazza, Calogero (ed.) (1976): *La prefettura apostolica del Congo alla metà del XVII secolo: la relazione inedita di Girolamo da Montesarchio.* Milan: Dott. A. Giuffrè Editore.

Pigafetta, Filippo (1970; first published 1881): *A Report of the Kingdom of Congo and of the Surrounding Countries, Drawn out of the Writings and Discourses of the Portuguese Duarte Lopez by Filippo Pigafetta.* Marguerite Hutchinson (ed. and trans.) London: Frank Cass & Co.

Pombo, Ruela (1944): *Anais de Angola, 1630–1635: época de decadência . . .* Lisbon: Emprêsa da Revista 'Diogo-Caâo'.

Primeira visitação do Santo Officio ás partes do Brasil. Denunciações da Bahia, 1591–1593 (1925). São Paulo: Homenagem de Paulo Prado (abbreviated as *PV*).

Proyart, Abbé (1776): *Histoire de Loango, Kakongo, et autres royaumes d'Afrique.* Paris: C. P. Berton & N. Crapart.

Purchas, Samuel (1905–7): *Hakluytus Posthumus, or Purchas His Pilgrimes, Contayning a History of the World in Sea Voyages and Lande Travells by Englishmen and Others.* Glasgow: James MacLehose & Sons; 20 vols.

Ratelband, K. (ed.). (1959): *De Westafrikaanse reis van Piet Heyn, 1624–1625*. 's-Gravenhage: Martinus Nijhoff.

—— (ed.) (1953): *Vijf dagregisters van het kasteel São Jorge da Mina (Elmina) aan de Goudkust (1645–1647)*. 's-Gravenhage: Martinus Nijhoff.

Ravenstein, E. G. (ed.) (1901): *The Strange Adventures of Andrew Batell of Leigh, in Angola and the Adjoining Regions*. London: Hakluyt Society.

Rebello, Amador (ed.) (1588): *Alguns capitulos tirados das cartas que vieram este anno de 1588 dos Padres da Companhia de Jesu que andam nas partes da India, China, Japão, & Reino de Angola* ... Lisbon: Antonio Ribeyro.

Reichardt, Charles Augustus Ludwig (1876): *Grammar of the Fulde Language*. London: Church Missionary House.

Ruyter, Michiel de, and Meppelen, Jan Cornelis van (1665): *Journael gehouden op 's landts-schip de Spiegel* ... Amsterdam: Jacob Venckel.

Sandoval, Alonso de (1627): *Naturaleza, policia sagrada i profana, costumbres i ritos, disciplina i catechismo evangelico de todos Etiopes*. Seville: Francisco de Lira.

Santiago, Diogo Lopes de (1943): *História da guerra de Pernambuco e feitos memoráveis do mestre de campo João Fernandes Vieira* ... Recife: Imprensa Oficial de Recife.

Saugnier, M. (1791): *Relations de plusieurs voyages à la Côte d'Afrique, a Maroc, au Sénégal, a Gorée, a Galam, etc.* ... Paris: Gueffier jeune.

Schouten, Willem (1618): *Journal ou description du merveilleux voyage de Guillaume Schouten, Hollondois natif de Hoorn, fait es années 1615, 1616, & 1617*. Amsterdam: Guillaume Janson.

Seydou, Christiane (ed. and trans.) (1991): *Bergers des mots: poésie peule du Mâssina*. Paris: Association Classiques Africains.

—— (1976): *La Geste de Ham-Bodêdio ou Hama le Rouge*. Paris: Armand Colin.

Silveira, Luís (ed.) (1945): *Peregrinação de André de Faro à Terra dos Gentios*. Lisbon: Officina da Tipographia Portugal-Brasil.

Smith, William (1967; first published 1744): *A New Voyage to Guinea*. London: Frank Cass & Co.

Soares, J. C. de Macedo (1958): *Livro primeiro do govêrno do Brasil, 1607–1633*. Rio de Janeiro: Imprensa Nacional.

Soh, Siré-Abbâs- (1913): *Chroniques du Foûta sénégalais*. Maurice Delafosse and Henri Gaden (trans.). Paris: Ernest Leroux.

Sow, Alfâ Ibrâhîm (ed.) (1971): *Le Filon du bonheur éternel, par Tierno Mouhammadou-Samba Mombéyâ*. Paris: Armand Colin.

Stone, Thora G. (ed.) (1924): 'The Journey of Cornelius Hodges in Senegambia, 1689–90', *English Historical Review*, 39/153, 89–95.

Tovar, Joseph Pellicer de (1649): *Mission evangelica al reyno de Congo . . .* Madrid: Domingo Garcia i Morràs.

Wilks, Ivor, Levtzion, Nehemia, and Haight, Bruce M. (eds.) (1986): *Chronicles from Gonja: A Tradition of West African Muslim Historiography*. Cambridge: Cambridge University Press.

SECONDARY SOURCES

Acemoglu, Daron, Johnson, Simon, and Robinson, James A. (2002): 'Reversal of Fortune: Geography and Institutions in the Making of the Modern World Income Distribution', *Quarterly Journal of Economics*, 117, 1,231–94.

Achebe, Nwando (2011): *The Female King of Colonial Nigeria: Ahebi Ugbabe*. Bloomington: Indiana University Press.

Adebayo, A. G. (1994): 'Money, Credit, and Banking in Precolonial Africa: The Yoruba Experience', *Anthropos*, 89/4–6, 379–400.

Adu-Boahen, Kwabena (2012): 'The Impact of European Presence on Slavery in the Sixteenth to Eighteenth-Century Gold Coast', *Transactions of the Historical Society of Ghana*, New Series, 14, 165–99.

Akinjogbin, I. A. (1967): *Dahomey and Its Neighbours, 1708–1818*. Cambridge: Cambridge University Press.

Alao, Abiodun (2016): 'Africa: A Voice to Be Heard, Not a Problem to be Solved', inaugural lecture at King's College London, 26 April 2016.

Alencastro, Luiz Felipe de (1980): 'L'Empire du Brésil', in Maurice Duverger (ed.), *Le Concept d'Empire*, 301–10. Paris: Presses Universitaires de France.

Alpern, Stanley B. (2011): *Amazons of Black Sparta: The Women Warriors of Dahomey*. New York: NYU Press.

Anderson, Robert Welson (1996): 'The *Quilombo* of Palmares: A New Overview of a Maroon State in Seventeenth-Century Brazil', *Journal of Latin American Studies*, 28/3, 545–66.

Appiah, Kwame Anthony (2010): *The Honor Code: How Moral Revolutions Happen*. New York: W. W. Norton & Company.

Apter, Andrew (2017): 'History in the Dungeon: Atlantic Slavery and the Spirit of Capitalism in Cape Coast Castle, Ghana', *American Historical Review*, 122/1, 23–54.

Aranzadi, Isabela de (2010): 'A Drum's Trans-Atlantic Journey from Africa to the Americas and Back after the End of Slavery: Annobonese and Fernandino Musical Cultures', *African Sociological Review*, 14/1, 20–47.

Araujo, Ana Lucia (2012): 'Dahomey, Portugal, and Bahia: King Adandozan and the Atlantic Slave Trade', *Slavery & Abolition*, 33/1, 1–19.

Argenti, Nicholas (2007): *The Intestines of the State: Youth, Violence, and Belated Histories in the Cameroon Grassfields*. Chicago: University of Chicago Press.

Arhin, Kwame (1995): 'Monetization and the Asante State', in Jane I. Guyer (ed.), *Money Matters: Instability, Values and Social Payments in the Modern History of West African Communities*, 97–110. London: James Currey.

Assadourian, Carlos Sempat (1966): *El tráfico de esclavos en Córdoba de Angola a Potosí, siglos XVI–XVII*. Córdoba, Argentina: Dirección General de Publicaciones.

Assunção, Matthias Röhrig (2005): *Capoeira: The History of an Afro-Brazilian Martial Art*. London: Routledge.

Atherton, John H., and Kalous, Milan (1970): 'Nomoli', *Journal of African History*, 11/3, 303–17.

Austen, Ralph A. (2010): *Trans-Saharan Africa in World History*. Oxford: Oxford University Press.

——— (1987): *African Economic History: Internal Development and External Dependency*. London: James Currey.

Austin, Gareth (2007): 'Reciprocal Comparison and African History: Tackling Conceptual Eurocentrism in the Study of Africa's Economic Past', *African Studies Review*, 50/3, 1–28.

Babalola, Abidemi Babatunde (2016): 'Rethinking Glass Bead Making and Interaction among Medieval West African Societies: Evidence from Ile-Ife, South-West Nigeria', paper presented at the African Studies Association Conference, Washington, DC, 1 December 2016.

Babou, Alhaji (2018): 'Sheriff Sheikhna Sheikh Mahfouz: the Man, the Myth, the Legend', manuscript presented at Banjul, ASAUK Writers' Workshop, 24 March 2018.

Bakchine-Dumont, Simonne (1979): 'Une inscription tumulaire hébraïque du Touat', *Revue des études juives*, 138/1–2, 143–6.

Balandier, Georges (1968): *Daily Life in the Kingdom of Kongo from the Sixteenth to the Eighteenth Century*. London: George Allen & Unwin Ltd.

Ballong-wen-Mewuda, J. Bato'ora (1993): *São Jorge da Mina, 1482–1637: la vie d'un comptoir portugais en Afrique occidentale*. Lisbon and Paris: Fondation Calouste Gulbenkian; 2 vols.

Balogun, Ismail A. B. (1975): *The Life and Works of 'Uthmān dan Fodio*. Lagos: Islamic Publications Bureau.

Barcia, Manuel (2014): *West African Warfare in Bahia and Cuba: Soldier Slaves in the Atlantic World, 1807–1844*. Oxford: Oxford University Press, 2014.

——— (2013): '"An Islamic Atlantic revolution": Dan Fodio's *Jihād* and Slave Rebellion in Bahia and Cuba, 1804–1844', *Journal of African Diaspora, Archaeology and Heritage*, 2/1, 6–17.

Barros, Philip Lynton de (2001): 'The Effect of the Slave Trade on the Bassar Ironworking Society, Togo', in Christopher R. DeCorse (ed.), *West Africa during the Atlantic Slave Trade: Archaeological Perspectives*, 59–80. London: Leicester University Press.

Barry, Boubacar (1998): *Senegambia and the Atlantic Slave Trade*, A. Kwei Armah (trans.). Cambridge: Cambridge University Press.

——— (1985): *Le Royaume du Waalo: le Sénégal avant la conquête*. Paris: Éditions Karthala.

Bathily, Abdoulaye (1989): *Les Portes de l'Or: le Royaume de Galam (Sénégal) de l'ère musulmane au temps de négriers (VIIIe–XVIIIe siècle)*. Paris: L'Harmattan.

Baum, Robert M. (1999): *Shrines of the Slave Trade: Diola Religion and Society in Precolonial Senegambia*. New York and Oxford: Oxford University Press.

Bay, Edna G. (1998): *Wives of the Leopard: Gender, Politics, and Culture in the Kingdom of Dahomey*. Charlottesville and London: University of Virginia Press.

Bazin, Jean (1974): 'War and Servitude in Segou', *Economy and Society*, 3/2, 107–44.

Becker, Charles, and Martin, Victor (1982): 'Kayor and Baol: Senegalese Kingdoms and the Slave Trade in the Eighteenth Century', in J. E. Inikori (ed.), *Forced Migration: The Impact of the Export Slave Trade on African Societies*, 100–125. London: Hutchinson.

Beckert, Sven (2014): *Empire of Cotton: A New History of Global Capitalism*. London: Allen Lane.

Bellagamba, Alice (2013): '"The little things that would please your heart . . .": Enslavement and Slavery in the Narrative of Al Hajj Bakoyo Suso (The Gambia)', in Alice Bellagamba, Sandra E. Greene and Martin A. Klein (eds.), *African Voices on Slavery and the Slave Trade. Vol. 1: The Sources*, 29–46. Cambridge: Cambridge University Press.

Bellman, Beryl L. (1984): *The Language of Secrecy: Symbols and Metaphors in Poro Ritual*. New Brunswick: Rutgers University Press.

Bennett, Herman L. (2003): *Africans in Colonial Mexico: Absolutism, Christianity and Afro-Creole Consciousness, 1570–1640*. Bloomington: Indiana University Press.

Benton, Lauren (2002): *Law and Colonial Cultures: Legal Regimes in World History, 1400–1900*. New York and Cambridge: Cambridge University Press.

Bernal, Antonio-Miguel (1992): *La financiación de la Carrera de Indias (1492–1824): dinero y crédito en el comercio colonial español con América*. Seville: Fundación el Monte.

Berzock, Kathleen Bickford (2008): *Benin: Royal Arts of a West African Kingdom*. New Haven and London: Yale University Press.

Bethencourt, Francisco (2011): 'Creolization of the Atlantic World: The Portuguese and the Kongolese', *Portuguese Studies*, 27/1, 56–69.

Bivar, A. D. H. (1961): 'The *Wathīqat ahl al-sūdān*: A Manifesto of the Fulani *Jihād*', *Journal of African History*, 2/2, 235–43.

Bockie, Simon (1993): *Death and the Invisible Powers: The World of Kongo Belief*. Bloomington: Indiana University Press.

Bolland, Rita (1991): *Tellem Textiles: Archaeological Finds from Burial Caves in Mali's Bandiagara Cliff*. Amsterdam: Royal Tropical Institute.

Boulègue, Jean (1987): *Le Grand Jolof (XIIIe–XVIe siècle)*. Blois: Édition Façades.

Boxer, C. R. (1973; first published 1957): *The Dutch in Brazil, 1624–1654*. Hamden: Archon Books.

——— (1952): *Salvador de Sá and the Struggle for Brazil and Angola, 1602–1686*. London: Athlone Press.

Bovill, E. W. (1958): *The Golden Trade of the Moors*. London: Oxford University Press.

Brandon, George (1993): *Santeria from Africa to the New World: The Dead Sell Memories*. Bloomington: Indiana University Press.

Brenner, Louis (1979): 'Muhammad al-Amīn al-Kānimī and Religion and Politics in Bornu', in John Ralph Willis (ed.), *Studies in West African Islamic History. Vol. 1: The Cultivators of Islam*, 160–76. London: Frank Cass & Co.

Brewer, John (1989): *The Sinews of Power: War, Money and the English State, 1688–1783*. London: Unwin Hyman.

Brivio, Alessandra (2013): 'Tales of Cowries, Money, and Slaves', in Bellagamba/Greene/Klein (eds.), *African Voices on Slavery and the Slave Trade. Vol. 1: The Sources*, 47–53. Cambridge: Cambridge University Press.

Brooks, George E. (2012): 'American Trade with Cabo Verde and Guiné, 1820s–1850s: Exploiting the Transition from Slave to Legitimate Commerce', in Toby Green (ed.), *Brokers of Change: Atlantic Commerce and Cultures in Precolonial Western Africa*, 307–32. Oxford: Oxford University Press for the British Academy.

——— (1993): *Landlords and Strangers: Ecology, Society, and Trade in Western Africa, 1000–1630*. Boulder: Westview Press.

Brown, David H. (2003): *Santería Enthroned: Art, Ritual, and Innovation in an Afro-Cuban Religion*. Chicago: University of Chicago Press.

Brown, Vincent (2008): *The Reaper's Garden: Death and Power in the World of Atlantic Slavery*. Cambridge, Mass.: Harvard University Press.

Budasz, Rogério (2007): 'Black Guitar-Players and Early African–Iberian Music in Portugal and Brazil', *Early Music*, 35/1, 3–21.

Cabral, Amilcar (1974): 'National Liberation and Culture', *Transition*, 45, 12–17.

Cabral de Mello, Evaldo (1998): *O negócio do Brasil: Portugal, os Países Baixos, e o Nordeste, 1641–1669*. Rio de Janeiro: Topbooks Editora.

Caldeira, Arlindo Manuel (1999): *Mulheres, sexualidade e casamento em São Tomé e Príncipe (séculos XV a XVIII)*. Lisbon: Edições Cosmos.

Candido, Mariana P. (2013): *An African Slaving Port and the Atlantic World: Benguela and Its Hinterland*. Cambridge: Cambridge University Press.

——— (2011): 'Slave Trade and New Identities in Benguela, 1700–1860', *Portuguese Studies Review*, 19/1–2, 59–75.

——— (2010): 'Different Slave Journeys: Enslaved African Seamen on Board of Portuguese Ships, *c.* 1760–1820s', *Slavery & Abolition*, 31/3, 395–409.

Candotti, Marisa (2015): 'Cotton Growing and Textile Production in Northern Nigeria: From Caliphate to Protectorate, *c.* 1804–1914'. London: School of Oriental and African Studies, PhD dissertation.

Capone, Stefania (2010): *Searching for Africa in Brazil: Power and Tradition in Candomblé*. Raleigh: Duke University Press.

Carney, Judith A. (2004): '"With grains in her hair": Rice in Colonial Brazil', *Slavery & Abolition*, 25/1, 1–27.

——— (2001): *Black Rice: The African Origins of Rice Cultivation in the Americas*. Cambridge, Mass.: Harvard University Press.

———, and Rosomoff, Richard Nicholas (2009): *In the Shadow of Slavery: Africa's Botanical Legacy in the Atlantic World*. Berkeley: University of California Press.

Carrigy, John (2017): 'Transcending Boundaries: John Dee's Imperial Literature in the Context of Elizabethan Scholarly Practice', paper presented at the conference 'Cross-disciplinary Approaches to the Study of Knowledge-making in the Early Modern World, 1450–1800', London, 14 October 2017.

Castillo, Lisa Earl, and Parés, Luis Nicolau (2010): 'Marcelina da Silva: A Nineteenth-Century Candomblé Priestess in Bahia', *Slavery & Abolition*, 31/1, 1–27.

Chasteen, John Charles (1996): 'The Prehistory of Samba: Carnival Dancing in Rio de Janeiro, 1840–1917', *Journal of Latin American Studies*, 28/1, 29–47.

Childs, Gladwyn M. (1970): 'The Chronology of the Ovimbundu Kingdoms', *Journal of African History*, 11/2, 241–8.

—— (1964): 'The Kingdom of Wambu (Huambo): A Tentative Chronology', *Journal of African History*, 5/3, 367–79.

Chouin, Gérard L. (2016): 'Rethinking the Chronology of Sungbo's Eredo: Recent Archaeological Investigations in Ijebuland', paper presented at the African Studies Association Conference, Washington, DC, 1 December 2016.

——, and DeCorse, Christopher R. (2010): 'Prelude to the Atlantic Trade: New Perspectives on Southern Ghana's Pre-Atlantic History (800–1500)', *Journal of African History*, 51/2, 123–45.

Cissoko, Sékéné Mody (1974): *Tombouctou et l'empire Songhay: épanouissement du Soudan nigérien aux XVe–XVIe siècles*. Paris: L'Harmattan.

Connah, Graham (1975): *The Archaeology of Benin: Excavations and Other Researches in and around Benin City, Nigeria*. Oxford: Clarendon Press.

Coolen, Michael Theodore (1982): 'The Fodet: A Senegambian Origin for the Blues?', *The Black Perspective in Music*, 10/1, 69–84.

Coquéry-Vidrovitch, Catherine (1971): 'De la traite des esclaves à l'exportation de l'huile de palme et des palmistes au Dahomey: XIXe siècle', in Claude Meillassoux (ed.), *The Development of Indigenous Trade and Markets in West Africa*, 107–23. London: Oxford University Press for the International African Institute.

—— (1969): 'Recherches sur un mode de production africaine', *La Pensée*, 144, 61–78.

Costa, Leonor Freire (2002): *O transporte no Atlântico e a Companhia Geral do Comércio do Brasil, 1580–1663*. Lisbon: Comissão Nacional para as Comemorações dos Descobrimentos Portugueses; 2 vols.

Curtin, Philip D. (1984): *Cross-Cultural Trade in World History*. Cambridge: Cambridge University Press.

—— (1975): *Economic Change in Precolonial Africa: Senegambia in the Era of the Slave Trade*. Madison: University of Wisconsin Press.

—— (1971): 'Jihad in West Africa: Early Phases and Inter-Relations in Mauritania and Senegal', *Journal of African History*, 12/1, 11–24.

Curto, José C. (2004): *Enslaving Spirits: The Portuguese–Brazilian Alcohol Trade at Luanda and Its Hinterland, c. 1550–1830*. Leiden: Brill.

Daaku, Kwame Yeboa (1970): *Trade and Politics on the Gold Coast, 1600–1720: A Study of the African Reaction to European Trade*. Oxford: Clarendon Press.

Dantzig, Albert van (1980): *Les Hollandais sur la Côte d Guinée, à l'époque de l'essor de l'Ashanti et du Dahomey, 1680–1740*. Paris: Société Française d'Histoire d'Outre-Mer.

Dewière, Rémi (2013): ' "Regards croisés entre deux ports de désert": l'enjeu des sources pour l'étud des relations entre Tripoli et le Sultana de Borno', *Hypothèses*, 16/1, 383–93.

Dobronravin, Nikolay (2016): 'Não só mandingas: *QaSīdat al-Burda*, poesia ascética (*Zuhdiyyāt*) e as *Maqāmāt* de al-Harīrī nos escritos dos negros muçulmanos no Brasil oitocentista', *Afro-Ásia*, 53, 185–226.

Domar, Evsey D. (1970): 'The Causes of Slavery or Serfdom: A Hypothesis', *Journal of Economic History*, 30/1, 18–32.

Dubois, Laurent (2016): *The Banjo: America's African Instrument*. Cambridge, Mass.: Harvard University Press.

——— (2004): *Avengers of the New World: The Story of the Haitian Revolution*. Cambridge, Mass.: Harvard University Press.

Duvall, Chris (2009): 'A Maroon Legacy? Sketching African Contributions to Live Fencing Practices in Early Spanish America', *Singapore Journal of Tropical Geography*, 30/2, 232–47.

Ekholm, Kasja (1972): *Power and Prestige: The Rise and Fall of the Kongo Kingdom*. Uppsala: Skriv Service AB.

Eltis, David (2000): *The Rise of African Slavery in the Americas*. Cambridge: Cambridge University Press.

Engerman, Stanley (2000): Contribution to '*AHR* Forum: Crossing Slavery's Boundaries', *American Historical Review*, 105/2, 451–84.

Evans, Chris (2015): '"Guinea Rods" and "Voyage Iron": Metals in the Atlantic Slave Trade, Their European Origins and African Impacts', paper delivered at the Annual Conference of the Economic History Society, 2015.

Everill, Bronwen (2012): *Abolition and Empire in Sierra Leone and Liberia*. London: Palgrave Macmillan.

Everts, Natalie (2012): 'A Motley Company: Differing Identities among Euro-Africans in Eighteenth-Century Elmina', in Toby Green (ed.), *Brokers of Change: Atlantic Commerce and Cultures in Precolonial Western Africa*, 54–69. Oxford: Oxford University Press for the British Academy.

Fage, J. D. (1969): 'Slavery and the Slave Trade in the Context of West African History', *Journal of African History*, 10/3, 393–404.

Fanon, Frantz F. (2008): *Black Skin, White Masks*. Charles Lam Markmann (trans.). London: Pluto Press.

Farias, P. F. de Moraes (2015): 'Muslim Oralcy: A Neglected Subject', Fage Lecture, delivered at the University of Birmingham, 11 November 2015.

——— (2007): 'Au-delà de l'opposition coloniale entre l'authenticité africaine et l'identité musulmane: l'œuvre de Waa Kamisòkò, barde moderne et critique du Mali', in Christophe de Beauvais and Mariella Villasante Cervello (eds.), *Colonisations et héritages au Sahara et au Sahel*, Vol. 2, 271–308. Paris: L'Harmattan; 2 vols.

——— (2003): *Medieval Arabic Inscriptions from the Republic of Mali: Epigraphy, Chronicles and Songhay-Tuareg History*. Oxford: Oxford University Press for the British Academy.

——— (1990): '"Yoruba Origins" Revisited by Muslims: An Interview with the Arọ́kin of Ọ̀yọ́ and a Reading of the Aṣl Qabā'il Yūrubā of Al-Ḥājj Ādam al-Ilūrī', in Karin Barber and Paulo de Moraes Farias (eds.), *Self-assertion and Brokerage: Early Cultural Nationalism in West Africa*, 109–47. Birmingham: Centre of West African Studies Monographs.

——— (1974): 'Silent Trade: Myth and Historical Evidence', *History in Africa*, 1, 9–24.

Farris Thompson, Robert (1984): *Flash of the Spirit: African and Afro-American Art and Philosophy*. New York: Vintage Books.

Faust, Franz X., et al. (2006): 'Evidence for the Postconquest Demographic Collapse of the Americas in Historical CO_2 Levels', *Earth Interactions*, 10, Paper No. 11, 1–15.

Fauvelle, François-Xavier (2013): *Le Rhinocéros d'Or: histoires du moyen âge africain*. Paris: Alma Editeur.

Fenske, James, and Kala, Namrata (2012): 'Climate, Ecosystem Resilience and the Slave Trade', CSAE Working Paper WPS/2012–23.

Ferreira, Roquinaldo (2014): 'Slave Flights and Runaway Communities in Angola (Seventeenth to Nineteenth Centuries)', *Anos 90, Porto Alegre*, 21/40, 65–90.

——— (2013): 'Agricultural Enterprise and Unfree Labour in Nineteenth-Century Angola', in Robin Law, Suzanne Schwarz and Silke Strickrodt (eds.), *Commercial Agriculture, the Slave Trade and Slavery in Africa*, 225–42. Woodbridge: James Currey.

——— (2012): *Cross-Cultural Trade in the Atlantic World: Angola and Brazil in the Era of the Slave Trade*. Cambridge: Cambridge University Press.

——— (2007): 'Atlantic Microhistories: Mobility, Personal Ties, and Slavery in the Black Atlantic World (Angola and Brazil)', in Nancy P. Naro, Roger Sansi-Roca and David H. Treece (eds.), *Cultures of the Lusophone Black Atlantic*, 99–128. New York: Palgrave Macmillan.

Fields-Black, Edda L. (2009): *Deep Roots: Rice Farmers in West Africa and the African Diaspora*. Bloomington and Indianapolis: Indiana University Press.

Filesi, Teobaldo (1968): *La relazioni tra il Regno del Congo e la Sede apostolica nel XVI secolo*. Como: Casa Editrice Pietro Cairoli.

Filipello, Marcus (2016): *The Nature of the Path: Reading a West African Road*. Minneapolis: University of Minnesota Press.

Fishburne Collier, Jane (1988): *Marriage and Inequality in Classless Societies*. Stanford: Stanford University Press.

Flynn, Dennis O. (1978): 'A New Perspective on the Spanish Price Revolution: The Monetary Approach to the Balance of Payments', *Explorations in Economic History*, 15, 388–406.

Flynn, Dennis O., and Giraldez, Arturo (1996): 'China and the Spanish Empire', *Revista de historia económica*, 14/2, 309–38.

——— (1995): 'Born with a "silver spoon": The Origin of World Trade in 1571', *Journal of World History*, 6/2, 201–21.

Fornah, Ibrahima, Fullah, Daniel, Kamara, Jesph S., Sesay, John, and Koroma, Augustine S. (2017): 'The Registers of the Rågbenle Society of the Themənɛ of Måtotoka of Tånɛ Chiefdom, Tonkolili District, Northern Sierra Leone', Working Paper presented at ASAUK Writing Workshop, Fourah Bay College, Sierra Leone, 3 May 2017.

Fortune, Stephen Alexander (1984): *Merchants and Jews: The Struggle for British West Indian Commerce, 1650–1750*. Gainesville: University of Florida Press.

Frank, Andre Gunder (1998): *ReOrient: The Global Economy in the Asian Age*. Berkeley: University of California Press.

Frank, Thomas (2004): *What's the Matter with Kansas? How Conservatives Won the Heart of America*. New York: Henry Holt & Co.

Fuente, Alejandro de la, with the collaboration of César García del Pino and Bernardo Iglesias Delgado (2008): *Havana and the Atlantic in the Sixteenth Century*. Chapel Hill: University of North Carolina Press.

Fromont, Cécile (2014): *The Art of Conversion: Christian Visual Culture in the Kingdom of Kongo*. Chapel Hill: University of North Carolina Press.

Garfield, Robert (1992): *A History of São Tomé Island, 1470–1655: The Key to Guinea*. San Francisco: Mellen Research University Press.

Gilroy, Paul (1992): *The Black Atlantic: Modernity and Double Consciousness*. Cambridge, Mass.: Harvard University Press.

Glete, Jan (2002): *War and the State in Early Modern Europe: Spain, the Dutch Republic and Sweden as Fiscal-Military States, 1500–1650*. London and New York: Routledge.

Godinho, Vitorino Magalhães (1969): *L'Économie de l'empire portugais aux XVe e XVIe siècles*. Paris: S.E.V.P.E.N.

Godinho Guarda, Ines (2016): 'European Slave Trade Middlemen in the Gold Coast, the Slave Coast and Angola, 1680–1720'. London: King's College London, PhD dissertation.

Gomez, Michael A. (2018): *African Dominion: A New History of Empire in Early and Medieval West Africa*. Princeton, NJ: Princeton University Press.

——— (1992): *Pragmatism in the Age of Jihad: The Precolonial State of Bundu*. Cambridge: Cambridge University Press.

Gómez, Pablo F. (2016): *The Experiential Caribbean: Creating Knowledge and Healing in the Early Modern Atlantic*. Chapel Hill: University of North Carolina Press.

——— (2013): 'The Circulation of Bodily Knowledge in the Seventeenth-Century Black Spanish Caribbean', *Social History of Medicine*, 26/3, 383–402.

Gonçalves, António Custódio (2005): *A história revisitada do Kongo e Angola*. Lisbon: Editorial Estampa.

——— (2000): 'A tradição oral na construção da história de Angola', in *Actas do seminário encontro de povos e culturas em Angola*, 415–28. Lisbon: Comissão Nacional para as Comemorações dos Descobrimentos Portugueses.

——— (1985): *Kongo: Le Lignage contre l'état: dynamique politique du Kongo du XVIème au XVIIème siècles*. Évora: Universidade de Évora/Instituto de Investigação Científica Tropical.

Graeber, David (2011): *Debt: The First Five Thousand Years*. New York: Melville House Publishing.

Gravrand, Henri (1983): *La Civilisation sereer: Cosaan, les origines*. Dakar: Nouvelles Éditions Africaines.

Green, Toby (2018b): 'The Challenges of Studying Inflation in Precolonial Africa: A Response to Klas Rönnbäck', *History in Africa*, 45, 19–28.

——— (2018a): 'From Essentialism to Pluralisms: New Directions in Precolonial West African History from the Oral History Archive at Fajara, The Gambia', in Toby Green and Benedetta Rossi (eds.), *Landscapes, Sources and Intellectual Projects of the West African Past: Essays in Honour of Paulo Fernando de Moraes Farias*, Chapter 16. Leiden: Brill.

——— (2017): '*Baculamento* or *Encomienda*? Legal Pluralisms and the Contestation of Power in the Pan-Atlantic World of the Sixteenth and Seventeenth Centuries', *Journal of Global Slavery*, 2, 310–36.

——— (2016b): 'Beyond an Imperial Atlantic: Trajectories of Africans from Upper Guinea and West-Central Africa in the Early Atlantic World', *Past & Present*, 230 (February 2016), 91–122.

——— (2016a): 'Africa and the Price Revolution: Currency Imports and Socioeconomic Change in West and West-Central Africa During the Seventeenth Century', *Journal of African History*, 57/1, 1–24.

——— (2015): 'Memories of Violence: Slavery, The Slave Trade, and Forced Labour in Greater Senegambia in the Past and the Present', *Mande Studies*, 16/17, 169–85.

——— (2013): 'The Export of Rice and Millet from Upper Guinea into the Sixteenth-Century Atlantic Trade', in *Commercial Agriculture, the Slave Trade and Slavery in Atlantic Africa*, Robin Law, Suzanne Schwarz and Silke Strickrodt (eds.), 79–97. Woodbridge: James Currey.

——— (2012b): *The Rise of the Trans-Atlantic Slave Trade in Western Africa, 1300–1589*. Cambridge: Cambridge University Press.

——— (ed.) (2012a): *Brokers of Change: Atlantic Commerce and Cultures in Precolonial Western Africa*. Oxford: Oxford University Press for the British Academy.

——— (2009): 'Architects of Knowledge, Builders of Power: Constructing the Kaabu "Empire", 16TH– 17TH Centuries', *Mande Studies*, 11, 91–112.

——— (2007): *Inquisition: The Reign of Fear*. London: Macmillan.

Greene, Sandra E. (2013): 'Oral Traditions about Individuals Enslaved in Asante', in Alice Bellagamba, Sandra E. Greene and Martin A. Klein (eds.), *African Voices on Slavery and the Slave Trade. Vol. 1: The Sources*, 15–28. Cambridge: Cambridge University Press.

——— (1996): *Gender, Ethnicity and Social Change on the Upper Slave Coast: A History of the Anlo-Ewe*. Portsmouth, NH: Heinemann.

Guerra, M. F., Sarthre, C. O., Gondonneau, A., and Barrandon, J. N. (1999): 'Precious Metals and Provenance Enquiries using LA-ICP-MS', *Journal of Archaeological Science*, 26, 1,101–10.

Guyer, Jane I. (2012): 'Soft Currencies, Cash Economies, New Monies: Past and Present', *Proceedings of the National Academy of Sciences*, 109/7, 2,214–21.

——— (2004): *Marginal Gains: Monetary Transactions in Atlantic Africa*. Chicago: University of Chicago Press.

Hair, P. E. H. (1967): 'Ethnolinguistic Continuity on the Guinea Coast', *Journal of African History*, 8/2, 247–68.

Hall, Bruce S. (2011b): 'How Slaves Used Islam: The Letters of Enslaved Muslim Commercial Agents in the Nineteenth-Century Niger Bend and Central Sahara', *Journal of African History*, 52/3, 279–97.

——— (2011a): *A History of Race in Muslim West Africa, 1600–1960*. Cambridge and New York: Cambridge University Press.

Hall, Gwendolyn Midlo (1992): *Africans in Colonial Louisiana: The Development of Afro-Creole Culture in the Eighteenth Century*. Baton Rouge: Louisiana State University Press.

Hall, Trevor P. (2015): *Beyond Middle Passage: Translated Portuguese Manuscripts of Atlantic Slave Trading from West Africa to Iberian Territories, 1513–1524*. London: Routledge.

Harling, P., and Mandler, P. (1993): 'From "Fiscal-Military" State to Laissez-faire State, 1760–1850', *Journal of British Studies*, 32/1, 44–70.

Haveaux, G. L. (1954): *La Tradition historique des Bapende orientaux*. Brussels: Académie Royale des Sciences Coloniales.

Havik, Philip J. (2016): 'Hybridising Medicine: Illness, Healing, and the Dynamics of Reciprocal Exchange on the Upper Guinea Coast (West Africa)', *Medical History*, 60/2, 181–205.

——— (2004): *Silences and Soundbytes: The Gendered Dynamics of Trade and Brokerage in the Pre-Colonial Guinea Bissau Region*. Münster/New Brunswick: LIT Verlag.

Hawthorne, Walter (2010b): 'From "Black Rice" to "Brown": Rethinking the History of Risiculture in the Seventeenth- and Eighteenth-Century Atlantic', *American Historical Review*, 115/1, 151–63.

——— (2010a): *From Africa to Brazil: Culture, Identity and an Atlantic Slave Trade, 1600–1830*. Cambridge and New York: Cambridge University Press.

——— (2003): *Planting Rice and Harvesting Slaves: Transformations along the Guinea-Bissau Coast, 1400–1900*. Portsmouth, NH: Heinemann.

——— (2001): 'Nourishing a Stateless Society during the Slave Trade: The Rise of Balanta Paddy-Rice Production in Guinea-Bissau', *Journal of African History*, 42/1, 1–24.

Hébrard, Jean, and Scott, Rebecca (2012): *Freedom Papers: An Atlantic Odyssey in the Age of Emancipation*. Cambridge, Mass.: Harvard University Press.

Hegel, G. W. F. (1956): *The Philosophy of World History*. John Sibree (ed. and trans.). New York: Dover.

Heijer, Henk den (1997): *Goud, ivoor en slaven: scheepvaart en handel van de Tweede Westindische Compagnie op Afrika, 1674–1740*. Zutphen: Walburg Pers.

Heintze, Beatrix (1989): 'A cultura material dos Ambundu de Angola segundo as fontes dos séculos XVI e XVII', *Revista internacional de estudos africanos*, 10–11, 15–63.

Henry, Clarence Bernard (2008): *Let's Make Some Noise: Axé and the African Roots of Brazilian Popular Music*. Oxford: University Press of Mississippi.

Herbert, Eugenia W. (1984): *Red Gold of Africa: Copper in Precolonial History and Culture*. Madison: University of Wisconsin Press.

Heusch, Luc de (2000): *Le Roi de Kongo et les monstres sacrés*. Paris: Gallimard.

Heywood, Linda M. (2017): *Njinga of Angola: Africa's Warrior Queen*. Cambridge, Mass., and London: Harvard University Press.

——— (2009): 'Slavery and Its Transformation in the Kingdom of Kongo, 1491–1800', *Journal of African History*, 50/1, 1–22.

———, and Thornton, John K. (2007): *Central Africans, Atlantic Creoles and the Foundation of the Americas, 1585–1660*. Cambridge: Cambridge University Press.

Hicks, Mary (2017): 'Panos como linguas: panos da costa, marinheiros libertos e escravos, e quitandeiras africanas em Salvador da Bahia, 1797–1850', paper presented at the conference 'Poder e dinheiro na era do tráfico: escravidão e outros laços econômicos entre África e Brasil', Universidade Federal da Bahia, Salvador, 15–17 March 2017.

Hilton, Anne (1985): *The Kingdom of Kongo*. Oxford: Clarendon Press.

——— (1981): 'The Jaga Reconsidered', *Journal of African History*, 22/2, 191–202.

Hiribarren, Vincent (2017): *A History of Borno: Trans-Saharan African Empire to Failing Nigerian State*. London: C. Hurst & Co.

Hiskett, Mervyn (1973): *The Sword of Truth: The Life and Times of the Shehu Usuman Dan Fodio*. New York: Oxford University Press.

Hobsbawm, Eric (1996): *The Age of Revolution, 1789–1848*. New York: Vintage Books.

Hogendorn, Jan, and Johnson, Marion (1986): *The Shell Money of the Slave Trade*. Cambridge: Cambridge University Press.

Hopkins, A. G. (1973): *An Economic History of West Africa*. Harlow: Longman.

Horta, José da Silva (2011): *A 'Guiné do Cabo Verde': produção textual e representações, 1578–1684*. Lisbon: Fundação Gulbenkian/FCT.

Hunter, Thomas C. (1976): 'The Jabi Ta'rikhs: Their Significance in West African Islam', *International Journal of African Historical Studies*, 9/3, 435–57.

Hunwick, John O. (1984): 'Ṣāliḥ al-Fullānī (1752/3–1803): The Career and Teachings of a West African 'Ālīm in Medina', in A. H. Green (ed.), *In Quest of an Islamic Humanism: Arabic and Islamic Studies in Memory of Mohamed al-Nowaihi*, 139–54. Cairo: The American University in Cairo Press.

Imbua, David Lishilinimle (2012): *Intercourse and Crosscurrents in the Atlantic World: Calabar–British Experience, Seventeenth–Twentieth Centuries*. Durham, NC: Carolina Academic Press.

Inikori, J. E. (2007): 'Africa and the Globalization Process: Western Africa, 1450–1850', *Journal of Global History*, 2/1, 63–86.

——— (2002): *Africans and the Industrial Revolution in England*. Cambridge: Cambridge University Press.

Insoll, Timothy (1996): *Islam, Archaeology and History: Gao Region (Mali), c. 900–1250*. Cambridge: Cambridge University Press.

Jackson, Rachel (2012): 'The Trans-Atlantic Journey of Gumbé – Where and Why Has It Survived?', *African Music*, 9/2, 128–53.

Jansen, Jan (2018): 'The Next Generation: Young Griots' Quest for Authority', in Toby Green and Benedetta Rossi (eds.), *Landscapes, Sources and Intellectual Projects of the West African Past: Essays in Honour of Paulo Fernando de Moraes Farias*, Chapter 14. Leiden: Brill.

——— (2016b): 'When Marrying a Muslim: The Social Code of Political Elites in the Western Sudan, *c.* 1600–*c.* 1850', *Journal of African History*, 57/1, 25–45.

——— (2016a): 'Beyond Mansa Musa: Rethinking the Sunjata Epic', paper presented at the African Studies Association Conference, Washington, DC, 1 December 2016.

Jatta, Daniel Laemouahuma (2014): 'The African Roots of the New World Banjo', seminar presented at the School of Oriental and African Studies, 1 December 2014.

Johnson, Marion (1970): 'The Cowrie Currencies of West Africa', *Journal of African History*, 11/1, 17–49, and 3, 331–53.

——— (1968): 'The Nineteenth-Century Gold "Mithqal" in West and North Africa', *Journal of African History*, 9/4, 547–68.

Johnson, Paul (2002): *Secrets, Gossip and Gods: The Transformation of Brazilian Camdomblé*. Oxford: Oxford University Press.

Jong, Ferdinand de (2008): *Masquerades of Modernity: Power and Secrecy in Casamance, Senegal*. Bloomington: Indiana University Press.

Kananoja, Kalle (2019): *Healing Knowledge in Atlantic Africa: Cross-Cultural Medical Encounters, 1500–1850*.

——— (2015): 'Bioprospecting and European Uses of African Natural Medicine in Early Modern Angola', *Portuguese Studies Review*, 23/2, 45–70.

——— (2012): 'Central African Religious Identities in Colonial Minas Gerais'. Helsinki: Åbo Akademi University, PhD dissertation.

Kane, Oumar (2004): *La Première hégémonie peule: le Fuuta Tooro de Koli Teŋella à Almaami Abdul*. Paris and Dakar: Karthala/Presses Universitaires de Dakar.

Kea, Ray A. (1982): *Settlements, Trade, and Politics in the Seventeenth-Century Gold Coast*. Baltimore and London: The Johns Hopkins University Press.

Keese, Alexander (2015): 'Colonialism and Fugitive Communities in West Central Africa, 1920–1955: Seeking Parallels with Maroon Societies', in Kadya Tall, Marie-Emanuelle Pommerolle and Michel Cahen (eds.), *Collective Mobilisations in Africa/Mobilisations collectives en Afrique: Enough is Enough!/ Ça suffit!*, 145–63. Leiden: Brill.

Kent, R. K. (1965): 'Palmares: An African State in Brazil', *Journal of African History*, 6/2, 161–75.

Klein, Martin A. (2001): 'The Slave Trade and Decentralized Societies', *Journal of African History*, 42/1, 49–66.

——— (1990): 'The Impact of the Atlantic Slave Trade on the Societies of the Western Sudan', *Social Science History*, 14/2, 231–53.

——— (1972): 'Social and Economic Factors in the Muslim Revolution in Senegambia', *Journal of African History*, 13/3, 419–41.

———, and Lovejoy, Paul E. (1979): 'Slavery in West Africa', in Henry A. Gemery and Jan S. Hogendorn (eds.), *The Uncommon Market: Essays in the Economic History of the Atlantic Slave Trade*, 181–212. New York: Academic Press Inc.

Kobayashi, Kazuo (2017): 'Indian Textiles and Gum Arabic in the Lower Senegal River: Global Significance of Local Trade and Consumers in the Nineteenth Century', *African Economic History*, 45/2, 27–53.

——— (2016): 'Indian Cotton Textiles and the Senegal River Valley in a Globalising World: Production, Trade, and Consumption, 1750–1850'. London: London School of Economics, PhD dissertation.

Konadu, Kwasi (2010): *The Akan Diaspora in the Americas*. Oxford: Oxford University Press.

Kriger, Colleen E. (2006): *Cloth in West African History*. Lanham: Rowman & Littlefield.

——— (1990): 'Textile Production in the Lower Niger Basin: New Evidence from the 1841 Niger Expedition Collection', *Textile History*, 21/1, 31–56.

Kuba, Richard (2015): 'Veiling and Unveiling Loropeni Mysteries', paper presented at the conference 'Landscapes, Sources and Intellectual Projects: A Conference in Honour of P. F. de Moraes Farias', University of Birmingham, 13 November 2015.

Kubik, Gerhard (1999): *Africa and the Blues*. Jackson: University of Mississippi Press.

——— (1979): 'Angolan Traits in Black Music, Games and Dances of Brazil: A Study of African Cultural Extensions Overseas', *Estudos de antropología cultural*, Lisbon, 10, 1–55.

Kuroda, Akinobu (2008): 'What is the Complementarity among Monies? An Introductory Note', *Financial History*, 15/1, 7–15.

——— (2007): 'The Maria Theresa Dollar in the Early Twentieth-Century Red Sea Region: A Complementary Interface between Multiple Markets', *Financial History Review*, 14/1, 89–110.

La Fleur, J. D. (2012): *Fusion Foodways of Africa's Gold Coast in the Atlantic Era*. Leiden: Brill.

Landers, Jane (2016): 'African War Captains of the Early Modern Atlantic', paper presented at the African Studies Association Conference, Washington, DC, 2 December 2016.

Last, Murray (2018): 'Slavery or Death in Sokoto and Borno: Tactics, Legalities and Sources', in Toby Green and Benedetta Rossi (eds.), *Landscapes, Sources and Intellectual Projects of the West African Past: Essays in Honour of Paulo Fernando de Moraes Farias*, Chapter 20. Leiden: Brill.

——— (1974): 'Reform in West Africa: The Jihād Movements of the Nineteenth Century', in J. F. A. Ajayi and Michael Crowder (eds.), *History of West Africa*, Vol. 1, 1–29. London: Longman; 2 vols.

——— (1967): *The Sokoto Caliphate*. London: Longman, Green & Co.

Law, Robin (2018): 'Fante "Origins": The Problematic Evidence of "Tradition"', in Toby Green and Benedetta Rossi (eds.), *Landscapes, Sources and Intellectual Projects of the West African Past: Essays in Honour of Paulo Fernando de Moraes Farias*, Chapter 5. Leiden: Brill.

——— (2016): 'The "Golden Age" in the History of the Gold Coast: The Seventeenth Century', paper presented at the University of Sussex conference 'African Economic History Network', October 2016.

——— (2013): 'The Government of Fante in the Seventeenth Century', *Journal of African History*, 54/1, 31–51.

——— (2012): 'Fante Expansion Reconsidered: Seventeenth-Century Origins', *Transactions of the Historical Society of Ghana*, 14, 41–78.

——— (1997): *The Kingdom of Allada*. Leiden: Research School CNWS.

——— (1995): 'Cowries, Gold and Dollars: Exchange Rate Instability and Domestic Price Inflation in Dahomey in the Eighteenth and Nineteenth Centuries', in Jane I. Guyer (ed.), *Money Matters: Instability, Values and Social Payments in the Modern History of West African Communities*, 53–73. London: James Currey.

——— (1991): *The Slave Coast of West Africa: The Impact of the Atlantic Slave Trade on an African Society, 1550–1750*. Oxford: Clarendon Press.

——— (1980): *The Horse in West African History: The Role of the Horse in the Societies of Pre-Colonial West Africa*. Oxford: Oxford University Press for the International African Institute.

——— (1977): *The Ọyọ Empire, c. 1600– c. 1836: A West African Imperialism in the Era of the Atlantic Slave Trade*. Oxford: Clarendon Press.

Lévi-Strauss, Claude (1966): *The Savage Mind*. Chicago: University of Chicago Press.

——— (1963): *Structural Anthropology*. New York: Basic Books.

Levtzion, Nehemia (1968): *Muslims and Chiefs in West Africa: A Study of Islam in the Middle Volta Basin in the Pre-Colonial Period*. Oxford: Clarendon Press.

Lewicki, Tadusz (1974): *West African Food in the Middle Ages according to Arabic Sources*. Cambridge: Cambridge University Press.

Linares, Olga F. (1992): *Power, Prayer and Production: The Jola of Casamance, Senegal*. Cambridge: Cambridge University Press.

Lindsay, Lisa A., and Sweet, John Wood (2013): *Biography and the Black Atlantic*. Chapel Hill: University of North Carolina Press.

Lopes, Carlos (1999): *Kaabunké: espaço, poder, território e poder na Guiné-Bissau, Gâmbia e Casamance pré-coloniais*. Lisbon: Comissão Nacional para as Comemorações dos Descobrimentos Portugueses.

Lovejoy, Paul E. (2018): 'The *Kano Chronicle* Revisited', in Toby Green and Benedetta Rossi (eds.), *Landscapes, Sources and Intellectual Projects of the West African Past: Essays in Honour of Paulo Fernando de Moraes Farias*, Chapter 19. Leiden: Brill.

——— (2016): *Jihād in West Africa during the Age of Revolutions*. Athens: Ohio University Press.

——— (2000): *Transformations in Slavery: A History of Slavery in Africa*. Cambridge: Cambridge University Press; third edition.

——— (1980): *Caravans of Kola: The Hausa Kola Trade, 1700–1900*. Zaria: Ahmadu Bello University Press.

——— (1978b): 'The Role of the Wangara in the Economic Transformation of the Central Sudan in the Fifteenth and Sixteenth Centuries', *Journal of African History*, 19/2, 173–93.

——— (1978a): 'Plantations in the Economy of the Sokoto Caliphate', *Journal of African History*, 19/3, 341–68.

——— (1974): 'Interregional Monetary Flows in the Precolonial Trade of Nigeria', *Journal of African History*, 15/4, 563–85.

———, and Richardson, David (2001): 'The Business of Slaving: Pawnship in Western Africa, *c.* 1600–1810', *Journal of African History*, 42/1, 67–89.

——— (1999): 'Trust, Pawnship, and Atlantic History: The Institutional Foundations of the Old Calabar Slave Trade', *American Historical Review*, 104/2, 333–55.

Luna, Kathryn M. de (2016): *Collecting Food, Cultivating People: Subsistence and Society in Central Africa*. New Haven: Yale University Press.

Macamo, Elísio S. (2017): *The Taming of Fate: Approaching Risk from a Social Action Perspective – Case Studies from Southern Mozambique*. Dakar: CODESRIA.

McCann, James C. (2005): *Maize and Grace: Africa's Encounter with a New World Crop, 1500–2000*. Cambridge, Mass.: Harvard University Press.

McCaskie, Thomas C. (2018): 'Dreamworlds: Cultural Narrative in Asante Visionary Experience', in Toby Green and Benedetta Rossi (eds.), *Landscapes, Sources and Intellectual Projects of the West African Past: Essays in Honour of Paulo Fernando de Moraes Farias*, Chapter 17. Leiden: Brill.

——— (1995): *State and Society in Pre-Colonial Asante*. Cambridge: Cambridge University Press.

McCulloch, Merran (1952): *The Ovimbundu of Angola*. London: International African Institute.

MacDonald, Kevin C., Gestrich, Nikolas, Camara, Seydou, and Keita, Daouda (2018): 'The "Pays Dô" and the Origins of the Empire of Mali', in Toby Green and Benedetta Rossi (eds.), *Landscapes, Sources and Intellectual Projects of the West African Past: Essays in Honour of Paulo Fernando de Moraes Farias*, Chapter 3. Leiden: Brill.

———, and Camara, Seydou (2012): 'Segou, Slavery and Sifinso', in J. Cameron Monroe and Akinwumi Ogundiran (eds.), *Power and Landscape in Atlantic West Africa: Archaeological Perspectives*, 169–90. Cambridge: Cambridge University Press.

MacGaffey, Wyatt (2005): 'Changing Representations in Central African History', *Journal of African History*, 46/2, 189–207.

——— (1986): *Religion and Society in Central Africa: The BaKongo of Lower Zaire*. Chicago and London: University of Chicago Press.

——— (1983): 'Lineage Structure, Marriage and the Family Amongst the Central Bantu', *Journal of African History*, 24/2, 173–87.

McIntosh, Susan Keech, and McIntosh, Roderick J. (1980): *Prehistoric Investigations in the Region of Jenne, Mali: A Study in the Development of Urbanism in the Sahel*. Cambridge: Cambridge Monographs in African Archaeology.

———, Susan Keech, and Thiaw, Ibrahima (2001): 'Tools for Understanding Transformation and Continuity in Senegambian Society, 1500–1900', in Christopher R. Decorse (ed.), *West Africa during the Atlantic Slave Trade: Archaeological Perspectives*, 14–37. London: Leicester University Press.

McLellan, David (ed.) (1977): *Karl Marx: Selected Writings*. Oxford: Oxford University Press.

MacLeod, William Christie (1928): 'Economic Aspects of Indigenous American Slavery', *American Anthropologist*, 30/4, 632–50.

McNaughton, Patrick (1993): *The Mande Blacksmiths: Knowledge, Power and Art in West Africa*. Bloomington: Indiana University Press.

Magnavita, Sonja, and Magnavita, Carlos (2018): 'All that Glitters is Not Gold: Facing the Myths of Ancient Trade between North and Sub-Saharan Africa', in Toby Green and Benedetta Rossi (eds.), *Landscapes, Sources and Intellectual Projects of the West African Past: Essays in Honour of Paulo Fernando de Moraes Farias*, Chapter 1. Leiden: Brill.

Malacco, Felipe Silveira de Oliveira (2016): 'O Gâmbia no mundo atlântico: fulas, jalofos e mandingas no comércio global moderno, 1580–1630'. Belo Horizonte: Universidade Federal de Minas Gerais, MA dissertation.

Mann, Charles C. (2005): *Ancient Americans: Rewriting the History of the New World*. London: Granta.

Mann, Kristin, and Bay, Edna G. (eds.) (2001): *Rethinking the African Diaspora: The Making of a Black Atlantic World in the Bight of Benin and Brazil*. London: Frank Cass & Co.

Marcussi, Alexandre Almeida (2016): *Diagonais do afeto – teorias do intercâmbio cultural nos estudos da diáspora*. São Paulo: Intermeios/FAPESP.

Mark, Peter (2014): 'African Meanings and European-African Discourse: Iconography and Semantics in Seventeenth-Century Salt Cellars from

Serra Leoa', in Francesca Trivellato, Leor Halevi and Cátia Antunes (eds.), *Religion and Trade: Cross-Cultural Exchanges in World History, 1000–1900*, Chapter 10. Oxford: Oxford University Press.

——— (2007): 'Towards a Reassessment of the Dating and the Geographical Origins of the Luso-African Ivories, Fifteenth to Seventeenth Centuries', *History in Africa*, 34, 189–211.

——— (1992): *The Wild Bull and the Sacred Forest: Form, Meaning, and Change in Senegambian Initiation Masks*. Cambridge: Cambridge University Press.

Martin, B. G. (1967): 'Unbelief in the Western Sudan: 'Uthmān dan Fodio's "Ta'līm al-ikhwān"', *Middle Eastern Studies*, 4/1, 50–97.

Martin, Phyllis M. (1986): 'Power, Cloth and Currency on the Loango Coast', *African Economic History*, 15, 1–12.

Masonen, Pekka (2006): 'Léon l'Africain et l'historiographie de l'Afrique soudanaise', *Studia Islamica*, 102/3, 71–89.

Matory, J. Lorand (2005): *Black Atlantic Religion: Tradition, Transnationalism and Matriarchy in the Afro-Brazilian Candomblé*. Princeton: Princeton University Press.

Mayer, Arno J. (1981): *The Persistence of the Old Regime: Europe to the Great War*. London: Croon Helm.

Mbembe, Achille (2016): 'Decolonizing the University: New Directions', *Arts and Humanities in Higher Education*, 15/1, 29–45.

——— (2001): *On the Postcolony*. Berkeley: University of California Press.

Meillassoux, Claude (1991): *The Anthropology of Slavery: The Womb of Iron and Gold*. Alide Dasnois (trans.). Chicago: University of Chicago Press.

——— (ed.) (1971): *The Development of Indigenous Trade and Markets in West Africa*, Introduction, 1–86. London: Oxford University Press for the International African Institute.

Meuwese, Mark (2012): *Brothers in Arms, Partners in Trade: Dutch-Indigenous Alliances in the Atlantic World, 1595–1674*. Leiden: Brill.

Miers, Suzanne, and Kopytoff, Igor (1977): *Slavery in Africa: Historical and Anthropological Perspectives*. Madison: University of Wisconsin Press.

Miller, Ivor, and Ojong, Matthew (2013): 'Ékpè "Leopard" Society in Africa and the Americas: Influence and Values of an Ancient Tradition', *Ethnic and Racial Studies*, 36/2, 266–81.

Miller, Joseph C. (2017): 'Crédito, cativos, colateral e moeda corrente: dívida, escravidão, e o financamento do mundo atlântico', paper presented at the conference 'Poder e dinheiro na era do tráfico: escravidão e outros laços econômicos entre África e Brasil', Universidade Federal da Bahia, Salvador, 15–17 March 2017.

——— (1997): 'Worlds Apart: Africans' Encounters and Africa's Encounters with the Atlantic in Angola before 1800', in *Actas do seminário encontro de povos e culturas em Angola*, 227–80. Lisbon: Comissão Nacional para as Comemorações dos Descobrimentos Portugueses.

——— (1988): *Way of Death: Merchant Capitalism and the Angolan Slave Trade, 1730–1830*. Madison: University of Wisconsin Press.

——— (1984): 'Capitalism and Slaving: The Financial and Commercial Organization of the Angolan Slave Trade, according to the Accounts of Antonio Coelho Guerreiro (1684–1692)', *International Journal of African Historical Studies*, 17/1, 1–56.

——— (1983): 'The Paradoxes of Impoverishment in the Atlantic Zone', in David Birmingham and Phyllis Martin (eds.), *History of Central Africa*, Vol. 1, 118–60. London and New York: Longman; 2 vols.

——— (1982): 'The Significance of Drought, Disease and Famine in the Agriculturally Marginal Zones of West-Central Africa', *Journal of African History*, 23/1, 17–61.

——— (1978): 'Thanatopsis', *Cahiers d'études africaines*, 18(1–2)/69–70, 229–31.

——— (1976): *Kings and Kinsmen: Early Mbundu States in Angola*. Oxford: Clarendon Press.

——— (1973): 'Requiem for the "Jaga"', *Cahiers d'études africaines*, 13(1)/49, 121–49.

Mitchell, Peter (2005): *African Connections: An Archaeologicial Perspective on Africa and the Wider World*. Walnut Creek: Altamira Press.

Monod, P. K. (1999): *The Power of Kings, Monarchy and Religion in Europe, 1589–1715*. New Haven: Yale University Press.

Monroe, J. Cameron, and Ogundiran, Akinwumi (eds.) (2012): *Power and Landscape in Atlantic West Africa: Archaeological Perspectives*, Introduction, 1–45. Cambridge: Cambridge University Press.

Moraes, Nize Izabel de (1998): *À la découverte de la Petite Côte au XVIIe siècle (Sénégal et Gambie). Vol. 3: 1664–1672*. Dakar: Université Cheikh Anta Diop–IFAN.

——— (1995): *À la découverte de la Petite Côte au XVIIe siècle (Sénégal et Gambie). Vol. 2: 1622–1664*. Dakar: Université Cheikh Anta Diop–IFAN.

——— (1993): *À la découverte de la Petite Côte au XVIIe siècle (Sénégal et Gambie). Vol. 1: 1600–1621*. Dakar: Université Cheikh Anta Diop–IFAN.

Morgan, Edmund S. (1972): 'Slavery and Freedom: The American Paradox', *Journal of American History*, 59/1, 5–29.

Mota, Thiago Henrique (2018): 'A grande jihad na África: história atlântica da islamização na Senegâmbia, séculos XVI e XVII'. Belo Horizonte: Universidade Federal das Minas Gerais, PhD dissertation.

——— (2016): 'Islã na África em perspectiva atlântica: instituições, agências, e práticas sociais na Senegâmbia, séculos XVI e XVII'. Belo Horizonte: Universidade Federal das Minas Gerais, MA dissertation.

Moumouni, Seyni (2008): *Vie et œuvre du Cheik Uthmân Dan Fodio, 1754–1817: de l'islam au soufisme*. Paris: L'Harmattan.

Mounkaïla, Fatimata (2008): *Anthologie de la littérature orale songhay-zarma: saveurs sahéliennes*. Paris: L'Harmattan.

Mpansu, Buakasa Tulu Kia (1973): *L'Impense du discours: 'kindoki' et 'nkisi' en pays Kongo du Zaïre*. Kinshasa: Presses Universitaires du Zaïre.

Mudimbe, V. Y. (1989): *The Invention of Africa: Gnosis, Philosophy and the Order of Knowledge*. Bloomington: Indiana University Press.

Muldrew, Craig (1997): *The Economy of Obligation: The Culture of Credit and Social Relations in Early Modern England*. Basingstoke: Palgrave Macmillan.

Nafafé, José Lingna (2012b): 'Challenges of the African Voice: Autonomy, Commerce and Resistance in Precolonial Western Africa', in Toby Green (ed.), *Brokers of Change: Atlantic Commerce and Cultures in Precolonial Western Africa*, 71–88. Oxford: Oxford University Press for the British Academy.

——— (2012a): 'African Orality in Iberian Space: Critique of Barros and Myth of Racial Discourse', *Portuguese Studies*, 28/2, 126–42.

——— (2007): *Colonial Encounters: Issues of Culture, Hybridity and Creolisation*. Frankfurt am Main: Peter Lang.

Naylor, Paul, and Wallace, Marion (2016): 'The Letters of Ayuba Suleiman Diallo: A New Chapter in the Diallo Story of Self-Emancipation', paper presented at the African Studies Association Conference, Washington, DC, 2 December 2016.

Ndâwla, Raphaël Batsîkama ba Mampuya ma (1999): *L'Ancien royaume du Congo et les BaKongo*. Paris: L'Harmattan.

Neto, Agostinho (1974): *Sacred Hope*. Maya Holness (trans.). New York: UNESCO.

Newson, Linda A. (2013): 'The Slave-Trading Accounts of Manoel Batista Peres, 1613–1619: Double-entry Bookkeeping in Cloth Money', *Accounting History*, 18/3, 343–65.

——— (2012): 'Africans and Luso-Africans in the Portuguese Slave Trade on the Upper Guinea Coast in the Early Seventeenth Century', *Journal of African History*, 53/1, 1–24.

———, and Minchin, Susie (2007): *From Capture to Sale: The Portuguese Slave Trade to Spanish South America in the Early Seventeenth Century*. Leiden: Brill.

Ngou-Mve, Nicolás (1994): *El África bantú en la colonización de México, 1595–1640*. Madrid: Consejo Superior de Investigaciones Científicas.

Nimako, Kwame, and Willemsen, Glenn (2011): *The Dutch Atlantic: Slavery, Abolition and Emancipation*. London: Pluto Press.

Northrup, David (1978): *Trade without Rulers: Precolonial Economic Development in South-Eastern Nigeria*. Oxford: Oxford University Press.

Nunn, Nathan (2007): 'Historical Legacies: A Model Linking Africa's Past to Its Current Underdevelopment', *Journal of Development Economics*, 83/1, 157–75.

Nwokeji, G. Ugo (2010): *The Slave Trade and Culture in the Bight of Biafra*. Cambridge: Cambridge University Press.

Ogundiran, Akinwumi (2016): 'The Chemistry of History: Decoding the Chemical Fingerprints of Yoruba Glass', paper presented at the African Studies Association Conference, Washington, DC, 1 December 2016.

——— (2014): 'The Making of an Internal Frontier Settlement: Archaeology and Historical Process in Osun Grove (Nigeria), Seventeenth to Eighteenth Centuries', *African Archaeological Review*, 31/1, 1–24.

——— (2009): 'Material Life and Domestic Economy in a Frontier of the Oyo Empire during the Mid-Atlantic Age', *International Journal of African Historical Studies*, 42/3, 351–85.

——— (2002b): *Archaeology and History in Ìlàrè District (Central Yorubaland, Nigeria), 1200–1900 AD*. Oxford: Archaeopress.

——— (2002a): 'Of Small Things Remembered: Beads, Cowries, and Cultural Translations of the Atlantic Experience in Yorubaland', *International Journal of African Historical Studies*, 35/2–3, 427–57.

———, and Ige, O. Akinlolu (2015): '"Our ancestors were material scientists": Archaeological and Geochemical Evidence for Indigenous Yoruba Glass Technology', *Journal of Black Studies*, 46/8, 751–72.

Ojo, Olatunji (2013): 'Silent Testimonies, Public Memory: Slavery in Yoruba Proverbs', in Alice Bellagamba, Sandra E. Greene and Martin A. Klein (eds.), *African Voices on Slavery and the Slave Trade. Vol. 1: The Sources*, 149–63. Cambridge: Cambridge University Press.

Okri, Ben (1991): *The Famished Road*. London: Vintage.

Oliel, Jacob (1994): *Les Juifs au Sahara: le Touat au moyen âge*. Paris: CNRS Éditions.

Osborn, Emily Lynn (2011): *Our New Husbands are Here: Households, Gender, and Politics in a West African State from the Slave Trade to Colonial Rule*. Columbus: Ohio University Press.

Palmer, R. R. (1959): *The Age of the Democratic Revolution: A Political History of Europe and America, 1760–1800*. Princeton: Princeton University Press; 2 vols.

Parés, Luis Nicolau (2016): *O Rei, o Pai e a Morte: a religião Vodum na antiga Costa dos Escravos na África ocidental*. São Paulo: Editora Schwarcz.

——— (2013a): 'Cartas do Daomé: uma introducão', *Afro-Ásia*, 47, 295–395.

——— (2013b): *The Formation of Candomblé: Vodun History and Ritual in Brazil*. Chapel Hill: University of North Carolina Press.

Parker, Geoffrey (2013): *Global Crisis: War, Climate Change and Catastrophe in the Seventeenth Century*, New Haven and London: Yale University Press.

Parreira, Adriano (1990): *Economia e sociedade em Angola na época da Rainha Jinga (século XVII)*. Lisbon: Editorial Estampa.

Paton, Diana (2015): *The Cultural Politics of Obeah: Religion, Colonialism and Modernity in the Caribbean World*. Cambridge: Cambridge University Press.

Patterson, Orlando (1982): *Slavery as Social Death: A Comparative Study*. Cambridge, Mass.: Harvard University Press.

Perinbam, B. Marie (1997): *Family Identity and the State in the Bamako Kafu, c. 1800–c. 1900*. Boulder: Westview Press.

Peters, Christabelle (2018): 'As Costas: Back to a Future Direction for Studying the Sociocultural History of the Atlantic World', paper presented at the conference 'Cross-Cultural Transformations in the Atlantic World, Sixteenth–Nineteenth Centuries', King's College London, 5 June 2018.

Phillips, Tom (2010): *African Goldweights: Miniature Sculptures from Ghana, 1400–1900*. London and Bangkok: Hansjorg Mayer.

Phillott-Almeida, Ralphina A. (2011): *A Succinct History of the Kingdom of Pachesi in the Empire of Kaabu*. Brikama: University of The Gambia.

Piketty, Thomas (2014): *Capital in the Twenty-First Century*. Arthur Goldhammer (trans.). Cambridge, Mass.: Harvard University Press.

Pitt-Rivers, Lieutenant-General Augustus (1900): *Antique Works of Art from Benin*. London: Harrison & Son.

Postma, Johannes Menne (1990): *The Dutch in the Atlantic Slave Trade*. Cambridge: Cambridge University Press.

Prange, Sebastian R. (2006): '"Trust in God, but tie your camel first": The Economic Organization of the Trans-Saharan Slave Trade Between the Fourteenth and the Nineteenth Centuries', *Journal of Global History*, 1/2, 219–39.

Pratten, David (2007): *The Man-Leopard Murders: History and Society in Colonial Nigeria*. Edinburgh and Indianapolis: Edinburgh University Press/Indiana University Press.

Price, Jacob M. (1991): 'Credit in the Slave Trade and Plantation Economies', in Barbara Solow (ed.), *Slavery and the Rise of the Atlantic System*, 293–339. Cambridge: Cambridge University Press.

Quinn, Charlotte (1972): *Mandingo Kingdoms of the Senegambia: Traditionalism, Islam, and European Expansion*. London: Longman.

Randles, W. G. L. (1968): *L'Ancien royaume du Congo: des origines à la fin du XIXe siècle*. Paris and The Hague: Mouton & Co.

Rashid, Ismail (2000): 'Escape, Revolt and Marronage in Eighteenth and Nineteenth Century Sierra Leone', *Canadian Journal of African Studies*, 34/3, 656–83.

Reid, Richard (2012): *Warfare in African History*. Cambridge: Cambridge University Press.

Reis, João José (2017): 'O tráfico negreiro e o escravo senhor de escravo: Bahia, 1800–1850', paper presented at the conference 'Poder e dinheiro na era do tráfico: escravidão e outros laços econômicos entre África e Brasil', Universidade Federal da Bahia, Salvador, 15–17 March 2017.

——— (2006): 'Domingos Pereira Sodré: um sacerdote africano na Bahia oitocentista', *Afro-Ásia*, 34, 237–313.

——— (1993): *Slave Rebellion in Brazil: The Muslim Uprising of 1835 in Bahia*. Baltimore: Johns Hopkins University Press.

Rentz, George S. (2004): *The Birth of the Islamic Reform Movement in Saudi Arabia: Muḥammad ibn 'Abd al-Wahhāb (1703/4–1792) and the Beginnings of the Unitarian Empire in Arabia*. London: Arabian Publishing.

Richard, François (2012): 'Political Transformations and Cultural Landscapes in Senegambia during the Atlantic Era: An Alternative View from the Siin (Senegal)?', in J. Cameron Monroe and Akinwumi Ogundiran (eds.), *Power and Landscape in Atlantic West Africa: Archaeological Perspectives*, 78–114. Cambridge: Cambridge University Press.

Roberts, Richard L. (1987): *Warriors, Merchants, and Slaves: The State and the Economy in the Middle Niger Valley, 1700–1914*. Stanford: Stanford University Press.

——— (1980): 'Production and Reproduction of Warrior States: Segu Bambara and Segu Tokolor, *c.* 1712–1890', *International Journal of African Historical Studies*, 13/3, 389–419.

Robinson, David (1975): 'The Islamic Revolution of Futa Toro', *International Journal of African Historical Studies*, 8/2, 185–221.

Rodney, Walter (1988, revised paperback edition; first published 1972): *How Europe Underdeveloped Africa*. Dar-es-Salaam/London: Tanzania Publishing House/Bogle Louverture.

——— (1970): *A History of the Upper Guinea Coast, 1545–1800*. Oxford: Clarendon Press.

——— (1966): 'African Slavery and Other Forms of Social Oppression on the Upper Guinea Coast in the Context of the Atlantic Slave Trade', *Journal of African History*, 7/3, 431–43.

——— (1965): 'Portuguese Attempts at Monopoly on the Upper Guinea Coast, 1580–1650', *Journal of African History*, 6/3, 307–22.

Rodrigues, Jaime (2016): *No mar e em terra: história e cultura de trabalhadores escravos e livres*. São Paulo: Alameda Casa Editorial.

Roese, Peter M., and Bondarenko, Dmitri M. (2003): *A Popular History of Benin: The Rise and Fall of a Mighty Forest Kingdom*. Frankfurt am Main: Peter Lang.

Roese, Peter M., and Smith, Ronald B. (2000): 'Cannon Known from the Former Kingdom of Benin (West Africa)', *Annals of the Náprstek Museum*, 21, 63–129.

Rönnbäck, Klas (2018): 'The Challenge of Studying Inflation in Precolonial Africa', *History in Africa*, 45, 5–18.

Roth, H. Ling (1968): *Great Benin: Its Customs, Art and Horrors*. London: Routledge & Kegan Paul.

Rufer, Mario (2016): 'A diáspora exorcizada, a etnicidade (re)inventada: historiografia pós-colonial e políticas da memória sobre o Daomé', in João José Reis and Carlos da Silva Junior (eds.), *Atlântico de dor: faces do tráfico de escravos*, 703–36. Cruz das Almas: Editora UFRB/Belo Horizonte: Fino Traço.

Ryder, A. F. C. (1969): *Benin and the Europeans, 1485–1897*. Harlow: Longmans, Green & Co.

Saccardo, P. Graziano (1982): *Congo e Angola, con la storia dell'antica missione dei cappuccini*. Venice: Curia Provinciale dei Cappuccini; 2 vols.

Saho, Bala (2012): 'Ritualizing and Domesticating Space: *Kañeleng* Women Coping with Childlessness in the Gambia', *Mande Studies*, 14, 99–126.

Sanneh, Lamin (2016): *Beyond Jihad: The Pacifist Tradition in West African Islam*. Oxford: Oxford University Press.

——— (1989): *The Jakhanke Muslim Clerics: A Religious and Historical Study of Islam in Senegambia*. Lanham: University Press of America.

Santos, Joice de Souza (2012): 'As embaixadas dos reinos da costa africana como mediadoras culturais: missões diplomáticas em Salvador, Rio de Janeiro e Lisboa (1750–1823)'. Rio de Janeiro: Pontifícia Universidade Católica do Rio de Janeiro, MA dissertation.

Santos-Granero, Fernando (2009): *Vital Enemies: Slavery, Predation and the Amerindian Political Economy of Life*. Austin: University of Texas Press.

Sarr, Assan (2017): 'Gender, Spirituality, and Economic Change in Rural Gambia: Agricultural Production in the Lower Gambia Region, *c.* 1830s-1940s', *African Economic History*, 45/2, 1–26.

——— (2016): *Islam, Power, and Dependency in West Africa: The Politics of Land Control in the Gambia River Basin, c. 1790s–1940s*. Rochester: University of Rochester Press.

Schultz, Kara (2016): ' "The Kingdom of Angola is not very far from here" ': The Río de la Plata, Brazil, and Angola, 1580–1680'. St Louis: Vanderbilt University, PhD dissertation.

Schwab, M. (1904): 'Deux transcriptions hébraiques', *Revue des études juives*, 48/95, 137–9.

Schwartz, Stuart B. (1992): 'Rethinking Palmares: Slave Resistance in Colonial Brazil', in his *Slaves, Peasants, and Rebels: Reconsidering Brazilian Slavery*. Urbana-Champaign: University of Illinois Press, 103–36.

Searing, James F. (2002): '"No kings, no lords, no slaves": Ethnicity and Religion among the Sereer-Safèn of Western Bawol, 1700–1914', *Journal of African History*, 43/3, 407–29.

Seck, Ibrahima (2016): 'Du Jolibaa au Mississippi, le long voyage des gens du Komo', *Mande Studies*, 18, 29–56.

Seijas, Tatiana (2014): *Asian Slaves in Colonial Mexico*. Cambridge: Cambridge University Press.

———, and Fredericks, Jake (2017): *Spanish Dollars and Sister Republics: The Money that Made Mexico and the United States*. Lanham, Mass.: Rowman & Littlefield.

Shain, Richard M. (2002): 'Roots in Reverse: *Cubanismo* in Twentieth-Century Senegalese Music', *International Journal of African Historical Studies*, 35/1, 83–101.

Shaw, Rosalind (2002): *Memories of the Slave Trade: Ritual and the Historical Imagination in Sierra Leone*. Chicago and London: Chicago University Press.

Shaw, Thurstan (1970): *Igbo-Ukwu: An Account of Archaeological Discoveries in Eastern Nigeria*. Evanston: University of Illinois Press.

Shumway, Rebecca (2011): *The Fante and the Transatlantic Slave Trade*. Rochester: University of Rochester Press.

Silva, Filipa Ribeiro da (2011): *Dutch and Portuguese in Western Africa: Empires, Merchants and the Atlantic System, 1580–1674*. Leiden: Brill.

Silva Junior, Carlos de (2016b): 'The Merchandise of Bahian Traffic: Cowries, Tobacco, and Other Products in the Eighteenth-Century Slave Trade between Bahia and the Bight of Benin', paper presented at the African Studies Association Conference, Washington, DC, 1 December 2016.

——— (2016a): 'Transatlantic Currencies and the Slave Trade: Tobacco and Gold Trade between Bahia and the Bight of Benin in the Eighteenth Century', paper presented at the African Studies Association Conference, Cambridge, 7 September 2016.

——— (2011): 'Identidades Afro-Atlânticas: Salvador, século XVIII (1700–1750)'. Salvador: Universidade Federal da Bahia, MA dissertation.

Sluyter, Andrew (2012): *Black Ranching Frontiers: African Cattle Herders of the Atlantic World, 1500–1900*. New Haven: Yale University Press.

Smartt Bell, Madison (2007): *Toussaint Louverture: A Biography*. New York: Pantheon.

Smith, M. G. (1997): *Government in Kano, 1350–1950*. Boulder: Westview Press.

Soares, Mariza de Carvalho (2014): 'Trocando *galanterias*: a diplomacia do comércio de escravos, Brasil-Daomé, 1810–1812', *Afro-Ásia*, 49, 229–71.

Soto, Hernando de (2000): *The Mystery of Capital*. New York: Basic Books.

Souza, Cândido Eugênio Domingues de (2011): '"Perseguidores da espécie humana": capitães negreiros da Cidade da Bahia na primeira metade do século XVIII'. Salvador: Universidade Federal da Bahia, MA dissertation.

Souza, Marina de Mello e (2015): 'Kongo King Festivals in Brazil: From Kings of Nations to Kings of Kongo', *African Studies Quarterly*, 15/3, 39–45.

Souza, Simone de (2006): *Le Domaine médico-magique et les Gris-Gris du Bénin*. Cotonou: Imprimerie Tunde.

Sparks, Randy J. (2014): *Where the Negroes are Masters: An African Port in the Era of the Slave Trade*. Cambridge, Mass.: Harvard University Press.

Spufford, Peter (1988): *Money and Its Use in Medieval Europe*. Cambridge: Cambridge University Press.

Stewart, Charles C. (2018): 'Calibrating the Scholarship of Timbuktu', in Toby Green and Benedetta Rossi (eds.), *Landscapes, Sources and Intellectual Projects of the West African Past: Essays in Honour of Paulo Fernando de Moraes Farias*, Chapter 10. Leiden: Brill.

Stewart, John, and Wilks, Ivor (1962): 'The Mande Loan Element in Twi', *Ghana Notes and Queries*, 4, 26–8.

Storrs, Christopher (ed.) (2008): *The Fiscal-Military State in Eighteenth-Century Europe: Essays in Honour of P. G. M. Dickson*. Farnham: Ashgate.

Strickrodt, Silke (2015): *Afro-European Trade in the Atlantic World: The Western Slave Coast, c. 1550–c. 1885*. Woodbridge: James Currey.

Sundström, Lars (1974): *The Exchange Economy of Pre-Colonial Tropical Africa*. London: C. Hurst & Co.

Suret-Canale, Jean (1964): *Essai sur la signification sociale et historique des hégémonies peules (XVIIème–XIXème siècles)*. Paris: Centre d'Études et de Recherches Marxistes.

Sweet, James H. (2011): *Domingos Álvares, African Healing, and the Intellectual History of the Atlantic World*. Chapel Hill: University of North Carolina Press.

——— (2009): 'Mistaken Identities? Olaudah Equiano, Domingos Álvares, and the Methodological Challenges of Studying the African Diaspora', *American Historical Review*, 114/2, 279–306.

Sylvanus, Nina (2016): *Patterns in Circulation: Cloth, Gender, and Materiality in West Africa*. Chicago: University of Chicago Press.

Tardieu, Jean-Pierre (2009): *Cimarrones de Panamá: la forja de una identidad afroamericana en el siglo XVI*. Madrid: Iberoamericana/Frankfurt am Main: Vervuert.

TePaske, John J. (2010): *A New World of Gold and Silver*. Kendall W. Brown (ed.). Leiden and Boston: Brill.

Thaler, Richard H., and Sunstein, Cass R. (2008): *Nudge: Improving Decisions about Health, Wealth and Happiness*. New Haven: Yale University Press.

Thiaw, Ibrahima (2012): 'Atlantic Impacts on Inland Senegambia: French Penetration and African Initiatives in Eighteenth- and Nineteenth-Century Gajaaga and Bundu (Upper Senegal River)', in J. Cameron Monroe and Akinwumi Ogundiran (eds.), *Power and Landscape in Atlantic West Africa: Archaeological Perspectives*, 49–77. Cambridge: Cambridge University Press.

Thornton, John K. (2012): *A Cultural History of the Atlantic World*. Cambridge: Cambridge University Press.

——— (2003): 'Cannibals, Witches, and Slave Traders in the Atlantic World', *William and Mary Quarterly*, Series 3, 60/2, 273–94.

——— (2002): 'Religious and Ceremonial Life in the Kongo and Mbundu Areas, 1500–1700', in Linda M. Heywood (ed.), *Central Africans and Cultural Transformations in the American Diaspora*, 71–90. Cambridge: Cambridge University Press.

——— (2001): 'The Origins and Early History of the Kingdom of Kongo, *c.* 1350–1550', *International Journal of African Historical Studies*, 34/1, 89–120.

——— (2000): 'Mbanza Kongo/São Salvador: Kongo's Holy City', in David M. Anderson and Richard Rathbone (eds.), *Africa's Urban Past*, 67–84. Oxford: James Currey.

——— (1999): *Warfare in Atlantic Africa, 1500–1800*. London: Routledge.

——— (1998b): *The Kongolese Saint Anthony: Dona Beatriz Kimpa Vita and the Antonian Movement, 1684–1706*. Cambridge: Cambridge University Press.

——— (1998a, second revised edition): *Africa and Africans in the Making of the Atlantic World, 1400–1800*. Cambridge: Cambridge University Press.

——— (1997): 'Sexual Demography: The Impact of the Slave Trade on Family Structure', in Claire C. Robertson and Martin A. Klein (eds.), *Women and Slavery in Africa*, 39–48. Portsmouth, NH: Heinemann.

——— (1991): 'African Dimensions of the Stono Rebellion', *American Historical Review*, 96/4, 1,101–13.

——— (1983): *The Kingdom of Kongo: Civil War and Transition, 1641–1718*. Madison: University of Wisconsin Press.

——— (1978): 'A Resurrection for the Jaga', *Cahiers d'études africaines*, 18(1–2)/69–70, 223–7.

———, and Mosterman, Andrea (2010): 'A Re-interpretation of the Kongo–Portuguese War of 1622 according to New Documentary Evidence', *Journal of African History*, 51/2, 235–48.

Tilly, Charles (2000): *Coercion, Capital, and European States, AD 990–1992*. Malden: Blackwell.

Tobin, James (2008): 'Fisher, Irving (1867–1947)', in Steven N. Durlauf and Lawrence E. Blume (eds.), *The New Palgrave Dictionary of Economics*, 412–21. Basingstoke: Nature Publishing.

Tocqueville, Alexis de (2010): *Democracy in America: Historical-Critical Edition of* De la démocratie en Amérique [1835–40]. Eduardo Nolla (ed.), James T. Schleifer (trans.). Indianapolis: Liberty Fund; 4 vols.

Torrão, Maria Manuel Ferraz (1991): 'Actividade comercial externa de Cabo Verde: organização, funcionamento, evolução', in Luís de Albuquerque and Maria Emília Madeira Santos (eds.), *História geral de Cabo Verde*, Vol. 1, 237–345. Coimbra: Imprensa de Coimbra; 3 vols.

Trevor-Roper, Hugh (1965): *The Rise of Christian Europe*. London: Harcourt, Brace & World.

Turner, J. Michael (2016): 'Escravos brasileiros no Daome', in João José Reis and Carlos da Silva Junior (eds.), *Atlântico de dor: faces do tráfico de escravos*, 653–69. Cruz das Almas: Editora UFRB/Belo Horizonte: Fino Traço.

Usman, Aribidesi (2016): 'Understanding Socio-Political Organization on the Niger–Benue Confluence: Recent Excavations at Oketekakini Palace Precinct, Idah, Nigeria', paper presented at the African Studies Association Conference, Washington, DC, 1 December 2016.

——— (2003): 'The Ethnohistory and Archaeology of Warfare in Northern Yoruba', *Journal of African Archaeology*, 1/2, 201–14.

——— (2000): 'A View from the Periphery: Northern Yoruba Villages during the Old Oyo Empire, Nigeria', *Journal of Field Archaeology*, 27/1, 43–61.

Usman, Yusufu Bala (1981): *The Transformation of Katsina, 1400–1883: The Emergence and Overthrow of the Sarauta System and the Establishment of the Emirate*. Zaria: Ahmadu Bello University Press.

Vainfas, Ronaldo (1995): *A heresia dos índios: Catolicismo e rebeldia no Brasil colonial*. São Paulo: Editora Schwarcz.

Van Wing, J. (1961–2): *Études Bakongo: sociologie – religion et magie*. Brussels: Office Internationale de Libraire.

Vansina, Jan (2010): 'A África equatorial e Angola: as migrações e o surgimento dos primeiros estados', in Djibril Tamsir Niane (ed.), *História geral da África. Vol 4: África do século XII ao XVI*, 623–54. Brasilía: UNESCO.

——— (2004): *How Societies are Born: Governance in West Central Africa before 1600*. Charlottesville and London: University of Virginia Press.

——— (1998): 'It Never Happened: Kinguri's Exodus and Its Consequences', *History in Africa*, 25, 387–403.

——— (1966): *Kingdoms of the Savanna*. Madison: University of Wisconsin Press.

——— (1963): 'The Foundation of the Kingdom of Kasanje', *Journal of African History*, 4/3, 355–74.

Verger, Pierre Fatumbi (1995): *Ewé: The Use of Plants in Yoruba Society*. São Paulo: Editora Schwarcz.

Vila Vilar, Enriqueta (1977): *Hispanoamérica y el comercio de esclavos*. Seville: Escuela de Estudios Hispanoamericanos.

Voeks, Robert A. (1997): *Sacred Leaves of Candomblé: African Magic, Medicine, and Religion in Brazil*. Austin: University of Texas Press.

Vogt, John L. (1973): 'The Early Sao Tome-Principe Slave Trade with Mina, 1500–1540', *International Journal of African Historical Studies*, 6/3, 453–67.

Vries, Jan de, and Woude, Ad van der (1997): *The First Modern Economy: Success, Failure, and Perseverance of the Dutch Economy, 1500–1815*. Cambridge: Cambridge University Press.

Wachtel, Nathan (2001): *La Foi du souvenir: labyrinthes marranes*. Paris: Éditions du Seuil.

Ware, Rudolph T., III (2014): *The Walking Qur'an: Islamic Education, Embodied Knowledge, and History in West Africa*. Chapel Hill: University of North Carolina Press.

Warsh, Molly A. (2010): 'Enslaved Pearl Divers in the Sixteenth-Century Caribbean,' *Slavery & Abolition*, 31/3, 345–62.

Webb, James L. A., Jr (1995): *Desert Frontier: Ecological and Economic Change along the Western Sahel, 1600–1850*. Madison: University of Wisconsin Press.

Weise, Constanze (2016): 'Kingdoms of the Confluence – Rituals and Politics in the Nupe Speaking Region', paper presented at the African Studies Association Conference, Washington, DC, 1 December 2016.

Wheat, David (2016): *Atlantic Africa and the Spanish Caribbean, 1570–1640*. Chapel Hill: University of North Carolina Press.

—— (2011): 'The First Great Waves: African Provenance Zones for the Transatlantic Slave Trade to Cartagena de Indias, 1570–1640', *Journal of African History*, 52/1, 1–22.

—— (2010): '*Nharas* and *Morenas Horras*: A Luso-African Model for the Social History of the Spanish Caribbean, *c.* 1570–1640', *Journal of Early Modern History*, 14/1–2, 119–50.

White, Bob W. (2002): 'Congolese Rumba and Other Cosmopolitanisms', *Cahiers d'études africaines*, 42(4)/168, 663–86.

Wilks, Ivor (1993): *Forests of Gold: Essays on the Akan and the Kingdom of Asante*. Athens: Ohio University Press.

Wright, Donald R. (2010, third edition): *The World and a Very Small Place in Africa: A History of Globalization in Niumi, The Gambia*. Armonk/London: M. E. Sharpe.

—— (1987): 'The Epic of Kelefa Saane as a Guide to the Nature of Precolonial Senegambian Society – and Vice Versa', *History in Africa*, 14, 287–309.

Yai, Olabiyi Babalola (2001): 'The Identity, Contributions, and Ideology of the Aguda (Afro-Brazilians) of the Gulf of Benin: A Reinterpretation', *Slavery & Abolition*, 22/1, 61–71.

Yerby, George (2008): *People and Parliament: Representative Rights and the English Revolution*. Basingstoke: Palgrave Macmillan.

Yoeli, Pinhas (1970): 'Abraham and Yehuda Cresques and the Catalan Atlas', *Cartographical Journal*, 7/1, 17–27.

Young, Jason R. (2007): *Rituals of Resistance: African Atlantic Religion in Kongo and the Lowcountry South in the Era of Slavery*. Baton Rouge: Louisiana State University Press.

Zhao, Bing (2017): 'Les Échanges sino-africains avant le XVIe siècle: une archéologie du commerce de la céramique chinoise', paper presented at the conference 'Les Mondialisations africaines dans l'histoire', Musée du Quai Branly, Paris, 20 April 2017.

——— (2012): 'Global Trade and Swahili Cosmopolitan Material Culture: Chinese-Style Ceramic Shards from Sanje ya Kati and Songo Mnara (Kilwa, Tanzania)', *Journal of World History*, 23/1, 41–85.

Notes

EPIGRAPH

1. Jansen/Duintjer/Tamboura (1995: 100–101).
2. Arnett (1922: 2).

FOREWORD

1. Axelrod Winsnes (1992: 60).
2. Farias (2007); Green (2018). In an important recent work, Gomez (2018: 66) suggests that in the distant past griots in the Kela region of what is now Mali may have drawn on written Arabic chronicles in circulation to formulate their narratives, in a form of 'feedback' between written and oral sources; nevertheless, it is clear that orature has subsequently evolved its distinctive modes of mediation and narrative.
3. It is also very relevant that when modern historical discourses on Africa began to develop in Europe in the late nineteenth century, they drew self-consciously on medieval European ideas of 'kingdom', 'fiefs' and 'serfs'; on this, see Hiribarren (2017: 48). We should remember, too, that this is by no means a problem limited to the history of West Africa: recent research suggests that compendia of 'primary sources' produced by famous English scholars of the Elizabethan era such as Hakluyt were modelled on intellectual traditions of structuring an argument through authoritative sources alone, constructing the pretence of not appearing to offer opinion. On the construction of Hakluyt, see Carrigy (2017).
4. For examples of these words in the Bamana, see Dumestre (1979: 146–7). I am grateful to Lucy Durán for confirming this hypothesis. For the example of totems in The Gambia, see Green (2012b: 243). For an eloquent championing of the use of microhistories in Atlantic African history, see Ferreira (2012: Introduction).

5. Fanon (2008: 169).
6. Mbembe (2016: 32–3).

INTRODUCTION

1. For a discussion of Kongo fashions in the 1640s, see Fromont (2014: 115–23); on Venetian pearls and diving in the Caribbean, Warsh (2010).
2. On the war for Brazil between the Dutch and the Portuguese, see especially Boxer (1952; 1973), Cabral de Mello (1998) and Calado (1648).
3. See Fromont (2014: 116–23) for a detailed discussion of the Eckhout sketches.
4. The most up-to-date account of the relationship between Dutch and Portuguese empires in Africa is Ribeiro da Silva (2011).
5. AHU, CU, Angola, Caixa 5, doc. 26, 28 July 1649.
6. On the import of *nzimbu* from Brazil, see *MMAI*, Vol. 6, 103, 342–3; and *idem*, Vol. 7, 504. On Dutch–Kongolese alliances, see Thornton/Mosterman (2010).
7. AHU, CU, Angola, Caixa 4, doc. 23, 23 February 1641.
8. ibid.
9. Miller (1988: 47–8); Thornton (1998a: 74).
10. See Heywood (2009) on the transformation of slavery in Kongo after 1491.
11. On the role of these phases of trade in triggering the Industrial Revolution, see Inikori (2002).
12. Graeber (2011: 114–15) has recently reminded us that 'markets aren't real. They are mathematical models, created by imagining a self-contained world where everyone has exactly the same motivation and the same knowledge and is engaged in the same self-interested calculating exchange.'
13. Camara/Jansen (1999: 72).
14. Some authors have written on this, but few have reached a wide audience, with the exception of Thornton (1998a) and *idem* (2012). On Dahomey's embassies to Brazil, see below, Chapter 9.
15. On rice, see Carney (2001; 2004) and Hawthorne (2010a and 2010b). On cattle-herding, see Sluyter (2012). On live-fencing practices, see Duvall (2009). On healing, especially Sweet (2011) and Gómez (2013; 2017); on 'bioprospecting', Kananoja (2015). On the role of African warfare, see especially Barcia (2014).
16. Mudimbe (1988); Mitchell (2005: 2); Macamo (2017: 11–13) also has a useful commentary on the construction of African identities through the experience of slavery and colonialism.

17. See Nimako/Willemsen (2011: 53) on the way in which the slave trade was part of a broader economic system in the early modern world; here I take Piketty (2014: 47–8)'s useful definition of 'capital' as including stores of value (such as gold) that do not have to be limited to their use in production.
18. The British Library, 'West Africa: Word, Symbol, Song' (November 2015–February 2016); Metropolitan Museum of Art, 'Kongo: Power and Majesty' (January–November 2015); Musée du Quai Branly, 'L'Afrique des routes' (February–November 2017). Of course, one major new change to this perspective is Michael Gomez's important recent book on late medieval empires in West Africa – see Gomez (2018).
19. For this quotation, Cabral (1974: 13); indeed, the concept of 'tradition' was directly connected to the reproduction of capitalist relations, as the Manchester School of Anthropology showed – see more recently Macamo (2017: 3)
20. Falconbridge (1788: 52).
21. Cf. Graeber (2011: 18), who shows moreover that credit systems for tabs kept in 'imaginary' financial units also often predate actual 'cash'.
22. Graeber (2011: 21–41) destroys the myth of barter; this pathfinding research in the 1970 and 1980s was conducted especially by Marion Johnson – see Johnson (1968; *idem*, 1970), and also Hogendorn/Johnson (1986). Professor J. E. Inikori is currently making a more systematized analysis of prices and currency imports in an ongoing project.
23. Piketty (2014: 46); Beckert (2014: esp. 60–61).
24. This excellent definition of hard currencies as retaining value over time is made by Guyer (2012: 2,214).
25. See, e.g., Marx's 'Theories of Surplus Value' in McLellan (1977: 393–414). For the role of Africans in economic growth in the Western hemisphere, see Inikori (2002).
26. On the relationship between currency imports, inflation and a lack of corresponding increase in trade goods, this is the classic theory on inflation of Irving Fisher – see Tobin (2008). For an application of this theory in African history, see Smith (1997: 56) on Kano. On cowrie inflation in Dahomey in the eighteenth century, see Law (1995: 55); on the dramatic rise in slave prices in iron bars in Gajaaga, Senegambia, in the eighteenth century, see Bathily (1989: 272); on the seventeenth-century pattern on the Gold Coast and in the Bight of Benin, Inikori (2007: 63).
27. On the different varieties of cowries, Ogundiran (2002b: 70).
28. On the 'sedee', Arhin (1995).
29. Ogundiran (2002a: 444–5); Sylvanus (2016: 94).

30. Jansen/Duintjer/Tamboura (1995).
31. See Guyer (2004: x) on the purported 'qualitative invariance of money'; and *idem*, 74–8, on the role of manillas in entry to the Ékpè secret society. See Imbua (2012: 17–24) on the relationship between Ékpè, trade and slavery.
32. Johnson (1937: 21).
33. Ogundiran (2002a: 448, 451); Usman (1981: 59–60). For the role of cowries in divination, see, e.g., NCAC, RDD, transcribed cassette 217C; on cloth in late-eighteenth-century Kongo burials, Fromont (2014: 96–7).
34. One of the key early texts promoting this view of external influence on African political change is Coquéry-Vidrovitch (1969); for a more recent critique of the ongoing problematic, see Konadu (2010). This approach still bedevils some economic theorists – Acemoglu et al. (2002) seem to equate economic and political development with the implementation of strong institutions by colonial outsiders. For an excellent critique of the assumption that European institutional frameworks are 'givens', see Austin (2007: 4).
35. Derive/Dumestre (1999: 73).

PART ONE

Causes: Economic Divergence in West and West-Central Africa

1 'THREE MEASURE OF GOLD': THE RISE AND FALL OF THE GREAT EMPIRES OF THE SAHEL

1. On the tumuli of Dô, MacDonald et al. (2018); on the ruins in Burkina Faso, Kuba (2015).
2. For Jenne-jenò, see the seminal work of R. and S. McIntosh (1980: 441–5); and for its later population by 800 CE, see Gomez (2018: 17); on the Upper Senegal, McIntosh/Thiaw (2001: 30).
3. Zhao (2012); on the Ethiopian ambassadors, Zhao (2017).
4. On the cave paintings with wheels, I am grateful to Gaëlle Beaujean's discussion of this feature at the Musée du Quai Branly on 20 April 2017; on the analysis of gold in North Africa as dating from the ninth century CE when West African in provenance, see Guerra et al. (1999); for a good discussion of the theories on an earlier trans-Saharan gold trade, see S. and C. Magnavita (2018); for the mints in North Africa and Siğilmāsa, see Spufford (1988).

5. Yoeli (1970).
6. On Jewish communities in Tuwāt, see Schwaab (1904), Bakchine-Dumont (1979) and Oliel (1994).
7. On the 'golden trade', see Bovill and Farias (1974); for the Bainunk narrative of the golden chair, an interview in Simbandi Balante by the author, March 2000.
8. Jansen/Duintjer/Tamboura (1995: 108).
9. This idea is Jan Jansen's, recently suggested by him in a quite novel interpretation of the Sunjata epic – see Jansen (2016a). On Sunjata as a master hunter, see Gomez (2018: 84).
10. La Roncière (1924–7: vol. 1, 157); see also Fauvelle (2013: Chapter 32).
11. On the Akan role in expanded gold production in this period, see Konadu (2010: 49–50).
12. Jansen/Duintjer/Tamboura (1995: 88).
13. On the transition from a credit economy to a bullion economy, see Graeber (2011: 308).
14. On the connection of the Al-Murabitūn coin to the *maravedí*, I am indebted to P. F. de Moraes Farias's Fage Lecture, University of Birmingham, 11 November 2015; see *Time Magazine*, 30 July 2015, 'The 10 Richest People of All Time', by Jacob Davidson.
15. Hunwick (1999: 9).
16. On the political projects of Al-Sa'dī in constructing this chronicle, see Farias (2003); on the broader role of political projects in these early chronicles, see Green/Rossi (2018); the best recent account of the pilgrimage, putting it in its local and global contexts, is Gomez (2018: 93–143).
17. *CEA*, 250.
18. ibid., 262.
19. On the belief in the need of miners for protection, see Jansen (2018).
20. On sacred geography, see Monroe/Ogundiran (2012: 18). For an important intervention on the creation of shared shrines, or 'shrine franchising', in the Empire of Mali, see MacDonald et al. (2018).
21. On smiths, see McNaughton (1993).
22. The work of the late John O. Hunwick is fundamental to much of this analysis. On the early growth of Gao, see Hunwick (1985: 3–7), and also Gomez (2018: 20–22); on the cotton trade *c.* 1300, see *CEA*, 210 (the evidence of Al-Dimashqī, 1256–1327); on the connections to Almería and Andalusia, see Insoll (1996: x); on the concentration of Islam among elites, see Hunwick (1985: 9).
23. Bobboyi (1992: 8–10).

24. For the gift of camels, Richmond Palmer (1936: 14); on the place of scholars in consolidating Kanem-Borno, see especially Bobboyi (1992). Michael Gomez (2018: 28) argues that the slave trade was fundamental in shaping the growth of Kanem, although this source suggests a more balanced framework.
25. Richmond Palmer (1936: 91); on merchants from Basra in Zawila, see Gomez (2018: 28).
26. H. R. Palmer (1928: 97). For a detailed analysis of the probable authorship of the chronicle by the Dan Rimi Barka of Kano, see Lovejoy (2018); Smith (1997: 9) argues that the sifting of oral evidence that went into the early chronicles took place initially *c.* 1500.
27. H. R. Palmer (1928: 109) on Kano; for Ibn Battūta, see *CEA*, 287. On the Wangara in Kano, see also Martin (1967: 57). On diasporas and early trans-Saharan trade in general, see Lovejoy (1978b) and Green (2012b).
28. NCAC, RDD, transcribed cassette 533A.
29. H. R. Palmer (1928: 107).
30. NCAC, RDD, transcribed cassette 566, p. 8; on Ibn Battūta, *CEA*, 295.
31. Jansen/Duintjer/Tamboura (1995: 126).
32. On Sunjata as the 'lion-thief', see Gomez (2018: 75).
33. *CEA*, 265.
34. ibid., 266, 290.
35. On the return of Mansa Musa and construction of the mosques, see Hunwick (1999: 10). On Al-Sahili, see Hunwick (2002: 10–11); one of the best recent works touching on these issues is Fauvelle (2013).
36. *CEA*, 283, for Battūta's quote. For a description of the riverine trade, see ibid., 299, where Battūta describes travelling on a small boat, and that 'each night we stayed in a village and bought what we were in need of in the way of wheat and butter, salt, spices and trinkets.' Ibn Khaldūn suggests this size for caravans, see Mitchell (2005: 160).
37. Hunwick (1999: 15). However, some scholars see this view of Al-Sa'dī's as reflecting a need to retroactively justify first the rise of Songhay and then the emergence of the 'Arma' states in the seventeenth century. Gomez (2018: 131–4) is, however, in no doubt as to the deeply hierarchical nature of Mali's power.
38. For Al-'Umari on Borno, *CEA*, 260; H. R. Palmer (1928: 105, 111) on details from the Kano Chronicle; on Borno and Kano, see Richmond Palmer (1936: 219).
39. *CEA*, 296.
40. Sanneh (1989: 1–2, 23–5); Sanneh (2016).

41. Lansiné Diabaté at the conference at SOAS, 24–6 June 2015, 'Identities in Greater Senegambia and Beyond: Interdisciplinary Approaches through History and Music in Dialogue' (convened by Lucy Durán and Toby Green); Ibrahima Galissá at the workshop at King's College London on 28 April 2017, 'Peacebuilding in Guinea-Bissau: Cultural Dialogues and Breaking the Impasse' (convened by Lucy Durán and Toby Green). This might especially be true in this region, from which, according to Lucy Durán, the kora originates.
42. On sorcery in general, *CEA*, 265; for Askia Mohammed, Hunwick (1985: 70 and 89).
43. On the open society in 1500, Hunwick (1985: 90); on this imperial state, see McIntosh (1988).
44. On Al-Kānemī, Hunwick (1995: 18); on Suware, Sanneh (1989: 23).
45. H. R. Palmer (1928: 110). On pre-Columbian slavery, see Santos Granero (2009). On slavery as Kanem-Borno's main export, see Candotti (2015: 100). As Gomez (2018: 57) puts it, 'slaving, together with Islam's continued rise, would constitute the double predicate upon which polity in the region would greatly expand over the next three centuries.'
46. On Kano and Borno sources for the horse–slave trade, H. R. Palmer (1928: 107); Richmond Palmer (1936: 29). On the horse in African history, more generally, see Law (1980).
47. For Askia Mohammed, see Hunwick (1985: 90).
48. For Al-'Umari on Borno, *CEA*, 260; on the adulteration of gold and silver, Hunwick (1985: 89–90).
49. *CEA*, 265.
50. Candotti (2015: 103); Wilks (1993: 5, 77); on Borno and Tripoli, see Dewière (2013).
51. Africain (1896–8: Vol. 3, 298–9); for a critique that he had never gone to sub-Saharan Africa, see Masonen (2006), although this is certainly tendentious, and, even if true, might suggest he had gained this information from traders who knew the region well.
52. Africain (1896–8: Vol. 3, 300).
53. Candotti (2015: 111–12) gives a good summary of this.
54. On Bighu, Africain (1896–8: Vol. 1, 14); on Mossi, Levtzion (1968: 5–6, 164); on Ijebu, Chouin (2016).
55. On the Dogon, see Bolland (1991: 14–15); the astronomical knowledge of the Dogon remains disputed, but is not to be discounted. I am also grateful to a personal communication from Gaëlle Beaujean of the Musée du Quai Branly in Paris; and Christopher Spring, then Curator of the Africa Collections at the British Museum.

56. On Djenné, see Hunwick (1999: 17–18); on Koli Tenguella's possible connection to the gold trade, see Kane (2004: 116–26).
57. Richmond Palmer (1936: 218–19, 222).
58. On the relative importance of the regional trade, see Usman (1981: 32). On the fifteenth-century transformations in general, see Levtzion (1968: 15–17).
59. H. R. Palmer (1928: 109).
60. On Queen Amina, ibid., 111; I am also grateful to personal communications from Nwando Achebe and Vincent Hiribarren on this point.
61. H. R. Palmer (1928: 109).
62. ibid.
63. I am indebted to the translation by Hiskett (1965: 116); on the 'Song of Bagauda' as sung in Kano in the 1990s, see Smith (1997: 8).
64. *CEA*, 281.
65. ibid., 299, for Battūta's purchases; on cowries' versatility, see Johnson (1970). For Duarte Pacheco Pereira, see Mauny (1956: 124).
66. Africain (1896–8: Vol. 3, 289).
67. For Al-Sa'dī, Hunwick (1999: 12); see also Africain (1896–8: Vol. 3, 291).
68. On Sonni 'Alī, Hunwick (1999: 91); Cissoko (1974: 51–2); on titles, see Hunwick (1999: 338–44).
69. Hunwick (1999: 91), for the description of Sonni 'Alī as a tyrant; on his death, ibid., 100; on his attitude to Islam, Cissoko (1974: 51).
70. For Al-Ouazzan's account, Africain (1896–8: Vol. 3, 295); for general descriptions of Songhay, see Hunwick (1999: 126, and ibid., n. 40).
71. Cissoko (1974: 43) on the shifting trade routes; see Green (2012b: 241–2) on the impact of the arrival of the Portuguese.
72. Africain (1896–8: Vol. 3, 284); on the details of the pilgrimage, Hunwick (1999: 104–5); on the creation of debt by Mansa Musa's pilgrimage, see Gomez (2018: 119–21).
73. Cissoko (1974: 88–95); on the lack of control over the goldfields, see Bathily (1989: 237).
74. Hunwick (1999: 187); on the insult to the Moroccan ruler, ibid., n. 11; on the seeking out of potential dissidents, Mota (2018: 337).
75. ibid., 193.
76. ibid., 190.
77. Wilks/Levtzion/Haight (1986: 46).
78. Camara/Jansen (1999: 44).
79. On the connection between Islam and trade in West Africanist historiography, see Hunter (1976: 450); this link is criticized from a religious perspective by Sanneh (1989: 8–9). For Shabinī, see Jackson (1967: 4). See also Bowdich (1966: 91).

80. On the Masūfa and Ahmad Baba, see Hunwick (2002: 1); on the Jakhanke, Sanneh (1989: 33–5).
81. NCAC, RDD, transcribed cassette 624B, p. 19 – M. Kuyate, Kalilu Fatty.

2 CAUSEWAYS ACROSS THE SAVANNAH: FROM SENEGAMBIA TO SIERRA LEONE

1. Hawthorne (2003).
2. For the dry and wet spells, see Brooks (1993); for Barry's intervention, see the film of the conference 'Identities in Greater Senegambia and Beyond: Interdisciplinary Approaches through History and Music in Dialogue' (convened by Lucy Durán and Toby Green) at https://www.youtube.com/watch?v=DMytlZcXRwA; on the later dry period, Webb (1995: 5–10).
3. The key article stressing this overwhelming import of currencies in the early decades is Inikori (2007: 63).
4. For the quote about cowries and divination, see NCAC, RDD, transcribed cassette 490A, p. 6; on the importance of dreams to the Ashanti, see McCaskie (2018); for a devastating critique of the Eurocentrism of much economic history of West Africa as it relates to land use, see Sarr (2016).
5. Personal communication, Daniel Laemouahuma Jatta, Bijilo, The Gambia, 6 November 2013.
6. Jatta (2014); Dubois (2016).
7. Jatta (2014); and discussion with Lucy Durán at this event.
8. See NCAC, RDD, transcribed cassette 566, p. 8; the term 'Greater Senegambia' is Boubacar Barry's – see Barry (1998).
9. NCAC, RDD, transcribed cassette 566, pp. 11–12; on Diogo Gomes, *MMAII*, Vol. 1, 194.
10. On the ways in which Senegambian oral histories repeat tropes over time, see Green (2009) and (2015); on the accounts of Koli Tenguella crossing the Gambia River in this manner, see Almada's account; on migration as a motive force in oral histories, see Green (2018).
11. NCAC, RDD, transcribed cassette 491B, p. 6; on the deep history of rice-producing in this region, see Carney (2001) and Fields-Black (2009).
12. NCAC, RDD, transcribed cassette 553A, p. 3; on the witch killed by Tiramakang's father, see NCAC, RDD, transcribed cassette 566, p. 8; on the phenomenon of 'cannibal witches', see Hawthorne (2010),

Austen (1999); on an analogous concept of 'eating' in Dahomey, see Dalzel (1967: 183).

13. *MMAII*, Vol. 3, 242; an excellent study of textual production in Portuguese about this region is Horta (2011). The best account of Kaabu probably remains Lopes (1999); see also Jansen (2016) and Green (2009). The best account of the 'Great Jolof' Kingdom remains Boulègue (1987).
14. On Jolof raids for Serèèr slaves, see Cadamosto's account of his 1455 voyage, in *MMAII*, Vol. 1, 316; on Kaabu Mandinga's intermarriage with local peoples, see Innes (1976: 77–9).
15. The fragmentation of Jolof is discussed in Boulègue (1987); one of the best sources is Almada's text in *MMAII*, Vol. 3, 234–5. On Serèèr alliances with the Portuguese, see T. Hall (2015).
16. The Dutch cattle-hide trade was carried out by Dutch Calvinist and Sephardic Jewish merchants trading on the Jolof coast. For examples, see GAA, NAA, Book 62, fol. 218v (1611); GAA, NAA, Book 117, fols. 181–182v; GAA, NAA, Book 129, fols. 163v–164r; and many others. The classic account of Nasir al-Din's attacks on the French in the 1670s is Barry (1985: 112–36); on Koli Tenguella, see Malacco (2016: 80–81).
17. On the connection of Askia Mohammed to the Senegal Valley, see Bathily (1989: 99); on the arrival of an Islamic cleric in Cayor by 1650, see Ware (2014: 105); on the relationship between Songhay and the maraboutic village of Pir in Cayor, see Webb (1995: 30).
18. On the relative profitability of the trade in manufactured goods by the 1680s, see Miller (1984).
19. *MMAII*, Vol. 1, 529, 534.
20. ibid., 531, 549.
21. NA, Inventarisnummer 43, MF 23: Journael van Willem Cunningham, 1625–6; I am grateful, too, to Ishmael Kamara of Fourah Bay College for showing me the way to this rock on 5 May 2017.
22. Gamble/Hair (1999: 139, 140). Jobson calls Saho 'Buckor Sano'. The Sahos are a famous trading family in Senegambia today, and so it is likely that this is a misspelling of Saho. 'Buckor' may be a version of *buur*, 'king' in Wolof – with 'Buur Saho' a moniker of those around him for the great trader. On proportions of taxes, Lemos Coelho tells us that the King of the Port of Gorée received around ¼ of exported animal hides in taxes – Peres (1953: 98).
23. For van den Broecke, La Fleur (2000: 39–40); for cloths from Gambia and Cape Verde at Cape Coast in 1687, see TNA, T70/659, fols. 56r, 63r.

24. On the road to Arrecife, La Fleur (2000: 98–9); on the goods for trade, Coppier (1645: 16).
25. *MMAII*, Vol. 3, 252.
26. On the landlords and strangers model, see Brooks (1993).
27. Purchas (1905–7: Vol. 4, 9).
28. Material from the account books has already been well used by Linda A. Newson – see Minchin/Newson (2007); and also Newson (2012) and (2013). A good account of Bautista Pérez more generally is Wachtel (2001). On the trip to Joal, Portudal and Rufisque, AGNL, SO-CO, Caja 33, doc. 349, fol. 23v; on Ziguinchor, AGNL, SO-CO, Caja 18, doc. 197, fol. 763v; and on Geba, and the general list of goods, ibid., fols. 809v–810r.
29. On the alcohol trade in Luanda, see Curto (2004); on bringing alcohol as gifts for *sobas*, personal communication from Mariana P. Candido, London, 11 July 2016; on the use of rum as a libation, I am grateful for this insight to Dr Samuel Adu-Gyamfi of Kwame Nkrumah University of Science and Technology, Kumasi.
30. For this account of Kelefa Saane, see NCAC, RDD, transcribed cassette 573A, p. 6. The classic analysis of Kelefa Saane is Wright (1987). On the sale of knives and swords, see AGNL, SO-CO, Caja 18, doc. 197, fols. 411v, 467r – this sword trade is well studied in Horta/Mark (2011: 103–34). On alcohol in Angola, see Curto (2004).
31. This process is well described for the North Bank Gambia Kingdom of Niumi by Wright (1987: 293); on the rise of the age-sets for rice production among the Balanta people of Guinea-Bissau, see Hawthorne (2003); these aristocracies were thus relatively new, as was the case, too, in Europe – on which, see R. R. Palmer (1959: Vol. 1, 29).
32. On Casamance shipwrecks, BA, Códice 51–IX–25, fol. 88v; on night-time robberies in Cacheu, BA, Códice 51–VI–54, no. 7, fol. 144r; on Cacheu in the 1660s, see AHU, CU, Guiné, Caixa 2, doc. 22 (6 March 1662) and 48 (26 September 1670); on De la Marche, Cultru (1913: 107–8).
33. On the Capuchins, see AHU, CU, doc. 12 (1 June 1686); on the two ill-starred traders, see Silveira (1945: 31).
34. Álvares's description is at SG, *Etiópia Menor e descrição geográphica da província da Serra Leoa* by Manoel Álvares, fol. 13r; for Donelha's, see *MMAII*, Vol. 5, 140. Brucama is located near to the modern town of Goudomp, in Casamance.
35. On rice production in general, in this region, see the important work of Fields-Black (2009) and Hawthorne (2003); on specific production

in the area ruled by Masatamba, see Green (2013); on the decline of rice production during the civil war, oral interview with Antonio de Silva Mango, Bula, 18 April 2011.

36. On Senegambian beliefs in European cannibalism, see *MMAII*, Vol. 1, 348. On beliefs in European cannibalism in Angola, see Miller (1988: 4–5), and, on Cameroon, Argenti (2007: 55).
37. For Almada's description of processes of enslavement, *MMAII*, Vol. 3, 274; for this description, ibid., Chapter 12.
38. For examples of branding and Bautista Pérez's assessment of these 'damages', see AGNL, SO-CO, Caja 2, doc. 8, fols. 1,332r–1,333r; for a gruesome description of the appalling conditions on these ships in the seventeenth century, see Green (2007: 280); for an example of the *livros dos mortos*, AGI, Escribanía 591A, Pieza 5.
39. Africain (1896–8: Vol. 3, 289); on *barafulas*, Curtin (1975: 237). Kwame Nimako and Glenn Willemsen (2011: 56) have suggested that Africa's greatest disadvantage in terms of global trade was 'the absence of an effective "money economy"'. However, there was plenty of 'ready money' knocking about in Greater Senegambia in the sixteenth and seventeenth centuries, as this paragraph shows. The idea that Africa did not have a 'money economy' owes something to preconceptions about 'archaic economies', ideas that assume that there is such a thing as 'primitive money', which should be contrasted with 'real' money. In fact, as David Graeber (2011) has shown, this is a myth.
40. The key work on identifying the standard size of the bar was done also by Curtin (1975: 241–2).
41. Dantzig/Jones (1987: 11).
42. For van den Broecke, La Fleur (2000: 28); for Bautista Pérez, AGNL, SO-CO, Caja 18, doc. 197, fols. 809v–810r (Geba) and 839r–v (Bijagós); for the Senegal, Jannequin (1643: 61); for the taxes at the Gambia, Moore (1738: 14).
43. The role of African demand in pushing up volumes of iron was noted first by the Guyanese historian-activist Walter Rodney, see Rodney (1965: 311); on the import of iron from Sweden, Peres (1990: 9–10). For Jobson, Gamble/Hair (1999: 160); on Cacheu, AHU, CU, Cabo Verde, Caixa 8, doc. 74 (16 May 1698).
44. Cultru (1913: 193).
45. See Miller (1988: 665) on this general relation; and also Miller (1984) on the profitability of manufacturing goods as opposed to enslaved Africans themselves.

46. Indeed, the situation was much as Roquinaldo Ferreira has described for Angola in the same period – see Ferreira (2012); on the Dutch trade goods, Moraes (1995: 241ff.).
47. On credit and the slave-trade system, see especially Price (1991).
48. On the *nyantios*, NCAC, RDD, transcribed cassette 491B, p. 13; on hierarchy, NCAC, RDD, transcribed cassette 23A, p. 3. On 'vital energy' in pre-Columbian and pre-Atlantic African economies of life, see Santos-Granero (2009).
49. Schouten (1618: 5–6). Schouten was captain of the Dutch ship that rounded and named Cape Horn on this voyage.
50. On a slave-trading ship at Magrabomba in 1561, see AGI, Patronato, 173, no. 1, Ramo 15, mention of a ship arriving in Hispaniola on 21 April direct from Magrabomba with captives; I am extremely grateful to Dr Stephen Ney of Fourah Bay College, University of Sierra Leone, for this insight on Banana Island and Newton – Freetown, 6 May 2017.
51. For the drought, see AHU, CU, Guiné, Caixa 1, doc. 23, 5 December 1641. This drought was part of a much larger ecological crisis across the world, which, as Parker (2013) has recently shown, led to major political changes from China to Spain and Portugal, via Angola. On the overthrow of the Sapes by the Manes, see Green (2012b: Chapter 8).
52. For Donelha, see *MMAII*, Vol. 5, 137. For Cissé's account, NCAC, RDD, transcribed cassette 466B, p. 29.
53. For inflation in 1616, AHU, CU, Cabo Verde, Caixa 2, doc. 78, *c.* 1616.
54. For Almada, *MMAII*, Vol. 3, 247. For Gambia cloth, AGNL, SO-CO, Caja 2, doc. 8, fol. 1,000; for cloth from Geba, AGNL, SO-CO, Caja 18, doc. 197, fol. 882v; for Jolof cloth, ibid., fol. 430v. On the use of *panos* as a standard unit of currencies, see ibid., fols. 405v (flagons of wine), 422v (buying paper) and 424v (buying couscous). On *panos* as a unit of account in the region, see Newson (2013). On the various descriptions of houses and clothing in Cacheu, SG, *Etiópia Menor e descrição geográfica da província da Serra Leoa* by Manoel Álvares, fols. 14v, 15r.
55. Moraes (1993: 71).
56. SG, *Etiópia Menor e descrição geográfica da província da Serra Leoa* by Manoel Álvares, fol. 4v; Ogilby (1670: 348); Cultru (1913: 28, 74).
57. On the Bautista Pérezes, see AGNL, SO-CO, Caja 2, doc. 201, fol. 2,300r, and AGNL, SO-CO, Caja 33, doc. 349, fol. 9r.
58. The research of Philip Curtin is important here – see Curtin (1975: 211–13). However, Curtin wrongly states that cloth and iron bars

became currencies because they had been a dominant import (ibid., 261) – in fact, both were currencies prior to the start of Atlantic trade.

59. For S. Manneh, NCAC, RDD, transcribed cassette 550A, pp. 63–4. See also NCAC, RDD, transcribed cassette 547A, p. 17 – 'the taxes were paid in the form / of strips of cloth'. For the account of *panos* and slaves, NCAC, RDD, transcribed cassette 309A, pp. 61, 67.
60. On the use of *barafulas* as a unit of account in 1641, AHU, CU, Cabo Verde, Caixa 3, no. 7 – a document of confiscation. On the governor in 1646 and *barafulas*, see AHU, CU, Guiné, Caixa 1, doc. 49, Anexos 1–6. See also SG, *Etiópia Menor e descrição geográfica da província da Serra Leoa* by Manoel Álvares, fol. 20v. On the Manjako use of cloth to differentiate themselves, see NCAC, RDD, transcribed cassette 432A, pp. 15–16.
61. The linguist Friederike Luepke argues that the multilingualism of this region emerged as part of this process – see her contribution to the 2015 conference 'Identities in Greater Senegambia and Beyond' at https://www.youtube.com/watch?v=DMytlZcXRwA.
62. On this important find, Landers (2016).
63. On maroons in Panamá and Cuba by the 1530s, AGI, Panamá 235, Libro 6, fols. 24v–25r, and Santo Domingo 1121, Libro 1, fols. 173v–174r; on maroon alliances with Drake, AGI, Patronato 234, Ramo 1.
64. AGI, Patronato 234, Ramo 6, fols. 208r–220r; on the stockade system at Bayano, see Tardieu (2009: 86); on the emergence of the *tabanka* in the late sixteenth century, see Hawthorne (2003: 121–7).
65. On the community for the maroons of Portobelo, see AGI, Patronato 234, Ramo 6, fols. 312v, 416v.
66. On the passage of African servants back and forth, see IAN/TT, Inquisição de Lisboa, Processo 2075, fol. 32r; on the Luso-African ancestry of Jorge Gonçalves Frances (a protagonist in this case), see the same trial.
67. See the seminal work by Mark (1992: 38–41, 62–3, 121–4).
68. On the *nomolis*, Atherton/Kalous (1970: 316). On the Luso-African ivories, Mark's work is also vital: see Mark (2007) and Mark (2014). The new research project 'African Ivories in the Atlantic World' will reveal much more information, https://africanivoriesul.wordpress.com/.
69. Interview with Ansumana Manga in Singuère, Casamance, May 2011.
70. NCAC, RDD, transcribed cassette 490A, pp. 6, 9.
71. On the relative cost of cloth and iron, see NA, Inventarisnummer 11, no. 92. The cost of the cloth was 35,625 florins, and of the iron bars, 21,000 florins.

72. On the value of slaves as at 150 *panos*, see AGNL, SO-CO, Caja 18, doc. 197 – see, e.g., fols. 467r (120 *panos* per captive) and 575r (150).
73. On the silver plates and mugs, see Moraes (1995: 241); on the King of Bawol, Peres (1990: 9); see also Dapper (1686: 240) and Jarric (1610–14: Vol. 3, 373) for gold in Gambia and Sierra Leone. On paper and kola nuts, Peres (1990: 23, 32); on kola, see also Jarric (1610–14: Vol. 3, 369).
74. See, for instance, Nafafé (2012)'s discussion of King Incinhate, who lived near Bissau in the late seventeenth century. Nafafé shows just how much more active Incinhate was in seeking free trade and access than his European trading partners, protesting at the various European nations' claim to an 'exclusive' right to trade.
75. See Kuroda (2007; 2008).
76. Peres (1990: 37–8); Moraes (1993: 71); AGNL, SO-CO, Caja 18, doc. 197, fol. 436r; on their equivalence with the *panos pretos* (dark cloths), see AGNL, SO-CO, Caja 54, doc. 425, fol. 314r: 'e asim me ficam mais de fora desta parsaria em mão de Anto rodrigez em hum conhecimento duzentos panos pretos de Cola que lhe vendi antes de fazer esta parsaria.'

3 READY MONEY: THE GOLD COAST AND THE GOLD TRADE

1. On the tendency of Europeans to label regions by commodities here, see, for instance, Daaku (1970: 21).
2. Phillips (2010).
3. ibid., 15.
4. A recent paper by Law (2016) casts doubt as to whether the increase in European trade both led to economic transformations for the Gold Coast and prompted the wars that facilitated the expansion of the trade in enslaved persons. Kay (1982) broadly suggests the gold trade facilitated an economic boom. This chapter shows how the boom built on existing foundations, and also offers several arguments to counterbalance Law's emphasis on purely internal conflicts driving the expanding trade in captives in the seventeenth century.
5. Santiago (1943: 472).
6. Dantzig/Jones (1987: 219); Kwamena Ansa is also Nana Kwamena Ansah, see Ballong-wen-Mewuda (1993: Vol. 1, 59).
7. *MMAI*, Vol. 1, 10–12; Konadu (2010: 59).

8. On the Castilian attack on Ribeira Grande in Cabo Verde, see Blake (1942: Vol. 1, 212–26); for a useful discussion of the reluctance to allow the Portuguese to build, see Ballong-wen-Mewuda (1993: Vol. 1, 60–67); on the power of Eguafo and the number of presents, ibid., Vol. 1, 90.
9. *MMAI*, Vol. 1, 12.
10. On the offer of payment of cloth and manillas, ibid., Vol. 1, 4; on Portuguese trade with other gold-producing kingdoms, see Ballong-wen-Mewuda (1993: Vol. 1, 104–12).
11. *MMAI*, Vol. 1, 13.
12. ibid.; for these descriptions of weaponry, see Jones (1983: 193–6).
13. *MMAI*, Vol. 1, 4–5.
14. On Denkyira's formation in the western forest, emerging from Takyiman, see Konadu (2010: 41); on the apogee of Akan power *c.* 1660, ibid., 64ff.
15. Daaku (1970: 22–3).
16. Green (2016a: 14).
17. Jones (1983: 66–7).
18. On inflation in fifteenth-century Portugal and the gold trade, the classic work is Godinho (1969: 149–63). On the profits accruing from the gold trade, see *MMAI*, Vol. 1, 5; on copper, see Herbert (1984); and on the role of expansion of the currency base in growing the market, see Green (2016a). Konadu (2010: 71) says that copper and manillas were never used as a currency on the Gold Coast, where gold dust was used; however, this is belied by the evidence of Pacheco Pereira on imports, and by the vast numbers of manillas spent by the English in their Gold Coast forts in the late seventeenth century – for this, see, e.g., TNA, T70/657, fol. 18v (25,329 manillas spent at Cape Coast in 1678); TNA, T70/658, fol. 51r, 10,718 manillas imported in 1687.
19. For this quotation on Fetu, see Jones (1983: 193). On the import of firearms in the seventeenth century, see also Law (2017).
20. BA, Cod. 51–IX–25, fol. 46v: 'e avẽdo escalla de negros loguo avera guerra entrelles e day avião de buscar ouro por mover guerra.'
21. These archaeological digs are the important work of the archaeologists Gerard Chouin and Christopher DeCorse (Chouin/DeCorse (2010): 129, 138–42). Chouin and DeCorse hypothesize that these changes were provoked by high mortality associated with the Black Death; however, it is equally plausible that they were brought about by relocations prompted by the economic and political changes analysed in Chapter 1.
22. On gold ornaments, Dantzig/Jones (1987: 34) and Jones (1983: 33); for the routes bringing gold from Asebu and Fante, Jones (1983: 84).
23. 'Its gold gives name to our coin', see Atkins (1970: 38).
24. Okri (1991: 1).

25. For the route from Anomabu, see, for instance, Bowdich's description, Bowdich (1966: 15).
26. On the baptism request, see *MMAI*, Vol. 1, 191.
27. On Akan influences on the Manding, see Konadu (2010); on Manding loanwords in Twi, see Stewart/Wilks (1962); on Islamic influence in the gold weights, Phillips (2010: 15).
28. On the variety of fruit trees imported, see *MMAI*, Vol. 3, 102; for Ruyters, Naber (1913: 74); on maize imports, see Kea (1982: 12) and La Fleur (2012).
29. On expanding states in the seventeenth century, see Daaku (1970: 28–9); on taxes and urban growth, see Kea (1982: 14–16, 18); on Fante, see Shumway (2011) and Law (2012); Law (2018) also argues that by the middle of the eighteenth century, Asante and Fante had effectively divided the Gold Coast between them; on the division of towns into *abrons* and on the *asafos*, see Konadu (2010: 60–61); for the date of the arrival of Fante leaders on the Gold Coast, I am grateful to Benjamin Kye-Ampadu during a visit to Winneba, although some historians place this earlier (e.g. Law (2018)).
30. Kea (1982: 23, 106–10, 206).
31. Jones (1983: 34–6); on the copper inserts, Phillips (2010: 14).
32. Purchas (1905–7: Vol. 6, 277–80). On the expansion of Dutch industry at this time, see Vries/Woude (1997).
33. Dantzig/Jones (1987: 26–7).
34. Jones (1985: 38).
35. Jones (1983: 34–6).
36. Acemoglu et al. (2002) and Nunn (2007), among others.
37. On distrust in the relations between Gold Coast and European peoples, Daaku (1970: 53); on Dutch cheating in the early cloth trade, Purchas (1905–7: Vol. 6, 280).
38. On De la Fosse, *MMAII*, Vol. 1, 472.
39. Dantzig/Jones (1987: 39, 58–9, 68).
40. The fundamental sources for this have been published by Adam Jones. On the gold rings of the people of Fetu, see Jones (1983: 33); on inflation in 1608, ibid., 90, n. 270; for Samuel Brun, see ibid., 90.
41. For the copper and brass trade at Elmina in 1510, see *MMAI*, Vol. 1, 210; on the enormous volumes of the 1500s, see Herbert (1984: 126); on the continuity from the trans-Saharan trade, ibid., 113–14.
42. On copper's use as commodity and store of power as well as currency, Herbert (1984: 184–5); on the different Akan words for cowrie, I am grateful to Mr Benjamin Kye-Ampadu of the Ghana History Teachers' Asssociation.

43. On the copper for gold trade at Great Zimbabwe, see Herbert (1984: 105–6).
44. On iron coins, Purchas (1905–7: Vol. 6, 288–9); on the growth of iron bars as a currency on the Gold Coast in the mid 1640s, see Ratelband (1953: 239–40). See also NA, OWIC, Inventarisnummer 52, no. 46, dated 6 April 1636.
45. For the 1510 report, *MMAI*, Vol. 1, 210.
46. IAN/TT, Inquisição de Lisboa, Processo 11041, fols. 1r–5r; to be published shortly in Konadu (forthcoming).
47. ibid., fol. 5v: 'era seo Deos ẽ q ella adorava'.
48. TNA, T70/656, fols. 9v, 15v.
49. On the despatch of children to the monastery in Portugal, IHGB, DL 98.06.01, 19 December 1564; for the 1572 account, *MMAI*, Vol. 3, 40, 97; on the incorporation of mixed-race children into lineage structures on the Gold Coast, see Everts (2012).
50. *MMAI*, Vol. 1, 190 (for Axim), 444 (for Duarte Pacheco Pereira, 1518–20); ibid., Vol. 4, 85, on the 1514 attack from Fetu.
51. On the 1577–8 war with Fetu, see Dantzig/Jones (1987: 91); on Komenda, Konadu (2010: 59); see Meuwese (2012: 3–4) for the alliance with Accra, and Den Heijer (1997: 13–14) for the alliance between the OWIC and the Fante chief Ambro in 1624; on the growth of a central state power by the seventeenth century for Fante, see Law (2013).
52. For the widespread planting of maize by 1572, see *MMAI*, Vol. 1, 102; and for a broader discussion of maize-growing and the Fante term *oborowi*, see La Fleur (2012: 91–3); for the import of maize from São Tomé, see Anonymous (1665: 14).
53. Dantzig/Jones (1987: 27).
54. For Ruyters, Naber (1913: 74): 'niet en Ox-hoost vuyl water halen, ofte moet het noch soo diere betalen, alst Bier in Nederlandt sonde costen'; on Elmina, Delbée (1671: 375); on Dixcove, Law (1997–2006: Vol. 3, 59).
55. On the English in Sekondi, Law (1997–2006: Vol. 2, 11); on the reliance on local servants, Daaku (1970: 38).
56. See for examples of these attacks on the European traders, e.g., De Naber (1931: 104–9), the attack of 1625 on the Dutch killing 442 men; Law (1997–2006: Vol. 1, 18) for the burning of Sekondi in 1683; ibid., Vol. 2, 158, 176, for the kidnapping of the Portuguese captain in Anomabu. On the import of firearms from *c.* 1650, Adu-Boahen (2012: 181); and, in 1600, Dantzig/Jones (1987: 92).
57. On the divergence in political and economic patterns, Daaku (1970: 49); on land ownership, Anonymous (1665: 13); see also Guyer (2004);

and I am grateful to Dr Sam Adu-Gyamfi for his assistance on this point related to land.

58. Camara/Jansen (1999: 43).
59. On slaves becoming Muslim at Elmina, *MMAI*, Vol. 1, 54–5; for the title *xerife* used in a 1503 document, ibid., 192. Konadu (2010: 62) mentions this title; and in further important new material that he has located (Konadu, forthcoming), the title is mentioned in other early-sixteenth-century Portuguese documents related to the Akan, showing that it was quite widespread at the time.
60. On the caps worn in a Turkish style, see Dantzig/Jones (1987: 34); on the war between Kano and Katsina, see Smith (1997: 22).
61. Dantzig/Jones (1987: 37).
62. On Songhay military structure, see Cissoko (1974: 109–12); on the Arma, see Hall (2011: 30–31).
63. On the rise of Katsina, see Usman (1981: 20–21) and Levtzion (1968: 18); on the Habe chiefdoms, see Hiskett (1973: 5–8); on Borno, see, e.g., Candotti (2015: 99) and Usman (1981: 34–5).
64. For the *dunamas* of Borno, Richmond Palmer (1936: 94–5); for a 1749 drought in Timbuktu, Abitbol (1982: 2); and for the 1740s drought in general, Lovejoy (1974: 566). More generally on the beginning of this dry period in West Africa and its longevity, see Brooks (1993).
65. Delbée (1671: 375–8); Ruyter/Meppelen (1665: 58); on the burning of Sekondi in 1695, Bosman (1967: 19).
66. Atkins (1970: 97–9).
67. Law (1997–2006: Vol. 1, 54) on the negotiation at Komenda between the English and Dutch of a price of 32 sheets per *benda* of gold; on the 1686 war of Akyem and Akron, ibid., Vol. 2, 192–3, and on the 1687 war of Fetu and Fante, ibid., 221–2; on the 1694 war of Akyem and Akwamu, ibid., Vol. 3, 523.
68. Bosman (1967: 5, 7); these sorts of divisions were commonplace, with, in 1695, the Dutch hiring Twifo to attack the King of Komenda, who was supported by the English – see Law (1997–2006: Vol. 3, 50, n. 180).
69. For the English factor's remark, Law (1997–2006: Vol. 2, 193).
70. Richmond Palmer (1936: 33–4); on the rapid growth of Borno's slave trade after 1650, see Candotti (2015: 99), and ibid., 103, on the pre-existing gold trade in the fifteenth century.
71. This key point on the interconnection of the two economic systems was made long ago in a key intervention by Paul Lovejoy – see Lovejoy (1974: 565).
72. Law (1997–2006: Vol. 2, 146).

73. *MMAI*, Vol. 3, 521.
74. ibid., 522–3, 600.
75. ibid., Vol. 2, 46; cf. Barcia (2014).
76. On the rise of São Tomé as a slave-exporting hub linked to Allada by *c.* 1605, see, for instance, AGI, Indiferente General 2795, [n.d.], letter of Gonçalo Vaz Countinho; and ibid., letter *c.* 1611 of Juan Nuñez Correa on the parasite infestation, and also for this BA, Cod. 51–IX–25, fol. 73v; on the early link of Elmina to São Tomé, see, e.g., *MMAI*, Vol. 1, 505.
77. On the English slave-trading ships, Ratelband (1953: 6, 7, 12, 24, 133); on Dutch and Portuguese laws, Dantzig (1980: 114–15); on a 1621 attempt to get the ban on the slave trade lifted, BA, Cod. 51–IX–25, fol. 46v; on the English trade as mostly for slaves, NA, OWIC, Inventarisnummer 11, no. 139 ('hare principalen negotie gesondert tot den slavsse handel').
78. TNA, T70/376, fol. 27v, for a 'dankra' [Denkyira] pawn; for canoemen as pawns by 1678–9, see TNA, T70/657, fols. 2v, 54r; on pawning in general, see Lovejoy/Richardson (1999) and (2001).
79. On the iron bars of the English, NA, OWIC, Inventarisnummer 11, no. 139; on the 125,000 pieces of *lijwaet*, see NA, OWIC, Inventarisnummer 11, no. 28; on the values in florins, NA, OWIC, Inventarisnummer 11, no. 61.
80. Vries/Woude (1997: 270, 281, 283–5, 670).
81. Evans (2015: 2–3, 9–14).
82. On maize, see, for instance, Purchas (1905–7: Vol. 6, 272), which describes the baking of maize bread at Elmina in 1600.
83. Ratelband (1953: 135) has a log report from 1645 of the cargo of the ship *Postpaert* carrying 213,035 pounds of grain.
84. Purchas (1905–7: Vol. 6, 281).

4 RIVERS OF CLOTH, MASKS OF BRONZE: THE BIGHTS OF BENIN AND BIAFRA

1. On the beginnings of the trade from Salvador to the 'Costa da Mina', see Souza (2011).
2. On the cultural borrowings between the Igbo and Igala, see Achebe (2011: 32).
3. Johnson (1937: 15–20); Ogundiran (2002: 433–4); Filipello (2016).
4. Alongside Babalola, the key work on these techniques is by the seminal archaeologist Akinwumi Ogundiran – see Ogundiran/Ige (2015); and Babalola (2016).

5. On potsherd pavements in many Edo and Yorùbá areas from the thirteenth to the fifteenth century, see Ogundiran (2002a: 54); on Nupe, Konstanze Weise has conducted important excavations – see Weise (2016).
6. On iron in Nupe, Weise (2016); for cloth, Kriger (1990) and Shaw (1970); on cloth from this region in Brazil in the late eighteenth and early nineteenth centuries, Hicks (2017).
7. The conceptualization of these links was formulated in part by the important work of Akinjogbin (1967: 16), who described an Aja–Yorùbá commonwealth. On the foundation of Enugu by a migrant from Benin, Achebe (2011: 31); for a critique of Akinjogbin's approach, Rufer (2016: 726–7).
8. Johnson (1937: xix).
9. Rufer (2016: 708); Parés (2016: 44); Filipello (2016).
10. Berzock (2008: 6); Roese/Bondarenko (2003: 18, 63).
11. Barros (1945: 90).
12. On the Ihogbe and Ogboka, Roese/Bondarenko (2003: 20). On the view of the bronzes as revealing European influence, Pitt-Rivers (1900). Pitt-Rivers's plates reveal swords shaped like leaves (Plates 1, 27); necklaces of leopards' teeth (ibid., 8); and the kings on horseback (ibid., 10). There is a large literature on *axé* in both Yorùbá and Brazilian contexts, where *axé* became central to the Afro-Brazilian religion of Candomblé. See on this, e.g., Henry (2008).
13. Barros (1945: 90).
14. On 'lost wax', see Berzock (2008: 6).
15. On the Ókìpò Wars, Ogundiran (2002a: 34–5); on the decline of Ilé-Ifè and these kingdoms in this period, see Ogundiran (2016); on the effect of the wars on the small Kingdom of Igala near Nupe, see Usman (2016).
16. Roese/Bondarenko (2003: 80–86); Ryder (1969: 8–10).
17. Ryder (1969: 8), on the interwoven kingdoms and dynastic transformations of Nupe, Oyo and Benin at this time. The date 1486 is confirmed in Rui de Pina's chronicle, *MMAI*, Vol. 1, 52.
18. *MMAI*, Vol. 1, 52; on the 1514 ambassador, ibid., 326.
19. Mauny (1956: 134).
20. On the 1515–16 conflict, see *MMAI*, Vol. 1, 370; on the disappointment of missionaries in 1539, ibid., Vol. 2, 79–80; on the economic problems with the trading post at Benin, see ibid., Vol. 1, 52. For a good overview of Bini–Portuguese relations at this time, see Roese/Bondarenko (2003: 127–8); and Ryder (1969: 33–49), who suggests

that it was independent Portuguese traders from São Tomé who supported the Bini in 1516, not the Portuguese crown.

21. Dantzig/Jones (1987: 228).
22. Roth (1968: 9–11).
23. For an example of such a depiction, Pitt-Rivers (1900: Plate 27). On words in Edo and Portuguese, Roese/Bondarenko (2003: 103, 348).
24. *MMAI*, Vol. 4, 619–20; see also Roese/Bondarenko (2003: 146–7).
25. Jones (1983: 24–5, 38).
26. Anguiano (1957: 36).
27. Roese/Bondarenko (2003: 25–6, 81).
28. Jones (1983: 24, 41).
29. Ogilby (1670: 470–71); Connah (1975: 32, 138).
30. Roth (1968: 91).
31. Nafafé (2007: 2); Berzock (2008: 5).
32. On casters' use of Portuguese designs for helmets and the attempts to reproduce cannons, Roese/Smith (2000: 97).
33. For Pacheco Pereira, Mauny (1956: 134); for the change to 1517, see Garfield (1992: 46) and Ryder (1969: 53); see ibid., 303, for the log of the ship *São Miguel* from 1522.
34. Connah (1975: 1–2).
35. Ogilby (1670: 470).
36. Ryder (1969: 61) – and for the inflation in the price of slaves and yams from 1522 to 1526, ibid., 63–4; Garfield (1992: 47); Roth (1968: 9); on the increasing prevalence of snail-shell motifs in the seventeenth century, Usman (2000: 58).
37. Roth (1968: 91, 132–3); Ogundiran (2014: 14–15); Ryder (1969: 61); Jones (1983: 41).
38. Ryder (1969: 60); Ogundiran (2002a: 436).
39. Law (1997: 18, 44); for more detail on African–European relations at Great Popo, see Strickrodt (2015).
40. Akinjogbin (1967: 10–14); Parés (2016: 114–18, 131).
41. Anguiano (1957: 52–3, and for the catechism, Appendix 3).
42. On Offra, Delbée (1671: 388).
43. On persons from Allada in what is now Colombia, see AGNB, Notaría Primera de Bogotá, Vol. 11, fol. 340v; and AGNB, Archivo Histórico de Boyacá, Notaría Primera de Tunja, Legajo 37, fol. 329r; on the 1582 contract, Vila Vilar (1977: 25); see also BA, Códice 51–IX–25, fol. 115v. Factors pushing the Sãotomense traders towards Allada included the fact that the slave trade from Angola was placed on a contract-holding basis after 1595.

44. Strickrodt (2015).
45. ibid., 244; Delbée (1671: 436).
46. Delbée (1671: 388–99); on the key Allada role in the emergence of maize-flour breads, La Fleur (2012: 113–22).
47. Delbée (1671: 440–41).
48. Purchas (1905–7: Vol. 6, 354); on markets and border areas, paper given by Professor Olukoya Ogen of Osun State University at the University of Birmingham, June 2009.
49. Purchas (1905–7: Vol. 6, 353–4).
50. On Jorge Fernandez Gramajo, see AGI, Escribanía 589B, fol. 2r; on the registers from San Juan de Ulúa, see AGI, Escribanía 12A, Pieza 7A; Ngou-Mve (1994: 43, 170); and Wheat (2011: 15, 19) makes a strong case for enslaved persons from Allada in Cartagena in the 1610s. For the voyages by Damião Ramires, see AHU, Conselho Ultramarino, São Tomé, Caixa 1, doc. 99, and also Northrup (1978: 51).
51. On 'Alladas' in Brazil, Calado (1648: 161); for Dutch ships going to and from Allada, Ratelband (1953: 36–7, 320); Delbée (1671: 437); on the growing seventeenth-century trade at Allada in general, Law (1991: 11).
52. On the export of cotton cloths from Allada by 1620, see BA, Códice 51–IX–25, fol. 74r; on the export to Luanda, see Jadin (1975: Vol. 1, 219).
53. Anguiano (1957: 244): 'esperando que el capitán del navío echase la ropa en tierra, que era lo que más atendían y de lo que principalmente cuidaban.' For a discussion of the decline in cloth exports from Allada by 1700, see Green (2016a). For evidence of trade of Allada cloths to the Gold Coast, see TNA, T70/657, fol. 38r (1678) and TNA, T70/659, fol. 20r (1687).
54. Anguiano (1957: 54); discussed recently in the context of religious practice by Parés (2016: 123).
55. On São Tomé, AHU, CU, São Tomé, Caixa 2, doc. 141, 15 January 1661; on an epidemic at Cape Lope Gonçalves in 1663, AGI, Indiferente General 2834, 22 March 1663; on Angola, see Miller (1982); on locusts in Nsundi, see Piazza (1976: 177); and ibid., 223–4, on epidemics in Kongo in 1655; on Osògbò, Ogundiran (2014: 2); on climate change and the slave trade, Fenske/Kala (2012).
56. Faust et al. (2006).
57. Roth (1968: 157–9).
58. Bosman (1967: 439–40).
59. ibid., 431, 461; Roth (1968: 157–9).
60. Law (1977: 33–41).

61. Usman (2000: 45–6, 49, 51); Usman (2003: 208).
62. The proverb is cited in Robin Law's important work on Oyo: see Law (1977: 198); for Oyo's seventeenth-century expansion and relations with Allada, ibid., 40–43, 151, 155.
63. Johnson (1937: 70–76, 164–6); Law (1977: 62–5); Ogundiran (2014: 13).
64. Bosman (1967: 462); on seventeenth-century obas, see Roese/Bondarenko (2003: 200–201).
65. On Dutch and English ships going to the Bight of Benin, Ratelband (1953: 36–7, 251, 259, 265); on Calabar, ibid., 54, 117, 165; on *ambasys*, ibid., 211; on the 1650s account of neighbouring settlements, Cavazzi (1687: 583).
66. For the 1670–71 report, see Moraes (1998: 294ff.); on the oba using Indian silk by 1700, Bosman (1967: 464); on the use of imported materials in weaving, see ibid., 433, where Bosman states that 'at our Arrival here, we are obliged to trust them with Goods to make Panes or Cloaths of'; nearly 300,000 ells of cloth were sent to Elmina alone by the Dutch in 1645, including damask, satin and silk (Ratelband 1953: Appendix K).
67. Dantzig (1978: 44–5); on Benin cloths at Cape Coast in 1687, TNA, T70/659, fol. 19r.
68. Dantzig (1978: 38). This conclusion is somewhat at odds with some of the historiography on this topic; historians such as John Thornton have framed the import of goods already manufactured in Africa as a choice, and yet the economic framework used in this book suggests that the push-pull factors were somewhat different.
69. Cavazzi (1687: 578).
70. Bosman (1967: 460); Ogilby (1670: 467).
71. Dantzig (1978: 89–90, 111).
72. ibid., 150.
73. ibid., 124–5.
74. On the recommencement of the slave trade, Roese/Bondarenko (2003: 221).
75. Bosman (1967: 339); Law (1997–2006: Vol. 3, 191).
76. See, on wider processes and the relative value of currencies, Austen (1987: 92). On this definition of 'hard' currencies, Guyer (2012). See Fromont (2014: 135–6) on the negative impact of the adoption of foreign textiles in Kongo.
77. TNA, T70/1213, Monday, 11 February 1677; TNA, T70/1214, the accounts of the ship *Morning Star*.

5 THE KINGDOM OF KONGO: FROM MAJESTY TO REVOLT

1. Ferreira (2013).
2. Cavazzi (1687): 179.
3. For more on Kongo ambassadors in this era, see Fromont (2014: 116–20) and Heywood (2017: 138).
4. For Sousa, *MMAI*, Vol. 8, 93; for 1652, AHU, CU, Angola, Caixa 5, doc. 101: 'aborreçem os Portugueses com odio capital'.
5. For Garcia's full name, BNM, MS 3533 (Antonio de Teruel), fol. ix; Garcia complained bitterly of the peace conditions, 'so hard and burdensome', e.g., AHU, CU, Angola, Caixa 5, doc. 26. One of the best general accounts of these wars in Angola remains Boxer (1952).
6. Tovar (1649: 20).
7. BNM, MS 3533, pp. 123–4.
8. On the early exchanges from 1606 onwards, see Meuwese (2012: 85–7); on the 1622 battle, Mosterman/Thornton (2010) is fundamental. On the Dutch and the Atlantic slave trade, Postma (1990).
9. On the despatch by the OWIC of Heyn, Naber (1931: 66); for Heyn's account of his trip to Luanda, Ratelband (1959: 3–9).
10. Mosterman/Thornton (2010: 244).
11. For Fernão de Sousa, *MMAI*, Vol. 7, 310–11; for 1638 and the fort at Mpinda, ibid., Vol. 8, 392; for 1638 and the offer to attack Luanda by land, AHU, CU, Angola, Caixa 3, doc. 44; for the 1660 account, AHU, CU, Angola, Caixa 7, doc. 55.
12. The phrase 'the struggle for Brazil and Angola' was the defining one of Boxer (1952). On British involvement in the Companhia do Brasil, see Costa (2002: Vol. 1, 127). This diplomatic involvement was very well known and appears in numerous documents and accounts – in addition to those cited elsewhere here, see Cadornega (1972: Vol. 1, 230). On 'sem Angola, não ha Brasil', see *MMAI*, Vol. 11, 428.
13. For Teruel's account, BNM, MS 3533, p. 27; for the ambassadors in the United Provinces, *MMAI*, Vol. 9, 64; for the ambassadors of Kongo and Nsoyo in Recife, Jadin (1975: Vol. 1, 394, 438); for the letters between Garcia II and Nzinga, see Heywood (2017: 149).
14. Nieuhoff's account is in *ACV*, Vol. 2, 42; the peace treaty of 1642, *MMAI*, Vol. 8, 585.
15. On the shared symbol of the cross that created a 'space of correlation', see Fromont (2014); see also Young (2007).

16. On Dutch and Kongos fighting together, AHU, CU, Angola, Caixa 4, doc. 22.
17. Haveaux (1954: 47).
18. One of the best books on pre-Atlantic formations south of Kongo, among the Bantu peoples of Angola, is Vansina (2004).
19. Vansina (2010: 635–6).
20. On sugarcane in Kongo, see *MMAI*, Vol. 1, 251, and in Benin as pre-dating the Portuguese, Roese/Bondarenko (2003: 116–18). As evidence of the role of long-distance routes and Arab regions in bringing sugar, there was also sugar in Gao and Kanem by the twelfth century – see Lewicki (1974: 115); on the link of the Kalahari to the Indian Ocean, Luna (2016: 186–90). On Kongo use of the crosses, see especially Fromont (2014: 65–108) and MacGaffey (1986: 43) and also Miller (1997: 238), who notes that cross-shaped ingots of copper circulated in Angola before the Portuguese arrival; for Edo use of crosses prior to the Portuguese arrival, see Pitt-Rivers (1900: 8) and Berzock (2007: 9).
21. On traders from Benin in Kongo in 1526, *MMAI*, Vol. 1, 479. Had these traders come via the Portuguese, it would most likely have been through São Tomé; at this time São Tomé traders were working especially in Angola, and less in Mpinda, which makes this not a certain route for the traders from Benin. For a preliminary discussion of the importance of a history of West and West-Central African seafaring, see Peters (2018).
22. For an overall argument as to the place of long-distance trade in economic growth, see Inikori (2002).
23. For Thornton's careful calculation of the origins of the kingdom in the later fourteenth century, see Thornton (2001: 106–7); on regional markets, Thornton (1983: 32–3); on iron, Cavazzi (1687: 5, 8).
24. Cavazzi (1687: 4, 5, 262); Miller (1983: 126–8) emphasizes the role of geographical boundaries in Kongo's trading networks. Miller (1997: 250) in this regard also notes that Kongo is located close to Mayombe's copper mines, salt from the Atlantic and forest products from the north. The importance of Malebo Pool to Kongolese trade is shown through the fact that the later word for trader in the Angola region, *pombeiro*, derives from it – Heintze (1985: 125). See also Hilton (1985: 33).
25. On the six seasons, see Parreira (1990: 30; Kitombi was in February and March); on the trade of cattle and oxen to Kongo, *MMAI*, Vol. 2, 502; on the annual floods of the river and the link of trade to the connecting of different ecologies, Vansina (2004: 188); on markets and rivers, Silva (2011: 188).
26. For Cavazzi on Loango and Kongo's hegemony (1687: 264–5, 564, 620–21); for the 1516 letter of the manikongo confirming influence

over Loango, Cordeiro (1881: 7); on the Kongo traditions of political supremacy, BA, Códice 46–X–12, fols. 270v–271r, and BA, Códice 51–IX–25, fol. 127v – see also, for instance, Brásio (1969: 47), and also Duarte Lopes's late-sixteenth-century evidence – Pigafetta (1970: 32); on the friendship of the King of Ndongo to Kongo, BA, Códice 51–IX–25, fol. 128r: 'O Rei de Angola era amigo e quase subdito do Rey de Congo e lhe mandava cada ano seu tributo'; on 'Pangelunga', Ngou-Mve (1994: 49); for the perspective of a contemporary historian on this, Gonçalves (2000: 420).

27. For Lucques, Cuvelier (1953: 140); and ibid., 81, for people's obeisance to those in superior rank if met on a path; also on the *mwissikongo*, Hilton (1985: 35–7); on iron, smiths and the connection to Kongo kings, see MacGaffey (1986: 66–7) and Balandier (1968: 36) and ibid., 176–7, on the hierarchies of daily life – see also Randles (1968: 54–5) on this.
28. On this dichotomy, Thornton (2000: 67) is excellent; see also Thornton (1983: 16). On sources for an original migration crossing the Congo, see Piazza (1976: 195–6) and Brásio (1969: 43–4); although Thornton (2001: 108) notes that there is a mythical element to such accounts.
29. For documents on women doing agricultural work, see, for instance, Cuvelier/Jadin (1954: 121) and Cuvelier (1953: 79). On gender as a key faultline and elder males seeking to control women, Miller (1983: 125). See also Hilton (1985: 5–6) and ibid., 8, on the patrifilial descent of spiritual identity and personality. On manikongos succeeding their uncles, see, e.g., *MMAI*, Vol. 8, 9, where Álvaro IV succeeded Ambrosio in 1631.
30. Balandier (1968: 13) puts it that the trade favoured 'the more powerful partner'.
31. MacGaffey (1986: 6, 43). As this great anthropologist of the BaKongo put it, 'it is only the nonbeliever who believes that the believer believes in God; to the believer his belief is knowledge, that is, perceived and experienced fact' (ibid., 1).
32. Bethencourt (2011); on witches in Loango, Ravenstein (1901: 48); on witchcraft and selfishness in BaKongo society, MacGaffey (1986: 171–4).
33. For the use of the cross on bowls made in South Carolina, see Young (2007: 89).
34. On the cross in Kongo symbolism, MacGaffey (1986: 43) and Young (2007: 88); and Thornton (1998b: 56). See also Kananoja (2012: 234). On Kongo crosses in the Americas, see, for instance, Farris Thompson (1984: 108–16), and on musical instruments, Dubois (2016: 68, 118–19).
35. *MMAI*, Vol. 1, 112.

36. ibid., Vol. 1, 113–14.
37. On the reluctance to sign up to monogamy, BNM, MS 3533, fol. vii; for the importance of polygamy for the *kandas*, see Hilton (1985: 52).
38. Hilton (1985: 53).
39. IHGB, DL 98.06.61.
40. *MMAI*, Vol. 1, 122, 132.
41. Cuvelier (1953: 67–8, 75–6, 79).
42. *MMAI*, Vol. 2, 78, 226–7; ibid., Vol. 4, 367; on 'Creole' Christianity in Kongo, see especially Heywood/Thornton (2007).
43. For the 1603 letter, *MMAI*, Vol. 5, 82; for the 1643 account, ibid., Vol. 9, 36; for the later account on Luanda, BA, Códice 50–V–37, fol. 245r [n.d.].
44. For more on the 'Creole' Catholicism practised by the *mwissikongo*, see Heywood/Thornton (2007).
45. Jadin (1966: 224); *MMAI*, Vol. 11, 190; on baptism and salt, Hilton (1985: 98).
46. On Beatriz Kimpa Vita, Thornton (1998b); on these episodes of spiritual renewal, MacGaffey (1986: 192–3).
47. See especially Fromont (2014: Chapter 1), on the *sangamentos*; on the water between the living and the dead in Kongo belief, MacGaffey (1986: 43).
48. On Kongo's embassy to the Vatican in 1539, *MMAI*, Vol. 2, 73; on Kongo ambassadors in the 1620s, *MMAI*, Vol. 7, 4; on the strategy of using the Vatican against the Portuguese, Filesi (1968: 22); on the gift of 1645, BNM, MS 3533, p. 32; for the letter of 1652 from Garcia II to the Vatican, *MMAI*, Vol. 11, 139–40.
49. On the Jesuit wealth, AHU, CU, Angola, Caixa 6, doc. 150, 5 November 1658.
50. *MMAI*, Vol. 1, 465–6, 470.
51. ibid., Vol. 1, 489–90.
52. ibid., Vol. 2, 59.
53. ibid., Vol. 1, 488–90; Vogt (1973: 458); Vansina (1966: 40); and Heywood (2009), a key work.
54. *MMAI*, Vol. 4, 21, 68, 82.
55. On the detail from 1516, ibid., Vol. 1, 378; on the 1530s, Vol. 2, 58; ibid., 199–205, on the volumes by 1548. See also Vansina (1966: 58–61) and Caldeira (1999: 22–4).
56. Vogt (1973: 460) on the certificates of the dead; for a comparative view on the growth of belief in witchcraft as related to the increase in the trade in captives, see Shaw (2002).

57. On 1515, *MMAI*, Vol. 1, 381; on the role of the Portuguese in defending Mbanza Kongo, Cadornega (1972: Vol. 1, 11); in general on Kongo as a middleman kingdom, see Hilton (1985: 58–60).
58. Hilton (1985: 66); for the Jesuit letter of 1552, *MMAI*, Vol. 2, 275.
59. Pigafetta (1970: 96).
60. ibid., 97; for the description of the Congo River, BNM, MS 3533, pp. 19, 28.
61. Pigafetta (1970: 11, 97–100).
62. The literature on the 'Jaga' and their identities is very large. For a good later summary, see especially Miller (1973) and *idem* (1997: 261), who argues that they represented a civil war; Thornton (1978), who disputes this and says the Tyo could not have been responsible (see also Miller (1978)'s response); and the key work to support the Kwango hypothesis, Hilton (1981: 193, 198) and *idem* (1985: 70). For a strong argument on the 'Jaga' as a Kongo faction, see Ndâwla (1999).
63. Jarric (1610–14: Vol. 2, 11).
64. On priests on the electoral council after 1568, see Vansina (1966: 43–4).
65. Cavazzi (1687: 164); Thornton (2003: 273).
66. Ravenstein (1901: 25–6, 30); the classic account of the Imbangala is Miller (1976), though Vansina (1998) casts doubt as to whether the migrations described by Miller in this work ever took place.
67. On infanticide and the adolescent military corps, Ravenstein (1901: 32). The best recent discussion of the term 'Jaga' is by Mariana Candido – see Candido (2013: 59–60); for the numbers leaving in 1576, *MMAI*, Vol. 3, 146, and for accounts of slave trading in Ndongo since at least the 1530s, ibid., Vol. 2, 268.
68. Cavazzi (1687: 201) on red wine; on the link of witchcraft, cannibalism, slavery and the Imbangala, Thornton (2002: 82–3) and *idem* (2003: 289); see also ibid., 282, on the 1627 account of Alonso de Sandoval from Cartagena, Colombia. That this belief was real is suggested by the fact that both he and Cavazzi noted this belief regarding 'oil' – see above, n. 65.
69. BNM, MS 3533, p. 101.
70. ibid., p. 117.
71. On 'calculative rationality', see Guyer (2004); on the privilege of gift-giving in classless societies, Fishburne Collier (1988: 215).
72. Felner (1933: 387).
73. ibid., 238, on copper in pre-Atlantic Kongo and Ndongo; on copper and the initial rise of Kongo, see Hilton (1985: 32); for Batell, Ravenstein (1901: 26–7); on the importance of copper currencies by the fourteenth century in Southern-Central Africa, see Luna (2016: 206–7).

74. On a 1627 gift of copper manillas, see *MMAI*, Vol. 7, 520.
75. On the general importance of mines to the Portuguese and Dutch colonial efforts in West-Central Africa, see Saccardo (1982: 327). On rumours of silver in Ndongo in 1520, *MMAI*, Vol. 1, 432; for smiths sent to mine Kongo's copper in 1536, ibid., Vol. 2, 59; on Portuguese royal interest in Kongo's silver and copper in 1556, ibid., 396; and on mines across the region in general in 1561, ibid., 476–9; on the silver connection to the foundation of Luanda, AHU, CU, Angola, Caixa 1, doc. 3A (published in *MMAI*, Vol. 5, doc. 101) – the same document (dated 1607) shows widespread continued interest in the copper, iron, tin and lead mines supposed to be widespread in Ndongo; miners accompanied a military expedition to Cambambe in 1587 (Rebello (1588: 63)), and rumours of silver mines persisted in 1626 (AHU, CU, Angola, Caixa 1, doc. 113); as late as 1628, royal instructions to the Governor of Luanda urged him to pressure the manikongo to open up mines of silver and copper (*MMAI*, Vol. 7, 569); and for the interest in Benguela, see ibid., Vol. 6, 31–3, and Heintze (1985: 136).
76. For Sousa's attempts in the later 1620s, ibid., 228–9; for his letter of 1633, *MMAI*, Vol. 8, 229; for the Jesuit letter of 1594, *MMAI*, Vol. 4, 550.
77. On copper currencies in sixteenth-century Portugal, *DHA*, Vol. 1, 101, 205. On the re-export of silver to China, see Frank (1998), Flynn (1978), and Flynn/Giraldez (1995) and (1996).
78. On copper's use for artillery in Pernambuco, Soares (1958: 45); and in Lima, KH, Collection Nassau-Siegen, A4–1454, fol. 183r; on copper's use in plantations (*engenhos*), see, for instance, the will of Antonio de Sá, of 1662, ASM, Maço 41, Livro do Tombo (2), fol. 156v. Moreover, copper *was* exported from Cacongo in the 1630s – see *MMAI*, Vol. 8, 93–5.
79. Neves (1854: 100). There is a huge and growing literature on Nzinga – see especially Heywood (2017).
80. BNM, MS 3533, pp. 32ff.
81. On the exchangeability to the *milreis*, Jadin (1966: 223); on being shaped like hearts, Cadornega (1972: Vol. 2, 269–70); for a summary of different measurements of *nzimbu*, Balandier (1968: 130). Curiously this vital element of the formation of Luanda in 1575 has escaped much discussion.
82. On Kongo governors at Luanda, *MMAI*, Vol. 4, 539; on trading for *nzimbu* at Luanda in 1553, ibid., Vol. 2, 354; on rich Portuguese in Luanda by 1574, ibid., Vol. 4, 554; on Novais's recognition of this importance, ibid., 537–9; on Kongo's administration of the island in the late sixteenth century, see ibid., 618.
83. Cuvelier/Jadin (1954: 263–4).

84. On royal seals on the *funda*, see Bontinck (1964: 44); on Kongo governors in Luanda in 1648, *MMAI*, Vol. 10, 236–7; on *nzimbu* being used in the 1690s, Bontinck (1970: 31).
85. On the inflation of the 1610s, *MMAI*, Vol. 6, 342–3 and 383, and Vol. 8, 143; the key work here is Hilton (1985: 106); on the lack of taxes paid on *nzimbu* imports in 1612, AHU, CU, Angola, Caixa 1, doc. 132 (republished in *MMAI*, Vol. 6, 108); on continued imports from Brazil in the 1620s, ibid., Vol. 7, 504. On Dutch exports of *nzimbu* from Brazil and the River Plate, Jadin (1975: Vol. 1, 122 and 170) and NA, OWIC, Inventarisnummer 58, no. 214; on the *nzimbu* trade from Ilhéus in the 1620s, Naber (1931: 58).
86. For the 1623 letter, Cuvelier/Jadin (1954: 454); on welcoming escaped slaves in the 1650s, AHU, CU, Angola, Caixa 7, doc. 11.
87. On the colours and weaving skills in the 1490s, *MMAI*, Vol. 1, 57; on the trade just for cloth, *MMAI*, Vol. 6, 438, and Heintze (1985: 197); on Momboares, *MMAI*, Vol. 15, 534 – an account of 1624.
88. On the trade of Kongo cloths to Angola, ibid., Vol. 6, 473; on the volume, see Heintze (1989: 32); Cadornega (1972: Vol. 3, 195).
89. On early cloth trade in Loango before 1595, see Ravenstein (1901: 9); on *libongos* as currency and the Portuguese trade in 1610, La Fleur (2000: 74–5, 95).
90. Cadornega (1972: Vol. 3, 195–6).

CODA TO PART ONE

1. Jansen/Duintjer/Tamboura (1995: 100–101).
2. On the link to the Indian Ocean, Luna (2016).
3. On Montesarchio and lions, Piazza (1976: 232); Cavazzi (1687: 10, 44, 670); on lions entering Mbanza Pemba, see BNM, MS 3533, p. 137; on the rise of wild animals and the collapse of the Native American population, see Mann (2005).
4. On the convertibility of *libongos* to *reais*, see BA, Códice 54–X–9, fol. 10v, *c.* 1657; cloth was described as 'the money of Angola' in a Dutch account of 1641, see NA, OWIC, Inventarisnummer 56, no. 270; on the various uses of cloth currency in Luanda, see AHU, CU, Angola, Caixa 5, doc. 93 (approx. 1663); on the extinction of the cloth currencies, see AHU, CU, Angola, Caixa 12, doc. 20.
5. On *libongos* and Kongo cloths as parallel currencies in 1649, see *MMAI*, Vol. 10, 312; on the different Kongo cloths, see Cadornega (1972: Vol. 2, 271), and on the red cloth from Loango already traded

by 1612, see AHU, CU, Angola, Caixa 1, doc. 132, and (in 1632) *MMAI*, Vol. 8, 124; on fraud and fraying of *libongos* by 1684, see AHU, CU, Angola, Caixa 13, docs. 9, 72 and 98 (which also documents the inflation after 1640).

6. On the fact that it begins as a currency in Loango, see AHU, CU, Angola, Caixa 13, doc. 98; on the greater profits on *libongos*, see Hilton (1985: 116); this central idea of inflation as a commonplace among currencies in this region is also advanced in Green (2016b); and criticized in Rönnbäck (2018); and responded to by Green (2018b).
7. On the 1699 ship, AHU, CU, Angola, Caixa 15, doc. 101; on the Dutch imports in 1642, see Jadin (1975: Vol. 1, 317–20), and on the demand from Kongo, see Jadin (1966: 228–9); on cloth as the major industry of Loango, see Parreira (1990: 53).
8. On candle manufacture, Bontinck (1964: 96); and on other types of manufacture, Tovar (1649: 64).
9. On wrapping bodies in cloth, see Cavazzi (1687: 116); on the mythic symbolism of the shell in Kongo, see Heusch (2000: 97); on wearing iron and copper, see Bontinck (1970: 128); on *takula* and its various uses in ritual practice and the constitution of power, see Cadornega (1972: Vol. 2, 47 – on the powder used as a dye for clothing and to cover the body with a special ointment), Cuvelier (1953: 137 – on the use of *takula* in bride-price negotiations), Miller (1976: 48 – on *takula* being given to young men by lineage heads as a sign of initiation), and BNM, MS 3533, pp. 117ff. (on painting sacred trees red with *takula*).
10. On Palmares, see especially Anderson (1996); Kent (1965), and Schwartz (1992).

PART TWO

Consequences: Politics, Belief and Revolutions from Below

PROLOGUE TO PART TWO

1. On this switch to the higher potential capital value of captive labour in the eighteenth century, see especially the pathfinding insights of Rodney (1988: 99).
2. ibid., 273; see also Marcussi (2016: 248) on contradiction as an attribute of colonial societies.
3. Bosman (1967: 48–9).

4. Smith (1967: 122–6).
5. Bosman (1967: 50–51).
6. For examples of inventories of provisions from São Tomé in the 1640s, see NA, OWIC, Inventarisnummer 42, MF 23, and Inventarisnummer 11, nos. 123 and 124; on the *Noorthollandt*, see NA, OWIC, Inventarisnummer, 64, nos. 105 and 134.
7. On the lack of food within 150 miles of Luanda, Jadin (1975: Vol. 1, 323); ibid., Vol. 1, 206, on the lack of means to start manioc plantations; ibid., Vol. 1, 390, and Vol. 2, 644 and 883, on lack of provisions as a key source of the failure of the Dutch in Luanda.
8. A new PhD dissertation on the connections between Angola and Buenos Aires in this period is Schultz (2016), who offers interesting analyses of the numbers of captives entering Buenos Aires, and the role of Africans entering the colonial Americas through this port.
9. On the 1623 taxes paid on the slave trade from Angola, AHU, CU, Bahia, Catálogo de Luíza da Fonseca, Caixa 3, doc. 301; on the movement of silver around Angola at this time, BA, Códice 51–IX–20; on the payment to the Dutch of Loango in silver, Heintze (1988: Vol. 2, 145); on the 1603 register, AGI, Charcas, 38, [unnumbered] doc. entitled 'Testimonios de todos los negros q an entrado por este puerto de Buenos ayres desde el año de 1597 hasta este presente de 1606'. Schultz (2016: 27–9) discusses Spanish complaints about Portuguese illegal access to silver through the slave trade.
10. On the relationship of New World silver to profits generated in China, see Flynn/Giraldez (1995: 211) and (1996).
11. On the declining profits in China, Flynn/Giraldez (1996); on seventeenth-century silver depreciation, see Hogendorn/Johnson (1986: 40).
12. On Kimpasi, see Hilton (1985: 26–8); and Kananoja (2019: Chapter 3).
13. AHU, CU, Angola, Caixa 10, doc. 2; also published in *MMAI*, Vol. 13, doc. 49.
14. ibid.
15. On the aftermath of Mbwila in general, see Thornton (1983: 76–96); on the link between Mbwila and the defeat of the ngola at Pungo Andongo, see *MMAI*, Vol. 13, 146–51; on the total lack of Portuguese influence, an interesting account of 1674 described how the manikongos were 'absolute lords without paying any tribute to Your Highness' (IHGB, DL 27, 10); on Mbanza Kongo as ruined and uninhabited, AHU, CU, Angola, Caixa 12, doc. 161.
16. On Beatriz Kimpa Vita and the Antonine movement, see especially Thornton (1998b), who argues it can be seen as a resistance against the trade; on Pedro IV and eighteenth-century Kongo, Fromont (2014: 7).

17. The apt phrase of 'the lineage against the state' is of Gonçalves (2005: 129–30) and (1985); on the purge of the manipemba's followers in 1657, *MMAI*, Vol. 12, 127.
18. *MMAI*, Vol. 12, 581.
19. On the Portuguese permission of Spanish trade in Luanda, Schultz (2016: 43); a sense of the real labour crisis provoked by the wars in the Spanish Americas is provided by countless documents in AGI, Indiferente General 284 and 2835; on the three platoons of infantry, *DHRJ*, Vol. 4, 133.
20. On the different *mbanzas* controlled by different factions, see Thornton (2000: 71); on the rise of the slave trade between 1665 and 1690, see Saccardo (1982: Vol. 2, 174–7); on the re-emergence of a weaker Kongo after 1709, see Vansina (1966: 151).
21. For the estimate of exports of captives, www.slavevoyages.org/estimates – data accessed 19 February 2018; on the proliferation of clans in Kongo, Mpansu (1973: 12–13).
22. On Kongo art in the eighteenth century, see Fromont (2014); Proyart (1776: 54, 162).
23. Candido (2013: 6, 250); on the Jaga Kakonda in 1687, see AHU, CU, Angola, Caixa 13, doc. 51; and in 1688, AHU, CU, Angola, Caixa 13, doc. 89; on the *soba*'s death in 1690, AH, CU, Angola, Caixa 14, doc. 38.
24. Candido (2013: 242–3) writes powerfully against the idea of a stable Ovimbundu ethnicity in these years; the emergence of new identities here after the seventeenth century is suggested in Childs (1964: 368) and Childs (1970).

6 'WITH BOOTS WORTH 3 SLAVES': SLAVERY AND VALUE IN THE EIGHTEENTH CENTURY

1. This impressive piece of research was conducted by Marion Wallace and Paul Naylor – Naylor/Wallace (2016); in their analysis, Diallo was not returned to Senegambia out of paternalistic concern, but because of the excellent trade connections that he held.
2. Curtin (1967: 37).
3. On slavery in Sokoto, see Lovejoy (1978a).
4. Curtin (1967: 39–40).
5. On the old discourse of Africa 'without history', see Hegel (1956: 99) and Trevor-Roper (1965); for a recent critique of the paradigm of 'Africa as a problem to be solved', see Alao (2016).

6. Austen (2010: 31–2). On the Bight of Biafra, Nwokeji (2010: 148). For this figure, see www.slavevoyages.org – data accessed 26 December 2017.
7. For pre-Columbian slavery, MacLeod (1928: 634–7). Nevertheless, many economic theories of slavery assume a core economic component – see especially Domar (1970). Moreover, many histories of Atlantic slavery also assume the fundamental normative role of economic production in slavery, such as Lovejoy (2000: 9–10).
8. On Angola, NA, OWIC, Inventarisnummer 58, no. 259: 'defendia el Gobernador que ningien fuera a benderle al Olandes presas de negros' (17 July 1643); and see also Cavazzi's report on Matamba from the 1660s in Cavazzi (1687: 165); on Senegal, Cultru (1913: 29, 70). On the 'institutionalization of marginality', and warfare as a means to incorporate outsiders, the classic account is Miers/Kopytoff (1977: esp. 14–16). On the comparison of warfare among Native Americans, Santos-Granero (2009: 123–8).
9. For this perspective on Africa, see especially Meillassoux (1991: 43, 85).
10. Law (1997: Vol. 1, 116).
11. For the quotation on kinship, affinity and vicinity, Meillassoux (1991: 33). On kinship and its relationship to forms of dependence, Miers/Kopytoff (1977: 10). See, however, Nwokeji (2010: 124) for a good example from the Bight of Biafra of enslaved persons retaining kin ties with their originary communities in the eighteenth century.
12. Law (1997: Vol. 2, 206).
13. The Jamaican sociologist Orlando Patterson was one of the first to delineate fully the relationship between slavery and honour – see Patterson (1982: 10–11, 93–5, 339). On the relation of the changing idea of honour to the Abolition movement, see Appiah (2010).
14. On the continuity of warfare into the New World, see especially Barcia (2014). On this account of the fears of Kongo slaves, see Cavazzi (1687: 164).
15. Dumestre (1979: 142–3).
16. ibid., 130–31.
17. On credit as originally a moral concept in early modern England, see Muldrew (1997); the analogous process in some parts of West Africa is indicated by the monetary value of goods used in religious forms, as with beads in Benin prior to the Portuguese arrival (cf. Chapter 4).
18. The 1499 case is at *MMAI*, Vol. 1, 161; on this early use of slaves as money, see Caldeira (1999: 22–3) and Vansina (1966: 52). On the 1516 convertibility of *nzimbu* to slaves, see Cordeiro (1881: 8); for the 1577 document, see *MMAI*, Vol. 3, 153–4.

19. For the 1610 case of Fonseca, AHU, CU, Angola, Caixa 1, doc. 10; for the 1613 letter, *idem*, Caixa 1, doc. 27; for the 1628 case, Heintze (1985: Vol. 1, 310); for the 1635 case, Pombo (1944: 61); for an example of cloth and slaves as parallel currencies in Luanda by 1635, see AHU, CU, Angola, Caixa 3, doc. 16.
20. On debts held in slaves, AGNL, SO-CO, Caja 2, doc. 201, fol. 49v ('devitos de negros'); on 'negros de fato', *idem*, Caja 33, doc. 349, fol. 6v; on the Sierra Leone mission from 1632, *idem*, Caja 54, doc. 425, fol. 314r; for Diogo Rodrigues de Lisboa, *idem*, Caja 2, doc. 8, fol. 715r: 'folgarei q en nhua maneira va devendo hũ real aningem principalmte de pesas'.
21. For Bautista Pérez's books, see AGNL, SO-CO, Caja 2, doc. 201, fols. 959v–960r and 1099v–1101v; on the relationship between credit and cash in purchases, see ibid., fol. 738r, with some purchasers offering only credit and no hard cash at all; for the link of credit and slavery between Salvador and Angola, see ASM, Maço 41, Livro do Tombo (2), fol. 345v.
22. On Garcés, Assadourian (1966: 37–8); for the 1609 account, AHU, CU, Angola, Caixa 1, doc. 4A; on Fernández d'Elvas, AHU, CU, Rio de Janeiro, Caixa 1, doc. 5.
23. AHU, CU, Angola, Caixa 3, doc. 5; for the 1653 note, AHU, CU, Angola, Caja 5, doc. 108 – 'tudo se compre fiado'; for the will of Pinheiro, IAN/TT, Cartório dos Jesuítas, Maço 38, doc. 39.
24. On credit in the Hanseatic League, Bernal (1992: 27–30).
25. On the long-standing relationship of credit and slavery, Sundström (1974: 35); for the Dutch document, NA, Inventarisnummer 52, no. 47, MF 4372, 24 October 1636.
26. On the flow of credit from Europe to the coast and then to the interior, see Austen (1987: 92).
27. Mounkaila (2008: Vol. 2, 180–81).
28. Some of the most significant work on pawnship is Lovejoy/Richardson (1999) and (2001).
29. Soh (1913: 25).
30. For this excellent analysis of *kindoki*, see Mpansu (1973: 29–30, 142–3); on beliefs identifying slavery with cannibalism and witchcraft, see Thornton (2003: 277).
31. On this transition from credit to a money economy, see (focusing especially on bullion) most recently Graeber (2011: 18).
32. ibid.; on the transformation of pawnship from a reciprocal mutual-aid system into chattel slavery on the Gold Coast, see Adu-Boahen (2012: 191).

33. MacGaffey (1986: 161–70); MacGaffey's work on the BaKongo remains fundamental for social and historical analysis of transformations in Kongo.
34. For an excellent study of this relationship in England, see Muldrew (1997).
35. On the 'natural alliance' between *kindoki* and trade in Kongo, see Heusch (2000: 122); on the expansion of witchcraft in many parts of Africa during the slave-trade era, see Paton (2015: 24).
36. Behrendt/Latham/Northrup (2010: 31–2).
37. ibid., 147, 173, 163; Lovejoy/Richardson (1999: 347–8).
38. On the relationship of Ékpè to slavery as a marker of social change, Imbua (2012: 20–24); on Ékpè as a means to spiritual advancement and not just material wealth, see Guyer (2004: 78).
39. On the relationship of long-distance Atlantic trade and the rise of London's banking sector, see Inikori (2002); for this example from Dahomey, see Akinjogbin (1967: 104).
40. Behrendt/Latham/Northrup (2010: 147, 155).
41. Curtin (1967: 151).
42. Camara/Jansen (1999: 76–7). For a similar example, see Dumestre (1979: 74–7), a section of the *Geste de Ségou* that describes *jòn* (captives/slaves) and their role in domestic labour for the elite of the Kingdom of Segu.
43. For Equiano's account, see Carretta (2003: Chapter 1). There is now also a lively discussion as to whether or not this account was accurate or rather constructed by Equiano from discussions in the New World – see also Sweet (2009).
44. See especially the essays in Lindsay/Sweet (2013).
45. Curtin (1967: 300–301).
46. On the payment of taxes in slaves in Senegambia, NCAC, RDD, transcribed cassette 167A, p. 76; on Fuuta Tòòro, www.aodl.org/westafrica/futa_mbem_fr.php – interview conducted on 23 January 1969.
47. On oral sources from Kongo, Mpansu (1973: 65), and the quote on the highest denomination is MacGaffey (1986: 39); on Kelefa Saane, NCAC, RDD, transcribed cassette 539B, p. 91; on Segu, Roberts (1980: 400).
48. Conneau (1977: 105); on slaves in Hausaland, Hiskett (1973: 22); on the widespread use of slaves as a currency in the trans-Saharan trade, see Prange (2006: 221).
49. On the eighteenth-century estimate, see www.slavevoyages.org – data accessed 26 December 2017.
50. On the sixteenth century, Green (2012b) and Heywood/Thornton (2007). On a slave from Mozambique as leader of a community of

maroon slaves in Panamá in 1582, see AGI, Patronato 234, Ramo 6, fol. 312v; and on another Mozambique slave in Tolima in 1578, AGNB, Negros y Esclavos, Tolima, SC43, Legajo 2, fol. 963v. On the slave trade from Asia, see Seijas (2014: Chapter 2). For an enslaved person from Arada (Allada) in Boyacá in 1582, see AGNB, Archivo Histórico de Boyacá, NT, Rollo 11, Legajo 37, fol. 329r; and *idem*, Rollo 16, Legajo 54, fol. 197v for 1592.

51. On Allada, AGI, Indiferente General 2795, letter of 27 May 1617; and see Calado (1648: 161) for the numbers of enslaved 'Ardas' in Brazil. On the rise of the slave trade in Benguela, see Candido (2013: 147–65). On the Dutch importance in the seventeenth century, see Den Heijer (1997: 11–29).
52. Law (1997: Vol. 3, 581); Bosman (1967: 365).
53. Behrendt/Latham/Northrup (2010: 159, 135, 145).
54. ibid., 149; for Isert, Axelrod Winsnes (1992: 76).
55. For the seventeenth-century report on cruelty, BA, Códice 50–V–37, fol. 245v; Van Wing (1961–2: 81 and 81 n. 34).
56. For an instance of this from the seventeenth century in Upper Guinea, and the violence involved, AGNSCL, Fondo Vicuña Mackenna, Vol. 77, Pieza 1, fols. 83r–v; Norris (1968: 10–11); Bosman (1967: 17).
57. On the road from Luanda to Matamba, see AHU, CU, Angola, Caixa 6, doc. 97; for the 1684 account, AHU, CU, Angola, Caixa 12, doc. 158; on the general depopulation around Luanda, see BA, Códice 50–V–39, fol. 41r.
58. On warfare in African history, see Reid (2012) and Thornton (1999). For the quote from the expedition of Bernardino de Távora, see BA, Códice 54–X–20 [n.d.]; on the use of people as porters, BA, Códice 50–V–39, fols. 40r–v; an example of the burning of palm trees by Portuguese armies comes in 1655 in Quissama, see AHU, CU, Angola, Caixa 6, doc. 25.
59. Camara/Jansen (1999: 45).
60. Demanet (1767: Vol. 1, 106).
61. Proyart (1776: 165); Conneau (1977: 104).
62. Gamble/Hair (1999: 108).
63. This remarkable account was located and analysed by Alessandra Brivio – see Brivio (2013: 52–3).
64. NCAC, RDD, transcribed cassette 309A, p. 61.
65. On Segu, Bazin (1974: 112, 118–19); for the proverb, Mounkaila (2008: Vol. 1, 195).
66. On iron bars at Komenda, Law (1997: Vol. 2, 90).

67. As Randles (1968: 174) puts it, it is 'the slave which is also the real money linking Africa with the outside world'; on Brazilian tobacco as currency, see Lessa (1957: 23), where the Brazilian priest buys a canoe for 68 rolls of tobacco near Elmina in 1796; on copper-rod currencies in Calabar, Antera Duke is very clear – see Behrendt/Latham/Northrup (2010: 135).
68. I am very grateful to Assan Sarr for this point on vulnerability to external shocks.
69. Dantzig (1978: 104); on the poor profits in Senegambia in the 1610s, AGI, Indiferente General, 2795 [n.d.]; for the 1622 document, AGI, Santa Fé 52, no. 172.
70. This idea of the relationship between the $ sign and slavery is expounded very significantly in Seijas/Fredericks (2017: 3, 70); I am very grateful to Tatiana Seijas for the gift of this book, which enabled me to make this link.

7 ON A WAR FOOTING: THE 'FISCAL-MILITARY STATE' IN WEST AFRICAN POLITICS

1. On the fiscal-military state, see Glete (2002) and Storrs (2008); and in the British case Brewer (1989) and Harling/Mandler (1993). I am indebted to Tony Hopkins for urging me to think further about the relationship of the 'fiscal-military state' to West African history.
2. This idea of a fundamental difference in historical trajectory is implicitly grounded in the long-standing anthropological and historical disjunction between 'primitive' and 'Western' societies and cultures. Those anthropologists such as Claude Lévi-Strauss who rather posited the parallelism between all societies and their worldviews (both 'magical' and 'scientific') were seen as highly controversial, especially by historians (for whom Lévi-Strauss had little time). To many, therefore, the finding of interconnectedness between African and Western historical processes advanced in this book will remain methodologically and conceptually controversial. Nevertheless, African philosophers such as V. Mudimbe recognize the value in Lévi-Strauss's ideas, and this concept of parallelism informs my approach. See Lévi-Strauss (1963) and (1966); Mudimbe (1988: 33).
3. I am very grateful to Benjamin Kye Ampadu of the Ghana History Teachers' Association and T. I. Amass Secondary School, Kumasi, for exploring this with me on a visit to Kumasi in March 2018.
4. Dumestre (1979).

5. Graeber (2011); Kuroda (2008).
6. There is a large literature on the 'predatory state thesis'. See especially Hawthorne (2001); Klein (2001); Fage (1969).
7. On the Nikky *mithqāl*, see especially Johnson (1968).
8. The key work on contraband gold imports to Dahomey is now being done by Carlos da Silva Junior. See Silva Junior (2016a and b); on the attacks on the Brazilian factors at Ouidah, see, for instance, APEB, Seção Colonial e Provincial, Série de Registro de Correspondência para o Rei, 1799, 139, doc. 665, fol. 248r (1799).
9. On Lambe, Dalzel (1967: 10); on Baillie's efforts, TNA, C113/276, fols. 76r–96r; for the gold ledger at Ouidah in 1724–6, see TNA, T70/1254, fols. 5v, 18v, 20v, and many other places; on the bequests of Adcock, TNA, PROB 11/617/56.
10. TNA, T70/1466, 190; TNA, C113/276, fol. 72r.
11. On the gift in 1730 from Dixcove, TNA, T70/1466, fol. 9; on a barter of Brazilian gold for East Indian Company cowries at Accra in 1730, ibid., fol. 141; on Asante's use of gold, see Lovejoy (1980: 14–15) and McCaskie (1995: 38–9).
12. On Asante gold exports in the nineteenth century, see Arhin (1995: 99).
13. Kingsley (2015: 531–2).
14. ibid., 537–8, on the Yorùbá; for Poro and Sandé, Bellman (1984).
15. Kingsley (2015: 541); on the spread of Ékpè to Sierra Leone, Northrup (1978: 109–10); on the secret societies of Sierra Leone, Bellman (1984: 17); on Ékpè and Abakuá in Cuba, see most recently Miller/Ojong (2013).
16. Bellman (1984: 107–8) on the role of secret societies in lineage-based societies; on the role of hunting people in initiation among the Balanta, see Hawthorne (2003).
17. For Biton Kulubali, Conrad (1990: 69, 79); on the link of iron and hunting to the Manding, see Derive/Dumestre (1999: 113–15); on the man–leopard murders, see Pratten (2007); on the leopard cult of Agassu in Dahomey, see Parés (2016); on the role of hunting and state formation, see Konadu (2010: 40) for the Akan, and Ogundiran (2002a: 29) for the state of Ìjèsà.
18. On Tiramakang as the son of a hunter, see NCAC, RDD, transcribed cassette 566; on the link of *nyantios* to monkeys, NCAC, RDD, transcribed cassette 491B, 12–13. I am grateful for this insight into secret societies to a discussion led by Ibrahima Thiaw at an event at the West African Research Association in Dakar, 1 July 2014.
19. On the problem of seeing hunter-gatherers as evolving into states, see Luna (2016: 9–10).

20. See, e.g., Pitt-Rivers (1900: Plates 1 and 4).
21. Lange (1987: 46); on Ghana's sacred forest, see Gomez (2018: 35).
22. On Anomabu in February 1687, see Law (1997–2006: Vol. 2, 196); ibid., Vol. 3, 31, for Dixcove in 1694.
23. On the 'suffrage' of the priests, Bosman (1967: 183); Ivor Wilks located this oral account on the capture of Takyiman from Asante: see Wilks (2013: 15–24).
24. See Bay (1998: 1–2); for this letter and response, see AHU, CU, São Tomé, Caixa 26, doc. 7; on the Dahomeys as originally 'Fons', see Dalzel (1967: 1).
25. Norris (1968: 102–3); for amulets, see Dalzel (1967: vi).
26. AHU, CU, São Tomé, Caixa 37, doc. 32; for a discussion of this letter, see Parés (2013a: 301); on the *yovo*, ibid., 330 n. 4.
27. For a discussion of the ways in which letters were composed in the Courts of the dadás, see Parés (2013a: 301), Soares (2014: 246) and Santos (2012: 95–104). On Onim's 1823 embassy, see Santos (2012: 21); on Dahomey as the first to recognize the Empire of Brazil, see Alencastro (1980); on Adandozan's letter about the transport of the Portuguese Court, see Araujo (2012: 9).
28. On Dahomey's distinction from Allada through militarized authority, see Law (1997: 64–5); Bay (1998: 60–63) on the vital importance of the pythons to the outcome of this battle – Bosman (1967: 228–9) notes that pythons are revered as the gods of Hueda; see an excellent discussion in Parés (2016: 159–61).
29. Akinjogbin (1967: 61–2).
30. For the argument on this purging of the Sakpata, see Sweet (2011)'s discussion of Domingos Álvares; a fundamental book for the transformation of religion in Dahomey is Parés (2016, esp. 68–91); on sacred groves and shrines, ibid., 99, and on Agassu, ibid., 162–79.
31. On divine right, see for instance Monod (1999); this is not just the case in Dahomey, of course, but also for instance in Angola, where, as the historian Linda Heywood has shown, the tremendous political power of Queen Nzinga of Ndongo was channelled by her through powerful religious idioms, which changed throughout the forty-one years of her rule to ensure her power – see Heywood (2017: 119–27).
32. For the description of the palace, Norris (1968: vi–vii); for the place of women in Dahomey's Court and army, see Bay (1998) and Alpern (2011).
33. Akinjogbin (1967: 110–32); on Truku, see Dalzel (1967).
34. Norris (1968: 95).

35. On the *ahisinon*, Bay (1998: 105); on the palace at Ouidah and the terms of trade, Axelrod Winsnes (1992: 97, 102).
36. Lessa (1957: 27, 109–15).
37. Norris (1968: 66–72).
38. ibid., 43, on the visits of the yovogan to the forts; Lessa (1957: 30) on the cavalrymen and troops greeting the Europeans.
39. Bosman (1967: 342–3); men were usually the weavers in West Africa, as Colleen Kriger has noted.
40. ibid., 339.
41. Dantzig (1978: 89–90, 104); on RAC stores, TNA, T70/1243, 12 March 1698.
42. On the unprecedented cowrie imports, see Law (1995: 56); on the rise of taxes in Allada in 1725, Dalzel (1967: 8).
43. On the use of gold to buy cowries in the 1730s, see TNA, T70/1254, fol. 4r; on the use of cowries to pay for the costs of the fort at Ajudá in 1795, see APEB, Seção Colonial e Provincial, Série Correpondência para o Rei, 138, fol. 326r; on the credit letters drawn against cowries in 1791, see AHU, CU, São Tomé, Caixa 26, doc. 7.
44. Norris (1968: 12–15) on the relationship of Dahomey and Oyo; on the logs from 1730, see TNA, T70/1466, fols. 185, 186, 189, 191.
45. Johnson (1937: 118–19).
46. Ogundiran (2002a: 429, 436–8) and (2009: 361–4).
47. Johnson (1937: 70–71, 75). The best modern account of the Oyo state is in Law (1977).
48. For the relationship of state power to currency control, see Graeber (2011). On the state as offering a monopoly of violence (or 'protection racket'), see Tilly (2000).
49. NCAC, RDD, transcribed cassette 491B, p. 8.
50. NCAC, RDD, transcribed cassette 434C, pp. 52, 79, 81; on the relationship of the household to state structures in Kankan, present-day Guinea-Conakry, see Osborn (2011).
51. On the Aro, the most important work is Nwokeji (2010); on Bassar iron production, Barros (2001).
52. For Saajo Mane's account of Kansala, NCAC, RDD, transcribed cassette 550A, p. 14; on the thirteen forts beyond Kansala, NCAC, RDD, transcribed cassette 624A, pp. 2–6; for Bakary Sane et al., NCAC, RDD, transcribed cassette 553A–B, p. 11; for the different smaller states and their relationship to Kaabu, Phillott-Almeida (2011: 8–10).
53. On Tamba Dibi, NCAC, RDD, transcribed cassette 123A, p. 36, and transcribed cassette 174C; on the tabo trees in the sacred grove of

Tamba Dibi, Phillott-Almeida (2011: 22); on Ghana's sacred royal snake, see Gomez (2018: 38) – Gomez also notes that the blacksmith-king and rival to Sunjata Keita, Sumanguru Kante, is said to have had a 44-headed supernatural snake (84).

54. On the sacrifices of bulls to shrines, see NCAC, RDD, transcribed cassette 554C, p. 33; on the empty bush around Bansang (near Basse in the Upper Gambia today), see NCAC, RDD, transcribed cassette 130A–B, pp. 52–3; on the burning of bush, see the narrative of the foundation of Brikama (in the Kombo region of Gambia), at NCAC, RDD, transcribed cassette 217C; see Sarr (2016), for a seminal discussion of the importance of spirit occupation of the bush to Senegambian worldviews.
55. On wealth as 'in a form of pagne' and traded alongside captives, NCAC, RDD, transcribed cassette 309A, p. 61; ibid., pp. 27–8, for the cultivation of cotton; on the use of Fulas to cultivate government farms for Kaabu, see NCAC, RDD, transcribed cassette 491B, pp. 1–2.
56. On matrilinearity of *nyantios*, see NCAC, RDD, transcribed cassette 554C, p. 9; on the 'feeding' of Kaabu on warfare, NCAC, RDD, transcribed cassette 550A, pp. 58–9; for intermarriage of people from Pachesi with *nyantios*, Phillott-Almeida (2011: 15).
57. NCAC, RDD, transcribed cassette 624B, pp. 40–41; on the Kanyeleng societies, Saho (2012).
58. On the Fula tax collection across the Fuuta Jaalo Kingdom, see NCAC, RDD, transcribed cassette 539A–B, pp. 54–5; on the Fula migration, NCAC, RDD, transcribed cassette 491B, p. 6; on the use of slaves in southern Gambia, see Bellagamba (2012: 40); on the enslavement of the local Jalonke population and resentment by them of the Fula, NCAC, RDD, transcribed cassette 490A, pp. 5–6; on the alliance of Fulas and the Europeans, see NCAC, RDD, transcribed cassette 466B, pp. 16–17.
59. The classic argument on the resistance and ingenuity of small communities such as the Balanta and Felupe is in Baum (1999) and Hawthorne (2003), which responded to earlier arguments as to the predatory state of Kaabu by Rodney (1970) and Barry (1998).
60. On the power of Islamic scholars to clear spirits from the land, and the relationship of this to agriculture, see Sarr (2016) and (2017).
61. NCAC, RDD, transcribed cassette 490A, p. 9.
62. For the argument on Oyo expansion and cowries, see Adebayo (2002: 381); on Abomey's storehouses, Norris (1968: ix); on the cowrie as the single largest import, Bay (1998: 123).
63. On English trade at Allada in 1686, see Dantzig (1978: 27), and ibid., 247, for the Portuguese trade from Mozambique, and 252 for

the trade from Accra in 1730; on the volumes by 1720, see Lovejoy (1974: 568).

64. Conrad (1990: 152).
65. On the lack of currency in early Segu, Conrad (1990: 90–91); on the absence of taxes before Segu, see MacDonald et al. (2018); Dumestre (1979: 184–5).
66. On the number of halls, ibid., 160; on the cavalry, ibid., 242; on the relationship of warfare to tax- and tribute-raising, Perinbam (1997: 171).
67. On this account of the *mithqāl* and *dègè*, see Conrad (1990: 111).
68. The best work on the Nikky *mithqāl* is by the pioneering historian of currency in West African history Marion Johnson – see Johnson (1968).
69. Conrad (1990: 112–13).
70. On warfare as a means of social production and reproduction, see Roberts (1980: 389, 401–2).
71. On the traditional view of state structures as static, see Bay (1998: 5); on the depreciation of the cowrie against gold stocks, see Law (1995: 57–8).
72. Bosman (1967: 440); on glass beads as early currency, Ogundiran (2016a).
73. On cowries on helmets, see Pitt-Rivers (1900: 4–5); on Ugi Evie, Roese/Bondarenko (2003: 26–7); on the importance of experience as a paradigm for constructing modernity, see Gómez (2016).
74. This was the SOAS historian Mervyn Hiskett – see Hiskett (1965: 114–15).
75. On the decline of Kano and the rise of the cloth industry in Katsina after 1730, see Smith (1997: 22–4); on credit in the cloth trade from Kano to Borno, Sundström (1974: 21); on Kano's growth and the expansion south to Kafaba, see Lovejoy (1980: 35–6); on the interconnection of the two trading systems, see Lovejoy (1974).
76. Hiskett (1965: 118).
77. Hallett (1964: 90, 92 fn).
78. For this episode, see the eighteenth-century chronicle published by Abitbol (1982: 12); on the horse in African history, see Law (1980).
79. Hiskett (1965: 120–21).
80. The key work on the model of the state in the household in precolonial Senegambia is the exemplary study by Osborn (2011).
81. Law (1997–2006: Vol. 1, 232ff.); ibid., Vol. 2, 122.
82. Bosman (1967: 433, 460, 461).
83. On the 1799 proposal for a military alliance, AHU, CU, Bahia, Caixa 213, doc. 12, fol. 2r.
84. Roth (1968: 93).

8 FEEDING POWER: NEW SOCIETIES, NEW WORLDVIEWS

1. Norris (1968: 125).
2. NCAC, RDD, transcribed cassette 494A, pp. 7–9.
3. On the relationship between the rise of a 'real money' economy and growing state power, see Graeber (2011: 45, 313).
4. On the process of pushback in Senegambia in the late sixteenth century, see Green (2012: Chapter 8).
5. I am grateful to my 2017–18 MA students from King's College London for their presentations and class discussion on this theme, which helped to clarify this point for me.
6. For the 1750s description of rice cultivations and houses, Adanson (1757: 89–91) – houses built in this style are still common in the region, and as far south as the Fuuta Djalon; for the description of the ricefields and cattle, see Moore (1738: 9).
7. The fundamental work on Mama-Jori/Mama-Jombo has been done by the important Senegalese museologist and historian Ibrahima Seck – see Seck (2016: 43–7); for Seck's description of Mama-Jori and Mama-Jombo, see the film of the 2015 conference (from 11:30 onwards) 'Identities in Greater Senegambia and Beyond: Interdisciplinary Approaches through History and Music in Dialogue' (convened by Lucy Durán and Toby Green) at https://www.youtube.com/watch?v=DMytlZcXRwA; on the transport of Africans from Senegambia to the ricefields of the Americas, see Carney (2001), Fields-Black (2009), and Hawthorne (2010a) and (2010b); on Africans in colonial Louisiana, see Hall (1992).
8. Curtin/Boulègue (1974: 271).
9. Moore (1738: 82).
10. Durand (1802: 307).
11. On the masculinization of rice production among the Balanta of Guinea-Bissau, see Hawthorne (2003); a classic study of the growing control of women's marriage choices in this era, and the erosion of their social power, is Greene (1996); for the case of women adopting male roles, see Achebe (2011: 13–14).
12. AHU, CU, Cabo Verde, Caixa 7a, doc. 133; on gambling, see AGNL, SO-CO, Caja 18, doc. 197, fol. 488v, an account from the 1610s of money owing from a bet.
13. For Ambrósio Gomes's testimony against Peres, see IAN/TT, Inquisição de Lisboa, Processo 2075, fol. 28v; on Gomes as Vaz's brother, see AHU,

CU, Guiné, Caixa 3, doc. 39. For an excellent comparative analysis of Peres and Vaz in Cacheu, see Havik (2004: III.2).

14. AHU, CU, Cabo Verde, Caixa 7a, docs. 75, 85, 133.
15. On Benguela, see Candido (2013: 129–35); on the Akan, Everts (2012).
16. For the 1699 case, AHU, CU, Guiné, Caixa 4, doc. 39.
17. On the Fula, Malacco (2016: 83); on Benin, Roth (1968: 131–2); on the ways in which elders allowed and sometimes encouraged Balanta women to marry European traders, see Hawthorne (2003).
18. On Nzinga's soldiers, Heywood (2017: 16, 58–9, 99); and on religious roles in Ndongo, ibid., 16, 32–3; see Phillott-Almeida (2011) on the female rulers of Pachesi in Senegambia; on the potential for female leadership among the Igbo, see Achebe (2011).
19. On increases in polygamy, see especially Thornton (1997: 44); on the wives of the Yovogan, Dalzel (1967: 95); for Pires's account, Lessa (1957: 59, 98).
20. The most remarkable study of the royal wives of Dahomey is Bay (1998) – here, see esp. pp. 8–9, 51, 67; on Dahomey's female soldiers, see Alpern (2011); on the strangling of the alafins of Oyo by their wives, Dalzel (1967: 13).
21. For a remarkable study of Dangbé in this context, see Parés (2016: 145–8).
22. Hiskett (1960: 567).
23. On the slaves of the Queen Mother of Borno, Richmond Palmer (1936: 33–4).
24. Bowdich (1966: 41); McCaskie (2018); on the role of the queen mother at the Asante Court, I am also grateful to a personal communication from Dr Samuel Adu-Gyamfi of Kwame Nkrumah University of Science and Technology in Kumasi.
25. NCAC, RDD, transcribed cassette 624B, pp. 29–32.
26. On Pachesi, see Phillott-Almeida (2011).
27. Moreover, changes to agricultural production in the nineteenth century with the adoption of cash crops such as groundnuts often had a negative effect on women's status in communities – see, for instance, Sarr (2017: 16–20).
28. On female traders in nineteenth-century Dahomey, Rufer (2016: 723); on female priestly power in Allada in the 1670s, see Parés (2016: 105); on the Kankurang, see Jong (2008), and also his discussion in the video of the 2015 conference (from 10:00 onwards) 'Identities in Greater Senegambia and Beyond: Interdisciplinary Approaches through History and Music in Dialogue' (convened by Lucy Durán and Toby Green) at

https://www.youtube.com/watch?v=DMytlZcXRwA; on the Igbo, see Achebe (2011).

29. The best study of this is Souza (2006: esp. 11, 64) – I am very grateful to Jane Guyer for the unexpected and hugely welcome gift of this book, which I would otherwise never have come across – the quotation in this paragraph is from this book. In a major work on plants and their medicinal properties in Benin, Verger (1995: 65, 76, 78, 90) also noted the role of malaguetta and its diverse uses. For the volume of malaguetta in 1687, see TNA, T70/659, fols. 61r–v; and T70/656, fol. 69r, for malaguetta purchases in 1674.
30. Souza (2006: 62) for a recipe using maize; Verger (1995: 37–8) for the use of maize.
31. Souza (2006: 56) for the use of cowries, and 62 for a recipe using maize; Verger (1995: 37–8) for the use of maize.
32. Falconbridge (1788: 9).
33. Corry (1968: 64); on honour, Appiah (2010); on Fuuta Tòòro, Kane (2004: 313–16); for the Gold Coast, Dantzig/Jones (1987: 97).
34. On this relationship of slavery and farming in Segu, see Roberts (1987: 35).
35. Dumestre (1979: 74–6).
36. On the role of the firearms trade in producing a coercive state in many parts of West Africa, see Adu Boahen (2012: 181); Imbua (2012: 13) suggests that farming in Calabar was mainly for local consumption, and, while this remained true, the accent towards trade did change over the period of Atlantic trade.
37. For the *Arthur*'s voyage, TNA, T70/1213; for the monthly purchases of corn in the 1670s, TNA, T70/656, fols. 43r, 46r; for the Gold Coast accounts, Law (1997–2006: Vol. 1, 32, 36, 64, 81); almost all factors discuss food, and similar information can be found for Anomabu (ibid., Vol. 1, 93); the factor at Anishan bought 200 chests of corn in January 1688 (ibid., Vol. 2, 148).
38. On the words for maize in African languages, see McCann (2005: 34–5) and La Fleur (2012: 92) for the Fante variant; for an important perspective on African contributions to the Columbian exchange, see Carney/Rosomoff (2009).
39. For Serèèr kingdoms in Siin, see Demanet (1767: Vol. 1, 110–11).
40. On Antera Duke, Behrendt/Latham/Northrup (2010: 145).
41. For an excellent discussion, see Carney/Rosomoff (2009: 52–66). On the relationship between cheap food and the slave trade, Demanet (1767: Vol. 1, 109); for the Dutch at Allada in 1687, Dantzig

(1978: 47); on the numbers of chests of corn for English ships, TNA, T70/657, fols. 43v–r; on estimates of food consumption in Fuuta Tòòro in the 1750s, Kane (2004: 319).

42. On the yam purchase at Calabar, Behrendt/Latham/Northrup (2010: 170 n. 144); on increased production among the Balanta, see Hawthorne (2003).
43. For the current estimates on figures, see www.slavevoyages.org/estimates – data accessed 20 February 2018. See Meillassoux (1971: 52) for an interesting discussion of how the Atlantic slave trade led to a subtraction of agricultural productive potential from coastal West African communities.
44. Lessa (1957: 9); Kup (1967: 105).
45. On the adoption of new crops, see Hawthorne (2003) and Linares (1992) for rice among the Balanta and Jola.
46. Cavazzi (1687: 695); Martin (1986: 5).
47. On canoemen as pawns, see TNA, T70/657, fol. 54r; on the relative weight of the slave trade in 1679 at Anomabu, Accra and Wyamba, see TNA, T70/657, fol. 41r – 2,035 enslaved persons were exported by the English from these ports in 1679.
48. Law (1997–2006: Vol. 2, 180, 181, 190, 216); for a good discussion of the role of caboceers, see Shumway (2011: 117–26); for the charges paid to the brafo in 1674, see TNA, T70/656, fol. 30r; on the brafo, see Law (2013) and (2018).
49. Graeber (2011: 45, 313). For Testefolle's will, TNA, PROB/11/644/92; for local reaction among the English trading class to his death, see TNA, T70/1466, fol. 182.
50. Park (1983: 252–63).
51. For sunblinds, AGNL, SO-CO, Caja 18, doc. 197, fol. 808v (the value of a *toldo*, or cloth, for use in a boat to Geba); many descriptions of this sacrifice on a trading ship are in the trial of Crispina Peres, IAN/TT, Inquisição de Lisboa, Processo 2075, e.g., fol. 13r; on singing, Kup (1967: 11), and on the flowers, Adanson (1757: 74).
52. Law (1997–2006: Vol. 1, 4, and Vol. 2, 327).
53. On the tendency for increasing trade to coincide with increasing inequality, see Piketty (2014).
54. For examples of payments to local kings, e.g., TNA, T70/659, fol. 5v, 1687, to the King of Fetu for ground rent of Cape Coast castle; TNA, T70/1214, October 1678, to the King and headmen of New Calabar; and to the rulers of the Akan, of Eguafo and of Sabo, TNA, T70/661, fols. 47r, 43r and 48r.

55. On the preponderance of iron bars over copper bars in the 1670s, see TNA, T70/1214 (Calabar), and T70/657 (Cape Coast); for the absence of copper bars, and continuity of iron bars by the late 1690s, see TNA, T70/659 and T70/661, fol. 16r; for the use of copper bars given at the Cape Coast to slave-trading ships in 1699, see TNA, T70/376, fol. 19r.
56. On these accounts in 1730, TNA T70/1466, fols. 1 (Dixcove), 34 (Sekondi), 62 (Komenda); on the manufacture of *perpetuanoes* in England, see, for instance, Haynes (1706: 81), and for a discussion of the origin in the seventeenth century, Yerby (2008: 113).
57. On the expansion of iron production, see Thornton (1998a: 45–7); cf. also Evans (2015).
58. On cowrie imports to the Kingdom of Hueda in 1699, TNA, T70/1243, many places – cowries are called here 'booges'; on the price of a house in Komenda as one ounce of gold, see Law (1997–2006: Vol. 2, 102); the factor at Sekondi protested in 1683 that the rise of the price of trade goods meant that he had lost 2 marks of gold in trade, ibid., Vol. 1, 4.
59. On the trade of powder for money, Law (1997–2006: Vol. 2, 186–7); on the importance of the RAC stamp on iron bars, ibid., Vol. 1, 43, and Vol. 2, 90; on the problem of shifting poor-quality bars, ibid., Vol. 2, 45; on the set prices of cowries against enslaved persons at Ouidah, ibid., Vol. 1, 223 (1681), and TNA, T70/1243 (1699); on the myth of the barter economy, see Graeber (2011: 21–41).
60. Law (1997–2006: Vol. 1, 54 and 6).
61. On the set rate in Cacongo in the 1770s, Proyart (1776: 151); set quantities of gunpowder, muskets and rum were added to these cloths.
62. Sarr (2016); for a manuscript in Ajami script that notes similar beliefs in Casamance, see Babou (2018: 16), where a marabout called Sherriff Sheykhna Sheikh Mahfouz was given land seen as infested by evil spirits.
63. Adanson (1757: 47).
64. On the view of this land as occupied by malign spirits, I am grateful to a personal communication from Ndane Faye.
65. Law (1997–2006: Vol. 1, 108).
66. Conrad (1990: 44–5).
67. On land as the property of the ancestors in Kongo, see Bockie (1993: 15–18); on sacred forests and public shrines to *vodunun*, Parés (2016: 133); Dapper (1686: 336) informs us that *nganga* adopted the name of the shrine that they served, drawing on a now-unknown source; on Loango, Thornton (2002: 77).

68. Law (1997–2006: Vol. 3, 418); a recent discussion of the participation of Europeans in African religious practice on the Gold Coast is found in Apter (2017).
69. For a useful discussion of the relation of land security, the enclosures and capital growth, see Fortune (1984: 4); for an economist's view of the link between land title and capital poverty, see also Soto (2000).
70. On Hupila Hudjenk, Baum (1999: 117); on the Otomporo masquerade, Ojo (2013: 161).
71. On the creation of a false discourse of 'the fetish' to ridicule African beliefs, see Parés (2016: 35–7).

9 TRANSNATIONAL AFRICAS, STRUGGLE AND THE RISING OF MODERNITY

1. Mudimbe (1989).
2. Dalzel (1967: 169).
3. On return movements in the nineteenth century, see especially the essays collected in Bay/Mann (2001); see also Turner (2016: 653).
4. On cattle herders, see Sluyter (2012); on rice, Carney (2001) and (2004). For stressing to me the value of this concept of influence, I am grateful to my student Ruby Taylor.
5. On African warfare techniques in New World conflicts, see especially Dubois (2004: 109) for Kongo in Haiti; Thornton (1991) on Stono; on Bahia and Cuba in the nineteenth century, Barcia (2014).
6. On the date of the red hat's incorporation into Gambian military uniforms, I am grateful to Hassoum Ceesay of the University of The Gambia; on the red hat in Jola authority in Casamance, see the film *Kásuumaay* by Xavier Puigserver and Jordi Tomàs.
7. Fanon (2008).
8. Rufer (2016: 706) notes that this was not the view of many immediate post-independence historians such as Akinjogbin (1967), who sought to valorize nineteenth-century African monarchies in terms of the needs of newly independent states – however, it is worth noting that even then others, such as Rodney (1988), wrote of the alliance of African and European elites at the expense of the African poor.
9. A pathfinding study of these manifestations of power is Fromont's important recent book. See Fromont (2014: 111–31) for cloth and the *mpu*; ibid., 23–4, 60–61, on the *sangamento*.
10. On the continuing importance of the red hat in Casamance, Senegal, today, see the film *Kásuumaay* by Puigserver and Tomàs.

11. *MMAI*, Vol. 1, 113.
12. Bosman (1967: 55).
13. For the 1750 embassy, Araujo (2012: 2–3); for the 1783 events, Dalzel (1967: 181).
14. AHU, CU, São Tomé, Caixa 27, doc. 45A.
15. Araujo (2012: 1–2); Santos (2012) has a good overview; Pares (2013a) has the best scholarly introduction and overview; Soares (2014) – see also AHU, CU, São Tomé, Caixa 27, doc. 45A, and *idem*, Caixa 39, doc. 1; on the Portuguese defraying of the costs of Nzinga's ambassadors to Luanda, see Heywood (2017: 50–51).
16. On Adandozan's letter of 1810 regarding the Portuguese royal family, see especially Araujo (2012: 14–15)'s excellent discussion; Soares (2014: 238–41).
17. For the gifts of cloths and ivory, see AHU, CU, Bahia, Caixa 213, doc. 12; for Portuguese gifts of silk, see AHU, CU, São Tomé, Caixa 39A, doc. 1; the best analysis of these material exchanges of gifts is in Soares (2014).
18. On the hat and jacket, Behrendt/Latham/Northrup (2010: 191); they argue (ibid., 135) that these references to time suggest a timepiece; for other examples of time, see ibid., 141, 145; for 'dressed as white men', ibid., 149.
19. Bosman (1967: 119); Parés (2016: 39).
20. On Agaja, Norris (1968: viii); on Cacongo, Proyart (1776: 77).
21. Axelrod Winsnes (1992: 94).
22. On Manoel I's use of elephants and rhinoceroses, Góis (1949–55: Vol. 2, 223–6).
23. AHU, CU, São Tomé, Caixa 27, doc. 45A.
24. On the son of the King of Bissau in Portugal in 1694, AHU, CU, Guiné, Caixa 3, doc. 89; on Calabari traders sending their sons to Britain, Imbua (2012: 48), and on Anomabu, Sparks (2014: Chapter 6); on the family from St Louis, Saugnier (1791: 177).
25. On the Great Popo trader, Axelrod Winsnes (1992: 90); and ibid., 102, on the multilingualism of the yovogan; on the King of Hueda understanding a little Portuguese *c.* 1700, Bosman (1967: 332); on understanding Portuguese at the Court of the King of Dahomey, AHU, CU, Bahia, Caixa 213, doc. 12, fol. 1v, and ibid., fol. 3r, on the death of the regent's uncle in Portugal.
26. On reading in Kumasi in the 1820s, Bowdich (1966: 144).
27. Rodney (1988); on the interplay of local and global agencies, Nwokeji (2010: xvii).

28. The consequences of this dismantling of aristocracies are something with which, as the Guinean historian Lansina Kabé has said, many West African societies are living to this day: Lansina Kabé, personal appreciation of award of Distinguished Africanist to Boubacar Barry of Université Cheikh Anta Diop-Dakar – Indianapolis, 25 November 2014.
29. On the Borno madrassa in Cairo, *CEA* 261, Al-'Umari's account of 1337–8.
30. On Kano and Katsina, Smith (1997: 22–4, 79); on Katsina and Al-Maghīlī, see Usman (1981: 22–3); on Indian goods and merchants in Kano, see Jackson (1967: 46); and ibid., 10, on marriage to local women by foreign traders in Timbuktu.
31. On the indigenous religious idiom for the installation of the sarkis of Katsina, see the seminal work of Usman (1981: 28).
32. Bowdich (1966: 56); on Lisá, Anguiano (1957: Vol. 2, Appendix 3).
33. AHU, CU, Guiné, Caixa 3, doc. 94.
34. Kup (1967: 74) on the Temne word for 'Hell'; on the use of wax from Senegambia in New World Churches, see AGNL, SO-CO, Caja 2, doc. 201, fol. 1,320r, a credit to someone for 24 measures of wax from Cacheu to be used in the feast of the Holy Sacrament; and ibid., fol. 2,083v, for 4 *quintals* of wax sold to the Jesuits in 1625; on the frustrated letters of Brazilian missionaries in Dahomey, see APEB, Seção Colonial e Provincial, Série Registro de Correspondência para o Rei, Maço 139, doc. 665, 1799.
35. On African presence in the *santidade*, see *PV*, 265, 276–7; on Noah, the 'pope', palm trees and baptism, ibid., 277. The best discussion of *santidade* is Vainfas (1995), and on African presence in it, see ibid., 77, 153, 221–2; and on the fundamental place of dance, see ibid., 60.
36. On the Malé Uprising in Salvador in 1835, see Reis (1993) and Barcia (2013); on the incorporation of plants and metaphysics from Africa in Candomblé, see Voeks (1997), and, in general on Candomblé, see Capone (2010), Johnson (2002), Matory (2005) and Parés (2013b); on Santería, see Brandon (1993) and Brown (2003); on Obeah and the role of spirituality in resistance in 1730s Jamaica, see Paton (2015: 35).
37. On the passage of free Africans back to Angola in the seventeenth century, see Green (2016b: 116), and on the continuity of this throughout the seventeenth and eighteenth centuries, see Ferreira (2012); on free Brazilians settling near Lagos, Turner (2016: 658).
38. On African crews of Brazilian ships, see Candido (2010), Souza (2011: 111–12), Rodrigues (2016: 106–26) and Silva Junior (2011: 85–7), who discovered the important records on the enslaved Africans on the

local ships in late-eighteenth-century Bahia; on the exile of slaves from Brazil to Angola, see, for instance, APEB, Colónia, Maço 2, docs. 62 and 71 (from 1692) – Ferreira (2012) shows that this was a practice that continued into the nineteenth century; on the medical importance of *sangradores* in colonial Cartagena in the 1630s, see AGNL, SO-CO, Caja 77, doc. 535, fol. 107v.

39. See especially Mbembe (2001).
40. On the auctions of slaves in Cartagena, AHN, Inquisición, Legajo 4822, Expediente 3, fol. 18v, and *idem*, Expediente 7, fol. 50r; on Sandoval's involvement, see AHN, Inquisición, Legajo 1608, Expediente 15, and his action on behalf of the Jesuits to recover debts lost to a slave trader arrested by the Inquisition. The best study of the trade from West Africa to Cartagena and Lima is Newson/Minchin (2007).
41. Sandoval (1627: fols. 38v, 61v).
42. On the Ndombe, Candido (2011: 60–61).
43. On ethnicity as an extension of political identity, see Lovejoy (2016: 25); on 'ethnolinguistic continuity', see Hair (1967).
44. On the relationship between the archaeological record and ethnic identities, see Ogundiran (2002a: 6).
45. AGI, Escribanía 2A, fol. 500r: 'un negro nombrado Manuel que dixo que hera criollo y era horro; un negro llamado hernando de tierra çape barbado que dixo que hera horro; otro negro barbado llamado amador lopez que dixo hera criado en la isla de Santiago y era horro.' For important discussions of the use of colonial law by Africans in pursuing rights in the New World, see Bennett (2003) and De la Fuente (2008).
46. For the evidence on endogamy in Mexico, see Bennett (2003: 83–90, 97–104); Fuente (2008: 167) shows similar evidence for Cuba; Hawthorne (2010a) shows that, in eighteenth-century Maranhão, people from Greater Senegambia often sought one another out in the same ways. For examples of 'Creoles' of these ethnicities, see AGI, Patronato 234, Ramo 6, fols. 418r and 419r (Serèèrs), 418v (Mandinka), 417v (Nalú). For the story of Francisco and Gaspar 'Bioho', see AGNL, SO-CO, Caja 77, doc. 535, fol. 107v.
47. On the role of Salvador in the emergence of Yorùbá identity, Reis (2017); on the emergence of a general language in Salvador, I am extremely grateful to a personal communication from Carlos da Silva Junior, 12 September 2017.
48. On the late emergence of 'Yorùbá' identity, see Law (1977: 5–7); for general background on communities of liberated Yorùbá in Freetown, see

Everill (2012); on language use in Ekiti, personal communication from William Rea, University of Leeds; see also Johnson (1937: xix–xx).

49. On the incorporation of different branches of the Yorùbá into Lucumí, see Brandon (1993: 55–6); on return of Candomblé priestesses to West Africa in the nineteenth century, see especially Castillo/Parés (2010), and in general on the return process, Yai (2001).
50. Sanneh (1989: 1).
51. On freedom and slavery in the United States, Morgan (1972).
52. Tardieu (2009: 16).
53. On Dahomey, Filipello (2016). On Sierra Leone, Kup (1967: 14); for an analysis of this and analogous communities in Sierra Leone, see Rashid (2000) and Lovejoy (2016: 41–2).
54. Kup (1967: 119–23).
55. On red as a colour restricted to the Dadá of Dahomey, see Parés (2016: 157); on red caps as insignia of office, see Mark (1992: 98), and also the film *Kásuumaay* by Puigserver and Tomàs.
56. On the Haitian Revolution, see especially Dubois (2005) and Smartt Bell (2007).
57. On the oral traditions of these Serèèr maroon communities, the pathfinding work was conducted by the late James F. Searing (2002); for an ethnographic study of the Serèèr, Gravrand (1983). On the mutual unintelligibility of different languages among the Serèèr, personal communication from Ndane Faye, 27 October 2016.
58. Ferreira (2014: 75–7, 80); on the first use of the term in Brazil, a personal communication from Carlos da Silva Junior.
59. For an interesting comparison of New World and African maroon communities in the twentieth century, under Portuguese colonialism in Angola, see Keese (2015); on hilltop settlements in eighteenth-century Igbominaland, Usman (2003: 205).
60. For Manecas Costa's view of *gumbe*, see the film of the conference 'Identities in Greater Senegambia and Beyond: Interdisciplinary Approaches through History and Music in Dialogue' (convened by Lucy Durán and Toby Green) at https://www.youtube.com/watch?v=DMytlZcXRwA; on the special importance of *gumbe* in communication, personal communication from Dr Carlos Cardoso, London, 11 October 2016; on *gumbe*'s return to Africa, see Aranzadi (2010) and Jackson (2012).
61. Gilroy (1992).
62. Moreover, way back in the sixteenth century, black guitar players were also often included in works of literature from Spain, in early novels and theatre, where already in practice they interwove musical

styles from Africa with the instruments and melodies more familiar to Spain – see Budasz (2007: 3–4); on Angolan musicians in Paraguay in the first decades of the seventeenth century, see AGI, Contratación 5403, no. 1; on Iberia as a cross-cultural space for musical transformation, see Dubois (2016).

63. On the influence of castle slaves in Elmina, see Adu-Boahen (2012); on domestic slavery in Cacheu, see, e.g., IAN/TT, Inquisição de Lisboa, Processo 2075, fols. 14v, 27v, 62r (on domestic slaves); 8v–9r, on traders moving back and forth between the two cities; and 32r, on a slave from Cacheu in Cartagena.
64. Budasz (2007: 9) for this song; on folk tales from Guinea-Bissau in the Alentejo, see Nafafé (2012a).
65. On the surname 'Senegal', personal communication from Ibrahima Seck, Director of the Whitney Plantation Heritage Museum; on Louisiana and the trans-Atlantic slave trade, Hall (1992); on the fodet and the xalam, Coolen (1982)'s pathfinding work, and in general on Senegambian influence on the Blues, Kubik (1999: 7–12); on the banjo and cross-cultural interchanges, Dubois (2016).
66. On Cuban influences on modern Senegambian music, Shain (2002); on Cuban music's influence in Zaire, see especially White (2002). Beyond Senegambia West-Central African flows tell of a similar story. In Brazil, the influence of music and dance from BaKongo and Umbundu cultures in West-Central Africa was profound. Traditions of war-games and militarized training coalesced in the north-eastern Brazilian martial art of *capoeira*, while music and dance from Kongo were reframed in the dances accompanying Catholic religious processions in the nineteenth century known as 'Dances to the King of Kongo'. Gradually, from these different forms, Samba would emerge, heavily influencing in its turn Latin music across the Americas. On the origins of Samba, see Chasteen (1996), and on Angolan traits in Brazilian music and dance in general, see Kubik (1979); on *capoeira*, see especially Assunção (2005: 6–7, 49–58); on Kongo dances in Brazil, Souza (2015).
67. Fanon (2008).
68. For this case, see AHN, Inquisición, Legajo 1602, Expediente 7, fols. 32r–34v.
69. On 'Eenie Meenie Maine Mo', Martinus (1998: 116).

10 WARRIOR ARISTOCRACIES AND PUSHBACK FROM BELOW

1. Tocqueville (2010: Vol. 1, 88).
2. Mayer (1981); R. R. Palmer (1959).
3. R. R. Palmer (1959: Vol. 1, 29) on the European aristocracies being new; ibid., Vol. 2, 327–63, on 1798 as the 'high tide of revolutionary democracy'. I am very grateful to Steven Pincus of Yale University for making this insightful comparison between African and European revolutions and aristocracies when commenting on a paper I presented there, 29 November 2016.
4. Lovejoy (2016).
5. David (1974: 102); Labarthe (1802: 49); see also Curtin/Boulègue (1974: 251–2), for a 1729 relation of this in Bambuk by Boucard.
6. For importance evidence of the rise of tobacco planting for the West Africa trade in Brazil by 1656, see *DHRJ*, Vol. 3, 315; for the complaints of the Dadá of Dahomey on the size of the rolls of tobacco from Brazil, APEB, Seção Colonial e Provincial, Correpondência Recebida pelo Governo da Bahia, Governos Estrangeiros, Maço 197, doc. 2; on Katsina, Usman (1981: 40).
7. For this saying, Dumestre (1979: 142–3).
8. On silver as the standard against which bars of merchandise were measured on the Senegal, Saugnier (1791: 205). For primary evidence of silver imports to Senegal, see TNA, T1/449, fol. 229r, 190 Mexico dollars imported in 1766; and TNA, T70/585, fol. 30, 30 Mexico dollars paid in annual customs at Podor in 1764. On the trade of silver *patacas* from the New World for gold in 1729, Curtin/Boulègue (1974: 274).
9. On depreciation of silver in Bengal, Hogendorn/Johnson (1986: 48); on the expansion in American silver production in the eighteenth century, Tepaske (2010: 76–82); on the silver trade to China in this era, Seijas/Fredericks (2017: 33). Some historians have argued that the fall in the silver trade to China was due to Europe requiring silver for its own use; however, Flynn/Giraldez (1995) and (1996) show the significance rather of the fall in silver's relative profitability in China.
10. On the melting down of silver for jewellery, Curtin (1975: 235); on the use of Spanish silver dollars in the Rio Pongo (Guinea-Conakry) in the 1820s, see Conneau (1977: 57); on the growing control of the kola forests after the early eighteenth century, Lovejoy (1980: 11).
11. TNA, T70/1240, in various places (no folios are used in these account registers).

12. Axelrod Winsnes (1992: 31, 71); beyond the Accra account, Isert has a telling account of a Danish officer commanding 'his army of Blacks' in a war 'to make another Black nation see reason'.
13. SG, *Etiópia Menor e descrição geográphica da província da Serra Leoa*, fol. 5r – on riding and playing at once; on the burials of griots into living memory, personal communication from Ndane Faye, 20 November 2017.
14. On this aspect of Gajaaga, see the important discussion in Bathily (1989: 17–8).
15. SG, *Etiópia Menor e descrição geográphica da província da Serra Leoa*, fol. 4v.
16. On payments of brandy to the griots at Fort Lewis, TNA T70/585, fol. 27 (April 1764); and TNA, T70/586, 31 May 1786; on the intellectual projects of griots and writers of Arabic chronicles, see the collected essays in Green/Rossi (2018).
17. On the importance of the *jeli* (griots) in spreading word of the fame of the new leaders of Segu, see Bazin (1974: 124); on the emergence of Bamako *kafu*, or state, from the Niare family, clients of Segu, see Perinbam (1997: 2).
18. Perinbam (1997: 168 n. 65) for the extent of Segu.
19. Park (1983: 149–50).
20. ibid., 150.
21. Mounkaila (2008: Vol. 1, 45, 53).
22. ibid., Vol. 1, 69.
23. ibid., Vol. 1, 84–5.
24. For these quotes on Kulubali, see Conrad (1990: 46–7, 90); the possible role of hunting in the formation of Segu is noted in Roberts (1987: 30).
25. Conrad (1990: 65–8); on the failed attempt by the faama to introduce Islam as the state religion, Roberts (1980: 405 n. 49); on the power that Islamic marabouts claimed to hold to clear the bush of djinns in the nineteenth century, see Sarr (2016); for the 1791 quote, Saugnier (1791: 129).
26. For this account of the rise of *tònjònw* and the Kulubali *tòn*, see Roberts (1980: 403–6).
27. Bazin (1974: 120); Conrad (1990: 160).
28. Conrad (1990: 98–9, 108); on Ngolo Jara's origins, Bazin (1974: 113–14).
29. Park (1983: 142).
30. Of the Jaras as descended from *jòn*, see Bazin (1974: 110, 114).
31. Roberts (1980: 406–8); see also MacDonald/Camara (2012: 174).

32. Adanson (1757); on Bambara slaves for service in Fort Lewis and as interpreters there, TNA, T70/586, fols. 41 and 47; Hallett (1964: 81).
33. Curtin (1967: 148).
34. MacDonald/Camara (2012: 175–7); Roberts (1987: 45).
35. On the slave origins of Kebbi, see Arnett (1922: 13); see also Lovejoy (2016: 41–2). On the role of griots in Dahomey, see Dalzel (1967: xxii).
36. Johnson (1937: 177).
37. Dalzel (1967: 12–13).
38. Johnson (1937: 178–85); Dalzel (1967: 156–7).
39. Law (1977: 150) for the decline of Oyo against Nupe in the 1780s.
40. Johnson (1937: 197–8).
41. Indeed, just as the Portuguese sought access to gold in the fifteenth century, some see the Moroccan invasion of Songhay in 1591 as motivated by a desire to control gold supplies and fund the war against Portugal – Mitchell (2005: 169).
42. Kobayashi (2016) is an excellent recent study on the trade in Indian cloth to the Senegal River Valley; see Saugnier (1791: 289); Labarthe (1802: 187) says that the iron-bar trade is specifically for millet.
43. Thiaw (2012: 54–7).
44. TNA, T70/586, fol. 70, for the payment to the ruler of Galam; for the 1764 customs at Podor, TNA, T70/585, fol. 30; see also Park (1983: 44).
45. TNA, T70/585, fol. 1, for the value of goods in 1763, and fol. 11 for the comparative value of trade goods in cloth and iron bars; TNA, T1/380/36, for the letter from Major Mason.
46. For the 1729 description, Curtin/Boulègue (1974: 257, 274); see also Duran (1802: Vol. 1, 235); for the influence of Fulani weaving styles on Asante cloth, I am grateful to a personal communication from Christopher Spring, then Curator of the Africa Collection at the British Museum, 13 December 2017; for the argument on ecology and decline in weaving, see Kobayashi (2017: 31–2).
47. On the status of indigo-dyed cloth as opposed to white cloth, see Kobayashi (2017: 45).
48. Park (1983: 47); for an account of the excavations of the French trading posts here, see McIntosh/Thiaw (2001).
49. On the choice of Indian cloth as reflecting Islamic clothing styles, see Kobayashi (2016); for a recent discussion of the demise of old warrior-blacksmith aristocracies and their replacement by Islamic worldviews at this time, see Sarr (2017).
50. On the frequent warfare between the two kingdoms, see Park (1983: 44).
51. ibid., 42–3.

52. For the excavations of Gajaaga and Bundu, see the important work led by Thiaw (2012: 62–4); on the Serèèr, Richard (2012: 94–5).
53. Moore (1738: 20); as Durand put it in 1802, 'almost all of them speak Arabic' (Durand 1802: Vol. 1, 304).
54. For the life of Al-Fullānī, see Hunwick (1984); for Karamoko Ba and other clerics from the Fuuta Jaalo with similar itinerant lives, see Hunwick (2003: 495–8).
55. On the place of dreams, see McCaskie (2018); I draw here also on a discussion with friends in Fajara, The Gambia, in May 2011, who stressed the importance of dreams to migration.
56. Reichardt (1876: 290).
57. Barcia (2014); Lovejoy (2016); Hobsbawm (1996).
58. Wilks/Levtzion/Haight (1986: 102).

11 LET THEM DRINK RUM! ISLAM, REVOLUTION AND THE ARISTOCRACY

1. Derive/Dumestre (1999: 276–7).
2. On the relationship of Islam, bush spirits and cash crops, Sarr (2016).
3. On the Rågbenle society, Fornah et al. (2017); on Poro and the secret language or Kpelle in Liberia, see Bellman (1984: 53–78); on Dangbé, Parés (2016: 146); on Islamic knowledge as open to outsiders, Farias (1990).
4. Corry (1968: 57).
5. ibid., 59–60.
6. Curtin (1975: 235–6).
7. On the Maria Theresa silver dollar, see, for instance, Candotti (2015: 122); on the resentment of paying tax to the Hausa kingdoms, a text attributed to Uthmān dan Fodio discusses this, see Hiskett (1960: 568); on the lack of tax paid at Kano in 1790, see Jackson (1967: 44).
8. For the evidence of the chronicle, Abitbol (1982: 26); on the value of cowries in Yorùbá lands, see Adebayo (1994: 381–3); for studies of the inflation of the cowrie in the nineteenth century, see especially Lovejoy (1974) and Hoendorn/Johnson (1986).
9. Bowdich (1977: 330–33); on currencies in Borno, Hallett (1964: 88); on cloth as a form of ritual gift like currency in Sierra Leone, see Kup (1967: 9); on the concentration of economic theorists on the links between Europe and the Americas in the emergence of capital, see Lovejoy/Richardson (1999: 333–4).
10. On the *ajo* and the *esusu*, see Adebayo (1994: 390–93).

11. Curtin (1967: 212).
12. NCAC, RDD, transcribed cassettes 573A and B; a superb analysis of the Kelefa Saane epic is Wright (1987).
13. On fetishes 'eating people', NCAC, RDD, transcribed cassette 554C, p. 33; on Bijini as a marabout town, see NCAC, RDD, transcribed cassettes 494A–B, p. 15 – and Giesing/Vydrine (2007); on the import of rum to Waalo for the use of the brac (king) in 1764, TNA, T70/585, fols. 21–3.
14. On Islam as a unifying feature that facilitated revolt, see Lovejoy (2016: 28).
15. Jackson (1967: 18 n. e); Lovejoy (2016: 133–65) puts forward an elegant argument on how, from the late eighteenth century onwards, Islamic leaders sought not to engage with the Atlantic trade where possible.
16. On imports to Cayor and Gajaaga, TNA, T70/586, fols. 59, 80; on Cidi Hamet and Fuuta Tòòro, TNA, T70/585, fol. 54; for a brilliant analysis of the conflict between Islamic and Soninké religiosity as symbolized by alcohol, see Mota (2018: 264–7).
17. Hall (2011a: 56) on the emergence of the *zwāya*; Klein (1972: 429); Gomez (1992: 49–50).
18. Barry (1998: 51); Becker/Martin (1982: 106); Curtin (1971: 23).
19. On madrassas in Barra, Cultru (1913: 191); on Bundu and Fuuta Tòòro, Curtin (1971: 18–20) and Gomez (1992: 35–9).
20. On Yusuf, Hunter (1976: 438–9).
21. Curtin (1971: 21–2); Lovejoy (2016: 41–2); and Gomez (1992: 50–54).
22. Demanet (1767: Vol. 1, 81); Saugnier (1791: 281).
23. Robinson (1975: 189–91).
24. This remarkable linguistic evidence was developed by the great historian of Fuuta Tòòro, Oumar Kane – see Kane (2004: 67, 74–5).
25. Soh (1913: 24–5).
26. Kane (2004: 515–27).
27. Robinson (1975: 198–204).
28. Demanet (1767: Vol. 1, 50–53).
29. Corry (1968: 14–17); on the wine bottles, McIntosh/Thiaw (2001: 30).
30. Richmond Palmer (1936: 275–6); see also H. R. Palmer (1931: 21).
31. Some accounts say the family migrated from Fuuta Tòòro eleven generations before the *jihād* ((Balogun (1975: 17) and Hiskett (1995: 53)); yet see also a text of Uthmān dan Fodio's brother Abdullāh from *c.* 1820–30, which states that the Fodio family had come six generations previously from Fuuta Tòòro to Sokoto – Hiskett (1957: 560).

What is most likely is that different branches migrated at different times, some in the late fifteenth century and others in the late seventeenth century.

32. On Songhay, Cissoko (1974: 57); on the *'ulamā*, Hiskett (1957: 572–6); on Mauritanian scholarly production, see Stewart (2018).
33. Richmond Palmer (1936: 33).
34. Curtin (1967: 150); Moore (1738: 22).
35. Abitbol (1982: 3, 3 n. 45); Last (1967: lxxix).
36. This assessment of Muhammad is made by Hiskett (1963: 8).
37. For the text on the *shaykh*, Hiskett (1957: 561).
38. Jackson (1967: 12, 22–5, 41–6).
39. ibid., 23, 32, 45, 54; on the rise of Fula power as connected with the booming leather trade, see Bathily (1989: 240), *apud* Suret-Canale (1964).
40. For the 'Song of Bagauda', Hiskett (1965: 118); for Timbuktu in 1758, Abitbol (1982: 5).
41. On Mâssina, Seydou (1991: 199 n. 11); on Timbuktu, Jackson (1967: 11); on Fuuta Tòòro, Kane (2004: 308–13).
42. On Baba Zaki, H. R. Palmer (1928: Vol. 3, 126).
43. On the musket imports, Hiskett (1973: 78–9) and H. R. Palmer (1928: Vol. 3, 124); on the cowrie exports from Dahomey to the Niger Bend, Law (1995: 54–5).
44. On Timbuktu, Abitbol (1982: 5, 12, 19) and also Stewart (2018); on Kano and camels, Jackson (1967: 38, 46).
45. Curtin (1967: 36–7); Hall (2011a: 69, 84–7); Hiskett (1960: 569); Jackson (1967: 34–5, 51).
46. Last (1974: 25); Malacco (2016: 83).
47. Hiskett (1963: 121–2).
48. The *Kitāb al-Farq* is attributed to Uthmān dan Fodio – see Hiskett (1960: 567–9).
49. Rentz (2004); Moumouni (2008: 59–60); Balogun (1975: 28–35).
50. On the hostility of Salafism to Sufi movements, Hunwick (1984: 149); on the hostility of Sufism to statecraft, Brenner (1979: 160–61); on Sufisim and the shehu, see Moumouni (2008); see also Hiskett (1973: 61); on Sufism in Borno, see Bobboyi (1992: 146–52).
51. See Moumouni (2008: 79–81) on the shehu's concern to encourage women to greater spirituality; on female scholars, Hiskett (1973: 26); for Bello, Arnett (1922: 20) and Balogun (1975: 27–8); on the weakness of the Ottoman grip on Arabia, Rentz (2004).
52. On the shehu's birth, Bivar (1961: 235); on his physical appearance, Hiskett (1973: 30); on the African religions of Sokoto in the fifteenth

century, Cissoko (1974: 51); on the pilgrimage to Mecca and return via Agades, Hiskett (1957: 563–4).

53. This moving analysis of Fula poetry is in Seydou (1991: 17).
54. Arnett (1922: 23); Hiskett (1973: 44–9); Last (1974: 5).
55. Hiskett (1963: 107).
56. Hiskett (1973: 70–74, 86–8).
57. Arnett (1922: 57–8).
58. Hiskett (1963: 114–15); on the question of whether there was, in fact, a high mortality, see Last (2018).
59. Arnett (1922: 6–7).
60. Richmond Palmer (1936: 52).
61. Curtin (1967: 207).
62. ibid., 208.
63. On drought and migrations in the eighteenth century, see Candotti (2015: 120); Hallett (1964: 92).
64. ibid., 87, 91; Bobboyi (1992).
65. Martin (1967: 59, 83); Bobboyi (1992: 10, 23–7, 165); see also Last (2018).
66. Brenner (1979: 162–5); Hiribarren (2017: 19–20).
67. On Oyo and Ilorin, Law (1977: 278); for Eisami and Crowther, Curtin (1967: 212, 299 n. 20).
68. On Mâssina, Seydou (1976) and Last (1974).
69. On Fulfulde poetry from Fuuta Jaalo, see Sow (1971); see also Conneau (1977: 69).
70. Hallett (1964: 131).
71. Quinn (1972: 32–3, 66–70).
72. ibid., 66, 110–11, on Tal's career.
73. The phrase 'the crisis of adaptation' is from Hopkins's landmark work (1973); the estimate of the slave population by 1850 is in Lovejoy (2016: 102–7); on the expansion of slavery in the nineteenth century in general, see Meillassoux (1972); and for the case of Dahomey, Coquery-Vidrovitch (1972: 116).
74. Conneau (1977: 115, 138).
75. Lovejoy (1978a); Lovejoy (1980).
76. El-Wakkad (1961: 28–30).

CONCLUSION

1. Dalzel (1967: 220–21).
2. Bowdich (1966: 106).

3. Frank (2004) on Kansas.
4. On the relationship of money as a universal value and other 'objective' equivalences, I am very grateful to my PhD student Joe da Costa for our discussions on this topic, and for making me see its importance, as developed with much more sophistication by him than me here in his doctorate.
5. For the letter of the ruler of Allada, Soares (2014: 264); the dispute between 'formalists' and 'substantivists' is dealt with at more length in Green (2018b); Piketty (2014) argues for an equivalence between 'wealth' and 'capital'.
6. Thaler/Sunstein (2008); on the interconnection of cultural and economic frameworks, Cabral (1974).
7. On Gold Coast swords, Axelrod Winsnes (1992: 39–40); on the manufacture of ink, bricks and soap, Kup (1967: 20, 107, 113).
8. On this visit in 1866, see Dobronravin (2016: 186–91).
9. On the rise of Lagos, see Parés (2013a: 300) and Reis (2006).
10. Brown (2003: 1).
11. On the practice of using local values to give new meanings to objects, see Parés (2016: 38–9).
12. Conrad (1990: 100).
13. Jansen/Duintjer/Tamboura (1995: 118).

List of Illustrations

Index

Note: page numbers in bold refer to illustrations

ALLEN LANE
an imprint of
PENGUIN BOOKS

Also Published

Ivan Krastev and Stephen Holmes, *The Light that Failed: A Reckoning*

Alexander Watson, *The Fortress: The Great Siege of Przemysl*

Thomas Penn, *The Brothers York: An English Tragedy*

David Abulafia, *The Boundless Sea: A Human History of the Oceans*

Dominic Sandbrook, *Who Dares Wins: Britain, 1979-1982*

Charles Moore, *Margaret Thatcher: The Authorized Biography, Volume Three: Herself Alone*

Orlando Figes, *The Europeans: Three Lives and the Making of a Cosmopolitan Culture*

Naomi Klein, *On Fire: The Burning Case for a Green New Deal*

Hassan Damluji, *The Responsible Globalist: What Citizens of the World Can Learn from Nationalism*

John Sellars, *Lessons in Stoicism: What Ancient Philosophers Teach Us about How to Live*

Peter Hennessy, *Winds of Change: Britain in the Early Sixties*

Brendan Simms, *Hitler: Only the World Was Enough*

Justin Marozzi, *Islamic Empires: Fifteen Cities that Define a Civilization*

Bruce Hood, *Possessed: Why We Want More Than We Need*

Frank Close, *Trinity: The Treachery and Pursuit of the Most Dangerous Spy in History*

Janet L. Nelson, *King and Emperor: A New Life of Charlemagne*

Richard M. Eaton, *India in the Persianate Age: 1000-1765*

Philip Mansel, *King of the World: The Life of Louis XIV*

James Lovelock, *Novacene: The Coming Age of Hyperintelligence*

Mark B. Smith, *The Russia Anxiety: And How History Can Resolve It*

Stella Tillyard, *George IV: King in Waiting*

Donald Sassoon, *The Anxious Triumph: A Global History of Capitalism, 1860-1914*

Elliot Ackerman, *Places and Names: On War, Revolution and Returning*

Johny Pits, *Afropean: Notes from Black Europe*

Jonathan Aldred, *Licence to be Bad: How Economics Corrupted Us*

Walt Odets, *Out of the Shadows: Reimagining Gay Men's Lives*

Jonathan Rée, *Witcraft: The Invention of Philosophy in English*

Jared Diamond, *Upheaval: How Nations Cope with Crisis and Change*

Emma Dabiri, *Don't Touch My Hair*

Srecko Horvat, *Poetry from the Future: Why a Global Liberation Movement Is Our Civilisation's Last Chance*

Paul Mason, *Clear Bright Future: A Radical Defence of the Human Being*